VINCENT PRICE
A Daughter's Biography

VINCENT PRICE—

A Daughter's Biography

VICTORIA PRICE

ST. MARTIN'S PRESS
New York

VINCENT PRICE: A DAUGHTER'S BIOGRAPHY. Copyright © 1999 by Victoria Price. All rights reserved. Printed in the United States of America. No part of this book may be used or reproduced in any manner whatsoever without written permission except in the case of brief quotations embodied in critical articles or reviews. For information, address St. Martin's Press, 175 Fifth Avenue, New York, N.Y. 10010.

Design by Lisa Pifher

Library of Congress Cataloging-in-Publication Data

Price, Victoria
    Vincent Price : a daughter's biography / Victoria Price. — 1st
  ed.
      p.   cm.
    Includes index.
    ISBN 0-312-24273-5
    1. Price, Vincent, 1911–1993.   2. Actors—United States Biography.
  I. Title.
  PN2287.P72P75   1999
  791.43'028'092—dc21
  [B]   99–15947
                                                CIP

First Edition: November 1999

10 9 8 7 6 5 4 3 2 1

To my family, my friends, and my teachers—
all along the way

AUTHOR'S NOTE AND ACKNOWLEDGMENTS

In undertaking to write this biography of my father, I spent almost two years travelling across the United States and Europe interviewing his family, friends, colleagues, and classmates. I sifted through the more than 66,000 items that comprise the Vincent Price papers at the Library of Congress, as well as the smaller Vincent Price collection at Yale University. I have reviewed his film, television, and radio careers and compiled a comprehensive record of his fifty years of public service to the arts. I have unearthed government documents, traced the Price family tree, and catalogued the Vincent Price art collection, as well as read the letters, jottings, journals, datebooks, clippings, and scrapbooks that remained among his personal effects after his death.

In taking his journey—literally and metaphorically—through his life, I relied on the generosity of many people who gave of their time and their recollections. I owe a debt of gratitude to all of them, and wish to record my sincere thanks, in no particular order. In London: Eileen Atkins, Frith Banbury, Alan Bennett, Dick and Marina Blodget, Felix Brenner and the late David Shipman, Adrienne Corri, Noel Davis, Sir Alec Guinness, Barry Humphries, Verity Lambert, Christopher and Gitte Lee, Jean Marsh, Jill Melford, Dame Diana Rigg, John Schlesinger. In Venice: Marcella and Victor Hazan. In Paris: Deanna Durbin and Charles David. In California: Eddie Albert, Wallace Albertson, Pat Altman, Sam Arkoff, Susan Blu, William and Shirley Brice, Isabelle Borchert, Carol Burnett, Tim Burton, David Capell, Charles Champlin, Jan and David Clive, Roger Corman, Hazel Court and the late Don Taylor, Johnny Depp, John and Kit Dreyfuss Michael Feinstein, the late Lily Fonda, Eric Harrison, Dennis Hopper, Sam Jaffe, John J. Larkin, Jr., Nina Lederman, Barbara Poe Levee, Norman and Peggy Lloyd, the late Robert Mitchum, Patricia Morison, Jane Russell Peoples, Sara and William Santschi, Tom Silliman, Bruce Villanch, Pearl Wexler, Jane Wyatt, Michael York. In New York: the late Cleveland Amory, Lauren Bacall, Susan Dillon, the late Fred Dockstader, Joan Rivers, Marti Stevens, Carlton Sedgeley. In Missouri: Ed and Nettie Carpenter, Bobbie Gay, the Honorable Franklin Ferriss, Mr. and Mrs. Dolph Boettler, Mr. and Mrs. Daniel Schlafly, Henry McIntyre. In Boston: Julia Child, Rebecca Eaton, Sandy Leonard. In New Mexico: Michael Childers, Lloyd Kiva New, Rini Price, Theo Raven. In Connecticut: Alvin Josephy, Elizabeth Kubler. In Oklahoma: Richard Cypher. In Florida: Ted and Sally Thomas. In Colorado: Ruth Maitland, Suzy and Gary Rubin. In Washington, D.C.: Letitia Baldridge.

Similarly, I am grateful for the invaluable resources (especially the human ones) of the Manuscript Division of the Library of Congress—and particularly archivist Laura Kells; the Sterling Library at Yale University; the Museum of Television and Radio; the Alumni Office at St. Louis Country Day; the Academy of Motion Picture Arts and Sciences Library; the Mander and Mitchensen Collection; CalebJ@aol.com and Mayflower Society; and the Los Angeles Public Library. My task was made immeasurably easier by Lucy Chase Williams, whose book, *The Films of Vincent Price*, was a wonderful source.

This book could not have been written without significant contributions from five very dear friends: the late Roddy McDowall, whose good word on my behalf opened countless doors and whose wonderful capacity for friendship and extraordinary depth of knowledge informed this book from the very beginning; Hank and Marin Milam, whose intimate and honest recollections of my father were essential to the writing of his biography; Wawona Hartwig, whose careful preservation of my father's records and whose faultless and loving memory filled in all the necessary gaps; and Reggie Williams, whose tireless research and witty, pointed recollections became this book's building blocks, and whose great generosity has been the mainstay of our family for more than a decade.

I am particularly grateful to my mother, Mary Grant Price, who selflessly shared her memories of my father, contributed crucial archival material, permitted me to use her wonderful photographs, and, as ever, lovingly and generously encouraged me; and to my brother Vincent Barrett Price, who shared his memories, read and reread the manuscript, gave me advice, and, as he has always done, unstintingly supported me in my work.

This book was shepherded to fruition through the collective effort of many people, particularly David Chalfant, Patrick White, Kathy Robbins, Tifany Richards, and David Halpern. But it would never have seen the light of day without Richard Cohen, who took a chance on an unknown writer and thereby made the publication of this book possible; and Cynthia Cannell, who is everything I could have wished for in an agent. Every writer should be so fortunate to have someone like Cynthia in her camp. My singular British editor, Robyn Karney, helped shape this biography through her insight, craft, and talent—not to mention her humor and friendship; I owe her a great debt of gratitude. Many people at St. Martin's have helped to guide this project to completion—including Rebecca Schuman and Kevin Flynn. But the lion's share of the effort fell to Cal Morgan, whose belief in both this project and in me brought a happy ending to a long, long story; and to Elizabeth Beier, who took the baton from Cal and carried it to the finish line.

Special thanks to Denis Adair, Jane Anderson and Tess Ayers, Mitchell Anderson, Sallie Bingham, Jim and Dottie Bradshaw, Paul Brown and Rick Mitz, Steve Coyne, Julie Cypher and Melissa Etheridge, Clay Grant Davidson, David DeNicolo, Electra Falliers, Mary Galloway, Joe Hardy, Chris Jakowchik, the Kennedy family, Pamela Lippert, Jim Phipps, Peggy Powell, Margaret Randall, Ilka and Frank Siegmund, Virginia Stevens, Henry and Inge Stölzle, Sharon Walker, Richard Wulfsberg; to the Department of American Studies at the University of New Mexico—especially Charlie Biebel, Gabriel Melendez, Vera Norwood, and Ruth Salvaggio—for their graceful tolerance of my idiosyncratic approach to an academic career; and to Cynthia Songé, who not only encouraged me to write, but actually bought me my first computer, all those years ago.

In 1992, Danae Falliers casually suggested that my father and I write a book about art, never dreaming that she would end up living through the daily and difficult birthing of this biography. I wouldn't have begun this project if it hadn't been for her, and I couldn't have finished it without her.

Victoria Price
June 1999
Santa Fe, New Mexico

VINCENT PRICE

A Daughter's Biography

PROLOGUE

Vincent Price was a man of glorious contradictions. He was a Renaissance man in an age of specialists, a Victorian aesthete who mastered the twentieth century's media. And although he is most vividly remembered as the cinema's King of Horror—indeed, his name is virtually synonymous with the genre—fewer than a third of the more than one hundred pictures he made in his fifty-five-year career as an actor were horror movies.

Under contract to Twentieth Century-Fox during Hollywood's Golden Age, he appeared in many films that have become screen classics, among them *Laura, The Song of Bernadette*, and *Leave Her to Heaven*. He also worked extensively in the theater, launching his professional career in a Broadway play and ending it over half a century later with an acclaimed one-man show. On radio, Vincent Price's famously distinctive voice brought him the title role in *The Saint*, and he was one of the first movie actors to find consistent work in television, where he appeared in shows as diverse as *Playhouse 90* and *Batman* and hosted the distinguished PBS series *Mystery!* But that is only part of his story.

Vincent Price created a life that knew few boundaries, because no one world could contain his expansive energies and enthusiasms. He was a gourmet chef who enjoyed nothing more than a hot dog at a baseball game, a trained stage actor who made commercials for bathroom tile cleaner, and a respected art historian who sold art for a department store, thus educating legions of his fans to share what was, in reality, the deepest passion of his life—the visual arts.

Intellectual and populist, art expert and the screen's master of menace, Vincent Price was loved and recognized in many worlds. He was also my father.

I was born at the height of my father's fame. Although he was just over fifty, he called me "the child of his old age." He loved me very much; during my childhood, however, he was busier than he had ever been, and often away from home. Thus, he floated in and out of my life, a teller of tales and a bearer of gifts. He loved to send me postcards. From Bangkok to Buffalo, from the Louvre to the Ann Arbor Municipal Library, he fired my imagination with news and images from around the world. Wherever my father went I followed him in my mind, and I devoured his stories when he came home. Every moment spent with him brought new adventures and exciting discoveries. He was a magical figure who radiated a spontaneous sense of fun, an immense capacity for joy, and an infinite curiosity about life and the world. I adored him.

After his marriage to his third wife, actress Coral Browne, when I was twelve, everything changed. Independent, willful, and with no sense of family, Coral had little tolerance for me, and the once easy relationship between my father and me became strained by her resentment of it. Although the love between us remained strong, its expression was often thwarted. After Coral's death in 1991, I longed for nothing more than to reestablish a close connection with my father and to know him better.

This desire grew out of twin needs, selfish and unselfish. I wanted my father back, but I also believed that he, too, needed to get to know me again. By the time of Coral's death, however, he was virtually bedridden, and it became the goal of all of us who loved him to find a way to make his last years compelling. I suggested to him that we collaborate on a book about art, which over the years had become our common ground—an almost sacred subject about which we could talk with the empathy and passion we had formerly shared, putting aside disagreements and disappointments. I believed that, in this way, we would come to understand each other better; I also felt that, in passing the legacy of his knowledge to me, he would round out his life. And so, once again, I found myself listening to his stories.

My father understood that in order to succeed in Hollywood you have to be good copy. Accordingly, in taking each event of his life and transforming it into a story, he was also crafting a good read in a publicity column, a hearty laugh at a cocktail party, a riveting anecdote for an interview. The poet Adrienne Rich writes, "The stories of our lives become our lives," and this was certainly true of my father, in whom the public and the private man had become inextricably entangled. He had long ago learned to hide his intimate self behind a glamorous façade. True intimacy, for my father, had become almost impossible. And although, by the end of our time together, much of our closeness had indeed been recaptured, for me there were still too many questions left unanswered.

Then, after my father died, it fell to me to put his affairs in order. As I sorted through his papers, I was frequently overtaken by a sense that I was searching for something. From time to time I stumbled across a little treasure. In a drawer filled with Peruvian pots wrapped in old newspaper, I found a small, well-worn, blue leather diary—his journal of his first European trip. A locked filing cabinet behind the air conditioner disclosed a black folder marked "Personal and Private" containing the letters written during Vincent and Coral's secret courtship. In the back of a desk drawer was a manila envelope marked "Keep," which held the FBI documents clearing Vincent of charges of Communism during the McCarthy era. With each discovery of a formerly hidden fragment of my father's life, I wanted to know more.

Whenever my father had a spare moment, he used whatever piece of paper was handy—an airline ticket envelope, a paper placemat, hotel notepads, and countless legal pads—to jot down his stories and his thoughts. Among these writings I uncovered two manuscripts of almost completed memoirs. Lastly, I transcribed over two hundred pages of taped conversations between my father and me, which capture his inimitable style of expression, witty and fluent. These recount his marvelously eventful life, telling of famous people, foreign places, funny incidents, and grand adventures. These are the stories he wanted me to hear and to tell others. They are his legacy to me.

And so I became my father's biographer, driven to the task, on the one hand, by needing to make sense of his life for myself and, on the other, because it became important to me to tell others about a remarkable man. Despite being plagued by the nagging question "How well can any child know the truth of a parent's life?" I have chosen to tread the fine line between daughter and biographer. In constructing this book as part biographical narrative, part personal memoir, I hope that I have succeeded in tempering passion with objectivity in telling the story of a life well lived.

I.

Renaissance Man

I BELIEVE IN YOU MY SOUL . . .
THE OTHER I AM MUST NOT ABASE ITSELF TO YOU,
AND YOU MUST NOT BE ABASED TO THE OTHER.

—WALT WHITMAN, *SONG OF MYSELF*

1

My father, Vincent Leonard Price Jr., was born in St. Louis, Missouri, on May 27, 1911, the fourth and last child of Vincent Leonard and Marguerite Willcox Price. He described his family as "well-to-do, not rich enough to evoke envy but successful enough to demand respect." But this sunny description belied a more complex financial legacy—one that had a profound impact on the lives of all the Price men. Thus, to tell my father's story, I must begin with the life of my great-grandfather, Dr. Vincent Clarence Price. His vicissitudes began a saga that became a cautionary tale to his famous grandson, who bore his name.

Although virtually nothing is known about his predecessors, family records confirm that Vincent Clarence Price was born in Troy, New York, on December 11, 1832. He was of Welsh descent, a fact borne out by his looks—he was, as my father would later write, "a wonderfully black-haired, black-mustached, 'black' Welshman." The earliest published mention of Vincent C. Price appears in the 1848 Troy City Directory, which lists the sixteen year old working as a clerk. His name appears in the directory again as a clerk in 1850, then as a bookkeeper at the American Hotel in 1852. During this time he attended medical college, from which he graduated in 1852. Indeed, by 1853, the city directory lists V.C. Price as a wholesale druggist.

In the fall of 1853, however, the young druggist moved to Buffalo to study homeopathic medicine and chemistry at New York College. Although his background was working class, Vincent C. was encouraged to further his medical education by Dr. Russell J. White, an analytical physician and father of his bride-to-be, Harriet Elizabeth, a striking young woman of patrician bearing and even-featured good looks.

According to Price family lore, Dr. White was not only a prominent citizen and a successful doctor but also reportedly a descendant of Peregrine White, the first child born as the *Mayflower* landed in Plymouth Harbor in 1620. Much was made of this distinguished heritage, particularly by Vincent Clarence himself, who left no record of his own family history but frequently referred to his wife's more illustrious origins. His enthusiasm for the White-*Mayflower* connection would be passed down through generations of the Price family, including to my father, who relished the idea of his American blue-blood ancestry. However, the Price accounts of the distinguished White lineage appear to be flawed; the purported family genealogy leading back to Peregrine White cannot be confirmed by *Mayflower* records.

Although he lived and attended school in Buffalo, Vincent C. frequently returned to Troy to visit his fiancée. On March 28, 1855, the couple were married at the White home in Troy. After their marriage, Harriet and V. C. set up residence near the college in Buffalo where, ten months later, their son Russell Clarence was born. That spring, Dr. V. C. Price graduated with an M.D. in pharmaceutical chemistry. A year later, Harriet gave birth to their second child, Ida Helena.

Numerous versions of the early years of Dr. Price's career have been passed down, undoubtedly mingling fact and fiction. As my father told it, after graduating from medical college with a wife and two young children to feed, the young homeopathic doctor and chemist began the hard work of establishing his own practice. He soon found, however, that he faced a serious impediment. Facial hair was in fashion in the mid-1850s, and young Price had always had difficulty growing a full beard—a deficit that emphasized his naturally youthful appearance. Prospective patients seemed wary of his youth, and he found it difficult to build a clientele. After a few rough years, the doctor, his wife, and their two babies were forced to move in with his parents. In his spare time, in an effort to help out around the house, he began experimenting with chemical formulas in an attempt to help his mother's neighborhood-renowned biscuits to rise more perfectly. In the process, Vincent C. Price invented baking powder. Realizing the commercial potential of his discovery, he patented his invention . . . then went out into the world to seek his fame and fortune.

According to his lengthy obituary in the *Chicago Tribune* of July 15, 1914, however, the man who would become "one of the housewife's best friends" was still in college when he invented baking powder. "It was more than sixty years ago that Dr. Price mixed the world's first cream of tartar baking powder. The doctor's mother had a reputation as a biscuit maker. But her biscuits were not for herself. She could not digest them. Price, then a student in a school of pharmacy, sat watching his mother one day as she kneaded biscuit dough. Then the great idea came to him. He returned to his laboratory and began a series of experiments, which ended with the discovery that the argols, left in the vats as the precipitation of the grapes in wine manufacture, when refined not only did away with the injurious effects of hot biscuit, but also greatly facilitated the work of making them. Soon after a new 'household help' appeared on the market—Price's baking powder."

Whatever the true story may be, after patenting his invention Vincent C., like so many nineteenth-century Americans, set out to find prosperity in the West. In 1861 he moved his young family to Waukegan, Illinois, a small but thriving Lake Michigan port city, forty miles north of Chicago, and established their home there. Waukegan had been founded by French explorers two centuries before. By 1860, Waukegan had become one of the busiest harbors on the Great Lakes, boasting over a thousand sailings a year; the city was well enough established to attract a visit from Abraham Lincoln, who spent a night there during his first campaign tour.

Dr. Price's intuition about Illinois proved correct. Not only was he able to establish both a family home and a thriving medical practice in Waukegan, he also pursued his dream of marketing his invention by establishing a business partnership with banker Charles R. Steele. Together they purchased a small factory in Chicago, where their company, Steele & Price, began to manufacture Dr. Price's Cream Baking Powder. According to the *Tribune* obituary, however, "Price did not create a market for his baking powder, enormous as the sales became in a few years, without great effort and many discouragements. His little Chicago plant turned out only a few pounds a day, but he had difficulty in disposing even of that. Personal appeals to grocers and finally a personal, house-to-house, back-door canvassing campaign at last built up a demand. Advertising did the rest." Indeed, within a few years, Dr. Price became a household name and his baking powder was sold across the country. His success led him to conduct other food experiments; soon he introduced cornstarch for culinary uses, patented the first fruit and herb flavoring extracts as well as vegetable colorings, manufactured breakfast foods, and even published popular cookbooks.

By his fiftieth birthday, Dr. V. C. Price was a multimillionaire. The small house he had purchased at 719 Grand Avenue was razed in 1888 and a larger, more modern home was built on its site for his ever-expanding family—a glorious three-story Queen Anne-style mansion complete with a castlelike turret, dormers, gables, ornate chimneys, and stained glass windows. In addition to Russell and Ida, Harriet had given birth to three more children: Emma Frances (in 1862), Guerdon White (in 1864), and Vincent Leonard (in 1871). In 1880, when Harriet was thirty-six and her husband thirty-eight, Blanche Castle was born, but just over a year later she succumbed to cholera. Dr. Price recorded his grief in the family Bible: "Our home is in mourning. Our home circle is broken. Our darling Blanche died last night."

Despite the loss of their youngest child, V. C. and Harriet found joy in the growth, education, and marriages of their surviving children. Dr. Price placed great stock in schooling. Russell was educated at Beloit College and Harvard Medical School before joining his father's company. Guerdon studied at Racine College before also joining the family business, and both the girls received a solid education. As Russell, Ida, Emma, and Guerdon came to maturity, their father built large homes for them and their families on adjoining properties on Grand Avenue, establishing the Prices as one of the most prominent families in Waukegan. Vincent Leonard, seven years younger than his closest sibling, also had meticulous attention paid to his education. After attending the Waukegan public schools, he was sent to the Racine College Grammar School in Wisconsin and prepared for college at the University School in Kenosha, Wisconsin. Among his classmates at the exclusive college preparatory academy was an impetuous and talented younger boy named Richard Head Wells. Price and Wells shared an interest in dramatics and took time away from their studies to put on an extravagant magic show for the school. Some forty-five years later, the younger sons of Price and Wells—Vincent Jr. and Orson (who added an 'e' to become Welles)—would work together as two of the rising young Broadway stars of the 1930s.

In 1884, Dr. Price had bought out his business partner and consolidated his holdings as the Price Baking Powder Company. His eldest son, Russell, had rapidly risen to the position of vice president. In the early 1890s, however, Dr. Price decided to sell his interest in the company, leaving Russell to continue as president. Dr. Price had hoped to retire a fairly young and very wealthy man; in the end, though, it would appear that his skill at invention was not matched by his skill at investment, and the Panic of 1893 virtually wiped him out—an event that, if one believes the family stories, had cataclysmic consequences for his youngest son, Vincent Leonard Price.

In 1893, Vincent Leonard, then twenty-two, was finishing his junior year at Sheffield Scientific School at Yale University when his father called him home. Although the handsome, mild-mannered young man had an aptitude for the sciences, he also evinced a strong interest in the arts, particularly English literature and poetry. Unlike his older brothers, Vincent was not sure that he wanted to follow in their father's footsteps and become a businessman. As a junior in college, he had been blissfully unconcerned with exact plans for his future. Nonetheless, with the catastrophic losses suffered by his father, he realized that he had no choice but to return home and find work.

According to my father, Vincent Leonard took an interest in one of Dr. Price's holdings, a company so deeply in the red that it was said even the creditors had over-looked it. But a detailed retrospective of the career of Vincent Leonard Price, published half a century later, notes that Vincent's career began in 1894 at the Hill-Rodda Company in Chicago, where he worked as a stenographer. Hill-Rodda Company, this account tells us, was later purchased by Dr. Price with his sons Russell and Vincent L., and other investors, when it was incorporated as the Pan Confection Company. Vincent L. Price acted as manager, secretary, and treasurer for his father, who by the turn of the century was president of the Lincoln National Bank and the Price Cereal Products Company, as well as Pan Confection. Despite his losses in 1893, apparently, the doctor did manage to retain some of his financial holdings; in his 1914 *Tribune* obituary, he was "reputed to be a millionaire several times over." And yet the story survived somewhat differently in the annals of family tradition: My father always maintained that Dr. Price lost all his money in the crash and died a poor man.

Whatever the precise circumstances of Vincent Leonard's removal from Yale, the end result was that he became a businessman. If he had harbored aspirations for a creative life, he dutifully gave them up to work, like both his brothers, for his father. But against all odds and counter to his dreams of a creative life, Vincent Leonard Price proved a shrewd businessman, going on to become one of the most respected leaders of the American candy business. Within the confectionery industry he was noted for his "kindness, generosity, and high ideals to the virtues of truth and love of his fellow man." So profound was his influence that twenty years after his death an article appeared in the newsletter of the National Candy Association, of which he had once been president, naming him one of the most respected industry leaders of the twentieth century. Despite Vincent Leonard's kindness, humility, and generosity of spirit, his own family would come to suspect that, in devoting his life to a successful business career, this remarkable man had been deprived of the life he had wanted to live. Decades later, his children still wondered, What if Dr. Price had remained a multimillionaire? What if their father had been able to pursue a career of his own choosing? And so the mythology of Dr. Price's moment of remembered failure, and its lasting effect on his family, took on a life that extended beyond that of his own children.

My father was enthralled by his family history. To him, Dr. Price was a fantastical figure. In his 1958 autobiography, *I Like What I Know*, Vincent Price wrote of his grand-father, "He had been very rich and, I gathered, rather racy. . . . I always regretted that my father's father had not lived long enough for me to know him. The history of his wealth and his vocabulary had made him my favorite relative. I also resented his dying poor." The stories of Dr. Price's financial failings became grist for the mill of many more Price family shortcomings, which his grandson both rued and recounted: "I vaguely recall something about a covered wagon from New York getting stuck in the mud in Chicago, and because that was a sign of some sort, these particular ancestors bought the adhesive spot, which, after they sold it, inevitably turned out to be the Loop—worth at least a million an acre. My family has a startling history of such misadventures. For instance, my father tried, nay pleaded with some of his friends to pool together and buy stock in Ford. Nothing. They didn't. He didn't. My grandfather was offered stock in every paying gold mine in the Western hemisphere and turned it all down to buy nonpaying ones anywhere. The only member of the whole outfit who hit the jackpot was a delightfully debauched uncle who bought half the state of Oklahoma (the right half), made millions, and was rumored to have owned half of a famous opera singer (the right half). Unfortunately, no one ever spoke to him; and my family, being honest, if not smart, only spoke about him after he made good. Proof of my family's misadventures came to light years later when we unearthed enough magnificently engraved but worthless stocks to paper a small room—which I did in a New York apartment. I hope none of them turn out to be good . . . I've moved."

Throughout his life, my father often returned to the tales of his grandfather's financial misfortunes and his own father's consequent self-sacrifice. Indeed, as a young man, Vincent Price's determination to make his career in the arts was heightened by his belief that his father's life had been irrevocably changed for the worse by his grandfather's monetary troubles. And throughout that career he maintained an uneasy relationship with money, forever juggling the fear of not making any, or somehow losing all of it, with the determination never to be forced into doing something that would denigrate his artistic integrity. Though he often joked about his grandfather, "I'll never forgive him for losing all that money," in truth, to Vincent his own family history was no laughing matter.

My brother, Vincent Barrett Price, maintained that "Dad always had his father and Vincent Clarence in the back of his mind. He was the youngest son in a family of men who were forced into doing exactly what they didn't want to do. It must have been terrifying for him, because he had this burgher mind about everything. He had these old tapes in his mind all his life—terrible fears. Fears of inadequacy, fears of poverty. He never was poor, but he always played like he was poor. I think he was under a huge amount of pressure." This troubled legacy would influence the whole course of my father's life.

Vincent Leonard Price's older brother Guerdon married Eunice Cobb in 1884. They lived on Grand Avenue, just down the street from the Price mansion. Tragedy struck in November 1891, when twenty-eight-year-old Guerdon, by then the father of two sons, was killed accidentally in Colorado. Three years later, however, Guerdon's younger brother, Vincent Leonard, married Eunice's Cobb Price's niece, Marguerite Cobb Willcox, giving both families something to celebrate.

Born and raised in Mineral Point, a wealthy county seat in the beautiful rolling hills of Southwestern Wisconsin, Marguerite Willcox descended from a family whose American roots went back over eight generations. Her illustrious ancestors included at least two soldiers who fought in the American Revolution, a fact of which Marguerite was particularly proud since it qualified her for membership in the Society of the Daughters of the American Revolution. On her father's side, Marguerite was a descendant of the Desnoyers family of Paris, France. Pierre, called Pepe, had crossed the Atlantic in the late eighteenth century, settling in what is now the Detroit area, and becoming one of the first silversmiths in the Midwest. He developed a reputation for fine workmanship and, more interestingly, for his ingenuity in creating artifacts inspired by his environment. Among these were small headbands of silver, complete with protruding silver feathers, which he used as barter with the local American Indian tribes on the Michigan peninsula.

On the maternal side, Marguerite descended from a line of strong-willed women with whom she turned out to have much in common. She was particularly intrigued by her great-grandmother, who had married the six-foot-eight-inch captain of a China clipper. He lavished all the silks of the Orient on his beautiful wife until she underwent a religious conversion and took to wearing only black. As my father recalled in *I Like*

What I Know, "From the gorgeous silks she made an endless series of patchwork quilts as penance. Mother cherished them all, as she cherished this legend, even though she would never have thought of emulating it, and the quilts were neatly folded at the foot of every Early American bed in the house."

Marguerite's own mother, Harriet Louise Cobb, a strong-willed and liberal-minded woman, married Henry Cole Willcox of Detroit on New Year's Day, 1874. Five months after the wedding, Willcox was tragically drowned, leaving Harriet four months pregnant. On October 28, 1874 she gave birth to a healthy daughter, Daisy Cobb Willcox.

A pudgy brown-haired girl with a resolute expression, Daisy showed her distinctive style and determination even when very young, telling anyone who would listen that she despised her name and that when she was old enough she would have it changed. Daisy, she liked to announce, was a name that should only be given to cows. And she was true to her words, striding into court at age twelve and succeeding in changing her name to the French Marguerite.

With the help of her own mother, Harriet Willcox raised her headstrong daughter alone for eleven years. Then, in December 1885, she remarried. Although one might imagine that Marguerite would have resented anyone who took away her mother's attention, she unreservedly adored her new stepfather. Born in Ireland, Hans Mortimer Oliver was an English sea captain who perfectly fitted Marguerite's idea of a worldly adventurer. Having never known her father, she idolized everything about Captain Oliver, not least his aristocratic English ancestry. His tales of world travels and his seafaring adventures gave young Marguerite her first glimpse of the glamorous world awaiting her outside of provincial Mineral Point. She immediately adopted his lineage as her own, dutifully hanging framed reproduction portraits of his ancestors in each home in which she lived throughout her lifetime. Her son would later write, "Mother called the reproductions 'The Pirates' just as a come-on to get the chance to explain further, which she always hastened to do. They were the elegantly dressed, in lace and armor, ruddy-cheeked, enormous-nosed antecedents of my British step-grandfather."

Marguerite certainly never intended to stay in Wisconsin, but her marriage into the wealthy Price family in Waukegan, forty miles from Chicago, was undoubtedly her first major step away from home. Apparently her own family was thrilled with the match, for as soon as Vincent Leonard and the twenty-year-old Marguerite were married, Harriet and Captain Oliver embarked on a series of journeys around the world. At first the union of this imposing young woman and the gentle and mild-mannered Price might have seemed an unlikely one, but Vincent Leonard Price would prove an ideal husband, and a perfect audience for his wife's dramatic approach to life. As their youngest son, my father, would later comment, "If ever there was a woman who knew what she wanted, it was my mother. Father was beatified by her the day she set eyes on him, and he became a full-fledged saint as the years rolled by. They were married for fifty-three years, until death did them part, and he sat back to wait out the few years until he could join her."

Marguerite and Vincent settled in Waukegan, and while Vincent commuted to work in Chicago, Marguerite gave birth to their first two children: Harriet, called Hat, in 1897, and James Mortimer, called Mort, in 1899. By the turn of the century, Vincent Leonard Price's business acumen had put him in a position to better himself financially. In 1902, he went into partnership with two St. Louis businessmen, arranging the merger of the Pan Confection Company with two other small candy manufacturers to form the larger National Candy Company. As vice president of a growing firm seeking to establish a national headquarters and build business, Price chose St. Louis, Missouri. The timing could not have been better. Two years later, in 1904, the city proudly hosted both the World's Fair and the Olympic Games. The National Candy Company set up a booth at the fair, flooding them with customers from around the world and starting them on the road to extraordinary success in the candy industry.

2

AT THE BEGINNING of the twentieth century, St. Louis exemplified the best of urban America. It was one of the fastest-growing cities in the United States, and businesses from all over the world were choosing to locate their national headquarters there. As the city's Business Men's League boasted, "As compared with the world, St. Louis has the largest railroad station, hardware house, drug house, woodenware house, tobacco factories, lead works, brickyards, and stove and range works. As compared with the United States, St. Louis has the largest brewery, shoe factory, saddlery market, street-car factories, hardwood lumber market, shoe output, finest streetcars and botanical gardens. St. Louis has 346 miles of electric street railroad. It was the first city to run electric mail cars, to sprinkle its streets by municipal contracts, and to light its streets and alleys uniformly by electricity."

This city, to which Vincent Leonard Price moved his wife and children, was very much a product of its history and its geography. Nestled where the Mississippi and Missouri Rivers meet, the place had attracted many settlers, the first of whom were the Hopewell people, who inhabited the area between 500 B.C. and 400 A.D. Also known as the Mound Builders, these Native American peoples constructed round earthen structures on both sides of the Mississippi in what are now Missouri and Illinois. Laid out along the lines of a compass, these structures were used as temples, forts, dwelling places, and burial grounds, and possibly as observatories for the study of astronomy. It is these mounds that gave St. Louis her first nickname—Mound City.

The first European settlers arrived in the late seventeenth and early eighteenth centuries—French Roman Catholic priests who built missions along the Mississippi. The French gradually settled the area, naming their small village after Louis IX, the Crusader King of France. Even after France ceded the territory to Spain in 1762, St. Louis prospered, settled by French, Spanish, and other European immigrants. For the remainder of the century St. Louis grew steadily, becoming one of the main trading centers on the Lower Mississippi.

In 1803 Thomas Jefferson engineered the Louisiana Purchase, choosing St. Louis as the site for the formal takeover of the territory by the United States. Ideally situated along the main waterway between North and South, the city came to serve as the starting point for many of the great Western expeditions, beginning with Lewis and Clark in 1804. It also became the gateway to the most popular (because the least dangerous and most temperate) route west, the Santa Fe Trail, and the starting point for the Pony Express, which carried mail into the Western Territories. Thus, St. Louis quickly earned her second nickname—the Gateway to the West. The city reached its peak as the fourth-largest city in the United States by 1870—a title it retained for almost forty years.

By 1910 this rapid growth had slowed somewhat, but St. Louis was still a bustling commercial center; it would remain the sixth largest city in the United States until the 1920s. With a large African-American population as well as diverse European immigrant communities, St. Louis was a prototypical American melting pot. Thanks to the 1904 World's Fair and Olympics, many fine public parks and municipal attractions had been built in the city, and residents took pride in an outstanding museum, a magnificent outdoor opera, a symphony orchestra, an excellent university, and a fine public school system. In addition, the city's immigrant and ethnic populations contributed strongly to St. Louis cultural life. The Germans brewed the best beer in the country, opened fine restaurants, and brought in well-known German musicians and singers; the Italian restaurants were equally good, as, of course, were their opera singers. And the city's Southern character was unmistakable, both in the many facets of African-American culture and in the riverboat trade that plied the Mississippi.

However, like many American cities, St. Louis was divided sharply along class and color lines. As the National Candy Company became increasingly successful, the Price family moved further away from the urban center and settled in an area where their neighbors were among the nation's leaders of industry—the Danforths of Ralston-Purina, the Queenys of Monsanto, the Stockstroms of Magic Chef Stove, and the scions of the Anheuser-Busch clan. Though St. Louis, like many other large urban centers, was rocked by racial conflict early in the century—in the summer of 1917, East St. Louis erupted in a devastating riot between African-Americans and the police—the suburban Prices were largely sheltered from their effects.

The St. Louis in which young Vincent Leonard Price Jr. was raised was one of country clubs and ladies' groups, private schools and summer homes. Upper-middle-class St. Louis society was a world to which young Vincent was perfectly suited, yet one from which he would always seek to distance himself. Nevertheless, throughout his life he identified fondly with his hometown, extolling its merits and its positive influence in his own life—among them the opportunities afforded a young man of means whose parents encouraged education and artistic exploration. As Vincent averred, "St. Louis was a fascinating place to start looking and, when possible, collecting. Being centrally situated at the crossroads of the two great rivers, things got brought to St. Louis from everywhere. I became fascinated with where I lived, my city, my state. There I found my way in the arts—before a great building, in a museum, listening to great music. I found this secret in St. Louis."

Vincent's wholly positive experiences of growing up in St. Louis were in radical contrast to those of a boy who would later become one of his theatrical peers. Thomas Lanier Williams III, born two months before Vincent Leonard Price Jr., arrived in St. Louis in 1918, after his shoe-salesman father had found a job there. The family remained in the city throughout Tom's high school years, moving from rooming house to rooming house and from dingy apartment to dingy apartment—this, in a place where, as Tom later wrote, "Location of residence was of prime importance." Edwina Williams, a former Southern belle and another Daughter of the American Revolution, desperately sought to ingratiate herself with St. Louis society, but found it a completely closed circle; though she also tried to enroll Tom and his sister in the finest schools, despite their creativity and academic excellence, their applications were refused.

Like the young Vincent Price, Tom Williams sought an outlet for his artistic aspirations in his hometown, but his social status prohibited access to the cultural circles Price would come to regard as the most important aspects of his youth. It would take Williams many years to find the means to leave his hated hometown and shed the constrictions under which he bridled while growing up in St. Louis. After he had gained fame as Tennessee Williams, the distinguished playwright would dismiss St. Louisans as "cold, smug, complacent, intolerant, stupid, and provincial."

As for Vincent, his own St. Louis upbringing left him easily impressed by money and status. In these early years he would learn from his mother a need for social approval; it was a tendency that would stay with him, even as he assumed a more bohemian attitude in adulthood, rejecting people and things he considered pretentious. These warring compulsions—a taste for the good life and an inclination to buck family expectations in favor of his own ideas—would instill a sense of ambivalence and conflict in Vincent Price that would remain with him all his life.

By 1911, Vincent Leonard Price Sr. had risen to a position of prominence in St. Louis. In *The Book of St. Louisans,* he was listed as vice president of both the National Candy Company of St. Louis and the Price Cereal Food Company of Chicago, as well as Chairman of the Executive Committee of the National Confectioners Association of the United States. A dedicated Republican, he was also a member of the Noonday, Racquet, Bellerive, City, Aero, and Automobile Clubs. A leader within his own industry, he also made significant contributions to his hometown. He was president of the St. Louis Advertising Club, Salesmanship Club, and YMCA, and vice president and director of the Chamber of Commerce. Furthermore, he was extremely active in the Episcopalian Church, serving as a warden and vestryman at St. Peter's for twenty-five years and as the treasurer of the Episcopal Diocese of Missouri for six years.

Following the profitable showing of the National Candy Company at the 1904 World's Fair, the growth of Price's business had been strong and steady. His family life had followed suit. In April 1904, Marguerite had given birth to their third child, Laralouise, called Lollie, in their comfortable home at 3748 Washington Avenue, in a well-heeled residential area near the large Forest Park. For the next seven years the Price children were raised and educated in a prosperous upper-middle-class household, even as the parents worked their way up the St. Louis social ladder. Thus, it came as something of a surprise to the family when thirty-six-year-old Marguerite announced that she was pregnant and, in May 1911, gave birth to their fourth child. Named after his father, the newborn was honored a month later at the annual convention of the National Confectioners Association, who pronounced Vincent Jr. the Candy Kid and presented his proud father with a small gold charm engraved to that effect. A year later, to accommodate their growing family, the Prices moved up the street to a massive three-story brick house at 5227 Washington Avenue.

The four Price children were all given nicknames, and Vincent Jr. was soon called Bink. Seven years younger than his closest sibling, Bink fell into the role of baby of the family, which allowed him to exercise his early penchant for drama and individualism. But because he came to regard his birth as an accident, an additional responsibility that hampered his mother's increasingly active social life, young Vincent sometimes felt unloved, yearning desperately—and, he thought, hopelessly—for Marguerite's love and approval. A few years before his death, he began a short essay entitled "Mother": "When

I think of her, if I think of her, it's mostly with regret that I knew her so little, so briefly. I was, as she joked, the child of her 'old age.' She was in her late thirties when I 'came along.' I never really thought I was born, she was so fond of saying 'came along.' Come to think of it, it sounds a little unwelcoming, as though I was a stranger at a late supper after a show. I dropped in, and her manners being polished enough, she said, 'Hello. Sit down. Have something to eat.' "

In *I Like What I Know*, Vincent had painted a different picture: "Good women can be dull, but she wasn't. She was fun for her children and fortunate for her husband. She had enough stamina for an Atlantic crossing, under her own steam, and she never let us get away with anything." The contrast between these descriptions typified Vincent's conflicted perspective: Only while writing for himself would he indulge in the expression of his deepest fears and insecurities. For the public, he put on the best possible face. Somewhere between the sometimes maudlin private self and the always positive public self lay the truth.

According to everyone who had met her, Vincent's mother was indeed a force to be reckoned with. But members of the Price family, many of whom themselves suffered under Marguerite's iron hand, maintain that Bink was, contrary to his private fears, the apple of his mother's eye. Though he always worried about pleasing her, his siblings recalled that Bink was allowed far more license than any of them. His niece, Sara Santschi, recalls her Uncle Bink's visits to St. Louis when he was in his twenties. "He would tell jokes and playact and my grandmother adored it; she would laugh so hard she could hardly stand it. And she would look at him as if she was in love with him. It was as if he was living out the life that she never got to have, because she was very much a drama queen. A real one. Smoked like a man, had her two stiff drinks every night. She was a character. I think only a saint like my grandfather could possibly have lived with her."

Indeed, by all accounts, Vincent Sr. was a man of compassion, intelligence, and great generosity. He is remembered as a kind and loving father and grandfather, who faithfully recorded family events in photographs, essays, poems, and even in early home movies. It is also clear that he was a loving and dutiful husband. In the countless photographs documenting their family life, whenever husband and wife are pictured together, the warmth and love between them is more than apparent. In one family photograph taken on the lawn of their summer home in Amherstburg, Ontario, overlooking the Detroit River, a smiling, blond, nine-year-old Bink sits cross-legged on the ground next to his thirteen-year-old sister, Lollie. On a wooden bench behind them sit his favorite grandmother, Granny Oliver, and his mother and father. Vincent Sr. smiles back at the camera, an unmistakably happy man surrounded by his family. Next to him, the often dour Marguerite also smiles for the camera, her arm around her husband's back, leaning against his shoulder. Behind her, her handsome eldest son, twenty-one-year-old Mort, and her twenty-three-year-old daughter Hat complete the family picture. Although all are dressed in their Sunday best, the men in three-piece suits, the women in long skirts, the photograph is neither stiff nor formal. They appear a truly happy family.

Bink's siblings adored their younger brother, but, in the case of Mort and Hat, it was largely from a distance. Hat was fourteen when Vincent was born, and by the time he was seven she had married Harold Reed Wilson; she gave birth to her own first child when Bink was only eight. Mort, who was twelve when his little brother was born, was a stronger presence for a while, until he left home for boarding school back East and then proceeded to Yale. It was Lollie to whom Bink felt the closest. On the occasion of her death in 1983, he wrote her daughter, Bobbie, "Lollie and I were, as you know, particularly close. She was my 'Little Mother' when I was growing up and my dear friend when I did."

From an early age, however, Bink seemed aware that he was somehow different than his siblings. In the first place, he looked different. While his brothers and sisters inherited their parents' dark good looks, Bink was very fair—towheaded, with hazel eyes that became lighter and lighter blue as he grew up. Furthermore, he was a very tall boy—by his teens taller than both his father and brother. But his looks were the least of it. Early on, it became apparent that the youngest Price was not quite like anyone else in the family. Marguerite encouraged all her children in the appreciation of music, paying for piano and singing lessons and taking them to the opera. Hat and Mort showed much talent and promise, and even Lollie loved to sing and play piano. Her youngest son, however, seemed to have little musical aptitude. As he later wrote, "At first I felt a little left out. I had a good baritone and could join in the music louder than everyone. But my musical instinct was more for caricature. I might have been a good singer if I hadn't always felt that the orchestra or the accompanist was bound to win." To a demanding woman like Marguerite, this would have likely been extremely troublesome—if it weren't for the fact that, from an early age, Bink displayed another interest. "As always in families," he recalled, "the one who feels left out—even if it isn't a fact—turns to his own devices, passionately. And passionately, I wanted to see."

Having stumbled across an art book left behind when his sister Hat had left home, Bink had begun to study its reproductions of great paintings with all the enthusiasm the others showed for music. "The reproductions were so small they could be used for postage, but I dug in with my youthful twenty-twenty until no fold or feature was unfamiliar. And there I found the world I knew I wanted to live in for the rest of my life—the world of man's creation—art." Realizing that art compelled him as did nothing else, he began to frequent the City Art Museum, already a fine local institution. Looking back on the beginnings of his passion for art, he reflected, "I think the first visual thing I was aware of was the beauty of the mother of Barbara O'Neil, who was a classmate of mine at the Community School until she was about eight years old. Her mother posed for one of the posters of the Red Cross nurses in World War I. She was a very *zaftig* lady, but extraordinarily beautiful, as Barbara was, too. And then I saw a reproduction of a painting by Andrea del Sarto, *Madonna of the Harpies*, and it did to me exactly what Barbara's mother had done to me."

Along with the treasures he discovered in books and in the City Art Museum, Bink found his own treasures just across the river from St. Louis, on day trips to the Cahokia Mounds. He later recalled, "My best friend was a boy named Freddie Roth. We went everywhere together because we were both crazy about American Indian stuff. We picked up arrowheads in fields, because St. Louis had been a great Indian meeting ground. Then, one summer, my mother and dad, who were then at the peak of their social existence and whose other kids were grown up or in college, sent me to a boys' camp in Colorado, and I had a miserable time because I hated horses and I had to ride every day and everywhere. But we were also allowed to go off on our own on these nags, and that was exhilarating. Quite by accident, I discovered a piece of pottery sticking up out of the soil, so I began digging with my hand and an old piece of wood, and I discovered a skull. And it turned out to be a burial ground of the Anasazi Indians who had lived at Mesa Verde. It was quite an important burial ground because it was a tribe of Indians who flattened their skulls with boards when they were babies. It was opened up later by archaeologists. Later there was a picture in the hometown paper of me, aged eleven years old, with this skull and a pot. And of course that did it—I was now Schliemann, the world's greatest archaeologist! . . . When you suddenly have that kind of interest when you're young, that kind of adventure, it's terribly exciting and it shapes your life. When my mother finally gave me an attic room to myself, I filled it with collections of everything." Although his parents were undoubtedly proud when their son's picture appeared in the *St. Louis Post-Dispatch*, it wasn't until a year later, when precocious twelve-year-old Bink came home one day and announced that he had purchased a first-state Rembrandt etching, that Vincent and Marguerite Price began to grasp the depth of their youngest child's passion for art.

There was only one art dealer in St. Louis during the early 1900s, a local man who paid his rent by selling popular nineteenth-century French prints and drawings. Occasionally, however, the dealer would risk offering an exhibition of fine engravings by masters such as Rembrandt or Dürer or contemporary artists such as Whistler. As Vincent recalled, "It was at one of these daring exhibitions that I fell financially in love with a work of art for the first time. *Two Nude Models, One Standing* by Rembrandt Harmensz van Rijn (1606–69)—price $37.50. First state from the A. Artaria collection." With five dollars down, it took the youthful aficionado a whole year of saving from his allowance, his paid summer jobs, and running errands, to earn the money and actually take possession of the etching. The subsequent pride of ownership he felt set an instant goal for the rest of his life. "My first privately-owned work of art, and by Rembrandt . . . *the* Rembrandt! Oh, joy; oh, rapture unforeseen, but now seen with the most loving pair of eyes ever to look upon a picture, I think." By age thirteen, Vincent Leonard Price Jr. was determined, among other things, to be a great art collector.

Vincent remained extremely close to his parents until their deaths, and always professed a great debt of gratitude for their support. His father was particularly encouraging toward his son, thwarted as he had been in his own artistic aspirations when he was called home from Yale decades before. Although he knew very little about the art that so ardently interested Bink, he was able to see right away that his boy had a passion and vision that needed nourishing. Marguerite must have also realized that her youngest child was somehow different. To her credit, she did her best to foster his artistic endeavors by taking him to the local museum and by introducing him to the St. Louis artistic set.

As Vincent later recalled, "There were two or three families up the street who were 'artistic.' They had connections with poets, painters, writers, musicians; and though they were not shunned by the straight social set, they posed a problem for my mother and her friends at dinner parties. It was her way of admitting that her other friends were a little 'square' by wondering whom to seat next to the artistic ones. But at those times Mother could usually solve it brilliantly by asking the bishop, who was a 'known' liberal and an extremely delightful conversationalist on any subject. Secretly, she approved of this fast-thinking set, for they were renegade Catholics. I loved these families, their way of life, and one of their daughters, Barbara O'Neil, whom I was engaged to off and on from the age of eight to thirty-eight. They were something out of another world. They used money as though it was meant to spend, not to sustain. They were frivolous. My little fiancée didn't dress like the other progressive children. She put a color or two into her middy-blouse wardrobe—a bow, a sash—to assure me, especially, that she was not only progressive but different. . . . Mother was delighted, if a little wary, that I had been 'exposed' to such interesting people. It was not so much the artistic qualities of these people that fascinated me, or that their lives were happier than ours—I seriously doubt they were. It was more their aura of excitement. I felt that they were taking some kind of chance with life—a chance to be different—to see differently and to think differently."

It was during these years that Vincent began to perceive a divergence between his evolving taste and that of his family. "As a family we had come to have *polite* vision. Our home and its decor, odd as it seems to me now, was indeed very politely correct. Our pictures were politely dull and our music was politely prosaic. . . . Mother and Father both disliked change. They worked hard to have their home the way she wanted it, and Father wanted it the way she made it. Home was their religion. If I poke fingers into the minor aspects of it that offended me, it's because I didn't want to get trapped in any one way of living—especially of *seeing*. They went along with my inquisitiveness, inch by inch, but their encouragement of, and interest in, my different approach to everything only spoke volumes of wishes . . . that I would one day become a standard American man and meanwhile, during that young moment, that I'd stop looking at new art and start practicing our old piano."

As the Prices' social position in St. Louis improved, Marguerite's dream was to build a home that would reflect their taste and status. Bink spent his early teenage years monitoring this daunting project with increasing humor and horror. He would later recall the new Price mansion: "Our home—that is, the one they were finally able to build after all the children, except myself, were educated and 'on their own'—was semi-pretentious. As our circumstances improved we moved farther out of town. Indeed, we helped start the ghastly rush into suburbia. Our final family home was on a lot carefully selected for its address, its view, and its trees—four pin oaks, sturdy, shaggy, and shady. The lot Mother chose was across from the university—not because of any hope that the view would rub off on us and we would slip across the street to higher education, but because the administration building was a squat elongation of Windsor Castle, and my mother's stepfather had been a British army officer. To her that made sense, just as the incorporation of a dozen or so broad *A*s into her much-better-than-average American enunciation made her: one, traveled; two, interestingly related; and three, slightly more cultured than some of her friends. . . . And when, two years after we moved in, the university saw fit to interrupt our view of Windsor Castle with an equally pseudo-Roman copy of a dubious Greek building for the Architecture School, Mother's pen emitted a six-month scream of protest to the president of the university, the architect, and finally to the mayor."

A further problem arose when Marguerite realized that the post office had had the unthinkable gall to mundanely name the new thoroughfare on which their lovely new lot was situated Forsyth Street. Located in the newest and most desirable district of town, Marguerite relished the air of culture lent by the university and her artistic neighbors. So she took it upon herself to quickly and permanently change their address to Forsyth Road, an appellation which, she believed, gave an air of "country," and she promptly sealed her decision by having several thousand sheets of stationery embossed in Yale blue to read Forsyth Road.

There remained only the question of architectural style. As my father recalled, "The house was to be American, no question about that. The architects, a pair of nice young American men, were very much in vogue, naturally, since my parents had waited all these years and were going to have the best. For Mother, there was always an excuse to have the best—and the best she always had. These two young men, I'm sure, matured rapidly as men and as architects after their endless losing rounds with Mother. Because she generously took into consideration my father's ten generations and our, so far, distinguished and unsullied Yale background, the facade was to be New England. Pure, authentic, classic New England. The two maturing architects were happy in this exterior triumph, but, unluckily for them, they wanted to carry it on inside. Here they met and fell before the whole eight generations of my mother's French-Dutch-English and American forebears, led by my great-great-grandmother, the sea captain's muted peacock wife."

Taking matters into her own hands, Marguerite transformed the interior into a faux-Oriental fantasyland that left the architects—and her son—appalled. "Mother and her decorator had created a sunroom that did have sun, thanks to the architects, but now was closer to a set for *The Shanghai Gesture* than anything else. The walls were green, a subtle split-pea green shot with gold. Real gold leaf tipped every bump of the plaster. The curtains were striped black and orange, reminding my father, not happily, of Princeton. The furniture was America's first attempt at Chinese Modern. It couldn't have been less Chinese or less modern. It was wood made to look like bamboo and richly enameled black, with every bamboo-like rung again gold. Tied on this frame of nondescript shape were lethal cushions of the same striped material as the curtains. Since house plants were the triumph of housewives in Missouri, Iowa, and, in fact, all of America, the room was alive with greenery. Leaf green fights with only one other green, and that green Mother had achieved on the walls—shot with gold. A bamboo (real, this time) cage sported the two angriest lovebirds in captivity. Quaint paintings of Chinese ladies in very tailored dresses by the Chinese branch of Peck & Peck were on the walls in black Chinese frames. And there was a brass bracket in the curly design of a dragon that held from his mouth a chain, at the end of which was a glass ball with that classic house plant, the philodendron. The rug was again imitation Chinese. It looked like a misshapen tweed coat, stretched out to accommodate the size of the floor. Two rubber pads finally had to be put under it to keep it from accompanying the family and guests as they left the room—or shooting them high into the air, to be blacked out on the terrazzo floor below." When her showpiece was completed, Marguerite invited the home's architects over to see what she had done with their New England–style home. "I think the architects never came back," my father recalled.

Clearly, her youngest son was dumbfounded by Marguerite's taste in decor. But what really concerned young Vincent was his family's collection of "art," comprised of a few family heirlooms, including "The Pirates" and what Vincent humorously referred to as their "masterpiece"—"an etching of three of the saddest cows ever seen, grazing in abject postures in a sepia valley which, to me, was always associated with the twenty-third Psalm—'Yea, though I walk through . . .'." He quickly came to realize, "As for the whole visual arts, the whole family was blind. They not only didn't know *how* to see, they didn't particularly want to. So my fight to learn to *see* was difficult, indeed. They were too nice to scoff at it, so their attitude was kind of, 'look and be damned.'" With only his mother's sorry melange of Shanghai flair and bathetic pastoral art to entertain his eye, Vincent must soon have realized that his future as an art connoisseur would inevitably lead him far from home.

And yet young Vincent Price was hardly an artistic outcast in Middle America. On the contrary, in many ways he was an all-American boy. Photographs show a good-looking young man with a big grin and a perpetual gleam in his eye. Early on, he evinced an easy gift for friendship and good fun, forming childhood clubs and theater groups to entertain the neighborhood. In retrospect, few of his childhood and schoolboy friends were surprised when he became an actor. For, in addition to his passion for art, Bink had early demonstrated a flair for drama.

Vincent's first theatrical venture occurred in 1914, when he was just three. St. Mary's School for Girls, which Lollie attended, was putting on an amateur theatrical written by one of Lollie's classmates, Grace Layman. Because his sister was in the play, Bink was given a part, as Layman later wrote, "for purely practical reasons only—we needed a curly-haired blond boy or girl slightly past infant stage." Bink never attended rehearsals since they interfered with his nap time, so the rest of the cast were, as Layman remembers, "nervous about our Water Sprite, completely lacking faith in his ability to carry off his role with no practice, although his sole actions were to sit or run about the stage." The big day came and Grace Layman, playing the Queen, came onstage holding Bink's hand. She would later describe the event in a letter to Vincent: "You were a dream and, to quote your mother as to your costume, 'a small sheer piece of pale green chiffon with Binkie inside.' I let go of your hand—my first horrible mistake—and beamed patronizingly down at you from my great height as the *star*. My and the rest of the cast's goose was cooked right then. We were all so tragically naive we never knew what was going on—thinking the marvelous applause was for each of us alone. *You effectively, without premeditation, completely, absolutely, and wholly stole the show.* Your enchanting antics and ad libbing brought down the house in spite of frequent shushes from the cast plus silent gestures that you *please* confine yourself to your lowly role."

The die was cast and, throughout childhood, Bink remained on the lookout for opportunities to exercise his interest in dramatics. One of his early playmates, Henry McIntyre, lived across the street and two doors east. He recalled, "Vinnie and I frequently put on 'plays' for our families. We charged two pins for admittance, although I cannot recall why we wanted the pins. We alternated between the living rooms at his house and mine, hanging a sheet to function as a theater curtain. All of the 'plays' were written, directed, and acted by the two of us."

Vincent's interest in drama naturally led him to seize every chance to go to the theater, the opera, or the cinema. He was a great movie buff from an early age. One of the first films he saw was the German silent *Der Golem*, a horror film about a stone statue that comes to life and goes on a murderous rampage. He loved the film, although he later confessed he was so terrified that "I wet my pants." Vincent subscribed to fan magazines and was an ardent admirer of many a glamorous movie star. He recalled, "The dream face of my extreme youth, my boyhood, was the dancer-actress Irene Castle's. She also made me aware that women wore something other than just clothes. In one of her serials, *Patrice*, she wore black stockings with white buttons up the back seam. My mother didn't, and my sisters couldn't be persuaded to copy her and, even if they had, sisters have a long way to go to be seductive to little brothers. But Irene Castle had that soft knowingness about her face; when she looked at me from the screen I knew she knew my secrets, most of which at that time were secrets even from me."

Among his other favorite actresses from motion picture serials were Marguerite Clarke, Ina Claire, Colleen Moore, Patsy Ruth Miller, and the Queen of Serials Pearl White. Even into adulthood he carried a small torch for his early idols, and hoped that he might chance upon one of them in the streets of the various cities to which they had gone after leaving Hollywood. These women were the sirens that first tempted Vincent Price into the world of acting, when they were "athrone that wonderful, truly make-believe, glamorous world I fell in love with and later became a part of long enough to see its glamour fade."

Like most boys of the early twentieth century, Vincent also kept up with the many new technological wonders, although he never did quite grasp how any of them ever worked. He later wrote, "The first radio set I ever had was wires wound round an oatmeal box. And then you had what was called a crystal set; you scraped this thing on it and somehow it worked. One day we got Chicago on it and I just about fainted. It sounded like Chicago was practically next door."

One of St. Louis's early claims to fame was its pioneering interest in the growing field of aviation. The city's Aeronautics Club (to which Vincent Sr. belonged) was among the first in the country. Many of the city's more successful businessmen took more than a passing interest in supporting the pilots and the development of aeronautical engineering. St. Louis attracted many air shows featuring the country's newest planes and best fliers. Most St. Louis boys knew a great deal about these planes and counted among their youthful heroes the most daring pilots, especially during and after World War I. Vincent was no exception. Like every St. Louis boy, he followed his city's sponsorship of a dashing young man named Charles Lindbergh, who hoped to be the first person to fly across the Atlantic. Huddled around the radio, Vincent and his friends listened as Lindbergh landed his plane, *The Spirit of St. Louis*, outside Paris, before joining the crowds who were celebrating their city's (and the nation's) great hero.

The Roaring Twenties was a decade of heroes. It was a boom time in America, when businesses prospered, cities grew, and work hours decreased. Americans not only had more leisure time on their hands, they also had more money to spend on recreation. By 1929, Americans were spending $4.9 billion annually on leisure activities, from listening to the radio and going to the movies to Sunday driving in the family automobile. Major sports were also attracting Americans—baseball, football, boxing, golf, and tennis—and St. Louis was the home of two Major League baseball teams, the National League's Cardinals and the American League's Browns. The Browns and the Cardinals played at the same field, Sportsman's Park, making it relatively easy for St. Louis fans to divide their energies between teams. Most enjoyed rooting for the Browns, even though (with the exception of the 1922 season when they finished one heartbreaking game behind the Yankees) they really never had much of a team. On the other hand, by the mid-1920s, the Cardinals—the Cards to their fans—had become one of baseball's powerhouse teams under the leadership of Branch Rickey, a man who came to be regarded as one of the sport's great geniuses. Rickey singlehandedly made a contender out of the lowly Cards by reviving the farm system and utilizing the minor leagues to develop young players. Rickey's club generally had a steady flow of star players, including the great Rogers Hornsby, who almost rivaled Babe Ruth as an object of hero worship, and certainly was the idol of many a St. Louis youth. In 1926 the Cardinals rose at last from baseball's basement, winning their first National League pennant and then crushing the Yankees in the World Series. For the next five years St. Louis had itself a team, and Vincent Price, like so many of his fellow St. Louisans, became a lifelong baseball fanatic. In 1944, many years after Vincent had left his hometown, the inevitable happened—the Browns won the American League pennant and the Cards the National League. Even from Hollywood Vincent followed his hometown teams with joy, rooting for the underdog Browns but rejoicing all the same when the Cards, led by Stan Musial, won. When he finally met Musial years later, the actor would crow, "I lunched with the great Stan 'The Man' Musial and had a flush of pride when he gave me an autographed baseball! I felt I'd really arrived!"

Thus, although the young Vincent Price fancied himself something of an aesthete, his interests were hardly confined to intellectual pursuits. Remembering his youthful journeys later, he said, "There were many joys which remained constant—the art museum, my earliest haunt; the zoo, one of the best; the municipal opera, the famous outdoor musical theater where many great stars got their start and which made all of us in St. Louis very knowledgeable musically about that great American art form, musical comedy. I loved being a part of this. Sports were always a major attraction in St. Louis and the ballparks became grander as the city's pride in its players grew. One can always say about St. Louis, it never stops trying."

3

THE SUCCESSFUL CAREER of Vincent's grandfather, Dr. Vincent Clarence Price, had proved—to others, but most importantly to himself—that in America, education was the great leveler, and he made sure to afford all five of his children the same opportunities he himself had had. His youngest son, Vincent Leonard Sr., also sought to impress upon his own children the importance of education. In this endeavor, he fortunately had a strong ally in his wife. As she was Marguerite and Vincent's first child, and a girl to boot, Hat's education received the least attention; like many upper-middle-class women of the time, she was encouraged as much to secure a good husband as to become a worthy member of society, and when she married a Yale man in 1919 she was deemed a great success. Mort, however, was groomed from the start to follow in his father's footsteps. He attended local public schools before being sent away to complete his preparation for his obligatory turn at Yale's Sheffield Scientific School. Lollie was able to attend the prestigious Mary Institute, though, like Hat, she was not expected to attend college, but rather to marry well. By the time Bink came along, though, the picture had changed; some more progressive notions about education, developed on the East Coast, had found their way to St. Louis—and into the purview of Marguerite Willcox Price.

Although Marguerite ruled her children's lives with discipline, she was also a woman of vision, and one who believed passionately in the importance of education and the arts. Like many of her friends, by 1914 she had become dissatisfied with the St. Louis public school system; that year, along with a number of other society ladies, she helped to found the Community School, dedicated to giving well-to-do St. Louis children a progressive education. The new school was built on an attractive lot on DeMun Avenue, chosen, as a 1920 brochure proudly proclaimed, "On account of the need of young children for sunlight, quiet, and fresh air. The school is equipped with large, airy rooms and full-length windows. In the center of the building is the large assembly hall, splendidly lighted and ventilated, with its stage, which makes possible school dramatics, group games, chorus singing, and gatherings of all kinds. Nearby woods give endless opportunities of nature study." The stated goal of the school was "to achieve for each pupil: abounding health, a highly developed sense of discrimination concerning social and moral values, a keen enjoyment of intellectual activity, and a disposition to be constructively active in promoting the best interest of any group with which he may become associated."

Vincent Price attended the Community School for seven years; that in itself made the youngest Price's education different from that of his siblings. Students there were allowed to read whatever books they wished, to listen to music, and to pursue other interests and hobbies as they developed—although movies were considered an undesirable form of entertainment. Playacting, however, was encouraged, and Vincent appeared in a number of school plays, including *Robin Hood* and *The Pied Piper of Hamlin*, in both of which he played the lead. He found one of the chief attractions of the school to be the presence of his beautiful classmate and school play co-star, Barbara O'Neil, but also found a fellow creative spirit in future author William S. Burroughs, with whom he would later carry on a correspondence.

In an open letter to the Community School written in the 1980s, Vincent recalled his years there, particularly his art classes with one Miss Stout, who gave her students a "chance to express yourself" and from whom he learned "creative freedom." He also noted that he "learned the importance of art, poetry, playacting at the Community School and not again until late in my college career," and fondly remembered the school's "very inventive wartime meals, especially peanut butter soup."

Vincent and Barbara graduated in the Class of 1922, but shortly afterward the O'Neils moved away, first to Paris, later to Connecticut. The young friends would not meet again for another eight years, for, unlike his brother who had been sent away to Eastern schools, Vincent would remain in St. Louis.

He would matriculate at the new St. Louis Country Day School, founded in 1917 by wealthy St. Louis fathers concerned about the local availability of quality education for their sons. Located on a large campus fifty minutes north of the city, St. Louis Country Day had attracted some of the nation's top educators, many of whom had taken undergraduate and graduate degrees from such institutions as Harvard, Yale, Williams, Amherst, Brown, and Columbia. In its first five years, the school had developed a topnotch reputation for both academic and athletic excellence. Boys from the "best" St. Louis families could now receive a well-rounded education, aimed at entry into the country's top colleges. In 1922, Country Day sent its first class of graduating seniors off to attend Harvard, Princeton, and Amherst; when Vincent Leonard Price Jr. graduated from the Community School that same year, his father felt complete confidence in sending his son to Country Day to prepare for college. A year later, Vincent Sr. would be invited to join the school's Board of Trustees.

Vincent Jr. entered Country Day in Class VI, or seventh grade. A number of the boys in his class had already been at the school for two years, but Vincent knew a few of his new schoolmates from his neighborhood and, in any event, he had an easy ability to make friends. His father's status as the primary candy maker in the area only helped his son's popularity. Once a year, Vincent Sr. would treat his children, their friends, and later his grandchildren, to a tour of the factory, during which, as Lollie's daughter Bobbie Gay recalled, "We would dive into large wooden barrels of maraschino cherries and eat ourselves silly. Then we would consume our fill of other candies, after which we would go home and vomit."

Though Vincent received a rigorous education, he was not regarded as a particularly serious student; his interests and talents clearly lay outside the classroom. In June of 1926, following his sophomore year at Country Day, his parents received a letter from Headmaster Robert Thompson informing them that their son's marks in English, History, French, and Latin were unsatisfactory. In fact, his only passing grade was in Mathematics, for which he had been marked "fair." In a class of twenty-nine students, Vincent Leonard Price Jr. ranked twenty-seventh. Due to this poor showing, the Prices were informed that their son would be required to repeat his sophomore year. Even in later years, Vincent would remember the devastation and shame he felt when told that he would not be allowed to continue on with his class. And if that weren't enough, the disappointment felt by his parents, who hoped that their youngest son would follow in the family tradition by attending Yale, made the next year of his life one of his worst. He watched his former classmates become juniors while he had to join a new group of boys and repeat a full year of classes under his parents' watchful eyes.

As his teachers had suspected, his poor grades had more to do with attitude rather than aptitude, and the humiliation of being left back did the trick. His marks quickly improved; by midyear he had raised his class ranking to thirteenth in a class of thirty-seven, receiving fair to good marks in English, Mathematics, and French as well as an "excellent" in History. Only in Latin did he remain unsatisfactory, and he was able to raise that to a "fair" by the following June. His attendance and tardiness levels also improved, and in June 1927 Headmaster Thompson was able to report, "Vincent has done pretty well this year and it did not seem necessary to impose a condition in regard to his Latin. He has an opportunity to clear the matter up by passing the Board examination, and in any case, I do not think it is necessary to count this failure against him. We feel that Vincent is a good citizen and is going to be a credit to the school."

Vincent was well built and taller than most of his classmates, who teasingly referred to him as the "Big Barbarian." His mother's cooking and the regular supply of candy had made him a big, strong boy, as he would later recall: "Recipes gleaned from all over the world from friends and relatives made meals a joy. Distorted as her sense of home decoration was, just as straightforward were her menus—brilliant for parties, healthy and toothsome for family fare. Since I was well on my way to a gigantic six-foot-four, the food side of my cultural background was most appreciated, and I have never regretted my knowledge of how to eat well. And eat well I did. Mother saw to it that each molecule, fiber, tissue, and gland was nourished." However, Gordon Browne, the head of the Country Day middle school, apparently felt that Vincent's height—by his senior year he was the tallest boy in the school—was more of a handicap than an asset, which may well account for his notoriously bad posture. Although his bearing on stage and in film or television would always be proud and erect, he habitually slouched whenever he was offstage. Vincent had always been taller than other children in his class; even in grade school he had to kneel in school photographs, and in high school photos, whenever he is pictured alongside another boy, Vincent slumps or leans. His height was a mixed blessing; although he frequently felt ungainly, his stature also gave him a certain distinction of which he was well aware, and which he would later use to advantage as an actor.

Vincent's years at Country Day happily coincided with a great interest in dramatics at the school. The Troubadours, a musical theater group, was founded in 1926, followed in 1928 by The Masque, a group for straight dramatics. Interestingly, he chose to join the Troubadours whose musicals were directed by Robert Reeve, a Ph.B. from the University of Chicago and Director of Music at Country Day since 1920. During his junior year, Vincent was given a starring role in their production of *All at Sea*. As classmate Franklin Ferriss recalled, "Because of Vinnie's fine acting and good singing, Robert Reeve chose him for major roles in the club's annual musical productions in both Vinnie's junior and senior years. I myself was just in the chorus those years, but I attended the rehearsals and can vouch that Vinnie worked hard to cooperate with Mr. Reeve's directions, which was not always easy to do." Vincent himself credited Reeve with having taught him "the divinity of music."

Country Day was also noted for its athletics; though it was a small school, it usually fielded winning teams. Vincent's chief athletic interests were track and soccer, although soccer teammate Daniel Schlafly recalled, "Neither one of us was very good. Vinnie ran something like a loping camel." Vincent was undoubtedly drawn to the track team because the coach was Eugene Hecker, the English teacher and a great favorite of all the boys. A graduate of Harvard, Hecker had taught at prep schools in the Boston area and fought in the army in the Great War before coming to Country Day in 1919. All the boys admired and respected Hecker, one of those rare teachers whose influence was remembered long after graduation. His great love was Shakespeare and he instilled that same passion in his students—including Vincent, whose lifelong love of the Bard was fostered at Country Day. He would later say that it was Eugene Hecker from whom he "learned respect of language."

Many of Vincent's closest friends were athletes, fellow members of the Troubadours, and boys who generally liked to have a good time. Among his classmates he was known as a good sport, a boy with a bawdy sense of humor. Franklin Ferriss remembered that "Vinnie was not generally considered a particularly serious student, but he was bright and made sure he did not flunk any of his courses. He was a pleasant, warmhearted, humorous classmate who loved to have good times with his friends. He liked to share bawdy jokes and his many sexy sketches of girls." More than anything, Vincent enjoyed a good time and was something of a prankster.

As a student at elite Country Day and the son of one of St. Louis's leaders of industry, Vincent was included in all of the city's finest social events. One of the most popular during his high school years was the Fortnightly Dance Club run by a Mr. and Mrs. Mahler. Founded in 1883, the club had taught generations of St. Louis boys and girls social deportment as well as the most popular dances of the day. The Mahlers often presented their students in small but dignified revues, in which both Lollie and Bink participated from a very young age. Vincent always enjoyed the dances, particularly the costume balls—Adelaide Schlafly remembered one event where he showed up as Dracula, playing the part with great gusto.

Boys and girls from the West End of St. Louis, where the Prices lived, often socialized together. Many attended churches, such as the Prices' parish, St. Peter's Episcopal, from which a number of popular social activities stemmed. With the lovely Forest Park nearby, spring and summertime brought picnics in the park, where Vincent recalled picking violets with his girlfriends. A popular winter pastime was skating at the beautiful Winter Garden, just a short walk away, but the highlight of the year was the Veiled Prophet Parade and Ball. Started in the mid-nineteenth century as an annual charity fundraiser, the Veiled Prophet became *the* event for St. Louis society. Each fall, a distinguished member of St. Louis society was chosen to play the robed and masked prophet and a weekend of festivities ensued. Vincent was particularly fond of the event because each year produced a new series of Veiled Prophet memorabilia—ashtrays, matches, and other souvenirs—all marked V.P. and the year. For Vincent Price, these became highly collectable.

Naturally, there were also less highfalutin pursuits available to teenage boys in St. Louis during the Roaring Twenties. Chief among these was visiting the burlesque houses. As Vincent later recalled, "In a town which got dramatic road shows, we boasted first run in burlesque. We had the famous Beef First Beauties, Carrie Finnell of the Tutored Tassels, and several strippers who taught us everything we knew. I remember one especially, Ann Corio—gleaming raven hair and even features set off a body that wouldn't stop, not that anyone wanted it to. What she started her strip in is of little matter; what mattered was the finished product and the chorus of screams, Takeitofftakeitalloff!" As his second wife, Mary Grant Price, would recall, even twenty years later "Vincent had that naughty-boy humor and was prone to scream 'Take it off' at the most inopportune moments! You really had to like him a lot to find it funny." He and his friends loved burlesque and Vincent was nicknamed "Carrie" by his classmates because of his infatuation with the aforementioned Carrie Finnell, she of the tutored tassels. "I used to worship Carrie," he remembered. "She was truly a great artist." In addition to the burlesque performers, the boys also expended considerable effort trying to get into the good graces of the chorus girls who passed through town from time to time. Vincent ruefully remembered "one chorus girl I tried to date but didn't get to first base with, named Ginger Rogers."

4

THE PRICES LOVED to travel, a habit they passed on to all their children, and particularly their youngest son. Marguerite and Vincent Sr. had been to Europe, and as their children grew older, whenever they could the couple took shorter trips to interesting cities such as New Orleans, Chicago, or New York, returning with "artistic" souvenirs for their new home. Occasionally, the two Vincents would go off together, making special father-and-son pilgrimages to New York or Chicago. The family also spent part of each summer at their home in Amherstburg, Ontario—a lovely two-story clapboard house on the banks of the Detroit River, where Bink in particular enjoyed swimming, and playing with cousins and friends.

Throughout his teenage years, Vincent had nurtured a consuming desire to go to Europe and see firsthand the works of art he had only been able to study in reproduction. During his junior year at Country Day he sent away to a travel company that offered trips to Europe and spent months perusing the twenty-four tours the brochure promoted. He finally decided on Tour 22, "Seven Capitals of Europe": "Whoever wrote the propaganda for Tour 22 had written it just for me. The sights which would be covered were my dreams come true. Where other tours included famous battlefields and natural phenomena, like rocks which look like ladies fast asleep, Tour 22 was heavy on the churches and museums, with just enough enticing treats to mysteries like the Catacombs outside Rome and castles like Chillon."

He pestered his parents, saved his own money and, most important, enlisted the support of his beloved Granny Oliver. Vincent had grown "delightfully and enrichingly close" with his maternal grandmother as she began living on and off with the Prices in her later years. Granny Oliver had traveled widely during a time when Europe was still accessible on a limited income, and as Vincent's dreams drifted toward the Continent, he found they shared "a rapport regarding the countries across the sea; a little lopsided to be sure, since it was comprised of endless queries from me and patiently understanding answers from her. I bent her ear for a description of every inch she'd covered, and she pictorially replied, in knowing prose. She told me tales of Mexico, of Spain, of Greece, and Egypt—whetting my appetite all the more. But I *had* to see for myself!"

Harriet Cobb Oliver recognized her youngest grandson as a kindred spirit who shared her great curiosity about the world, and encouraged his parents to allow him to travel. At the end of each summer during Bink's teens, he took the train to visit Harriet near San Diego, California, where he developed what would become two more lifelong passions—deep-sea fishing and swimming in the ocean. Since childhood, Bink found in Granny Oliver the maternal affection that had always been hard to come by from his mother. The boy unreservedly adored his grandmother, and learned from her one of his most important lessons. As the baby of the family, one of his chief means of getting his way had always been to display his prodigious temper. One day, after he had thrown a particularly awful tantrum during one of Harriet Oliver's visits, she calmly told him that if he continued to do so he would never see her again. He later told his wife Mary that the fear of losing this beloved woman was so terrifying that "I learned to control my temper."

Harriet Oliver now became the greatest champion of Vincent's European dream. Despite any protests his mother might have lodged about her "baby" going alone to Europe, "With Grandmother pitching on my behalf, whatever objections Mother might have had dissipated, for their relationship was one of deep devotion and mutual respect." Once he received his parents' permission, all that was left was to save enough money for the trip. As he had done after spotting the Rembrandt, Vincent scrimped and saved, but came nowhere close to the amount he needed until his father came to the rescue. (It was, incidentally, around this time that Vincent Sr. sold the summer home at Amherstburg and decided to contribute additional funds to his son.) Vincent wrote, "He understood my need to fulfill my curiosity and made it possible for me to go to Europe. His generosity was so subtle that he made me feel that I'd earned the right to go, as well as most of the money, by teaching me to save."

In early July 1928, a few weeks after the end of Bink's junior year at Country Day, Marguerite and Vincent Price accompanied their youngest son by train to New York City, whence he would depart alone on his voyage to Europe. They arrived on the morning of the Fourth of July; immediately upon reaching the posh Biltmore Hotel, Vincent Jr. made reservations for four Broadway shows. In his new blue leather journal, bought specially to record his trip, he noted that Florenz Ziegfeld's lavish production of *Show Boat* was "tres bon," while his first visit to the Metropolitan Musuem was the start of a lifelong affair.

On July 6, the seventeen year old realized all at once that he was on the verge of leaving his parents and his country. In his journal he wrote, "When I woke up a sinky feeling overtook me, for I was going abroad alone!" Nonetheless, the Prices spent the day shopping and then took in two movies, *Wheels of Chance* and *The Big Killing*, both of which the articulate young critic thought were "darn good." He was most impressed, however, with the movie theater itself, New York's palatial Paramount. For Bink's farewell dinner the Prices dined at the Cascades atop the Biltmore; then it was down to the harbor, where Vincent boarded Cunard's *Caronia*. His journal records: "I sailed at 12:00 on the dot with a big lump in my throat as I left my mother and father." Describing that first night at sea, he later wrote: "I was Columbus, vice versa, Marco Polo, young Leonardo—going to see the wonders of the world. I stood on the upper deck like the seagoing hero in the last scene of a movie, with hair awind, watching the magic city disappear."

From the start, Vincent Price loved being at sea. He thoroughly enjoyed the amenities of the luxuriously refurbished liner, the novelty of his surroundings, and the pleasure of meeting his fellow passengers, many of whom he found attractive or otherwise interesting. Tour 22 consisted of "ladies of all ages, accents, costumes and, with all the world of ladies, one thing in common—that ugliest of headgear, the suffocating cloche; that hat which, in the twenties, turned females into warriors of old, cut the chance of conversation right in half, and leveled noble brows to idiocy. The men were standard, in plus-fours, slacks, and caps, if not in age. They ranged from my seventeen to eighty-four. But male and female, boy and girl, we had a purpose and a goal: Europe."

The crossing took seven days, the first few of which routed them through the warm Gulf Stream waters. Vincent enjoyed swimming in the ship's pool but, by July 9, he had "an awful sunburn" and was "in misery with it," so was glad when the weather turned cooler. But without swimming, the crossing quickly became interminable. "Today is dull and dreary," he reported on July 10, "and so far there is nothing to do." Thus, the highlight of each day became the evening, when Vincent found many able dancing partners and jitterbugged (often uphill) late into each night. By the 13th, however, things were looking up as he had "met a swell girl who I like a lot and I had a good time with her. I am going to have a date in London too."

On arrival in London from Plymouth, the group checked into their hotel on Cromwell Road in South Kensington. After supper, Vincent and a few of his more eager new acquaintances caught the bus to Piccadilly Circus and took in the sights. The next morning, he went by underground to St. James' Park and then walked to Westminster Abbey, where he attended a service before seeing the various statues and monuments. In the afternoon, he paid his first visit to a building in which he would spend a great deal of time during his life—the British Museum. "There is really only one mysterious museum in the world: the British Museum," he later wrote. "Nothing can touch it for clutter, for atmosphere, for gravity of purpose, that purpose being to collect civilization complete under one roof. It is the home of discovery." The next three days were spent at popular tourist attractions in London and surrounding areas—the Tower of London, St. Paul's Cathedral, Hampton Court, Windsor Castle (where Vincent particularly noted the paintings by Rubens and Van Dyck), and Stratford-on-Avon. At last on July 20 there was a free day, and Vincent took the opportunity to have a date with a girl named only as "K" in his journal. He later wrote that he "took London on like the biggest hick ever to hit a big city."

From England, Tour 22 crossed the channel to Holland. After a day of sightseeing in the Hague and Amsterdam, Vincent came face to face with the first works of art on the tour that truly took his breath away—Rembrandt's *The Night Watch* and *The Anatomy Lesson*. After years of staring at tiny reproductions, he could hardly believe their scope and size. The tour stayed at the Grand Hotel on the North Sea, where Vincent walked out to the shore and stood alone, "thinking of home. Mother had been reading a lot about 'thought transference,' and we'd agreed to try it while I wandered about Europe. It was a good idea, for the ache of homesickness dulled away as I remembered home, itself. I thought of happiness at home; my sisters and brother; Father and Mother; of how lucky I was to have them there, and yet how lucky I was to be here. It wouldn't have been half as much fun being here if they weren't there."

For most of the next week, Tour 22 traveled through Belgium, Germany, and Switzerland. Vincent wrote in his journal, "I like Germany more than I have dreamed of, it is so beautiful." He particularly marveled at the Cologne Cathedral, but in truth more of his attention during the following week was taken up with his first love affair, involving a fellow traveler named Lucy. She was a "toothsome blond, the only contemporary appetizer on Tour 22. This girl, with a lovely semi-Southern accent, was the only one of the ten assorted ladies on our tour anywhere near my age, yet there was a decent difference in her favor and, I felt, in mine, for I hoped she'd lead me to the garden of delights and crown my young years with conquest. I tried hard, God knows, and she almost complied, but it would have to be a night in Nice, some weeks later, before my quest was satisfied."

Although Vincent's intended goal had been to see as much art as possible, he was still his parents' son, and in his journal entries he seems almost as taken with the beautiful shops and glamorous hotels of Europe as he was by the great works of art. Furthermore, like his father, he made home movies of his journeys—a habit that would continue well into his forties, even though the films were rarely shown after they were developed. After a tour of Switzerland—where he admired the scenery and caught up on his swimming at the luxury resorts—it was off to Italy, where his art appreciation would begin in earnest.

First stop was Milan where, after seeing the famous cathedral, the group went to "the small chapel where the *Last Supper* is. It is gorgeous." From Milan, they moved on to Venice by train—the tour's first disappointment for Vincent. The hotel, far from the heart of town, was deemed "miserable" by the young sophisticate and, despite a gondola ride after supper, the intense heat gave him a restless night. The next day Vincent and three friends—Lucy, Helen, and Elizabeth—wandered off to see the glassblowers and the lacemakers, ending up in St. Mark's Square, where Vincent thought the cathedral "very ornate, but beautiful . . . saw the stone on which the transfiguration took place and another on which St. John was beheaded. Saw Madonna of the golden foot." A photograph of Vincent and his girlfriends shows them in front of the cathedral surrounded by the square's ubiquitous pigeons, each of them holding one. Though the day may have been unbearably hot, the women all wear long sleeves and cloche hats; Vincent sports a suit, tie, and hat. Later that afternoon, he would make his first acquaintance with an artist he would admire throughout his life—Titian. The love affair was instant; in his journal he called the artist's *Assumption* one of "the most beautiful paintings in the world."

So eager was Vincent to reach Florence, the cradle of the Renaissance, that he left Venice ahead of the group. Once he arrived, he set out on a shopping mission—to find a work of art for his parents. "I had saved a small amount with which to buy Mother and Dad a present, and Florence would get that money. I was determined to get it on the Ponte Vecchio. I shopped and thought of silver, of leather, of everything sold on that bridge, but nothing really said "Buy me." Back and forth I searched, and finally found it—a little bronze fountain figure. Twenty-five dollars. He was a cutie, holding a fish out of which the water squirted. There are hundreds of figures like this, but I'd never seen them, and somehow I felt sure that the shopkeeper's information about its being modern was just to spoof me—that this was an original Donatello-Verrocchio, undiscovered until now by *me*! I bought it, lugged it to a packer, sent it home via collect freight, and sighed with delight that I had found a treasure in Florence and that my parents would have it forever—in the Middle West of America.

"They received it in good order. The collect freight was sixty dollars. Then my father was forced into building a pool for it to fountain into. This cost two hundred and fifty dollars. The entire family spent two years dragging rocks back from the Ozarks to make the surrounding rock garden. The final blow came when Mother decided to import three hundred and fifty dollars' worth of rare bulbs from Holland to set the whole thing off, and as a background two mature willow trees were brought in, employing six workmen for three days. Then I decided to grow water lilies, but soon found out that they must be planted in rich, preferably fresh, cow manure—under the water. This murky operation caused the death of twenty-five high-priced, fan-tailed goldfish and yearly saw me up to my armpits in fresh cow dung." After his parents' death, Vincent couldn't bear to part with the beloved fountain and had it sent to California, where the whole procedure commenced all over again.

Vincent's next stop was the Uffizi, where he saw "so many famous pictures that I was lost. The best was *Madonna of the Harpies* by Del Sarto." Indeed, decades later he still vividly recalled the momentous instant when he came face to face with the favorite painting of his youth: "Suddenly, I came upon a room and there she was. My own personal Madonna . . . Oh beautiful, serene, soft-eyed, and glamorous—she's not the Virgin Mother, not the Woman of Sorrows—she's the Queen of Goddesses, a woman to worship as a woman. She is beautiful, and she's in love with all mankind. Especially with me. And there I was, standing in the Uffizi with a watermelon in my throat and two painful jets of warm salt water spurting out of my eyes. Then I heard a soft voice, over my shoulder, say: "Come over here. I'll show you the one that makes me cry." I blew my nose, blotted my eyes, buried as much of my face as I could in my handkerchief, and blurted out a feeble: "Sorry . . . something in my eye." The voice said: "Yes . . . beauty."

Vincent and the group spent two more days in Florence, the first city in Europe that truly transfixed him. He noted in his journal, "If you look any way around you in this city you find something interesting. Such marvelous pictures I have never seen." Then it was on to Naples, to Pompeii, and then to the Amalfi Coast; following a "beautiful and cool" boat ride to Capri, they headed to Rome. In Rome, Vincent's journal entries, largely perfunctory till then, become poetic and almost rapturous, prefiguring his lifelong devotion to the city. On the center of each page of his little blue journal is pasted the tour itinerary, surrounded by his copious and exuberant notes: "Rome the eternal city, the mother of Christianity, the center of antiquity consumes four days well deserved." He made detailed notes of everything he saw—the Sistine Chapel, the Pantheon, St. John the Lateran, St. Peter's, the Guido Renis in the Caputian church, the Forum of Trajan "where eighty-five cats now live," St. Mary the Greater "with a ceiling of solid gold brought by Columbus from his first trip to America," St. Peter in Chains. Enraptured by the city's many churches, one "massive," another "very beautiful in its simplicity," Vincent found Rome overtaking Florence in his eyes; on this trip his lifelong wish to live in the Eternal City was born.

With ten days of the tour remaining, the group took in Pisa, Genoa, and Nice. By this point, Lucy seems to have been replaced in Vincent's affections by Marie, with whom he went dancing at Maxim's until three in the morning. But the next night, his date was with Helen—"dancing again." He later wrote, "I spent those two days in Nice not in the pursuit of the beautiful (though she was very pretty), but in the study and exploration of the human body. Since I had dedicated myself to the world of art, I could hardly do better than to study seriously art's greatest source of inspiration—the female form."

Finally it was on to Paris—the last stop. Tour 22 had scheduled tours of Versailles, the cathedral at Rheims, and the battlefields of the Great War. Vincent later wrote, "We saw the trenches and the rows of crosses in Flanders fields, so peaceful now. But I could sense the anguish in the people, still—and when two of our Tour 22 requested that we visit at the graveyard of their son, I was brought up short by the individuality of the war. I had been too young to remember much of World War I, except the flags, food restrictions, saving tin foil, and the gaiety of the armistice. But these two people, standing at the gateway to the graves with heads bowed, their secret silent in themselves, I wouldn't forget."

Vincent had three days in Paris—and, as he would later admit, he hated it. "The whole effect was a forced laugh," he remembered, "and I only learned to appreciate it years later when my own laugh was a little forced too, and hers seemed more familiar." But his journals reveal little of this impatience; Vincent noted dozens of sights, from the *Mona Lisa* to the Galeries Lafayette to the junk shops along the Seine, where he purchased three small etchings for a mere six cents.

But the nights were a particular success. Vincent and his friends went to a show at the Moulin Rouge and to the Folies Bergère, "which were nuder than Moulin Rouge, and not nearly so well put on." Then came a more culturally enlightening but equally interesting outing. "Tonight we went to the Paris Opera house, a thrill of a lifetime. *Thaïs* was playing and with that marvelous opera house staging it was wonderful beyond description."

August 24 was Vincent's last full day in Europe and he was determined to make the most of it, spending the day shopping and the evening absorbing more of the city's nightlife. "Tonight we went to the Casino de Paris. I am bound to see Paris even if it breaks me. We went to a place called Paradis and there lay before you Paris. Smoke so thick you could hardly see, an accordion wailing some wild tunes and Negroes dancing with whites both ways. Girls try to pick you up, but you say 'J'ai une femme' and then they go, saying 'Quelle dommage!' but it's Paris. After this we went to Florence's, entirely run by Negroes. Oh boy such dancing. Back at 6 A.M. That's good by Paris nightlife."

The next day, Vincent boarded the *Tuscania* for the States. The eight-day return crossing was turbulent and left everyone seasick, except those like Vincent "with cast iron stomachs." On July 5, in the front flyleaf of his journal, he had written, "Forward. My first trip abroad will be, I hope, just a starter on a long life filled with voyages." Now, at the end of his first trip abroad, on the back flyleaf next to a pull-out map of the world, he echoed his earlier sentiments. "I would that this map could determine only a small part of my voyages, that I might explore into unknown places." The St. Louis boy's transformation into international sophisticate had begun.

5

DURING HIS JUNIOR year at Country Day, Vincent had kept up his grades as promised, but had slipped somewhat in the class ranking due to a failure in German. Fearful that this might hold his son back from becoming a senior or being accepted by Yale, Vincent Sr. wrote to Headmaster Thompson. The reply was only partially encouraging. Thompson assured Price that his son's failure in German "will not be counted as a condition for advancement, and he is promoted to Class I." Then came the bad news. "I should like, however, to call your attention to the fact that his prospects for passing all of his Board examinations, judged by his showing on our finals, are slim."

Aware of his pupil's summer trip to Europe, Thompson encouraged Vincent Sr. to engage a private tutor for his son or send him to a tutoring school near New Haven, in order to prepare him should he be forced to retake the Boards in September. While their son was in Europe, however, Vincent and Marguerite were informed that their son *had* passed all his Board exams after all, except for one—Plane Geometry. Vincent had hoped to attend football camp with his Country Day classmates upon returning home from Europe; instead, his parents sent him to the Milford School near New Haven for an intensive two-week course in Plane Geometry. The experience only furthered Vincent's resolve to succeed academically; and by the time he took his examination in Plane Geometry at Yale on September 17, it seems clear that the aspiring young art student had finally grown serious about returning to New Haven for college, in the Price family tradition.

During his senior year of high school, Vincent was only required to take three courses per semester, leaving him time for the many extra-curricular activities with which he would occupy himself until he could become a Yale man. He played on the soccer team as a fullback, served as treasurer of the Troubadours in addition to performing lead roles in their two major productions, and acted as manager of the track team. In the latter capacity, it was noted that he was "quite a talker and the workouts often turned into bull sessions." But it was his job as art editor for *Codasco*, the Country Day yearbook, which he took most seriously. Throughout the yearbook, he created illustrations for every class and activity as well as caricatures for each of his classmates on their senior pages.

During his senior year of high school, however, Vincent made a sobering discovery about his future in the arts. "When I got back from Europe I had only one year left before going to college," he recalled. "Inspired by the trip, I determined to become an active artist. In that one year I learned a fact that I wasn't about to admit for five years. I had no talent at all. I tried painting, sculpting, and woodcutting, to no avail. My greatest humiliation was a portrait I did of Mother, which she loved because I did it, so she had

it expensively framed and prominently hung in her living room. For many years it reminded me that none of the great painters' talents had rubbed off on me, despite my
love for their works."

But however discouraged he may have felt, Vincent nonetheless worked hard at his
art. His niece Sara Santschi remembered Vincent's third-floor attic in the house on Forsyth Road. "It was a garret, a real garret. It had this uncomfortable bed, a big old wooden
bed, and it looked like someplace Van Gogh would live in, or Gauguin. Oh, it was so
French Impressionist. And he painted all these big, kind of El Greco–type heads, elongated heads, which looked like him, of course, and sculptures and things. He had a real
elongated style." The influence of El Greco was undoubtedly due to one of the City Art
Museum's more notorious acquisitions—notorious, at least, by the standards of 1920s St.
Louis society. While Vincent was still in high school, the museum had the opportunity
to acquire a superb El Greco portrait for which they paid a good sum of money. As
Vincent later wrote, "No sooner did the news break of this good fortune but a long line
was formed around the City Hall with placards that demanded to know who the hell
this Greek was, and how come he got so much money for painting a picture of himself!"

Senior year passed quickly; Vincent kept up his grades, and took his place among
only twenty of his classmates in the yearbook, where a profile described him as "The
artist of the senior class. His ability in this line has not only won him a post on the
Codasco, but also makes him the central attraction in the study period when he rapidly
distributes pictures of good-looking girls. 'Carrie's' good acting and musical talent have
earned him success when handling major roles in the Troubadours' last two productions;
and as for his athletic ability, that is the main reason why many [rival school] Burroughs
supporters had to add another moral victory to their collection after a spirited encounter
between the schools on the soccer field. He is also well known among his schoolmates
for his inexhaustible supply of stories about his European trip last summer." In class
voting, Vincent received mention in one category, coming in second, ten votes to four,
as the handsomest person in the Class of 1929.

Graduation took place on June 6. Vincent Price matriculated solidly in the middle
of his class, and looked forward to meeting up with other members of Country Day's
Class of '29 again at Yale in September. After an address by the senior orator, class
president Henry McIntyre presented the class gift—a concrete bench. Vincent had lobbied to persuade his classmates to give the school a set of prints by Joseph Pennell, but
had lost; he would have the last laugh later, when the bench cracked during a winter
cold snap.

In June 1929, Vincent took his final College Board examinations before leaving St. Louis
for Ontario, where he would spend the summer with his parents' friends, the Tuppers,
and their two teenage daughters. He occupied his time swimming and making home
movies. The best of these featured Vincent, blond and bathing-suited, rescuing a
seaweed-covered maiden from the surf and carrying her to the dunes, where he performs
mouth-to-mouth resuscitation, only to be discovered by his girlfriend, who runs away
in distress with the youth in hot pursuit.

On July 29, he received a telegram from his father. It read, "You have been admitted
to Yale with no pull exerted. Don't break any furniture in your excitement. We are all
very happy and send love and congratulations. Dad." Despite his casually jocular wire,
Vincent Sr. was surely relieved that, after years of worry, his youngest son had finally

been admitted at his own alma mater. In a letter to the Yale Board of Admissions, Vincent Sr. confessed that the admission to Yale "certainly brought me a lot of happiness. You know I have always been a staunch Yale supporter and had that natural desire of every Yale man to have his son go to Yale. In these times of struggles to get boys to work and make the grade, the old man does a lot of worrying and hoping and now for the time being, at least, my worries are over. I really believe my son, Vincent, is going to make good, as he certainly has taken a new lease on life during the last year."

Over the course of the summer, Vincent Sr. took care of all the details of his son's fall registration—sending in his fall fees ($200 for tuition and $87 for board), applying on his behalf for a single room, supervising the packing and sending of his trunk, and marking what he felt were the appropriate pages his son should study in the *Eli Handbook*. In some fathers this could have seemed like meddling, but Vincent Sr. had a way of showing support without smothering his son.

As for Vincent himself, although he had always assumed he would make it into Yale, the knowledge that the next four years of his life were spoken for was welcome indeed. He later wrote, "I wanted to be a 'Yale man.' I looked forward to this four-year journey that would make me a *man*. In going to Yale, I thought I was going to the Athens of America. Great paintings and statues would be everywhere; the buildings would be classic, as befitted the alma mater of my father and brother and, particularly, as befitted the college where I was going to spend four years, then graduate a cultured, *gentle* man . . . I hoped."

But Vincent's initial reaction to Yale was one of "wide-eyed disappointment." With the buildings of Europe fresh in his mind, he was horrified by the campus architecture, a mishmash of "Nathan Hale, Georgian, Gothic, Roman, Greek, war memorial, nineteenth-century, nothing-style dormitories, plus isolated (thank God) examples of Swedish Modern and bastard Bauhaus concentrated on an implacable modicum of land called the campus." Even worse, the Yale men themselves failed to meet his expectations. Although the Yale College Class of '33 contained a wide spectrum of students, including a number of brilliant intellectuals and talented athletes, most of Vincent's classmates were old-money Easterners who had been educated at the prep schools of New England. As Vincent later described it, "Yale was a place where it was one hell of a help to be from an *Eastern* prep school. They'd scouted those schools and knew all the top boys in them long before the boys got to New Haven. So it was no small job to push your way from the Middle West into any of the top social or athletic endeavors in the East." In the beginning, the Midwestern boys stuck to themselves, finding it hard to break into the Eastern prep school cliques. Eventually, of course, they came to know one another as the cliques broke down.

All of the young men who would become Vincent's closest friends were unique individuals–Herman "Fritz" Liebert, George Kubler, and Ted Thomas. Although they had very different backgrounds as well as diverse academic interests, all four shared a love of learning, particularly in the areas of art and literature, and, in due course, they were all elected to the Elizabethan Club, an honorary society whose members excelled in English literature.

Vincent met Fritz Liebert during the first few days of their freshman year. "The first thing [Liebert] uttered was a long quotation from Boswell. How a boy of eighteen could have managed to sustain an interest in the eighteenth century, I'll wonder all my life. But here was a complete scholar in his own field, entering Yale. He was so fascinated with the Johnson circle that he seldom spoke of anything else, and while he was enormous fun and always stimulating, many of his close friends (especially me) were put off Johnson forever." Liebert became a lifelong Johnson scholar and returned to Yale to serve as the university's chief librarian.

George Kubler was another brilliant classmate who returned to Yale, in his case to help launch the school's art history department. Vincent and George shared a wide-ranging interest in the visual arts, particularly in the art and architecture of New Mexico, Mexico, and South and Central America. Kubler's book *The Shape of Time* remains a classic in the fields of anthropology and art history.

Ted Thomas was Vincent's closest friend at Yale. Another midwesterner, he had briefly attended St. Louis Country Day, but in the class below Vincent, so the two had not known each other well. When Thomas's parents died within a year of one another, he and his three sisters had gone to live with relatives in Pittsburgh, where he had continued his schooling. After their freshman year, Ted and Vincent decided to room together for their sophomore year. Vincent wrote home to his family, telling them how very fond he was of his friend: "I'm sure we'll get along swell. We both like the same things and aren't too much alike to be boring to one another."

The two spent plenty of time horsing around. Ted would later recall that one day, while mock wrestling on the stairs outside their dorm room, he tried to get his roommate into a headlock and accidentally smashed Vincent in the nose. Thomas heard it break, but as blood started to ooze down the young man's face, Vincent simply "took his three fingers and molded it all back." In fact, he had broken his nose twice before in high school and had fixed it in a similar manner; the third break left him virtually unable to breathe, though, and that summer he finally consented to the first of his nose surgeries.

Most of their fun, however, did not have such disastrous results. Because Prohibition was still in effect, the pair devoted a certain amount of time and energy to brewing up their own alcoholic concoctions. Vincent fondly remembered rigging up a still in their bathtub and making "our own booze called Love in a Punt." Ted Thomas remembered a more problematic occasion: "Vinnie and I bought a large cask of grape juice. The label on the cask said, 'Warning. Do not turn this plug one-quarter to the right because this will allow air inside and cause fermentation.' That was the legal way to teach you how to make wine. Well, we did just that and left the cask in our closet. One day, it exploded and the smell of sour wine almost drove us out into the street. We had to send all our clothes to the cleaners, and we never tried to make bootleg wine again."

But having fun was not the first order of business during the early fall of 1929. On Tuesday October 29, 1929, just over a month after Vincent's first Yale semester had begun, the stock market crashed—just as it had done in 1893 when his father was at Yale. This time, however, the collapse was far more serious. Vincent later wrote, "1929 was hardly a vintage year for America, but I've always believed that the Great Depression was the best thing that happened to all of us children of affluent parents. Entering Yale that year with its wellborn, often extremely rich scions of old and new rich parents was no joke. People were hurling themselves out of windows at an alarming rate and oddly enough the jumpers included some of the boys about to enter the big three Ivy League colleges. I guess the thought of being poor or even comparatively so was more than they could face. It seemed to me and most of the other survivors ridiculous." Vincent remembered his frequent excursions to New York during his college years—trips that, under the restricted financial conditions of the Depression, seemed to bring out the bohemian in him. "If you couldn't afford to take your girl to a classy restaurant and show, the Village was cheap and so were movies, especially art movies. You could see

Cocteau's *Blood of a Poet* or the latest René Clair film. There was always a Nadick's nutbread and cream cheese sandwich or Horn and Hardart's palatial slot-machine, food-vendoring marble rooms to get a nosh, and it didn't take long for the college crowd to make them more than acceptable, even chic."

During the first years of the Depression many boys were pulled out of school for financial reasons; but Vincent Price Sr. was not about to do to his younger son what had been done to him. Unlike his own father, Vincent Sr. was a shrewd businessman and a canny investor. Furthermore, he made his living in one of the few industries that would remain virtually unaffected by the Depression. As a manufacturer of penny candy, the National Candy Company provided America with one of the few luxury items it could afford. Thus, while the lives of many of his classmates changed forever that autumn, Vincent Leonard Price Jr. began his career at Yale with no financial worries.

Vincent Leonard Price Sr. and his elder son James Mortimer Price had both attended Sheffield Scientific School at Yale University. Naturally, the youngest Price also enrolled at Sheff. Over the course of his freshman year, he completed his basic course requirements and also tried out a variety of extracurricular activities. He elected to row crew, putting his six-foot-four-inch frame to good use on the freshman team, and he submitted a cartoon to the Yale humor magazine which, to his great joy, was accepted. He later remembered, "It showed a freshman, riding on a train, going to New York—writing home. The caption: 'Dear Mother and Dad. The first few days were hell, but I'm beginning to find my way around now.' For one lovely moment I thought I was going to step into Peter Arno's shoes [the *New Yorker* cartoonist was also a Yale man], but the next half dozen drawings I submitted were not only dull in wit but in draftsmanship. There were some very clever cartoonists in the class of '33."

During the spring of his freshman year, Vincent faced his first major decision at Yale: choosing a college. Eager to please his father by following in his and Mort's footsteps, at first Vincent leaned toward the science-oriented Sheffield, but soon after he declared for Sheff, his interest in art and literature got the better of him and he changed to Academic. He wrote home, "I'm crazy about Sheff life, but I'd be miserable taking courses that I have avoided and hated all my life. I don't know whether I'll make a frat in Ac[ademic], but I'd rather get through my studies successfully than be a social lion. Of course, I hope to make a frat. I hate to break the family tradition but from now on the Prices will have a choice." He closes his letter with a brief postscript scrawled in large letters over the bottom of the page—"My son won't go to Harvard or I'll beat the H--- out of him!" Shortly thereafter he received a letter from his father congratulating him on his decision and reassuring him that it made no difference to him or Mort that they were Sheff "as we are all Eli Yale and so what else matters."

As his freshman year drew to a close, Vincent considered his summer plans. He wrote home that "Ted wants me to go to Europe and stay in a *pension*(?) and tour from there around France on bicycles." Although Ted promised his friend that their trip would only cost eight hundred dollars, Vincent was unsure of what he wanted, or could afford, and wrote home to ask if his family was still planning a trip through the Canadian Rockies, assuring them, "I would love to do that with you or anything you want me to do." In the end, he opted to spend the summer with his family, first in St. Louis, where he had his nose surgery, and then on a trip through the Rockies ending up in Glacier and Banff. If the photos are any indication, nineteen-year-old Vincent Price Jr. made the right choice. Snapshots reveal him at various St. Louis garden parties holding court with family and friends. In Glacier, he poses for the camera on the log porch of a stone hunting lodge overlooking the Rockies. He is wearing a beret and polo shirt, and is holding a cigarette, a rifle crooked in his arm. In Banff, he once again holds court, his hair blond at the end of the summer, his face tan; wearing a white suit, white shirt, and white tie, he laughs with two young ladies who gaze up at the six-foot-four young man with admiration.

6

PRICE RETURNED TO Yale, rooming with Ted Thomas during his sophomore year. Pursuing his interest in writing, he joined the staff of the *Yale Record*, and also began to work more seriously at poetry, which his sister Hat eventually compiled into a collection for the family in 1932. Like his father's writing, Vincent's poetry tended to be flowery and, given his burgeoning interest in Shakespeare and English literature in general, rather heavily influenced by the great English poets, including Tennyson, Shelley, and Matthew Arnold.

Although only an average student, Vincent tried to adapt his course of study to his many interests, and his choice of subjects even then reflected a wide-ranging eclecticism. During his sophomore year he took classical civilization, economics, chemistry, and English; by his junior year, he had found his two favorites, history of religion and Shakespeare. He liked the former because through it he gained a better understanding of many of the great Renaissance works of art he had seen in Europe. The latter, as he later recalled, "was taught by a handsome, somewhat pedantic, dignified man named Carl Young. He didn't miss much in his exploration of that universal genius, but he approached the Bard as literature rather than theater, and the one thing I missed was the magic of performance. It was not until Mr. Young came to *The Tempest* that he allowed himself to impart to us the spirit of Shakespeare and not just the word. He took flight in the beauty of that play, and took me right with him. He showed me a 'brave new world,' one that I knew I must try to be a part of, but I also knew that it would take me time to find out how to enter it."

In hindsight, Vincent would discern that "my two secret ambitions—to be an artist or to be an actor—were keeping their secret, even from me, during the first years at college. Little glimpses kept coming through that made me sure one or the other would eventually become a fact. In those days Yale was not the kind of university that set itself out to create actors or artists. Rather, its aim was to give you an all-around education and, by the simple act of having created a Yale man with a diploma, make you a possible leader in your community, socially or otherwise—if you cared to chance the otherwise." One of these "glimpses" came during his junior year, when he took his first formal art course. It proved a disheartening experience. He recalled, "When I saw what I could do to make a charcoal drawing of a plaster cast look like a child's rendition of Frankenstein's monster, I gave up, then and there."

Fortunately, he could still find enrichment in the study of art. "One of the few things that you could afford to do that was really fun was to go down to New York and stay in terribly cheap hotels, and go around to the galleries. Everything was so cheap because nobody had any money at all. I used to go into the great galleries like Knoedler and Durlacher, very famous name galleries, and I became friends with these people, because they had nobody else to sell art to. They were so delighted to see a student who might someday have enough money to buy something." One gallery that became a favorite was run by one Antoinette Krauschauer, with whom Vincent became close friends; later he would make his first major purchase from her—a Modigliani drawing that he bought for fifty dollars and which now resides in the Museum of Modern Art. During his college days, Vincent's art collection grew to include a self-portrait by French artist Alphonse Legros, which he bought for one hundred dollars, and a small bronze by the American Harriet Frishmuth. Whenever he laid out the money for a work of art, he scrimped by living on the delicious barley soup at the Waldorf Cafeteria on High Street in New Haven. He later wrote, "I still have the Legros, but barley soup I can't drink more than once a year."

In addition to his consuming interest in the visual arts, Vincent remained a great movie buff, and he rarely missed a feature at New Haven's movie palace, the Fox Poli. Of all the many films he saw there, the highlight for him was hearing Garbo speak for the first time in *Anna Christie*. He would later remember sitting in the dark, trembling in anticipation of her first words: "Gimme a visky baby, ginger ale on the side." In those days, he felt, "Of all the actresses in the world, Garbo was the one for me." But he didn't limit his affections to the Swedish star. On a lark, he sent Tallulah Bankhead a telegram inviting her to attend the Yale-Princeton game. "Never a thought entered my mind that the lady would answer my telegram, but she did, and although it was in the negative, she had a devoted fan forever." New Haven was also famous for its Shubert Theatre, where many Broadway shows tried out before braving the New York critics and audiences. During his time at Yale, Vincent saw many of the great actors and musical comedy stars of the day, among them Helen Hayes, Clifton Webb, Mae West, Fred Allen, Bert Lahr, Kate Smith, Beatrice Lillie, Ed Wynn, Al Jolson, Ethel Barrymore, Paul Muni, Eugenie Leontovitch, and Charles Laughton. He would remember Yale as a parade of "chorus girls and raccoon coats. We used to stay at the revues at the Shubert until two or three A.M. I didn't miss many concerts, plays, or revues."

He also became an inveterate fan-letter writer to anyone whose work he enjoyed, and a keen autograph seeker. He wrote English author A. J. Cronin to tell him how much he liked his work and to ask him whether he had been influenced by Thomas Hardy and the Brontë sisters. Cronin wrote back to thank him for his letters and answered his questions. Price's pleasure in receiving responses from those few who took the time to write back undoubtedly became the foundation for his generous response to anyone who later asked him for an autograph. He never said no, and always answered his fan mail himself. When he returned to Yale in 1984 for the Vincent Price Film Festival, a line of autograph seekers spontaneously formed in the restaurant while he was eating dinner, and extended out around the block Vincent signed each person's autograph and spoke with them. By the time he returned to his meal forty-five minutes later, it was cold.

Despite his secret ambition to be an actor, curiously Vincent Price decided against joining the famous Yale Dramat. As he explained, "I went over to see about it as a possible way to try out one of my secret schemes—to be an actor. But it seemed sort of precious, and also, while I knew that someday I'd have to take a crack at the theater to get it out of my system (or make it my life's work), the drama school climate didn't appeal to me at all, and never has." In the fall of 1930, however, his childhood "fiancée",

Barbara O'Neil, whose parents lived nearby in Connecticut, enrolled in a playwriting course at the school of dramatic arts. Within a few months, she was cast in a small part in one of their productions. She remained at Yale through the spring, appearing as Hermione in the spring production of *The Winter's Tale*. She then left to audition for the University Players of Falmouth, Massachusetts, and Princeton, New Jersey. During her year at Yale, Barbara reconnected with Vincent, who indulged his theater fantasies vicariously through his childhood sweetheart.

Despite his reluctance to join the Dramat, Vincent's penchant for drama frequently surfaced during these years. George Kubler's wife, Elizabeth, recalled meeting Vincent at a costume party. She was a native of New Haven and, with her friends from Vassar, had come down and raided her parents' attic for turn-of-the-century dresses to wear to the event, where they joined other similarly costumed young men and women. Vincent, however, stepped out of the period and came as Robin Hood, clad completely in green, tights and all, and spent the afternoon climbing the ivy-covered walls and playing the part to the hilt. He also continued to make home movies, coercing his friends into helping him—silent films replete with abductions and rescues of various damsels in distress tied to railroad tracks.

In his sophomore year, however, he found a legitimate outlet for his yen to perform. He and Ted Thomas were among the many undergraduates who auditioned for the popular Yale Glee Club, led by Marshall "Barty" Bartholomew. Barty had taken over the leadership of the Glee Club in 1921, transforming it from an informal group that sang folk and popular songs to one of the finest male singing groups in the country. The group still performed both popular and folk music, but Barty added serious classical music to the repertoire. Although Vincent continually maintained that he was not as musically gifted as his three siblings, he possessed a pleasing enough voice to make the cut, as did Ted. The Glee Club traveled frequently, performing at other Ivy League schools or at group recitals in Boston and New York; by the summer of 1932, at the end of his junior year, the group had set its sights on a trip to Europe. Ted by this time had left the group, but Vincent, of course, participated. A few of his friends went so far as to insinuate that he had joined the Glee Club simply to be able to go to Europe again.

On June 24, 1932, the Yale Glee Club, comprising sixty young men, sailed from New York on the S.S. *Volendam*. The trip was promoted as a goodwill tour with all concerts, two of which they gave during the Atlantic crossing, performed for charity. The Yale Glee Club arrived in Boulogne on the Fourth of July and went straight to Paris. After two performances, the group took the train to Zurich for an overnight stay; from there it was on to Innsbruck, where their outdoor concert was rained out. Train rides from Austria to Hungary and back were tedious—eight hours at a stretch in third-class compartments—though, as Vincent wrote his parents, "Beer and bridge help."

In Germany, Vincent went down with a severe bout of tonsillitis and had to miss the last three concerts of the tour. When the rest of the Glee Club left for the States, Vincent went back to Paris with a few friends and took up residence at the Hotel Marigny until he had fully recovered. From there, he planned to travel around Europe alone. He wrote his family that this summer in Europe was "the grandest present I could have and I appreciate what all of you have done to give it to me. I do love you so and wish you could be here with me. Imagine the mad Prices together here. Someday we may be. I will repay you by getting all I can out of this. I think I am."

Once recovered, Vincent traveled back to Vienna with the intention of studying German. Away from the rowdy Glee Club group, he brushed up on his language skills and visted the museums. He spent an entire day at the marvelous Kunsthistorisches Museum—a nineteenth-century building fairly bursting with European masters. In his letters home, he made particular note of the many paintings by Rubens, an artist he had difficulty appreciating. There were, he wrote with some hyperbole, "one billion Rubens fifty feet high. That man must have been inexhaustible. Everywhere he fills half the museums." He would later write that at first he found the painter's subjects— "big fat dames," he called them—less than appealing. "But eventually I realized that Rubens was an enormous influence on almost every artist who lived after him and I began to discover why in his sketches, where you could really see his composition." The Kunsthistorisches also contained a work he thought was one of the "sexiest paintings in the world": Correggio's wonderfully sensual *Jupiter and Io*, in which Jupiter as a cloud fairly smothers a voluptuous Io.

It was during his week in Vienna that Vincent first became aware of the changing social climate of 1930s Europe. On August 9 he wrote his parents, "If you ever had a trouble in your life, here it would seem a miracle of joy. These people are so poor not only in money but in health, mental and physical. What was once a country of sixty million is now six and their access to the sea is gone." Even, alas, the nation's burgeoning anti-Semitism had begun to infiltrate his thinking. "They are ruled by Jews who tax them to excess. I befriended a nephew of the woman who owns the *pension*. He is twenty-six and has a doctor's degree, but he can't get work. I thought this might make our national Prohibition troubles look smaller to you. We want beer; they want a new mental attitude, health and work. They say we are all rich; they are right. They don't mean money but in standard of living." Vincent's experience at Yale, where he was surrounded mostly by pampered boys from wealthy families, had only served to underline his St. Louis conservatism, and he began to swallow the German National Socialist propaganda whole. It would be some years before he would begin to question his inherited right-wing inclinations.

But Vincent expended little time thinking about politics. In Vienna, he spent his nights devouring twenty-five-cent all-you-can-eat-and-drink dinners and taking in music at the famous Viennese Staatsoper and a number of local clubs, indulging in his lifelong fondness for both opera and German *Lieder*. Naturally, he found time to visit as many art galleries as possible and managed the lucky purchase of two lithographs by the great French political artist Honoré Daumier at a mere dollar each. Then it was back to Venice, a city he once again found hot and the language difficult. He occasionally resorted to using German while in Italy, not always with much success. On his previous trip, he had found that the Italians undercooked their eggs; this time, speaking German (which the waiter professed to understand) he ordered two eggs cooked six minutes each. The waiter returned rather too quickly—with six eggs, cooked two minutes each. Vincent threw the eggs in the canal and headed for the French Riviera.

Back at Yale for his senior year, Vincent learned that Ted Thomas, his roommate for the past two academic years, had decided to move out because he was not getting enough studying done. For his senior year, then, Vincent roomed with another good friend, Gerrard "Pee Wee" Lee. Nevertheless, Ted ruefully recalled that he spent most of his senior year in Vincent and Pee Wee's quarters, where all the fun was. There was a new addition to the circle of friends, a young Cambridge University exchange student named Alistair Cooke. And then there was Lisa. Pee Wee and Vincent spent most of their weekends at Pee Wee's parents' house nearby, where Vincent fell sincerely and mutually in love with the Lees' dachshund, "a shiny stovepipe of a dog with saddle-colored spots." When she was bred and produced a litter of puppies, the family gave Vincent one whom he named Lisa and who spent senior year living "a cloistered existence in Harkness Quadrangle."

Friends and dogs aside, fun would slowly be put on the back burner. On his return from Europe, Vincent had realized that the time had come to begin thinking about his future. "Yale was a place to learn to learn. First you had to survive the boredom of repeating your high school subjects. And if there wasn't any freedom of choice, at least they dangled elective subjects like art before your eyes—the reward for getting good grades. I was no great student, but I had a pair of eyes that wouldn't stop. A picture was worth a thousand words, even if I had to read ten million words to get to see more pictures."

At the end of his junior year, he had finally made the Dean's List, which allowed him to begin taking his coveted art history courses. "The art faculty at Yale must have felt the dichotomy in their audience," he later reflected. "Some were there just to get through it, others to get as much out of it as possible. I came to the conclusion that art is man's history, or at least the highest level of it." For the first time he became an A student, completing his degree that June with a major in English and a minor in Art History. However, with the country still in the grip of the Depression his degree left him yet another well-educated young man without prospect of work. "I don't think I would have been so determined to make something of myself if it hadn't been for the Depression," he admitted later. "When my brother, Mortimer, graduated fourteen years before, the world was his oyster. When I graduated, there were no jobs. The world was not your oyster but a very small pebble you had to push around with your nose. I realized you have to seize every opportunity that comes your way."

Over the course of his last few semesters at Yale, Vincent's social circle had expanded to include some of the artists and writers who were living nearby in Connecticut. As he later recalled, "Connecticut was, at that time, a place where you lived when you couldn't afford, or didn't want, to live in New York. It was full of artists and writers and a lot of the *New Yorker* magazine crowd." One of the members of this set with whom he became the closest was James Thurber, who was living nearby with his first wife, Althea. Price described Thurber as "a wonderful man to whom I became enormously attached—not only as a writer, but as a draftsman of great ability." When Vincent celebrated his twenty-second birthday on May 27, 1933, a few weeks before he graduated, Thurber presented his young friend with a marvelous cartoon. "In that enchanting line, so uniquely his, he drew me a birthday card that profoundly, humorously was the story of that time of wondering if the American dream was for real. It showed me and my roommate as blobs beneath the signpost of our education—Yale, 21, Harvard, 0, with Hitler as a winged ogre prophetically hanging over our heads. J. P. Morgan is high-silk-hatted, creeping toward the grave occupied already by Calvin Coolidge. My dachshund represents loyalty, another blob is named 'Youth' and a self-portrait of Thurber is called 'Envious Age.' Althea, Jim's wife at the time, is proposing a toast, and an enigmatic circle in one corner seemed to tell me by its label, 'Ball,' that that was just what life could be if you used your talents to the fullest."

7

IT WAS CLEAR to twenty-two-year-old Vincent Price that using his talents to the fullest would mean deciding against a return to St. Louis to work in his father's business. During his four years at Yale, his desire for an artistic life had become greater than ever. "Abstractly, I knew that my adult life had to be in the arts, but how, I hadn't the slightest inkling. In some way I wanted to apply my education, self-taught and school-taught, to making a life and a livelihood . . . as an artist." The truth of the matter was that, for all of his traveling and experiences at Yale, Vincent had never been a committed academic; nor had he settled on any other professional goal. His abstract notions of a future in the arts were fueled as much by his desire to avoid the family business as by any real under-standing of what role the arts might hold for him. Thus, when his sister Hat heard of an opening for an apprentice teacher at a well-respected private school in Riverdale, New York, he applied and was accepted. It was a temporary solution that would give him some time to figure out his next step—while placing him just across the river from New York City, where he could spend weekends exploring art galleries and seeing plays.

After his graduation Vincent traveled back to St. Louis, then to New York with his parents, who left on a trip to Europe a few days later. The day after their departure, he commenced his new life—the first of many such new lives that he would embrace in the coming years. In a letter he left with his parents, he wrote, "All you have done for me externally and internally, all the great spirit of you both that should, and I pray will, find itself in me, I can only repay deep in my heart and by trying my best in action. If I can only give these little brats something of the great stuff that has become mine from you, I will be happy."

The first part of Vincent's job at Riverdale Country School entailed working as a coun-selor at the school's summer camp on Long Lake in the Adirondacks in upstate New York. There he met a couple with whom he would form a lifelong friendship and who would become his first significant mentors—Marc and Cecil Baldwin. Marc Baldwin had come to America from England, where he had studied to be a medical doctor, but now taught Latin at the boys' school. He had met his wife Cecil, now headmistress of the girls' school, in Vienna, where he had spent a year studying. Both became lifelong educators. The Baldwins were beloved by their students and they had a similar effect on on Vincent. As he later wrote, "These two remarkable people, who have remained close friends, gave me the keenest insight into the teacher's philosophy by letting me share in their dedicated and lively excitement at being privileged to inspire young people in the desire to learn. They were both more than distributors of prefabricated knowledge. They were prophets of what education can mean to students who would let themselves be made aware that the truth can make you free and that freedom from ignorance is the highest good to which man can aspire."

Marc and Cecil Baldwin, along with Cecil's sister Hildy, were "the kind of people who were interested in everything, who were curious about everything," and they quickly recognized the young college graduate's own omnivorous curiosity. Furthermore, they appreciated the spirit in which he had joined the staff of Riverdale, despite the school's limited means. When he arrived at Riverdale from Yale, he was told by Hildy that he might not receive a salary that summer. It was, after all, still the Depression. Hildy, an artist herself, showed Vincent her paintings of Long Lake; years later she remembered Vincent telling her that the money was unimportant "if Long Lake was as beautiful as I had painted it." The Baldwins took Price under their wing and treated him like family, even taking to calling him "*unser Sohn*—our son."

Riverdale Country School was much like Vincent's own high school in St. Louis, and he soon found his niche. As an apprentice teacher, he performed myriad duties, including driving the school bus, teaching English, coaching soccer, and even playing the occasional role in a school play. But his great interest lay in trying to incorporate the teaching of the visual arts into the standard curriculum. The headmaster, Frank S. Hackett, the founder of the school and an innovative educator, allowed Vincent to visit other teacher's courses and illustrate what the class was studying through examples from the visual arts. For example, "In the Latin course I showed the students what Cicero and his contemporaries looked like through the magnificent school of Roman portrait sculpture. Where de Maupassant and Zola were being read, I let them examine the visual report of their time through the eyes of the many superb nineteenth-century painters, some of whom were intimately connected with the writers, like Zola and Cézanne, Baudelaire and Delacroix." The experiment was a success. Many of the students had had no idea of what the periods they were studying looked like or, indeed, that they had any "look" at all. The apprentice teacher also gave an art appreciation class in which he tried to show his students how to look at art through the eyes of the artist. By demonstrating that almost every artist tries to make a unique statement, eschewing the past in an effort to be "modern," Vincent was furthering his own artistic education as well as his students'.

Despite his success at Riverdale, Vincent found his first year out in "the real world" quite difficult. He realized that his Yale education had given him the basic tools with which to make something of himself, but still he felt largely unprepared. Furthermore, having had to abandon his goal of becoming a great painter or sculptor, he knew he had to make a concrete decision regarding his future. His passion for the visual arts made him yearn to continue his career in education, and the extraordinary example of the Baldwins suggested that he might make a life for himself in the field.

However, he still harbored a secret dream of a life as an artist—if not a visual artist, then a performing artist. At the end of April he appeared as Captain Corcoran in two performances of HMS *Pinafore* with the Riverdale Players. Gleefully, he wrote his parents with a report on his progress, "How quickly the whole work is at an end. All is over but the shouting and that is very loud and complimentary and very flattering to my ego. But do not worry, I am at ease. I wish you could have seen it and I missed not having you out front to sing to. I do love the stage, and never before have I realized how much at home I am on it. I simply must try it some day and prove to myself that I can't do it or can do it. So don't be surprised if I join a stock company this summer if I get a chance. (Save the clippings.)"

He didn't join any stock company that summer, but during his visits to Manhattan Vincent did, in fact, knock on the doors of a few theatrical agents. His efforts met with little or no response, though, and when he got up the courage to ask his friends whether he should give acting a serious try, all encouraged him to stick with teaching and his interest in art history. Even James Thurber gave him no encouragement; later he would wryly admit his mistake after Vincent had his first success.

Price himself looked back on the period with mixed emotions. "Periods of discovery about yourself are seldom fun. It's tough to realize how little you know just when you think you ought to know a lot. That period immediately after graduation from college, when you suddenly realize for the first time that 'commencement' means beginning, and actually you are just beginning to learn—to live—it comes as a terrible blow to your ego. You become aware that all you really learned at college was *how* to learn and that continued learning is the true key to all existence. My year of teaching taught me that whatever I was going to do or be, I had to know more."

When his youngest son graduated from Yale, Vincent Sr. had presented him with a check for eleven hundred dollars, accompanied by a letter stating that this was the precise amount of a junior membership at his country club—carrying a postscript promising that if his son ever used the check for that purpose, he would be disowned. With this tidy sum in hand and encouraged by the Baldwins, Vincent applied for admission to a new but already distinguished graduate program in art history at the Courtauld Institute at London University.

One of his chief reasons for applying to the Courtauld, as opposed to an American program, was his desire to get away—to leave the United States and, more important, to live in Europe. As he later admitted, "In my escape from the beginnings of being a teacher into a foreign world of further learning, the emphasis was on the foreign. I simply wanted to get away . . . from family somewhat, from the U.S. Depression more, but mostly from the good old USA. The trouble was that, in my juvenile estimation, it wasn't old enough. My tastes of the Old World had left me hungry. Now I wanted to live somewhere over there, even if it meant studying. I found the perfect solution for all my needs in an art magazine mention of the Courtauld Institute of Art in London."

On September 14, 1934, Vincent Leonard Price Jr. set sail for England for the third time in just over five years. As he stood on the railing of the S.S. *Olympic* watching the New York skyline fade from view, he reached into his pocket to open an envelope containing two letters. The first was from Vincent Sr. who had written some very paternal words of advice: "This is a great adventure for you and it will be something that will remain with you all your life. Make up your mind in the start that you will fill it full of memories which will contain no regret for which you may be ashamed. The past, as you grow older, is the time you look back upon as the time of opportunity and you look back upon opportunities as something gained or something lost. If gained, they are yours for life, if lost they may never be recovered. This is a great opportunity for you to prepare yourself for the future work you want to do, and the reason Mother and I are willing to help you in it is because we not only love you, but have faith in your ability and your honesty of purpose. Keep this faith in your mind, and that which it will mean to you and to us to have you fulfill it. As I told you when you went to Yale, the greatest safeguard from temptation is the right kind of friends. You have chosen well in the past, don't change. Don't be tempted toward foolish extravagances. We want you comfortable and to live well, but we are making financial sacrifices for you and need your help. We love you so. If you have the confidence in yourself which we have in you, you are sure to succeed. You are not only my son but my namesake. What little of the name I have made stands for something I want you to add to."

From his mother, he received an equally long letter in which she, too, gave voice to her feelings. "Before you were born," she wrote, "I prayed for a son, that he might be fine and strong and have a singing voice. My Heavenly Father was surely good to me. The dividends from you have been a great boon to your mother and father." Little did they, or he, know the extraordinary future which lay ahead, just across the Atlantic.

8

VINCENT PRICE BELONGED to that certain breed of Americans who feel a particular affinity for all things British. Throughout his life he would often return to England, nurturing his Anglophilia and establishing firm friendships along the way. Of his three wives, two were British, and he was himself often thought to hail from Great Britain. In the early years of his film career, publicity pieces sometimes referred to him as "the Englishman from St. Louis," a sobriquet he did nothing to discourage.

Although his ardor for England, particularly London, had been kindled on Tour 22, the love affair commenced in earnest during his year at the Courtauld in 1934–35. Looking back on that year, Vincent wrote, "London in 1934 was one of the glories of the civilized world. What was left of the Empire was considerably less than in its Victorian heyday; it was an atmosphere rather than a climate and, for an American, still glamorous. Above all, it was still more for your money than anywhere in the English-speaking world. London! My God, what a city. Established, stolid, cold and warm, wet but never dry— maybe of modern cities the greatest, the most entertaining."

Vincent arrived in England in late September and moved into lodgings at 20 Upper Wimpole Street, tucked between beautiful Regent's Park and the shopping on Oxford Street. After settling in as quickly as possible, he paid his first visit to his new school. The University of London art history program had been founded only two years earlier with a bequest from Samuel Courtauld, a wealthy textile manufacturer and art collector. In addition to a large endowment, Courtauld left his mansion at 20 Portman Square, the elegant eighteenth-century Home House designed by the Adams brothers, along with a celebrated art collection that included paintings and drawings by Cézanne, Modigliani, Van Gogh, Daumier, Degas, Mantegna, Manet, and other masters old and new.

In a syndicated art column from 1968, Vincent conveyed his excitement at having been a part of this new program over thirty years before. "Can you imagine the sensation this tall, wide-eyed midwestern art lover had when we were assembled in the drawing room for registration? The Missouri boy, sitting day after day at the feet of the masters, and the excitement was still on them, as it was on me. It was Mr. Hitler's moment in Europe. Because of him, all those terribly 'dangerous' art historians who just could not get along with his Aryan theory of art and people left Germany, and Europe in general, either by command or desire, and an enormous percentage of them ended up as lecturers at the Courtauld, where, if you could keep your eyes straight front, you could hear more about art than perhaps at any other time in history."

These sentiments reflect a mature adult who, with the hindsight of history, had long since recognized the debilitating influences of fascist thought. At the time, however,

Vincent was politically untutored and thus easily swayed by the fashionable thinking of whichever circle he enthusiastically embraced. While studying at the Courtauld, he signally failed, for example, to make any connection between the presence of the learned academics he encountered and the reasons they had fled Hitler's Germany.

Beginning his course of study with great seriousness and enthusiasm, Vincent showed a sense of dedication that outstripped his performance at Yale. After his first lecture he wrote home ecstatically to his parents that he was now "carded" into every museum, collection, and library in London. He immediately felt that he had found a home at the Courtauld and, after years of academic struggle, a mode of study to which he was perfectly suited. "This is very unlike the American idea," he wrote his mother and father. "You learn only as much as you care to—they don't give a damn if you ever go to the lectures—but if you miss something that's your bad luck. I won't miss a thing. Every man that lectures leads in his field. I am superbly happy. This is how I love to study."

His first task was to find an advisor for his proposed thesis on Albrecht Dürer and the School of the Danube. Since discovering Dürer in Austria and Germany, Vincent had been fascinated with the artist, whom he believed had singlehandedly changed the course of art in Northern Europe. He felt that Dürer's greatest contribution to the Northern Renaissance was the draftsman's series of detailed studies from nature, and his intention was to study these drawings in order to see how they influenced the artist's finished paintings, woodcuts, and engravings. It didn't take him long to find the ideal tutor for his graduate work. Campbell Dodgson, the world's leading authority on Albrecht Dürer and perhaps the whole German Renaissance, had just joined the faculty of the Courtauld.

Working with Dodgson proved the highlight of Vincent's time at the Courtauld. He later wrote of his mentor, "He was a monument to scholarship in every way. You had only to see him walking down the street to know he was someone special. He shot like a bent arrow from one place to another with the determination only the British have—on their feet—to get where they are going. He had no age, but you suspected he had been born old, like a dwarfed Japanese pine tree, and just got more beautifully gnarled as the years went by. He knew so much of Dürer, having written more about him than anyone else, that next to meeting Dürer himself, I couldn't have done better than to have Campbell Dodgson as my guide to get to know that genius. His name proved to be an open-sesame for all my research, both in London and all over the continent."

Indeed, through Dodgson, who had been the curator of prints at the British Museum, Vincent gained admission to some of the great private libraries and collections in Europe. But it was through W. G. Constable, then the head of the Courtauld, that he was given a letter of introduction to an incomparable resource. Vincent had told Constable that he was having trouble researching some of the lesser-known painters of the School of the Danube, whereupon Constable gave him a letter of introduction to Sir Robert DeWitt, who housed one of the greatest art research libraries in the world in the basement of his great home.

Vincent visited the DeWitt estate, where he found thousands of files on hundreds of artists awaiting him, all meticulously maintained by two or three secretaries employed by DeWitt for the purpose. Vincent was able to find all the information he needed on the more obscure painters of the School of the Danube. When he next saw Constable, he expressed not only his gratitude but his amazement at the scope of this private collection. Constable informed Vincent that such libraries and collections existed all over the world, noting that there was hardly a single subject to which somebody somewhere had not devoted single-minded amateur scholarship. The notion had an extraordinary impact on Price: the idea that amateur scholars would devote their life to the pursuit of a single field of research—without thought of monetary reward or society's approval—struck him with awe.

Vincent later wrote that, upon graduating from Yale, he felt as though he was expected to give up the intellectual curiosity he had spent four years nurturing and go out into the world to earn a living—the intellectual and the professional being, for most Americans, mutually exclusive. If visiting the DeWitt collection first opened his eyes to a different set of values, the time he spent in England, where he met poets, scholars, painters, and actors who made of life a passionate intellectual and artistic adventure, allowed him for the first time to begin honoring his own curiosity without continually worrying about what he was going to end up doing for a living. Not that he banished that worry for good; as the offspring of two self-made men, he would always be concerned with making a name for himself, with becoming a financial success. And success for Vincent Leonard Price Jr. would always mean being a good provider for his family, as his father was. But in London he caught his first glimpse of a world of arts and letters in which success was not necessarily defined by external rewards.

The Vincent Price who was beginning to emerge during these years was a curious mix: part bohemian, part social climber, part intellectual, part starstruck kid. He was able to move in many worlds, but always felt most at home among creative artists of every field. His life as a twenty-four-year-old in London found him struggling to weed through his many personas, to find a combination that worked. Here was a man who could never have been just one thing: He could no more have been only an art historian than he could have been only an actor. He could not have lived a solely bohemian life, nor could he have survived exclusively in high society. As a young man, he sensed this about himself instinctively; as he grew older, he came to realize that he had to find a way to make the many pieces of his life fit together. He came to be called a modern Renaissance man by many commentators, and perhaps he was. But, talented though he was, it was not really the case that an overflow of talent took him into the many worlds in which he felt at home. Rather, it was his curiosity and sense of wonder that motivated him; his talents merely supported his interests. Often, as a young man and a student, his capacity for fascination led him (and certainly his friends and parents) to fear that he might never settle down and make something of his life. But whatever his self-doubts, he inevitably allowed his curiosity to lead him wherever it might.

Thus, despite his passion for the fine arts, he was soon easily enticed by many other attractions that were to be found in London in 1934. Like so many Americans, the young man from Missouri was strongly impressed with British royalty and the aristocracy. One of his first good friends in London was a man named Stanley Dunn, who worked for the publisher John Murray. Vincent had been introduced to Dunn by his Yale roommate Ted Thomas, and through Dunn he began meeting people outside of the Courtauld—society people as well as artists and writers.

In early October he was asked to tea with Mr. Dunn at the home of Lord and Lady Gorrell. Lord Gorrell, the head of the Air Club, business partner of John Murray, and "a poet of some standing," soon became a close acquaintance, and saw to it that Vincent was invited to a host of toney social events. Soon Marguerite and Vincent Sr. were receiving newsy letters from their son, describing his social adventures in beguiling detail.

Although his father might have worried that his son's socializing would distract him from his studies, his mother relished every last tidbit of news about London society, and the fact that her handsome son was proving such a success.

He wrote home of playing bridge with the Honorable Maude Ackland-Hood and winning every rubber; of dining with Mrs. Piers Warburton; of being invited to meet a Miss Hoste, "who is young and I hope attractive." Thanks to his great success at cards, the Honorable Miss Ackland-Hood and her brother Lord Saint Aubreys invited the young student to a bridge party given by Princess Mary Louise, where he was thrilled to think of himself playing cards in tails. At the party, the winner at each table received a prize. Vincent won—a box of chocolates. To his immense pleasure, the princess herself called him over and told him that she "hated to see a young man with a box of candy and that she wished me to have something else. So she gave me a book and everyone signed it."

Vincent also began meeting many artists and writers. One memorable occasion found him invited with Stanley Dunn to Mrs. Bram Stoker's house for tea. Although the name of Bram Stoker is now synonymous with his novel, *Dracula*, the story had not achieved its reputation until sometime after the author's death in 1912. In fact, Stoker had not even considered himself a writer; he had dedicated his life to managing the career of his idol, Henry Irving, considered the greatest English actor of the nineteenth century. As Irving's manager, Stoker was said to have been almost slavishly devoted to the actor, a fact his wife was rumored to resent bitterly. As *Dracula* grew increasingly popular after its creator's death, Florence Stoker not only reaped the financial rewards, but was able at last to come into her own after a lifetime in the shadow of her husband's enthrallment to Irving.

Among the other guests were a pair of adventurers, one of whom, according to Vincent, was "Tschiffely, the man who rode on horseback from Buenos Aires to New York." Writing home, he noted, "But the one is Mrs. Bram. All over the house there are the most wonderful things, including a portrait of her by Burne-Jones. She was considered, along with Lily Langtry, one of the two most beautiful women of that age. Oscar Wilde was one of her closest friends and gave her the only watercolor of his that he ever thought good enough to keep. And it is lovely, though more interesting than beautiful. She is eighty, but what spark and a lovely sense of humor, and she is very fond of me and has asked me again."

His closest friend during these first months was a young man named Wilfred Russell, in whom he found a kindred spirit for his hijinks. When the two of them dressed Vincent up as a German baron and crashed a party at the Dorchester, Vincent proudly wrote his parents, "Did I make a mark! Such temperament. I was in my element." But Wilfred was leaving for a new job in Bombay after Christmas, and so when two new friends— David Babbington-Smith, "Etonian and o-o-h so reserved," and Wake Thring—asked Vincent to share their flat at 33 Baker Street, he accepted their offer as much for the flat as for the company.

He moved into 33 Baker Street in early December. Babbington-Smith, a Cambridge man, the grandson of a well-known financier, and an avid theatergoer, took his new friend to see John Gielgud as *Hamlet*. Vincent was transfixed by the performance and was thrilled to be introduced to the actor backstage—where he found Gielgud eager to impress the importance of Shakespeare's language on Vincent. "Gielgud cautioned me to see his Hamlet many times and he was so right. As the enormity of his performance grew on me in the eleven times I saw it, so did the mind-blowing, overwhelming genius of Shakespeare." Soon Vincent was spending as much time at the London theater as in the London museums.

Just before Christmas, Campbell Dodgson asked his young American protégé to dinner at the home he shared with a male companion in Montague Square. Dodgson, like Vincent's roommates, and several other young men in the fashionable circles in which the American was moving, was homosexual. In an age when such proclivities constituted a criminal offense, affairs were conducted with the greatest discretion, even secrecy; however, Vincent not only was unjudgmental about the lifestyles of these men, but he also was undeniably intrigued by and drawn to them intellectually and, on occasion, emotionally. His response to their cultural and artisitic sensibilities was profound. He wrote home of his impressions of the eclectic Dodgson household, filled with letters from Tolstoy, rare first editions, Christmas cards from artist Muirhead Bone, Holbein prints, and other gems. Here was a man whose tastes and interests were as diverse as his own. Since boyhood, Vincent had squirreled away hundreds of improbable items that had attracted his wide-ranging attention—a piece of bone from the catacombs in Rome, a potshard from a southern Colorado Anasazi burial ground, a first edition of *Tom Sawyer* found in his sisters' bookshelf, Indian-head pennies, pressed flowers, seashells. Although his family certainly had their own cluttered collection of "whatnots," there was nothing in Vincent's experience to this point to suggest that his own curious sort of stockpiling was anything other than somewhat eccentric. Yet here, in the home of his mentor, he found an aggregation of objects that seemed to affirm his own.

Vincent accepted an invitation to spend Christmas 1934 in Graz, Austria, with Wally Reichenberg, an Austrian friend of the Baldwins. The daughter of an Austrian baroness, Wally was in her late thirties, divorced from her first husband, and working on her doctorate in child psychology and psychoanalysis at Duke University and in Vienna. Vincent had liked her immensely when he had met her at Riverdale the year before, and her invitation brought an opportunity to spend some time in his beloved Vienna—and to tour Germany on his return.

A week before Christmas the twenty-three year old took a train to Austria, traveling third-class on uncomfortable wooden seats (shades of the Glee Club tour) and was met at the station by Wally waving a Yale flag. The two friends spent the first three or four days in Vienna where Vincent returned to the Albertina Museum—this time armed with a letter of introduction from Campbell Dodgson to the curator of the Dürer collection, Frau Doktor Spitzmüller. Spitzmüller took him to lunch and personally guided him through five boxes of Dürer drawings. A few days before Christmas, Vincent accompanied Wally to her family home in Graz.

Although he was welcomed warmly by the Reichenbergs and accorded generous hospitality, Vincent was homesick. For all his enthusiasm about living overseas, he had never been away from his family for such a long time. While at Yale and Riverdale, he had frequently visited his sister Hat in nearby Westchester County or returned home to St. Louis to see his parents. This was his first Christmas spent away from home, and he missed his family desperately. He wrote his parents, "This may be a great experience, but not right at this point—I no like it!"

On Christmas morning Wally surprised her young friend with a big American breakfast. Later that day, the whole family walked ten miles out into the country to visit some Russian friends, a dethroned prince and princess who, as Vincent wrote home, were now "little more than Russian peasants." Once again Austria was affording him some perspective on the privilege of his upbringing, although his innocence, and his conservatism, still show through in his remarks to his parents. "The wife was a relative of the Tsar and is without exception the handsomest woman I have ever seen. They still think Russia will be restored to them. I hope it will be! If these people made up Russia's aristocracy, Russia is missing a great deal now. More and more I think America is the land of the chosen, but we could use some of their courage."

After Christmas itself was over, Vincent's spirits improved. Over the New Year's holiday he and Wally traveled to the Austrian resort town of Spit am Semmering to ski, trekking for four hours to a cabin high in the Austrian Alps with a panoramic view of the whole Tyrolean range. On New Year's Eve Vincent and Wally attended a party where the young American was the life of the party—"I sang Negro songs for an audience of two hundred people not one of whom understood a word, but they did like the tunes!"—and also taught an older Austrian man some of the songs. This same man apparently kept the whole town awake by wandering through the streets until six A.M., playing his accordion and shouting, *"Wo ist Mr. Price?"*

On January 2 Vincent headed back to Vienna, while Wally returned to her family in Graz. His brief vacation over, Vincent immersed himself in his research. He spent another whole day at the Albertina, where he found a drawing for the Rembrandt etching he owned, about which he made copious notes. From Austria he traveled north into Germany to continue his research. His first stop was Bamberg, where he visited the famous cathedral. "The cathedral," he wrote, "is beyond beyond! The sculpture is so fine that it grasps the whole significance of the Gothic age at once, and gives the beholder an emotional elevation as I imagine absolutely true and pure love would." Upon arriving at the cathedral, however, he had found the beautiful Romanesque building completely covered in scaffolding. "After all those centuries against the wind and the rain, they were checking it for repairs . . . on my time! Much as I approve of the preservation of great works, my disappointment was acute. But then I thought of something. If I could climb those scaffolds, I'd be among the very few who'd ever seen the sculpture as the artist had when he created it."

This, however, was easier thought than done. After finding a cleaning lady whom he addressed in halting German while gesturing toward the scaffolding, she dubiously referred him to the *Landamt*. Nonplussed by the unfamiliar word, Vincent was stymied until a hot meal and a glass of vermouth emboldened him to say somewhat timidly to his waiter, *"Landamt?"* Vincent was eventually guided to the Bamberg City Hall, where the elusive Land Office was located. He walked in and explained his cause awkwardly to an official who, without a word, wrote something on a piece of paper and handed it to him. So armed, Vincent walked back to the cathedral and clambered up the scaffolding, spending hours examining the famous *Fürstentor—The Last Judgment* tympanum over the main entrance and as much of the spectacular Romanesque façade as he could take in. No one ever asked him for his letter of permission.

From Bamberg, he went to Dürer's hometown of Nuremberg, where he spent the day working "never so hard or so gladly" at the museum. In later years, after he had grown vociferously liberal, Vincent liked to tell friends that his visit to Nuremberg had coincided with the famous National Party Day rally immortalized by Leni Riefenstahl in *Triumph of the Will*, that he had heard Hitler speak, that the mesmeric power of his oratory had both transfixed and chilled him. In fact, that infamous Nuremberg rally had taken place the previous September. But Nuremberg was a notoriously pro-Nazi town, so it is entirely possible that Hitler might have spoken there during Vincent's visit. What is clear, however, is that Vincent did see the effects of Nazism already sweeping the country—and, in his youthful ignorance, appeared to approve. From his hotel room in Nuremberg he wrote his parents: "Three hundred small boys called the *Hitlerknabe* are marching outside and singing. From the spirit here and faith in the man and the lack of faith in Austria, which is completely under the control of the Pope and Judea, I feel he must be right, and at least it is a direct appeal to the right emotion in man, love for his brother!" Clearly, the irony of his sentiments escaped him.

Conservative St. Louisans of the time tended to be prejudiced against non-Protestants, particularly Catholics and Jews. Of the city's many immigrant populations, the substantial German community was by far the best respected, their most prominent members having injected much wealth into the city. Vincent Price had grown up with an anti-Semitism that was heightened by his own affection for German culture. In contrast, his prejudices did not extend to African-Americans; the Republican Party was, after all, the party of Lincoln, and the Price family strongly supported Negro rights.

In April 1933, shortly before Vincent's graduation from Yale, Adolf Hitler became chancellor of Germany, and began enacting the laws which barred Jews from holding official positions. Jewish shops and businesses were boycotted; the infamous book burnings began. By August of the following year Hitler had combined the offices of chancellor and president, declaring himself *Reichsführer*. Separated from Europe by a vast ocean, most Americans had scarcely reacted to his rise to power. In contrast, by 1934 Winston Churchill was already warning the British parliament of the German menace. Many young Londoners kept thoroughly abreast of each new political development in Europe as fascism began sweeping across the Continent. At the Courtauld, Vincent was taught by a number of scholars who had already fled Hitler's Germany, and who in their newfound freedom spoke out against the fascist laws in the Third Reich. But for the time being Vincent Price seemed impervious to their message, and his conservative politics remained unaffected by his surroundings. His friends in London were largely upper-class young men who showed more concern for money and social position than for the storm clouds swelling on the Continent. It would be a while before he began to challenge the beliefs with which he had been raised.

9

THE WINTER SEMESTER back in England brought a measure of disappointment; a number of the more distinguished professors were on sabbatical, leaving Vincent with a limited roster of classes. Instead of attending as many lectures as he had during the fall, therefore, Vincent concentrated on his thesis. And with fewer hours spent in the classroom, there was more opportunity for other activities—most notably theatergoing.

In a 1945 interview, Vincent told columnist Inez Wallace a colorful story concerning his initial motives for attending graduate school in London. During his spare time while at Riverdale, he claimed, he would "hound the theatrical agencies looking for a job on the stage. Hollywood, I must admit, never entered my mind. And New York gave me the cold shoulder. I noticed, however, that every time a boat arrived from abroad, some ham actor walked down that gangplank and was instantly hailed by producers as a talented new discovery! Almost overnight I decided to go abroad for a year and acquire a European background. Off I went to London—by the simple process of telling Dad I wanted to take my master's degree over there. But I spent much less time at the British Museum than in the stalls of London theaters." Vincent was always a great one for embellishment. He had certainly harbored secret aspirations regarding the theater while at Riverdale, but his decision to go to London had had nothing to do with trying to further his acting career; every shred of contemporary evidence confirms that he went to London sincerely committed to a career in art history. And yet the events of 1935 quickly changed all that.

In later years, Vincent often spoke of John Gielgud as having been among the first to encourage him to pursue his dream of becoming an actor, and he long treasured a copy of Stanislavsky's *An Actor Prepares* given him by Gielgud. But, as legend has it, his first foray into serious acting came about when one of his flatmates, David Babbington-Smith, read a notice for auditions for a controversial play by Maurine Watkins called *Chicago*, to be produced at a private theater club known as the Gate. Knowing of his friend's infatuation with the stage, Babbington-Smith dared Vincent to audition, assuring him that, with his American accent, he would be a shoe-in. Sure enough, he was given two small roles—as Charles E. Murdock, a gum-chewing police sergeant, and as a judge. Vincent enjoyed crediting his ability to chew gum as the sole reason for being chosen; chewing gum was virtually unknown in England at that time, and the candymaker's son was recruited to teach the cast how to chew gum and talk at the same time.

Vincent could not have picked a better time or place to make his entrance into the London theater, which was enjoying a golden period in the mid-1930s. In addition to Gielgud's *Hamlet*, the 1935 season saw a production of *Romeo and Juliet* starring Laurence

Olivier, Peggy Ashcroft, and Edith Evans, while at another small private theater a young W. H. Auden was seeing his first plays produced. Paul Robeson was also appearing on the London stage that spring in two plays, *Basalik* and *Stevedore*. In the first, a young Australian actress named Coral Browne received good notices from the *Observer* for her "cool and stylish" performance. Although *Basalik* only ran three nights, Vincent might well have seen the play; its cast also featured Margaret Webster, who was playing Velma in *Chicago*. Miss Webster, the daughter of Shakespearean actor Ben Greet and famous actress Dame May Whitty, would later become one of the leading Shakespearean directors of her time.

On February 26, after he had been cast in *Chicago*, Vincent wrote his parents, "How happy I am—there is nothing in the world like the profession to me. But don't worry dearests, I am not slacking in my work. But please don't be angry as I can no more leave it alone than I can give up my love of life for it is so wonderful. Pray that I make a go of it!" *Chicago* opened in early March, and the experience overwhelmed the aspiring actor. He loved everything about the theater: playing a role, winning over an audience— above all theater people themselves, who seemed the best he'd ever met, full of spirit and life. The notices for the play were good, and Bink raved to his mother: "I am so tickled about the show. It is really very good and though my part is small, it is a start and the people are so grand—there are no people so much fun as theater people. My how they do work and what experiences they have on tour and in town—a real life of ups and downs, excitement and dejection."

Located on Villiers Street just behind Charing Cross station, the Gate had become an extremely popular theater club since it had been taken over by producer-director Norman Marshall in 1934. By its second season under Marshall, it had already attracted a loyal audience which, Marshall always felt, was its primary attraction for the actors who worked there. For Vincent, therefore, his initiation into the London theater was a fortuitous one. Marshall maintained that the Gate had "the reputation of the best audience to play to in London. It differed from the ordinary West End audience in being on the whole a younger audience. Partly this is explained by the nature of the plays and partly because of the very low cost of theatergoing at the Gate." The most expensive seats went for five shillings, the cheapest for two shillings and fourpence. Marshall called the Gate "a thoroughly democratic theater. One went there in a pullover or a white tie and felt thoroughly at home. The mere fact of paying an annual subscription had a subconscious effect on a member of the Gate. He felt to some extent that it was his theater. So there was no need for the actor to spend the first twenty minutes of the play 'settling' the audience. The audience was disposed to be 'with' the actors from the beginning."

Chicago opened on March 13, 1935 to good notices and ran for a full month, while Vincent "ran around like a bird dog between the play and the Courtauld." But already his attention had shifted from art to acting. Through his new friends in the cast, he began pursuing other opportunities, auditioning for other plays and for radio work. However, the reawakening of his dream of a life in the theater also reawakened the doubts that had bedevilled him in America. He wrote his parents, "It is very alarming how one suddenly feels old! I do now and see behind me so much happiness, I wonder if there can be any ahead. I realize how little I have done, and so if any chance comes to prove myself, believe you me I'll take it, regardless of anyone's objections or reasons. I am a man now!"

That chance came almost immediately. Casting notices were posted at the Gate for a new play by Laurence Housman called *Victoria Regina*. Over a period of years, Housman, the brother of poet A. E. Housman, had written a series of short plays about the life of

the Queen. These had been published and well received, but they had never been produced on the stage because of a ruling by the Lord Chamberlain that "in deference to
the wishes of His Majesty the King, the impersonation of her late Majesty Queen Victoria
and His Royal Highness the Prince Consort on stage, including pageants, should not be
permitted during the present reign in plays submitted for licence." Yet as a private club,
the Gate was exempt from the ban and the young American auditioned for the part of
the Prince Consort as soon as he learned of the production. Vincent bore an uncanny
resemblance to Albert, and his travels in Germany and Austria enabled him to mimic a
perfect German accent. Director Norman Marshall, having been forced to cast a relatively
unknown actress, Pamela Stanley, as Victoria, faced another difficult casting decision in
Albert. "The choice was limited by physical appearance, as the Prince Consort was an
exceptionally tall man. In the end I gave the part to a young and almost totally inexperienced American called Vincent Price, who had not only the height and looks for the
part but was able to put on an extremely convincing German accent."

Vincent set about preparing for his first major role methodically and with great
passion. He visited the Victoria and Albert Museum to learn everything he could about
his character. He found out that the Prince Consort had achieved his remarkable posture
by wearing a corset with Toledo steel stays, so he bought himself a golfer's waist support
and fastened it as tightly as he could—though he gave up the idea after he fainted halfway
through rehearsal. Most extraordinarily, however, Vincent translated his entire role into
German, so that he would think in German, as Albert would have done. He was determined to get to the heart of Albert's character. He came to believe that "Albert was
inflexible in mind and body and was determined to save the monarchy from softness and
the country from moral and mental deterioration." He believed that in many ways Albert
was a truer symbol of the age than Victoria herself.

In her memoirs, Hermione Gingold recalled meeting Vincent in London just after
he had been cast as Albert. Gingold herself had made her first big success at the Gate in
a revue six months before. She remembered, "As the prince, he had to play 'Drink to
me only with thine eyes' on the piano, and as he had never played before, I took him
up to my flat in the Adelphi to teach him how to sing and play. He proved to be a very
able pupil." Marguerite had once told her son, when he was a young boy, that she would
give him five dollars if he could ever learn to play and sing a song. On May 10, he wrote
her that she owed him the money.

Well before opening night, Marshall began generating publicity for his new play.
Because of the ban on public performance, he was readily able to interest the press. His
leading lady, Pamela Stanley, was easy to promote—she was herself a daughter of the
British aristocracy, which lent some piquancy to her playing Queen Victoria—but the
matter of an unknown twenty-four-year-old American playing the beloved Prince Consort was more problematic, and Marshall found himself inventing facts about his star. In
one early publicity piece, Vincent was touted as "an English actor who had played a great
deal in Germany and is therefore able to simulate the German accent to perfection." In
another, the writer claimed that "Norman Marshall was lucky enough to find a young
English actor to play the part. One could use the word 'discovery', if Mr. Price had not
already had wide experience in America and on the Continent." Meanwhile, a nervous
novice prepared for his first big opening night.

*   *   *

There were other significant developments in Vincent's life. In many of his letters home during this period, Vincent mentioned a woman named Dotty. In October 1934, he wrote his father, "I hear from Dotty every week and it seems that she has a place for me and I certainly have a great place in me for her. I know I love her and that is a surety to hold any man up." In late January, he sent her a ring, "a lovely jewel, while not expensive, does have great brilliance." He wrote his parents, "I suppose I am madly in love with her. Well, I see it this way! I love her and more than anyone I've ever met, she has all those qualities of dignity and poise which my three womenfolk have brought me up to look for—you Mommy, Hat, and Lol. She is not so young as I should fall for, but I have never been fond of people younger than myself and she understands what a lot there is to do and would like to do it instead of stagnate! So, I love her and you are all sweet to love her too—though I can't see any reason not to. I am not thinking of another burden yet, so Dad, don't worry!" But after January, there is no mention of Dotty again.

Then, in a letter written in early March, he alludes to being "very upset about something. You see I am capable of adult feelings, too." Whether Dotty refused the ring is unclear. We know nothing about her—how they met, who she was, what she ended up doing with her life—and she is never mentioned again in his letters. In a photo album of early publicity shots, however, there is a typed scrap of paper attached to a photograph of Vincent as a young man, naked from the shoulders up, his wavy hair mussed and damp, his pensive face glistening with water. The paper reads, "Gag photo for Fiancée because she called me Tarzan because of my love for swimming. Had agreed with photographer he could use one photo for commercial purposes thereby saving expense. Three weeks later found this one photo three times life size in Piccadilly Circus advertising deodorant."

A few weeks before the opening of *Victoria Regina*, Vincent fell seriously ill. He had struggled through the winter with bouts of colds and flu, but this time a more serious intestinal flu had put him out of commission. He lost a great deal of weight, and was confined to bed for almost a week after the doctor pronounced him on the verge of severe jaundice. He was nursed back to health over the Easter weekend by a woman named Margaret Fraser, who was stage managing *Victoria Regina*. Fraser, a very witty and attractive woman with dark, almost Spanish features and yet (as described by director Frith Banbury) "very pukka English in her manners and mores," had begun her theatrical career in the early 1930s; by mid-decade she had become a well-respected stage manager, working for Robert Morley and Banbury in their London productions. Banbury described Fraser as "an acquired taste, utterly unsentimental, quite tough in her estimate of people; she only liked those she liked and she cottoned on to them—no trouble was too much for those she cared for." One thing we know about the mysterious Dotty was that she understood "what a lot there is to do and would like to do it instead of stagnate." Margaret Fraser appears to have been another of the strong and independent working women to whom Vincent was attracted. By May they had begun a passionate affair.

On May 1, 1935, the inexperienced amateur stood anxiously in the wings awaiting his first cue. That morning he had written his parents, "Well today is about the most exciting day of my life—my first taste of stardom." That night his friends and fellow cast members heralded the arrival of a great new actor. The papers did the same. The *Daily Mail* called the piece "a notable production. In the acting it impresses us chiefly because of the convincing impersonation of Prince Albert by a young American actor, Mr. Vincent Price. We should hear of him again." And while the *Evening Standard* critic found Pamela Stanley's Queen Victoria "a little sentimental," he found that "Vincent Price made an excellent study of the Prince Consort." And the *Times* noted, "The Prince Consort, as Mr. Housman interprets him and as Mr. Vincent Price plays him, is more interesting than the Queen. The performance owes much to Mr. Vincent Price for so completely catching the conscientious stiffness, the gentleness, and the pathos of the Prince."

Vincent wrote home about his opening night almost as soon as it was over. "The show opened to cheers and screams, something so unusual here that we all stood on the stage and wept. Then Thursday the papers were simply unbelievable. They loved it and us." He enclosed clippings from the London papers, noting that the *Times* notice "is all for me." Vincent Sr. and Marguerite had neglected to send a telegram for opening night. In his letter to them, Vincent appears concerned that they were either not taking his acting seriously or were displeased with him, and so makes a point of telling them, rather plaintively, that he is still working hard at the Courtauld and "having fun doing both." A few days later Marguerite and Vincent Sr. wired that they had been out of town and sent their congratulations. (Never again would they neglect either to wire or attend one of their son's opening nights.) Already publicity conscious, Vincent closed his letter with a postscript asking his parents to get one of his London notices placed in the St. Louis papers.

The production attracted considerable publicity, although it eventually made a profit of only five pounds. Marshall later wrote, "Although the critics were enthusiastic, a large proportion of the Gate audiences stayed away. At that time interest in Queen Victoria was at its lowest ebb and those who came to see the play were mainly people old enough to remember the Victorian days." Although the show had run only a month, Vincent's life had already changed. He was invited to dinner parties, country homes, even given tickets to the King's Silver Jubilee. But equally important was the fact that he was making a name for himself in the theater, that he was coming to be regarded as an equal by the theater people he had so long admired.

10

WITH WORD OF this exciting new actor filtering throughout London, producers and casting agents began approaching Vincent Price with job offers, and he decided to withdraw from the Courtauld and devote his efforts solely to finding work in theater or in film. It was a *volte face* he was at pains to explain to his parents, "Honestly, the Courtauld has turned out to be like the majority of American art schools for dilettantes and debutantes," he wrote. "Both of which I shrink from—lectures too specialized. This is no complaint, but the honest truth."

Flushed with success, Vincent envisioned himself at the start of a long and fruitful theatrical career in England. He decided it was time to make a real home for himself in London, and the first step was to visit the famous pet department at Selfridge's, where he bought a whimsical cat. As he later wrote, "His face was typically Siamese, but from about an inch below his neck to the base of his tail the fur became gradually more and more striped until his rump was pure tabby. He was christened Albert the Good, not only because I had just made a success playing the part of the Prince Consort, but also because Albert was a really good cat."

During the run of the play Vincent had received a great deal of publicity, but an undoubted highlight of his fledgling theatrical career came when he was chosen by producer and critic Sydney Carroll for his yearly list of "discoveries." As Vincent later wrote, "Each year Carroll picked one young man and a usually younger woman and gave them an onstage party plus a much more welcome feast of publicity. My younger co-honoree was the eighteen-year-old beauty, Vivien Leigh. She had made her West End debut in *The Masque of Virtue*, a bit of period fluff made dazzling by her beauty. When I met her at our gathering, I flocked to that beatific beauty like every other male present. It was impossible not to—the skin, the nose, the shape of her face. I was so taken by it I almost forgot I was the other recipient of the prize. Vivien Leigh was the prize."

On May 27, 1935, his twenty-fourth birthday, Vincent had received a call from Carroll asking him to come down to Regent's Park to audition for their prestigious summer Shakespeare repertory season. That evening he got the news that he had been selected for the role of Orsino in *Twelfth Night*, and thereafter for Orlando in *As You Like It*. He could hardly believe his good fortune, and he celebrated his new success as well as his birthday with the cast of *Victoria Regina* on stage after their performance. But his jubilation was short-lived. As an American student, Vincent had permission to live and to study in England—but not to earn money. The young actor had assumed that if he refused the salary he would be spared, but after the London papers reported that an American had been cast at Regent's Park he was refused a work permit, pay or no pay.

Carroll countered by offering to contribute Price's salary to charity; Lord Gorrell offered his help; but it was all to no avail. To Vincent's great dismay, the company had to let him go.

Marguerite and Vincent Sr. had been discussing whether or not to come to England to spend the summer with their son. On receiving his disheartening news, they decided to sail over on the *Majestic* on June 29 for a two-month trip. Their arrival couldn't have been better timed; the aspiring young theatrical star was suddenly and completely at loose ends. Barred from theater work except at private clubs such as the Gate (which was closed for the summer), yet having quit school to become an actor, he had almost nowhere to turn.

His only hope now lay with playwright Laurence Housman, who had been contacted by two American producing powers, the Shuberts and Gilbert Miller, regarding the rights to *Victoria Regina* for a Broadway production. During the London run Vincent had received a letter from Miller asking after the play's potential for Broadway. Not surprisingly, Vincent's response was completely enthusiastic. He spoke highly of Housman's work and offered to facilitate a meeting between the two men. He also mentioned that, since Miller's interests were both in England and America, "being an American, I may be of some use to you."

Laurence Housman had become fond of his American Albert during the run of his play. He quickly became a mentor figure (he liked to sign his letters to Vincent "your loving godfather"), and had nothing but praise for his portrayal of the Prince Consort, telling the actor that he was his "own idea of an idealized and humanized Albert." When he heard of Vincent's predicament with the British government, Housman told him that if he sold the play to America, he would do everything in his power to make sure Vincent was given the role in New York. Housman spent much of the summer in negotiations with the Americans while Vincent escorted his mother and father on a driving trip through the British Isles—all the while agonizing about his future. Twenty-five years later, he confessed that those months of waiting were the hardest of his life.

In mid-August, when Vincent returned from his travels, he received a letter from Housman telling him that "an exuberant letter of praise has been written to Gilbert Miller about you." Because Price had brought Housman and Miller together, Housman had sold the Broadway rights to him instead of to the Shuberts. Now he indicated to the producer that he wished Vincent to be cast as Albert, writing that "the choice of any other actor will have my severe disapproval." If any one person can be credited with Vincent Price's auspicious Broadway debut, it would be Housman. His powers of persuasion must have been prodigious: by late August Miller had agreed to hire Price, pending, of course, the approval of his star, Helen Hayes.

Gilbert Miller was a distinguished and influential figure in the theater, having made a name for himself with such productions as *Ethan Frome, Dodsworth*, and *Design for Living*, both in New York and London. He had bought *Victoria Regina* as a vehicle for Helen Hayes, who after three years in Hollywood was eagerly returning to Broadway to reclaim her title as the First Lady of the American Theater. In early September she and her young daughter, Mary, along with actress Ruth Gordon, came over to London and took an apartment at Claridge's. On September 11, Helen Hayes wired Vincent Price, asking him to tea. After their meeting, she immediately wrote Laurence Housman: "I am delighted about Mr. Price. Albert seemed such a serious problem to cast. You can't imagine what a relief it is to solve it so simply." In later years, Miss Hayes would aver that Housman had told her quite simply that he would not sell the play to anyone who would not also take on his young protégé as Prince Albert. During Miss Hayes's visit, Vincent took the actress to an antique-jewelry shop near the British Museum where she purchased copies of Queen Victoria's gems to wear in the Broadway production. Later Miller, Hayes, Housman, and Price had another tea during which an ecstatic Vincent signed a contract for a two-hundred-dollar starting salary, to increase to three hundred dollars if the play ran. Miller and Hayes then returned to New York promising to wire once the production schedule had been set.

In order to stay busy during his last few months in England, Vincent again auditioned at the Gate for a role in *Anatol*, a Viennese light comedy written by Arthur Schnitzler and adapted by Harley Granville Barker. He was cast as Max, Anatol's best friend who provides the satirical commentary throughout the action of the play. Stage managed by Margaret Fraser, with a cast that again included Pamela Stanley, the lead was played by Sir Basil Bartlett, who Stanley Dunn described in a letter to Vincent's parents as "a stagestruck wealthy baronet who is the World's Worst Actor in any and every part which he has tried." Dunn reported that, as Anatol, Bartlett had "the flirtatious lightness of a hippopotamus with a headache. His actions on the stage remind one of a dyspeptic stork stalking frogs in a marsh." Despite Dunn's disastrous assessment of Bartlett and his agreement with the *Times* that the play should not have been revived, he believed the experience to have been a valuable one for his young American friend who, he wrote, "shone last night despite Bartlett. And now he knows how to act before an audience which is fidgety and looking at its wristwatch while the ninety-second minutes drag their way into ninety-minute hours, whereas before he was only aware of interest and enthusiasm before his face."

Vincent later recalled the disastrous opening night. "One scene was a wild dinner party, and since the stage was right in the audience's lap, it was difficult to fake the food. Oysters were part of the dialogue and the menu, so real oysters they had to be—not halves of grapes or any other substitute. Oysters are terribly expensive in England (at least the good ones are), and since all Gate productions were done on a shoestring, we were not given those delicious Ostend or Whitstable varieties, but the kind that are sold 'incognito' by street vendors. Opening night, in the gusto of the first performance, the three of us involved in the scene ate two dozen between us, and if the notices the next day were bad (which, indeed, they were), they had nothing on the oysters. We were all violently ill. In my theatrical experience nothing has ever topped the dejection of the three of us the second night of that play. Bad notices and bad oysters are guaranteed to build any actor up to a big letdown."

Indeed, the reviews were barely passable. Pamela Stanley came off the best, with Vincent pulling in mixed notices. The *Times* wrote that "Mr. Vincent Price was an amiably epigrammatic friend, but too often failed to flourish the cynicism which twists the tail of the situation." It is fair to say that Vincent did not give *Anatol* his all. He recalled one evening when, while performing in a very clipped British accent, he realized he had slipped into his native St. Louis drawl, and then decided, much to the amusement of the audience, that he had better keep it up through the rest of the show. By this time, though, he might have been forgiven for being distracted; as late September rolled around, New York and London papers were reporting that Vincent Price would soon be heading back to the United States to star on Broadway opposite Helen Hayes.

*　　*　　*

In early October, having received confirmation of his contract from Gilbert Miller, Vincent prepared to return home. However, he was almost completely broke, and wired Gilbert Miller for an advance on his salary. Miller apparently thought that Vincent, whom he regarded as a successful London actor, was fooling, and responded rather tersely that Price should quit kidding and get going. So, get going he did, the only way he could afford to—steerage on the *Aquitania*. Basil Bartlett and Margaret Fraser drove him to Southampton, where they saw him off. Vincent and Margaret's affair had continued through the summer, but by the fall his attentions were directed toward Broadway and he was more concerned with his career than with romance. Although Margaret maintained a stiff upper lip at his departure, three years later she would write him, "You won't believe me probably when I tell you that I miss you *every* bit as much as the day you went away . . . I had no idea that anyone could leave such a hideous blank in my life. I wonder if I'll ever see you again? . . . Oh darling, you never knew you were—and still are—my whole life, did you?" Though she professed that she would kick herself for sending the letter and teased him about her comments swelling his head, she signed "I love you always."

Standing on the deck of the *Aquitania* in October 1935, with his feline companion, Albert the Good, by his side, Vincent Price could only smile as he reflected on the curious events of the past year. He had come to England on a third-class passage, envisioning two years in London and a life ahead of him as an art historian. Now he was returning home just over a year later and, although demoted to steerage, had the prospect of starring on Broadway opposite one of the greatest of American actresses. As the English coastline faded from view, he turned his sights toward America.

On November 5, 1935, Gilbert Miller invited the New York press to the docks to witness the arrival of his new star. He and a corps of newspapermen waited at the gangplank for the first-class passengers while, unbeknownst to them, a lanky twenty-four-year-old, two overcoats draped over one shoulder, a pair of shoes with their laces knotted together over the other, and a bedraggled and fairly anxious cat tucked under one arm, disembarked with the rest of the steerage passengers, cleared customs, and hailed a cab into the city, where he checked into the Dryden Hotel on East 39th Street.

Miller was furious. When the actor reported for rehearsal the next day, he screamed at him in front of the entire cast, accusing him of "pulling a Garbo." It took some convincing before Miller believed Vincent's story but, after this inauspicious beginning, everything else seemed to go quite well. Although Price was an amateur in a cast of experienced actors, he had the advantage of knowing his part inside out. This naturally made his first few weeks of rehearsal fairly easy, despite being intimidated by his surroundings. More importantly, Vincent Price and Helen Hayes hit it off immediately. Not only did the actress feel that the role of Victoria was the perfect choice for her return to Broadway, she also believed that the love story between Victoria and Albert was the crux of the story. She knew that if she did not establish a strong working relationship with her leading man the play would fail, so she took Vincent under her wing and immediately made him feel welcome.

Victoria Regina rehearsed for four weeks in New York. On December 1, Vincent wrote home that Helen Hayes was "building up a very great performance, and Miller has been so fine I think my part will be far more polished (if less in character) than in London. Hayes has helped me a great deal and I think everyone is pleased with my work. Anyway, I have applied a great deal of molasses and have caught the whole cast to my side—which never hurts." Throughout his lengthy career, Vincent made the "application of molasses" almost a ritual, and developed a reputation as one of the nicest people in the business. In contrast to his insecurities, Vincent seemed suprisingly confident in writing his parents that "The movie people are already after me, and it means that there is interest in me, but I know that my heart is here and so I have specified already that if I do any movies it will be so that I can work here half the time."

On December 9, cast and crew headed to the Auditorium Theater in Baltimore, where they gave their first performance on December 12. The house sold out a week before their arrival, and the early reviews held out the promise of a long Broadway run. Donald Kirkley of the *Baltimore Evening Sun* captured the essence of the piece as written and played: "Victoria the woman, rather than the Queen, is the subject of the play. Politics, the manners and customs of the era, affairs of state, are introduced only as far as they illustrate the character of the sovereign . . . Many significant facts of her long reign are introduced, but it is the progress of Victoria herself through the sixty years that gives unity to the work." Indeed, the play focuses on the transformation of Victoria from a strong-willed girl into an extraordinary ruler through her relationship with Albert. This metamorphosis is initially played out as a battle between Victoria's will and her love for the Prince Consort. It was under Albert's influence, Housman believed, that Victoria became a great queen.

Along with praise for the play, reviewers for the Baltimore papers glowed that Helen Hayes gave "a flawless performance" and that Vincent Price created a "splendid portrait of Albert." Indeed, from the beginning, Vincent held his own against the experienced Miss Hayes. Norman Clark of the *Baltimore News* wrote that his work "is exceptionally good. He imparts charm, intelligence, a gentle firmness . . . and humor to a fairly difficult role."

Both Vincent's family and his English friends were following his American debut. Stanley Dunn and Margaret Fraser cabled him from London and then went out to dinner in his honor. Upon reading the Baltimore notices in the London papers, Stanley wrote to Vincent Sr. and Marguerite that he "had the same sense of satisfaction that anybody in the crowd had when the 'Queen Mary' was launched without sticking on the slips, or crashing into the mud." Naturally, Laurence Housman also followed the proceedings with great interest and with equally high hopes for his play as for his young friend.

From Baltimore, the show moved to Washington, D.C., which was Helen Hayes's hometown. Like many actresses, Hayes had certain superstitions. Chief among these was her belief that it would bring a production good luck to try it out in D.C. before taking it to Broadway. Thus, the play opened at Washington's National Theater on December 16, 1935, to a command performance for First Lady Eleanor Roosevelt. Columnist Sylvia S. Freeman reported that "It was like a tennis match . . . the very important audience kept glancing from Mrs. Roosevelt in one box to Secretary [Henry] Morgenthau in another and sat with frozen faces, waiting for a cue to laugh from either one." Politics aside, the reviews were once again excellent. Nelson B. Bell of the *Washington Post* proclaimed, "Helen Hayes . . . soars to new heights of histrionic perfection." And Don Craig of the *Washington News* noted, "Price, as Prince Albert, gives a characterization second only to Miss Hayes. He is always the prince, yet never a king. It is a distinction that few actors could maintain. (When he died at the end of the second act, the feminine portion of the audience wept almost as much as Victoria.)"

After receiving such glowing notices, Miller and the cast felt the show was more than ready for their New York opening on December 26, 1935 at the Broadhurst Theater. They would be joining a season that was already showing great promise. Broadway had been struggling to recover from the Depression, but the critics unanimously felt that this season might be the best since 1929. In that same week Helen Hayes's great rival, Katherine Cornell, would open in *Romeo and Juliet* supported by Florence Reed, Ralph Richardson as Mercutio, and a young Maurice Evans making his American debut as Romeo. *The Petrified Forest*, starring Leslie Howard, was already a hit that season, as was *The Taming of the Shrew* with Alfred Lunt and Lynn Fontanne. But the publicity on Broadway was all for Hayes, whose return from Hollywood had been eagerly awaited by the New York press.

Opening night proved a tremendous success. Vincent received telegrams from Pamela Stanley, Margaret Fraser, Norman Marshall, Stanley Dunn, numerous St. Louis Country Day classmates, Ted Thomas, Pee Wee Lee, his brother Mort, and his sister Lollie. Thus fortified, and with his parents and his sister Hat and her husband in attendance, Vincent Price took Broadway by storm. He could hardly believe his good fortune. Neither could his parents, after so many years of being both worried and intrigued by their son's intense but unfocused artistic goals. After the Washington opening, his mother had enthusiastically written, "Do please stay on the stage—you will go far and have the gift for great success. I have known this, my boy, for many years, but they say mothers are queer animals about their young. Be that as it may. You know, Bink, I will not be quite sure this wonderful thing has really happened until I see you as 'the Prince.' It seems like a fairy tale." Twenty-two curtain calls later, the fairy tale had come true.

On opening day, *Time* magazine hit the newsstands with the First Lady of the American Theater gracing its cover. The next day the newspaper and trade reviews for Helen Hayes, for Vincent Price, and for the play were tremendous, and Miller knew that he had a huge hit on his hands. The *Evening Post*, who were among Miss Hayes's many admirers, found Vincent to be "no less good and no less authoritative as Albert. Newcomer though he is, Mr. Price has astonishing ease, genuine presence, an ingratiating manner, great dignity, a rich singing as well as effective speaking voice and who, in this first real opportunity which has come to him, shows exceptional promise as an actor." Columnist Euphemia Van Rensselaer Wyatt enthused, "What Mr. Vincent Price adds to *Victoria Regina* is incalculable. He has the height, the elegance, and profile that made Victoria so jealous of his beauty. He is also able to convey the patient but insatiable conscientiousness which consumed the youthful German." Even the notoriously hard-to-please *New York Times* reviewer, Brooks Atkinson, found that "Price's gentleness of manner as an actor is completely winning" and that he "plays the part beautifully enough to evoke all the romance that lay under the surface of a singular royal marriage."

Naturally, there were bound to be a few detractors. Some felt that the play did not constitute a fully realized drama. Despite his praise for the star performances, Atkinson felt the piece to be "a succession of literary scenes," and, although most reviewers acclaimed Miss Hayes's performance as a tour de force which took the actress from a twenty-year-old princess to an eighty-year-old queen, several criticized her choice of a German accent for the monarch. Hayes defended herself, saying that, while interviewing one of the late queen's granddaughters, the Marchioness of Milford Haven, she had asked whether the queen had spoken with an accent. "Ach, no! She het no more eggzent den you or me!" was the purported response. Many, including most of Vincent's English friends, disagreed with the actress's assessment. There were also those who found her performance perhaps a tad too royal. Percy Hammond wrote, "Helen Hayes suffers from fallen archness." And yet, despite the smattering of negative reviews for the leading lady, there were none for her untested costar.

Vincent Price was all at once the toast of the town. He was praised by critics, actors, and theatergoers equally. Those who saw him on Broadway never forgot his performance. One scene in particular stood out for almost everyone who saw the much lauded production. Actress Jane Wyatt recalled, "Nobody will ever forget that shaving scene. He did it just the right way." Although it's difficult to believe nowadays, the sight of an actor actually shaving on stage, complete with all the accoutrements of the task, and in the presence of an innocent nineteenth-century queen who had never before been in such intimate circumstances with a man, made an enormous impact. Indeed, in the highly-anticipated premiere issue of *Life* magazine published on November 23, 1936, with Margaret Bourke White's now famous photograph of the Hoover Dam gracing its cover, the largest feature article was about Helen Hayes—and one whole page was given over to reproducing the dialogue of the shaving scene. Accompanying the text was a half-page full-color photograph of the scene. The rage for the play, and for this scene in particular, even spawned a dressing-gown craze; a copy of the elegant striped robe worn on stage by Vincent soon appeared in the windows of Bonwit Teller's department store, and the fad spread throughout the country.

Despite the overwhelming excitement of being the star of Broadway's hit show, Vincent's first experience in the American theater was swiftly colored by doubt and disappointment. Norman Marshall came over from London to see the new Broadway production, and during his visit Vincent overheard him say that with the kind of break that he and Gilbert Miller and the critics had afforded the young actor in his first play, he thought Price would last no more than four or five years. Vincent later credited this remark as one of the galvanizing forces in his decision "to survive the vicissitudes of the theater instead of fading into that oblivion of people who had had such a break and then drink themselves to death." Nonetheless, during the run of *Victoria Regina* he often feared that he might prove to be a one-play sensation, a flash in the pan. Certainly no one could dispute the mastery with which he handled his role; but after all he looked just like Albert, he could speak German, he had lived in England. It was a perfect fit. But what would this inexperienced actor do when faced with a more demanding role?

Along with the many naysayers he encountered, Vincent also faced the continuous warnings of his family, who frequently reminded him not to let the attention go to his head. Early on, instead of revelling in his new success, he found himself frequently consumed with worry and self-doubt. The effort it took to conquer his own insecurities about his viability as an actor, as well as the doubts of others, would be remembered and rued throughout his life. Of his first years in the theater, he later wrote, "This familial warning took a lot of the fun out of everything and especially it took away whatever joy I might have had from the company of my fellow actors. I could see in my imagination, and often in truth, the expression in their eyes of 'who the hell does he think he is?' Nevertheless, my heart was so full of gratitude that I had so early on found what I wanted and loved to do."

Over the course of his first year, many nagging fears plagued the young actor. Among these was a growing disillusionment with the American theater. More disheartening even than the petty jealousies of other actors in regard to his meteoric success, Vincent initially found his American colleagues boring, comparing them unfavorably with their English counterparts. "There developed a question during the long and successful run—what did I really want to do? Did I want to act or to be a personality, or, even more abstract, did I want to use a career in the theater as a stepping stone to a life in the arts overall? I met actors, many of them who seemed to shut their art-receptive lives behind them at the stage door, behind a curtain of devotion to one art at the expense of the others. English actors, who had been my first theatrical contacts, had been very different. They knew what was going on in most of the other arts."

Thus, even during those early, exhilarating days of success, Vincent struggled with the pull between his two vocations—the public world of the theater, and his private, intimate, and personal passion for the visual arts. This conflict of choice, with which he was already familiar, had, for a time in London, appeared to resolve itself with his decision to become an actor rather than an art historian. In reality, the conflict would follow him throughout his career.

Vincent's most immediate solution was to devote his days to art, exploring the galleries and museums, getting to know local artists, and adding to his growing collection. "I sought refuge from theater talk in art talk and, happily, I was persona grata in every gallery in New York, either because I was in a hit play . . . or because what little publicity had filtered through all the glamour crap of a 'new find,' said that I had been a serious art historian at the Courtauld. I couldn't have cared less. I loved the art dealers and their wares and, especially, I loved the fact that they never thought me successfully rich and thus helped me to collect what I could afford." And still he worried that by making a commitment to acting as a profession he might in some way be deceiving himself and depriving himself of his one true love.

It was Helen Hayes who assumed the role of Vincent's first important acting mentor, and who taught him how to find the tools with which to make a successful career. She offered him the wisdom of her experience. Most important, she said, he needed to know that to choose the life of an actor was to choose the life of a public servant. An actor, she frequently reiterated, is nothing without his or her audience—advice Vincent quickly took to heart. She warned him, too, of the perils of instant fame, of becoming a one-part actor; instead of denigrating his potential, though, she encouraged him to go out and learn his craft. When pre–air-conditioned Broadway closed for the hot New York summer, she suggested he try his hand at summer stock, taking on as many different roles in as many different kinds of plays as he could.

Vincent later wrote, "I owe so much to Helen. It was she who taught me just how hard I had to work to 'learn the business' after my beginner's luck. Every summer I did stock—five plays in six weeks, and half the time I fell flat on my butt. That's when I realized the best training is just to keep acting, working, with other actors. I also took acting classes. But I didn't tell Helen I was taking classes. I'd been portraying Prince Albert as a rather simple, straightforward fellow. Then, as our teacher suggested, one night I played him in a more emotional way. After the first act, Helen stopped me backstage. 'What's come over you?' she asked. 'Whom do you think you're playing, the Russian Tsar?' "

Although critics and audiences alike certainly felt he had mastered the part of Albert, Vincent himself felt that he was continually endeavoring to learn more about acting. "I learned the importance of moving gracefully and developing absolute ease onstage. That's one of the most difficult things for an actor to learn. In a sense, I had the advantage, or the disadvantage, of being very tall. When I was fourteen, my brother, who was much smaller, made fun of me for being such a tall, gawky thing. I paid no attention to him but secretly resolved to prove that just because I was tall I didn't have to be gawky. Ever since then I have tried to move with the dignity that becomes a tall man and now I realize how important that was."

Hayes also offered advice on technique. In early interviews, Vincent shared pieces of her wisdom: "Miss Hayes told me once that if you let yourself be dominated by the character, your performance will lack conviction. The actor should always have the upper hand, and he can do this if he is convinced of the value of his interpretation. The star is already well established in the audience's mind, and it is the task of any supporting actor to establish himself in his relative importance to her. To gain the audience's sympathy with the character you portray is, I have learned, most essential. In the case of Albert, this is almost done for him by the author."

Of course, Helen and Vincent's friendship during the Broadway run was mutually advantageous, although the most obvious gain was Vincent's. As Helen Hayes's leading man and sometime escort, he was introduced to the glamorous side of the theater world. He later remembered, "One of the many nice things Helen Hayes did for me was to invite me down from my dressing room two flights up, to her onstage one to meet the great of the world which I had entered (again with her help) with such a bang. I met real royalty—the Queen of Spain, heroes—Admiral Byrd, personalities like Irene Castle. Mrs. Castle was one of the great thrills, as childhood idols almost always are. She lived up to her short-lived legend—a dear, now handsome face full of the same warmth, the allure. I was thrilled—beauty always does it." However, Miss Hayes also stood to gain from her leading man's attentions. Vincent's friend, Roddy McDowall remarked: "He became her watch fob. She was married to an irretrievable drunk. And so when Vincent became the talk of the town, the young hope, it was safe. He escorted her everywhere. It was a mutual convenience. She opened the doors to all of this society and he took care of her without being a sexual threat. Helen was an iron butterfly and the keeper of her flame. She certainly wouldn't allow anything to spoil her reputation or her morals. She was dedicated to that. She was royal, actually. She lived in the 'we' term."

In addition to his friendship with Helen, Vincent became good friends with George Macready, the young actor who played Albert's brother, Prince Ernest. Like Vincent, Macready had been educated at an Ivy League school, Brown University, and had become an actor quite by accident, having trained in journalism. He was the only other young man in the cast, and Vincent had written home, "The boy who plays my brother and is my understudy is a swell egg and I thank God for him." The two actors quickly found they had more in common than their youth. They were both art lovers and often haunted the galleries together during the day, laying the foundation for future art ventures together on the West Coast.

All in all, despite Vincent's fears of failure, his first year on Broadway proved a heady and rewarding experience, and it was to his credit that he managed not to become overwhelmed by sudden success. Perhaps most important in this regard was his family, who remained supportive and nurturing. Still only twenty-four, Vincent relied on his father to help him make all of his artistic and business decisions. But most of all, Vincent relied on his family's love and humor to help him keep his head.

Just after the opening of *Victoria Regina*, Vincent Sr. wrote his youngest son, "Since you have become famous it has added greatly to your father's duties at home, at office, and socially. I spend much time interviewing individuals who desire to share your wealth—so far my list includes: 32 Life Insurance Agents, 62 Bond and Share Pushers, 9 Book Agents—who have books which will land you in Hollywood or in Jail, 2 Tailors—who want to make your clothes, 1 Matrimonial Agent who wants to know if you would be interested in marrying a rich widow, 52 who would just love an Actor, 3 Winners of local beauty contests who want you to further their ambitions, 9 Chauffeurs who know all about Actors and Rolls-Royces, 2 Artists who want to paint your portrait while you are still young and beautiful, 1 Yale Professor who needed financial assistance and explained what a difficult time he had getting you through your exams. I trust my services are satisfactory and that you will reward them by writing often."

In the summer of 1936, when Broadway closed its doors during the heat of summer, Vincent followed Helen Hayes's advice and took on the challenge of summer stock. But first, on June 29, he flew to Hollywood for a screen test for producer David O. Selznick. Although the press reported that Selznick was interested in the actor's services, by mid-July Vincent returned to the East Coast, having stayed in Hollywood just long enough to get a glimpse of its glamour. On this first trip, he had a letter of introduction from Helen Hayes to Joan Crawford, whom Hayes liked very much. She told Vincent "there was nobody more glamorous that I could meet in Hollywood or more fun to be with," he remembered. "So, I sent the letter off when I got there but, quite honestly, never expected to have an answer to it. One Sunday morning, the hotel phone rang and a cheery voice chirped, 'Hello, Vincent. This is Joanie!' Now, I did not say 'Joanie who?' but it did take me a gulping moment or two to figure out who Joanie was." Crawford invited him to come over that evening for a quick swim followed by an informal pot luck. Naturally, he accepted.

As he drove up Sunset Boulevard to Crawford's house, he couldn't believe his good fortune—a pot luck with one of the biggest stars in Hollywood. As he later reflected, "In Missouri, pot luck means you get what's left over. It's almost always cold: stuffed eggs in a variety of flavors, cold meats, salads, dessert, and you eat them all off your lap. Needless to say, Joan Crawford's Pot Luck was spelled with capital letters and turned out to be a sit-down dinner for over twenty. It was an extraordinary afternoon. Everybody you ever heard of was there. Joan was in a fabulously form-fitting bathing costume adorning her fabulous form and swam like a goddess. And we swam together. I raced her up and down the Olympic-sized pool until she left me lying limp on the lip of the pool. Then she slipped into a little something designed by Adrian or Orry-Kelly and, covered with star sapphires, glided down the curved staircase looking more like Joan Crawford than one could imagine." Crawford's brand of casual glamour entranced Vincent. "She was a star without trying. She just was. And her promise of an informal afternoon somehow also was. Other famous people arrived informally and Joan just welcomed them. It did not matter if she was dressed to kill or swim. She was glamorously informal. After dinner, we were locked into a theater and had to watch two Spencer Tracy films, who she thought was the best actor in the business. That was how Joan entertained her guests."

*   *   *

Despite the temptations of Hollywood, Vincent was resolute in his decision to spend the summer learning his craft. His first stock role was in an old J. M. Barrie chestnut, *What Every Woman Knows*, at the Westchester Playhouse in Mount Kisco, New York. His costar was another rising Broadway star, Mildred Natwick. The local papers raved over Vincent. One (female) critic gushed, "It is difficult for this reviewer to be able to understand how the show could ever have been a success without Vincent Price as the hero. He makes it all so understandable; the dour Scot, minus humor, plus consummate ability, ambition, intelligence, driving force—but it's Vincent Price who adds to this the looks that simply slayed every female in the audience under twenty, and many of those over twenty admit, grudgingly, that the young man is very handsome and quite the actor." Going from success to success, a week later Vincent opened in *Elizabeth the Queen* at the Ridgeway Theater in White Plains, New York. He played Essex, again opposite Mildred Natwick as Elizabeth. Notices were good, and Price and Natwick took the play back to the Westchester Playhouse a week later.

One of the great perks of these jobs was the proximity of both of these theaters to the home of his sister Hat, her husband, Reed, and their two daughters, Marnie and Anne, in Scarsdale. Vincent was a loving uncle who often took his nieces on short trips or invited them to spend time with him in New York or wherever he was doing summer stock. For all of the Prices family was terribly important and they eagerly threw themselves into Bink's career. Hat and Reed saw all of his plays in the New York area. His parents came up frequently, and also subscribed to the New York papers and national magazines, as well as a clipping service for newspapers around the country that might interview or even mention Bink; they even received the trade magazine *Stage*, so that they could learn more about the theater in general. Vincent Sr. meticulously filled embossed leather-bound scrapbooks detailing his son's career from his first days at the Gate.

For his last show of the summer before returning to Broadway and Albert, Vincent went back to Mount Kisco, this time to the Suffern County Theater, for *Parnell*, a play by Elise Schauffler about the great Irish leader Charles Stewart Parnell and his romantic devotion to Katie O'Shea, which eventually caused his political downfall. The director was the future Hollywood director Joshua Logan, then a young man from Princeton University's Triangle Club and the University Players. To play Price's love interest Logan brought with him a fellow Princetonian, Barbara O'Neil—Vincent's old classmate and first love.

Barbara was the daughter of David and Barbara Blackman O'Neil, the former a poet, the latter a great beauty and well-known suffragette. Although Barbara always felt that everyone was disappointed that she was not as beautiful as her mother, in fact, the two women were quite similar. An interviewer described Barbara as "almost like her tall, graceful mother, with her high-bridged short straight nose, brilliantly flashing dark eyes, lofty eyebrows and head held high, her dusky hair and high-bred voice, and her warmth of manner the same as which her mother used to enfold people." Whether she knew it or not, Barbara was commonly regarded as a very striking young woman, whom Josh Logan had dubbed "the statue of Athena brought to life." After graduating from Sarah Lawrence, she had briefly enrolled at the Yale School of Dramatic Arts before joining the University Players Repertory Theater in Princeton, New Jersey and in Falmouth, Massachusetts, where she worked with James Stewart, Margaret Sullavan, Henry Fonda, Mildred Natwick, Myron McCormick, and Logan, who was then also an actor. Barbara returned to Broadway with the Princeton company in 1932 in their hit play *Carry Nation*, and continued to work in the theater throughout the mid-thirties.

Shortly after appearing in Logan's production of *Parnell* with Vincent, Barbara was called to Hollywood, where Sam Goldwyn had slated her for a featured role in King Vidor's *Stella Dallas* with Barbara Stanwyck. But in playing the historic Irish lovers, Vincent and Barbara had rekindled their own passion—and, although Barbara continued to divide her time between Hollywood and Broadway, she and Vincent began a courtship that would soon be chronicled by gossip columnists on both coasts.

11

THE SECOND BROADWAY season of *Victoria Regina* opened in mid-August, with the original cast intact. In late November, *Life* magazine reported that the play had grossed over one million dollars since opening night, of which Miss Hayes had made $100,000. During Vincent's second year on Broadway, rumors began circulating about movie contracts for the handsome young star; finally Warner Brothers came through with an extraordinary deal—one million dollars for seven years. It is hard to imagine any young actor who would turn down such an offer—particularly one earning $350 a week—but Vincent was determined to achieve long-term success in his career. He knew that he had a great deal to learn before he could truly consider himself an actor; furthermore, he saw himself as a character actor, and he worried that in Hollywood he would be made over into a male ingenue. So he turned for advice to his mentor, Helen Hayes, who encouraged him to reject the offer, counseling him to go out and learn his craft. He took her advice, though he later admitted that it "nearly killed me . . . it would have been very exciting to go out and do Hollywood in that way."

Nonetheless, starring in a Broadway hit certainly had its advantages. Among those who visited Miss Hayes backstage during the second season was Hollywood director George Cukor. At the time, Cukor was conducting a highly publicized casting search for the lead actress in his next film, *Gone With the Wind*. Vincent had heard that he was under consideration for the part of Ashley Wilkes. When the actor spoke with Cukor after the show, he greeted him in his regular, somewhat Southern Missouri accent, instead of the German-English Prince Albert blend the director was expecting. Although Vincent later tested for the part, he always believed that Cukor had thought he was putting the Southern accent on. "I didn't get the part, of course. I wish I had. I think I would have been better than Leslie Howard, because I never thought he was anything but English. He was just wrong. Everyone else was perfect . . . Gable, Olivia de Havilland, and Vivien Leigh. It would have been fun." (Cukor himself was later taken off the film; it was completed by, and credited to, Victor Fleming.)

While appearing in the play, Vincent used his spare time to hone his skills. He took acting lessons at Benno Schneider's Theater School, where his classmates included Burgess Meredith, Britain's Peggy Ashcroft, and the beautiful Mexican singer-actress Margo, who would become one of Vincent's dearest friends. Born in Mexico City, as a little girl Margo had trained as a dancer with Eduardo Cansino, Rita Hayworth's father. She had begun performing with her uncle Xavier Cugat's band, and came with him to New York where they triumphantly introduced the rhumba at the Waldorf Astoria. Soon she began working as an actress on Broadway, appearing in such hit plays as Maxwell Anderson's

Winterset with Burgess Meredith, and in Hollywood, where she starred opposite Ronald Colman in *Lost Horizon*. Margo later married actor Eddie Albert, who had also made a much talked-about Broadway debut in 1936 in *Brother Rat*, rivalling Vincent for the critics' attention as Broadway's newest young male star. Eddie and Margo would be among the few acquaintances of Vincent's New York years who would become lifelong friends when they all settled in Los Angeles.

In an interview for the *Yale Daily News* on April 1, 1937, Broadway's new star reported that his "high spots" thus far in New York were meeting and getting to know a host of the contemporary stage's leading lights: John Gielgud, Judith Anderson, Lillian Gish, Emlyn Williams, Ruth Gordon, Beatrice Lillie, Noel Coward, Burgess Meredith, and Laurette Taylor. Some, like Gielgud and Williams, he had already met in London; others he knew through Helen Hayes or had worked with briefly during summer stock. Always starstruck, Vincent reveled in being part of this glamorous circle.

Helen Hayes, however, took celebrity less calmly. Vincent remembered: "Helen, a star since she was a child, would attest to predictable nausea opening nights. But it didn't stop there. After months of triumph as Queen Victoria, she called me into her dressing room as I came into the theater. 'Before he makes up,' she demanded. My by then great friend took my hand in her firm grasp and plaintively announced, 'I won't go through it alone. I've been sick all day. I wish people wouldn't tell me who's going to be in front.' Resigned to this familiar routine—she'd almost had to cancel the performance when the ex-Queen of Spain was to be in the audience—I said, 'And who is it tonight, Helen, the Queen of England?' 'Oh, no, that would be easy. You can't ask her if she liked the performance and she won't tell you. This is different and twice as difficult.' . . . Then she blurted it out, 'Noel Coward, that's who. Noel Coward.' I couldn't resist asking, 'Why Mr. Coward? I've always heard he was a very kind man.' 'Oh, he is, but even if he likes it, everyone will quote what he might have said.' And she fled to the john to disgorge what little she'd been able to eat all day."

During the second season of *Victoria Regina*, producer-director Guthrie McClintic brought Gielgud's *Hamlet* to New York, unwisely setting it in the period of Charles II. Starring Judith Anderson, and Lillian Gish, the New York production failed to match the high standards of its London predecessor. Through Gielgud, however, Vincent met both Lillian Gish and Judith Anderson for the first time, both of whom he would later work with in films. When Gielgud, Anderson, and Gish gave a garden party at One Fifth Avenue shortly after their play opened, Vincent was invited. Years later, he recalled his first meeting with Anderson. "I was standing nervously by the refreshments waiting to be introduced to the great lady. Suddenly I spied her coming toward me and then I was being offered her hand. It took me off my feet, quite literally, for I retreated a step and with her hand firmly in my grasp, found myself seated in the punch bowl. I think I felt like crying, but I was wet everywhere else. But whatever I felt other than wet, suddenly I found myself joining peals of joyous laughter coming from the great lady's lips. As the laughter subsided and as I peeled a lemon slice from the seat of my pants, I thought, 'Well, she's never had anyone fall for her this way.' At that moment I fell in love with Judith Anderson."

During his first years in the theater, Vincent came to know many of the great American leading ladies. One of his favorites was certainly Tallulah Bankhead, whom he first met at the bar of the El Morocco in the late 1930s, when she tackled him and practically threw him to the floor. Over the years they remained good friends, often working in radio together. Tallulah loved to shock people, but those who became her friends were inevitably those who took her outrageous behavior in stride. Early in their friendship, she had dropped by Vincent's dressing room at the Westport Playhouse. She chatted for a while and then he noticed, "She was sitting on my washbasin, and suddenly I realized that she was taking a leak. You know, if she hadn't been, I'd have been terribly disappointed. Because that was part of the Tallulah legend." Vincent loved strong, outspoken women. He said of Tallulah, "She was magnificent. There ain't nobody like her. In her heyday nobody had a bigger ball. She had that magnificent beauty that is ugly in a funny way. Judith Anderson and Laurette Taylor had it too. They came off being the most beautiful women in the world through an illumination of their own personality. I've seen Tallulah look absolutely dreadful, then take a shot of ammonia and Coca-Cola and turn into a beauty." When she died in 1968, Vincent was writing a weekly syndicated column about art. That week he devoted his column to an appreciation of his friend, "Tallulah: A Work of Art."

As Helen Hayes's sometime escort, Vincent was regarded as a charming and convivial man-about-town. There was one person, however, who had held Vincent's attention for many years. After his reunion with Barbara O'Neil during the summer of 1936, they had begun to correspond regularly and to date whenever she returned to New York. Vincent seemed able to bare his soul to Barbara as to no one else. During the second season of *Victoria Regina*, he briefly felt a strain with his leading lady, which he expressed to no one but Barbara in a letter: "I have done something to get into Hayes' bad book though I don't know what! But I think she resents me terribly—she has been giving stinking performances lately, and I haven't! Maybe that's it!" The letter continued, "My God! but I love you—and have mulled everything over in my head and have come to the conclusion that I have never loved anyone before. Did you show your family the ring?" The ring Vincent sent Barbara in the spring of 1937 doubtless carried some meaning, but it could not have suggested a firm commitment; throughout this period, and despite his declarations to Barbara, Vincent continued to date other women. Among my father's possessions, for example, there survives a letter from this period, addressed to "My dearest Albert" and signed "MW". It reads, "I love you darling with the very best and sweetest side of me—my crazy side has nothing to do with you. That is why I am capable at the same time—alas—of loving nobility (you) and the *dregs* (him). Both so infinitely attractive. But dearest stay the way you are. You are going to be famous and do the world good for having lived in it. And (don't laugh at me) I am too. We've both got something really good to give—more than others, most of the others we meet. And I wish you the greatness that will be yours." It seems reasonable to surmise that the letter was from Margaret Webster, the English actress-director with whom he had worked in his first play in London. She was in New York to direct Maurice Evans in her acclaimed production of *Richard II*, which opened in February 1937, and became the surprise sensation of the new Broadway season.

The summer of 1937 brought the end of the two-year Broadway run of *Victoria Regina*. The show would go on to tour nationally—but without Vincent Price. Following Hayes's advice, Vincent decided to break away from the part with which he had become so closely identified and make his name as a well-rounded actor. To ease the transition, he opted to spend the summer once again doing stock. (For many years, however, he continued to identify with Albert, wearing a ring he had found in London which had belonged to the Prince Consort and was inscribed with his name. In 1947, columnist Louella Parsons reported that a London jewelry firm was reputed to have offered $10,000 for the ring on behalf of a client who wished to give it to Princess Elizabeth's bridegroom-to-be, Prince Philip, as a wedding gift. As Parsons noted, "The only hitch is that Vincent hasn't yet made up his mind whether or not he wants to part with the valuable piece of jewelry.")

In mid-June, Vincent arrived at the Lakewood Theatre in Skowhegan, Maine, to try his hand at serious drama as Halmar Ekdal in Henrik Ibsen's *The Wild Duck*. Playing his wife, Gina, was one of the great ladies of the theater, Blanche Yurka, an opera singer who had become a dramatic star on Broadway during the twenties. Vincent admired Yurka, a legendary leading lady of his youth, and rose to the dual challenge—a complex role, a formidable costar—and garnered excellent reviews.

Vincent liked Skowhegan. Nestled in an idyllic lakeside environment, the Maine summer theater saw itself as an artists' colony of sorts, promoting new playwrights and young actors as well as attracting major stars. On *The Wild Duck*'s closing night, Vincent drove to Boston, chartered a plane, and reached New York in time to do a broadcast of a scene from *Victoria Regina* with Helen Hayes. He then flew back to Boston and caught the night train to Maine to begin rehearsals for his next play—a second crack at *Parnell*, this time opposite the famous and accomplished Edith Barrett.

Edith Barrett was a star of melodrama and one of the first Broadway actresses to support summer stock. She had played Lakewood in 1933 and was now returning as one of their most popular performers. She had begun her career as a child star and become a famous actress in the twenties; her grandfather was Lawrence Barrett, a business and acting partner to Edwin Booth, with whom he was one of the cofounders of New York's famous Players Club. Edith herself had debuted on the Broadway stage as a flower girl in Walter Hampden's Broadway production of *Cyrano de Bergerac* which opened November 1, 1923 at the National Theater; from there her career saw a steady assent. By the 1930–31 Broadway season, when Barrett scored an extraordinary success in the title role of *Mrs. Moonlight*, chronicling the life of a woman who never wanted to grow old, the *New York Times* had voted her the leading ingenue of the season—at the age of twenty-six.

When twenty-six-year-old Vincent Price met Edith Barrett, she was in her early thirties, though she claimed to be almost a decade younger. A pretty woman with sharp features, a fair complexion, and large, luminous, brown eyes, she had reached a plateau in her career. Increasingly typecast as a Barrie-esque leading lady, in the kinds of gutless parts she called "Winnie the Pooh roles," Barrett was determined to show that she could succeed in more serious dramas. "It makes me so damn mad," she said. "Nobody ever thought of me in anything but those kinds of parts—you know, saccharine or whimsical, however you want to call it." Her first step was to return to summer stock during the mid-1930s, where she proved herself in more substantial roles; finally, during the spring of 1936, she was cast in Guthrie McClintic's Broadway production of *Parnell*, which was hailed as perhaps the best performance of her career. When she arrived at Lakewood, it was to repeat her New York success.

Edith and Vincent hit it off immediately. They spent almost every day together, taking time off to swim in the lake or go into town for meals when not rehearsing their roles as doomed lovers. The production of *Parnell* was well received and both were easily persuaded to stay an additional week to perform in *Eden's End* by J. B. Priestley. Photographs from Lakewood show Vincent and Edith clowning around during the day, swimming, their friendship clearly developing into a romantic relationship. At the end of the second week, however, Edith left on a previously planned trip to Europe, while Vincent went into a play opposite yet another theatrical legend, the great fan dancer Sally Rand. For a boy who was bred on burlesque, this was almost as exciting as working with Helen Hayes.

Riding high on good notices and his heady few weeks with Edith Barrett, Vincent returned to the Westport Playhouse, where he had played the previous summer, to star opposite the exotic Hollywood actress Anna May Wong in a dramatic adaptation of Puccini's opera, *Turandot*. A Californian by birth, Anna May Wong had quickly risen to great heights in Hollywood playing exotic Asian sirens. Having recently returned from her first trip to China, she was trying her hand in the East Coast theater for the first time, and opening night drew a gathering of Broadway's greatest leading ladies, eager to see what this screen actress could do on stage. One catty reporter noted that Tallulah Bankhead, Ethel Barrymore, Ina Clair, Eugenie Leontovitch, Alla Nazimova, and Princess Nathalie Paley spent the evening "bowing to each other and hiding in every available spotlight."

When the curtain rose, Anna May Wong came off moderately well, but she left room for her costar to steal the show. Once again, reporters gushed over Vincent's physical presence and theatrical aplomb. "Mr. Price surpassed all my expectations," wrote one local reviewer. "Physically, he is a child of the gods. Exceptionally tall, he is exceptionally handsome, and exceptionally graceful. He is one man who can be called beautiful in the sense that a thoroughbred of seventeen hands is beautiful. Garbed as an Apollo king of the near East, his presence brought glory to the stage. For these gifts, Mr. Price deserves little credit. But for the way he handled himself on the undersized stage and for the thrilling way in which he gave his lines, he merited acclaim and got plenty of it. These showed art and show he's been hard at work at the task of becoming an actor."

Radiating in the acclaim, Vincent enjoyed a memorable week in *Turandot*, which also brought a brief affair with his costar. More important, though, Vincent was contacted by Rufus Phillips and Watson Barratt, producers looking to capitalize on his success in *Victoria Regina* by casting him in their next Broadway vehicle. They had the rights to *Jean*, a romantic comedy by Hungarian playwright Ladislaus Bus-Fekete, and had chosen Hollywood sensation Elissa Landi to play the female lead. When they offered Vincent the title role, he eagerly accepted. It was a demanding part: The play concerns a butler to the Hungarian prime minister who is elected to a parliamentary position on the opposition ticket, but is obliged for financial reasons to continue working for the prime minister, even as he opposes him in the government.

Publicity for the Broadway-bound play focused on Vincent Price, who was being touted as a matinée idol, and Elissa Landi, a rumored descendant of European royalty, who took the role of the prime minister's daughter. Whether or not Landi was indeed the offspring of her mother's affair with a member of the Austrian royal family, she was undeniably beautiful. Vincent later described her as "a wide-eyed wonder of womanly perfection. Even in her maturity, she had a young girl's stance and stare. This innocence was real, and I felt she hid a certain shyness by pretending to act, which she did rather diffidently and not too well." Whatever her shortcomings as an actress, however, Vincent affirmed, "One couldn't help liking Elissa. Even my mother, not given to liking actresses by the piece or by the bolt, liked Elissa, and I think sensed her frailty—she died of cancer not long after we worked together."

Vincent breezed through his last two summer stock obligations, returning to Lakewood to perform in a mediocre comedy, *The Lady of La Paz*, then obliging the producers at the Westport Playhouse by taking the leading role in *Romance* opposite yet another legend, Eugenie Leontovitch. A notoriously difficult actress, Leontovitch had rejected her first costar, leaving the producers in the uncomfortable position of having to find another actor on very short notice. Vincent was perfect: Popular with local playgoers, he also happened to be easygoing and a very quick study. Leontovitch's reputation preceded her, but Vincent was still unprepared for the intensity of her attacks. He later described his ordeal: "She was probably the most difficult woman to work with on stage in the world. They claimed that more men took to drink after doing a play with her than anyone else. She would upstage you. She would do the most terrible things. I thought she'd be good to me because I'd done her this great favor, but she murdered me. She was a killer, but she was brilliant. She was a great actress. She didn't need to do any of that nonsense."

Vincent was eager to get to work on *Jean*, perhaps because it was slated to open first at the Shubert Theatre in New Haven, scene of so many of his theater fantasies in his college days. Helen Hayes and the touring company of *Victoria Regina* had played there for the three nights prior to *Jean*'s arrival, and she left Vincent a sweet note of encouragement, as had the rest of the company. He wrote his parents, "It made me a bit homesick for *V.R.* and what a tour it is going to be—$10,600 in three performances here. But what the hell, we must never stagnate, but go ahead." Many of his friends turned out for the opening, including Ted Thomas and Barbara O'Neil's family. Audiences and critics alike fell for the show, while *Variety* gave the advance word that "Price walks away with top acting honors, offering a highly polished interpretation of a meticulous role. Lad should make a great catch for Hollywood, possessing as he does both looks and ability." Vincent's friends also encouraged him in his work, although they didn't think so much of Elissa Landi, who, Vincent commented, was "inclined to overwork." Still, his hopes were high as the company headed to New York. "Everything, I think, will iron itself out and come out a good show. It has charm and so many laughs and such delightful comedy and pathos—we had them in tears and laughing."

Critics continued to lavish as much praise on Vincent's looks as on his thespian abilities. "After last night's performance," one wrote, "one could almost predict a return to the 'matinée idol' days of long ago. Mr. Price, as handsome a blond God as this reviewer has ever encountered, evoked rhapsodic gushings from the feminine portion of the audience, formerly reserved for Robert Taylor." Certainly there was a growing feeling within the profession that Vincent was, indeed, destined to follow in the footsteps of such stars as Taylor and Gary Cooper. With his wavy blond hair, full lips, and strong, straight features, he had become strikingly good-looking; he also had the aristocratic bearing and easy grace of one on whom success sat easily.

Even his family had grown to think of their youngest son as star material. When he had first received the script for *Jean*, Vincent had sent it to his father to get his opinion. In early July, Vincent Sr. had written his son, "I'll admit what I know about plays, especially from reading the script—could be put in a gnat's eye—but there is one thing I'm going to stick to and that is your exploiting your good looks to the utmost along with your acting. You have a double asset few have."

With its title changed to *The Lady Has a Heart*, the play opened at Broadway's

Longacre Theatre on September 25, 1937. On opening night Helen Hayes sent Vincent a telegram which read, "Do you remember a fellow named Albert? Well make a bum out of him tonight." And yet, despite everybody's high hopes, the play was a flop. Although the first-night audience gave it a standing ovation, for the first time in his brief career Vincent experienced failure with the New York critics. They were far tougher than the out-of-town press had been, disliking the play and, what was worse for the young actor, attacking his "comically ponderous acting." Brooks Atkinson gave him his first of many negative notices over the years, declaring that "the acting has fallen under the otiose spell of Hungarian dramaturgy. As the precocious valet, Vincent Price looks handsome enough to give a maiden apoplexy. Every hair is perfectly turned and his carriage is exquisite. But the immediate reticence that was so winning when Mr. Price was the Prince Consort in *Victoria Regina* is merely monotonous on this pasteboard occasion. For all his charms, Mr. Price is going to be a dull actor unless he can learn how to give himself to a play."

Vincent was wounded deeply by the attacks. He had turned down the national tour of *Victoria Regina* only to wind up in a flop. He wrote his parents, "All our elation over the opening went down the drain with the critics. They panned me in the morning papers and were fair and kind in the evening, but all panned the play." Then, with a touch of defiance, "I had a feeling they would gun for me. They hate to have a young actor come into prominence too quickly. I suppose I'll have to job hunt soon, but success is built on failure, so here's hoping. I feel pretty low today, but now am quite reconciled to it and realize that it had to be; it would have been just too good to be true."

There was, however, one sector of the population with whom, despite his notices, Vincent was only becoming more popular—young women. Journalist Harry Mines reported him to be "the heart-throb of thousands. The girls adore him frankly and openly. There's always a crowd of feminine gapers to be found at the stage door of the Longacre. Pandemonium breaks loose and all reserve is thrown to the wind when the actor looms on the threshold leading from the realms behind the scenes, and attempts to make his way to the street." But although eighty percent of the audiences for *The Lady Has a Heart* were adoring women, Vincent fought his growing sex-symbol status; what he wanted was the respect of the theater community, though, according to Mines, and despite his recent spate of negative reviews, the actor already had this in hand: "If you ask any of the folks in the theater, they will tell you that Price is hard working, eager to absorb, quick and intelligent when it comes to finding out about the job of acting. He studies voice and diction, singing, in fact anything to improve himself. Sincerity is his strongest characteristic . . . Added to this is a fine vein of seriousness. With all his sudden success, Vincent has managed to keep his feet on the ground."

Anticipating another long run on Broadway, Vincent had taken a small basement apartment on 53rd Street between Fifth and Sixth Avenues. He was thrilled to have his own place at last and soon found that, although it was tiny, it had two great advantages. From an apartment overlooking his, "strains of heavenly music occasionally burst forth which always came to an abrupt stop before the song was sung out. I knew it was vocalizing but whose I didn't know until one day I saw Isolde enter the building." The great Wagnerian soprano Kirsten Flagstad, it turned out, lived nearby; Vincent rushed home and wrote the diva a fan letter; a few days later a signed photograph arrived, which he framed and hung in every house he lived in until his death. Besides the proximity of

Flagstad, another favorable feature of the small flat was an outdoor patio, which Vincent gradually transformed into a garden. Walking home at night after a performance, he would scour his neighborhood for discarded houseplants and trees and carefully nurture them back to health. "It really was a wonderful garden," he later reminisced. "I also bought an old bathtub, which I put in the center of the garden and put flagstones around and made into a lovely fishpond."

Harry Mines, the journalist who became a lifelong friend, interviewed Vincent during this period, and his profile captures the flavor of the actor's first months in his new home. "Armed with an irrepressible sense of humor, Vincent dwells like a happy bohemian in a white-walled suite of rooms on West Fifty-Third Street. He has a garden, a band-box affair, in which some worried-looking plants fight valiantly for air which has been pretty well shut off by a surrounding cluster of buildings. Price's roommates are a bulldog with sad eyes by the name of Johnny and a cat, armed with wanderlust, who answers to the call of Albert. Neighboring fish markets are a constant lure to Albert and Vincent spends most of his free hours conducting frantic one-man hunts for his pet tabby."

Albert the Good, Vincent's cat, had spent the past two years as the gypsy cat of a gypsy owner. But now that the two had settled down, the family expanded. Vincent's new neighbors included a pet shop, which he walked past daily, knowing that "sooner or later . . . a wistful pair of dog eyes would stare up at me out of the straw and Albert and I would have a new roommate." A few days after the dismal opening of *The Lady Has a Heart*, Vincent "wandered down Sixth Avenue in that critically induced state of amnesia in which all actors forget themselves when connected with a failure. In my lostness I was drawn to the pet shop window, and there, of course, was something more lost than I was. A brown-patched, white English bulldog puppy reeled around the cage on his gnarled legs. His jaw was as far out as mine in a determination not to let life get him down. His price was twenty-five dollars. I had twenty-five dollars, but I had no right to spend it with the imminent closing of the play staring me in the face. But everyone has a way (or many ways) of counteracting the blues. Some people get drunk. Others go off on a trip. I have two steps: art and animals. Art always cheers me up, even if I can't or don't buy it. It gives me courage to see the creative products of others. Animals cheer me up because they are so dependent on man, and most men are completely willing to take them on as dependents."

Meanwhile, Vincent's romance with Barbara O'Neil seemed to be hopelessly stalled. Although Walter Winchell reported that "Vincent Price is the new Romeo with Barbara O'Neil," and other gossip columnists noted that he had spent forty-two minutes on the phone with Barbara after opening night—as well as sixty percent of his weekly income on regular phone calls to her—Vincent was downhearted to be sure. He had hoped that they would spend the following summer together in Los Angeles, but he now was worried that the play's failure might affect his chances in Hollywood. Writing to Barbara, who was still in Los Angeles, he professed himself "very upbeat, though the reviews are not all good and it's looking like a short run. I'm afraid the public likes me, but not the critics. I took the expected pokes about Albert, etc. So obvious!" Nonetheless, he conceded, "My white bulldog fights Albert all the time. I'm a nervous wreck. No sleep."

On November 29 the producers moved the play to the 46th Street Theatre, hoping to cut their losses in the smaller house, but the show closed on December 18. To make matters worse, Albert had run away for good. Vincent spent days looking for him, until he received an eerie note in his mailbox informing him that the cat had a new and happy home, but he would be returned if Vincent got rid of his dog. Out of work and unsure what to do or where to go next, a depressed Vincent could only hope that Albert was happier where he was; accompanied by Johnny, the out-of-work actor drove to St. Louis to spend the holidays. From there he flew out to Hollywood again, where he was tested for the romantic lead in MGM's *Marie Antoinette*, starring Norma Shearer. But he still did not feel ready to go into movies, particularly so soon after his recent disaster. He was offered the role but turned it down, and he told his parents would continue to turn down movies until he "felt sure of himself." In his dejected frame of mind, Vincent decided to leave Johnny in St. Louis with a friend who owned a big farm. In early January, he returned to New York, alone and with little idea of what the future would hold.

12

THROUGHOUT THE RUN of *Victoria Regina*, Vincent had continued to frequent the art galleries he had discovered while a student at Yale, and to seek out new ones. His most frequent companion was George Macready, who was almost as adventurous as he in the pursuit of art. He also frequently accompanied Helen Hayes to the galleries, and though her taste was fairly conservative, he took pleasure in introducing her to modern artists.

Through Helen, Vincent came to know comedienne Bea Lillie. He found her art collection even more pedestrian than Helen's, and was distressed that a comic actress's collection could be so humorless. He determined to find her a painting with humor. Months later he saw it. "In a gallery sat the most charming Modigliani in the whole world. It was a little blond boy, pudgy and arch, with blue eyes which gave you the feeling you were looking straight through his empty fat head to the sky on the other side. I found myself laughing out loud, standing in the street. This picture belonged to Beatrice Lillie. It was a wicked comment on youth, the kind of comment she might make on a particularly repulsive English boy." Vincent convinced the comedienne to purchase the painting—but he always thought "she bought it because she had to admit it was amusing, but not because she really liked it." A decade later, Vincent encoutered Lillie, and the topic arose again. "I had almost forgotten the Modigliani, but she came over to say hello and reminded me of the incident. She thanked me and said, 'Dear me, it's worth a lot of money now, isn't it?' I allowed as how it was and that it hadn't even begun to hit its top. Miss Lillie listened to my predictions of the future art boom and said, pertly, 'Well, that may be, dear—but I still don't like it.' "

During this period, Vincent's success in the theater also brought him into contact with many artists and writers who were politically active in Spanish Civil War relief efforts. When Franco's fascist troops marched on their compatriots in July 1936, the workers had responded by fomenting a revolution whose effects extended far beyond the boundaries of Spain. Around the world, leftist and liberal forces joined in support of the workers and against fascism. In the United States, artists and writers joined communists and liberals in organizing Civil War fundraisers.

By 1938 Vincent, like many of his colleagues, had begun attending meetings concerning various social and political causes sponsored by socialist, communist, and other left-wing activist groups. Inspired by new friendships with theater people whose wide-ranging interests mirrored his own, Vincent began for the first time to question his parents' politics. Vincent Sr. and Marguerite were, as their son later reflected, "As Republican as you could be. My dad was really a very clean, neat-thinking man in all ways, in religion and politics and every other way. He wasn't active in politics, but he was a Republican, and I guess my mother was, too, if she thought about it at all. The man in the White House who was their bête noir was Roosevelt. I was brought up in that atmosphere, but I didn't really have a point of view one way or the other. My first vote was for Wendell Wilkie, but when I finally came to my senses, I was a rabid Rooseveltian."

As Vincent came to spend more time in New York art circles, meeting a group of men and women whose commitment to social issues compelled him to learn more about their ideas, he soon shed his early negative feelings about the insularity of Broadway actors. Their enthusiasm for such New Deal programs as the WPA (Works Progress Administration), which sponsored public art, led him to examine all of Roosevelt's policies, which, in turn, led him to a deep sense of loyalty to the president. (When the radio announcement came in 1945 that Roosevelt had died, Vincent fell backward off the couch, sobbing.)

Vincent soon became more actively involved in fundraising for left-wing political causes. Because he was known as an art collector, he was asked to be the auctioneer at the downtown ACA Gallery for a Spanish Civil War relief benefit. All of the hot New York painters of the day donated work—Paul Burlin, William Gropper, David Burliuk, and Yasuo Kuniyoshi among them. This event also brought him into contact with prominent leftists in the New York theater community such as Paul Robeson and Lillian Hellman, with whom he became friends. In 1938, Vincent helped Lillian Hellman and Dorothy Parker organize a benefit for Spanish Civil War relief by persuading a group of artists to do the plates for an illustrated limited edition of Hellman's play *Watch on the Rhine*. For the first time since returning home from London, Vincent had found a means of integrating art and theater, often serving as a liaison between the two worlds.

Meanwhile, Vincent's own art collection grew. In 1936, Helen Hayes had given him a small landscape by Alexander Brook for Christmas; Vincent didn't particularly admire it, and with Helen's permission he traded it for Toulouse-Lautrec's poster, *May Belfort*. Everyone thought he was crazy to exchange a known quantity like Brook for the work of a then relatively unrecognized graphic artist, but both he and Miss Hayes were pleased, and became more so as Lautrec grew in importance. Around this time Vincent also bought an oil painting of a flower arrangement by Vlaminck for $400, a George Bellows crayon of *Girls By a Lake*, and a few Goya etchings.

Through his connections to the art world, his collection began to encompass new interests. During the brief run of *The Lady Has a Heart*, one of his favorite galleries was just a few blocks away on 56th Street. "They had Mexican and Peruvian furniture and silver, and a few wonderful drawings by Central and South American artists. It was run by a woman named Alma Reed, who was José Orozco's mistress. She was also his biographer, and had a painting of his called *Zapata*, which was about seven feet high and five feet wide. A really fabulous painting of Zapata, standing in a cave entrance with the daylight behind him, and the people begging for deliverance. The blues, browns, and reds were superb, and it spoke eloquently for the freedom of the Mexican people. It moved me a great deal." One day, on a lark, Vincent asked Reed how much the painting was worth. "She told me it was $5,000. That meant nothing to me, because I couldn't afford anything close to that. Still I used to go in all the time to talk to her. And she kept saying to me, 'Why don't you buy this painting?' And I said, 'Alma, you know I'm just a young actor at the beginning of my career. I haven't got a pot to piss in.' But she said, 'Well, for instance, what could you pay for it?' I told her I had about $750 in the bank and that I could pay that, but I'd have to do it by making a down payment of one hundred dollars and then maybe fifty dollars a month. And she said, 'Sold!' I thought, 'My God, now what am I going to do?' "

And so Vincent Price found himself struggling down Fifth Avenue carrying the enormous canvas back to his apartment. Happily, he found one wall on which it just fit; but then, to his chagrin, he realized that the painting's perspective was such that it could only be properly viewed from below; anyone who wanted to appreciate the piece fully was obliged to clamber beneath his kitchen table. As word got out that the Broadway actor had bought the Orozco masterpiece, he received calls from students at the New School, where the painter had taught, asking if they could come see it. Vincent always graciously welcomed the students into his small apartment, then went about his day while they lay for hours underneath his kitchen table. Not long afterward, Vincent loaned the painting to the Museum of Modern Art; later he sold it to the Chicago Art Institute, where it hangs today.

13

DURING THE 1937–38 season, two theater troupes were the talk of Broadway. The Group Theater was performing new work by playwrights such as Clifford Odets, while John Houseman and Orson Welles's Mercury Theater was revitalizing the classics. After the dismal failure of *The Lady Has a Heart*, Vincent was thrilled when Welles invited him to join the Mercury Theater company in early January 1938, and he gladly signed a five-play contract. Because he had already made a name for himself, he was given a leading actor's salary—seventy dollars a week. It was a significant pay cut from the $350 a week he had received in his last year of *Victoria Regina*, but the Mercury Theater was the place to be that year. Welles's company had quickly developed a reputation for theatrical innovation and high standards, bringing the classics back to Broadway, yet making them accessible to a contemporary audience.

Determined to develop his skills and enlarge his reputation as an actor by shedding his matinée idol image, Vincent realized that working in a repertory company would be the ideal situation. Except for a few older character actors this was a group of brash young men, and Vincent quickly found his niche in the troupe, forming lifelong friendships with fellow actors Norman Lloyd and Joseph Cotten. Lloyd remembered: "Vincent came into the Mercury as a star. We were just scruffy individuals. Here comes this long drink of water. Oh this guy's a star, is he? Gonna take all the leading parts from us, is he? That was just our attitude. But he was such a charmer that at the end of the first day it was as if he was just another scruffy individual, which of course he never was. It was great chemistry and everyone had a great time with each other."

Perhaps unsurprisingly, a certain preoccupation with appearances gave Vincent and Lloyd a point in common. "Vincent was afraid that he was going to lose his hair and I was afraid that I was going to lose mine, and I was indeed righter than Vincent, because I did lose mine. So, Vincent was always discovering either new ointments or places you go where you have your scalp burnt off. All of which I did, at Vincent's encouraging. 'Oh,' he said, 'this one is great!' And then they'd burn off your scalp and put a foul-smelling ointment on your hair. Well, I must have done four or five, all of which Vincent had done first. And he always came back with his hair looking good. And I thought, well, that's for me, you see. So, that gave us something, a great common ground. The aesthetics came later."

Initially, Vincent Price and Orson Welles also got along well. They seemed to have much in common—two intelligent and talented Midwesterners who had made names for themselves fairly quickly, and whose strikingly mellifluous voices were fast becoming as famous as their faces. And, of course, their fathers were old friends. But Vincent soon grew disenchanted with Welles's capricious and petulant behaviour, both as a director and an actor. Welles had the common affliction of so many geniuses—his greatest concern was for himself. In planning his season and casting his plays, he treated his actors like royalty when he needed them and then forgot about them completely when he did not, shifting them from one play to another at whim, promising them roles and then reneging on his offers if something or someone better came along. Almost all of the actors in the original company ended up disappointed, and some fell into outright conflict with Welles. For the always-disciplined Price, such unprofessional behavior went against everything he believed the theater should be. He later wrote of Welles, "I'm sorry I never got to know Orson Welles better, but he became a legend before his time. He could have been one of the greatest American theatrical and cinema directors, but he had to act. Whether he directed or acted, a play was his show and finally, for that reason and for the fact that he ignored contracts and gave no one else any credit, the Mercury fell apart."

Vincent joined the Mercury following its triumphant first production, a modern-dress *Julius Caesar* that was immediately hailed as the solution to all that was wrong with Broadway. His initial hopes were high; here, he felt, was a company that could form the foundation of an American national theater to rival the best in England. Despite his eventual disillusionment with Welles, their first production together proved a success. Vincent recalled, "Orson was twenty-one years old, and to work with him was so exciting. He was fresh and new with wonderful ideas, and it was an exciting time in the theater." Vincent himself turned in a fine performance as Master Hammon in the Elizabethan classic *The Shoemaker's Holiday*. Norman Lloyd recalled, "He was lovely in *Shoemaker's Holiday*. And Joe Cotten and I were really rather unruly in it. Vincent was beautiful in it, because he played this very elegant fellow with all these rats running around him and he was imperturbable. You know, he was the greatest guy in tights because of those legs that went eight hundred feet high. So, he put on those tights and cape and, as they say, he brought class to the joint."

After three years of performing with some of the great ladies of the American stage, Vincent relished an opportunity to act along with his peers. Although only twenty-six, he had earned a reputation as a mature and reliable performer. Now, for the first time, he had the opportunity to have fun on stage. Norman Lloyd told of a woman in *The Shoemaker's Holiday* named Marion Waring-Manley who "weighed close to three hundred pounds and Orson called her Marion Whoring-Boring Manley. She was a nice lady, but she had a bad habit of chewing Dentyne gum and pasting it on the back of the set where we all entered, before she came on stage. After a while, we had this whole mural of Dentyne gum. We requested that she cease and desist, but she wouldn't. Joe Cotten and I had these brooms of faggots, and the groundcloth of the stage was made of rope, so every time she had a laugh line, we would sweep and sweep and make this terrible sound. And we said we'd only stop when she stopped posting her gum. Now, Vincent was on stage the whole time that we did these things and he said, 'Go right ahead. It's quite all right with me.' So, we all had a very enjoyable time."

Providing a happy remedy to the disastrous reviews of Vincent's previous New York outing, the critics loved his performance as Master Hammon. Even previous detractors like Eugene Burr of *Billboard* allowed, "Certainly no one could overlook the Hammon of Vincent Price, a performer hitherto regarded not too highly in this corner. Mr. Price comes through to give a polished performance and a series of really beautiful readings, turning in the best among a stageful of excellent jobs."

Though joining the Mercury had given him a chance to find his professional footing once again, his malaise of the previous fall still lingered. In addition to his growing displeasure with Welles, his increasing involvement with the artists' community on behalf of Spanish Civil War relief caused him, once again, to question his commitment to the theater. In early February, he wrote Barbara O'Neil, "I often wonder if there isn't something great for every man to do during his life, and that if we try hard enough and prepare ourselves well enough the genius will not one day enter us and demand to make itself heard. I have always had a feeling that there was something for me to do, and I knew that I must give pleasure to people. The theater seemed the way to do that but now, more and more with the heat of maturity burning in me, I feel there is also something else, something much more important than that, but I don't quite know what it is, so I am preparing myself for the day when the spirit will enter me. It must sound very foolish, but it is true, and it may not come for many years, but I want to be ready." The reality of being in the theater was starting to dispel his initial idealism about the profession. "We are not happy people; painters are, musicians are, their instruments are always at their disposal. Ours is locked up by Equity, by critics, and by egos that belong to us and to those we work for or with. The more shows I see here the more I think that [motion] pictures, in almost every case, have it all over them. The stage could be so grand, but it just isn't and I have no cure to recommend for it, unless there was a theater like the Mercury that was the private enterprise of one man. Orson is a genius, and a grand guy, but I fear that the Mercury is his, and that all others are disregarded, even the actors working with him. Someday perhaps there will be such a theater and then we will be able to prove ourselves, and to have real theater once again."

Whatever the difficulties in their romantic liaison, Vincent was still best able to pour out his heart to Barbara. To the outside world he showed himself as the charming young actor or the happy bohemian, but underneath he could be self-doubting, even maudlin. That season he wrote her: "Gosh—I do miss you darling and don't see anyone. You have made all other company seem very dull and unless you hurry back or I hurry out I am going to become a confirmed bachelor." And yet he seems to have known even then that there was no real hope for the two of them. His letters betray a frustration that may have been sexual: "I love you, but you have fear of me, or rather your relations with me, both mental and physical. I have never been in love, and I am not quite sure that I know what love means. It certainly doesn't mean for us what it meant to my mother and father. I would love to think myself an ordinary individual, but I am not; I have never been allowed the pleasure of thinking as others do, and therefore all my life have been separated from others. I have separated myself, I have thought everything out for and by myself, and now I want to join with you, if you will let me. I am very afraid that we don't really love each other, but I do think that we need each other, for some reason or other and in some strange way or other . . . I think you will agree with me." He goes on to implore Barbara "to come out of your little little shell and tell me so . . . I really think that perhaps you are my ideal human being, I have searched everywhere for someone to take your place and have found no one that can even approach you, and now I have given up, and don't see or search anymore."

There is no record of Barbara's response, but soon after this outpouring Vincent appears to have given up all hope of their union. A few years later, Barbara O'Neil married director Joshua Logan. In his autobiography, Logan describes their brief and ill-fated marriage, saying that within a few days of their wedding, "We both knew the marriage was a mistake. We liked each other and that was all." Logan and O'Neil were divorced and she never remarried.

But Vincent would not remain desolate for long, for he had been joined in the Mercury Theater by his leading lady from two summers before. Edith Barrett, auditioning against type, had won the role of the bawdy maid, Sybil. For Edith, the Mercury proved a rejuvenating venture. Critics lauded her gutsy performance; the *New York City Telegraph* noted, "What is more stunning than, actually, the Welles spirit in this enterprise is the Welles magic for setting alight actors who up to now have been, let us say, wooden. Let us consider Miss Edith Barrett, unfortunately the victim of too many treacle shows . . . Here she is a light, dashing, and winning actress, afire with zeal for her role, obviously happy in the lines and having a hell of a good time. It is good to see her released from the syrup pot and to discover that she can grin like a gamin and act like one."

Although Welles's direction and the magic of the Mercury might well have been responsible for the excellent performances of Vincent and Edith, an additional factor may have been at play. In confused despair over his relationship with Barbara, Vincent began pursuing Edith and the two renewed their summer romance, this time with a great deal more seriousness. Completely enamored with everything about the theater, Vincent fell in love as much with Edith's family background and acting persona as he did with Edith herself. He sent her poems and flowers, took her to museums and galleries, encouraged her painting, and idolized her acting. Edith, in turn, basked in his attentions. Still insisting that she was in her late twenties, she turned thirty-four during *The Shoemaker's Holiday* and had reached the point where she could no longer be considered an ingenue. Marriage to a younger man whose star was clearly in the ascendant must have promised a kind of rebirth.

Although Edith already evinced a kind of unsteadiness that would later develop into full-blown mental instability, Vincent viewed this as simply an essential element of her creative genius. Roddy McDowall, who worked with Edith when he was a boy, recalled, "I was very put off by her as a child. I can vividly remember her on the set and my memories are of terror. She was like somebody out of the attic. But you know, there's a strange thing—when people are young, insanity is really a quite attractive quotient in one's peers, because you say, 'Oh well, she's young, she'll grow out of it.' She didn't grow out of it; she grew into it. She looked like a bird. She had this strange birdlike quality, and before age took over it must have seemed awesome because it must have appeared to be ephemeral. I'm sure she was extraordinary when she was young—deeply appealing and very moving, and I'm sure that life force could be very attractive, especially to someone like Vincent, who I'm sure thought he could help her."

During March 1938, Vincent continued in *The Shoemaker's Holiday* while rehearsing for the next Mercury production, George Bernard Shaw's *Heartbreak House*. Sometime during the middle of the run, it became apparent to the cast that something was happening between Vincent Price and Edith Barrett. Norman Lloyd remembered, "We all knew he was madly in love with Barbara O'Neil. We knew she was his girl. And then this romance developed on the show. I found Edi very strange, but very attractive. Edi had a wonderful sort of acting face and was very good in *Shoemaker's Holiday*. She was very right for it." After six months of gloom, Vincent found himself reinvigorated by the romance. He gave a garden party in his little patio and, in honor of the famous actress he was courting, "I hired an organ grinder and a monkey, which I though was great fun to have. Laurette Taylor, the greatest American actress; Blanche Yurka; Florence Reed; and all these wonderful ladies came to the party wearing spring dresses and big hats. There was one thing I didn't foresee about having an organ grinder. The moment he started to play, everybody in the big tall buildings around me threw up their windows and threw pennies down. We were all nearly killed."

Early on the morning of March 31, a telegram was delivered to Vincent Price at 53 West 53rd Street. It read, "To are honey I dream not oh I love you good morning. Edith." In Vincent's meticulous hand, we can read the transcription of the telegraph operator's bastardized verse: " 'Tis an honor I dream not of . . ." Vincent Price had asked Edith Barrett for her hand in marriage. But he had to ask more than once, although his first proposal was undoubtedly the most romantic: He sang her a song, "Here Am I," at Child's Restaurant. In early April, Edith accepted. A letter from Vincent Sr. to his son dated April 6 reads, "Your telephone message made us both very happy—and we feel you are a very fortunate young man to get a girl like Edith—everything seems just as it ought to be with you two and we know the loneliness you both must have experienced will be replaced by a mutual interest in things, in living, and in each other. It's just ideal— and I might add that I think Edith is getting a fine man. How I love you. How proud I am of you."

On Saturday, April 23, 1938, the company's day off between the closing of *Shoemaker* and the opening of *Heartbreak House*, Vincent Price married Edith Barrett in an elegant church ceremony in the chapel of St. Thomas' Episcopal Church on Fifth Avenue. In addition to Vincent Sr. and Marguerite and their daughters Hat and Lollie, two hundred relatives and friends attended the wedding. Also present were Walter Hampden, Blanche Yurka, Orson Welles, Laurette Taylor, Skowhegan friends Owen Davis and Harold Gould, and the cast and crew of the Mercury Theater. Norman Lloyd remembered, "I see him walking down the aisle of St. Thomas' and we were all shunted to the back because we were scrungy-looking in all that makeup on from last night and he came down the aisle and looked at us, and I could see what was going through his mind, 'They're going to do something, these guys.' But we didn't; we behaved. And we all chipped in, as they say in the theater, to get him a silver tray with an inscription on it, 'From the Mercury Players.' " Newspapers printed a picture of Vincent, in a navy blue double-breasted pin striped suit; Edi was on his arm, wearing a simple knee-length blue dress with a white pattern, a large blue straw hat, and a corsage of lilies of the valley. They reported (incorrectly) that the bride was twenty-six; the groom *was* twenty-seven.

It seems fair to surmise that, after so many years as a single woman living the itinerant life of a constantly working actress, Edith, in deciding to marry Vincent, hoped to settle down to a more stable existence. Her hopes were buoyed after meeting her new in-laws, particularly Vincent's father, of whom she was immediately enamored. As soon as the Prices left for St. Louis, Edith began corresponding with them as "Mommie and Daddy," informing them of her and Vincent's activities, even planning a trip to St. Louis. For his part, Vincent later admitted that a large element of his infatuation with his new wife was his image of her both as the granddaughter of Lawrence Barrett and as a great melodrama star. He believed that Edith loved the theater and that this love would provide the foundation for their lives together as two career actors. Vincent and Edith had begun their marriage with high hopes—they had a great deal to learn about each other.

Two days after a wedding party on the stage of the Mercury, Vincent opened in *Heartbreak House*. It was an ambitious production, with twenty-three-year-old Welles taking on the extremely challenging role of the aged Captain Shotover. According to Vincent, "Orson was not very good in it, because he never rehearsed with us. The company was marvelous; it was an all-star cast, as they call it. He was completely undisciplined. He never showed up for rehearsal." On the other hand, Welles gave a great deal of his directorial attention to the debut of a young Irish actress named Geraldine Fitzgerald. As Vincent remembered, "Orson directed her with such affection and care that she stole almost every scene from him . . . We all felt he could have lavished a little more direction in his own direction."

Disgruntled with Welles, Vincent nonetheless kept his dissatisfaction quiet, while privately amusing himself with a bet as to the date of the disintegration of Welles's monumental plaster makeup; he was convinced that, when the moment finally came, the stage would have to be excavated from the massive debris. (For better or for worse, it never happened.) As for the production, most of the reviews were lukewarm, although Vincent generally came off well. Co-producer John Houseman later wrote that he had had many trepidations about the production and "felt lucky" to have received even the passing notices it got. The season was ending on a flat note, but Vincent was no longer concerned. All of a sudden, his sights were set on Hollywood.

14

THROUGHOUT VINCENT PRICE'S early stage career, it was frequently reported that he had been offered sizeable Hollywood contracts. Before his marriage he had turned them all down, believing that he should make a name for himself in the theater first. However, by the summer of 1938, he felt it was time to give Hollywood a try, and in mid-June the optimistic young actor, accompanied by his bride, flew to California.

The couple stayed at the elegant Chateau Elysée in Hollywood, where Vincent began the process of negotiations for his film future. Having received offers from Universal and MGM, he played off one against the other in order to get the best possible contract. On June 30, he wrote his parents that he was "almost a movie actor" and that he would be signing with Universal later that week, having succeeded in getting the deal that he had hoped for—six months in Los Angeles shooting at least two pictures and six months on Broadway, with a clause protecting him from having to work in any B-pictures and ensuring him of the best possible directors and productions. This, Vincent believed, would allow him "to see what I think of pictures in the best possible way."

In the late 1930s, Universal was still considered a major studio, albeit one without any big name stars. Nonetheless, "Uncle Carl" Laemmle, who had founded the studio, had a handful of top directors under contract, among them James Whale, John Stahl, and William Wyler, who could attract stars from other studios. Universal also had a stable of popular character actors—W. C. Fields, Boris Karloff, Bela Lugosi, and Basil Rathbone among them—who kept the studio out of the red by appearing in a steady stream of comedies and horror films. Their biggest star, however, was a young woman who almost single-handedly rescued the studio from bankruptcy in 1937: a teenager from Canada named Deanna Durbin, whose remarkable soprano singing voice and fresh personality made her a household name overnight when her first film, *Three Smart Girls*, grossed $2 million. In signing Vincent Price, the studio hoped it had found a leading man with comparable appeal—a figure who could rival other studios' A-list actors, such as Robert Taylor and Gary Cooper.

Vincent immediately took to Los Angeles. Since the summers he had spent near San Diego visiting his grandmother, Vincent had loved the ocean and the beach; now he longed to share this passion with Edi. Their first visit to L.A. was a roaring success; the couple even saw a lot of Barbara O'Neil, and Vincent wrote home that "All is well and she and Edi get along well and we are all great friends! *Grace à Dieu!*" Standing on the threshhold of a movie career, married to the woman of his dreams, Bink told his father, "Next to you, Dad, I must be the luckiest man in the world!"

In early July, Edi left for the East Coast to fulfill her summer stock obligations, while

Vincent stayed to sign his contract and prepare for his first assignment. Universal had told him that they wanted him for *The Sun Never Sets*, an epic about the Bengal Lancers, but allowed him to test for the part of the Emperor Maximilian in Warner Bros.' *Juarez*, starring Paul Muni and Bette Davis. (Brian Aherne got the part.) On July 13, he inked his deal—$1,000 a week with a six-week guarantee for two pictures a year. At this point, *The Sun Never Sets* appeared to be off the agenda, with Universal instead slating him for a James Whale movie, *SOS*, to be followed by another opposite Danielle Darrieux. After a week or two, that plan, too, seemed unsure. Vincent had hoped to join Edi in New York, but now he was obliged to remain in Hollywood while Universal searched for the right vehicle for their new acquisition. In early August the studio finally green-lighted *Service de Luxe* for Vincent, a romantic comedy they hoped would bolster the sagging career of Constance Bennett, a vivacious blond who had originally made her name as a silent screen star. The decision came none too soon for Vincent, who wrote home that he was "very much in need of work as I had to lay out a lot of cash for doctor, clothes, and car. I'll be glad to get back to the security and more to work. I hate being idle."

By the time filming on *Service de Luxe* began, Edi and Vincent had been apart for almost two months, almost as long as they had been married. In a letter, he said, "I know Edi and I will be able to work this out—being apart. I feel she must work and that for her happiness and mine, the greatest thing is a success for her on the stage. She feels very lonely, but that is natural and too much thought about it is bad." Clearly Vincent was too preoccupied with his first film to be very lonely himself. Indeed, throughout his long career, work would not only come first: It almost always helped to assuage the difficulties of long absences from friends and family.

In making his screen debut in *Service de Luxe*, Vincent responded enthusiastically to the director, Rowland V. Lee, whom he described to his parents as "a gentle and superb director who is very interested in me and will work to make my start as good as possible." After a career as a proficient director of silent films, Lee had broken into talkies in 1929 with the unanimously praised *The Mysterious Dr. Fu Manchu*. Having gracefully made the transition to sound, he had directed a number of swashbuckling epics before trying his hand at romantic comedies.

Filming on *Service de Luxe* began on August 15, 1938. Driving to Universal, Vincent found himself behind a flatbed truck carrying an entire building. As he poked along behind the large vehicle, the compulsively punctual young man began to worry that he would be late for his first day of his first film job. And here he was, stuck behind a house. Unable to get around the truck, he followed it for miles through the hills to Universal, where it—and he—turned on to the lot and proceeded to the sound stage for *Service de Luxe*. The "building" was Constance Bennett's dressing room.

Vincent spent four or five days in wardrobe and makeup where his "romantic leading man look" was perfected. His hair had begun receding at his temples when he was in college; now he was fitted with two small hairpieces which, he wrote home to his parents, made him look "very purty." He enjoyed watching the more experienced actors at work, and tried to take in everything he could about making movies. He quickly noted that "everything out here is done by someone else. Even your voice has to be controlled by the sound man." Finally, his first moment before the camera came, which he described to columnist Harry Mines a few weeks later. "This is my first picture and, naturally, I was pretty wound up in knots the first day I worked. Blew lines and all that. Miss Bennett was swell. Took take after take without a murmur until I calmed down. Then I had a scene where I was supposed to knock her hat off with a fish rod. My mistake, I bopped her pretty hard on the head. She laughed off the incident and told me to forget the whole business when I started to apologize." However, after seeing the first day's rushes, Mines reported that the Universal executives "believe they have a valuable property in this new actor from the theater."

The Hollywood publicity machine was operating at high gear during Price's first excursion into picture making. He gave countless interviews about the daily details of filming, and much was made of the relationship between leading man and leading lady. He was always gracious about Constance Bennett, telling reporters that although he had been "warned" about Bennett, she had been wonderful about "showing him tricks— how to be seen better, how to use screen makeup, how to use his voice." Only later was he more forthright: "Constance Bennett invented thinness. She had a figure like a slice of bent Melba toast, crisp and tasteless, but she wore clothes like a perfectly shaped coat hanger. Her hair was long and blond and her unpretty face was made up to be the epitome of what a current star should look like . . . But two things were in her favor, she could act and was nice, and she accepted me as, if not an equal, a competent new-comer."

Any mishaps or comical stories were quickly picked up by the press. Vincent had grown a mustache for the role—"the first one that had ever come in all one color"— but they made him shave it off and then pasted on one that was exactly like it "except that it had more hairs than any man—I don't care who he is—could ever grow." In one scene, the papers reported that he had been "making love to Joy Hodges and while kissing her, half of his prop mustache had stuck to her upper lip." But most of the publicity centered on the actor's viability as Hollywood's newest leading man. One long article in *Screen and Radio Weekly* refered to him as the "It Man" and went on to catalogue his various physical attributes: "Hollywood's latest importation from the New York stage: tall, dark, and not too handsome. His blue eyes, wavy brown hair, 180 pounds distributed nicely over 6 feet 4 inches of well proportioned stature, and a beguiling voice give him the Sex Appeal. Note the capitals. S.A. is the *sine qua non*. If you haven't got it, you haven't got a thing. Price has it. Price has IT."

In September, Edi returned to Hollywood and she and Vincent rented a furnished house on Canon Drive in Beverly Hills, just off Sunset Boulevard. For the first time since their marriage at the end of April, the couple would share a home, but with both ready to pick up and leave for New York whenever work beckoned it almost seemed as though they were playing house. Vincent told interviewer Jon Stokes, "I asked my agent to find me a little house, something cozy. Mrs. Price hasn't lived in a house since she was four years old. I wanted her to get used to it gradually. The place is cozy as a circus tent. It has four bedrooms, each large enough to play badminton in. It is furnished in the early Sid Graumann period—porcelain cats, ivory elephants, bronze bookends, crystal cigarette trays, chromium andirons. I said to the agent, 'Do you call this cozy?' 'It hasn't got a swimming pool, has it?' he argued. I guess that proves it's cozy." Vincent went on to give some domestic details of their new life. "Mrs. Price is learning to cook. I like steaks, fried chicken, beans, frankfurters, sauerkraut, wiener schnitzel, scrambled eggs and bacon, hamburgers and onions, and any salad made with garlic. When she can cook these to my taste, I don't care if she doesn't learn to cook anything else." A far cry both from the gourmet cook and liberated, sharing husband of later years.

Vincent went on to share his opinions about life in the movie capital. "I like the hospitality of the gas station attendants, the slacks on the waitresses in the eat-in-your-car-drive-in restaurants and I dislike the idea of having to be seen anywhere with anybody. The funniest thing about Hollywood is finding out what you are doing from someone else. Everyone knows before you do, if they know anything at all. I like to eat in Hollywood drug stores, hot dog wagons, barbecue stands, and chili con carne parlors shaped like bean pots, Dopey, or castles on the Rhine." The article goes on to list a dizzying array of his favorite diversions: fishing, trains, amusement parks, circuses, gardening, driving, collecting anything, conversation, listening, opera, singing, painting, writing, reading, art galleries, junk shops, cards, window shopping, sightseeing, and movies. Over the years, this list would hardly change at all.

Although pleased with his film career and life in Hollywood, Vincent pined for his old connection with the art world in New York. He wrote his parents, "I am very enthusiastic about the possibilities of California, but it will take time and a great effort culturally to make it what it should be. Bad taste is more apparent here than in any other part of the country. They are years behind the times in architecture and what modern efforts they've made are too extreme. But the climate has limitless advantages—it should make things easier for the culture to flourish." In the same letter, a far less noble note was sounded again—the inherited anti-Semitism of his Missouri upbringing. "The only setbacks are the Jews and their power here. They are in command in all fields and they, of course, as always, are responsible for the bad taste." It was one of the last such comments he would make: As he became friends with the many Jewish people with whom he worked, he came to recognize the error of his beliefs.

By the mid-forties, as he became increasingly active on behalf of liberal social and political causes, organizations such as B'nai Brith and the Jewish Anti-Defamation League were among the groups he regularly supported. (During the fifties, a prominent Southern California Jewish organization honored Vincent for his efforts on behalf of their community. At the banquet, he sat on the dais as the master of ceremonies introduced the guest of honor as "that great actor, that great humanitarian, that great art collector, that great man, that great Jew, Vincent Price.")

Whatever Vincent's reservations about his cultural environment, however, they were more than compensated for by his excitement about being in the midst of star-studded glamour. Even without Edi, during the summer he had made the most of the Hollywood social scene. In mid-August he attended the Tailwaggers Ball, a charity event for the seeing-eye dogs organization hosted by Bette Davis. His date for the evening was Myra Kingsley, a popular Hollywood astrologer; his dinner companions were the Basil Rathbones, whom he had originally met in London. He wrote home that although the evening was hot and the event dull, "The crowd made it fun for me—the old sightseer. Everyone was there—Gary Cooper, Robert Taylor, Mary Pickford. I had a lovely talk with Norma Shearer about Marie Antoinette." For the star-struck St. Louis boy who had spent his youth subscribing to fan magazines, it was a dream come true.

As a young, attractive and, for a time at least, geographically single actor, Vincent had soon been invited to many interesting soirées. One he particularly remembered took place at Mrs. Jack Warner's house. "She was one of the great hostesses in town. She invited me to another pot luck that turned out to be a sit-down dinner for eighty. And when I got to the house, which was a spectacular mansion that you got to by driving up this endless driveway full of wild and wonderful trees, I looked around the living room and sitting room and den, and there was this extraordinary collection of pictures. There were Renoirs and Bonnards, really quite a nice collection. But the thing was that they all looked slightly familiar, although I couldn't think of having read a book about the Warner collection of Impressionist painting. And suddenly I realized that I'd seen them a few days before in a gallery downtown. She must have called the owner and told him that she was having a party and that she'd like to show some pictures. Of course, it would have been great publicity for him, if she had ever admitted that they weren't hers. I went back to the gallery about three days later, and there they all were. Mrs. Warner also had the great Cabishaw emerald surrounded by diamonds. And when Clifton Webb met her, he said, "I'm so pleased to meet you, Mrs. Warner. I see you wear your swimming pool."

Price's status as a young man of sophistication and culture accorded him a few rather unique assignments. Mrs. Warner called him one day and asked him to pick someone up to take them to a benefit she was giving at the Biltmore Hotel ballroom in downtown Los Angeles. Vincent had hired a chauffer-driven car for the evening and directed the driver to the address in Brentwood that Mrs. Warner had given him. As he liked to tell the story, Vincent climbed the steps to the simple bungalow, suddenly realizing that he had forgotten to ask who he was fetching. "I rang the doorbell and was met by a woman who was dressed in black tulle wound around her legs and around her bosom and around her neck and then around her head with a great red rose at the top of this masterpiece. It had all been sewn on for the occasion. It was Marlene Dietrich. I had to carry her down and lift her into the car, because the dress would have torn, which she thought was wonderful and funny. Then we drove downtown to the Biltmore and it was very sort of *gemütlich*, despite the outfit. She was a lovely lady, very German, very housewifely, but still the great star. When we got there, I had to get her out of the car and up to the ballroom where she made an entrance and stopped the show, of course. And there I was with her, which was great fun."

If the glamour of Hollywood naturally held a decided fascination for the movie buff, he found it equally thrilling to spend his weekends at the ocean. He often fished for hours from the Malibu pier, and those who knew him well felt that he was perhaps never happier than when fishing, preferably deep-sea fishing on a boat. In mid-September, he invited actor Mischa Auer and his wife to come down to Del Mar with him. There they chartered the *Glorietta*, a boat that his family had often hired when he was a boy. If being a movie star meant being able to rent a fishing boat for the weekend, it was well worth it.

Service de Luxe was released nationwide in late October 1938. Vincent and Edith attended the Hollywood premiere. Vincent was naturally nervous, but as Edi reported to his parents, "When he came on screen there was a beautiful reception for him. It is not a great story or part, but it was beautifully played and everyone out here feels he has a great future in pictures as well as theater." And yet she noted that her husband "was depressed for two days" until he realized that, for his first picture, he had done a perfectly good job. Edi's own reaction to Hollywood seems to have been similarly muted. "It's such a strange world out here," she wrote, "but V really seems to love it."

Although reviewers appreciated Vincent's acting ability, it was generally felt that he had been handicapped by the material. The film was viewed as a "Class B plot in a Class

A setting." My father, however, failed to understand that *Service de Luxe* was a typical bread-and-butter studio product of the kind that were churned out by the dozen every year and always referred to his first film as a signal failure. When I finally saw *Service de Luxe* I was surprised to find it neither more nor less than a pleasing romantic comedy in which my father came across as a rather charming romantic lead. I later came to realize that his disillusionment was a reflection of his unrealistically high expectations and his naïve failure to realize that Hollywood was not Broadway.

He, however, decided that he had been miscast and blamed Hollywood for attempting to trivialize his dramatic potential by making him into a frivolous romantic lead. He determined to surmount this setback by showing Hollywood what he could really do. "I hope to make another picture and get a serious character role. That's when acting is fun, when you must convince an audience that you're someone else. Here everything is individuals, and their personalities are never hidden for fear the great public won't take it."

15

WHATEVER THE ENTICEMENTS of Hollywood, after the disappointing experience of *Service de Luxe* Vincent was eager to return to Broadway. In mid–November, en route to New York, he took Edi home to St. Louis for the first time. The couple spent most of their three-day visit socializing with family and friends. Edi, it seemed, felt at home with the senior Prices right away.

After the couple's arrival in New York, Vincent auditioned successfully for a plum role in *Outward Bound*, a play by Sutton Vane. The production would mark a return to Broadway for Laurette Taylor, one of the most celebrated actresses of the age, who had been absent from the stage for almost ten years. One of the leading ladies of the teens and twenties, she had become a household name through her hit *Peg O' My Heart*, but when her second husband, playwright Hartley Manners, died suddenly, she fell into a period of alcoholism—or what she referred to as "the longest wake in history." Laurette became so unreliable that no one would use her, and she had faded from public view. By the time she was offered the part in *Outward Bound*, she was ready to return to the stage, and although the role of Mrs. Midget, a kindly scrubwoman, was hardly a leading part, Taylor saw its possibilities for both pathos and comedy.

The actor and producer Bramwell Fletcher was slated both to direct and to play the part of Mrs. Midget's son. But before long it became clear that Taylor, who seemed extremely nervous, was unable to take direction, and Fletcher replaced himself with Viennese director Otto Preminger, who had a reputation for being able to handle temperamental stars. Because the producers feared that the pressure of returning to the stage might drive Taylor back to the bottle, one of the producer's wives, Grace George, attended rehearsals as an understudy. When Preminger took over, he invited Laurette to lunch and frankly told her what he had heard about her. His candor earned her respect, but she also put him to the test, telling him that having Grace sitting in the back of the theater was humiliating. Laurette felt as though everyone was waiting for her to fail, but Preminger reassured her strongly: "I'm in charge now. I assure you that no one will play your part but you. No one will study your lines. There will be no understudy. But if I do this for you, you must come through for me." He then said that he knew she had difficulty memorizing her lines and that that added to her nervousness. He told her to go home and not to come back until she had memorized her part, whether it took a few days or two weeks. Laurette returned in three days, and while the rest of the cast read from their scripts and struggled through their parts, she was word-perfect.

From then on, Taylor and Preminger got along brilliantly and the rest of the cast witnessed the regeneration of a great actress. *Outward Bound* is a fantasy about a shipload of people who discover, to their shock and horror, that they are dead and are bound for Eternity. Mrs. Midget, a dowdy, self-effacing charwoman, is initially snubbed by the other passengers but later becomes a heroine of sorts when their destination is revealed. In addition to Laurette Taylor, Bramwell Fletcher, and Vincent Price as the kindly Reverend William Duke, facing Eternity doubtful of all that he has preached, the cast featured a number of other excellent actors. Among them were Helen Chandler and, also returning to the stage after an absence of six years, the superb Florence Reed.

The play opened on December 22, 1938 to the longest standing ovation in recent New York history. Laurette Taylor's daughter later described the scene. "In porkpie hat, black alpaca cape, and tippet of fur, holding a capacious knitting bag, Laurette made her entrance, backing cautiously through stage door left. Most of the cast was assembled onstage and had received their hand. On sight of the nondescript little figure sidling backwards through the door the audience burst into thunderous applause. Laurette turned to say her first lines but it was of no use. The ovation continued, gathering momentum. People shouted and whistled and wept; they beat their feet on the floor; here and there groups rose, until finally the whole audience was standing . . . It was obvious that Laurette was shaken—shattered, almost—by the prolonged ovation, but also evident was the delicate poise, the established inner equilibrium of the artist that cannot be swayed by emotional turmoil within or without. She tried to stop them every way she knew how, but it was hopeless. For ten solid minutes shock waves of sound buffeted the tiny figure on the stage." At the end of the night, there were twenty-two curtain calls and Miss Taylor was called upon to make three short speeches. One reviewer went so far as to say, "There is no more brilliant actress in the world than Miss Taylor and her long absence from the theater is one of the tragedies of the American stage." She was back.

Vincent and Laurette had quickly become close during rehearsals. Laurette, whom Vincent described as having "eyes like a rolltop desk," had long been friends with Edi; now she was made to feel comfortable by Vincent's easy charm. After her spectacular reception that night, as she walked arm in arm with the Prices to dinner at their apartment, she said, "It really wasn't a good performance." But as the production went on, her confidence grew. For Vincent, who by now had worked with an impressive lineup of the early twentieth century's most famous Broadway actresses—Helen Hayes, Eugenie Leontovitch, Florence Reed, Edith Barrett, Blanche Yurka, as well as such up-and-coming stars as Mildred Natwick and Geraldine Fitzgerald—working with Laurette was a kind of culmination of his stage career to date.

Vincent, of course, was also thrilled to find himself once again in a hit Broadway play. Though most of the attention had been given to Laurette, the production as a whole had fared well at the hands of the critics and he himself had come away with good reviews. On January 30, the company took the train to Washington, D.C., where they had been invited to give a benefit performance for infantile paralysis on Roosevelt's birthday. The president and the first lady were in the audience and, after another lengthy ovation, Taylor made a birthday speech to the president, after which Otto Preminger and the cast went to the White House for supper. For everyone present this was an extraordinary honor; for Vincent, who by now worshipped Roosevelt, it was one of the highlights of his life.

*   *   *

While Vincent was appearing in a hit, Edi was looking for a job. Big names shone on Broadway marquees—Raymond Massey as Abraham Lincoln, Maurice Evans as Falstaff, Robert Morley as Oscar Wilde, Tallulah Bankhead in *The Little Foxes*, and Katharine Hepburn in *The Philadelphia Story*—and still Edith continued to wait for the right role to come along. Despite her discouraging situation, she and Vincent treasured the opportunity to be on the same coast at the same time. But Hollywood beckoned again. As with Broadway, 1939 was a spectacular year for Hollywood. Clark Gable and Vivien Leigh starred in *Gone with the Wind* and Judy Garland in *The Wizard of Oz*; Garbo laughed in *Ninotchka*; John Wayne drove John Ford's *Stagecoach*; and that was just for openers. That spring, Vincent's understudy stepped into *Outward Bound* while Price paid a flying visit back to Hollywood to test for a part opposite Irene Dunne in *A Modern Cinderella*, but the role went to Charles Boyer and the film was eventually called *When Tomorrow Comes*. Edi remained in New York, where she finally had a job, costarring in a new production of *Wuthering Heights*. Vincent wrote his parents, "Of course she is carrying on simply stinking about my going away, but she does understand that it will always have to be this way with us if we are to keep on in the theater."

On April 27, 1939, Edith Barrett opened at the Longacre Theatre as Cathy opposite John Emery's Heathcliff. Unfortunately, however, the film version of *Wuthering Heights*, starring Laurence Olivier and Merle Oberon, had been released earlier in the year and was still playing near Broadway at the Rivoli Theater. While the film had been pronounced an instant classic, the Broadway production suffered by comparison. Brooks Atkinson called the stage production "overpoweringly dull" and was no kinder to the acting, which he said "drugs a theatergoer into a state of insensibility." Thus, at the moment her husband was enjoying the attentions of Hollywood while appearing in one of the most successful plays of the season, Edi was having just the opposite experience—an awkward situation that that would plague the couple throughout their marriage.

In June 1939, Vincent left the cast of *Outward Bound* and returned to Hollywood to begin shooting his second film. Universal had loaned him to Warner Bros. for the epic period piece, *The Private Lives of Elizabeth and Essex*, starring two-time Academy Award winner Bette Davis as Queen Elizabeth I and megastar Errol Flynn as Robert Devereaux, Earl of Essex. Also cast were Olivia de Havilland, Alan Hale, Donald Crisp, Leo G. Carroll, John Sutton, and Nanette Fabares (later Nanette Fabray). Vincent was cast as Sir Walter Raleigh, a supporting role, but one which gave him the opportunity to work with a stellar cast on a prestige production. The director was Hungarian emigré Michael Curtiz, one of Warner Bros.' most prolific and successful directors during the 1930s, and a man both greatly feared and much respected.

Having considered his screen debut in *Service de Luxe* a failure, Vincent relished the opportunity to play a character part in a period piece. As usual, in preparing for his role he did his homework, this time referring to the historical portraits of Raleigh, particularly those he knew from London's National Portrait Gallery. But when he arrived on the set, he discovered that the studio had a different look in mind altogether. Their idea of the character derived from the likeness of Raleigh which appeared on a tobacco can. Claiming that that was what America would expect the nobleman to look like, they asked Vincent to disregard any more authentic likenesses in working on his character. He already knew better than to argue.

In addition to his character preparation, Vincent felt he should take lessons in film acting. "I went to a woman called Laura Elliot. Everybody in theater who came out to Hollywood went to her to study the technique of film acting. It involved learning how to control your face, because when you are thrown up on a huge screen, and your face is twenty feet high, when you start to talk it can suddenly look like you're eating the screen—and a lot of actors do! So, she taught us how to control our face, so we don't mug, because actors from the theater tend to mug a bit. She was invaluable, and we learned a great deal from her. One of her recipes for all of us was to go and see two actors . . . Charles Boyer and Ronald Colman. So, I went to see every film I could, to learn, and I found that Ronald Colman was the master of his craft."

In his second round with Hollywood, Vincent determined to take hold of his film career in the way he had done in the theater. This proved more difficult, however, because, as a Universal contract player, he was subject to the whims of a studio that could use him in any projects they chose, as well as loan him out to any other studio. Realizing that he stood the best chance of getting good roles as a character actor, Vincent worked hard to learn his craft. He strove to emulate actors such as Colman, and even began trying to mold himself after them in an attempt to define himself in the eyes of Hollywood. Norman Lloyd, who worked with Vincent many times during his career, observed, "I always felt that to a degree, or maybe more than to a degree, he was influenced by Barrymore, who was the great influence of our generation. The mustache and everything, that's Barrymore. Vincent did what all of us did, but he did it successfully—we saw what the going thing with actors was. Vincent had a couple of heroes. Ronald Colman was one—Colman with the pencil-thin mustache. It was the going thing and you had to find a way to get a job."

Vincent hoped that playing Raleigh in *The Private Lives of Elizabeth and Essex* would give him a chance to display his technique, but the adventurer received insignificant treatment in the film, and Vincent was forced to make the best of a mediocre role. Though he looked elegant in his doublet and hose, designed by Orry-Kelly, he had little to do in the film and even less to say. With two stars as notoriously temperamental as Bette Davis and Errol Flynn, tensions ran high on the set—particularly as everyone knew that Davis's first choice for the role had been Laurence Olivier. Director Curtiz grew rapidly frustrated with Flynn's erratic behavior; the swashbuckling star was frequently late and usually unprepared. Because Vincent had played Essex in summer stock in the Maxwell Anderson play, Curtiz often turned to him to feed Flynn the lines. Vincent realized that the director did this in an effort to shame the star into learning his lines, but he hated being thrust into the middle of their contretemps. The situation finally came to a head when Curtiz warned Flynn that if he wasn't prepared the next day, he would give the part to Price—a gambit that apparently did the trick. Vincent did his best, in the meantime, to remain friends with the mercurial Flynn; gossip columnists reported finding the two playing tennis on the studio court one day, still in costume.

Immediately after filming on *Elizabeth and Essex* was completed, Vincent returned to Universal for *Tower of London*, a bastardized version of Shakespeare's *Richard III*, which reunited him with director Rowland Lee. Starring Basil Rathbone as Richard and Boris Karloff as an invented character called Mord, the film was made as part of Universal's ongoing horror cycle. Taking the role of Richard's ill-fated brother, the Duke of Clarence, Vincent found himself working once again with Barbara O'Neil, as well as with his friend Basil Rathbone. The film also saw the beginning of his working friendship with Boris Karloff, one of the most important of Vincent's life. Karloff had been a household name since the extraordinary success of director James Whale's *Frankenstein* in 1931 and, despite the lifelong typecasting he had to endure as a result, he remained grateful for the opportunity which that film had given him. Vincent later noted, "It was something that plagued him all his life, as a good part plagues every actor, but he was so thankful for it, because it gave him enormous fame. He knew he had gotten stuck on something, but he had great pride in it."

Vincent got a real kick out of working with Karloff and Rathbone. "We had this scene where Basil and I had to drink to the kingdom of England. Rowland Lee didn't like the dialogue, and neither did we, because the more we drank, the less we could remember. It was only Coca-Cola, but Coke is stimulating, too. Well, over in one corner was a huge vat of malmsey wine in which I was to be drowned. Boris and Basil, knowing I was new to the business, thought it was great fun to throw everything they could into that vat of wine, which was actually just water. You know, old Coca-Cola bottles, cigarette butts, anything they could find to dirty it up, because they knew at the end of the scene I had to get into it. There was a handrail at the bottom of the vat, so I could dive down and hang onto it. I had to stay under for a full ten counts, and then I was yanked out by my heels. Well, when I came out I got a round of applause from the crew, but was disappointed not to see Boris and Basil. Then a few minutes later they reappeared and were very nice to me. They congratulated me on playing the scene so well for a newcomer, and then presented me with a case of Coca-Cola!"

While he was making *Tower of London*, Universal took advantage of Vincent's presence in Hollywood to cast him in their new James Whale film, *Green Hell*. A reviewer later offered a telling survey of the plot: "Half a dozen glycerine-sweated explorers dodge a million movie-insects and prop snakes to paddle through the crocodile-infested headwaters of the Amazon so they can reach an Inca treasure-temple—and what do they find? Right!—they find Joan Bennett . . . Her sex lure busts up the explorers' sextuple camaraderie, and blow-gunning aborigines bust up the expedition with the result that Doug Fairbanks, Jr. gets Joan, George Bancroft goes back home to Texas and his Lena, and George Sanders and Vincent Price are eliminated. Let's just forget the whole thing." Vincent played Joan (sister of Constance) Bennett's husband, but never even met her during filming; his character met an early demise after succumbing to the effects of a poison arrow. Given the fact that the movie was shot on a 45,000-square-foot interior jungle set during the worst heat wave Los Angeles had experienced in over forty years, his premature death was merciful.

Despite Whale's strong reputation as a director of such diverse and successful films as *Show Boat* and *Frankenstein*, *Green Hell* was quickly recognized by cast and crew alike as potentially one of the worst pictures ever made. In fact, Vincent, with his sharp sense of the ridiculous, was always rather proud of appearing in a movie about which Frank S. Nugent quipped in the *New York Times*, "We cannot remember when we have had a better time at a worse picture." Vincent himself later said, "About five of the worst pictures ever made were all in that one picture. The story was so preposterous. There was a scene where Joan is brought in after having been lost in the jungle. She had one very neat smudge, that's all. A week in the jungle, she got a smudge. And Alan Hale, Sr. who was the doctor of the expedition, leaned over her and said, 'It's all right, fellows, it's just a coma!' The audience fell apart."

Notwithstanding his apparent good spirits about *Green Hell*, Vincent's Hollywood experience was clearly not living up to his expectations. But although he learned to develop a sense of humor about the vicissitudes of being a film actor, he continued to hope that if he took his profession seriously, he would eventually be rewarded with a breakthrough role. It was something that, over the course of a hundred-film career, he would never lose—a reserve of eternally optimistic faith in the quality of every new role.

Vincent and Edi had rented a beach house in Malibu for that summer of 1939, and his parents came out to stay for two weeks, during which time their son gave them a grand tour of Hollywood. While they were still there, he took a role at the Lobero Theatre in Santa Barbara for their summer pageant, Fiesta Week. *The Mistress of the Inn*, a Goldoni play about Spanish nobles, also featured Universal player Mischa Auer, and Harry Mines reported that, after a few days of rehearsal, the cast "frolicked happily, if not always smoothly, through the bawdy farce." Because Vincent was working, Edi spent a great deal of time with his parents, an arrangement which suited all three. Marguerite and Vincent Sr. had grown to love their daughter-in-law and Edi loved being a part of a real family at last.

In October, Vincent was back at Universal. The studio was winding down its celebrated cycle of horror films, through which Boris Karloff, Lon Chaney, and others had become household names. One of their most successful pictures had been James Whale's 1933 classic *The Invisible Man*, which had launched Claude Rains's successful film career. In an effort to capitalize on that earlier success, the studio proposed a sequel—*The Invisible Man Returns*, with Vincent Price replacing Rains in the title role. The film was originally to be directed by Rowland Lee, but Universal finally decided on German director Joe May. Shooting began in October 1939, with Sir Cedric Hardwicke receiving top billing. Of Joe May, Vincent said, "He was very difficult, mainly because he didn't speak English. He would try to give me a direction and I'd say, 'For God's sake, Joe, tell me in German, because I can get along better with you in German than I can in English,' I don't think anyone in the cast ever understood a word he said!" Because Vincent's character was largely invisible, the film became a showcase for his extraordinary voice, which all the reviewers appreciated. Opening night of the film, he later recalled, was "the only premiere I ever enjoyed. When, at the end of the film, I reappeared vein by vein, artery after artery, a weary drunk in the seat in front of me said to his friend, 'That'll teach me not to drink cheap whiskey!' "

Vincent's next film (and his last under contract to Universal) proved his best yet—a screen adaptation of Nathaniel Hawthorne's *The House of the Seven Gables*, starring George Sanders and Margaret Lindsay and directed by Joe May. Six-foot-four Vincent was joined by Sanders at six foot three and Gilbert Emery at six foot two and a half; the papers soon reported that "carpenters were hurriedly called in to heighten every doorway at least three inches in the 'House of the Seven Gables' after the final cast was selected." Vincent played Clifford Pyncheon, haunted by a family curse—a demanding role which allowed him to tackle a dramatic romantic lead and to age over twenty years.

The film opened as a double world premiere in Chicago on February 29, 1940, paired with *Black Friday* starring Bela Lugosi and Boris Karloff, and then moved to its West Coast premiere in San Francisco. Lugosi and Price attended the Chicago premiere and Karloff, Lugosi, Price, and Sanders the San Francisco screening; it would be the first of many times these men would find themselves on the same stage. Of his work in *The*

House of the Seven Gables, Silver Screen felt "Vincent Price has at last hit his stride as one of the screen's most romantic leading men." And the *Los Angeles Examiner* noted that Sanders, Margaret Lindsay, and Price had turned in "brilliant characterizations, climbing several steps higher in the Hollywood performance ratings." Price's stock in Hollywood, slowly but finally, was on the rise.

16

NOW THAT EDITH Barrett Price had joined her husband in Hollywood, she began to contemplate, for the first time, the possibility of making a film career for herself. But any such plans were put on hold when, in December 1939, she learned that she was pregnant. She and Vincent were overjoyed. The next nine months would be among the best of their marriage. The couple set up a new home on Chevy Chase in Beverly Hills, where they drew and painted together and socialized with friends. Among their first close friends were actress Janet Gaynor and her husband, the designer Adrian. As Vincent later wrote of Gaynor, "She was my first real close genuine movie-star friend. She and her husband chose Edi and me to be best friends. Adrian once told me that we were safer and more apt to be lasting because we were not superstars. He was honest enough not to add a conciliatory 'yet.' He obviously thought we would be what he preferred for friends, 'working actors,' not mega-personalities. Both Janet and Edi were pregnant and wags in Hollywood referred to Janet's pregnancy as an immaculate conception because Adrian, as a costume designer, was taken for granted as being gay."

When Vincent's contract with Universal expired he negotiated a similar seven-year deal with Twentieth Century-Fox, giving him six months off a year for the theater. During the 1940s, Darryl F. Zanuck's studio maintained a high profile, boasting a stable of top stars such as Shirley Temple, Tyrone Power, Alice Faye, Gene Tierney, Roddy McDowall, and Betty Grable, and directors of the caliber of John Ford, Rouben Mamoulian, Otto Preminger, and Henry King. So for Vincent, the move could only be regarded as a step up.

Throughout the past year Vincent had been nagged by throat problems, and in late March he finally had his tonsils removed before starting his first film for Fox: *Brigham Young*, starring Tyrone Power, Linda Darnell, Dean Jagger, and John Carradine. Vincent played Joseph Smith, the early prophet of the Mormon movement, whose trial as a heretic and eventual lynching in Missouri in the 1840s provided the impetus for the Mormons' westward journey to Utah. The film was shot in late April and early May of 1940 and was released in late September. Price's reviews were solid, and for the rest of his life he would remain immensely popular in the state of Utah.

Fox had nothing lined up for Vincent after *Brigham Young*, and with the prospect of another mouth to feed, he began pursuing possibilities in the theater. Worried about leaving Edi alone during her pregnancy, he contemplated sending her to his family in St. Louis. Marguerite even offered to come out to Los Angeles to be with her daughter-in-law after Edi's doctor warned her off such a strenuous trip. But Vincent Sr.'s arthritis, which had been troubling him for years, was steadily worsening, and the two couples decided that it would be best for Marguerite to remain at home.

Meanwhile, Vincent had been invited to appear at the famous Municipal Opera in St. Louis. He was overjoyed at the prospect of performing at the biggest theater in his hometown and had looked forward to being there with Edith for the occasion. Now, however, he was faced with the choice of going alone or remaining at home with his pregnant wife. In the end the need to earn a living won out, and on June 4 he opened in *The American Way* to an audience of nine thousand at the Muni.

In this patriotic revue by George S. Kaufman and Moss Hart, Vincent played German immigrant Martin Gunther. Vincent Sr. wrote Edi: "It was a thrilling sight to see and to hear their enthusiasm. Bink was a trifle nervous before the first performance so Mommie gave him a massage and we doped him up with bromides." Bink stayed with his parents for the two-week run, spending his days swimming at the country club and seeing family and old friends.

Ever since college days, he had dabbled in writing poetry and had, in fact, written a play called *Poet's Corner*, which he had recently sent to his friends at the Lakewood Theatre in Skowhegan, Maine. While in St. Louis, he got word from Melville Burke, the director of the Lakewood Players, that he would produce the play that summer provided Vincent appear in it and two other plays in the season. And so, instead of heading home to Edi as might have been expected, he traveled on to Skowhegan.

As Vincent had said in an interview in St. Louis, "Playwriting is one of my ambitions, but I wrote this mainly to get it off my chest." Largely autobiographical, *Poet's Corner* is the story of an American family, the Mortimers. Jim, the practical, understanding father, had wanted to write but has had to earn a living for his family, while his wife, Lily, though outwardly flighty and given to incongruous remarks, is actually a shrewd woman who completely controls her family. After daughter Laura settles for marriage, the family places its hopes in their son Peter, a poet. When Jim becomes sick, Lily calls the family home by magnifying her husband's illness, but it is clear that what she really wants is to see her son. Peter returns, bringing with him Judith Francis, to whom he has been engaged three times since childhood. Judith has been waiting for Peter "to find himself," but has been growing unhappy. At the family reunion, the talk becomes a discussion of life's motives and meanings and Peter, unable to face the conversation, slips away. In the third act, he returns to report that he understands both himself and his family better than he ever had. While Peter is home, Jim is stricken with an attack and is forced to take it easy. While doing so, he writes and sells his first story.

Local reviewers seemed to respond well to the piece, and the papers reported that two Broadway producers were negotiating for the rights. Vincent had intended to play Peter in the production but he felt unsure of his decision, and when Edi pointed out that his stage manner was all wrong for Peter he took a minor part. *Poet's Corner* clearly addresses the concerns of Vincent's youth. Lily (Marguerite) is scatterbrained and easily upset, and although she loves her son somewhat smotheringly, she always means well; Jim (Vincent Sr.) is an understanding and encouraging father figure who knows how to love his son and yet let him go. Laura (Lollie) abandons any ambitions to marry a hometown boy; and Peter (Bink) worries that he will drift through life without ever discovering what it is all about, while becoming engaged on and off to Judith (Barbara O'Neil). Vincent was pleased with the response to the play and clearly hoped that it might go further; though it never did, the very fact that it was produced at all was gratifying.

While Vincent was at Skowhegan, Darryl Zanuck sent a wire asking him to return to Hollywood to test for the lead in Fox's new film, *Hudson's Bay*. He flew out as requested, which allowed him a few days with his wife, all expenses paid. Returning to Maine, he wrote his mother from the plane, "Edi is fine, but has to be very quiet from now on in and she is resigned to it. Our friends especially Janet and Adrian, Rachel Field and Allen Kenward, have been simply wonderful to her. She's had quite a whirl—and now the quiet is not so bad."

Back in Maine, he appeared in another new play, *Mr. and Mrs. North* by Owen Davis, and then once again as Essex in *Elizabeth the Queen*, opposite Ann Mason as Elizabeth and with Hume Cronyn as the Fool. However, his thoughts were not with his work, but rather with his wife in the last month of her pregnancy, and with his father, whose arthritis had finally forced him to consult a specialist. On August 1 he wrote his father, following Vincent Sr.'s fifty-ninth birthday, "I had so many wonderful thoughts for you on your birthday . . . The play this week has gone over very well—and it has been sort of a justification to me playing Essex again, as I never felt very good in it four years ago—but this time I really have done a good job. I leave Sunday for the coast and Edith and will I be glad to get there."

Vincent returned home in early August to spend the last month of Edi's pregnancy with his wife. He wrote his parents, "It's so wonderful to be back! I have been basking in gratitude and have sorely neglected my other loves. The time approaches and the last month is pretty wearing for Edi; she is uncomfortable, but fortunately not too big. The doctor says September 8th sees us proud parents, and will we be glad—one, to have it over and two, to look it over! I can't wait, and at the same time I feel all lost about it, all bewildered, all excited and strangely enough defeated—suddenly to have to pass on what I know, what little I've learnt makes me feel I've neglected so much. Perhaps I can catch up and, when it is become sensible, I'll have enough sense to know what to do."

On August 30, 1940, at Hollywood's Good Samaritan Hospital, thirty-six-year-old Edith gave birth to her first and only child, a son, by Caesarean section. He was christened Vincent Barrett Price, but his parents soon took to calling Barrett or Boo Boo. Though very small at birth, he quickly gained weight and, with his blond hair, big hazel eyes, and serious expression, he favored both his parents. The newspapers reported the event and Vincent and Edi celebrated it. Though Edi remained in the hospital for almost two weeks and Vincent started filming *Hudson's Bay* in early September, they had found another house, this one in the San Fernando Valley near their friends Janet Gaynor and Adrian, whose baby had also just been born. For a time, at least, their fantasy family seemed to have materialized.

On September 12, Vincent wrote his parents, "Things certainly move fast once they start. I have been in a state of utter confusion since the day the baby was born. The picture started and everything else—but I did have a breather of a few days to enjoy Edi and the baby. He'll be the joy of the world to you when you see him—he's so sweet, and looks more and more like Edi I think—with eyes and forehead like mine. I hope I can mean as much to Vini IV as Vini II and Marguerite I mean to me—to both of us."

Although he would have preferred to spend more time with Edi and their baby, Vincent was nonetheless glad to have work. His role in *Hudson's Bay* was not the one he had tested for, which had gone to Paul Muni. Instead, Vincent was cast as the foppish King Charles II, complete with wig and spaniel. Despite his disappointment at losing the lead, he thought it "a very nice part, though not too big, and I hate being idle more than anything." He turned in a good performance which he hoped would raise his stock with

Zanuck, but the film itself did not fare well, being generally criticized for having too much dialogue and too little action. And yet Vincent's reviews stood out; the *New York Morning Telegraph* went so far as to say, "Only Vincent Price, as King Charles himself, sets an example of what good acting should be." Also appearing in a small role in the film was a young Gene Tierney, who would become a renowned beauty, one of Fox's biggest stars of the forties, and one of Vincent's favorite and most frequent leading ladies.

After *Hudson's Bay*, the actor entered a dry spell. With a new baby to feed, the timing couldn't have been worse. After four months without work, during which time the studio was not obliged to pay him anything, in late January 1941, a very tense Vincent went off to spend four days at Yucca Loma Ranch in the Mojave Desert by himself. He returned in a slightly more optimistic frame of mind, writing his parents, "Things have been pretty gloomy out here and I haven't had a picture in four months and no offers in sight, so I got myself into a fine stew and decided to go away and relieve Edi of my stewing presence—it did me a world of good and I'm back now trying to be patient about this hectic business. I changed agents last week and hope that may do some good, but I'm at a loss as to what more to do." But it would be another four months before Vincent would find any work at all, months that forced him to learn to sit still with himself—a difficult task for a man as restless as he.

During Barrett's first year of life, Vincent had the chance—for perhaps the first time since leaving London in 1935—to contemplate the choices he had made thus far in his adult life and career. In their small rented home in the valley he tended his garden which, during the rainy winter of 1941, produced an abundance of calla lilies, roses, poppies, lupine, and other lush and fragrant flowers. Living in Los Angeles, where whole gardens can seem miraculously to bloom almost overnight, Vincent became an avid gardener. His green thumb offered him a welcome creative outlet in the midst of his professional dry spell. After almost three years on the West Coast, he admitted, "I am delighted with this state of California, and am definitely decided to spend my life out here with a year now and then in New York. I do miss London and the wonderful life I had in Europe. Of course, whoever wins, it can never be the same—everyone will be so poor and so nerve wracked—it will be a miracle if they are sane." Indeed, World War II, which was by then raging in Europe, occupied his daily thoughts, and the specter of his former "hero" Hitler loomed large as the United States contemplated whether or not to get involved in the mounting conflict. He wrote, "We get very upset about the world, and are full of wonder at what is going to happen, but there doesn't seem to be much we can do about it—so we are trying to do our best in our minds to be prepared for the worst."

After eight months without work, Vincent took a three-week gig at a regional theater in Del Monte, performing in *The Constant Wife* with Helen Gahagan. He changed agents again, increasingly anxious to find movie work. Meanwhile, he took advantage of his free time to fly to St. Louis to visit his parents; his father's health, after a year of hospital visits, changes of doctors, and spa cures, at last seemed to be improving. Vincent and Edi also moved yet again, this time back out to the beach, where they spent hours playing with their son in sand and surf. They enjoyed the cool summer out in Malibu, where friends such as Charles Laughton and his wife Elsa Lanchester, Louis Hayward, Ida Lupino, Rachel Field, Janet Gaynor and Adrian came out to spend the day, have picnics, and cook campfire dinners on the beach. As Vincent confided to his father, "I am trying with all my heart to get back to the simple things of life."

After their restful summer, Vincent was asked to join the West Coast touring company of *Mamba's Daughters*. During the 1920s, Broadway had seen a wave of plays featuring black actors. Dramatists such as Eugene O'Neill had begun exploring "the Negro condition," and their work gave African-American actors such as Paul Robeson the chance to rise to the top of their profession. The Depression had drawn attention away from race issues; nonetheless a few black actors continued to work on Broadway, and chief among these was Ethel Waters, who after a number of successful theater and film comedies, had taken Broadway by storm in 1938 as Hagar in *Mamba's Daughters*. On opening night Eleanor Roosevelt and Helen Hayes had gone backstage to congratulate Miss Waters, sparking a wave of adulation for the actress. A few days later an advertisement appeared in the New York papers which read, "The undersigned feel that Ethel Waters' superb performance in 'Mamba's Daughters' at the Empire is a profound emotional experience which any playgoer would be the poorer for missing. It seems such a magnificent example of great acting, simple, deeply felt, moving on a plane of complete reality that we are glad to pay for the privilege of saying so." Among the signatures were those of Judith Anderson, Tallulah Bankhead, Norman Bel Geddes, John Emery, Oscar Hammerstein, Burgess Meredith, and Carl Van Vechten.

As Vincent had always relished working with the great actresses of the theater, he accepted the part of the sympathetic plantation superintendent who befriends Hagar. Of course, the prospect of earning again made the offer doubly attractive. The cast also featured Fredi Washington, who had made a name for herself as the tragic daughter of Louise Beavers in the 1934 film of *Imitation of Life*. After playing to sold-out houses in Los Angeles, the company traveled to San Francisco and Seattle, once again luring Vincent away from Edi and his new son.

After recovering from Barrett's difficult birth, Edith had decided to go back to work—and, for the first time, it seemed her prospects in Hollywood were looking up. In the spring of 1941 she was cast by director Charles Vidor in his film version of the play *Ladies in Retirement*, a thriller starring Ida Lupino, Louis Hayward, and Elsa Lanchester. Her husband was thrilled at the possibility of Edi finally having the opportunity to "be back on her way again to being the actress she wants to be." During the filming, he was away doing the play in Del Monte, but he wrote his father, "Edith is blooming in her work and loves pictures now—it looks as though it's going to be swell for her—and I feel it's the beginning of a new career." Undoubtedly Vincent was also relieved that someone in the family was bringing home a Hollywood paycheck.

As the batty Louisa, Edith had been given a character role she could sink her teeth into, and the critics lauded her sympathetic performance. Jimmy Starr voted Edith Barrett, along with Red Skelton, Donna Reed, Veronica Lake, Carmen Miranda, and Dana Andrews, one of the best "discoveries" of the year. In addition, he praised her performance in *Ladies in Retirement* as one of the best of the year, placing her alongside Bette Davis in *The Little Foxes*, Gary Cooper in *Sergeant York*, Greer Garson in *Blossoms in the Dust*, and Joan Crawford in *A Woman's Face*. This was the break Edith had long been hoping for. In October, she and Vincent's one time costar Blanche Yurka began filming *Lady for a Night* starring Joan Blondell and John Wayne. Playing Blanche's inhibited sister, Edith had a tremendous courtroom scene in which her character, after years of living in fear, summons the courage to accuse her sister of a double murder. After watching her film the scene, *Los Angeles Daily News* drama editor Virginia Wright reported that Edith

Barrett's "screen career is likely to follow the track beaten for her previously in the theater."

In the spring of 1941, however, Vincent and Edi had seen a three-handed melodrama called *Five Chelsea Lane*, at a small theater in Hollywood. They had liked the piece tremendously and had gone about securing the Broadway rights for themselves. Set in nineteenth-century London, Patrick Hamilton's play is a thriller in which a psychopath named Manningham marries a wealthy woman and then drives her mad in order to get her to reveal the location of the jewels he knows she has hidden. The play works because the audience truly does not know who the crazy one is for quite a while—the husband initially appears not only benign but urbane and charming, whereas the wife seems fragile and on the verge of a breakdown. By autumn, Vincent and Edi had found a producer who would underwrite their return to Broadway; but then, at the last minute, Edi withdrew from the project, claiming illness.

In fact, it seems that Edith chose to stay in Hollywood to find more film work. After struggling to break into films, she faced a difficult decision—to return to the Broadway stage to star opposite her husband, playing another period role in another melodrama, or to remain in a Hollywood that, as Virginia Wright noted, had "just learned to appreciate her talents." There is no record of Vincent's reaction to her decision to stay in Hollywood, but it's likely that he supported her choice; he had married Edith because she was an actress, and he always respected the decisions she made regarding her career. Her decision meant that he would be leaving his wife and year-old son behind, but it was never in question that he should go. And so, in November 1941, Vincent left Edi and Barrett, and once again traveled back to Broadway.

With Edi out of the picture, the producers hired Judith Evelyn, the Canadian actress who had played the part in the Los Angeles production, to take her part. They also decided to change the name of the play to *Angel Street* for its Broadway opening at the Golden Theater. Joining Price and Evelyn was Leo G. Carroll, the well-respected character actor with whom Vincent had worked in Hollywood. After three weeks of rehearsal the play opened, to little advance enthusiasm, on Friday December 5, 1941. Melodramas, it was feared, were passé, and tickets were printed for only three more shows. On opening night, however, the audience was so enthusiastic that the small cast was obliged to take eight curtain calls; even so, cast and crew went on to Sardi's with little hope that they would survive the notices. Vincent was particularly downcast, remembering his experience with *The Lady Has a Heart*, another show adored by its opening-night audience—but panned by critics.

Vincent always maintained that the notices for *Angel Street* were terrible, and liked to tell the story that the show was saved from its predicted three-show doom by America's entry into World War II, which came with the bombing of Pearl Harbor on December 7, 1941—two days after the play's opening. As he chose to remember it, the Pearl Harbor headlines had diverted the New York theater world's attention. And yet this tale seems to have been just so much self-deprecating fiction: In fact, *Angel Street* collected a set of phenomenal raves.

Burns Mantle in the *New York Daily News* wrote, "Watch me closely, ladies and gents! I think I am about to teeter off the deep end. I have just seen the theater really come alive for the first time this season. A London thriller called *Angel Street*, at the

Golden, is responsible. But don't get me wrong I mean the THEATER. Not the important theater. Or the theater of social significance. No, no—not the intellectual theater. Or the pseudo-educational theater. Just the good old emotional hokum theater in which your interest is definitely challenged along about 9:15 and held taut until 11 o'clock." He went on to note that the piece—"a pretty exciting game"—is "about as well acted as it could be" and praised Price for playing "the suave Manningham with distinction," Evelyn for giving "a striking performance," and Leo G. Carroll for his "deft, convincing, perfect performance." George Freedley of the *New York Morning Telegraph* also sang Vincent's praises: "Vincent Price gives perhaps his best performance as the husband. His brutality, his silken villainy, his honest sensuality, his domination of his wife is perfectly portrayed. His presence is never absent from your mind whether he is onstage or not." And even the ever-critical Brooks Atkinson of the *Times* praised Hamilton's play, the production, and the actors. He wrote, "As the unpleasant Mr. Manningham Vincent Price is giving an excellent performance of unctuous-voiced, assured, dissembling gentleness."

Whatever caused Vincent to read critical success as disaster, *Angel Street*—which became the longest-running melodrama in Broadway history, playing for 1,293 performances—undoubtedly found a measure of its immense popularity in the climate of the times. With the country at war, audiences sought out escapist entertainment to take their minds off reality. And escapist theater this certainly was. As the curtain went up, theatergoers were enmeshed in a nineteenth-century London household and the psychological drama that played itself out there. The play's atmosphere was perfect for live theater presentation, and yet, retitled *Gaslight*, it was successfully filmed twice—by Thorold Dickinson in Britain the previous year with Diana Wynyard and Anton Walbrook, and by George Cukor in Hollywood in 1944 with Ingrid Bergman and Charles Boyer.

Even if Vincent chose to forget the critical raves, he would always remember the joy of again being in a hit show on Broadway. For the first time, he felt that he had found his stride. He loved playing the evil and elegant Manningham, relishing the palpable effect of his stage presence as he struck fear into the hearts of the delighted audience. "I was launched as a villain—a sadistic heavy, a suave killer, a wife-beater, a sexy extrovert, a diabolical introvert—take your pick!" As usual, he had taken an intellectual approach in preparing for his role, reading Krafft-Ebing and studying reports about madness and psychopathic behavior, all of which he gladly shared with interviewers who asked about his first foray into villainy.

Angel Street ran through the summer, despite the fact that the Golden Theater was not air conditioned. When he was offstage, Vincent often went out into the alley by the stage door to get some air, have a smoke or a soda, and listen to the sounds of Gershwin floating out of the stage door of the Majestic Theater opposite, where a revival of *Porgy and Bess* was playing. He soon became friends with many of the actors in the production across the way, so visibly that the *New York Times* featured a cartoon that summer entitled "When 'Catfish Row' Meets 'Angel Street.'" The caption read, "Vincent Price, of 'Angel Street,' comes out for a chat with Todd Duncan, of 'Porgy and Bess,' in the alley between acts. Others of the cast, including Porgy's goat, emerge for a breath of fresh air and refreshments." Vincent and Porgy's goat became quite close; he took to feeding the animal leftovers, even bringing him vegetables from Sardi's. Now and again he even bought an Eskimo Pie from a nearby ice cream vendor, eating half and giving the goat the rest—until, one night while biting into his pie, Vincent dislodged a cap on his front tooth. Rushing back onstage, he found a way to plug the hole with a wad of tape. But in his very next scene Vincent had to sip from a glass of milk before launching into another series of accusations against his wife. As he later recalled, "The milk dissolved what little hold the adhesive had on my other teeth, and, instead of the vocal report designed to make her confess her guilt, a wad of tape shot from my mouth and across the stage, hitting her square on the cheek. The rest of the scene was helplessly lisped, and limped to an undramatic conclusion. There's nothing more innocuous than trying to be menacing with a drooping lip and a missing tooth." Although the dentist fixed his tooth the next day, Vincent's friendship with the goat fell off sharply thereafter.

Apparently the flying wad of tape was not the only problem that occurred between Vincent and Judith Evelyn. Among his papers is a letter from 1943 in which she paints a bleak picture of their working relationship. "I cannot blame you for leaving *Angel Street*," she wrote. "Indeed, I would have done so as far back as the summer had I had any other means of earning a living as immediate prospect. My playing Mrs. Manningham from the early spring until December 7, 1942 was a ghastly nightmare. I was extremely sorry that you took such a violent dislike to me—not for myself—but it ruined what had been a lovely artistic thing between us. As far as I am concerned, you and I never gave a performance worth a damn from the moment you began thinking of Mr. Manningham as a sole creation of the part of Vincent Price—irrespective of and oblivious to any intermingling thoughts and actions between the two characters. A real artistic achievement is only possible between two people when they are friendly enough to discuss a scene without rancor and in an honest endeavor to help one another—not hinder."

This barrage of criticism must have stung Vincent, and it seems likely that he took it to heart; from then on, he seems to have developed a reputation as the soul of consideration to his costars.

During his year on Broadway in *Angel Street* Vincent, as ever, used his days productively. Edi and Barrett had stayed in Los Angeles for Christmas and well into the new year before coming to spend a few months with him in a house he rented in Riverdale. Alone in New York and ever eager to work and to learn, he quickly found a niche doing radio work. Some years later, a character on the comedy radio series *Duffy's Tavern* would say of Vincent, "He's got that sweet sooooooothing kind of a voice; you don't know whether to listen to it or pour it on a waffle." Indeed, his immediately recognizable voice and his aptitude for learning his lines fast made Vincent a natural for radio, where actors were often asked to work with scant rehearsal time, disorganized or unfinished scripts, and cramped conditions. Actors who could master the medium often found they were in high demand. Vincent loved radio, calling it "a wonderful combination of the stage and movies." During *Victoria Regina*, he had appeared with Helen Hayes in a number of broadcast scenes from the play; after that he was asked to read a variety of other parts, and even took part in the first around-the-world radio broadcast, along with such luminaries as the Lunts. Vincent recalled, "It was beamed from New York to Miami, from Miami to South America, and from South America to Dakar, from Dakar to Cairo, Cairo to Bombay, Bombay to Bangkok, and then on to Japan, and then the Hawaiian Islands, and then L.A., and then back to us in New York. It was the first time it had ever been done. It was a kind of a trick, but it was interesting to be a part of it. We all did our little bits. I did a speech from *Romeo and Juliet*."

While *Angel Street* was on, he often appeared unbilled on one of the daytime radio soap operas such as *Valiant Lady* and *Helpmate*, claiming "they were such fun and you learned a whole area of acting you were never trained to do." As well as the soaps, he also participated in numerous weekly series. One of his favorite radio ventures was a serial called *Johnny Presents* with Tallulah Bankhead, who frequently asked Vincent to appear on the show. No matter the project, the producers, or the sponsors, Tallulah refused to be anyone but herself. A February 19, 1942, *Chicago Sun-Times* article showed a photograph of Vincent and Tallulah together in rehearsal and noted that Tallulah had "talked her cigarette sponsor into letting her wear slacks at rehearsals and during actual programs. In fact, she's a slacks-addict since Katharine Hepburn gave her her first pair." But, as Vincent remembered, slacks were the least of sponsor Philip Morris's worries. "I had many a good time with Tallulah. She was a talker, full of ribald gossip, true and, better than true, made up. The humorless men from Philip Morris always insisted that if we smoked it had to be their cigarettes. Tallulah smoked only English Gold Flakes. She would dump the Philip Morris cigs in the john and then fill the pack up with English ovals. No one was fooled—the smell of her Virginia tobacco knocked you down, but the pack protected her."

Vincent also donated his radio time to the war effort on such programs as *Heirs of Liberty*. New York stage actors lent their abilities to the war effort in a variety of ways, among the most popular being the Stage Door Canteen. Created by the American Theater Wing War Service, the Canteen was housed in the basement of an old theater just off Times Square. A July 1942 article in *The American* magazine featured a spread about this "Hot Spot for Heroes: A star-spangled Stork Club where Broadway celebrities entertain and feed 2,000 service men every night." Seven nights a week, servicemen from all of the allied nations could dance with Broadway starlets and chorus girls, see live entertainment, and be served coffee, doughnuts, cake, and milk by actors such as Katharine Cornell, Lynn Fontanne, Alfred Lunt, Tallulah Bankhead, Bette Davis, and Vincent Price. A highlight for many of these enlisted men (officers weren't welcome) was the opportunity to dance with such stars as Paulette Goddard, Dorothy Lamour, and Loretta Young. Another Stage Door volunteer was a young girl whom Vincent had befriended during the run of *Angel Street*. Starstruck sixteen-year-old Betty Perske had taken a job as an usher at the Golden in order to be as close to the theater as possible and became a frequent visitor in Vincent's dressing room. A year later, she took Hollywood by storm as Lauren Bacall in *To Have and Have Not*.

One of the war benefits Vincent most enjoyed took place at Madison Square Garden in February 1942, when he and Jack Haley, Ray Bolger, Danny Kaye, Bobby Clark, and other Broadway dancers and comedians performed an elaborate striptease à la Gypsy Rose Lee, down to their briefs (daintily ornamented with large shamrock leaves), shoes, and socks. The event was such a success that it was repeated in November 1942, at *Cheer China*, a midnight to four A.M. benefit for Chinese relief. This time the group, who called themselves the Floradora Sextet, included Ed Wynn, Danny Kaye, Clifton Webb, Bobby Clark, Charles Butterworth, and Vincent Price in full drag. *Time* magazine, which featured a fetching photograph of the six men doing a kick routine, reported that the "pretty maidens almost broke down the stage with their feathery steps, almost brought out the fire department with their dimpled charm. They also brought out the beast in their mannishly dressed swains (Elsa Maxwell, Peggy Wood, Benay Venuta, Luella Gear, Lili Damita, Luise Rainer)."

But perhaps even more than the star-studded benefits, Vincent enjoyed taking performances of *Angel Street* to nearby army and navy bases. For the young servicemen facing an imminent departure for the European front, the entertainment provided by these Broadway stars provided a welcome respite not only from their daily routine but from their thoughts about what lay ahead. Long after the war, Vincent continued his tradition of performing at military bases. Richard Cypher was a young ensign from the Midwest stationed in Providence, Rhode Island, when Vincent played there during the early 1950s. Cypher would always remember that Vincent Price did more than merely perform. After the play, the actor came out and spent a couple of hours talking with the men, telling them about the theater and about the stars he had met, but also listening to them talk about their own lives, their hopes and fears. For young soldiers like Cypher, this one-on-one attention meant a great deal and had a profound effect. As Ed Sullivan reported in his September 21, 1942 *Daily News* column, "Nobody does so much so graciously."

For years Vincent had struggled to find an identity for himself, both as an actor and as a person. Now, at thirty-one, as a husband and father, with a Broadway hit on his hands, and flexing his muscles in myriad pursuits, for the first time in his life, he finally felt as if all the pieces had begun to come together.

17

AFTER A SUCCESSFUL year in *Angel Street*, Vincent Price decided it was time to return to Los Angeles. Having achieved more than he had hoped in his triumphant return to Broadway, he hoped to parlay his newfound confidence as well as his recent positive publicity into a full-fledged movie career. "I felt it was time for a real try at Hollywood. My short and bitter taste of failure in *Service de Luxe* made me know I had to go to Hollywood in a different way, not as a condescending stage 'star' deigning to do a film now and then, but to jump into it up to my ears. A term contract was the way to do it and hopefully to convince the studio that I could make a mark as a character actor."

For his journey home to Edith and Barrett, Vincent took the Twentieth Century Limited out of New York to Chicago and the Super Chief on to the Coast—with a pair of international celebrities as company. He would later refer to his journey as "about as eventful as any I would ever take. The fun of the trip was the company of two famous figures traveling west. The three of us made up the only celebrity population so in self-protection we drank and ate and stayed up late together. Strangely enough, I was as recognizable as the others because the one was a writer primarily and the other, though certainly one of the most famous faces of all time, was disguised by age and lack of makeup. Time had whitened his hair and the famous twitching little black mustache had been a prop all along." Just days before their journey, Charles Chaplin had come out openly for the Left at a forum at Carnegie Hall; not many months later, he would virtually be exiled from his adopted country. The third member of their improvised party provided an unlikely counterpart—Clare Boothe Luce, "a classy dame if there ever was one, playwright [she wrote *The Women*] and wife of the publisher of *Time*, as right of center as Chaplin was left of it." Vincent found himself somewhere in the middle politically, but all three enjoyed each other's company immensely. After dinner, Chaplin would entertain in the club car. "He'd do all the famous schticks, his walk, every gesture, all with running commentaries from past performances. Other occupants of the club car were amused, but several had no idea who this distinguished-looking little man had been or was. It was, I'm sure, much more fun for me, as I'm highly impressionable in the company of big names of any kind."

Back in Hollywood, Vincent resumed his screen career with one of the most prestigious films he ever made. *The Song of Bernadette* was a very popular novel by Austrian Franz

Werfel, who had fled the Nazis for France and was then forced to flee again in June 1940 when the Nazis occupied Paris. Upon reaching Lourdes, Werfel heard the story of Bernadette Soubirous, a peasant girl who claimed that the Virgin Mary had appeared to her in a nearby grotto in 1858. After being persecuted by the local authorities and spending most of her life in a convent, Bernadette was canonized in 1933. Werfel was taken with her story and vowed that if he escaped alive, he would "magnify the divine mystery and the holiness of man" as evidenced in the life of Saint Bernadette. After a harrowing trip over the Pyrenees into Spain and then across the ocean to America, Werfel kept his promise.

Fox purchased the rights to Werfel's novel in April 1942, before it was published, and invested a great deal of time and money in the production. Many young women were tested for the title role, but the part finally went to a twenty-three-year-old actress named Phyllis Isley. She had made a few forgettable films in the late 1930s, so the studio changed her name to Jennifer Jones for this, her "official" film debut. Under Henry King's direction, Jones would be supported by a strong cast—William Eythe, Charles Bickford, Lee J. Cobb, Gladys Cooper, Anne Revere, Blanche Yurka, Linda Darnell, and, as a village woman whose crippled infant is healed through faith in Bernadette, Edith Barrett. Vincent Price received fourth billing for his role as Imperial Prosecutor Dutour, a cynical man determined to stamp out religious fanaticism and disprove Bernadette's story. Still bearded for the film, Vincent was cold and handsome, clearly bringing a little of Manningham to the role. The action of the film takes place over a few decades during which Dutour eventually succumbs to throat cancer and, by the end of the film, a pale and wasted Dutour joins the line of worshippers at Bernadette's grotto and implores the girl he once persecuted to pray for him.

Fox released *The Song of Bernadette* at the end of December 1943, in time for Academy Award consideration. It garnered eleven nominations of which it won four, including Best Actress for Jones. Vincent was not nominated but his reviews were strong. More important, his performance attracted the attention of Darryl F. Zanuck, who proceeded to slot him in for increasingly interesting parts in the studio's pictures.

Vincent next appeared in a war movie, *The Eve of St. Mark*, directed by John Stahl and top-lining William Eythe and Anne Baxter. During the war, all the studios produced a great many features depicting and supporting America's war effort. Although Zanuck had joined the army himself, he instructed his deputies to put their maximum effort behind war-related films. Thus, Fox spent $300,000 to purchase Maxwell Anderson's blank verse play, from which the script for *The Eve of St. Mark* was derived. Vincent played Private Francis Marion, a gentle yet cynical Southern poet, who deflects his fears and doubts by spouting poetry to amuse his friends and seduce his women.

Vincent always claimed that the role of Marion was "one of the best parts I ever had and one of the best performances I ever gave. It was one of the first times that I was allowed to play a contemporary person." He had acquired the confidence to play the role, which utilized his unique ability to speak verse. Years later, British actress Diana Rigg said of him, "What people don't know is what a wonderful verse speaker he was. And I think what a great classical actor he would have been. He had a wonderful voice and he had a perfect command of the verse form." The universally excellent reviews reflected Vincent's satisfaction with the role. The *New Yorker* noted his strong work as "the hero's poetic pal from the deep South" and reminded its readers of the diversity of roles in his career, "which demonstrates a nice flexibility"; the *Hollywood Reporter* pronounced that "Vincent Price scores a rich hit as the sorrowful Southerner with a weakness for Cuba Libres," and the *New York Daily News* felt he gave "an arresting performance in the role of a poetry-spouting soldier."

After the wrap of *The Eve of St. Mark,* during the first half of 1944 Vincent worked more or less concurrently on three strongly contrasting projects: *Wilson, The Keys of the Kingdom,* and *Laura.* Much time and money went into *Wilson,* a biopic of the twenty-eighth United States president, which took almost five months to shoot, from November 1943 through mid-March of 1944. A patriotic and sentimental depiction of Wilson's two terms as president, the film was nominated for ten Academy Awards, winning five. Alexander Knox played the title role, supported by a cast of fine actors including Charles Coburn, Geraldine Fitzgerald, Sir Cedric Hardwicke, William Eythe, George Macready, and former silent screen idol Francis X. Bushman. Vincent played William Gibbs McAdoo, Wilson's Secretary of the Treasury, who later married the president's daughter. He appears on screen for less than seven minutes and is given little to do other than deliver a few well-timed lines and stand in the background. With his hair slicked flat to his head, Vincent looks remarkably like his own father.

The Keys of the Kingdom, adapted from A. J. Cronin's best-selling novel about the life of a Scottish missionary in China, was directed by John Stahl, produced and cowritten by Joseph L. Mankiewicz, and starred Gregory Peck. Vincent received prominent billing as Monsignor Angus Mealy, a pompous, worldly cleric. Although he was initially set to appear in a number of scenes, his part was whittled down during editing. The strong cast again featured Sir Cedric Hardwicke, as well as Anne Revere, Roddy McDowall, and Edith Barrett in another small role. Vincent's chief enjoyment in the film was playing "a *fat* priest." He noted, "I had to starve all through *Eve of St. Mark* so I could look heroic. I ate nothing but rabbit food during *Song of Bernadette.* I had some more of the same in *Wilson* so I wouldn't be giving a bay window to William G. McAdoo. Then came this picture with me turning into a big fat bishop, and I started to eat. Boy did I eat."

His binge, however, was short-lived. In early March, the United States Navy informed Twentieth Century Fox that it would induct thirty-two-year-old Vincent Price into service on March 24. This sent the director and producers into a turmoil. A Chinese village had been erected on the lot and a cast of over seventy-five Asian children were being employed. There were three more weeks of shooting scheduled before the scene in which Japanese planes bomb the village and destroy a church and orphanage. Because there was a final shot in which Vincent was to survey the ruins, the studio was forced to demolish church and village twice so they could show Monsignor Mealy being wheeled through the rubble by Chinese coolies. After destroying everything with blow-torches, crowbars, and dynamite in order to shoot the sequence, the whole village was reconstructed at considerable cost.

While rushing to complete Vincent's scenes in *The Keys of the Kingdom,* Fox executives scurried around to make sure that they had enough footage of him for *Wilson.* Vincent was in heaven, telling reporter Harold Heffernan, "This is simply wonderful. I never felt so important in my life. Here is John Stahl shooting just my scenes, and Gregory Peck and Rose Stradner, the stars, are waiting around so they can be handy. And over there in the projection room right now Zanuck is running *Wilson* just to see if they've got all of Price that they need in it." Having been more or less ignored by Hollywood just a few years before, Vincent was thrilled to be the center of the studio's attention. There was only one small problem—he had to leave to fight a war.

And yet, in the end, Vincent Price never joined the navy. In later years he claimed that color blindness had prevented his induction, although in truth, the navy knew about his color blindness and he had passed his vision test. Though no confirmation exists, it seems possible that the studio may have interceded on Vincent's behalf—after all, their ranks of male stars had been sorely depleted by the call-up. From the beginning of World War II, most of Hollywood's leading men joined the forces. Those who didn't—even those who were legitimately exempt from the war due to age or injury—often felt a great deal of public pressure to join. Spencer Tracy, forty-one when the war began, was heckled for draft dodging; John Wayne, thirty-five, a married father of four, felt so unhappy about not being able to enlist that he flew to Washington to demand a commission, but was turned down due to a bad shoulder. Vincent Price was thirty years old and a married father of one when the war began. He had worked for the war effort in New York and in Hollywood, and had never considered enlisting. By 1943, however, he began to state publicly that he hoped to join the navy. Never one for extreme physical activity, he plainly admitted that he would not be well-suited to army life but, as a good sailor, he would welcome the opportunity to serve his country in the navy. When the opportunity escaped him—for whatever reason—Vincent continued making films for Fox.

His next project became a film noir classic: _Laura_. Fox had originally intended to have Rouben Mamoulian direct this stylish mystery with Otto Preminger producing, but after viewing the early rushes both Preminger and studio head Darryl F. Zanuck were unhappy with what they saw. Everything that had been shot would be scrapped—along with Mamoulian, his cameraman, his designer, and a portrait of Laura painted by Mamoulian's wife. Preminger then took over.

Laura featured a superb ensemble cast—Gene Tierney as the mysteriously disappeared Laura, Dana Andrews as investigating detective Mark McPherson who falls in love with Laura's portrait and, notably, Clifton Webb as radio personality Waldo Lydecker who regards the beautiful Laura as both his creation and his property. Vincent played Laura's suitor, Shelby Carpenter, a shallow, Southern playboy; Judith Anderson took the role of Laura's aunt and Shelby's would-be lover.

Excellent actors all, these were also all good friends, and they were delighted with the opportunity to work together. And the Mamoulian fiasco only meant they got to work together longer. Vincent said of Webb, "Clifton was the kindest man I ever knew in my life. I first met him in New York when I was in _Victoria_. He and Maybelle one day took me out to dinner. He said, 'You need publicity. You're the top young actor in New York today, and you need to be included in all of the things here.' Clifton would always put me in any kind of benefit that he had a chance to." Webb, a fixture on Broadway who had made a few silent films, made his talking picture debut with _Laura_ and earned an Oscar nomination for Best Supporting Actor. If Vincent enjoyed working with Webb, he loved working with Judith Anderson. As he recalled, he and Judith "got hysterical all the time. We were thrown off the set day by day."

Vincent would always regard _Laura_ as the best movie he had made. He considered it "one of those few pictures that is perfect. Not pretentious, very simple, just brilliant. Certainly way and away the best thing Otto Preminger ever did, and I think Otto thinks that as well. I once asked Otto why he did so much better with _Laura_ than Rouben. He told me, 'Rouben only knows nice people. I understand the characters in _Laura_. They're all heels, just like my friends.' Having worked with Preminger in _Outward Bound_ on Broadway, Vincent got along easily with [the director, who had a reputation for making things difficult on movie sets.] "I may be one of the few people in the world who like Otto Preminger," he admitted, "but I do." This was characteristic of Vincent, who found a way to get along with almost everyone he worked with.

In his opinion, it was Gene Tierney's "odd beauty" and underrated acting ability that made *Laura* so popular. He felt her beauty was both timeless and imperfect. The two made four films together and grew quite close until she withdrew from Hollywood in the 1950s. The film went through a number of changes before its release, including the editing out of a "smart set" party scene where Vincent, seated at the piano and surrounded by a bevy of beautiful women, sang the Sinatra number "You'll Never Know." But no matter what ended up on the cutting room floor, the film contained at least one pleasant surprise for its cast. Vincent recalled, "When we all went to see *Laura* on opening night, we had never heard the score! That was written long after the film was finished. So we sat there and thought 'Isn't that marvelous.' " David Raksin's haunting score is one of the most famous movie themes ever written, and when joined with words by Johnny Mercer, it went on to become a massive popular hit, famously recorded by Sinatra. The film itself, despite initially mixed reviews and an inexplicably lukewarm audience reception, is now regarded as one of the great examples of the genre.

Fox kept Price busy with one project after another. His next film, *A Royal Scandal*, was also fraught with director troubles, but brought him the chance to work with his old friend Tallulah Bankhead, cast as Catherine the Great. Ernst Lubitsch, whom Vincent, along with many others, considered "the greatest comedy director we ever had," was down to direct, but was recovering from a lengthy illness. The studio arrived at a compromise, arranging for Lubitsch to work in conjunction with Otto Preminger—a collaboration that proved disastrous. As Vincent recalled, "Unfortunately Lubitsch had had a heart attack and they wouldn't let him direct, so he had to watch Otto Preminger, who had the sense of humor of a guillotine. Gave him another heart attack!" The result was an unfunny failure: Vincent played a bewigged French ambassador with quite a bad French accent, and the entire cast looked as though they were struggling in vain to overcome Preminger's plodding direction.

Happily, in early 1945 Vincent moved on to another of his favorites, the eighteen-carat Technicolor melodrama *Leave Her to Heaven*. Based on a recent bestseller by Ben Ames Williams, it was directed by John Stahl with Gene Tierney, Cornel Wilde, and Jeanne Crain. The film marked Tierney's first in color, prompting Vincent to tell an interviewer, "That means that audiences will get the full force of those Tierney eyes. Now maybe they'll understand why scriptwriters have me go off the deep end every time I'm in the same picture with her." The star played an obsessively jealous woman who lies, cheats, murders, and contrives her own miscarriage in an effort to hold on to her husband (Cornel Wilde). When he falls in love with her sister (Crain), she kills herself in such a manner as to frame her sister for murder. Vincent played Gene's ex-fiancée who, despite her cruel dismissal of him, remains in love with her. He had only a few scenes, but the last of them was a tour de force in which he is the prosecuting attorney in the case against Crain. His performance brought praise; the *Los Angeles Times* suggested that his "portrayal merits attention as contending for the Academy supporting honors."

Having completed seven films (and six successes) for Fox since his return from New York, Vincent was rising in the ranks of Hollywood actors. He had resisted the matinée idol image the industry had wished to impose on him and struggled to find a persona with which audiences could identify. Now his strong showings in a variety of roles were attracting critical and audience attention and, most important, that of the producers at his studio, who intended to continue promoting him. But even as he began to earn the respect which he had coveted for so long, Vincent was once again beset with doubt. "I loved being a Hollywood actor working toward being a star. The work was hard and rewarding, although the life you led to make it work was difficult on the life you wanted to lead at home. If you had any sensitivity at all about normalcy, you could feel the trap closing around you, dragging you into the much-publicized muck that makes up a lot of Hollywood life. This isn't as true in the theater—you have days in which to live and, if it's New York, a city to live them in. In Hollywood, you led a studio life. Hollywood then was a hick town. It is, after all, not a town at all, it's a state of mind, a condition. And particularly under the studio system, it was a very cliquey condition, very juvenile in many ways, very exciting, and very dangerous. Still, even knowing the dangers, there was an excitement about being part of something that really was a world commodity. I knew I was stuck."

One of Vincent's antidotes to being "stuck" was to allow himself idiosyncrasies in his personal life. In fact, he began exaggerating them. Hollywood reporter Michael Sheridan spoke with him in 1945: "One of the tallest actors in the movies, Vincent Price, at 33, is a man of very definite likes and dislikes. In the matter of clothing, for instance. He dislikes hats, umbrellas, gloves, loud ties, imported English socks, tight-fitting coats, and suspenders. He likes best flannels, shirts one size too large, and he always wears a tie in place of a belt." Indeed, for an actor who made a living playing erudite and well-dressed men, Vincent was at best a casual dresser, at worst a mismatched slob. During his first months in Hollywood, he had succumbed to hiring a publicist in an effort to combat his matinée idol image. He liked to joke that it took his publicist two years to get a mention in the papers and, when she finally did, it read, "Who wears Vincent Price's clothes before he puts them on?"

Vincent's notoriously casual approach to dress extended to his automobile. In a town where you are what you drive, Sheridan reported, "Whenever Price drives his dilapidated, tumble-down midget car, which he calls The Bug, he sings at the top of his voice in a rich baritone. He was singing 'Ride of the Valkyries' the afternoon his car caught fire, and with fumes and flame belching forth from the belly of The Bug, his entrance into the nearest garage was dramatic to say the least." The Bug soon gave way to a 1923 Ford pickup truck that had once belonged to the Brunswick Drug Company and still had their logo emblazoned on the doors. The more Vincent became entrenched in Hollywood, the more he rebelled against its conventions. It was as if, by wearing rumpled, ill-matched clothes, he could prove that he hadn't sold out to its demands. Nonetheless, as much as he might have worried about his artistic integrity, as much he was subject to his own conflicts of interest, he would never be able to sacrifice being in the public eye. He loved it, and would never give up Hollywood. But he did realize that he would have to find a way to nourish his earliest and most fundamental passion—art.

By the mid-forties, Vincent Price was a firmly established movie actor, but he desperately missed the buzz of the New York art world. Los Angeles in the forties was still a provincial town in many ways, despite an abundance of money generated both by the film and the war industries. The town, however, was still run by Angelenos with old money—the men who owned the railroads and the newspapers and their wives who supported standard cultural institutions such as the museum and the opera. Nonetheless, the war years saw exciting changes arrive; the continuing influx of European wartime refugees filled the city with renowned writers, artists, musicians, and intellectuals, infusing Los Angeles with a thriving cosmopolitan culture it had previously lacked. Among their numbers were talented filmmakers whose exile led them to the Hollywood studios.

Buoyed by the European presence as well as that of Easterners who had come West after war broke out, the arts in Los Angeles gradually developed a place in the life of the city. It was in this atmosphere of change that Vincent decided to start an art gallery. Together with his old friend and *Victoria Regina* costar George Macready, he opened the Little Gallery in Beverly Hills in the spring of 1943.

Price and Macready had rented a tiny shop on Little Santa Monica Boulevard for sixty-five dollars a month. Situated between Martindale's Bookstore and Del Haven's, a very popular bar, the partners figured, correctly as it turned out, that they would catch a mixed clientele of erudites and inebriates. Their stock consisted mostly of paintings and drawings they had purchased in New York, selections from their own collections, and works by California artists they were newly discovering. They launched the opening show with vodka martinis dripped out of a silver-plated porcelain-lined urn that Vincent's mother had given him for serving iced tea. As he recalled, "Most of our friends liked martinis, especially free ones, and we drew an overflow crowd who hadn't the slightest intention of buying anything. A few idle pricing passes were made, but no purchases; but the main joy was that we were launched and art was back in our lives."

With his degree in art history from Yale and a year of study at the Courtauld, Vincent was accepted as a legitimate art connoisseur and was warmly welcomed into the Los Angeles art world, such as it was. He swiftly earned a reputation as an innovative dealer and an enthusiastic patron. As artist and lifelong friend, William Brice recalled, "George was a very urbane and very attractive man, but he obviously didn't have the full passion and commitment that Vincent had. You knew he was interested, or he wouldn't have been doing it, but he really lived in the aura of Vincent's passion. I remember coming to Los Angeles in 1937 and what was really present was the Laguna Watercolor Society and marine landscapes were very prevalent. There were only a few dealers who had artists from outside the country or even from outside the state. So what Vincent was doing was really quite adventurous."

By starting a gallery, Vincent came to know most of the significant members of the small Los Angeles fine arts community, as well as many of the European expatriates. He had met Igor Stravinsky when the composer asked him to do the narration for a production of his ballet, *L'Histoire d'un Soldat*. Although the ballet was never produced, Vincent remained on good terms with the composer who often came into the gallery to see the work and to visit. On one fondly remembered occasion, "Stravinsky came in and said, 'Do you mind if I wait here because some friends of mine are going to join me here? We want to see your show and then we're going to go next door.' And in came Thomas Mann, and he introduced me. And then in came Franz Werfel. Well, I knew Franz Werfel because I had done *The Song of Bernadette*. And in came Aldous Huxley and I met him. Then Rachmaninov came in and Schoenberg, and I took one look at them and I thought, 'My God, this is an all-star cast.' "

The Little Gallery soon became a fixture in the Los Angeles art and social scenes. Jane Wyatt recalled, "It was a great, fun gallery. It was the place to go and meet and mingle. There was nothing else like it around. It was a wonderful place." Customers soon included Tallulah Bankhead, Woolworth heiress Barbara Hutton, Fanny Brice, Katharine Hepburn, and even the notoriously reclusive Greta Garbo who, Vincent remembered, "dropped in to look and, if anyone else was looking, dropped out—quickly." Charles Laughton was an early patron of the Little Gallery. The versatile and talented character actor also had a great eye for art. He collected selectively and owned a few genuine masterpieces, including Renoir's *Judgment of Paris*. Laughton's great passion, however, was the Northwest Coast painter Morris Graves. He collected the painter's work assiduously and boasted twenty or more pieces from Graves's bird and tree periods. When the Little Gallery had a Graves show, Laughton bought another superb pine tree and asked that Vincent keep in touch with him regarding their future shows and acquisitions. When Vincent came across two original posters by Jean Cocteau of Karsavina and Nijinsky, created for their debut in *Le Spectre de la Rose*, he called Laughton, thinking he would love them. When Laughton came into the gallery, Vincent recalled, "For some inexplicable reason, he looked at them and flew into a tiny tantrum. 'They're too homosexual,' he screamed and left the gallery. They were certainly by one and of one, but they were beautiful and, after all, great works of art with extraordinary associations with ballet and music and a period of unique artistic history. I never did understand what Laughton was going on about, but felt that if the shoe fit . . . I sold them to the very macho Otto Preminger."

As Vincent's name became more publicly identified with art, he began receiving letters from artists who wished to be given shows at the Little Gallery. One such letter, which arrived during 1943, had been posted from just up Beverly Glen canyon by a struggling artist who enclosed a sample of his work, saying that, if Vincent liked the piece, he had only to send a tube of vermilion and a pair of socks in return. The painting was a watercolor, loosely painted, quite primitive, and clearly influenced by Matisse and particularly by Chagall. The letter was signed Henry Miller.

As for many men of Vincent's age, Miller had been an important figure of the actor's youth. While on Tour 22, he had bought Miller's books—then banned in the U.S.— to bring back home. "One of the things that I remember about going to Europe," Vincent said, "was that you tried to bring back his books because they were dirty books, you know. And he was enormously famous. People thought he was a very good writer except for those dirty words. So, of course, I bought his books and smuggled them in. I remember I was terribly impressed when I read them."

Not only did Vincent like Henry Miller's work, he also was intrigued by the idea of this great writer becoming a painter. When Miller returned to the United States from Paris, he had settled in Hollywood, hoping to earn a living as a screenwriter. With his books still banned he was broke, but after working for a short while at the studios, he became so disgusted that he quit, feeling he would rather starve than prostitute his gifts. He began painting and showing his work to friends and to other artists. One of the first people outside his own circle to respond to his work was Vincent, and soon they began a regular socks-for-art exchange. Miller wrote Vincent whenever he became desperate: "I need dough immediately for rent and groceries—overdue. Just as soon as I can breathe easily again, I'll breathe out a half-dozen for you to show around. It's understood that I can always let you have some—*you're my friend*. Like Christ, I choose the humble ones for the inner circle."

Vincent never did give Miller an exhibition at the Little Gallery, but he helped to interest another dealer with a gallery on Hollywood Boulevard, who eventually gave Miller a show. Vincent bought eight or ten of Miller's pieces, which ran between forty dollars and one hundred dollars at that show, and at one time had accumulated about twenty of them. Margaret Neiman Byers recalled, "Henry always gave the paintings away except when Vincent Price got involved. Then it got to be more fun, and he sold a few." Vincent liked Miller a lot, because "he was a real bohemian, you know, the real McCoy. I really enjoyed him. I ended up with a very large collection of his paintings because no one else was really collecting them. I felt they were a very private discovery of mine."

Despite the success of the Little Gallery and the untold pleasure it afforded its proprietors, George and Vincent soon realized that they couldn't run the business and have movie careers at the same time, so when the landlord raised the rent they called it quits. Vincent later admitted, "I really didn't have the time. And, as much fun as it was, it was really kind of a dilettante's approach to it, which it shouldn't be. We broke even because the rent was so cheap, but we never really made money and neither of us could ever afford to keep it going for the fun of it." His experience of a day-to-day interaction with the art world, however, had served to whet his appetite for more. Although Vincent Price would never again own a gallery, from the mid-forties on, he would always remain actively involved with the visual arts.

In 1944, Fox bought the rights to Anya Seton's best-selling novel, *Dragonwyck*. A Gothic melodrama set in the Hudson River valley during the early nineteenth century, Seton's book tells the story of a wealthy landowner, Nicholas Van Ryn, whose wife is unable to bear him an heir. He secretly poisons her and then marries his beautiful young cousin. But Van Ryn's drug addiction drives him to increasingly erratic behavior, until he finally dies a tortured death.

Joseph L. Mankiewicz was slated to direct *Dragonwyck*. Van Ryn was a role Vincent desperately wanted; having made such a success of the villain in *Angel Street*, he was convinced that to play a similar role on screen would be a great boost to his career. But first he had to convince Mankiewicz and the studio heads. This was not that easy. "I had to fight like the devil for this part. My bosses kept remembering me as the good-natured guy in *Laura* and I insisted I wasn't that type." Furthermore, Mankiewicz, who had produced *The Keys of the Kingdom*, could only think of Vincent as the portly prelate he had played in that film—a long shot from the tall, dark, handsome Van Ryn he had in mind. Determined to convince Mankiewicz, Vincent lost all the weight he had gained, auditioned, and won the coveted role.

Dragonwyck began shooting in February 1945. Starring Vincent and Gene Tierney, in their fourth film together, the cast also included Walter Huston, Anne Revere, Spring Byington, Henry Morgan, and a young Jessica Tandy playing a crippled Irish maid. Gene Tierney was married to designer Oleg Cassini, but their relationship was steadily deteriorating. One day during shooting, Mankiewicz instructed her to turn slowly and look into the camera. She would later write in her autobiography, "I turned and found myself staring into what I thought were the most perfect blue eyes I had ever seen on a man. He was standing near the camera, wearing a navy lieutenant's uniform. He smiled at me. My reaction was right out of a ladies' romance novel. Literally, my heart skipped." The eyes belonged to John F. Kennedy and soon the two were seriously involved. As their romance continued, Tierney sought to obtain a divorce from Cassini, convinced that Kennedy would marry her. But, as the scion of one of the country's most prominent Catholic families, Kennedy could never attempt such a union. A few years later, a heartbroken Tierney would take up with Aly Khan, and when he left her she collapsed. Shortly thereafter, Fox put her on suspension and she left Hollywood for Texas.

Following the successful release of *Dragonwyck* in 1946, for which Vincent received excellent reviews and a Box Office Blue Ribbon Award, Hollywood reporters began to write about Vincent Price as potentially one of Hollywood's biggest stars. In February, Virginia MacPherson optimistically reported, "There's a lot of talk among Twentieth Century-Fox bosses these days that maybe they have a big star in Vincent Price and maybe they better start doing something about it. And it couldn't have happened to a nicer guy. This six-foot-four giant thinks it might be nice to be up there in the top bracket with the rest of the movie stars. But the money isn't what's putting the sparkle in his eyes these days. It's the fact that now he's where he can ask for the parts he wants."

In April 1946, Louella Parsons devoted an entire "In Hollywood" column to Vincent Price, complete with a full-color photograph of the actor as Nicholas Van Ryn. Parsons, maker and breaker of reputations, wrote that Vincent "has reached the pinnacle of his success. His Nicholas Van Ryn . . . is his top performance. It is an extremely difficult role because the man is a charmer, even though he is a snobbish rogue. Also, he is a case for a psychiatrist. The role of Van Ryn calls for a lot of acting and Vincent admits he's a ham and loves to act all over the place, but the fact that he has restrained himself and doesn't over-emote is a tribute to his ability." Price, Parsons believed, had settled down to playing villains and would continue to do so with great success. For his part, the actor hoped for rather more diversity and challenge.

Vincent was next cast in *Forever Amber*, an adaptation of Kathleen Windsor's best-selling period romance, and was thrilled to be playing the best friend of the hero, "the only sane person in the book . . . I want to have a chance to play an occasional role where I am not motivated by wickedness." Darryl Zanuck had big expectations for the film which began shooting in the summer of 1946 with Peggy Cummins and Cornel Wilde starring. Over half of the film had been shot when Zanuck became dissatisfied with both the director and his female lead. By the time Otto Preminger once again had been called in to take over and Cummins replaced by Linda Darnell, Vincent had been cast in something else. (He was replaced by Richard Greene.)

Vincent's high hopes for more quality roles were short-lived. The film he was moved to during the disruption of *Forever Amber* was *Shock*, one of the studio's 'B' unit productions. He and his costar, Lynn Bari, were chosen for the eighteen-day shoot by producer Howard Koch because he knew they were the quickest studies and the most reliable actors on the lot. Admittedly, Vincent had the leading role—that of a sinister psychiatrist who kills his wife and goes on to more murder and mayhem—but *Shock* might just as well have been titled 'Schlock.' And yet the reviews for this low-budget thriller, which played on its star's *Angel Street* persona, were surprisingly positive, and he came out of it especially well, with one reviewer describing him as "terrific, smooth, menacing, and as dangerous as a tiger's paw."

Pleased with the picture's unexpected success, the studio next cast Vincent in *Moss Rose*, another period mystery-romance. For him, the highlight of this project was the opportunity to work with another grande dame of the American theater, Ethel Barrymore. He later wrote, " 'Working with' was the operative term. Just meeting or knowing an actress is not enough. To appreciate them fully, you must work with them; one is rarely disappointed with the 'person' once you have known their 'personality.' Ethel Barrymore was no exception. Off camera, she was pleasant and chatty, especially because during the filming one of her two great passions—baseball—was on the air. She was a famous fan of our National Sport." Indeed, it was rumored that when Miss Barrymore first came to Hollywood, her contract stipulated that she didn't have to work during the crucial games of the World Series or during broadcasts from the Metropolitan Opera, her other great passion. Naturally, she and Vincent got along superbly, discussing their favorite operas and keeping up with the 1947 baseball season.

Vincent described Ethel Barrymore as having "one of those faces that became a theatrical shrine. As she grew older, it was so open, like the front of a theater that had seen a huge audience pass through." His scene in *Moss Rose* with this doyenne of her profession was filmed in a greenhouse filled, not surprisingly, with moss roses. When he asked her afterward if she was going to see the rushes, she exclaimed, "My God no, my dear! I never had to see myself on the stage. Why should I have to see myself on the screen?" Struck by her wisdom, Vincent, too, stopped watching rushes; forever after, he would only sit through his own films under duress.

Moss Rose was the last film Vincent Price made under contract to Fox. By the late forties, the studio system had begun its eventual collapse. In 1938 the U.S. Congress had begun an investigation into the production, distribution, and exhibition monopolies held by the major studios, but the war had interrupted the inquiry. In the years after the war, Congress renewed its efforts to bring anti-trust suits against the studios, and in 1948 RKO announced that it would divest itself of its theater interests. Under increased pressure from Congress the other studios followed suit, gradually allowing their players' contracts to expire gracefully. Without the backing of a studio, Vincent was consigned to a string of mediocre roles in mediocre films but, as ever, for him the work was the thing, and he felt he had to take whatever was offered. Back at Universal, where he had begun his Hollywood career, he played another suave villain in *The Web*, a dull melodrama starring Edmond O'Brien, then went to RKO for a project that, on paper at least, looked somewhat more promising.

Directed by Anatol Litvak, *The Long Night* was a remake of Marcel Carné's 1939 French film, *Le Jour se Lève*. This version co-starred Henry Fonda and Broadway star Barbara Bel Geddes, making her screen debut. The plot had Fonda as an ex-soldier, falling in love with Bel Geddes and goaded into fatally shooting Price, a philandering nightclub magician with whom she is involved. In the event, the picture *Film Daily* called "an unsavory spectacle" was a box-office disaster, losing RKO a cool million dollars and bringing no credit to its cast.

In the fall of 1947, Vincent returned to Universal for *Up in Central Park*. The film starred the now twenty-six-year-old Deanna Durbin, making her penultimate screen appearance before retiring to France with her director husband Charles David. A pointless bowdlerization of Sigmund Romberg's Broadway musical, the movie was another disappointment for Vincent, wildly miscast in a role originally created by Noah Beery, that of the short-statured, corrupt nineteenth-century New York mayor Boss Tweed. He did his best, but few disagreed with *New York Times* critic Thomas Pryor that "the juicy role of Tweed is played by Vincent Price and a more inappropriate choice could hardly be imagined. This is not meant to reflect on Mr. Price's acting ability; it's merely a case of the actor not fitting the character." The ill-fated enterprise did, however, bring Vincent and Deanna Durbin the compensation of a firm friendship that lasted until his death over forty years later.

Now a fixture in the Hollywood he had set out to conquer five years earlier, Vincent had acquired a popular fan base, and an official Vincent Price fan club—the first of many—had been formed. His name regularly appeared in the movie magazines; he had charmed a number of gossip columnists, including the queenly Hedda Hopper, into a lasting friendship. One of his biggest admirers during this period was writer and syndicated columnist Inez Wallace, who described her May 1947 interview with the star thus: "It was so grand being with him again—I really have a crush on that St. Bernard, with that courtly manner and that doggone smile of his which is like the sun breaking through the clouds. Of all the actors I know, Vincent Price is the only one about whom one never hears an unkind word."

18————————————

THE YEARS FOLLOWING 1945 were a time of victory celebration and postwar tranquility for most of America. For Vincent Price, though, they would become among the most trying of his life. Although by the mid-forties his career had achieved a steady momentum and his name was becoming increasingly well-respected in the art world, his home life had fallen apart. In a 1946 column devoted to his personal life and acting career, Louella Parsons noted, "Two years ago Vincent and his actress wife, Edith Barrett, parted and it was expected they would get a divorce. He was in New York in a play, and she was here, and after a series of misunderstandings, there was a cessation of all pleasantries, which led to many gossip items that the Prices were washed up for good. 'Then,' said Vincent, 'I suddenly realized I couldn't get along without Edith. We had always been in love but the distance between Hollywood and New York is too great for any man and wife. So I'm saying to people who are happily married—'Don't ever stay apart. Don't ever give up the ship while there's a chance of saving it, and never, never let your wife live in one place while you are in another!' " He went on to tell Parsons that although he considered Edith a great actress, after their separation they had decided that she would give up her career, "so that we need never be separated again. Don't think I don't know what that means with her talent and her love of the theater. But we figure if we're to have any happiness it is better for her just to stay home and let me do the breadwinning. So far it's worked out beautifully."

Given Vincent's desire to have his public always think the best of him, his comments to Parsons about his marital problems must be taken with a grain of salt. Indeed, Vincent and Edith had separated in 1944; however, Vincent was not on the East Coast, but involved in his heavy shooting schedule in Hollywood. Meanwhile, following her success in *Ladies in Retirement*, Edith landed a few plum jobs, the best of which were a supporting part in Jacques Tourneur's 1943 horror classic *I Walked With a Zombie* and the role of Rochester's housekeeper, Mrs. Fairfax, in the Orson Welles-Joan Fontaine version of *Jane Eyre*. These small but significant parts gave the actress something to take pride in, but they were the best of a sorry bunch of films that also included two Andrews sisters musicals and a number of other B-pictures during the early 1940s. Thus, while her husband's career was steadily climbing, Edith found herself relegated to increasingly inferior roles in increasingly inferior films. That she was obliged to take minor character parts in *The Song of Bernadette* and *The Keys of the Kingdom*, in which her husband had major roles, could only have added to her frustration.

By 1944 Edith, who had lived the life of a Broadway star from a young age, realized that her movie career was anything but flourishing. An eccentric woman, she had used money to buffer her loneliness and to support her idiosyncratic habits. For example, for reasons unclear to anyone but herself, Edi had always refused to cross Fifth Avenue by foot. She would hail a cab to take her across the street. Money meant little to her. One day, en route to a social engagement, she found she had left home without her white gloves. She asked her cab driver to stop outside Bonwit Teller, handed him a hundred-dollar bill, and sent him in to get all the white gloves a hundred dollars could buy. He returned laden with gloves from which she picked a few pairs that suited her, then gave the rest to the driver to give to his wife. At the height of her fame, Edith had had a retinue of servants and retainers who helped her to live in the style to which she had so rapidly become accustomed.

After her marriage to Vincent, things were different. During their first few years together Vincent and Edith often struggled to make ends meet, and after Barrett was born Vincent carried the burden of providing for his wife and baby. He was always conscious of the pressure to live up to the standards to which he had been raised, and held his father up to himself as a constant example. Whenever he finished shooting a film, he dutifully headed down to the unemployment line to collect his first check, barely containing the panic that he might never work again. It was particularly difficult for him during Barrett's first year, when he was not working at all. It was during that year, as he was standing in the unemployment line, that he saw a limousine drive by, glanced at the woman inside—and saw it was his wife. When he got home, she told him that yes, she had received a sum of money from a relative, and had hired a car and driver and gone out shopping. Vincent would later admit that, for him, this had been the beginning of the end.

Certainly, the couple had widely differing views about money. Vincent lived with the inherited fear that, no matter how much money he made, one stroke of bad luck could cause him to lose it all. Although he liked to live well and could be extremely generous, he was always very aware of money, and fluctuated wildly between munificence and penury. Edi, however, was simply profligate.

But perhaps even more than these differences, Vincent's love for Edi began to erode when he realized that the theatrical legend he had married actually hated the theater. He claimed that this discovery changed everything for him. "I think she really got married to get out of the theater. Here I was goggle-eyed to be married to this actress, and it was a terrible blow to me. It didn't do our marriage any good, I'll tell you that."

In fact, the truth seems to have been a bit more complicated. As her hopes of a significant movie career faded, Edi began to talk about retiring in order to raise Barrett and to support Vincent's career. She took up painting in a back studio of their house in Benedict Canyon—and she took to drinking. Friends recall spending evenings at home with Vincent and rarely seeing Edi, who often only emerged to make herself another pitcher of martinis to take back to her room. Vincent's longtime friends Bill and Shirley Brice remembered, "She was quite reclusive. Edith could be in the house, but we wouldn't see her. She would occasionally come out of her room, but she was a bit adrift. She had an etherealness, a non–terra firma–ness. You just sensed that this was an extraordinarily sensitive actress, fragile, volatile. She also projected a sense that she needed help, that she needed people around her to help her. She didn't seem strong."

Edi's behavior grew increasingly odd. She claimed she had always hated the theater and wanted nothing more than to have a family and to paint, but her actions belied her assertions. Edith Barrett was a tremendous stage actress who, like so many other Broadway stars, found that the camera did not like her face. After her hugely successful Broadway career—twenty-five plays in as many years—the B-movies in Hollywood took it all out of her. She began to fall apart and Vincent couldn't handle it. He hated a show of weakness, either in himself or in those he loved, and he couldn't bring himself to support a woman who had given up everything to drink and paint in a back room while he went out and faced the world. What he did want was a family. He could be a good provider, as long as Edi held up her part of the bargain.

During this difficult period, Vincent finally confessed his difficulties to his father. He told him of his troubles with Edi, his worries about money, his loneliness in a marriage that wasn't working. Vincent Sr. responded with surprising candor: "I think I can appreciate your feelings because of my own—I'm lonely also. I have no one to go to with things that are troubling me—and oh how I long for someone, but have had to school myself to carry on without it. Mother would do anything for me—but she just doesn't understand and I haven't the courage to make her—it upsets her so. I don't blame you for drowning within yourself and I know how you suffer the torments of hell when you do, and this is hard for any one with Edith's temperament to understand. She has been so long by herself and loves you desperately and wants to possess you body and soul. That's perfectly natural, Bink—and I'm sure she'll learn to understand. Tears—oh I know what they are and how Edith's sink you into the very depths—but they're her safety valve. How often I wish I could have a good cry and get it over with—but I'm pent up within like you are and it's horrible." Nonetheless, he encouraged Vincent to "stick with it."

Vincent tried to follow his father's advice. In 1944, reunited after their separation, Vincent and Edi had found a new house—an unoccupied and slightly run-down, though atmospheric, adobe nestled in the trees of Benedict Canyon. Barrett Price remembered being taken to look at it. "It was a big thing. They were really excited about it; it was a wonderful place, sort of like this Valhalla where everyone was going to be together, with Edi painting in a little place up behind. She was an Impressionist of some sort. Christmas of '46, he gave her a car and it was all very, very jolly. It was our most intimate and happy time."

After the couple bought the Benedict Canyon house, things seemed to look up for a while. As Barrett recalled, "Parties were heaven. He was always cooking bouillabaisse or something. They were friends with Janet Gaynor and Adrian and Louis Hayward. Tallulah Bankhead was a wonderful blowsy broad. And, of course, George Macready and crusty-voiced Lew Ayres. Helen and Ed Carrere were their best, best, best friends. He was an art director at a big studio, Cuban, a beautiful man and Helen was a Swede and Bobby Lee was their son. He was a little bit older than me. Deanna Durbin and Joe Cotten. Broderick Crawford, Rachmaninov, and Huxley, and all that Pacific Palisades crowd. Thomas Mann. But I was too young to get it."

In 1943, Vincent and Edi had bought ten acres in Malibu. Located on the bluffs above Point Dume, their land boasted three hundred trees and a precious three hundred feet of oceanfront. Vincent outlined his fantasy to Inez Wallace: "That's the place I expect to be our permanent home when all this show business is over. Right after the war, when building is again permitted, I'm going to build a house for us. We have one baby, three years old, and would like about two more. I never want my wife to go back into show business though." In 1946, Vincent Price and Ed Carrere began to build a small house on the property. It seemed, for a time, as if Vincent and Edi might be able to make a home and have a happy family together. At least, they seemed to have found some kind of peace.

Then, in October, 1946, Marguerite Price died quite unexpectedly. Two years before, Vincent and Marguerite had celebrated their golden wedding anniversary by renewing their vows before their family. Although Vincent Sr. was increasingly crippled by arthritis, Marguerite maintained her vigor, despite being a heavy smoker. In April 1946, she and her husband came out to Hollywood to visit their son and his family. During their visit, Vincent gave his parents a tour behind the scenes at Fox, introduced them to his movie friends, and took them out to the most glamorous restaurants. A photograph shows Marguerite and her son at Sugie's Original Tropics restaurant, a Hawaiian-style restaurant; Marguerite, wearing a flowered, veiled hat and a black lamb coat smiles at the camera as Vincent, neatly dressed in a suit with a bow tie, smiles dotingly on her.

Marguerite's sudden death only six months after that visit devastated her husband, who wrote his youngest son that he could no longer imagine living in the house in which he and Marguerite had spent so many wonderful years. He intended to close the place and move to a sanitarium, where he could be treated for his increasingly painful arthritis. But Marguerite's death proved equally traumatic for her youngest son. Edi later told Barrett that after her mother-in-law died, her husband had fallen apart; he had begun to rethink his life and question everything. According to her, it was then that everything changed for Vincent.

Ever since he was a boy, Vincent had tried to please his mother, to meet her demands, even as he had often resented what he saw as her lack of attention. Thus, his perpetual conflict between the need for an audience and his deeper artistic aspirations were, in a sense, a playing out of the conflict in his relationship with Marguerite—the clash between her conventional values and his more individualistic beliefs. Her death brought a kind of release, but it was a release into an unknown and sometimes frightening world of other possibilities. He was now free to make decisions that would please him, without the restraint imposed by worrying about his mother's reaction. In short, he could be his own person, even if who that person was remained to be discovered.

In April 1947, Bink flew to St. Louis to help his father close up the house. His niece Sara Santschi recalled his visit. "Uncle Bink had just finished doing a film and he called and said he was coming out to see his father. His mother had just died and his father was alone in the big house. He flew out still wearing the suit and makeup from the set. That's the kind of thing he would do. He was a real bohemian. He just didn't care. He didn't have any agenda and he didn't follow any rules and he certainly didn't want anyone to lay any on him. He was very, very anti-agenda. I went to Mary Institute and it was the time of my junior prom. And I had a date with a guy. But Uncle Bink said, 'I'm going to take Sally to her dance.' So, my mother got me a forest-green dress and it was strapless with netting over taffeta or something. It was perfectly plain and very attractive. I went to my grandfather's house and Uncle Bink put me up on this stool and he said, 'Don't move a muscle until I tell you to.' And so I stood there and I thought I was going to faint. He had ordered from the florist a huge box of gardenias and camellias and daisies, all white. And he carefully pinned all of these over the whole dress, underneath the lace, and he designed this being and then got the big car that the chauffeur drove, the Packard, and drove me out to the country to Mary Institute. And when we walked in all my girlfriends just died because they didn't know that was going to happen. And I was shaking like a leaf and he was shaking like a leaf. He said, 'I feel like I have stage fright.'

And all my girlfriends fell madly in love with him and all the boys were furious because he was so handsome. And that was the turning point in my life. I knew that I couldn't stay in St. Louis. I had to go where he went. I knew I wasn't him, but I had to go out there, go out to California and find gold."

That trip marked Vincent's last visit to his childhood home. A few weeks later, Vincent Sr. came out to visit his youngest son. Although still grieving over Marguerite's death, he enjoyed spending time in Hollywood, where his son introduced him to many of his fellow actors and showed him around the Fox lot. A gossip columnist reported the visit and claimed that Vincent Price Sr. was his namesake son's number one fan. Price, the article notes, had seen his son in *Victoria Regina* twenty-eight times and had seen his new film, *Shock*, thirty times. The article also noted that Fox would be giving the actor two weeks off from the *Forever Amber* shoot to take a car trip through California and Arizona with his father. In fact, Vincent Sr. was looking for a new place to live. Bink had tried to persuade him to move to Hollywood, but after their two-week trip, the elder Price settled on Tucson, feeling that the warm, dry desert climate would be the best thing for his arthritis. He found a sanitarium and brought Matt Smith, who had worked for the Prices in St. Louis for years. Until Vincent Sr.'s death, father and son would spend much time together, the older man sustaining the younger during the disintegration of his marriage, the younger helping the older through his physical struggle.

Interestingly, although Marguerite and her son certainly shared a great many traits—a flair for drama, a love of social occasions, travel, collecting anything and everything, a sense of humor—it was Vincent Sr. whom my father quietly but most significantly resembled. Both men set extremely high standards for themselves in both their personal relationships and their professional dealings. These standards continually motivated them to excel in their daily lives, but also plagued them with continual doubts and fears. When he had retired early in 1945, Vincent Sr. had written his youngest son, "You know how you have felt when you were not busy—hopes seem to vanish and life gets pretty depressing—even with all the nice things my children and friends say about me, I have many regrets that I didn't do some things differently. But one thing I haven't done is to bring any disgrace to my family. One thing consoles—providing as I went along and not getting into debt was best."

Vincent Sr., a man described by all who knew him as a saint, had spent his life worrying about money. His son inherited his financial concerns, but took them one step further—he constantly feared that he was teetering on the brink of major financial hardship, even when this was patently not the case. This perpetual terror had the unfortunate consequence of making Vincent feel that he had to take whatever work he was offered, and it would lead him to compromise the artistic integrity he held so dear. Meanwhile, with the marriage to Edi in collapse, he feared he might never live up to his expectations of himself.

By the beginning of December 1947, relations between Vincent and Edi had so deteriorated that the couple once again separated. Barrett recalled, "My mother came into my bedroom and told me that they were going to get a divorce. I was seven and I thought the end of the world had come. She was in tears and he wasn't anywhere and we moved out of the house." Barrett and his mother left to stay with friends. As Vincent later wrote: "Christmas loomed a couple of days ahead, like the funeral of hope. By mutual agreement my wife and I had parted. She took our seven-year-old son and went to stay with friends, and Christmas walked out with my boy, leaving me unseasonably and unreasonably desolate. No . . . not unreasonably." It went from bad to worse. Vincent's favorite holiday was Christmas, which he admitted to seeing through the rose-colored glasses of his childhood. He loved everything about it and looked forward to it each year. But, as he wrote, that year he looked forward "to only one thing: having it over with. It seemed that the whole world was sinking around me and I was alone, a monument to loneliness beneath those canyon sycamores laden with mistletoe, with only misery tall enough to reach my height and kiss me." All he had were their two dogs—a gold and black brindled bitch whom Barrett had aptly named Golden Blackie and one of her puppies, whom Barrett had called Panda because he was a black and white furball. With only the dogs for company, Vincent nonetheless decorated the house in anticipation of his son's visit on Christmas Day.

By midday on Christmas Eve, Vincent had had a beer or two and felt "a little blurred," falling asleep on the floor. He woke to the sound of screeching brakes. He rushed out the door and met a woman running toward him, mumbling apologetically. Goldie lay on the neighbor's lawn with a broken leg. "Somewhere out of the leftover terror of being awakened by that screech—out of my beer-bruised brain—out of the burden of that new aloneness—came the longest continuous line of curse words I've ever mustered up in my life. This careless carful of people had hurt my dog and I damned them with every word of hate I'd ever heard." He called the vet who arrived, gave Goldie a shot and splinted her leg before taking her to the hospital for a week or two with the assurance that she would be fine. After calling the friends with whom Edi was staying and asking them to tell her about Goldie, Vincent downed a whiskey, which had the curious effect of sobering him up completely. He realized that it was time to feed Panda, but the puppy didn't come when he called and he went looking for him. "Up on the back terrace, sticking out from under a pitisporum bush, bent with its Christmas splendor of red berries, I spied his large black plume of a tail. I snuck up on it and gave it a gentle yank. No wag. I lifted a berry branch and there was the rest of him, quiet as he'd never been . . . dead. He'd been hit and had taken off on the impulse that he was still alive, only to die a hundred yards away . . . I buried him near the bush, and then I sat down on the ground and cried—for about an hour. My God, how it hurts for a man to cry! Not from masculinity abused or from vanity or fear that someone will see you. It just plain hurts. This time it hurt so much that I didn't even think of doing what I always had done the few times I'd cried before: look at myself in a mirror. This was a sadness I didn't want to see and I certainly didn't want to remember."

Even as he couldn't wait for the few precious hours he would get to spend with his little boy, Vincent dreaded Barrett's arrival on Christmas, knowing that he would have to tell him that Panda was dead. "This boy was my dream come true. Blond, loving, sensitive, and completely boy. My profession had kept me away from him enough that my responsibility to him weighed pretty heavily. But now I would have to live without him, with only the usual 'normal visiting rights,' every-other-weekends in which to try to be a father; odd holidays to make desperate passes at his affection." This Christmas was the first of these holidays, and Vincent was desperate to connect with his son knowing that Barrett was confused about everything that had so recently happened. In the event, the emotion of seeing one another became the day; Barrett went home having forgotten to ask about the dogs and Vincent having subconsciously forgotten to tell him.

The next day, Vincent had a mission "to get back on the horse of happiness, which had so violently thrown me two days before. I wanted another dog." With Goldie going to live with Barrett and Edi, "I felt deeply that if my house were to keep any identity as a home, even a part-time home, for my son, a dog-tag would give me at least some license to his affections . . . Anyway, I wanted a dog for my own needs as well as his and ours." In a pet store on Pico Boulevard, he found his dog, "looking like a miniature Trafalgar Square lion. I knew instantly that this was my dog and that his name was Joe . . . Dog of dogs. Short-legged, slightly bowed in the front and splay-foot behind, curl-tailed, with ears like a flying fox and a face that, if there are dog angels (and I'm sure there are), was an angel dog's face." And so Vincent took Joe home to start their new life together.

On New Year's Eve, Deanna Durbin invited Vincent Price to a party at her house. At Deanna's suggestion he took the costume designer from *Up in Central Park*, Mary Grant, as his date. Although there was generally not much fraternization between cast and staff in Hollywood, Vincent later recalled that he had noticed Mary Grant immediately because "she actually designed clothes that fit comfortably and allowed action. She was the first designer I'd met who thought that actors, like movies, should move." As for Mary, she said, "I never cared much for actors, and I remember our meeting mainly because Vincent seemed less troublesome than most men about the business of fitting. Usually actors are either too nonchalant or too fussy. He was the first one I had worked with who hit the happy medium."

After their initial meeting on the set, Vincent had encountered the designer at a dinner party at the Bel Air home of art collectors Leslie and Ruth Maitland. A woman of great taste and social skills, Mrs. Maitland had met Vincent through mutual art-collector acquaintances, and the two had become good friends. She had invited Mary Grant to her home at the request of her son's fiancée, Ruth Vollmer, who was Mary's best friend in New York. Sensitive to the fact that the young designer had just come to Hollywood from New York and wouldn't know many people, she seated Mary next to Vincent. After they had chatted for a few minutes, he earnestly told her that he had never really met anyone from Brooklyn before. She burst out laughing and then told him that she was really British, but that she had lost her accent after a few months in New York in an effort to better fit into her surroundings. Having spent much of her early apprenticeship in the garment district, she had simply mimicked what she heard around her and now spoke with a Brooklyn accent. (A few years of living in California eventually erased all but the slightest traces.)

A slim, pretty, blond, free-spirited, and highly creative woman with a great sense of style, Mary Grant had come to New York in the late 1930s to work as an apprentice to a fashion designer and, in less than a decade, had carved out a successful career for herself as a Broadway costume designer. The youngest of three children, she was born in South Wales to a Scots father and an English mother. Her father, Captain Reginald Grant, served in the Scots National Guard during World War I, surviving the terrible battle at Gallipoli. After the war, the family moved to Shanghai when Captain Grant was offered a job running the famous Cultee Dairy for the company that brought pasteurization to China. Mary was five. After six years in Asia, the family left for Victoria, British Columbia, where Captain Grant was able to renew the career in landscape design for which he had been trained at the University of Edinburgh.

As a teenager in provincial Victoria, Mary aspired to go to the United States and become a dancer, but her family couldn't afford lessons, and so she sewed clothes and worked odd jobs, saving her money in the hope that she might someday study dance in the well-respected department at the University of Washington in Seattle. The opportunity came when her older brother, John, who had been living in Seattle for a number of years, was able to send for her. After a year of training, Mary and a number of her classmates earned scholarships to spend the summer studying with Martha Graham protégée Dorothy Herman at Mills College in San Francisco. After a week of classes, she realized that she had begun training too late ever to reach the level she had hoped to attain. Devastated, she called her brother, who suggested that she take advantage of her time in San Francisco to join a design class being taught there by Rudolf Schaeffer, an eminent color theorist. There, Mary found that she had a great aptitude for design and, hearing of an apprenticeship in New York, decided to go there at the end of the summer with some of her dancer friends who were driving across country. Meanwhile, with her friend and classmate Merce Cunningham, she took the opportunity to visit Los Angeles.

Staying in a rooming house in Silver Lake, the pair had enough money for a hot dog and a shake a day, and trolley fare to the beach in Santa Monica, where they headed on their first day. On their way back they passed the Ambassador Hotel and because they had no money and were dressed for the beach, they decided to climb over the back wall into the pool area so they could see the movie stars. They were promptly thrown out. Down to their last dollar, they decided to enter the dance contest at the Hollywood Palladium where big-band leader Gene Krupa and his band were performing. Merce Cunningham and Mary Grant beat out all their competitors and won the first prize cup. They devoutly wished the prize had been food.

With the little money she had left, Mary left with her fellow students to drive cross-country in a Model T. By the time they reached Oklahoma City, however, she was completely broke and her friends abandoned her there. She wired her brother for money and eventually arrived in Brooklyn, where she stayed with some maiden cousins and took an apprenticeship with clothing designer Elizabeth Hayes, for whom she worked for six months learning the garment business. For her birthday that year, one of her Seattle friends took her to see *One for the Money* on Broadway. Mary was so impressed with the look of the show that she wrote a fan letter to its designer, Raoul Pene DuBois, in which she noted that if he ever needed an assistant she would be honored to work for him. Months later, literally down to her last rent check, she received a call from DuBois, offering her a job at $25 a week. She took it. DuBois would later tell her that he had received hundreds of letters from Yale School of Drama graduates and the like, but that he had decided to hire her because she hadn't come on strong. He soon knew that he had made the right choice. Mary proved to have an accurate eye for color, and was also absolutely reliable. As for her, she knew that she had finally found her niche.

Mary quickly became a favorite of many New York directors, including John Murray Anderson and Billy Rose, and, as well as working for DuBois, she began working for Miles White, Broadway's other top designer. Both men soon realized that they could leave her in charge of whole areas of design; for *Oklahoma!*, Mary Grant designed and executed all of the men's costumes, while White did the women's. In just a few years she had became known in the theater as a talented and dependable costumer. She began applying for her own shows, and soon got her first Broadway assignment, Cole Porter's *Mexican Hayride*, for which she received extraordinary notices: One critic said he left "whistling the costumes."

Mary Grant went on to work on a number of major stage musicals during the forties; but, by 1947, when Hollywood beckoned, she was ready to switch to the movies. After almost ten years in New York, she was eager to go out to the Coast. As an inveterate sunbather she relished the idea of the glorious Southern California weather; more important, as a lifelong learner, she saw the move as an opportunity to apply all that she knew about design to a completely new medium. In the event, her transformation from diehard New Yorker to "native" Angeleno was indeed swift.

Despite a pleasant New Year's Eve with Mary Grant at the Durbin party, the beginning of 1948 loomed fearfully and emptily ahead for Vincent. Alone in the Benedict Canyon adobe, with only his houseman, Will Lawson, for company, Vincent was virtually starting his life over again. But slowly, with the raising of Joe, visits with Barrett, and a new movie underway, the year lurched into gear. The advantage of being a weekend father, of course, is that every visit seems like a special treat, at least to the child. On January 3, Vincent brought home four Westerns to show his son. Because of the polio scare, Edith was concerned about letting her son go out in public places. Vincent solved that by buying a projector and bringing home films from the studio. This gradually became one of father and son's favorite pastimes. He even showed Barrett one of his own pictures— *Return of the Invisible Man*—a curious choice since he is invisible throughout most of the film. When Barrett asked his father how he disappeared, Vincent told his son that every morning on the set the director made him drink a special potion that made him invisible.

Meanwhile, fittings were underway for Vincent's first role of the year, Cardinal Richelieu in MGM's new production of *The Three Musketeers*. It starred an athletic Gene Kelly as D'Artagnan and the beautiful Lana Turner as Milady, Countess de Winter. Directed by George Sidney, the new Technicolor production also featured June Allyson as Kelly's love interest and a young Angela Lansbury as Queen Anne. The studio chose to play down the Cardinal's religious affiliations by dressing Vincent in a decidedly unclerical manner; his Richelieu became a dashingly dastardly villain in scarlet doublet and hose in this camped-up screen adaptation of the Dumas classic. As Angela Lansbury remembered, "We laughed a lot. I think Vincent and I took it all with a big grain of salt. This was MGM's idea of the court of Louis; we just did our best to make it as palatable as possible." The reviews were merely passable, but Vincent received another Box Office Blue Ribbon Award for his work on the film. In April, he made *Rogue's Regiment* for Universal, another atmospheric spy thriller, in which he played a German gunrunner disguised as a white-suited Dutch antiques dealer.

Vincent also had his radio work—a thirteen-week stint that winter playing the title role in the immensely popular series, *The Saint*. A staple of popular fiction since the late twenties, the Saint had been impersonated by George Sanders in a series of movies during the thirties and forties, and a number of actors on the radio had followed suit. Although Leslie Charteris, the creator of *The Saint*, always claimed Brian Aherne was his personal radio favorite, Vincent was undoubtedly the most famous radio Saint. He lent his cultured voice to the role for four years; his first episode aired in July 1947 on CBS, who carried the series through June of the following year, then continued the role on the Mutual Broadcasting System and later on NBC.

Each episode of *The Saint* was introduced by the sound of footsteps followed by the Saint's signature whistle. Each week the masterful Simon Templar, a modern-day Robin Hood whom Vincent described as the suavest character he had ever played, would engage in a new adventure, "The Doll with a Broken Head," for instance, or "The Case of the

Confused Cadillacs." At the end of each episode, the actor addressed his radio audience as himself on behalf of a variety of causes from the Red Cross and voting to CARE and civil rights. At the end of "The Color-Blind Killer Case" in September 1949, he said, "Ladies and gentlemen, in a prejudice-filled America, no one would be secure—in his job, his business, his church, or his home. Yet racial and religious antagonisms are exploited daily by quacks and adventurers, whose followers make up the lunatic fringe of American life. Refuse to listen to or spread rumors against any race or religion. Help to stamp out prejudice in our country. Let's judge our neighbors by the character of their lives alone, and not on the basis of their religion or origin." Now one of the most outspokenly liberal actors, Vincent had clearly come a long way from the conservatism and bias of his upbringing.

Early in 1948, two significant meetings took place that would have tremendous impact on Vincent's life. On January 6, he invited an artist friend and his wife to dinner. Vincent had "discovered" Howard Warshaw when he was a young animator working at Disney. In *I Like What I Know*, he described their first encounter. "A hairy, black, Teddy-bear of a man came into the gallery. He had the charm of a great puppy and an undiscovered intensity which gave great promise. We looked at his portfolio of drawings and made a date to see the rest of his work at his home, where we bought as many as we could for our stock, and I bought one for myself. Howard took the money and went to New York to live, and paint us a show. A year later he and the rest of his first show returned to California."

Howard and his wife, Helen, were looking for a place to live and Vincent thought of offering them the apartment over his garage. After talking it over at dinner that night, they accepted and moved in. Howard set up a studio at the back of the house where Edith had once had hers. Their friendship would help to buffer Vincent's loneliness following his separation from his wife, while their daily presence helped the actor increasingly to balance his life in the movies with his life in the visual arts.

Vincent later spoke of Warshaw as "one of my proudest discoveries. Well, I didn't discover him, because nobody discovered him—he was already quite an extraordinary talent, but in a different way. But I did lead him into things that were much more interesting than what he was doing as an apprentice cartoonist at Disney. He was fascinated with surrealism and he studied Dali and Man Ray and people like that. I told him to look for surrealist literature to illustrate. And I commissioned him to do a series on the *Song of Solomon*. It was a series of gouaches, brilliantly executed."

Despite Howard's obvious talent as an artist, he was completely uncoordinated and clumsy—a circumstance that added a measure of humor to the new living arrangements at 1815 Benedict Canyon. Vincent recalled, "Whatever he touched he would break. One time I brought a very delicate little figure back from Mexico—two thousand years old. And I showed it to Howard, who thought it was beautiful. And he asked to hold it. And I said, 'Oh, Howard, you know what will happen. I can't.' But he begged me and so I let him. And he held it in his great big hands and one of the legs just fell right off. It was so sad because he loved beautiful things. One time, I rented a backhoe to do some work on the front of the house. I was out front with the thing and Howard came out to watch. And he thought it looked like such fun so he asked me if he could drive it. I thought, 'Oh my God.' But for some reason I got out and showed him how everything worked. But I told him not, under any circumstances, to lift the backhoe. So, of course, the moment he got in the thing, the hoe went straight up in the air, twirled around, got caught in the wires and took out all the electricity in the whole canyon!"

A week after his dinner with Howard and Helen, Vincent drove halfway across the city to meet with a Miss Judith Miller who taught art at East Los Angeles Junior College, which Vincent described as being "two Quonset huts on a mud flat." At this two-year college in a largely Hispanic area of the city across the river from downtown Los Angeles, Judith Miller had begun an art department which impressed Vincent with its ambition. He gave a brief talk to her students and began a correspondence with her. He would return to give a lecture that would open the door to one of the most rewarding aspects of his life.

That January 1948, Vincent also flew to Tucson to visit his father at the sanitorium. Vincent Sr. had grown increasingly feeble and their visits together were limited by his lack of energy. This left time for one of Vincent's favorite pursuits—art shopping. Upon spying a beautiful black and white Anasazi pot in a store, he went in to price it. When the store owner said five dollars, Vincent took it. Then the man asked, "You like this crap, do you?" When Vincent replied in the affirmative, the owner took him down to the basement, where there were thousands of similar pots and bowls. Vincent recalled, "He was, I think, very little better than a grave robber, or somebody with him had been a grave robber, because he also opened up baskets and suitcases full of pawn jewelry. And I bought two hundred pots from him, really just to get even with Ralph Altman. I never had more fun in my life."

A week later, when the parcels arrived from Tucson, Vincent invited Ralph and Pat Altman to dinner and they spent the evening unpacking the pots. Ralph Altman had come to Los Angeles by way of Germany, where his father had been the director of the Hanoverian State Theater. He had been educated to be a medical doctor, but that was curtailed by the Jewish pogroms. Ralph and his sister got out of Nazi Germany and he married his second cousin, Pat, who lived in Oregon. The couple came to Los Angeles to open a gallery and Vincent first met them there during World War II. "I was driving down La Cienega Boulevard one day and I saw an African figure in a gallery window and I nearly fainted because I hadn't seen anything like that on La Cienega. I jammed on the brakes and backed up and parked and went in and introduced myself." Throughout their friendship, Vincent and Ralph had a spirited, good-natured competition to see who could discover the most exciting things for the least amount of money. Vincent had "a kind of rivalry with him, in that I had a little more money than he had, so I kind of threw my weight around." When Ralph had sold Vincent an eleventh-century black and white Anasazi cup from Mesa Verde, Vincent responded with the Tucson cache. He later recalled, "When I unloaded them one by one in front of Ralph, I thought he was going to die." Not long after Vincent's serendipitous find, Ralph made his own discovery of Native American artifacts in Ojai where he and Vincent and Pat spent a lovely Sunday examining prehistoric pottery. But, as Vincent duly noted, "He had an outlet in his store. I didn't, so I got stuck with two hundred pots which I then began to give to museums."

It was an exciting time in Southern California for an art collector; not very many people were tuned in to the visual arts so it was an open field for those who were. Pat Altman remembered, "We found things with practically no effort. Had there been fewer pieces stashed hither and yon we probably would have made more of an effort, but we didn't because things came to us. There weren't very many places to sell things in those days. No one wanted it." Indeed, Ralph taught his friend a great deal about African, Oceanic, Pre-Columbian, and Native American art and artifacts. Vincent remembered, "It was great fun with Ralph. I bought some of the most interesting things and learned a tremendous amount from him because he was a great scholar. And when he didn't know about it, he learned. I remember finding in another store little Indian drawings that were Sioux courtship drawings. And I told Ralph that there was a great cache of them somewhere and then he walked around every junkshop looking for them."

After his separation from Edi, friends such as Howard and Helen Warshaw and Ralph and Pat Altman became increasingly important to Vincent. For most of his twenties he had been too unsettled, too busy, and too focused on his career to make very many long-lasting friendships. When his *Angel Street* co-star, Judith Evelyn, had written to him in 1943, she had upbraided him regarding his ability to make and to keep friends: "I hope you will now spend a little time making friends instead of another thousand acquaintances, for if you don't, my dear, you are due to reap a fallow crop in later years. For you cannot make friends without giving true friendship and it is only by giving of yourself honestly and faithfully that you will add depth to your character. Your multitudinous acquaintances can only be superficial and that, in time, stamps itself upon your individual character. You have such generosity, Vincent, in your nature, that it seems a dread shame to expend the whole of it in showy incidentals. Perhaps the proximity of Edith and Barrett will prove needed stabilizers for you and you will no longer be aggravated by conflicting obsessions which cause you to be uncannily cruel without reason to others and thus only hurt yourself." Ironically, it was the absence of Edith and Barrett that at last motivated Vincent to settle down, not in the fantasy of married life, but in meaningful friendships that would last a lifetime. Vincent had always had a vast capacity for closeness and generosity. Now, alone at thirty-six years old, he had to face himself and learn to give and to take real friendship.

Fortunately, he began meeting people who not only moved through the world with a curiosity equal to his, but who also shared his sense of fun and adventure. Although a few of these people had ties to the movie industry, most of his closest friends were connected to the art world—artists, collectors, dealers, and scholars. Vincent sought the company of Eddie and Margo Albert, who had moved out to Los Angeles, along with Mildred and Sam Jaffe, Barbara and James Poe, and Shirley and Bill Brice.

Sam Jaffe, one of the biggest agents in Hollywood, represented the likes of Humphrey Bogart and Barbara Stanwyck, and had been Vincent's agent for a time. He was married to a beautiful and intelligent woman, Mildred Gersh, and the couple had a marvelous art collection, consisting of extraordinary paintings by most of the great late nineteenth- and early twentieth-century European and American artists, as well as tribal art from Africa, Oceania, and the Americas. Many of Vincent's closest friends were women, with whom he felt able to talk more openly; over the almost forty years of their friendship, Mildred was often the person to whom Vincent turned in times of need.

The same held true of Barbara Poe. Married to screenwriter James Poe, Barbara was the daughter of New York art collectors and dealers Bernard and Becky Reis. She had grown up in a home filled with modern art and had met many of the leading contemporary European and American painters. She had come to Hollywood with her husband and continued to work as an artist. It was Vincent who helped her to get her first show. Barbara had invited him to her first dinner party in L.A., with German director Fritz Lang and the popular Japanese-American dancer Sono Sato, among others. Barbara recalled, "I was getting ready for dinner and Sono said that Gene Kelly and his wife would love us to come over after dinner. Everyone thought that was a good idea except Vincent said nothing, and I said nothing, because I was on the verge of tears thinking I had done all this work and suddenly everyone's going to go over to someone else's house, especially a house where I didn't feel comfortable because they never said hello to you. It was always an open house, terribly progressive, but there were no introductions which was terribly hard for me. And Vincent said, 'I'm not going.' And I said, 'Well, I'm not going either.' And then I asked him why he wasn't going. And he said, 'Because I can't bear to walk into a room where no one introduces you.' And from that moment on, I knew we were kindred spirits."

Vincent felt the same. As with Mildred Jaffe, he felt he could really talk to Barbara. He believed, "You must be around curious people to be curious because they generate curiosity. And most of my friends really are curious people. Barbara is an infinitely curious person and she always has been. She's the kind of woman who doesn't miss a thing. She never misses an opportunity to whet her curiosity, and curiosity needs whetting all the time."

William and Shirley Brice were teenagers when they first met Vincent, through Bill's mother, the famed comedienne Fanny Brice. Bill and Shirley later said of their friendship with my father, "When we talk about people who make a significant contribution to us in our lives, and there is that sense that when you know someone in your formative years and they continue to make a contribution, they're a kind of light in your life. Vincent was certainly that for us." As for Vincent, he found it exciting to become friends with what he saw as the next generation of artists and art lovers. He loved Bill and Shirley and valued their friendship separately and together. In Shirley he found another close female friend, and in Bill he saw someone who had the same appetite for learning. In *I Like What I Know*, he wrote of his friend's work, "He will not, I think, grow stale in sight, to see a single world when all the world is his to look at and, through him, for everyone to look at, too—and love."

Along with his old friends the Carreres, it was the Altmans, Warshaws, Brices, and Poes who formed the nucleus of Vincent's new family. He spent most of his free time with one or another combination of the group at picnics on the beach or looking at art or finding new treasures.

On June 15, 1948, Vincent placed a call to Tucson, and learned that his father's condition had deteriorated. He caught a plane the next day, and stayed with his father until he passed away two days later. Vincent Sr. had been so proud of his namesake son, and during the hardships of his last years had loved being close enough to Los Angeles to see more of him.

After one of their last meetings, Vincent Sr. wrote that he and Matt had "watched your plane until it was out of sight. Your visit put me on tops with hope and pride. I am so proud of you and your kindness to all here has greatly raised my stock in trade. You surely made a hit. I did love your visit every minute and I do love you so. Will count the days til you can come again or I can come to you." As Vincent somberly took care of all the arrangements and put his father's body on the train to St. Louis, he felt as though his whole life as he had known it was over. His parents were both gone and his divorce from Edith was imminent. It was time to start over.

19

CONSTRAINED BY HIS filming schedule, Vincent Price was not able to attend his father's funeral, which was held in St. Louis. But work proved a real antidote to the sorrow he felt over his father's death. In *The Bribe*, billed fourth below Robert Taylor, Ava Gardner, and Charles Laughton, he played a racketeer of war surplus goods in the Caribbean. In an effort to make him seem older than Taylor, the studio greyed Vincent's temples and he looked heavier than usual. He relished the chance to work with the ravishing Ava Gardner, whom he later described as the only leading lady who "ever seemed to me to live up to her reputation as a sex object." He chuckled, "My God, she was sexy, let me tell ya."

As soon as *The Bribe* wrapped, Vincent and Barrett flew to San Francisco where they boarded the S.S. *Lurline* bound for Honolulu. Edith had permitted Vincent three weeks of vacation with their son and he was determined to make the most of it. They stayed on Waikiki, where they swam and fished. Through a college friend, father and son were introduced to legendary surfer, Olympic gold medalist swimmer, and mayor of Honolulu Duke Kahanamoku, and his wife, Nadine, and they were also taken on a flight in a bomber over Pearl Harbor. They returned home on Barrett's eighth birthday.

After the Little Gallery closed in 1944, Vincent had become involved in another even more exciting project. Walter Arensberg was a famous, though notoriously eccentric, man who had begun a great modern art collection at the Armory Show of 1913. By the forties, he was looking for an institution in which to house his now priceless mostly Dadaist paintings. Having met Vincent Price at the Little Gallery, Arensberg was impressed with the actor's knowledge and enthusiasm. He offered him a challenge: If Vincent could organize a modern museum in Los Angeles, Arensburg would loan his collection, perhaps even donate it permanently. Feeling that this was an incredible opportunity for the city, Vincent threw himself into the project.

To head the board of trustees Vincent suggested Kenneth MacGowan, "one of the nicest men in the world," who would later start the UCLA film school. MacGowan and Price, who was named vice president, assembled a remarkable team for the board— Arensberg, of course, who was joined by Henry Dreyfuss, Leland Hayward, Aldous Huxley, Wright Luddington, Clifford Odets, and Edward G. Robinson. In addition to these famous names, there were a number of women who, it is fair to say, became the heart and soul of the Modern Institute of Art. Among them were Caroline Adler, Shirley

Brice, Mildred Jaffe, Ruth Maitland, and Barbara Poe. The board elected a young and talented art historian named Kenneth Ross as their director.

They began with high hopes and a great spirit of adventure. Having found a loft in Beverly Hills, they proceeded to turn it into a museum. At one particularly memorable board meeting, the group settled down to decide on the color scheme. Vincent recalled, "Fanny Brice, who moonlighted from Baby Snooks as an interior designer for her friends," had come to the meeting "in an impeccably tailored warm beige suit and we all decided it was just the right color. Off came the skirt and Fanny left the meeting wrapped in a fur coat but skirtless, her skirt hung on a scaffold for the painter to match."

For their inaugural exhibition, the Board was able to solicit loans and donations from a number of extraordinary collectors including the Crocker family of San Francisco, George Cukor, the Ira Gershwins, the Averell Harrimans of New York, the Sam Jaffes, Knoedler and Co. of New York, the Charles Laughtons, Wright Luddington, the Leslie Maitlands, Price himself, and Edward G. Robinson, then the premier collector among film actors. This first show, curated by Kenneth Ross, was called "Modern Artists in Transition" and featured the work of many of the best artists of the twentieth century. Aldous Huxley wrote the preface for the catalogue, capturing the high hopes of the board for this new and crucial artistic venture.

The Modern Institute of Art opened in Beverly Hills in 1948. During the two years of its existence, in reciprocal cooperation with the Museum of Modern Art in New York, the Institute put on ten high-powered, extremely impressive shows, including the Arensburg collection, a Paul Klee retrospective, and French Impressionism from California collections. They saw themselves as a wider cultural center and sponsored readings and concerts by many emigrés, among them Thomas Mann, Stravinsky, Schoenberg, and Rachmaninov, as well as offering classes taught by Edward G. Robinson, Clifford Odets, and others.

Although supported by many of the Southern California society women and by all the universities, the Modern Institute was ultimately unable to find sufficient financial backers to keep it afloat—which infuriated Vincent. He found the narrow-minded, provincial attitudes of Los Angeles big business, including the film industry, unbearable. Without the money to back them up, the Institute was forced to close, despite a last-minute student campaign that raised almost half the amount needed. Vincent later wrote, "In two years we built a membership of five thousand, and an annual attendance of forty thousand, but by the end of the second year we were doomed to close. The public, especially the students, could not do without us. There were torchlight parades to protest its closing. Ten thousand students put their signatures on a petition which was sent along to all the big business firms and the heads of motion picture studios; most of the original founders were bled time and time again for additional contributions, but the good, rich people of Los Angeles wouldn't come through, so we closed."

Shirley Brice recalled that one of the events which precipitated the closure was Arensburg's decision to give his collection elsewhere, noting, "We all felt tremendously hurt." And Barbara Poe remembered, "We were even given a piece of park land. The city of Beverly Hills offered us that little strip on Santa Monica Boulevard where they sometimes show sculpture. But Walter Arensberg didn't fork over his collection. We would also have gotten the Gelke Scheier collection, which is now at the Norton Simon Museum." Bill Brice said, "I think the Modern Institute was too sophisticated for most people here in town. They didn't even go to New York to buy paintings. They just weren't involved with art. Although the membership was enormous, it was student membership mostly. And the shows, my God, they were terrific shows, but they just didn't attract the people who could have supported a museum."

The closure of the Modern Institute of Art was one of Vincent Price's greatest disappointments, but it galvanized him into action. He had found a cause in which he believed profoundly and for which he was determined to fight. It became a personal crusade for him to turn Los Angeles into an important center for the visual arts. What stood in his way and particularly enraged him was what he saw as the willful ignorance of the moneyed men who ran Hollywood. In an interview given at the time, he said, "You can sell 'em sin and you can sell 'em sex but when you try to peddle 'culture' you run smack into a solid wall of stupid ignorance. I probably shouldn't say this, but I'm going to. I get so blankety-blank mad. They scream to high heaven about the reputation Hollywood's getting from people like Robert Mitchum, but when you try to get 'em to support something cultural they shrug their $5,000-a-week shoulders and brush you off."

Over the next ten years, Vincent's crusade led him to sit on (and eventually chair) the UCLA Arts Council, which became the most powerful force in the California visual arts for over a decade. He also came to serve on the board of trustees of the Los Angeles County Art Museum, involved in the construction of their new building and the expansion of their collection. But, perhaps most important, he began to go out and see the work of local students and painters, encouraging them in their work and becoming in the process one of the greatest champions of the visual arts in California. This, in turn, gave his life the coherence and meaning for which he had long searched.

Vincent Price and Mary Grant had continued to see one another sporadically through the beginning of 1948, getting together with Deanna Durbin or the Maitlands. But both also dated other people. Naturally, after Vincent's separation from Edith, the press eagerly probed the dating activities of the newly eligible actor. Because Vincent and Deanna Durbin saw each other often, gossip columnists made much of their friendship but, as Miss Durbin said, "There was nothing romantic between us, although I certainly found him attractive." Indeed, at thirty-seven, Vincent had matured into his dark, handsome looks. In May of 1948, Walter Winchell wrote, "Reports that Vincent Price of H'wood is mad about Deanna Durbin are debunked by his steadying with a lady medica." Dorothy Kilgallen also reported, "Vincent Price, whose romance with Deanna Durbin hit an iceberg, is getting his pulse back to abnormal with Dr. Lorraine Kramer, a Coast physician. They met over a case of Virus X. (He had it, she cured it!)"

For a brief moment, Vincent had harbored the fantasy that he might finally get together with Barbara O'Neil. They had remained friends throughout his marriage to Edi and, after the split, had begun to spend more time together, perhaps even briefly reigniting their love affair. Vincent had continued to idealize Barbara as the great love of his life, but although she was devoted to him, she never indicated for a moment that she wanted to be anything more than a friend and, perhaps, a sometime lover. Indeed, soon after they reconnected, she left Hollywood for the East Coast, and Vincent once again found himself in the position of pouring his heart out to her by phone and letter. In the late spring, he wrote, "I can't begin to tell you how really miserable I am. I feel my whole mixed up life has been a failure as far as making anyone happy. I think I have rejected love in a foolish belief that it would possess me and I would not be able to have wings. Then on looking into my heart, I find I really have loved only one person—you! Loved, that is, the way I think love should be—free . . . without restrictions. I believe if we ever get together I would devote my whole life to you—probably would swamp you with this fantastic complex personality of mine—and you would run screaming. How would you like a devotee? Next time I love it's for keeps—everything."

But by the fall of 1948, Vincent's main date—if indeed there were ever any serious others—was Mary Grant, who had stayed on in Los Angeles having decided to leave costume design for a field in which she would have more autonomy. She hoped to start her own fashion design business in L.A. During the summer, Vincent had taken to dropping by Mary's house on Canon Drive in Beverly Hills with increasing frequency. Then, with her finances dwindling, the free-spirited blonde moved to a small bungalow in Brentwood in the same complex as two of Vincent's good friends, art dealer Frank Perls and his wife Ann. It was there that Vincent and Mary's relationship began to get more serious. Bill Brice recalled, "That was the beginning of when we would see Mary and Vincent. I remember very, very well because she wore a white cotton shirt sort of open at the bottom and tied at her waist and she wore khaki shorts. She had a great sort of casualness about her."

Barbara Poe recalled, "I remember when I first met Mary, he was very secretive about her. He would whisk her in and out of the Modern Institute. She was very glamorous. Mysterious glamorous. There was an aura of mystery about her." This mystery stemmed from Vincent's caution about both Edith's and Barrett's reactions. He needn't have worried about Barrett. In November 1948, he arranged a fishing trip for the three of them along with the Altmans, the Warshaws, and the Carreres and their son, Bobby Lee. Happily, when Vincent introduced Barrett to Mary for the first time, they immediately took to one another.

Although Mary Grant had always professed a dislike for actors, she was impressed by Vincent's generosity and intelligence, not to mention his good looks. For his part, as the year wore on and they began to date more seriously, he was increasingly struck by Mary's inventiveness, her originality, and a sense of adventure that equaled his own. But perhaps even more than her innate qualities, he valued what she saw and brought out in him. With Edith, Vincent had come to feel deceived and misunderstood, and he desperately wanted to be with someone who could be both a lover and a partner. In Mary, it seemed, he had found both.

The first order of business for 1949, however, was to resolve matters with Edith. Both Edith and Vincent wanted custody of Barrett, but Vincent was concerned about Edith's capacity to raise a son and they engaged in a vicious battle over him. Barrett remembered that their divorce proceedings were continually chronicled by gossip columnists Hedda Hopper and Louella Parsons: "There were court fights that went on into my eighth year. He's fighting for custody, she's accusing him of cruelty in court and in the papers. He gives her a house, a car, and what he thought was a lot of money. There're thousands of visits, it seems to me, with psychologists. In the meantime, she's having serious alcohol problems and nobody knows this except me and her doctor. And I couldn't tell anyone because he enlisted me in his war and she enlisted me in her war. I don't think he really wanted custody of me. I was a big load. I was crying and screaming and homesick and miserable. He didn't know what the hell to do with me. I was really upset and probably no fun." Barrett was forced to go to a court-appointed psychiatrist to determine which parent would be more fit. As for his parents, they spent an unbecoming amount of time slinging mud at each other. It is difficult to imagine Vincent Price engaged in a venomous battle, since he was a man who hated confrontation and avoided it at any cost. Nonetheless, the arguments raged back and forth for years. In the middle was Barrett, torn between protecting his increasingly fragile mother and wanting to be with his adored father. Through the stress of the separation and of living with Edith, Barrett developed a stutter. As the son of an actor, particularly one who was famous for his speaking voice, he felt a horrible failure—a feeling that was only exacerbated as his father blamed Edi for the changes he saw in his son.

The previous summer, Edith had changed lawyers. She had already postponed the divorce hearing three times, constantly changing her demands regarding both the financial settlement and arrangements affecting their son. Vincent wrote Barbara O'Neil, "I want to be someone of whom Barrett can be proud, and yet almost everything I do would seem to be done in a conscious effort to destroy myself. She wants more and more—of Barrett and the wherewithal to keep herself in her own hopeless brand of confusion. I'm through with her completely." On top of it all, Vincent Sr., whose will had stipulated that one eighth of his estate should be left to his daughter-in-law, had neglected to change the document before he died. He had told Vincent, however, that he no longer wished Edith to have the money but intended to leave it to Barrett. Fearing that Edith would squander the money, Vincent had tried to talk with her about it. When she refused to respond, his father's lawyer also sent her a letter. Finally, Vincent's brother Mort contacted his sister-in-law and she relented, allowing the $45,000 left to her by Vincent Sr. to be put into trust for Barrett, with the provision that she could benefit from the income on the principal. After this agreement was reached, Vincent was hopeful that Edith would finally settle matters between them peaceably.

Suddenly, however, on Christmas Eve, Edith refused to let Barrett spend Christmas Day with his father, as had been planned. Although they did spend New Year's Day together with Mary, by the next weekend Edith again suddenly refused to let Vincent see his son. Fearing that Edith's toying with his visitation rights might be a prelude to losing his son altogether, Vincent decided not to fight Edi in her divorce suit. Nonetheless, during the six months between January, when she filed for divorce, and June, when it was granted, she wouldn't relent, playing Barrett off against his father.

Edith's divorce suit, filed early January 1949 in Santa Monica Superior Court, charged that he had inflicted "grievous mental suffering without justification." Edith's attorney Peyton H. Moore urged his client to plead that her husband had been guilty of extreme cruelty for the past two years. The proposed settlement would give Edith custody of eight-year-old Barrett, although his father would retain full visitation rights. She would receive $660 a month in alimony and child support—$330 for each.

Despite the vicious court proceedings, Vincent endeavored to get his life under control. For the second year in a row he attended January commencement ceremonies at East Los Angeles Junior College, later recalling that "I was invited to come and give a lecture at East Los Angeles Junior College, I think because I had shot off my mouth a lot about art around town and somebody had read about it. The student body had selected a topic for me called 'The Aesthetic Responsibility of the Citizen.' But I think it was selected by Judith Miller. Regardless of who selected it, it challenged me and it was a wonderful idea. And I do think that the citizen has an aesthetic responsibility. At the time of the lecture, when Los Angeles was spreading its wings and beginning to have public fountains and things like that, it was fun to promote the idea of each person's aesthetic responsibility." Once again impressed by Judith Miller's work on the campus, he offered to help her in any way he could.

Shortly afterward he left for his first trip to Central America and Mexico. Through Walter Arensburg he had got to know the pre-Columbian dealer Earl Stendahl. Barrett remembered, "Stendahl smuggled stuff out of Latin America and I was there when he brought the last box of Costa Rican gold. They opened up drawer after drawer of eagles and bells and rabbits that they had taken out of sarcophagi down there." The treasures Vincent saw in Stendahl's shop only made him want to see the art *in situ*. He later wrote, "I've had affinities with certain places, places that have been very important in my life. For example, I first went to Mexico because I found myself talking about it like it was a part of my life. And I didn't know them at all first hand."

Vincent visited Guatemala City and Quiriga in Guatemala; St. Cristobal, Merida, and the Mayan ruins at Chichen Itza and Uxmal in the Yucatan; then Teotihuacan and Mexico City before heading home. The highlight of the trip was his arrival at Chichen Itza under a full moon. He later described his adventure: "The ruins are closed at night, but I begged one of the attendants to let me see them by the light of that moon. He agreed, and we trudged along the road, climbed a fence, and instantly I was a Mayan, too. The great pyramid, with its ninety steps, loomed ghostly white out of the night. Following my guide's instructions, I panted to the top and up the five more steps that, with the ninety on four sides, make intentionally the three hundred and sixty-five of our calendar. Breathless, I saw below me the great open plaza; to one side, the ball court; to the other, the Temple of Warriors. It was not a view of details, for the moon cast silver shadows, and you could not see Chac-Mool atop the warrior temple, or the frieze of jaguars or skulls of plumed warriors on columns. None of this was visible. But if you looked through your romantic eye, the ancient people soon appeared and marched with solemn steps across the great expanse. A rattle and flute made mystic music, and a quetzal feather turned peacock blue in the path of the moon. Chichen Itza is one of the wonders of the world." Vincent would return to Mexico many times, always able to find something new to marvel at in this most magical and romantic of lands.

Back home again, Vincent accepted a guest spot on the Jack Benny radio show. Columnist Harrison Carroll reported that Price had wired the notoriously stingy Benny: "I accept, but what am I going to do with Confederate money?" Vincent and Jack Benny got along well and the pair quickly developed a repartee that would enliven future radio episodes as well as Benny's television program during the 1950s, where Vincent was a frequent and favored guest. As a foil for his own purported lack of education, Benny traded on Vincent's image as an erudite and well-educated actor. In one of their most famous episodes, which would also later be used on television, Benny gets word that Vincent has been cast in a new film opposite Irene Dunne. Benny feels that he has been unfairly excluded from the film and somehow manages to get himself invited to a rehearsal with Dunne, Price, and director Gregory Ratoff. Price, Ratoff, and Benny arrive at the same time and, while they are waiting, they begin to banter with one another. What followed was a wonderful bit that became one of Jack Benny's favorite jokes.

Jack Benny tries to convince Ratoff to use him instead of Price, saying, "Look, Mr. Ratoff, why don't you have me and Vincent compete for the part, and you can decide who is the best actor." Price objects, not only to this idea but also to Benny's grammar:

"You mean *better* actor, not *best*. If three or more were competing, then *best* would be correct. But since only two of us are involved, you should use the comparative, and *better* is correct. Not *best* actor, but *better* actor. I therefore suggest that before you think of competing with me for an acting assignment, it might be well if you first learned to speak English." A few minutes later, after Irene Dunne has joined the men, a butler enters to serve coffee. Only Benny and Dunne accept the coffee. Jack sips his and announces, "This is the *better* coffee I ever tasted." Price turns on him, "You mean the *best* coffee." To which Jack responds irately, "There are only two of us drinking it! Make up your mind!"

On June 3, 1949, Vincent and Edith's divorce case finally went before Judge Stanley Mosk. The next day, the *Los Angeles Times* reported that Judge Mosk had granted Edith "an interlocutory decree after she stated that Price had constantly criticized her, told her it was none of her business where he had been when he came home at four or five A.M., and many times said he was sorry he had married her." The *City News* reported that Mrs. Price received the alimony she had requested along with "a residence in Santa Monica, a ranch in Ventura County, numerous art objects, a $25,000 life insurance policy and various bank accounts and bonds aggregating more than $20,000." Despite the considerable cost of the settlement, Vincent was relieved to have everything over and done with and his relationship with his son legally protected. Vincent never disputed Edith's claims of cruelty. As the marriage had disintegrated, he had indeed felt angry and threatened. His temper sometimes flared and he took his disappointment and guilt out on his wife in bitter and cruel words. Now all he wanted was to move on.

During the summer, Vincent began filming *Bagdad*, a Universal-International release with Maureen O'Hara in the lead. A mediocre saga tracing the nineteenth-century power struggle for Bagdad, the film featured Vincent, third-billed, as the villainous Turk, Pasha Ali Nadim. When the film was released many of the reviewers commented on his choice of playing his character with one drooping eye; but this was no actorly affectation. Just before starting work on the film, Vincent and Mary had attended a student fancy-dress ball for the Modern Institute of Art. Feeling the necessity to go all out, they went as a "space couple in long underwear, dyed black, with black stocking caps that fitted like helmets, down into the neck. We were black from head to toe, with black masks over our eyes and, on top of our heads, a triple-tiered set of strobolite plastic propellers." During the ball someone offered Vincent a cigarette; holding the matches close to his mask to light one, he accidentally lit the whole book on fire, and the flames flared up into his right eye. He ignored the pain and went on with the party, but two days later he found himself in absolute agony, unable to tolerate any light. For days he sat in darkness, nursed by Mary and watched over by an extremely concerned Joe, who sat *on* the feet of his injured master and steadfastly refused to move for five days. When Vincent began work on *Bagdad*, Maureen O'Hara recalled, "It was terribly painful; he couldn't open his eye, so he had to play the role with it swollen closed. But halfway through the movie it started to get better, and he had one helluva time trying to keep it closed. He really should have put a patch on it and then he wouldn't have had so much trouble. He was complaining and laughing. He made a big, big joke out of the whole thing."

As for the place of *Bagdad* in his own personal recollections, Vincent remembered the film for only two reasons. One was the opportunity to work with Maureen O'Hara; the other was the onset of an unlikely (and one-sided) love affair. Filming in Lone Pine,

California, nestled in the Eastern foothills of the Sierra Nevadas, director Charles Lamont and his crew did their best to replicate the Arabian desert. Aside from the requisite palm trees, the chief prop aiding this unlikely transformation was a herd of camels. Vincent described what transpired: "All through one week's filming in the blistering sun, take after take was being ruined by the inhuman howls of a lady camel. No one could make her stop, and the furious reprimand by the sound man to the animal owner brought out the news that the camel must have fallen in love with one of the cast. Since there were only three men, including myself, in the company and lady camels fall only for human men, it must be one of us.

"Unbeknownst to me, the undignified suggestion was made that the three of us be presented to the camel in question. I was elsewhere when my coworkers were paraded before her. I walked onto the set at the end of this unlikely spectacle. They apparently had caused her no emotional upset whatsoever, but the moment I appeared the great lumpy beast gave forth with the most disturbing screams of passionate anguish. I was the object of her affection and also the friendly derision of the entire company." It was a story he retold for years: "It's not every man who could find a camel willing to walk a mile for him." Then, almost before he knew it, he would find love again—a love of a far more auspicious (and human) kind.

In late August 1949, Vincent asked Mary Grant to join him on a trip to San Diego, where he had been invited to help judge an art show. There they met up with one of his acquaintances, Perry Rathbone, the director of the Museum of Fine Arts in Boston, who had met Vincent when Rathbone had been the director of the City Art Museum in St. Louis and was now also sitting on the jury. Vincent later described their weekend together. "Mary and I had been 'going together,' as that lovely American expression goes when two people want to get married and don't quite know how to accomplish it for various reasons. It's also a period of great lightheartedness, and the addition of a person with mutual interest is more acceptable then than ever again in a marriage. So, we took Perry on to show him the sights of California, including the fabulous San Diego Zoo. One thing led to another, and Tijuana being across the border from San Diego, our thirst took us there. Perry adored it, and the wild kind of abandon that happens once you're out of your own land happened sooner than usual this time. Before he knew what hit him, he was our best man! Poor Perry left Los Angeles in a state of shock—and especially so, because he was not allowed to tell anyone our secret, both of us feeling slightly guilty to have done this without telling our families, who incidentally couldn't have cared less or more one way or the other." Their spontaneous marriage would last twenty-four years.

20

THE EARLY FIFTIES proved a turning point in Vincent Price's career and in his personal life. Buoyed by a happy marriage and a creative partnership, he finally found the support he had needed for his various endeavors. From the beginning, his relationship with Mary was in complete contrast to his marriage with Edi. In the first place, with Mary there were no surprises. Unlike Edi, who had hidden her feelings, her idiosyncrasies, and even her age, Mary was frank from the start. When they were first dating, the costume designer had told Vincent quite plainly, "I usually hate actors." He always enjoyed her candor, and his wife's antipathy toward his profession even became a joke between them.

But more important than her frankness was her talent: Mary was Vincent's creative equal. Bill and Shirley Brice, who had met Vincent while he was still married to Edith, believed that "Mary was good for Vincent. Mary did projects. She brought a kind of structure to Vincent's life. Vincent had always diffused not only the arbitrary distinction between high and low art but also between one's life and art. He believed that one's life is a work of art. He really lived that way and, for that reason, wherever Vincent was there was a perpetual project. And Mary was just brilliant at that." Barbara Poe first met Vincent while he was still married to Edi, whom she thought "peculiar and very, very fey." But she believed that "Vincent had the best life with Mary. That was my impression. They had the most fun together and Mary took the most interest in his career." Vincent acknowledged that interest. At the end of his life, he said, "God knows Mary was enormously important in my life. Enormously important. And I knew that. She did a tremendous amount for me to establish me in people's minds. She was a follow-upper." Indeed, during their years of marriage, Vincent Price made sixty of his one hundred films, appeared on countless television programs, established himself as a viable force in the visual arts, and wrote seven books.

After they were married, Mary worked sporadically as a costume designer, but also branched out into fashion design. With the talented Edward Sebesta as a partner, she opened a company called the Workroom, which specialized in clothes and costumes for performers and for motion pictures. In addition to making clothes for Peggy Lee, Angela Lansbury, Jane Russell, and Diana Lynn, she also made her husband one of her most frequent models. Her first creation, for which Vincent had modeled and Mary garnered some publicity in November 1947, was a cross between a zoot suit and mechanic's overalls. In February 1951, the couple followed up with a one-piece tuxedo, inspired by the flying suits of World War II pilots. Mary's inventiveness was equaled only by Vincent's—during these years he wrote and proposed a host of screenplay concepts to various studios, including a film based on the life of Sir Arthur Conan Doyle and another about

Grandma Moses, as well as a story called *Sir Sagebrush*, about an Englishman forced to hide from the law in Texas. He was also reported to be marketing inventions, such as a sail-in theater for boats and an alarm clock which featured his dulcet tones instead of a harsh bell.

The couple set up home in Vincent's house in Benedict Canyon. During these early years, the transformation of the house became their most absorbing shared occupation. When Vincent had bought the place for $16,000 in the mid-1940s "there were ninety broken panes and rags stuffed in every one, to say nothing of canvas tacked on most of the doors." Vincent had begun decorating during the period when he was being paid for *Forever Amber*; after moving in, Mary threw herself into further refurbishing. Her first project was to execute Vincent's idea for a greenhouse dining room. To this end, she traveled the length and breadth of Southern California, unearthing wonderful sources for buying marvelous (but always bargain-priced) items. In 1951, *Los Angeles Daily News* reporter Darr Smith described the transformation: "In the house are two noticeable fireplaces, a glass-enclosed outdoor dining room, and several patios, 18 dozen-odd pieces of sculpture, and a vast library covering most aspects of art. The walls of the house are covered with drawings." A reporter for the local *Canyon Crier* noted that the Prices live "midst Indian pottery, African masks, flowing jungle vines, and early Modiglianis, in a half-hidden, Spanish mission-style, once-deserted house."

Mary recalled, "From the outset of our marriage, Vincent was away a great deal of the time. So, there were small projects on which we worked together. But there was one major one, which Vincent never failed to use as an example of what his 'designer wife' had been up to. The existing floor plan, in my opinion, did not work very well, so I moved the front door several feet to the right. When Vincent arrived, the previous entrance had been bricked in, which caused him some consternation. He never stopped laughing about that. He found it so funny." Their home became their fondest joint project, and over the years they filled it with the artistic spoils of their many tours abroad.

Immediately after their impromptu Tijuana wedding, Vincent had returned to work; there was no time for a honeymoon. A few months later, though, a wonderful opportunity for a few weeks away together presented itself: The Hollywood Foreign Correspondents had begun to organize themselves into a cohesive group and were sponsoring goodwill tours to various countries. Among the first of these was a trip to Peru, which was organized by the Chilean Maria Sisternas, the leading Spanish-language columnist in Hollywood. His well-known interest in South and Central American art garnered Vincent an invitation, and he and his new wife eagerly accepted, deciding that this would be the honeymoon they hadn't had.

They arrived in Peru in late November where they met up with their Hollywood contingent for a two-week tour. It soon became clear to Vincent that he had been touted as an authority on Peruvian art, though, as he later admitted, "I didn't know Nasca from Chimu. But I got to their museum and got every book I could and started to look things up. I soon learned because fortunately I'm inquisitive." Accompanying her husband, the new and attractive Mrs. Price received lots of attention. It was the first time that Mary found herself in the spotlight as Mrs. Vincent Price, a task to which she gamely took, though it was at odds with her more retiring nature. They toured the country, being photographed and interviewed by the Peruvian press.

The Prices spent most of their time with Barbara Britton, another actor along for the ride. Vincent had just wrapped a film, *Champagne for Caesar*, in which the young actress had also appeared. Mary and Barbara bought some of the brightly-colored alpaca peasant skirts which, however itchy they were, both women wore with, as Mary said, "great enthusiasm until we realized our legs were being dyed fuschia." In Lima, Vincent found that the U.S. ambassador to Peru happened to be a St. Louis man and a friend of his family. Ambassador and Mrs. Harold Tittman threw a big party for the Prices, and Mrs. Tittman was subsequently able to show them some of the better antiquities galleries in Lima. There Vincent bought his usual great gross of pots and had them shipped back home so he could gloat to Ralph Altman.

From Lima, the group traveled to the ancient cities of Pachamac, Cuxco, and Saxouman, and finally to Machu Picchu. Mary and Vincent both reveled in each new day's adventure. Indeed, for the first time, Vincent was married to someone whose curiosity matched his own. The trip proved an ideal honeymoon for the Prices: It was the first of many such tours they would undertake together over the next twenty-four years.

Although Mary and Vincent had been married on August 28, 1949, they did not announce their nuptials in the press until late September. Vincent, of course, was particularly concerned about Barrett's reaction. But he needn't have worried—his son had liked his new stepmother from the moment he had met her. The new Mrs. Price felt the same way. She later recalled, "I first saw Barrett on the set of *Up in Central Park* which he and his mother came to visit. He was a handsome little boy with an understandably anxious expression. Later on, when we became integral parts of each others lives and he had a sense of permanency and place, he and I really became Best Friends."

After Vincent and Mary were married, Barrett spent every other weekend, and part of each vacation, with them. This was a difficult time for the shy, blond, nine-year-old boy. Every time he left to be with his father and his stepmother, Edith would break down in tears and beg her son not to leave. Although he enjoyed his weekends away, he dreaded leaving Edi and then dreaded returning home.

Barrett's home life with his mother was rapidly deteriorating. As he recalled, "Edi was chronically broke. As it all turns out, part of that money did not go to booze but to amphetamines because we were all getting hooked on them. It started when I was eight or nine and went on until I was twelve or thirteen. Dad didn't know about it. I didn't know about it. I thought I was taking calcium shots." Two or three times a week, Edith took her son to a fashionable Beverly Hills physician, who would intravenously inject them both with pure Benzedrine. Barrett told of the experience. "It was terrible; it was wonderful, delicious. After a full dose, I would literally rearrange my comic books and toys all night long. And Edi was in her room doing something, probably rearranging her shoes. I don't think she knew. Mrs. Maitland was the one who found him out, I believe. She was an old woman and he was her doctor and she'd been on them a terribly long time. I think another heart physician told her they were pure Benzedrine." After the unethical doctor had been found out, Vincent made sure that both Edi and Barrett stopped going to get shots but, as Barrett recalled, "The withdrawals were quite severe for both of us and for everyone else. Dad is the one who told me a long time afterwards what was going on. I didn't understand why I felt like shit and why I was so desperate. By that time, I was a total wreck. I couldn't talk and I was furious at being contained. Edi would come down to the playground in her nightgown and drag me off the ballfields. She was abusive to me, because she was angry. It was terrible. Dad had to have known how bad she was because I'm sure all her friends were calling him, as they were always calling me when I got older. They wanted him to do something about it and he said, 'I pay her $660 a month—I am doing something about it.' " Unable to confront Edith, Vincent was wracked with guilt about his son.

For Barrett "Dad was very much like a wonderful uncle. He did his best to take care of me. He took me on trips, we'd go to movies. We went to Mexico a lot and we'd hang out there. It was really quite sublime. But he was more like an uncle than a dad in a way. I didn't really want him to be a dad. I asked him if I could call him Vincent, and he wanted me to call him Dad. I was ten. He wanted to be Dad, I think." Indeed he did: Vincent felt trapped by his separation from his son, yet equally trapped by his own compulsion to work and to keep a schedule that made him very much a part-time father. Still, he sought to recreate what had been special in his relationship with his own father. Vincent later wrote, "Till the day he died, I never left off kissing my father goodbye and hello. There is a tenderness in the father-son embrace untasted in any other. It is an unspoken agreement, an undiscussed closeness." Vincent would try to pass this and many other intimate and loving customs onto Barrett.

Among Vincent's favorite activities with Barrett were their trips to Ocean Park—an old-fashioned and somewhat run-down amusement park near the Santa Monica Pier, complete with fun house, con games, penny arcade, wooden roller coaster, and other gravity-defying rides. "My son and I both thought of Ocean Park as something sacred, a projection into the ocean of our desire to be together. At the same time, we were both conscious that its tawdriness and tangled trap of things to do were a bulwark against too much discussion of our plight as separated son and father. Here we could play together with public toys and be unashamed in our love of them. . . . We let our handwritings and our accents be analyzed, our weights be guessed, and his chin and my mustache be gummed up by huge pink clouds of cotton candy. Over the years our prowess yielded us dozens of plaster dolls, Japanese porcelain toys, unusable utensils, pennants, and even a smoked ham, which by pooling our wins we joyously lugged away from a short-lived new game of chance, the odds of which were too much in favor of the customer."

For Vincent, the best part of the Ocean Park experience was riding the great old wooden roller coaster (or rolly coaster, as he called it), but Barrett had gotten sick on his first ride and flatly refused to join his father on the rickety wooden contraption again. Yet Vincent wouldn't be denied his own boyish fun, so Barrett would stand at the exit watching his father as he plunged down the daredevil descents; it became a regular part of their Ocean Park ritual. When the announcement appeared in the paper that the park was finally closing down, father and son planned a farewell pilgrimage to the shabbily glamorous old place; Barrett still refused to hazard the roller coaster, though, and so Vincent too decided to forego his favorite ride.

The next morning Mary heard that a pile of weathered old woodblocks were being given away somewhere nearby, and she and Vincent set off to find them. "Before I knew it," Vincent remembered, "we were in the parking lot at Ocean Park. The lumber was pointed out to me, pieces of old pilings, well-weathered indeed, by years of wind and sea, and suddenly the awful fact that Ocean Park was being torn down, roped out of the sea and sand forever, was brought back to me." When they passed the roller coaster, Vincent couldn't help clambering onto the ride he'd missed the night before. "I was about to climb in when a voice said, 'Hey, buddy, the fun's over. Ain't you heard we closed last night?' I was about to leave when he appeared and said, 'Ain't you that actor, what's your name?' I said, 'Any chance at one last ride?' And with that coup de grace all good Americans love, the handshake with a palmed buck in it, I was in and off on the great adventure." Vincent had just turned forty, and he found himself linking the passing of the park with the passing of his own youth; now, as he coursed around the rails one final time, he experienced a rapture that would come swimming back to him years later when he recalled the incident in his autobiographical writings. When he was through, "the forty-year-old juvenile who had pouted about missing the last ride on the old roller coaster at Ocean Park tiptoed down the miles of catwalk into the arms of his giggling wife" and was happy at last.

Despite the inherent difficulties in his relationship with Barrett during the early years of his marriage to Mary, Vincent and his son endeavored to find a common ground. Mary was instrumental in this. She tried not only to become involved in Barrett's life, but also to create a sense of family. Because she had moved so often during her childhood and into her twenties, she, like Edith before her, relished the opportunity to have a home. She particularly enjoyed holidays, recalling, "I had never had the opportunity to celebrate special occasions. On our first Easter, I cooked a ham, and a traditional cake in the shape of a lamb for Barrett, and Vincent was so carried away." For the first time, he had a sense of home, for himself, and for his son.

Not only did Mary and Barrett quickly become close, but Mary also easily fitted in with Vincent's friends. As she recalled, their family circle was ever-expanding and their door always open to a new group of art-collecting friends. "After we were married, I became part of an extended family of the Carreres, the Warshaws, the Brices, the Poes, and the Altmans, who made me feel a part of their lives from then on. When the Warshaws left Los Angeles, Pat and Ralph Altman moved into the upstairs apartment. At any moment, any or all of us seemed to be driving to Santa Barbara, Julian, San Francisco, or Tijuana/ Ensenada, which in those days was the ultimate source with a capital *S*. Somewhere it must be written that 'Thou shalt not leave Baja empty-handed.' We never did. Nothing was ever too heavy, too large, nor were there too many. There is another unwritten accumulator's rule, i.e., whoever first sights a treasure gets to acquire it. Pat and I had no problem with this. Not so Ralph and Vincent: To the most devious went the most spoils. What wonderful times those were."

Despite the ease with which Mary became integral to Vincent's life, there was one key member of the household with whom she often found herself at odds. As Vincent later recounted, "From the time Mary and I were married and Joe found himself with a 'mother,' their relationship has been one of the joyous banes of my existence. It's been a ten-year tug-of-war between the two, and, up to now, even the Marquis of Queens-berry, while abhorring the tactics used on both sides, would have to call it a draw. They are evenly matched, histrionically, temperamentally, endurance-wise, and, though the battle they wage is an all-out war, the ambushes and sallies, direct advances and retreats, the diplomacy used in inviting allies to one side or the other, the subterfuges and ruses, delays and prognostications make it one of the most fascinating tactical maneuvers to watch in the history of modern cold warfare. I am the innocent battleground on which this war is waged. Since Joe already had an unequivocal ally in me and a mercenary in my houseman, Will, Mary inherited, through marriage, a small enemy army she was perfectly capable of conquering single-handed."

Pets became an ongoing drama in the Price household during the 1950s. Because Mary wanted a pet of her own, some friends gave her a cat, which she gamely named Josephine. But Joe taught the cat to roam the canyon and one day she simply never returned; Mary was devastated. Then, to make matters worse, Joe became somewhat of a celebrity when Vincent Price was sued for $13,193 in damages by a local eccentric after Joe allegedly knocked him off his bicycle. On January 23, 1951, Los Angeles Superior Judge Caryl M. Sheldon heard the case against Joe, who was accompanied to court by Vincent. As the prosecution attempted to establish the nature of Benjamin's injury, they called a doctor, who displayed Benjamin's X rays for the jury. Vincent later recounted, "At this point Joe decided to sit up in his best food-begging manner, and that did it. The idea of a dog sitting up at the sight of the X rayed bones, though of course it wasn't the bones at all, simply his genius for dramatic timing, undid the courtroom and even the judge couldn't keep a straight face." The jury decided in favor of Joe—and Vincent.

Joe continued to rule the roost until a friend offered Mary a puppy. One of Mary's chief complaints about her husband's dog had always been his undistinguished appearance—her preference was for a pedigreed dog. And so Prudence, an Oxford-grey standard poodle, entered the Price household—the first of a long line of animals whose names would all begin with P—for Price. Although singularly devoted to Mary, Prudence managed to win over both Vincent and Joe. The two dogs became fast friends, and at long last peace reigned in the Price household.

With the pet problem finally resolved and with Barrett adjusting to his new lifestyle, the Prices were becoming a family. Life began to settle into a happy rhythm at 1815 Benedict Canyon, and even the fact that Vincent never stopped working didn't alter anyone's happiness, at least not during those early years. Despite his workaholism, Vincent never drifted too far away from home. When away on location or on a lecture tour, he kept in continual contact with Mary and Barrett; when in Los Angeles, he always let his wife know where he would be for the day and when he expected to be home, calling if he thought he would be fifteen minutes late. None of this was at Mary's behest; she was hardly the type of wife to hang around the set waiting for her husband or watching his behavior with his glamorous leading ladies. She trusted him because she understood that he was a curious mix—a career man whose commitment to his work and his desire for creative independence kept him frequently away from home, and yet nevertheless a family man who liked his wife to know just what he was doing at all times. He relished his travels as much as he looked forward to coming home and puttering around in his garden. And because Mary understood this, for the first time Vincent had both the freedom and the sense of home that he had long desired. Everything worked.

A few weeks after marrying Mary, Vincent had begun work on *Champagne for Caesar*, a film that he loved. In danger of becoming typecast as a heavy, he seized this opportunity to play something completely different—comedy. Vincent's friends, family, and costars had long enjoyed his ribald sense of humor and devastating wit, but he had had few opportunities to show this side of himself in his acting until his good friend, the director Richard Whorf, gave him this chance to break away from his usual assortment of villains.

In *Champagne for Caesar*, Vincent played Burnbridge Waters, the pompous president of Milady Soap Company. He gave a wildly funny characterization, complete with "brainstorms"—self-induced trances into which Waters frequently slipped. The film was a delightful comedy, and a box office success. Vincent collected a number of good reviews for his outrageous comic turn, which he certainly hoped would lead to other similar roles. But what he most relished was the opportunity to play opposite his longtime screen idol, Ronald Colman, and he professed to being tongue-tied upon their first meeting. Happily for Price, Colman more than lived up to his reputation. He was both a marvelous actor and a gracious man. He and his wife, the lovely actress Benita Hume, were known in Hollywood as an elegant and glamorous couple, and during the shoot they invited the Prices to dinner.

Mary and Vincent were overjoyed to be asked, but, as Vincent later admitted, "We were a bit nervous about it. After all, he was a huge star, and Mary wanted to be sure to wear the right thing. And so I asked Benita, who said she would be wearing 'just a little black.' Well, Mary, the costume designer, made sure to get just the right thing—a little black dress, which looked fantastic on her. But we had a bit of an argument before we left because I wore a foulard, sport coat, and slacks, which is what all the men were wearing at the time. I thought I was dressed just right but Mary was convinced I was totally underdressed. But at least we knew that she was in just the right thing.

"So, we set out for the Colmans. Of course, we hadn't bothered to ask directions because everyone knew that Ronald Colman lived next door to Jack Benny, and we knew where Jack lived. For years and years on the *Jack Benny Show*, that had been a running gag. So, we went to the house next door to Jack's and rang the doorbell, and a complete stranger came to the door, who looked at us as though we were mad when we asked for Ronald Colman. As it turned out, Ronald Colman did not live next door to Jack Benny, nor did he live anywhere near him. And we had no idea where to find him because we hadn't brought the phone number with us. So, we had to ask people, and you can imagine their skepticism. But we finally found the place, which was miles from Jack Benny's house. And later, when we explained why we had been late, no one seemed to quite see the humor in it."

With a born storyteller's license, he continued, "So, Benita and Ronald came to the door and she was dressed for the opening of the Paris opera—to the nines. And I knew Mary was just mortified. But Benita was gracious enough to announce, 'Ronald says I look just like Brunhilde.' But Ronald was wearing exactly the same thing as I was—a sport coat, slacks, and foulard. Then the next guests came—Merle Oberon, dressed for the opening of the opera in Vienna, wearing a dress with a train, and about seven million dollars worth of jewelry, and George Cukor, wearing a sport coat, slacks, and foulard. The fourth couple were Clark Gable and his wife. She was dressed for the opening of the Cairo opera, with a diamond necklace the size of golf balls. And you know what *he* was wearing. So, 'a little black' became a running joke between Mary and me after that night!"

Immediately after wrapping *Champagne for Caesar*, Vincent started work on another film that gave him a chance to try his hand at something different. *The Baron of Arizona*, directed by Sam Fuller, was a quasi-fictional account of one man's scheme to swindle the U.S. government out of the territory of Arizona during the 1870s. A bearded Price starred as the baron of the title, otherwise James Addison Reavis. His character was a loveable rascal, who not only romanced numerous women at the same time but also posed as a monk before being found out and sent to prison. The role allowed the actor to display some versatility, which pleased the critics. George H. Jackson of the *Los Angeles Evening Herald and Express* felt, "Vincent Price was a happy choice for the title role. He carries it off to perfection and is believable throughout." The *Los Angeles Times* concurred, noting that "Vincent Price makes the Baron a brilliantly resourceful, fascinating fellow, and his adventures absorbing."

In addition to adulation for Price, the film itself was well received. The world premiere was held on March 1, 1950, in Phoenix, Arizona, where crowds broke all records for the Paramount Orpheum Theater. For the occasion, a large cake was baked in the shape of Arizona. A second and identical cake was later presented to the Prices. True collectors, they preserved it in their freezer for years, even taking it with them when they moved—unwilling to throw out something made with such care.

During the winter of 1950, Vincent filmed *Curtain Call at Cactus Creek*, directed by Charles Lamont for Universal-International. A spoof on the "they went thataway pardner" school of movies, it paired Vincent with the famous screen wisecracker Eve Arden. Hollywood columnists soon reported the two had hit it off so well that they were developing a comedy routine to use at benefits. In the film, Vincent had to ride a horse, one of his most unhappy requirements in movies. Hollywood was always trying to get a saddle under him, but Vincent Price hated horses. As he later wrote, his lifelong relationship with the animal had been a troubled one: "The horse and I just don't see eye to eye. In the first place, the top of a horse and my bottom don't fit. My legs are too long and my torso too short—in short, I look ridiculous on top of a horse and I suspect that it feels ridiculous under me. Maybe the situations should be reversed." Aside from the riding, the film, which also starred Donald O'Connor, Gale Storm, and Walter Brennan, allowed Vincent another opportunity to explore his gift for comedy. Playing ham actor Tracy Holland, he spouts Shakespeare, spoofs the cowboys, plays a vaudeville villain, and participates in countless theatrical skits. Reviewers appreciated his gift for travesty; *Newsweek* opined that "Price wading pompously through an old-time melodrama called 'Ruined by Drink' is alone worth the price of admission."

21

DURING THE FILMING of *Curtain Call at Cactus Creek*, Vincent had been approached by Howard Hughes who, in 1948, had bought a controlling interest in RKO Studios. RKO had produced some fine pictures in its history, including *King Kong, Citizen Kane,* and the Astaire-Rogers musicals. Although Hughes had assured the studio's head of production, Dore Schary, that he would not interfere with day-to-day operations, he lost no time in firing and hiring talent. Barbara Bel Geddes was canned, while Hughes's ex-lover Jane Greer was kept on salary but not allowed to work; Jane Russell, under personal contract to Hughes since the early 1940s, was given starring roles, as was Robert Mitchum, who along with Russell became one of the studio's two biggest names.

In 1950 Hughes signed Vincent Price, and immediately cast him in a picture starring Russell and Mitchum. Vincent would later recall, "I have a tender place in my heart for Howard Hughes. For all the jokes and barbs, Hughes was quite a fellow. When he bought RKO, he arrived one day to inspect his purchase, walked silently all over the lot, toilets, stages, shops, and left with only two words to the cowering entourage: 'Paint it!' That's what I call a man of few words. I was one of three actors under personal contract to the great eccentric, and he actually was credited with writing a scene for me because he liked my character and, after the film was finished, he still wanted more."

As it happened, *His Kind of Woman* would be over a year in the making. As Robert Mitchum recalled, "We started off on the picture with John Farrow and John Farrow was sadistic. I mean, he was a sadist. But he was sort of an invitee in this situation. I mean, we were the teacher's pets. That was everyone's opinion. We had no more influence than anyone else. People approached us tenderly. So Mr. Farrow never vented his spleen upon us. We finished it up and it was a very decent film. And apparently somebody, and everyone says it was Mr. Hughes, saw the picture and said it was a very good picture, but now we're going to make it a *great* picture. So we started all over again. They brought in Richard Fleischer, and it became an entirely different film. The comedy thing happened the second time around. First time around it was more dramatic, a tighter film."

Vincent was hilariously funny and rather touchingly vulnerable in *His Kind of Woman*, playing a popular but second-rate movie star who is having a casual affair with Russell's lounge singer. After completion of shooting, Hughes decided that the last reel needed more action, and more comedy from Vincent, whose performance he much enjoyed. An entirely new ending was created, largely authored by Hughes, with Vincent's intentional ham acting as the focal point.

Reviewers generally applauded Vincent's on-screen comedy gifts, while off-screen, cast and crew alike enjoyed his ribaldry and dry wit. Jane Russell remembered "how amazed I was meeting him and finding out what a marvelous sense of humor he had, because he had always played the 'proper' young man, and if they wanted a 'proper' young man—sophisticated, almost British—they got him. Then this wild humor comes out and you think, 'Why aren't they using some of that?' That's why he had a lot of fun at the end of *His Kind of Woman*, because he got to let go and be a ham actor with the cape and all that."

His Kind of Woman received mixed reviews. Tom Coffey in the *Los Angeles Mirror* headlined his piece "Price Steals the Show," remarking that although Mitchum was "a strong personality on the screen" and Russell "very pleasant to watch," neither was the star of the picture: "Vincent Price has stolen it from them in an extravagant comedy role." Darr Smith of the *Los Angeles Daily News* dwelt on what he felt to be the confusion wrought on the film by multiple changes in director and script, but conceded that "the best part of the picture, as far as we are concerned, is Vincent Price, deliciously funny as the ham actor."

Vincent's routine at RKO proved a welcome relief from moving around from studio to studio as a freelance actor. Although he was still loaned out elsewhere, he had the security of knowing that he had a "home" and a steady income.

After the lengthy shoot of *His Kind of Woman*, Vincent was set to start his next film, *Adventures of Captain Fabian*, in August 1950 in the South of France. A period swash-buckler starring an aging Errol Flynn, French star Micheline Presle (called Prelle in the U.S.), Vincent, and Agnes Moorehead, the film ran into trouble well before shooting began. First the French Labor Department withheld work permits for the American actors; then Warner Bros. claimed that Flynn's appearance in the Republic Pictures film was a breach of contract. Finally, Flynn, as Vincent later wrote, "was disengaging a princess at that point, and she was apparently hard to break off with. Her royal blood, I suppose. But if that match was not made in heaven, the results for us were heaven-sent. Errol arrived a month late, and since he was co-producer and cowriter, plus star number one, we could hardly start the picture without him."

Adventures of Captain Fabian was hardly bound to be a positive career move for Vincent, but it afforded him one of the only kind of vacations he would ever think to allow himself—a paid one. He later confessed, "I sort of hate to admit it, but I've accepted a lot of parts in pictures in order to go places, because I never earned enough salary to take time off. So I would do pictures in Rome and in France and in places I would like to be. A lot of people do that but very few of them say they do it for that reason." "*Adventures of Captain Fabian*," he claimed, "should have been a very good picture. I thought it would be great fun. Mary did the costumes. And so we went over there to get the costumes made, because they were being done by a famous house in Paris. We got there two weeks before the shoot. We were there on Bastille Day, and we had this wonderful experience of running into Barbara Poe's mother and father, Bernard and Becky Reis. They took us to several galleries and to lunch with one of the great art dealers in the world. We sat in his dining room, which was the most beautiful dining room I'd ever seen in my life, completely painted. I asked, 'Who painted this room?' And it was Bonnard. Then we went to the opening night of Darius Milhaud's opera, *Bolivar*. The sets were done by Leger and we were there with him.

"So there we were in France and we were ready to begin to shoot and Errol failed to show. They had to keep us there, in France, on salary, for a month. It was right after the war, so the French were not rich and smug. They were open and delighted to get rid of things. I found a Delacroix drawing on the Rue de Seine. We didn't know it, but it was a last gasp for the middle-income collector. Five years later the prices began to soar, and all kinds of art and art objects were vacuumed from European shops by the collectors of the world at large." While Vincent searched for drawings, Mary accumulated an extraordinary collection of copper culinary molds; husband and wife were so equally single-minded in their desire to make a find that, as Mary told it, "from junk stores to galleries, we would pore over every nook and cranny and often bump into each other and say excuse me—we were both so intent on not missing a single stitch."

When they realized that their trip would be indefinitely extended, the Prices bought a tiny second-hand car and scoured the countryside for treasures to add to their collection. In Vincent's words, they "came back with some lovely loot—about twenty drawings, fifty copper molds, enough white faïence china for a sit-down dinner for thirty, and two of the most precarious objects ever brought to these shores—a delicate little Greek angel of the fifth century and a monstrously heavy sixteenth-century bronze king from Benin."

In the tradition of Vincent's teenage Florentine fountain, these latter objects would be the first of many pieces, unwieldy or extremely fragile, that Vincent and Mary would somehow manage to bring home from abroad. Vincent recalled, "The angel we found our last day in Nice, after the picture was completed, and we carried it everywhere we went, packed in a little wicker basket with yards of cotton around it—by plane, train, car, and foot, until it landed on our mantelpiece at home. The Benin bronze we acquired on our last day in Paris, too late to ship. We were crazy about it and, not having had it long, wanted to see it the minute we got it home. I was afraid of getting it through the French customs, as it could have been considered a national treasure, in which case they could have paid me what I paid for it and kept it. I needn't have worried, for Benin is in the British part of Africa, not the French, and they couldn't have cared less. But I always look on the gloomy side of every customs transaction, so I rolled it up in the trousers of my best suit and put it in the overnight airplane bag. I got it through the French customs by pretending it was my quota of brandy, then I paid one hundred and twenty-five dollars excess weight to take it on the plane. Everything was in control until we started for the plane, whereupon it dropped through the bottom of the overnight case and spread my pants before it like a carpet as it rolled down the ramp. Everything was retrieved, no one was nabbed by the police, but in New York, some fifteen hours later, the customs man, questioning my right to bring it in duty-free, declared it was neither old nor a work of art and that I would have to leave it there, rolled up in my best pants, until an expert could examine it. We might just as well have sent it around the Horn by canoe. It, and my pants, arrived four weeks later, and even then I had to take my friend Ralph Altman to expertize it and get it released into my custody."

After a glorious month exploring Paris, the surrounding countryside, and the great cathedrals at Chartres and Rheims, the couple headed to Nice where they moved into the Negresco Hotel on the Boulevard des Anglais during filming. There they met up with Agnes Moorehead, who proved an amiable addition to their collecting expeditions. Vincent would later say that he, Mary, and Agnes "covered Europe like three vacuum cleaners." The film itself was rather less remarkable than their trip. Although only two years older than Vincent, Errol Flynn had led a debauched lifestyle that aged him dramatically, and he failed to carry off the role of the swashbuckling Captain Fabian. The *New York Times* speculated, "Possibly to give authentic Gallic backgrounds and flavoring to this heavy-handed tale of Old New Orleans, producer William Marshall packed the stars off to France . . . Neither the trip nor this foundering fiasco was necessary." Although Vincent might have agreed with the critical sentiment, on entirely separate grounds the trip had certainly been worthwhile.

Back from France, Vincent began his second film for RKO, *The Las Vegas Story*, which reunited him with Jane Russell and added Victor Mature. During the shoot, the studio put the stars and their spouses up in Vegas. It was "very jolly," according to Mary, and the whole company enjoyed the brand-new ambiance of Las Vegas, taking advantage of the casinos, lounging by the pool, and watching the nightclub acts. Price and Russell, a pair of tall, dark, and handsome stars, played husband and wife in the film and made a very attractive couple.

The plot concerned Lloyd and Linda Rollins, who, en route from the East Coast to L.A., make a stopover in Vegas where Linda had once been a nightclub singer. There, Lloyd racks up serious gambling debts and finds himself in trouble with the law—Sheriff Andrews (Mature) who also happens to be Linda's ex-lover. The plot thickens: Lloyd ends up in jail, his wife back in the sheriff's arms. However, Vincent felt that his part as written was insufficiently developed. According to Jane Russell, "He wasn't pushy. He didn't play the star, but he was a little unhappy. He just told me, he wouldn't tell the director [Robert Stevenson] or anybody else. He would say, 'It seems very peculiar. These people are supposed to be married and there's no place where it shows that they separate or have an argument.' But he wouldn't go fight for it. He wanted to get along, just get along. He wanted to please the director."

During the early fifties, Vincent hoped to redirect his career away from villains and heavy dramatic roles, and with three comedies behind him, he was optimistic that things were changing. In a 1951 guest column for the *Los Angeles Examiner*, he wrote, "Whenever I used to sit down at producers' desks in Hollywood to argue I could play comedy roles, it was like standing on a dark stage watching the audience leave for the night. Before getting that vague, I've-got-some-very-important-business-to-attend-to look on their faces, they would tell me that I was crazy to seek anything but dramatic roles. Typecasting is an actor's bugaboo. Of course, you may say, at those prices who should complain? But being typed is like digging yourself deeper into a rut. First thing you know you're in so deep nobody can see the top of your head. And then you have no worries; you have no career."

Yet this was hardly a fallow time for Vincent Price; at one point he received two offers in the same week. One was for a lead in a Broadway play, the other a lead in a movie, and in the end, his perpetual concern with money won out over higher aspirations and he chose the movie. The play, *We're No Angels*, was a comedy directed by Jose Ferrer; with Walter Slezak starring, it became a smash hit. After playing at the Morosco for years, it was made into a movie with Humphrey Bogart and Peter Ustinov, not to mention costumes (much to her husband's chagrin) by Mary Grant. Vincent often reflected on his decision with some regret, wondering what direction his career might have taken had he found himself in another Broadway hit. Would he have succeeded in resurrecting a distinguished Broadway reputation?

The film he chose instead would send his career in a far different direction. *House of Wax* was a Warner Bros. remake of the 1933 horror classic *The Mystery of the Wax Museum*, but with a uniquely fifties twist—it was to be photographed in 3-D. Touted as "the film technology of the future" by Warner (who hoped the gimmick would lure television viewers back into theaters), 3-D required the audience to don special glasses in order to get the impact of the trick photographic effects. Vincent felt that *House of Wax* was saved from being unrelieved schlock only by the faulty vision of its director, Andre de Toth, who had only one eye and therefore no depth perception. Since the 3-D effect was lost on him, de Toth never really understood what all the fuss was about, and limited his use of the gimmick rather than shamelessly indulging it the way a man with normal eyesight might have done. It was de Toth's relative restraint, Vincent believed, that helped make the film a classic.

House of Wax marked Vincent Price's first role in a pure example of the horror genre. In the end, the film's lasting power had less to to with the 3-D effects than with its leading actor's subtle, nuanced portrait of a good man gone bad, a chilling villain who nonetheless evokes audience sympathy. *House of Wax* succeeded on Vincent Price's talent as an actor, on his ability to use his voice and his eyes to draw a character of many facets—a man often at odds with himself. Combining elements of comedy, pathos, and evil, Vincent Price crystallized in this film a character whose outlines were already evident in films such as *Dragonwyck*—and unexpectedly took his unsought place as a master of the horror genre.

The plot of *House of Wax* concerns Professor Henry Jarrod (Price), an idealistic sculptor who creates life-size and, more significantly, lifelike wax models for a small museum of which he is co-owner. When his business partner burns down the museum for the insurance money, Jarrod is left for dead, but later reappears in a wheelchair. Although he looks normal, the sculptor has, in fact, created a wax mask to hide his hideous facial burns, and is mentally as well as physically scarred by the destruction of his life's work. He opens a new museum—this time a Chamber of Horrors—but, having lost both his ability and his gentle nature in the fire, he creates his pieces by murdering people with a likeness to the originals and dipping them in wax. Phyllis Kirk played the heroine who barely escapes this appalling fate; as Jarrod's assistant, Igor, the film featured a young actor named Charles Buchinsky, later to become better known as Charles Bronson.

Much was made in the Hollywood press of Vincent's extensive makeup for the film, created by George and Gordon Bau. "The makeup director spent weeks studying people who had been burned, then he stuck pieces of rubber on my face with pure alcohol," Vincent recalled. "Two doctors supervised it to be sure the burns were as real as could be. It took almost three hours to put on and as long to take off, and both processes were very painful. I couldn't eat because my mouth was partially 'scar tissue,' so I drank many liquids and because of the running around in makeup, I fainted one day from lack of oxygen. It took my face months to heal because it was raw from peeling off wax each night." The first time Vincent walked into the studio commissary with his gruesomely realistic makeup, he wryly remembered, "The girl at the cash register turned green and almost fainted. Then the patrons got up and headed for the door." He spent the remainder of the thirty-day shoot eating lunch in his dressing room.

The 3-D format required the use of two cameras for every shot. One of the downsides of the new technology—at least as far as Vincent was concerned—was that with two cameras rolling at all times, he had to perform all his own stunts. "It wasn't fun," he recalled, "because in one scene I had to run under a falling balcony, which was two thousand pounds of steel and timber, and the damn set caught on fire."

House of Wax proved to be an instant moneymaker for Warner Bros. The studio launched a huge campaign for the April 1953 opening of its 3-D extravaganza, and around-the-clock screenings were held in L.A. Aging horror star Bela Lugosi, complete with Dracula cape, was even trotted out for the New York opening, which Mary and Vincent attended. The always good-natured Vincent promoted the film around the country. He even participated in a publicity stunt at the Buena Park Wax Museum near Anaheim, taking the place of a wax figure of himself from a scene in the movie. He recalled, "I was standing in a menacing pose with a hypodermic needle. As the people came closer to look, I squirted water from the needle at them. It was great fun."

In turn, the film brought Vincent a great deal of publicity. Headlining at movie theaters around the country, the forty-two-year-old actor was discovered by a whole new generation—teenagers. Vincent got a real kick out of his new fans. During the thirty-week run of *House of Wax* at New York's Paramount Theater, Vincent was working in New York. As he loved to tell the story: "I was doing a play down the street so I'd walk right in and sit among the audience. Once I sat down behind two teenage girls who seemed to be enjoying the picture immensely. When I finally died in the picture—I rarely died the first time out—I was plunged into a vat of boiling wax. Moments later as 'The End' flashed up on the screen, I bent over the two girls and said, 'Did you like it?' They went into orbit!"

Despite his choice of *House of Wax* over *We're No Angels*, the early 1950s did bring Vincent a return to the theater. During the previous decade, his time had been largely taken up with his career at Fox and his work for the Little Gallery and the Modern Institute of Art. He had tried, however, to keep his hand in the theater and, in 1947, had participated in an evening of one-act plays by fellow St. Louisan Tennessee Williams for the Actor's Lab at the tiny Las Palmas Theatre. He played an old-time traveling salesman in *The Last of My Solid Gold Watches*—a role originally conceived with character actor Sidney Greenstreet in mind. Although Vincent received good notices, as did Jessica Tandy who appeared in *Portrait of a Madonna*, the Actor's Lab became a center of controversy for other than artistic reasons. Vincent recalled, "The group was a great success. Each play had a different director. Mine was Jules Dassin, who did *Never on Sunday*. And he was very left-wing, so we found ourselves in the midst of accusations about Communism. Jules Dassin had to leave the country. But our organization had nothing to do with politics." The *Hollywood Citizen-News* reported, "In view of the leftist views of some of the big names identified with the Lab, some patrons might have expected plays dealing directly with the basic conflict between totalitarianism and democracy. Since Actor's Lab is accredited as a training school for war veterans, the presence of well-known leftists on its executive board stirs the suspicions of those who understand communists. This reviewer failed to find anything alarming in Williams' trio of tragedies."

In 1950, Vincent returned to the Las Palmas Theatre to star opposite Jane Wyatt in Terence Rattigan's *The Winslow Boy*, about a schoolboy mistakenly accused of stealing. Vincent played the lead role of Sir Robert Morton, the lawyer who interrogates the boy but ends up proving his innocence. The part allowed him to hone his acting skills and provided a welcome respite from Hollywood in a production that was very successful.

But the real fulfillment of his desire to work in the live theater came in the summer of 1951, when he was asked to appear at the prestigious La Jolla Playhouse. Director Norman Lloyd described the genesis of this unique theater company. "The La Jolla Playhouse came about at a time when there was no television. There were actors in Los Angeles who had worked in the Broadway theater and missed it; some of them had no opportunity to go back to New York to do a play. . . . The theater in those days seemed very remote when you were a Broadway actor in Los Angeles making movies. Actors felt a kind of guilt and had a feeling that they had deserted their true calling. Several actors under contract to David O. Selznick loved the theater and wanted to have one. They were Gregory Peck, Dorothy McGuire, Joe Cotten, Jennifer Jones, and Mel Ferrer. Greg Peck came up with the idea of using his old high school in La Jolla. There was an auditorium with a stage that was usable at best. The actors went to Selznick, who shrewdly saw the value of it; it would allow them to let off steam. He loaned them fifteen thousand dollars, and Greg went to the La Jolla authorities and got permission to use their stage." Founded in 1948, the attraction of big Hollywood names, good plays, and the location of the lovely seaside town of La Jolla, just two hours south of Los Angeles, soon made the playhouse one of the most respected theater companies outside of New York City. Mel Ferrer managed the theater until 1953, when Dorothy McGuire's husband, photographer John Swope, whom Lloyd described as "a man of impeccable taste, great warmth, and charm who had much compassion for people," took over.

Norman Lloyd had been brought in to direct at the playhouse in 1948 and returned in 1951 to direct *The Cocktail Party* written by the St. Louis–born poet and expatriate T. S. Eliot. Lloyd immediately thought of Vincent for the lead role. The two men had remained friends since their Mercury Theater days. Lloyd not only suspected that Vincent was right for the part of medical specialist Sir Henry Harcourt-Reilly, a role originated by Alec Guinness at the Edinburgh Festival in 1949, he also knew that Vincent was always eager for a new challenge: "The great thing about him, you see, is he believed in work. You announced a play and Vinnie would call you and say, 'On what street corner? I'll be there.' " Lloyd also cast Patricia Neal, Estelle Winwood, Harry Ellerbee, and Rose Hobart in what was only the fourth production of the play worldwide to that date. (While some even today find the piece inaccessibly highbrow, the author regarded his verse play simply as a "sophisticated comedy of marital misunderstanding.")

That fall Lloyd's successful La Jolla production traveled up to the Curran Theatre in San Francisco where Marsha Hunt took over the role of Celia Copplestone from Patricia Neal. The rest of the La Jolla cast, including Estelle Winwood, remained in place. Winwood, by then getting on in years, had the unenviable task in the first act of delivering a very long monologue which sets the scene and identifies the characters. Vincent described it as the type of speech actresses approach with "that tell-tale look of 'here it comes' and then promptly forget it." Estelle fell prey to just such amnesia, frequently leaving the audience "none the wiser as to who was who, while the other actors sat dumbfounded and desperately ad-libbed their own identities . . . But nevertheless Estelle was enchanting in the play and a joy to be with on the road. She was an avid and demanding bridge player, but if she couldn't find a foursome, she commandeered our dapper little stage manager, or anyone else his age, to take her dancing after the show. The poor little fellows were, we all said, troopers or fools, which according to one of Noel Coward's songs are the same thing. She wore from next-to-nothing to nothing in the dressing room and as she was well into her seventies, she was not the most provocative lady on the block. But with Estelle, her conduct or lack of it didn't matter."

Following the San Francisco run of the play, the company toured the Northwest. During a one-night run in Tacoma, Vincent collapsed after the curtain call and was hospitalized with what was diagnosed as a minor perforation of a duodenal ulcer. Mary flew up to take care of her husband, and Reginald Denny, who had a minor role in the company and understudied the lead, replaced Vincent for the rest of the tour. Vincent returned home and recovered in a few weeks, but this was only the beginning of stomach troubles from which the actor would suffer for a good deal of his life.

In the summer of 1952, he returned to the La Jolla Playhouse to appear in Christopher Fry's *The Lady's Not for Burning* with Marsha Hunt and Beulah Bondi. Once again Norman Lloyd directed. He remembered, "In these plays that Vinnie and I did, a kind of bond was formed, because when you go through these kind of things together—it's very interesting about the theater—there is an emotional attachment among the cast if it's favorable. If it isn't, it's hate. But Vinnie was very funny. I'll never forget in one of the rehearsals, he came back from lunch and he had bought in a bakery a bread in the form of an alligator. And he came in and put it on the director's table. And I said, 'What's that?' And he said, "That's what you are when you direct.' "

This production, too, went to San Francisco for a limited run in the fall of 1952. Vincent always relished every opportunity to visit San Francisco, which he considered a far more cultured city than Los Angeles. On these trips he was often accompanied by Mary, whose mother had settled in the city after the death of her husband. Like many transplanted New Yorkers living in Southern California, the Prices loved traveling to the city by the bay. In addition to its great beauty, they enjoyed the cosmopolitan atmosphere, the innovative restaurants, the many art galleries and, perhaps most of all, the sophisticated and devoted theater audiences.

Later that summer the Prices went east to Boston and Newport, where Vincent appeared in *Goodbye Again*, a three-act comedy. A standard of the repertoire since the 1930s, the piece afforded him another opportunity to exploit his comic skills on stage. A Newport review noted, "We had never suspected it, but the tall, distinguished-looking actor is a clown in the grand manner. His facial expressions, his mastery of zany stage business, his way with a witty line, and his obvious enjoyment of his role (his making the bed in his hotel room is one of the funniest sequences we have seen in a long time) all contribute to a comic portrayal that gave us the most laughs we have yet enjoyed this season."

Vincent would appear in two more La Jolla Playhouse productions, a revival of *The Winslow Boy* in 1954 and *Billy Budd* a year later, both directed by Lloyd. The former, in which he starred with Dorothy McGuire, opened in late June in La Jolla and then toured around the country throughout the summer. Vincent adored touring—he loved people and had a soft spot for small-town audiences. Clearly those audiences reciprocated the affection. In Hinsdale, Illinois, where he played for two weeks, a local reporter effused, "Mr. Price possesses a kind of magnetic vigor that comes singing over the floodlights like a warrior's arrow to stab an audience into quivering awareness."

Billy Budd was one of the Playhouse's more ambitious productions. The play was originally adapted from Herman Melville's novel for a 1949 Experimental Theater production in New York. The La Jolla production featured Charles Nolte, who had been the original Billy Budd, playing the role again, with Vincent as Vere. He was well received as the captain torn between his duty and what he knows to be right. The production also featured a first-time young actor named James Coburn.

Vincent's four productions at the La Jolla Playhouse afforded him a kind of professional satisfaction he sorely missed in film work. Of Vincent, Norman Lloyd noted, "I loved directing Vinnie. He was a most conscientious and disciplined actor. He was very serious about acting. No jokes. Just great. He cared as an actor very much and that's not true of many actors. He was totally immersed in the theater. He loved the theater. I know he had the whole art world out there, but as an actor, he really cared. He never mocked anything in the theater."

Vincent's decision to return to the theater brought him a number of exciting challenges. In the fall of 1952, while appearing in San Francisco in *The Lady's Not for Burning*, he was invited to take over the role of the Devil from Charles Laughton in the national touring company of George Bernard Shaw's *Don Juan in Hell*, which Laughton had also directed. Vincent worked into the part under Laughton's direction for a short run in San Francisco's Curran Theatre; then, for three months, he toured the United States to rave notices in company with Charles Boyer, Cedric Hardwicke, and Agnes Moorehead. As Vincent later found out, however, the circumstances of his casting were peculiar. "Laughton, who had put the piece together, had made a pact that the original cast would stick together. On this third, fabulously successful twelve-week tour, he wanted out to do a film and, for some obtuse reason, decided to do it in an underhand way by rehearsing me in it without telling anyone else—except Agnes. She was the confidante of Laughton and the producer, and I was the ignorant, stupidly innocent party. I knew nothing of the original agreement, nothing of Laughton's film—he told me he was ill; I only knew it was a great part and that to work with Hardwicke and especially with Boyer was a dream come true. And Laughton's personal direction night after night during the San Francisco run was one of my greatest theatrical excitements. He was a superb, if eccentric, man and actor, but an enlightenment as a director.

"When I finally learned the truth about my takeover, I often wondered if, had I known about the double-cross, would I have turned it down? I came to the conclusion that I would have done it at all costs, but mainly because Boyer and Hardwicke were so wonderful to me. It destroyed their respect and friendship for Laughton, but I made two of the best theatrical partners I ever had. I am afraid Agnes's part in the whole affair, even though I later discovered she had suggested me to replace Charles, did nothing for her relationship with any of us. I always suspected the good notices I got in the part were almost bitterly received by Aggie. Our long friendship was chilled to the bone and it was a bone never entirely buried. I should have been grateful to her for suggesting me for a great experience. Instead, I sympathized with the others' feelings of betrayal." Years later, when a friend told Vincent that he had seen graffiti near Moorehead's star on Hollywood Boulevard, which read "Agnes is God," Vincent replied, "Indeed, she thought she was."

As usual, for Vincent, the touring was half the fun. This time, the pleasure was increased by the company of Hardwicke, Boyer, and even Moorehead. He later recalled, "We all read mysteries as we traveled. We had a tacit understanding that if the girl wasn't seduced by page fifteen or if there hadn't been a murder by page ten, the book was thrown out the window." However, although the tour was a success, Laughton's departure haunted the company; they arrived in each new city to find Laughton's name on the marquee, as the producers one after another "forgot" to change the billing. The *Seattle Post-Intelligencer* reported this deception: "Price substituted for Charles Laughton. The change, known days ago to the California director of the tour, was inexcusably hidden from the public here; even the company manager was not apprised of the change until 11 o'clock Monday night. But Price is a fine actor. He drew a tremendous round of applause for his first significant reading."

A year later, Vincent accepted the invitation of his old friend Margaret Webster to appear in her new production of *Richard III*, starring Jose Ferrer. He received second billing as the Duke of Buckingham, with Florence Reed as Queen Margaret and Maureen Stapleton as Anne. Scenic design duties were taken on by artist and *Champagne for Caesar* director Richard Whorf. Produced by the New York City Theater Company at the City Center, the limited-run production opened in early December 1953 to largely positive reviews. Webster was uniformly praised for her excellent staging and her astute understanding of the play, as was Whorf for his brooding designs. However, Ferrer was criticized for a performance that took the malevolence of Shakespeare's villain to a level approaching absurdity. Never a consistent admirer of Vincent's, Brooks Atkinson judged that, "As Buckingham, Vincent Price gives a weak performance in a style that is almost conversational." Others disagreed. Wolcott Gibbs of the *New Yorker* felt "Vincent Price as Buckingham is remarkably handsome and satisfactorily detestable." And Richard Watts Jr. of the *New York Post* noted, "Vincent Price seems to me an extraordinarily good Buckingham."

Although the play ran only through the month of December, Vincent was ecstatic to be back on Broadway and even more thrilled to play Shakespeare. As a young man, he had harbored an ambition one day to play all of the Shakespearean greats such as Hamlet, Macbeth, and eventually King Lear. And yet he was rarely asked, except for one occasion when "Eva Le Gallienne called me from out of the blue to ask me to appear in her production of *Hamlet*. I floundered around in mock modesty and managed to blurt out that I doubted I was yet ready to take the big leap and face the ultimate challenge of the role. 'No, dear boy,' she admonished. '*I* am playing Hamlet.' "

Indeed, one of the big disappointments of Vincent's career was never having played any of the great Shakespearean leads. Nonetheless, the early 1950s proved a fruitful time for the actor, who embraced every opportunity to work on the legitimate stage. There are many people who feel that Vincent Price's best work was done in the theater, a medium that allowed him to make use of his unique ability to communicate and connect with an audience. But perhaps more important, he was possessed of a persona that was almost larger than life—a quality that on film can come off as campy, even over-the-top—while the theater offered a venue grand enough to contain his presence. According to Norman Lloyd, "Vincent needed that space that he had in the legitimate theater. He needed it to project, because in the theater it is the actor who projects; in pictures the lens projects. That is to say, as an actor, you have to be giving something, but the lens does it for you. In the theater, you have to be giving with your whole being and Vincent could do that."

22

AFTER FOUR YEARS of living at 1815 Benedict Canyon, Mary and Vincent's atmospheric little adobe was overflowing with *objets* from their mutual collecting. Finally, after buying a large abstract canvas by California painter Richard Diebenkorn and realizing the only empty space was on the ceiling above their bed, Mary—to Vincent's dismay—began looking for a new home for the couple.

Aside from its inadequate size, Mary had always had one complaint about 1815— the lack of light in the canyon, where the house received sun for only about four hours a day. But she loved its traditional Spanish architecture and was eager to find another in the same style, so she began by looking in the hills above Sunset Boulevard. Mary was, by this time, the in-house costume designer for Hecht-Hill-Lancaster, assigned to such films as *Sweet Smell of Success* and *Separate Tables*, as well as working for Pat Duggan at Paramount. Now house-hunting occupied a great deal of both her free time and thought. One day in Bel Air, she spied a great wall with tiled roofs in the distance. She tried to see behind it, and when that proved easier said than done she called her realtor and announced she had found the perfect place. The next day they drove out to the estate, but when they arrived the realtor looked at Mary incredulously—what she had stumbled on was the south wall of the Bel Air Hotel. Not much later, and not far from her "perfect place," she did find their new home—a large Spanish colonial mansion on half an acre in the exclusive community of Holmby Hills, an area of rolling hills, large trees, and spacious estates between Bel Air and Beverly Hills.

Built in 1927 by an adoring father for his daughter (who hated it) on the occasion of her marriage, 580 North Beverly Glen was the quintessential Spanish mansion from a period noted for its Spanish mansions. In the early fifties, though, these houses were seriously out of fashion, and Mary was able to buy it for $50,000. From the driveway, a multi-leveled staircase led up ninety-two steps to the massive front door, which opened onto a two-story hall. To the right was a vast living room—forty-five feet long, thirty feet wide, with a beautiful twenty-two-foot-high beamed ceiling. With spacious grounds, an Olympic-sized swimming pool, and a paddle-tennis court, no one could deny it was spectacular—no one, that is, but Vincent, whose taste ran to the small and cozy. In the end, though, he reluctantly agreed to leave his little adobe and from the moment they moved in the house became Mary's project.

In the last years at 1815 Benedict Canyon, Will Lawson had left, and Mary and Vincent had found they enjoyed doing their own cooking; but 580 North Beverly Glen posed a different set of problems for the busy couple. Mary recalled, "Moving into what was subsequently referred to as the 'big house,' I blithely rose above the fact that someone was going to have to clean all nine thousand-plus square feet of it. Reality took hold and we began calling every known domestic agency and were told it would take three people to run a house that big. We interviewed people of every known age and nationality and were at our wits' end when the agent called and said he had just interviewed someone and had never seen a man as neat, clean, shiny, and sparkling. His references were vague, but the agent felt we should see him anyway. Best of all, we were told he really wanted the job. When I met Harry I asked him, 'Do you like to clean?' which he found funny. He said he liked to clean, but not to cook. He had been with us a long time, like a year, before I found out that he had never had a job in his life. He was forty-five-years old and a gambler, a pool hustler. He played a certain kind of pool and people bet on him. He had been a great star in his youth, which I can understand, because he did everything so well with his hands. And he took the job with us because he needed the money to get his teeth done. Harry became a dear friend, and there never was a harder worker. He always threw himself into the projects and would work till two A.M. saying, 'If you're gonna do something, do it.' Everybody loved Harry and he became a part of the family. He had faultless timing and we formed a great team. On top of all of that, he was neat as a pin and very handsome."

Harry Mullen soon became an important member of the household. Mary set to work transforming 580 into an architectural showpiece and a marvelous home. Barrett remembered that "The fifties were one great big sort of Y camp, with Mary as the director. It was divine. The house was the project. It was like we were building the City of Light in Cordoba. There was a lot of esprit de corps and there was a sense of family, except for the fact that everyone was always hiding the expenses from Dad." In fact, although Vincent was appreciative of Mary's work on their home, he worried perpetually about the money being spent on it. He was immensely proud of his wife's reputation as a costume designer who always brought her projects in under budget and on time, but he still couldn't stop himself from worrying about the money she spent on the various projects around the house. Although he knew she was a notorious bargain shopper—she amassed a vast quantity of beautiful Tiffany shades, never spending more than eight dollars per shade, and once made a curtain for their Moroccan-themed room by stringing together thousands of wooden toy parts to create an exotic beaded effect—Vincent continually struggled with the sense of fiscal responsibility he had learned from his father. Mary remembered, "When we first got married, he made a comment to me about being a 'good provider' and I almost burst out laughing until I realized how serious he was. It was an odd thing to say, but it was central to his being, and he certainly was one."

Vincent's complicated attitude toward money was exacerbated by his need to see Mary in a certain light—a trait that had previously surfaced with Edith in his tendency to pigeonhole her as a fellow theater lover. He respected Mary's design talent and achievements, but as the house took up more and more of her energy, he grew concerned that her spending habits might get away from her. And yet, as Mary told it, though Vincent himself was "penurious about a great many things, the last thing he was was ungenerous. For example, he hated spending money on cars, clothes, mortgages, taxes, utilities, and all the other nuts and bolts of daily living. He never thought twice, however, about spending money on pictures, things, and, above all, presents for other people. Furthermore, he invariably picked up the check in any restaurant. Presents were a way of life in our household and where the rest of us would delight in finding and saving something marvelous for a birthday or a Christmas, when Vincent found something, he couldn't wait to give it to the recipient, thereby having to go out and find something else when the actual occasion rolled around."

In the long run, Mary believed that "Vincent grew proud of the big house. No one was doing anything like what we were doing. People would come into the house and shake their heads in wonder." Jane Russell described "shelves everywhere to hold pre-Columbian art and gold leaf church artifacts from Mexico. And, of course, paintings everywhere. They were both marvelous cooks and it was a joy to visit them and see what had been done there since I had been there last." Indeed, all of their friends as well as the many visitors who came to the big house acclaimed the Price residence as one of the most beautiful and unusual homes anywhere in the world.

What made 580 so special was that it was not just a showcase—it was also very much a home. Vincent had gone out of his way to make sure of that. From the moment he laid eyes on the enormous living room he feared they would never be able to make it cozy, but after playing around with the furniture he realized that the cavernous space should be transformed into a series of small areas where one could readily sit down and have a conversation or read a book. Once he solved that problem, he knew anything was possible. Of course, it helped that the house was generally full of friends and family. In addition to Harry, who lived downstairs, Barrett came on weekends, and Vincent's niece Sara, called Sally, had followed her uncle to California and was a frequent and welcome guest. Good friends often came over and spent weekend days by the pool, and Vincent and Mary's families and out-of-town friends were always welcome to take up one of the many guest rooms.

Barrett was given his own room overlooking the swimming pool for his weekend and vacation visits, but his home life with Edith had by now become untenable. Ultimately, it was Mary who came to the rescue. By the time Barrett was thirteen they had grown close, and she began to notice how he dreaded going home to Edith. Finally, one day Mary asked him about it, and he admitted how he felt. She then told him that when he turned fourteen he could go to court and sue to come live with them. She made sure that he knew it would have to be his decision, but that if he made that decision, she and his father would support him completely. Barrett remembered this time of transition, "Mary became my champion, my friend. I loved her. I knew that she somehow wanted me." Barrett did go to court, and in the fall of 1954 came to live with his father and Mary. Away from a life surrounded by alcoholism, drug addiction, and confusion, Barrett bloomed under Mary's guidance. She encouraged him in his studies, taught him how to be more disciplined, took note of his interests, and became involved in his life. He ran track throughout high school and college, and it was Mary who came to all of his high school track meets. "I adored Mary beyond anything. She could ask me to do virtually anything and I felt I had to do it. She was enormously powerful. She got her own way and I always loved that. She's the one I think about, not Edi. Always. I think of her as the person who raised me." Mary enjoyed having her stepson living with them: He was a well-mannered and gracious teenager who easily fell into step with their lifestyle. As Mary noted, "Our friends loved him, perhaps because even in his extreme youth he really listened to what others had to say."

The "big house" was steadily filling up. In the early 1950s Hank Milam arrived. Vincent and Mary had met him at the La Jolla Playhouse, where he had worked as the prop boy. Barrett reminisced, "The first thing that I ever did alone in my life was to take a bus from Santa Monica to La Jolla to go and spend the week with Dad. It was a thing that he must have fought tooth and nail for me to do, because I was eleven or so. And while he was working, he hired Hank as my sitter. I just loved him; I idolized him. And then he came to live at the house and we were tight as ticks. He was the big brother I never had. As I got older, we went to San Diego a lot together and to Tijuana and got drunk a lot together. He taught me how to smoke. It was all really quite spectacular."

After his brief stint at the La Jolla Playhouse, Hank Milam had served in the Korean War, after which he enrolled at UCLA. He recalled, "I came back from Korea in 1953. I had gotten a Christmas card from Mary and Vincent that gave their new address somewhere near Westwood. So, I called and said I was going to be up there and asked if they could have lunch. They said yes, but asked me to come by first and see the house. At some point I said that I was going to have to look for a place to live. And they said they had what had been at one point the chauffeur's quarters. They said, 'Until you find a place, it's something you could use.' Of course I stayed nine years, until I got married. They said they liked having someone else on the property. They liked the fact that a car would be coming and going and there would be lights on. And they were generous about encouraging me to use the pool and things like that. Of course, for me it was so fortuitous and just a wonderful thing. We really had great fun."

Because Vincent was often away on location or on tour, Hank, Harry, Mary, and Barrett formed a harmonious alliance, whose chief preoccupation was to work on the house. Although the work was hard, both the result and the camaraderie were wonderfully rewarding, particularly for Barrett, who had never really had a sense of family. "Mary and Hank and Harry was family. I still have a little St. Christopher medal that Mary made for me when I went to Europe. It was a locket, except it was on a key chain and you opened it up and there was a picture of Hank and Harry and her and dad. Really terribly touching."

Each new project, many of them undertaken as "surprises" for Vincent's homecomings, was embarked on with a wonderful combination of seriousness, inventiveness, and fun. Hank noted, "When Mary wasn't working she was very quick to get involved with a project. We would go down to Mock's wrecking yard or we would go to a tile place and look through all the seconds and Mary would design something to fit in with what was available. Vincent was never one for sourcing and Mary always went to such extremes to keep him in the background and to keep anyone from knowing about him. If we went up to Santa Barbara to go to an antique store and have lunch on a weekend, she made Vincent either wait in the car or around the corner, because she was just determined the price was not going to go up."

One of everybody's favorite projects was the poolhouse tiles. The Olympic-sized pool came complete with a compact underwater viewing chamber beneath the diving board. The pool was situated a short distance from the house, and Mary set to work opening up the poolhouse so that it became another outside room, complete with its own kitchen. Next to the pool, there was a fifteen-foot sandbox above which was a paddle-tennis court. Mary explained how "Vincent always felt that the semi-circular rim of the sandbox would look well with a stand of classic columns. These turned up in one of my favorite wrecking yards and so became one of the surprises we got ready for him when he came home." Once she had the basic design of the poolhouse settled, Mary decided to decorate part of the exterior with large, brightly-patterned tiles. "One of my accumulations was an eight-foot long professional kiln. Bill Brice very generously agreed to design and execute eighteen various-sized tile panels, depicting butterflies." Bill Brice remembered, "That was just a great time. Everybody was painting tiles—Shirl painted, Vincent painted, Mary painted, we all painted."

Although Mary and Vincent had a great deal in common, there was at least one area where their temperaments were diametrically opposed. Hank observed, "There were times that Mary and Vincent did not always agree with respect to social occasions. Vincent could run into someone on the street that he hadn't seen in six years and his impulse was to say 'Let's go have a drink' or 'Stop by on your way home.' And if the doorbell rang and Harry was in the hall vacuuming, Vincent would just say, 'Don't trip over the cord.' But Mary would be standing at the top of the stair frozen at the thought. She wanted Vincent to appear in the most knowledgeable and attractive light, not for herself, but because she is so visually oriented. I think she thought she should do everything she could do to perpetuate that, to reinforce that. If he was going to open the door to somebody and say come have a drink or come for lunch, it should look just as beautiful as it could."

Vincent Price was a people person, who enjoyed talking to the man on the street just as much as to a learned professor of art history; he was remarkably unjudgmental, and was just as happy having a ham sandwich on a park bench with a total stranger as wearing a tuxedo to a formal sit-down dinner for fifty. Mary, on the other hand, was given less to spontaneity than to loyalty. She valued long-term friendships and enjoyed cultivating and building new ones. As a much shyer person than her very gregarious husband, she never understood his impulse to invite a perfect stranger to drop in. Vincent found her attitude a little rigid, but for the most part they managed to find social compromises that worked for them both. To most dinner parties or social functions, Mary and Vincent invited a core group of close friends, along with a smattering of new faces or visitors from out of town.

The couple became well known in Hollywood for their extraordinary hospitality and their extravagant dinner parties. Hank recalled, "For some of the dinner parties, we would bake ceramics in the kiln so that there would be a motif. Big-time How to Set a Table. And the food was always so wonderful. Of course, by the time Harry and Mary and Vincent and I got through lighting all those frigging candles, it looked like a religious ceremony in Sardinia. I think it always gave Vincent enormous pleasure that things were wonderful but I also think that there was a frustration sometimes because it was too regimented and produced."

Barrett agreed. "At 580 there were these enormous state occasions, huge. Everything had to be 'done.' The dining room wasn't done and so it had to be done for this party and so everything had to be glazed and thrown and tiled and potted and grouted and cemented. It seemed like there was a party a week. Mary and Vincent were, at least to my knowledge, a font of good times for everybody. Mary was not the kind of jovial person that Dad was, but everyone benefited from her extraordinary and exquisite care. They all adored her."

Another difference between Mary and Vincent, which was resolved when it became a running joke, was their divergent attitudes toward fashion. As Hank Milam put it, "You could never say that there was any vanity about Vincent in his dressing, because I can remember Vincent saying that he was going to the studio or he was going to have lunch with somebody and Mary saying, 'You cannot pull out of the driveway. I'll tie myself to the gate to prevent the car from leaving.' And he might be wearing a plaid shirt or he might pick out one of those awful Lamar Alexander flannel shirts that he happened to have left over from some time that he was going to go fishing, but he would put a silk tie on with it. It was just what was handy and available and the first thing when the closet door opened that was easy to get to."

Mary thought, "Vincent looked like an old laundry bag all the time—the more crumpled the better. But because Vincent had such a good time with his work and was so well-liked and so jolly on the set, he was very popular with everyone on the set. Out of fondness for their friend—rather than excellence of choice—the costumers decided to give him the Best Dressed Actor award. There's no need to describe the humor that this announcement engendered. On the night of the big event, Vincent came down with non-matching socks, black tuxedo trousers, and something that was very fashionable at the moment, a midnight blue jacket. All you could say about the ensemble was that the shirt was well-ironed. Happily this was caught before he left the house."

Shirley Brice recalled a particular visit to Benedict Canyon: "There was one thing about Vincent that I never got over. There was no morning or noon or night or afternoon with Vincent. Everything was just all the time. You know, some people you think of being a night person or a day person. Vincent was just every time, everything. It's like going to Las Vegas. There's no time in Las Vegas either. I remember in Benedict Canyon dropping by at 9:30 in the morning and we had seen each other the evening before and it had been quite an evening and we maybe hadn't gone to bed until two in the morning and now he was out in the garden and he had a dinner suit on. He just woke up and put on the first thing he saw."

Vincent's sartorial carelessness bordered on the rebellious. He found it funny that Hollywood pictured him as the kind of man who wore ascots and smoking jackets when in fact he usually wore an old pair of pants held up with a necktie. His color-blindness prevented him sometimes from distinguishing dark colors—blacks from navy blues from forest greens—so he often didn't match. Furthermore, he had notoriously difficult feet, so he took to wearing tennis shoes whenever possible. Somewhere along the way this became his way of proclaiming himself anti-Hollywood, anti-glamor. Of course, Mary didn't care what Vincent wore around the house, in the garden, or at the beach, but as a costume designer, she knew that her husband, a well-known actor with a reputation for playing sophisticated gentlemen, ought to look his best when left the house to appear in public. After all, it was her job.

Vincent and Mary Price became one of Hollywood's marvelous partnerships, a couple well known and widely admired around town. Their instinct for hospitality may have been their closest bond, and naturally this generous streak extended to the animal world. Mary recalled, "A friend rescued a turtle from being run over by traffic and gave it to Vincent. Word got out around Hollywood about this and every time one got saved, we got it. Soon we had a whole family of turtles on the grounds." When Mary took a shine to parakeets, Harry was enlisted to build an oblong aviary that ran between two rooms—and then to erect shades for it when they found the birds alarmed guests dining nearby. Mary even kept pigeons in a dovecote above the garage and trained them to walk around with her. A school of goldfish was rescued from a movie set and given a new home in the Price's backyard pond—which eventually led to the construction of two more gold-fish ponds. And then there were the dogs: Mary already had her grey poodle Prudence, but she'd always longed for a white one, and one day (some weeks after a visit from a friend's white poodle) Prudence presented the Prices with eleven puppies—none of them, much to Mary's dismay, white in the least. Nine survived, and Mary named them all at once: Paderewski, Pinto, Pansy, Patience, Penelope, Picayune, Percival, Pablo, and Pasquale. (To protect his feelings, Joe was rechristened PJoe.) The Prices knew they'd have to parcel out the litter among their friends, but there was one Vincent couldn't bear to part with: Pasquale, who won his heart by being edged out of the food-bowl sweepstakes by the others. The menagerie, at least for the moment, was complete.

So the Prices settled in—with PJoe, Prudence, Pasquale, the birds, the fishes, the turtles, and Hank, Harry, Barrett, Vincent, and Mary. With a large home and many mouths to feed, Vincent was counting on his RKO contract to bring him steady work, and on the good publicity from *House of Wax* to revive his star status. All signs seemed to point to good times ahead. And yet, as it happened, he was about to enter a profoundly difficult period—a time from which he would emerge thankfully whole, but quite changed.

Although 1953's *House of Wax* proved a huge box-office hit, initially it appeared to do nothing for Vincent Price's career, and in the years immediately following its release he would make only a few mediocre films. These included *Dangerous Mission* for RKO, *Casanova's Big Night* for Paramount, and *The Mad Magician* for Columbia, all in 1952, and a return to RKO for *Son of Sinbad*.

The first of this lackluster group, *Dangerous Mission*, was directed by Louis King for producer Irwin Allen, the future disaster-film king. The film was a weak thriller, with Vincent as—yes—the villain, albeit an uncharacteristically bespectacled and blue-jeaned villain; as in so many of his films, he was killed off at the end, this time by an avalanche. Filmed in 3-D, the picture fared badly both in the making and its release.

In his next film, *Casanova's Big Night*, directed by Norman Z. McLeod, Vincent was unbilled—though he took what was actually the title role—in a starry cast headed by Bob Hope and Joan Fontaine and featuring Basil Rathbone, John Carradine, Lon Chaney Jr., and Raymond Burr. Publicity pieces made much of Vincent's guest appearance as a special favor "to his good friend Hope" in this lavishly dressed period comedy, but the chance to work with Hope and Joan Fontaine must have been the only reward he found in the otherwise forgettable vehicle.

He starred next as *The Mad Magician*, a horror programmer in which he goes insane and eventually dies in a crematorium of his own invention. John Brahm directed this deeply second-rate attempt by Columbia to cash in on the success of *House of Wax*. Returning to RKO in the spring of 1953, he then appeared in a movie he always recalled with great glee as an absolute dog—*Son of Sinbad*. (He readily acknowledged that he had done more than a few real stinkers.) Along with 1940's *Green Hell*, *Son of Sinbad* topped the list of his "best" worst films. For Howard Hughes, the film had amounted to a way to get a list of old commitments off the books: Over the years the producer had awarded dozens of contracts to girls from all over the country, guaranteeing them at least one film appearance, and now he had found a way to fulfill them all in one fell swoop. The solution would be a film about the son of Sinbad (Dale Robertson), and as Vincent later wrote, the script would call for "girls, girls, girls! Instead of the forty thieves, we had the daughters of the forty thieves in a cave. Every marketplace was wriggling with girls, selling their wares, among other things. Twenty girls who had won a Midwest Hughes-inspired beauty contest at least ten years before were rooted out of their happy homes. The prize had been a part in a movie—now they were to have their unwonted chance. They were exported from the Midwest to Hollywood, installed in gated luxury in various motels, and flung onto the set embarrassed to death in the flimsiest costumes and for exposure in 3-D no less. I was asked to pose with them and got their stories firsthand; most of them couldn't wait to get back home. On meeting Kim Novak, after she had become a star, she reminded me that she was one of the band. A few others became famous, but most retired before they began."

Hughes's producers had sent Vincent the script—he would take the part of the poet Omar Khayyam—and called him in a few days later to ask his opinion. He told them it was just about the worst thing he had ever read. Apparently delighted, they said, "It *is*, isn't it? But it serves our purpose!" Under contract, Vincent couldn't refuse the assignment. He recalled, "For some reason Hughes liked me, though I never met him. He used to call me from Las Vegas—he was deaf as a post, so I had to shout—and he'd say, 'What happened on the set today?' With 250 starlets on the set, I always had a lot to tell him." Vincent himself never saw the film, but the reviewers who did seemed to enjoy it—in a manner of speaking. Ruth Waterbury of the *Los Angeles Examiner* warned, "If for one split second you take *Son of Sinbad* seriously, you'll go out of your mind. But if you follow the line of its advertising, which admonishes you to 'hold on to your turban' and regard it as a big, colorful, crazy romp, you'll really have a ball."

In the summer of 1953, Vincent's career suddenly and inexplicably appeared to stall. Shortly thereafter, film and television offers stopped altogether, and before long he began to panic. He was always anxious about getting work—as soon as he signed for a picture, he began to fear it would be his last—but this was different; this was more than the usual ebb and flow of the movie business. For the first time in his career, he faced a serious threat to his ability to continue earning his living as an actor.

From the mid-1940s, the House Committee on Un-American Activities (HUAC) had been hunting down alleged Communists across America. In 1947, ten of Hollywood's most talented writers and directors were brought up before the committee and accused of being communists. Although the film community initially seemed united in their support of the Hollywood Ten, with stars such as Humphrey Bogart, Lauren Bacall, Groucho Marx, and Frank Sinatra organizing under the banner of the Committee for the First Amendment and flying to Washington to attend the hearings, once Congress voted to cite the Ten for contempt, the picture changed. Fifty top movie executives flew to New York for two days of meetings, and though the consensus in Hollywood had been that the studios would never back the blacklist, when they emerged it was announced that the Ten would be suspended without pay and that the movie industry would no longer employ any known Communists or other subversives. For the next eight years, Hollywood was a town divided into "friendlies" and "unfriendlies," riddled with suspicion, accusation, and conspiracy. Anyone who had ever been affiliated, however harmlessly, with a left-wing organization, lived in fear that their past might be dredged up by the HUAC, which by the early 1950s had the full cooperation of the studios. Actor Eddie Albert, whose own wife, the Mexican actress Margo, was blacklisted by the studios, never forgot the poisoned atmosphere engendered by Senator McCarthy's witchhunts, when "everyone was so full of fear. Many people couldn't support their families, or worse, their lives were ruined and they had to go out and do menial jobs. Some even killed themselves."

Acting was the center of Vincent's life, and he was terrified when word filtered down that he had been named on McCarthy's list of Premature Anti-Nazi Sympathizers. (He derived some little comfort from the fact that Eleanor Roosevelt's name also appeared on the list.) For almost a year, Vincent could get no work in films or television. Friends in radio and the theater tried to help him, and Mary encouraged him to work on various writing projects. Barbara Poe recalled, "Mary got him through that terrible time when he was almost blacklisted; she saw to it that he kept busy. Mary knew he had to work. My Jim did a good thing too—he wrote a radio show for him and he fought to have him in it. There was a greylist and Vincent was liberal. Didn't matter who you were, they just were going to attack you. You needed people to get you through it. Jim was in a position of doing that because of a script. Mary did it because she was his wife and knew all these things that he could be doing. She was very industrious. It was a hard time, but he had a lot of projects going and I don't think Mary allowed him to become depressed. You could hear Mary's voice saying, 'Get on with it.' "

Vincent relied on the help of his wife and his friends. One of Mary's New York friends was a marvelous older woman named Mildred Coombs who had come out to visit the Prices many times in Los Angeles. Mary said of her that "she was happy, positive, and had a wonderful jolly disposition along with being a very fine thinker, and Vincent liked her from the moment they met." Mildred became a kind of spiritual mentor to the actor, particularly during this difficult time. Although he outwardly kept his spirits up, the rumors surrounding his name filled him with despair, particularly as he witnessed the lives of certain friends and colleagues begin to fall apart. Looking back he said, "I'll never get over finding out who was on that list. The entire world was on it, except for Mc-Carthy. If you were against the Nazis before we went to war with them, that made you a Communist. Unbelievable. And terrible. Just terrible. It hurt some of my friends very badly. A lot of people just disappeared off the face of the earth." Vincent Price had been greylisted—his name had been circulated and studios were advised not to use him, but, as yet, he had not been approached by the FBI or the HUAC.

By the end of 1953, Vincent was paralyzed by the situation; he didn't know what to do. He reviled those actors who had "worked against Communism out here—John Wayne and Adolph Menjou and Ginger Rogers and Robert Taylor and Barbara Stanwyck. An extraordinary group of people who were informing on everyone." But he knew he had to find a way to clear his name with the studios. His agent suggested bringing in a friend of hers who she thought might be able to help him—the very Republican Mrs. Mabel Walker Hildebrandt, former assistant United States Attorney General. After interviewing both Mary and Vincent, Mrs. Hildebrandt concluded that the Prices should voluntarily contact the FBI and submit to an interview in order to clear themselves, implying that she would support them. Vincent agreed and, as Mary recalled, "Two straight-arrow, buzz-cut, young FBI agents came to the house. They interviewed us, and shortly thereafter we were exonerated." According to both Mary and Vincent, this was the end of it.

After my father's death, however, a manila envelope surfaced among his papers, containing a five-page FBI document, signed and dated 6 March 1954, in which Vincent described all his political activity and refuted any charges of Communism. In the document, my father not only stated that he had never been a Communist, but also declared that he believed anyone who pleaded the Fifth Amendment was un-American. Along with this document, he carefully preserved a letter dated September 30, 1955, addressed to the head of CBS, which he had sent, along with the FBI document, in an attempt to clear himself to work for the television studio again.

When I was in high school, I became fascinated by the McCarthy era. I asked my father about it and he told me about the Premature Anti-Nazi Sympathizer list, ridiculing its very idea. He also decried those actors who had turned evidence. And that was all. From time to time over the years we talked about McCarthyism, but his response never varied from the lighthearted shrugging-off I had first encountered. Then, near his death, the name of Mrs. Hildebrandt suddenly emerged as "a nice Republican lady I knew who helped me out." But again, that was all. So I was shocked when I found the documents; shocked that he had saved them all those years; shocked that my liberal father had declared "un-American" those people I considered heroes, those who pleaded the Fifth, refusing to name names. I wanted—needed—an explanation. But when I asked my mother about the document, she, too, was genuinely surprised. "I didn't know he signed any kind of paper," she said, "but I think everyone would have done that. Vincent was always scared that he wouldn't work again." It was my "Uncle" Eddie Albert who finally put it all into perspective. When I expressed my disapproval at what I saw as my father's act of cowardice, Uncle Eddie's usually jovial face became very stern. He looked me in the eye and pointed his finger: "You have no right. You have no right to judge. You don't know what it was like."

When Vincent Price was asked to speak out publicly about the McCarthy era, he professed anger at his peers who had given names, sorrow for his friends whose lives had been destroyed, and admiration for those who had stood up to McCarthy. But he kept his own story to himself, just as he kept all of the documents. My father often warned me of the dangers of becoming too politically active, lest my name become associated with any sort of list. I can only surmise that he lived in fear of another witchhunt, just as he lived with the guilt of having betrayed his own principles.

Early in 1955 word filtered out in Hollywood that Cecil B. DeMille was returning to make an epic film. *The Ten Commandments* would be the legendary director's Technicolor reprise of his 1923 silent epic of the same name. Everyone who was anyone wanted to be a part of the production, and Vincent Price was no exception. The actor later recalled, "I think all of us, you know, Eddie Robinson, myself, Judith Anderson, we all really wanted to be in a DeMille picture. We really felt that you couldn't call yourself a star unless you had been in a DeMille picture! So we all took these sort of small, but rather arresting parts." Of course, having not worked in Hollywood for so long, Vincent was desperate to act in a film again; with his name now officially cleared by the FBI, he lobbied hard for a role and was cast as Baka, the master builder of the pharaoh's pyramids. Edward G. Robinson and Judith Anderson also got their wish, joining him in a cast that boasted Charlton Heston, Yul Brynner, Anne Baxter, Yvonne DeCarlo, Debra Paget, John Derek, Sir Cedric Hardwicke, Nina Foch, and John Carradine.

Vincent admired the veteran director enormously. "DeMille was a wonderful director to work with, unlike any other in the business. He was one hundred percent visually minded. Really, his stories were very thin, but the visual effects he pulled off were marvelous. The script was of secondary importance to him. What he was interested in was what was on the screen—the use of crowds, particularly. He was really fond of putting hundreds, even thousands, of people in a shot and then pulling it off. Spectacle! That was DeMille." Vincent learned a great deal from the experience, and he often told the story of being given direction by DeMille while shooting a particular scene. "I had a scene where I climbed up on a pyramid. I came up on this big parapet, looked over this huge cyclorama, and said to Charlton Heston and Yul Brynner, 'Yonder is the city of Sethi!' DeMille came over to me and said, 'You're not reading that line with much conviction.' And I told him, 'That's because I haven't the slightest idea what I'm talking about.' There was nothing for me to react to; a scene had been shot somewhere else that was going to be added into the picture later. So DeMille said, 'You're right! Let's go into the projection room and I'll show you.' He did. It was thirteen thousand people carrying an obelisk up the Valley of the Kings against a matte on which they had painted the whole of ancient Egypt and superimposed it on the real location. It was one of the most impressive scenes ever photographed. After seeing it, I changed my reading."

Although the film garnered mixed reviews, it became an immediate staple of popular epic cinema and is still shown on television each spring. Vincent's reviews were adequate, but several critics echoed the sentiments of Dick Williams in the *Los Angeles Mirror News,* who felt that "Villains, under DeMille's characteristic flowery approach, inevitably become unbelievable blackguards of an old and outdated school of melodrama. Edward G. Robinson, as the evil Hebrew informer Dathan, looks ludicrously like Little Caesar in a turban. Vincent Price, as the effete, whip-cracking master builder Baka is equally overdone." But these minor criticisms were quickly lost in the star treatment the film was, and has continued to be, accorded. As for Vincent, though he had invested a great deal of time and energy in trying to re-establish himself in the minds of producers, directors, and audiences as something other than a villain, he played his part with gusto. After a long drought, he was once again on screen in a major Hollywood movie.

Having broken back into the ranks, during 1955 Vincent slowly but steadily re-emerged as a working actor. His next film was directed by Fritz Lang, with a grade-A cast that included Dana Andrews, Rhonda Fleming, George Sanders, Howard Duff, John Barrymore Jr., and Ida Lupino. Produced by RKO, *While the City Sleeps* was promoted as a classic film noir thriller featuring "Ten Top Stars! Ten Peak Performances!" It proved, as the *Hollywood Reporter* noted, "A very commercial attraction . . . proven staple fare." Vincent was pleased with his role as Walter Kyne, the pampered but ambitious playboy son of a newspaper magnate determined to make his mark in his father's business. It was a compelling film that included all the "musts" of the genre: greed, betrayal, murder, blackmail, and adultery. If not up to the standard set by Lang himself, a master of noir in earlier pictures, the film is undeniably entertaining and well-directed and was counted a success on all fronts.

Vincent moved straight to Warner Bros. to take a part in *Serenade,* a film based on a 1937 novel by James M. Cain, and starring Joan Fontaine and Mario Lanza. Lanza played a grapepicker in Northern California whose voice attracts the attention of wealthy socialite Fontaine and well-known concert manager Price. Fontaine's character has a history of finding talented young men and dumping them just as their careers are taking off. The novel, the rights for which were originally purchased by the studio in 1944, had actually depicted a relationship between two men and was thus shelved for many years due to the controversy about homosexuality on film. In this watered-down version, the singing of Lanza and of opera stars such as Licia Albanese and Norman Zimmer drew strong notices. The acting, however, fared less well, with only Vincent emerging with good reviews for his delivery of what the *Hollywood Reporter* termed his "scintillatingly witty dialogue." The film's relative lack of success was outweighed by Vincent's relief at having resurrected his career when so many of his friends would never work in Hollywood again. For the remainder of his working life, he would seize upon any acting opportunity with such gratitude that he was almost always able to surmount his disappointment when the films weren't a success.

In January 1957, Vincent commenced the year reunited with Ronald Colman in the all-star lineup for Warner Bros.' *The Story of Mankind*. Irwin Allen's handling of this portentous historical-philosophical epic bordered on the ludicrous. The most startling aspect was the size of the cast assembled, not to mention the bizarre apportioning of roles: Edward Everett Horton as Sir Walter Raleigh, Virginia Mayo as Cleopatra, Harpo Marx as Sir Isaac Newton; best of all, the sultry Hedy Lamarr as Joan of Arc. Also present were Agnes Moorehead, Peter Lorre, Cesar Romero, Charles Coburn, Sir Cedric Hardwicke, John Carradine, a young Dennis Hopper, and Helmut Dantine, with one-time silent star Francis X. Bushman wheeled out to play Moses and George E. Stone as a waiter! A moral debate about the H-bomb was at the center of this adaptation of Hendrik van Loon's book, with Colman arguing, before a court assembled in heaven, for the salvation of mankind, and Price counter-arguing that the human race is inherently evil and deserves to annihilate itself. These two came off best and, for Vincent, anything that allowed him to work with Ronald Colman again was worth the trouble.

Although Vincent was once again working after his greylisting, the pace of his career had slowed noticeably. As with many actors in their late forties, Hollywood had a hard time finding a niche for him other than in a variety of character roles. Very few actors, of course, were surviving the transition to middle age. Swashbucklers such as Errol Flynn and Douglas Fairbanks Jr. seemed ridiculous as aging pirates while other leading men of yesteryear found it hard to persuade the powers-that-were that there was still an audience for their aging matinée-idol good looks. Only actors such as Jimmy Stewart or Cary Grant, whose personas were so firmly established in the minds of their audiences that they transcended age, or genre actors like John Wayne or Gary Cooper, whose age made little difference, continued to find work. But aside from a general association with villainy, Vincent had yet to find a particular image to fall back on, and his career floundered as he was forced to take whatever came along.

What came along in 1958 was the movie version of a story that had been named *Playboy*'s best story of the year in 1957—*The Fly*, a film destined to become a late-night TV staple and a cult classic. It is a wonderfully absurd story of a scientist who is mistakenly transformed into a fly-man hybrid by a scientific experiment gone awry. The rights to the story, written by science-fiction author George Langelaan, were bought by Twentieth Century-Fox, who hired James Clavell, later of *Shogun* fame, to write the screenplay.

Vincent played Francois Delambre, brother of the mutated scientist (Al Hedison) and a sympathetic character who spends much of the picture attempting to console his sister-in-law (Patricia Owens), who has been jailed for killing her husband. Herbert Marshall played the inspector who, with Vincent, discovers the other fly-man entangled in a spider's web and mercifully kills it. In the film's famous final scene the fly, complete with a miniature human head, screams "Helllp meeee!" over and over again until finally heard by Price and Marshall. While filming the scene, neither actor was able to maintain a straight face; according to Vincent, the more they tried to regain their professional composure the more ludicrous the whole thing seemed, and they dissolved into helpless giggles. Each successive take only made it worse, until both men were sitting on the ground with tears of laughter streaming down their faces. Nobody knows exactly how many takes director Kurt Neumann required to finally get it right. This low-budget feature, made for half a million dollars, went on to gross well over three million.

In 1958, Vincent also starred in the first of two films for a quirky but brilliant director named William Castle. Castle was in many ways more showman than film director, using every trick in the book to reel in his audiences. In his largely apocryphal autobiography, *Step Right Up! . . . I'm Going to Scare the Pants off America*, he reveals that his own infatuation with horror films began at age thirteen, after seeing Bela Lugosi in a stage version of *Dracula*; two years later, he joined the production as a backstage assistant. He talked his way into directing B-pictures at Columbia, eventually producing his own films. Since the advent of 3-D, the studios were eager to find new gimmicks that would lure young people away from their television sets and back into the movie theaters. Castle had scored a singular success with his debut effort, *Macabre*, which issued audience members thousand-dollar life insurance policies for attending his film. Allied Artists encouraged him to make a second; happily, he had one up his sleeve—*House on Haunted Hill*, complete with a flying-skeleton gimmick publicized as "Emergo."

Castle's meeting with his new leading man was a fortuitous one. He ran across Vincent eating a slice of pie at a coffee shop near Goldwyn Studios and proceeded to pitch him his idea: A millionaire, Frederick Loren, invites five strangers to a "haunted house party" and offers $10,000 to anyone who will stay in the house through the night— if they survive, that is, since in the hundred years of its existence seven people have been murdered in it. What ensues are a series of hauntings and spookings which reach fever pitch when Loren's wife tries to throw him into a vat of boiling acid. Vincent liked William Castle, whom he described as "one of the last great 'characters' in the movies. A witty man who loved a gimmick and knew how to make them work sometimes."

House on Haunted Hill was released in December 1958, and much was made of the Emergo setup, whereby glow-in-the-dark skeletons were rigged up in the movie theaters and run on wires out into the audience when a skeleton appeared on screen. The film scared the pants off every child in America who lined up around the block to experience Emergo, and created a new generation of horror fanatics. Filmed for $150,000, it reputedly went on to gross over $4 million, becoming a cult classic in the process and confirming Vincent Price's place in the horror firmament.

It is to the late fifties that scholars and fans of horror movies look back as the beginning of the renaissance of the "Gothic" film. During the 1930s, the studios, most famously Universal, made great profits on horror classics such as *Frankenstein, Dracula*, and *The Mummy*. The first great stars of the genre were Boris Karloff, Bela Lugosi, Basil Rathbone, and Lon Chaney Sr., but by the 1950s they were all but gone. During the late 1950s, Hammer Productions in England almost single-handedly resurrected the genre. The British studio had been making low budget "quota quickies" for the U.K., mainly shown as curtain-raisers in a double bill with Hollywood features. In 1951, a co-production deal was struck between Hammer and American producer Robert Lippert, guaranteeing the British studio American distribution for its product. Hammer company head James Carreras made a name for himself making films about whatever he thought the public wanted to see. He once said, "If people liked Strauss waltzes, we'd be in the Strauss waltz business." Accordingly, during the mid-fifties, he had jumped on the science-fiction bandwagon, achieving a healthy success with films such as *The Quatermass Xperiment*. In 1955, the deal with Lippert expired as the interest in sci-fi seemed to be waning: Audiences were turning to television and to increasingly lavish and spectacular films shot in CinemaScope and Technicolor. In 1956, Hammer made *The Curse of Frankenstein*, taking a gamble by shooting it in color. Shown to Warner executives in New York, it was immediately purchased by Jack Warner, who also bought its worldwide distribution rights—a first for a British picture since before the war. *The Curse of Frankenstein* went on to become one of the most successful British films to that point in movie history, grossing $7 million worldwide on a film shot for between $200,000 and $300,000. The critics largely deplored it. The *Hollywood Reporter* claimed to be "nauseated" and English reviewers were similarly offended, while the *Observer* called it one of "the half-dozen most repulsive films I have ever encountered." This only served to bring in the teen audience in droves.

Horror aficionado Bruce Lanier Wright noted, "Hammer's first Gothic does display a kind of verve, an exuberant glee in its own wickedness, which was quite unlike anything else in the cinema of the day. Part of the shock it delivered came simply from the film's obvious professionalism. This was no crude torpid grade Z flick, but a quite polished-looking production, with a star-quality performance from Peter Cushing . . . *The Curse of Frankenstein* is fast-moving and ruthless, with nothing whatever stately or Germanic about it. And that sumptuous color! The ruby splashes of blood! Those sleek, improbably buxom women, in their flimsy bodices! There was a fleshy, sensual quality immediately apparent in the film that quickly became a Hammer trademark!"

It is fair to say that the American revival of the Gothic genre was a natural byproduct of the political climate during the fifties. On the one hand, the United States had entered an era of unmitigated prosperity; on the other hand, the country was engaged in a Cold War of terrifying proportions which threatened annihilation at the hands of its own increasingly destructive weaponry. The first wave of Gothic horror films had largely been produced and directed by German filmmakers living through the rotting decadence of the Weimar Republic, and then fleeing the rise of Nazism to the Depression-era United States. This second wave of films was similarly a response to the apocalyptic nightmares to which modern warfare was driving the world. These dark visions of reality gave expression to the subconsciously fearful preoccupation of audiences, and the studios were quick to recognize their huge box-office potential.

It was in this climate that Vincent made a second film with William Castle in 1959. *The Tingler* featured Vincent as a mad scientist, literally out to scare his friends to death. The cult status of the movie was guaranteed by Castle's newest gimmick, "Percepto," in which electric devices were fitted to selected seats in the theaters, causing them to shimmy and buzz and causing the occupants to scream—or even faint—in shock.

One of the major benefits that Vincent derived from his work with Castle was the acquisition of a new young audience. He wrote, "The world can never grow old for me as long as there are young people, seeing it differently every second of every day, for all my days." Vincent always sought to stay abreast of what was current, popular, hip—not in that I-want-to-act-young-so-that-I-can-pretend-I'm-not-growing-old escapism that afflicts many people nearing middle age, but rather because his keen curiosity kept him young, continually interested in what was new and in what other generations thought and saw. It was a happy result of this that, by the end of his life, when many of the big stars of his own generation were all but forgotten, the name of Vincent Price was known and loved by moviegoers of all ages.

In 1958 he also appeared in *The Big Circus,* another Irwin Allen extravaganza, this time directed by Joseph Newman and top-lined by Victor Mature, Red Buttons, and Rhonda Fleming, not to mention "the World's Greatest Circus Acts." In this mystery story set against the backdrop of a three-ring circus, Vincent played the ringmaster, the red herring of the story. The plot failed to support the dark intimations of his dastardy— the ringmaster was not a bad guy at all, and, as Hedda Hopper noted after visiting the set, "No circus ever had a ringmaster like Vincent Price, whose six-feet-four in top hat, scarlet coat, white tights, and high black patent boots, literally stops the show."

Vincent's last two films of the decade continued his association with the burgeoning genres of horror, mystery, and science fiction. Although he was less than thrilled with the script, he nonetheless agreed to appear in *The Return of the Fly,* a mediocre sequel that played to America's new fascination with fear. The poster urged audiences to "Scream at the human terror created by atoms gone wild! Scream at the ghastly fly-monster as he keeps a love tryst! Scream at the desperate search for the fly with the head of a man!" In a similar vein, he joined his frequent costar Agnes Moorehead in *The Bat,* adapted from one of Broadway's top-grossing thrillers of the 1920s. Already immortalized on film in three different versions, this production attempted to modernize the material, but failed dismally. Vincent played the title role, that of a doctor who is also a murderer. *Variety* noted, "As in every other film he has made over the past two years, Vincent Price casts enough furtive glances to register as the ghoul when, indeed, he isn't." Indeed, by the end of the fifties, Vincent's firm association with audience-appealing villainy was unshakeable, although most of the films he was being offered were rather mediocre fare. It would remain to be seen whether the new decade would give him the opportunity to capitalize on his increased identification with horror, mystery, and sci-fi, or whether, as a fifty-year-old actor, he would become a victim of a slow fade into small character roles.

23

WHEN TWENTY-SIX-YEAR-OLD Vincent Price had married thirty-four-year-old Edith Barrett, his fantasy had been to recreate the big, loving family of his childhood. Now, entering the second decade of his marriage to Mary and nearing fifty, Vincent seemed at last to have fulfilled that need. Not only was Vincent and Mary's marriage strong and their home a happy one, but they were surrounded by a circle of exceptional friends. Other than the Warshaws, who had left Los Angeles when Howard accepted a position as professor of art at the University of California, Santa Barbara, most of their friends from the early years of their marriage—the Brices, the Poes, the Altmans, the Jaffes, and the Milams—continued to form the nucleus of their ever-expanding circle, which was enriched by many extraordinary people.

Interestingly, many of the couple's closest friends were not involved in the film industry. Through Vincent's ties to the Los Angeles art world, the Prices became close friends with Frances and Sidney Brody, two of Southern California's most prominent collectors and patrons of the visual arts. Charles Collingwood, Edward R. Murrow's brilliant protégé who became chief White House correspondent for CBS, and his wife, actress Louise Albritton, were another couple the Prices greatly enjoyed spending time with, while Henry and Doris Dreyfuss became among the closest of their friends. Henry Dreyfuss was one of the most famous industrial designers in America, responsible for the designs of Twentieth Century Limited, the Standard Bell telephone, the John Deere tractor, the Polaroid camera, and countless other iconic American inventions. He had married Doris Marks, a brilliant woman in her own right, who not only managed her husband's design firm, but was a noted philanthropist. Vincent had originally met Henry on the board of the Modern Institute of Art, and they found common ground in their mutual interest in pre-Columbian art. Three of Mary's best friends from her years in New York became intimate members of the Price circle: actress Martha Hodge, who married author Cleveland Amory; dancer Ruth Vollmer, who married Walter Maitland, the son of Vincent's friend and fellow art collector, Mrs. Leslie Maitland; and Hugh Wheeler, the third of the New York trio and a writer who later came to collaborate with Stephen Sondheim on *A Little Night Music* and *Sweeney Todd*.

Both Vincent and Mary set much store by their friendships. No matter how busy they were, they managed to throw parties and picnics, to sneak away to Tijuana and Ensenada, in order to spend time with the people who meant something to them. After having been somewhat remiss in his early friendships, Vincent became known in Hollywood as a man who took pride in being a good friend.

The Prices also did make many fascinating friends through their work in film and in the theater. Within their vast social circle, those that counted as real friends read like a who's who of the currently famous. Aside from Margo and Eddie Albert, the Ronald Colmans, Clifton Webb, Jane Russell, Norman Lloyd, Jane Wyatt, and Dorothy McGuire and her husband John Swope, were Mary Wickes, Joseph Cotten and his wife Patricia Medina, Edward G. Robinson, and Joan Fontaine and her sister Olivia de Havilland. Then, of course, there were Helen Hayes, Boris Karloff, Joan Crawford, Greer Garson, and Hans Conried, as well as TV stars Ozzie and Harriet Nelson and Art Linkletter, and comedians Danny Kaye, Lucille Ball, Jack Benny, and Red Skelton. Stripper Gypsy Rose Lee came into their orbit, along with Hope Lange and, from Hollywood's British contingent, Cathleen Nesbitt, Gladys Cooper, Deborah Kerr, Angela Lansbury, David Niven, and Peter Ustinov. Among the many directors to whom they were particularly close were Martin Manulis and Mary's colleagues Delbert Mann and Alexander Mackendrick, who had directed *Marty* and *Sweet Smell of Success* respectively for Hecht-Hill-Lancaster. Producer Frank McCarthy and his close friend, Grace Kelly's publicist Rupert Allen, were other Price intimates; unusual for an actor, Vincent even numbered gossip columnist Hedda Hopper among his good friends.

This last was in many ways a curious relationship. Hedda Hopper was as staunch a Republican as Vincent was a Democrat. It was said of her that her politics were somewhere to the right of Genghis Khan, yet she nonetheless adored the Prices. Of this feared and sometimes venomous columnist, Mary acknowledged, "She was a loyal and generous friend. She would have punched anyone in the nose for a friend. She was extraordinary. There was a total mutual respect and affection, despite the fact that we were on opposite ends of the political spectrum. For example, she invited us to watch the Kennedy-Nixon debate at her house with Lucius Beebe. We sat in front of her television set with a great deal of champagne and caviar. It was very funny—we all had a lot to say, and we were all saying very different things."

In her June 22, 1964 column, Hedda Hopper wrote, "Did you ever see a Clark Cortez? It's Chrysler's compact mobile home that rides almost like a Rolls, sleeps four, has shower, icebox, stove, air-conditioning, and can be parked beside the roadway. When one drove up to my house, I thought the man in the white suit had come to get me, rushed out to see, and there was Vincent Price getting out the champagne. Then we motored down to Jim Poe's home for dinner."

The Prices' Clark Cortez became a favorite of family and friends. Mary remembered, "I was as surprised as anybody when Vincent suddenly said to me at lunch, 'There's something that I've just found which I think is just wonderful. Shall we go and see it?' To my profound amazement, there was something that looked like a brown milk truck. By the end of the afternoon, Vincent had signed the papers and we were driving away in one of the first RVs ever invented. This purchase was so atypical because he hated anything and everything mechanical. I loved it instantly and so did all of our friends. It became one of the great joys of our life. We went on short trips and long trips. We never stopped going to Tijuana in it or parking on the edge of Pacific Coast Highway, eating a delicious lunch in our own private room with a view."

Hank and Marin Milam also introduced Mary and Vincent to a number of their friends, which brought a younger crowd into the house. These included director Don Taylor and his wife, actress-sculptor Hazel Court, who would costar with Vincent in two films during the 1960s, and a young man named Dennis Hopper. As Vincent remembered, "Dennis used to come to the house a lot and because he was curious about modern art, I would always invite him when somebody interesting like Tamayo would be coming over. He was very young but he was as intense as he is now as an actor. He was intense in his determination to discover everything. It was fun having him there because he represented a new generation. I was the older generation, Billy Brice was the next generation, and Dennis the next. It was very exciting."

Mary recalled that "When Dennis discovered the kiln in the garage at 580, he made a great many deathless tiles. From there, he branched out into large abstract paintings that were left flat on the driveway to dry. He was more than distressed when our Harry accidentally backed over them on the way to the market. Happily this didn't deter him from becoming the fine artist that he is. I also remember that Vincent was presenting an art direction award at the Oscars one year and it occurred to me that it would be great fun for Dennis to be part of the occasion as my escort. Little did we know how many times in the future he would be attending that same ceremony."

Although Vincent now lived his life among the famous, there were still occasions when he reverted to being the star-struck fan of his younger days. In a 1988 article for the *Yale Review*, he recalled his meeting with a screen legend. He had been rehearsing a television show with Cathleen Nesbitt and Gladys Cooper, after which he and Mary, along with the two British actresses, went to a dinner given by Bill Frye and Jim Wharton, "two producer friends who knew everybody. They collected people, and being their guest always meant being in good company . . . Several other old friends were invited, including Brian Aherne, who called almost as we arrived to say that he was working very late, had an early call next morning, and so could not come to dinner. But could his house guest come alone? Of course, Bill and Jim agreed, without asking who it was. And she arrived. I have been around famous people most of my adult life, and here I was in the company of two of them, Gladys and Cathleen. But the advent of this surprise guest shot the place down, wrapped it up, no, packaged it! Whatever fame and beauty had been present was now eclipsed, for there stood an apparition. Do I go too far? No, worshippers can't go too far. It was Garbo.

"After a lot of inane chitchat from the common folk who surrounded the legend, I was designated by room position to talk to her. I had a hard time taking my eyes off the fabulous face: the eyes, the straggly blond hair, the mouth with its tiny lip lines, and the nose—above all, the nose—a whole personality in a nose! When she laughed that almost raucous Ninotchka laugh, the lips curled as the head went back, and the jaw sharpened above the turtleneck of the sweater, worn, I suppose, to disguise her barely discernible wattles. And then I laughed, too, but at my own inadequacy and stupidity.

"No matter, I had her attention and so had to say something. But what? 'You're not divine, you're human!' Silly. 'I loved your last picture!' No, it was terrible. 'I hear you like home-baked bread.' There, yes, she had said so a dozen times in print. She was a health-food addict . . . So, I started in, and what could have been an unleavened few moments turned out to be magic—for me, at least. And she seemed to enjoy it, too. I told her of my disgust with people who give in to arthritis when all they had to do was knead some bread and stay the pains with Nature's remedy, yeast. She laughed a lot but turned serious when we discussed the perfumes of baking bread . . . I had almost exhausted the subject before dinner. Then I found, to my delight and horror, that I was seated next to her. I mean, one can bake only so many loaves of bread over cocktails and dinner! I sat there, grinning stupidly, and she started it all up again. Had I ever had herb bread toast? Had I ever! Why, that very day I'd made a loaf and planned to let it sit overnight for toast in the morning. What herbs had I used? I recited them like a rosary, starting with rosemary. Did I grow my own herbs? Of course! What kind of a baker

Successful St. Louis businessman
Vincent Leonard Price Sr., 1904.

Twenty-year-old Marguerite
Willcox Price on her
wedding day, 1894.

Vincent Leonard Price Jr.,
the Candy Kid, age three.
St. Louis, 1914.

The Price family at their summer home in Amherstburg, Ontario, 1920.
Clockwise from top left: Mort, Marguerite, Hat, Grandmother Oliver,
Lollie, Bink, Vincent Sr.

Ten-year-old Bink (center with feather in cap) in his first starring role,
as Robin Hood at the Community School, St. Louis, 1921.

Fifteen-year-old Bink cuts a
dashing figure in his beaver
coat at the house on Forsyth
Road. St. Louis, 1926.

On Bink's eighteenth birthday, at the time of his graduation
from St. Louis Country Day, 1929.

Camping it up for the camera.
San Diego, 1931.

Graduation from Yale.
Vincent, Pee Wee Lee,
and Ted Thomas.
New Haven, 1933.

The summer after graduation: Alistair Cook (en route to Hollywood) stops in
St. Louis to visit Vincent and Ted (taking picture), 1933.

The young aesthete,
London, 1934.

My father wrote of this
picture: "Gag photo for
Fiancée because she called
me Tarzan because of my
love for swimming. Had
agreed with photographer
he could use one photo for
commercial purposes thereby
saving expense. Three weeks
later found this one photo
three times life size in
Piccadilly Circus advertising
deodorant." London, 1935.

Pamela Stanley and Vincent Price in *Victoria Regina* at the Gate. London, 1935.

Helen Hayes and Vincent Price in *Victoria Regina* on Broadway, 1936.

Vincent gazes adoringly into the eyes of his lover and costar
Anna May Wong in *Turandot*. Westport Playhouse, 1937.

Vincent was always tickled by Tallulah Bankhead.
With Charles MacArthur at the Stork Club, New York, 1938.

Organizing for Spanish Civil War relief with Paul Robeson, 1938.

Barbara O'Neil.

Edith Barrett Price, Hollywood, 1939.

The happy couple visit Vincent's childhood home. St. Louis, 1938.

Hollywood's newest matinee idol. On the set of *Service de Luxe*, 1938.

Constance Bennett and Vincent Price in *Service de Luxe*, 1938.

A delighted Marguerite with her movie star son and daughter-in-law, escorted to a Hollywood party by a proud Vincent Sr., 1939.

Costarring with the extraordinary Ethel Waters in the West Coast tour of *Mambo's Daughters*, 1941.

The next Errol Flynn? Vincent goes Hollywood, 1938.

Vincent doing very little as Sir Walter Raleigh in *The Private Lives of Elizabeth and Essex*—but looking dashing in his Orry-Kelly doublet and hose. Hollywood, 1939.

Vincent as the evil Mr. Manningham with Judith Evelyn in *Angel Street* on Broadway, 1942.

"Take it all off!" Vincent, third from left, doing a striptease for a World War II benefit, with members of the Floradora Sextet, 1942.

Vincent as Inspector Dutour with Jennifer Jones in *Song of Bernadette*, 1942.

Clifton Webb, Gene Tierney, and Vincent as Shelby Carpenter in *Laura*, 1944.

Vincent, Barrett, and Edi in the Benedict Canyon adobe, 1946.

Father and son on a fishing trip, 1948.

Vincent and Deanna Durbin in *Up in Central Park*, 1947.

Designer Mary Grant preparing for the Broadway production of *Polonaise*. New York, mid–1940s.

A rare earnest moment on a Tijuana toot. Mary, Hugh Wheeler, and Vincent, 1950.

Vincent, Mary, Joe (sitting up), and the ill-fated Josephine at home in Benedict Canyon in the early 1950s.

Mary and Vincent in Palm Springs, taken by their friend Roddy McDowall, 1951.

Hank Milam, Vincent, and Barrett with the spoils of a trip to Tijuana on top of the station wagon, mid-1950s.

Vincent and Jane Russell make a handsome couple in *The Las Vegas Story*, 1952.

Vincent with Charles Buchinsky (later Bronson)
and Frank Lovejoy in *House of Wax*, 1953.

On the town with (from left) Charles Collingwood, Martha Amory, Vincent, Louise Albritton Collingwood, Cleveland Amory, Mary. The Stork Club, mid-1950s.

Under the Brodies' new Matisse. From left Francie Brody, Vincent, Sidney Brody, Jane Wyatt, Mary, and Frank McCarthy.
Los Angeles, 1953.

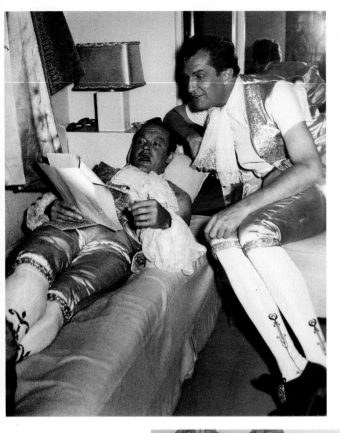

Bob Hope and Vincent learn their lines for *Casanova's Big Night*, 1953.

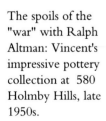

The spoils of the "war" with Ralph Altman: Vincent's impressive pottery collection at 580 Holmby Hills, late 1950s.

Extended family: Vincent with Marin and Hank Milam. Southern California, late 1950s.

Mary and Vincent in front of the totem pole, shooting Edward R. Murrow's *Person to Person*. Holmby Hills, 1958.

Four old friends: Basil Rathbone, Vincent, Peter Lorre, Boris Karloff on the set of *The Comedy of Terrors*. Los Angeles, 1963.

The hypersensitive hero in *The Tomb of Ligeia*. London, 1964.

My hip Daddy-O in *Dr. Goldfoot and the Bikini Machine*, 1965.

As the eggstraordinary Egghead on *Batman*.
With "Chief" Edward Everett Horton and Adam West. Mid-1960s.

Selecting the Vincent Price Collection for Sears, Roebuck Company on the
living room floor at 580 Holmby Hills, early 1960s.

Mary and Vincent on the *France*. New York City, mid-1960s.

Dad and me in our matching outfits at the beach house with **Mary Wickes**. Nicholas **Beach**, mid-1960s.

Dad and me in our matching bolo ties, somewhere in the Southwest, mid-1960s.

Barrett's birthday, at the poolhouse at 580 Holmby Hills, late 1960s.

Easter Sunday in Santa Barbara, 1974.

My wicked stepmother (as Coral jokingly called herself) with Tiggy and me with Maile, on a sunny southern California Christmas Eve. West Hollywood, 1975.

A dreamy Vincent and Coral in their caftan period. Los Angeles, mid-1970s.

Vincent and Coral with Julia Child at an American Food and Wine Institute benefit. Los Angeles, late 1980s.

Vincent, Coral, Roddy McDowall, and Joan Rivers. Bel Air, 1990.

A tour de force as Oscar Wilde in *Diversions and Delights*, late 1970s.

Bette Davis, Vincent, Lillian Gish, and Ann Sothern (from left) in *Whales of August*. Maine, 1987.

The urbane host of *Mystery!*
Boston, late 1980s.

Caviar to the General: Coral
as she wanted to be seen.
Los Angeles, late 1980s.

In Vincent's garden. Barrett,
Rini, and Vincent.
Los Angeles, 1993.

Old and new friends at Roddy's: (sitting from left) Vincent, Mona
Malden, Jessica Tandy, Karl Malden, Carol Kane, and Roddy
McDowall. (standing from left) Lisanne Falk, Christopher Hewitt,
and Winona Ryder. North Hollywood, 1992.

A soirée at Roddy's: (from left) Blake Edwards, Licia Albanese,
Eva Gabor, Julie Andrews, Vincent, Christopher Hewitt, Merv
Griffin, and Michael Feinstein. North Hollywood, 1991.

Vincent and Johnny Depp in *Edward Scissorhands*. Los Angeles, 1990.

Vincent and Tim Burton on the set of *Edward Scissorhands*. Los Angeles, 1990.

Father and daughter at a Vincent Price Gallery opening at
East Los Angeles College. Monterey Park, 1992.

Curtain call. Hollywood, 1990.

would I be if I didn't? So I had an enchanting evening . . . Lap dissolve, as we say in movies. I am walking down Third Avenue about two weeks after having dined with Garbo . . . At the corner, one foot in the gutter, I felt a hand on my shoulder. Looking around with that forced smile one prepares in advance for taps on the shoulder, I saw it was Garbo. 'Wasn't that a lovely dinner at Bill and Jim's?' My practiced smile was instantly erased and, in its place, that look of wonder reserved to such special encounters. 'Yes, I enjoyed myself,' I managed to say. 'I hope I didn't bore you with bread talk?' 'No, I loved it. I hope we meet again!' And she was gone, swallowed up into a crowd which had no idea what treasure it bore."

It was undeniably a glamorous, interesting, and fulfilling life the Prices led. They were the honey pot around which the bees of their large circle buzzed. But if it appeared idyllic, it was not without its shadows. Despite the many satisfactions of Vincent and Mary's home life, the scare of Vincent's greylisiting in the fifties had galvanized him into working harder than ever. Mary understood her husband's need to work. After all, she herself remained extremely busy as a costume, fashion, and architectural designer. But as his commitments increasingly took him away from home, she grew concerned about their marriage and began suggesting that he try to spend more time at home with her and with Barrett. On those rare occasions when she complained about his workaholism, Vincent would turn on her. His childhood temper, which he had so studiously learned to check, would suddenly flare. Out of control, he would scream at his wife, telling her that if she wasn't happy she should leave. These outbursts, though occasional, were not easy to forget, and surfaced whenever he felt threatened or when he had had too much to drink.

Vincent could be a mean drunk. Mary sometimes dreaded coming home after a party where her husband had had a lot to drink. Vincent always wanted to show his best face in public, so he sometimes took his fears out on his family. Barrett recalled, "Dad was a mean drunk; he would turn on me. He didn't get drunk a lot. This was not his problem at all. But he'd act cruel. He had a cruel streak, though he only turned it on me when he felt I wasn't being efficient enough. It was so strange to be hanging around this charming man. He was fun, enormously fun, but also terrifying. You just adored to be with him and yet you were scared of doing something wrong. I could always tell when he was starting to go off a little bit. He would get a little high, pre-nasty thing. Yet, at the same time, he was expansive. He wanted you to have fun, to have a good time and he would do virtually anything to make sure of it. So I adored him and I was afraid of him."

Of course, during those party days of the 1950s, everyone drank quite a bit. But, as Hank Milam noticed, "At some point, I don't know at what point, it became a problem; but I know that Mary was never very happy about Vincent's drinking. We all drank a lot. We used to do a pub crawl going to Tijuana—Mary, Vincent, Marin and I did. Sometimes we would drive out on Sunset Boulevard as far as the beach, where we would have our first drink. Then whenever there was an off-ramp with a bar we would stop and have a Bloody Mary in the Clark Cortez. Then we'd get in the car and drive another thirty or forty minutes so that by the time we got to Tijuana, we'd just be bombed." Marin Milam concurred, "My impression was that it wasn't so much that she minded his drinking, although he did drink quite a bit—we all did—but I think she was so terrified that if he drank so much in an ensemble he might do or say something that would reflect badly on him, not so much on her. I think he could be sort of nasty." Hank added, "Mary always wanted to ensure that he appeared in his best light. We all drank a lot because it was fun, but I do think that Mary was very protective of the appearance. I only saw evidences of nastiness a couple of times, but he could be nasty."

Vincent Price was always extremely concerned with what people thought of him—a trait he had learned from his mother. To the outside world, he wished never to seem anything other than content and grateful for his life, but in truth, he frequently struggled with feelings of inadequacy, failure, guilt, and terrible, terrible worry. When the stresses of his busy life mounted, he often became moody and depressed. Among friends, he liked to put on a perpetually happy face, but as a result, he often bottled up his feelings. Sooner or later, he always brought his troubles home, where he tried to sort them out in safety with his family. But in doing so he sometimes took them out on those he loved. My brother reflected, "He was so frightened. He seemed to me to be a man out of control of his life, always. Whereas I feel as though I am someone who is obsessed with keeping control of the rudder of my life, Dad always let movies take him someplace, let television take him someplace, let his wives take him someplace that he didn't want to go. He was constantly complaining that he was being forced to do things, that things that looked like opportunities were really not opportunities, and although he really tried to doctor it up and laugh it off, it used to seem to me that he never was doing what he ought to be doing. But I don't think he *knew* what he ought to be doing.

"From very early on, he took this strange approach to me. He would tell me his troubles. A lot of them. He was always confessing to me his unhappiness. Like he was worried about his work, he didn't think he was making good movies; he wanted to paint, he wasn't painting; he didn't think he was being creative enough. The older I got, the more confessional he became. I was flattered by it. It was always something with work, something with how he perceived himself as a person trying to fulfill his potential, and he always felt that his potential wasn't fulfilled. I think that was the great object lesson of my life—I did not want to feel that way about myself."

Driven by these demons, Vincent became the master of his public persona—the one he displayed to audiences, reporters, and even to friends. The genuine kindness, humility, grace, and charm could provide a buffer between himself and his guilt and fear and worry. It was more complicated, however, with family and friends. Intimacy seemed to demand an honesty of which he felt incapable. Even as he tried to love, he was never sure that he could succeed. As Barrett has said, "Throughout his life, as in most people's lives, love, or the absence of it, shaped his character, and the risks he took for love and the risks he didn't take are crucial to everything, because you learn the most from those you love." At the end of his life, my father wrote, "I have loved too few people. I say that because, in truth, I find love harder to define than life. I've loved but have never been quite sure what loving meant."

Whatever difficulties Mary and Vincent faced in their marriage, they were regarded in Hollywood as an extraordinarily compatible couple who had formed a loving and creative partnership. According to Roddy McDowall, "Mary and Vincent were an institution. They brought a partnership in elegance and creativity to Hollywood that the town had never seen." Along with the many extraordinary aspects of their public lives, they enjoyed many things at home together—cooking, gardening, entertaining, and, of course, their animals. They also had a great deal in common away from their home.

One of their favorite mutual pastimes was baseball. Vincent had long been a fan, and he passed his love of the game on to his wife. When the Dodgers moved to Los Angeles from Brooklyn in 1958, there were never two more enthusiastic supporters. Both loved watching their team on TV as well as attending games, first at the Los Angeles Coliseum and later at Chavez Ravine. But Vincent took particular pleasure in listening to the games on the radio, because they were broadcast by a man who he considered to be a great American treasure—the voice of the Dodgers, Vin Scully. He loved to listen to Scully's brilliant and witty play-by-plays and counted himself among his fans.

A trip to the ballpark was one of the great treats of life for the Prices. For Vincent, "No hot dog ever tastes as good as the ones at the ballpark. It is a question of being just the right thing at the right time and place. At that particular moment when the crack of the bat signals a hit, and the white uniforms move gracefully against the green outfield, at that very moment a hawker stumbles up your aisle and your wife taps you on the arm and asks you to buy her a hot dog. You miss the play, but you gain the world. Even at that crucial moment, there is nothing more soul-satisfying than the first succulent bite into the juicy frankfurter. Whether you slather your hot dog with mustard, relish, and onions, or eat it purist style with just a delicate dab of mustard, it is, in that brief time, the perfect food."

Traveling together continued to be a great joy to Mary and Vincent. However, because both of their schedules were usually so full, they often had to content themselves with brief local excursions, of which the highlight was exploring junk stores, antique shops, and museums. But their collection was not limited to objects of art. They loved to eat anywhere from a gourmet restaurant to a taco stand, collecting recipes wherever they went. Nurseries were also a favorite stop. The extensive gardens at 580 reflected their wide-ranging interest in horticulture, and after visiting the famous Huntington Gardens in Pasadena, the couple embarked on what they referred to as their "cactus period." They combed nurseries all over Southern California, collecting various cactus specimens until they discovered the ultimate source, Cactus Pete's. Vincent also grew cymbidium orchids, poinsettia, geraniums of all shapes and hues, and many of the local wildflower varieties.

One of the Price's favorite weekend getaways was their beach house on Malibu Road, which they bought for $25,000 in the early fifties. Whenever life permitted, however, they grabbed the opportunity to take longer trips. In the summer of 1951, Vincent took Mary on a lengthy tour of Haiti, Bermuda, the Yucatan, and Oaxaca. Mexico was one of their best-loved destinations. In 1959, Vincent wrote, "My wife, my son, and I take off for Mexico whenever we can. We have made incomplete surveys of the Toltecs, Aztecs, Mayas, and the exuberant baroque art and architecture of colonial Mexico. Of all the countries I've visited, I think Mexico still has more hidden charm than any place else and more in the open, too."

Hawaii was another favorite port of call, where visits with the famous and respected Duke Kahanamoku were a highlight of their island sojourns. During their initial visits, the couple generally stayed at the Surfrider, one of the earliest elegant and modern hotels on Waikiki. But over the years, as jet travel shortened the journey, they began to explore other islands, eventually visiting all of them. They especially loved staying at Hana, the quiet village on the rainy leeward shore of Maui, with its lush vegetation and the beautiful taro plantations.

In 1952 they took their first journey to the Southwest, visiting Mesa Verde and the spectacular national parks of southern Utah. Over the twenty-four years of their marriage,

Vincent and Mary frequently visited the Southwest, often arranging their stay around the Gallup Indian Ceremonial where they watched the tribal dancing and the Indian rodeos and collected jewelry. Long before wearing the turquoise and silver jewelry of the Navajo and Pueblo Indians became fashionable, Mary and Vincent started an impressive collection. They visited reservation trading posts where a barter system, originally conceived by white merchants who profited by it, formed the backbone of the Southwestern tribal economy. Rugs, blankets, and jewelry were traded, pawned, or bartered, and dead pawn—jewelry that the original owners no longer wished to redeem or could not redeem because they had died—became an increasingly rich source for collectors. Throughout his life, Vincent wore a heavy Navajo watch of silver and turquoise; such items became part of his unique personal aesthetic.

As their schedules became more pressing, Vincent and Mary found themselves with less time to drive, and the couple took great delight traveling on the Super Chief to the Southwest. Vincent loved to reminisce, "The greatest breakfasts either of us could ever remember having eaten were served in a railroad dining car. . . . Mornings should be bright and crisp and immaculate as the new day, holding promise of new adventures. The dining car of the Super Chief, with its gleaming silver, white napery, and the colorful Western landscape rolling past the window, is all those things. Besides, it smells deliciously of breakfast. The aroma of coffee and bacon greet you at the door, as do the white-coated waiters whose gentle solicitude is just what you need to start the day right." The couple considered little more romantic than watching the beautiful red deserts roll by their picture window while they enjoyed the incomparable Super Chief French Toast.

Generally, though, their journeys were organized around Vincent's work. When he was on location, Mary would try to join him for the last two weeks of the shoot; when he toured the country in plays, she joined him in their favorite cities. Often they were able to tag a few days of vacation on the end of a tour and visit friends and family. Occasionally, though, Mary and Vincent did manage to take a real vacation; during the mid-fifties, for instance, they visited England together for the first time. It was also the first time Mary had returned to the land of her birth. After visiting London, the couple made a tour of the stately homes of England and Scotland, ending up in the part of the country from which Mary's clan, the Grants, hailed. It was a marvelous trip, with high tea taken every afternoon in a different stately home.

In 1958, the couple planned their first trip to Greece. They were brimming with excitement as they boarded one of the first transatlantic jets. Although he was by then a seasoned traveler, it took Vincent a little while to get used to jet travel. He preferred to be able to see the movement of propellers, which reassured him that something was running out there attached to the wing. On one early jet trip, while traveling through severe weather he confessed his fear to the gentleman sitting next to him, asking, " 'What keeps these big goddamn things up in the air?' He was a nice man, whose face I never bothered to look at as I sat enthralled with a brilliant explanation he was giving me of the theories and principles of flight. When he had finished, I understood at least that, chances were, airplanes were here to stay and that nothing could be more logical than that they should fly. When we finally made Los Angeles and I introduced myself and honestly thanked him, he said, very calmly, 'Not at all, Mr. Price, I enjoyed it. My name's Rickenbacker.' "

By the time Mary and Vincent headed for Europe in the fall of 1958, he had all but got over his fear of flying, and whatever minor trepidations still remained were erased by his anticipation of seeing Greece. He had long felt an affinity for Greek culture and couldn't wait to discover the country for himself. "I don't know exactly what I expected to have happen to me when I first set foot on Greek soil, but of one thing I was fairly sure—I wouldn't be given the gift of tongues, and, indeed, I wasn't. I couldn't understand a syllable." The couple took in as much of Greece as possible—the Acropolis and the superb museums of Athens, Thebes, Delphi, and Mycenae as well as a visit to Crete. "Greece, even in the short time we were there, withheld none of its beauty. The light is unlike the light of any other land, as has been said a thousand times, and, bracing yourself against the lashing winds in the temple at Sounion, you feel a part of that tough, ancient world which gave more to the mind of man than any other era."

The Prices' travel agent had included two tickets to Istanbul in their itinerary, "with the curt advice that we'd be near it—so *see* it." Vincent was faintly interested in the prospect of seeing some of the great Turkish mosques, but Mary, who had been partially raised in Shanghai and whose forebears had created the first tea plantation in Darjeeling, India, was, as her husband put it, "carried away with the dream of Istanbul as the entrance to the East, as the bazaar of bazaars; and since I didn't have anything but a few mosques on my sightseeing menu, we played it her way. But we soon found out that there was nothing to buy in Istanbul, and that prices were extremely high and the merchandise very inferior." But all was not lost. "We decided to take the advice of Mildred Coombs, our dearest friend, and hire her private Turkish guide for our three short days in Istanbul." It was a wise decision. As Vincent wryly noted, "Mary's disappointment over the bazaars and their goods had to be assuaged, so our delightful and informative guide took us just outside one of them where they make the copper and brass 'antiques' they sell inside. Here she purchased, over my dead body (it's been dead so many times and stepped over by her, I wonder how I've survived), an enormous copper brazier, brand-new, but dated 1874. This we had to take with us on the plane to Rome, then ship it from there, as the Turkish government, for some unexplained reason, frowns on exports and imports of anything."

So with their thirty-five pound copper brazier in hand, they flew from Istanbul to Rome. Ever since Vincent had "discovered" Rome on Tour 22, it had been one of his favorite places in the world. A few summers before he had introduced Mary to the Eternal City over the course of a two-week visit, and she had found it as glorious as he did. This time they only had a few days to revisit their old haunts, among them the Piazza Navona where Mary took in an art fair featuring hundreds of Christmas nativity scenes from around Italy, and the Villa Giulia with its famous collection of Etruscan art. Mary sneaked away to buy Vincent what would become one of his most treasured Christmas presents— a beautiful piece of black Etruscan pottery. In order to hide it for the rest of the trip, she had to persuade the shopkeeper to rebreak the pot along the lines where it had previously been repaired so that it would fit undetected in her hatbox. This must have taken some convincing, but she managed it, knowing how Vincent loved to repair things. Over the years he had pieced together countless pots from various cultures, which other people had claimed were beyond repair. This one would be easy by comparison and, as a large and otherwise pristine example of the ancient pottery, a wonderful addition to their collection.

They hired a chauffeur-driven car to tour Umbria and Tuscany before continuing to Venice by train. Although the driver turned out to have absolutely no sense of direction, they made it to the glorious golden city of Orvieto, where Vincent particularly wanted to visit the great cathedral, and then to Arezzo to see the Piero della Francesca frescoes and where Mary was able to buy one of the crèches she had been coveting since the Piazza Navona. Next it was off to the small town of Borgo San Sepolcro thirty miles away to view the other great Piero. It took hours to get there as the driver had never heard of Piero della Francesca and when his clients were finally able to explain that he was a painter and to persuade him to ask someone about his great *Resurrection*, they were driven to a large statue of the artist. Finally, they arrived at the town hall where the painting was housed, only to find that it was closed. Vincent described the situation. "I have one special idiosyncrasy in a case like this: I suddenly throw myself on the mercy of the police. Even with no Italian, I got my message across, and one of the strong arms of the law was induced into reaching out for the keeper of that little city hall. After a freezing half-hour, the man arrived and we were allowed to see a painting worth waiting a lifetime to see—Man humiliated and dignity reborn!"

The next stop was Florence where they crammed a week of art into two days before taking the train to Venice. Vincent's two previous visits to Venice had been less than successful and he had no higher hopes for this one. "I suspected winter in Venice would not be a postcard, so I'd reserved a room in the Royal Danieli. The room I wanted in this old converted palace, next door to the Palace of the Doges, was on the third floor overlooking the Grand Canal. Years before, when I was a starving student, I met up with a couple of rich American girls who had this room, and the comparison between it and the one I had at the time—a back canal room near the station—gave me the ambition to move upstream the next time I came to Venice. The room was ours, and whatever misgivings we'd had about Venice in the winter were immediately dispelled. The canals seemed to rise out of their stone-lined routes and cover the entire city, and the palaces and churches dripped, poured, and gurgled on, seemingly underwater. The Venetians, bless them, being half duck by this time, apparently couldn't have minded this weather less. The gaiety of the people was infectious, and we had more fun those few wet days in Venice than anywhere on the trip."

Mary agreed that, despite the persistent rain, those few days were among the best of the entire vacation. Vincent was able to introduce his wife to some of his most revered artists—Titian, Tiepolo, Veronese, and Tintoretto. Of the latter he wrote, "I've loved Tintoretto ever since I first made his acquaintance in St. Louis with a not too great one called *The Finding of Moses*. I'd seen a lot of them since, but it is in the Scuola di San Rocco where he's completely alive. The entire two floors of this enormous building are Tintoretto from top to bottom; ceiling, walls, everything. Someday, if you want proof of how lazy you are, go see every Tintoretto in Venice, just in Venice. You'll never believe that one man could cover this much canvas with paint, let alone recreate with inexhaustible brilliance heaven and hell, the entire Bible, and the history of every saint who ever lived."

After this experience, anything would have been hard put to compete, but they hoped Madrid might. They both loved Mexico City and had longed to visit its Spanish counterpart. Sadly, it fell very short of their expectations. To begin with, their three-hour flight from Rome ended up taking eighteen by way of a broken-down engine and an emergency landing in Barcelona. After a quick tour of the Gaudi buildings in Barcelona, everything went downhill. Vincent catalogued his disappointment. "I thought Madrid an old city. It isn't. I thought it was cheap to live in. It isn't. I thought it was one of the great shopping centers of the world. It isn't. I even thought it was beautiful. It isn't. The only welcome we felt was in the Prado, and in a gallery we chanced into where there was an exciting exhibition of a young Spanish painter named Lucio Muñoz."

Vincent and Mary were immediately taken with the dark, brooding abstracts of

Muñoz and promptly bought two. Their pleasure was heightened immeasurably when they realized that the young man showing them the canvases was Muñoz himself. Through the young artist, they were able to meet, and to view the work of, other young painters who were trying to make their artistic presence felt under the grim thumb of Franco. Vincent, who had previously considered Spain "artistically dormant" since the thirties, was thrilled to see that there was a great deal going on. In the end, although as a city Madrid had been a disappointment, Vincent had discovered its true artistic life and was able to share it with others.

Vincent also took advantage of the opportunity to look at the work of some of the historically great Spanish artists. Since his purchase of two Goya etchings in his college days, he had longed to see more of the master's work, and marveled at the Prado collection which takes the viewer from the beginning to the end of Goya's career—from the hopeful, almost frivolous early scenes of Spanish life to the nightmarish darkness of the artist's last years. But the big surprise was Velázquez. "Here is absolute truth in painting. It is unsentimental, unemotional, completely mental—pure, unadulterated truth. Velázquez takes no personal liberties with his subjects. They existed, and he merely allows them to exist forever by his genius. He is credited with being the first artist to use oil as an absolute medium. A detail of Velázquez will give you more insight into the freedom of modern painting than a Jackson Pollock." Vincent always claimed that he would never have appreciated the true genius of Velázquez without seeing his great works at the Prado. It was for precisely this reason that he so loved to travel. He valued breaking through his own limitations, and believed that if one could approach everything with open eyes and an open mind, life would always return a reward.

The Prices were home in time for Christmas. Vincent later wrote, "Besides the fun and excitement of seeing so much in so little time, we left Europe with feelings of regret but with even greater feelings of joy to be coming back to America. It wasn't just to be home by Christmas, but to be home in a country that, all around, holds the greatest promise to be found on earth today." Vincent strongly believed that America was moving to the forefront of the visual arts by the late 1950s, and felt that he personally had something unique to offer in communicating an understanding and appreciation of the visual arts, and his belief in their importance to his fellow Americans. Travel had allowed the Prices to synthesize visual experiences so that they could share them with others. The objects they purchased were not only integrated into their collection, but their new world views and life experiences informed their philosophy of living. "Most of the *great* things of life involve the creative act, thinking, and hard work," he once wrote. "The need for the arts is growing every day, therefore the need for the artist. It is not easy; it never was, but then it isn't easy to be good at anything. The best demands the greatest effort. Wherever I go—and I'm sure this applies all over the world—I will find talent. It isn't just there for one to *find*—it's *there*—and anyone who wants to see it can."

24

ALTHOUGH IN HIS film career Vincent Price's name was becoming increasingly associated with villainy and horror, during the 1950s this began to be offset by his growing identity as an art expert. After the Modern Institute of Art had closed, Vincent continued to dream of establishing a world-class art museum in Los Angeles. In 1958, he became involved in the effort to move the Los Angeles County Museum of Art from its lackluster space near Exposition Park to a brand-new modern building in the more centrally located Miracle Mile area of Wilshire Boulevard. He recalled, "The County Museum had a lot of problems because it was mainly social, like most museums are. The old museum had been founded by a small group of people and the original board had no one who was out of the social swim in Los Angeles." A new board was formed which featured some of the biggest cultural movers and shakers in the city, including Charles E. Ducommon, Edward W. Carter, Sidney F. Brody, and Dr. Franklin D. Murphy. Vincent was pleased to be asked to join this powerful group and he encouraged the others to enlist the help of the motion picture industry. To that end, Tony Curtis and Merle Oberon were asked to become the co-chairs of the Motion Picture Industry Committee, and for the first time it seemed as though Hollywood was ready to join forces with the L.A. visual arts world.

At that time, Los Angeles was the third largest city in the United States, but its museum was ranked only sixteenth in the country. The board of trustees raised funds for gallery donations from some of the great moneyed families of California. Many of the largest businesses made contributions, and among the key donors were, at long last, some important names from the film industry, including the Goldwyn Foundation, Alfred Hitchcock, the Mervyn LeRoy Foundation, and Spyros P. Skouras. Vincent could only be relieved that ten years after complaining that Hollywood didn't give a damn about the visual arts, his community had finally responded with gusto. The Los Angeles County Museum flourished in its new premises, which continued to expand and grow into the early 1990s, when LACMA boasted the second largest membership in the country after New York's Metropolitan Museum.

One of Vincent's more rewarding artistic associations during this period was his work with the UCLA Arts Council. In 1953, the University of California at Los Angeles Arts Council was formed by a group of dedicated women, including Mrs. Sidney F. Brody, Mrs. Charles Ducommon, Mrs. Harold Hecht, Mrs. Leo Bing, and Mrs. Sam Jaffe. The goal of the organization was to create a world-class program for the visual arts on the West Los Angeles campus. To that end, the UCLA Art Galleries were created and, supported by Chancellor Franklin D. Murphy, the Arts Council worked to put together exhibitions from around the world. As Bill Brice described it, "It was a wonderful time, a time of unlimited ascendancy of the university. It was pre-Reagan. The university had a reputation of being a model of state education that would vie with the best of Eastern schools. In terms of budget, it seemed unlimited. It coincided with the coming of Franklin Murphy to the university. He was an enormously capable man and that was an enormously fortunate moment."

Vincent Price was asked to join the Arts Council a few years after its inception, and soon the group took on more Price friends—Barbara Poe, Bill and Shirley Brice, Rupert Allen, and Frank McCarthy. Vincent was elected president of the organization in 1958. Along with Frederick S. Wight, who had been named director of the UCLA Art Galleries, the council planned exhibitions and was involved in the appointing of key figures in the UCLA arts administration. Among the shows Vincent helped to bring to fruition were one on the history of sculpture, and another on Spanish Masters. Because the campus was situated less than five minutes away from 580, the Prices often opened their house to tours for students and to benefit the arts council. Furthermore, they made their collection available for seminars, and for at least one semester during Vincent's tenure on the board, an art history class was held every Tuesday night in the Price home.

As a member of the UCLA Arts Council, Vincent was approached about donating parts of his collection to the Westside campus, but he always had an eye out for those people and institutions that were overlooked by mainstream patrons of the arts. After speaking at East Los Angeles Junior College in 1948, Vincent had remained in close contact with art department head Judith Miller. A few years later, he and Mary attended a graduation on campus. Impressed by the multicultural composition of the student body and the academic excellence that was being achieved, Mary suggested to Vincent that they look into donating part of their collection to the school. He thought the idea a brilliant one. Having long admired Miller and her students, he warmly embraced the notion of giving these young people the opportunity to encounter original works of art first-hand.

Judith Miller was thrilled by the offer, and after obtaining the support of the college the Prices donated some ninety pieces from their collection, establishing the first "teaching art collection" at a community college in the United States—the Vincent and Mary Price Gallery. In 1957, a young professor named Tom Silliman came to work at the college and, after Miller's retirement, took over the directorship of the gallery. With Silliman at the helm, the Prices became even more involved in the gallery—not only did they donate additional pieces and solicit donations from friends and colleagues, but, most importantly, they remained actively involved with the students and the daily operation of the gallery.

Tom Silliman has described how Vincent would call him at seven in the morning to ask about various pieces in the collection, or to support his efforts on behalf of the gallery when the politics of running a community college subject to the whims of administrators, presidents, state governors, and educational boards became trying. "He talked about ideas for shows and with the constant political strife at East L.A.—jealousy and lack of funding—many, many times I would be down and out, ready to throw in the towel, and he'd give me a pep talk. He'd say, 'Go get 'em.' He was really proud of the gallery and I think that's the one thing that I draw the greatest satisfaction from, that I was able to build the gallery up in everything we did, from our exhibitions to our exhibition design to our posters, so that it was a gallery and an image that he was proud to be associated with. He was my mentor and I was almost like his other son—he made me feel that way and I loved him for it."

In the late 1990s, over forty years after coming to East Los Angeles, Silliman was still there. "What's really kept me there, of course, is the gallery, is my association with Price, and seeing the impact the gallery has, to this very day, on the kids. You can see it! You walk in there you see how they work, how they look, and virtually every one of those kids would never ever have had a chance to handle genuine, valuable works of art, firsthand, all by themselves, learn how to do it properly. These are kids off the streets of East L.A. It's wonderful! It still thrills me." Indeed, the gallery at East Los Angeles proved to be one of the great success stories of Vincent Price's life.

While striving to help make Los Angeles a world-class art center, Vincent had not neglected his own collection, which continued its considerable growth. Collecting, for him, was never about acquiring big names to display on a wall, but rather "a way of learning." As he explained, "Everybody who collects art has some adventure. There's no question about it—whether it's paying a lot of money for a picture and hanging it in exactly the right spot, or whatever it is. There's never a day goes by in my life that I haven't looked at the things I have. And that's all my life because I started when I was twelve. I don't look at everything, of course. I don't go around and count them. But there are certain things that I have that bring back the whole minute when I first saw them, the impression I had, the things that made me want them."

Vincent always remembered with joy and precision almost every detail about finding each piece in his collection. One of his favorite acquisitions occurred virtually in his own back yard. He loved to tell the story: "Many times in Los Angeles, they have tried to make a center for the arts, to get the galleries all in one place, as they used to be in New York on 57th Street. But they've never really been able to do it. Finally, somebody had the idea of having a night walk for all the galleries on La Cienega Boulevard. An Art Walk they called it. And one night a month, you'd go down and have dinner there and walk around all the different galleries, which all stayed open. It was lovely and everybody had a glorious time, but they didn't buy much art. But it seemed to have a good effect on the community in that it brought some new galleries into town because they thought the Art Walk would do something for them.

"One of these new galleries belonged to a woman named Helen Bruce, whom I had met in New York through some society ladies I knew from Yale. She supplied all these ladies with beautiful porcelains and she was really very famous for her shop on Madison Avenue. She had decided to open a little shop out here and it was filled with beautiful porcelains, which really are something that leave me rather cold. I admire them as works of art and as works of craft, but they're not something I particularly want unless I have enough for a sit-down dinner for fifty. In any case, I went in to say hello and to welcome her to the community. She remembered me, so we had a lovely talk and I looked at some of the things. And as she showed me around, on top of one cabinet I saw a tiny horseback rider in bronze. It was an Ashanti goldweight. I love Ashanti goldweights, and it tickled me to see this silly little thing sitting on top of a Louis XV vitrine with seventeenth, eighteenth, and nineteenth-century china in it. So, I said to her, 'That's hysterical. Is it a good luck piece?' And she said, 'No. It's just one of the last remnants of my late husband's collection, the son of a bitch. We lived in Paris for a long time and he loved this African stuff. He was one of a group of young painters who "discovered" African art and was very much influenced by it.' And I thought, 'Now that sounds familiar.' Of course, I was intrigued and I engaged her in conversation to find out more.

"As it turned out, she hated her husband a treat. They had had a son together, but had eventually divorced. Later he had destroyed a lot of his paintings and in the end had committed suicide, because he was a very mixed-up fellow. His name was Patrick Henry Bruce. So, of course, I said, 'Have you got anything else of his?' And she said, 'Oh, well, there might be something in here.' She rummaged through a bottom drawer of a bureau and pulled out this old, dead-tired brown manila envelope. Inside it was a ravishing drawing, really ravishing drawing, pen and ink of a bearded man. And it said 'À' Bruce. Henri Matisse.' It was from about 1906. Of course, I bought the drawing for very little money, because she really wanted to get rid of his things.

"Well, naturally, I was tickled. And I got to know more. A group of artists had all lived in a big house of studios. One of the artists was Matisse and Bruce was another, and Matisse had given him this drawing as a present. Well, I didn't know who Patrick Henry Bruce was to save my life. I'd never heard of him. So, twenty-five years pass and I never hear another thing about him, until suddenly I begin to see the name in art literature. And in 1979, the Museum of Modern Art had a retrospective. I went back and saw it—a very interesting show. He was the first American Cubist and they called him the precursor of Abstract Expressionism. Then I slowly began to see some of his earlier work, where he was kind of floundering around to make some kind of final statement. And you could understand why he felt he wasn't succeeding and maybe why he did away with himself. But the Matisse drawing was one of the great adventures in my life because it was considered to be one of the greatest of all his self-portraits."

Vincent's collection was full of treasures gleaned from such improbable places. Like his wife, Vincent had his own "sources" among which were decorators' shops. He explained, "In Santa Monica, there used to be a shop that had used furniture, pretty good used furniture, that was run by a couple of fellows who had good taste. I found a number of great things there. And then I met the director of the great collection of Chinese art in Kansas City, which is really one of the great collections in the world, who said, 'I always go into every decorators' shop because they have great taste and very little knowledge. They pick up a bowl or a pot and sell it to some lady to put a plant in or something—and it's a Ming.' He showed me some of the things in the museum that he had found in decorators' shops. So, there's never a decorators' shop I don't go in."

Though she lacked her husband's artistic education, Mary was blessed with an excellent eye, and she unearthed a few treasures to add to their collection. Chief among these was the classic late nineteenth-century Haida totem pole which graced their homes in both Benedict Canyon and in Beverly Glen. Mary was in the famous back room of the Altmans' shop when two men came by. They had seen a small slate totem pole in the gallery and inquired as to whether the Altmans would be interested in buying something similar that they had found on a piece of land they were developing. They began to discuss the details when, as Mary remembers, one of the men mentioned that it was "twenty-eight feet high. Well, Ralph could hardly contain himself but he said that he thought he might be able to free up a little time that evening to go see it. Of course, he would have gone right then. And because I was there, they had to invite me to see it. Vincent was out of town, but we later bought it from Ralph."

As Vincent told the story, "John Barrymore had died and this great piece was on his estate. He had had a yacht in which he used to take people up to British Columbia and cruise around the islands. He came to one village and there were all these totem poles *in situ*. He asked if he could buy one, but they were burial posts and mom and dad were bundled up and put in the pole, so naturally he was refused. That night he sent some sailor ashore and they cut it open and threw mom and dad in the drink, presumably, and they sawed the pole in three pieces and brought it away with them and erected it in his house up in Beverly Hills. They put a water pipe inside it and it sprayed out the top and over the pole. We had to spend quite a bit of money to have it preserved because of the water damage."

Another prominent item in their collection, which Vincent called their greatest "find," also came about through Mary. He wrote, "My wife is British-born, and she has one quality in common with another British product, the English setter, in that once she's on the scent of something, the chances of her coming back from the hunt with it are very high." An artist friend in Laguna had told the Prices about a woman there who owned a few large stone sculptures from Mexico. The couple was intrigued and pressed their friend for details, but he proved unforthcoming. "But Mary never stopped thinking about it or trying to get it out of him. One lovely day in Los Angeles she suddenly announced that we were going to Laguna and we were going to find that lady if it took us the whole week."

As Mary told the story, "We went to Laguna where we talked to a dealer who had heard about this woman. He gave us vague directions and we worked out the rest. The timing was fortuitous because the woman had been recently widowed and the five-foot Huastecan figure had been her husband's property when he had been an engineer with an oil company in Central America. The statue had been unearthed by an earthmoving machine. At the end of the job, he elected to bring it home to Laguna where it stood in a very small back yard for all those years. She had been recently widowed and her entire life she had wanted to travel to Europe. The price of the Huastecan figure was predicated on the amount she felt she would need to take her long-awaited tour. A great many dealers in Los Angeles were unhappy that we had been the ones to make this acquisition."

Like so many Californians, the Prices loved to visit the art galleries whenever they were in New York. Among their favorites was one on 57th Street that sold African art. Mary recalled, "One day our arrival coincided with the uncrating of a large African mask. The price was astronomical but neither of us could get it out of our mind. So each time we went to New York we went to visit it. One day they gave us the sad news that it had been purchased by the head of display for Neiman Marcus in Dallas. Sometime later, when we went back, our friends greeted us with the news that because the mask depicted too many nude African women, Neiman Marcus decided it would be offensive to the Dallas clientele. Therefore, they had returned it to the gallery, forfeiting their deposit. It was with great joy that our friends told us that now they thought we could afford it, which indeed we could, and it came to live at 1815 Benedict Canyon. When word trickled up to Stanley Marcus, who is himself a great collector of tribal art, he was not very pleased. Over the years, it continued to be a sore but humorous subject whenever we met." The mask is a classic Yoruba Epa mask, which African art scholar Robert Ferris Thompson later took as the subject of his Yale doctoral dissertation. Aside from its size and striking beauty, what makes the mask truly unique and special is that it is the work of Bamboya, one of the last true Yoruba sculptors, who carved the piece with a pocketknife and an adz during the first decade of the twentieth century.

Vincent and Mary always enjoyed buying the work of unknown artists. They went to the first show of a young painter who had taught at the University of New Mexico in Albuquerque and had returned to his home state of California to continue his work. An abstract painter with a penchant for deeply saturated color fields, Richard Diebenkorn would go on to become the best-known of the California Abstract Expressionists. At Diebenkorn's first show in the early 1950s, Vincent bought a large canvas from the artist's *Albuquerque* series—an abstract in rich ochres, browns, and oranges, reflecting the colors of the Southwest. Vincent wrote of this purchase, "In his early work he has a sense of space and color and pattern which seems to have intrigued our midcentury painters more than anything else. When I first saw his work, I had the wit to ask myself (and no one else), 'What is it? Why does he see like this? Why is there no identifiable form, why no virtuosity, dash, or amble in the brushstroke?' And I didn't have an answer. But I liked it—in fact, I was terribly excited by it—so I bought one and had the hysterical experience of trying to take it home in my Hillman Minx, the canvas being five feet by six feet and the Hillman very little bigger. I drove one-handed with the top down and held onto the crossbar of the stretcher with the other. A sudden gust of wind caught the canvas and took me out of the seat as the car sped along a few hundred feet with me standing straight up, my foot down on the accelerator and no hands on the wheel. But safely home with the Diebenkorn and having obliterated a wall by hanging it, we fell deeply in love with the painting, and the love has grown. I'll tell you why. The painting demands nothing from you but enjoyment of it. It doesn't say, I'm a landscape, portrait, or even an abstraction of reality—it just hangs there to be looked at like an ever-present and ever-changing sunset. My wife, when once asked the title of it by a group of visiting ladies, summed it up. She said, 'It's called *We Like It!*' " In fact, they liked it so much that, for an anniversary present, Vincent bought Mary a canvas from Diebenkorn's *Berkeley* series—this one equally large in saturated and vibrant green with touches of yellows, blues, red, and brown.

As a champion of Abstract Expressionism, Vincent also supported the artists of the New York school. He bought a small Jackson Pollock, a burnt orange canvas with Pollock's trademark black-and-white drippings. Unlike most of Pollock's canvases, however, this one was quite small—approximately eleven by fourteen inches—and Mary liked to refer to it as their postage-stamp Pollock. As a collector, in buying a controversial artist like Pollock Vincent saw himself as a liaison between mainstream America and the art world. He later noted, "I've had these wonderful experiences of talking to people about contemporary modern art when it needed explanation. Pollock said, 'Because painting has a life of its own, I let it live.' And people have come up to me saying, 'Until I heard that statement, I never realized what he meant by just swinging a paintbrush.' And I said, 'You try it someday and you'll make a mess. But *he* didn't make a mess.' "

Vincent didn't limit his collection to fine art and tribal art. He was curious about anything and everything. He believed, "Probably the most impressive 'discovery' I ever made was made secondhand, but it could not have been sent to me through more capable hands than the fabulous book dealer, Jake Zeitlin, in Los Angeles." This item, called *The Modern Spirit and Catholicism*, was one of four books written by Paul Gauguin while living in Tahiti and was a vehemently anti-church treatise. "He wrote ninety meticulous pages in longhand and bound it in a handmade cover, beautifully designed and lavished with drawings, front and back, of the birth of Christ, in which he portrayed himself as an angel. On the insides of the covers he pasted two unique woodcuts, across one of which he wrote, in exquisite print, 'Paradise Lost.' "

When Gauguin died, the book was sold to a sea captain who in turn sold it to a doctor in Honolulu. This doctor had it translated and upon reading it decided that it was so violently anti-Catholic that he locked it away in his vault for twenty years. When Zeitlin was finally able to get him to sell it, the book was in pristine condition. Vincent bought it and later donated it to the City Art Museum in St. Louis, as a memorial to his "mother's worrisome apprehension about the Pope wanting to rule the world. I knew this would tickle Mother, while it might have upset Dad—for he and I shared many a snicker over her worries about Catholicism."

Vincent took his role as a collector very seriously. He felt that "the collector has a very important role in art. There's no question about it, because not only is he the supporter of the arts, he's also a mentor of the artist." Vincent's collection was never valued at hundreds of millions of dollars, but that was never the point; instead it reflected its collector's philosophy of life and his all-encompassing passion for art. "The moment that you see a work of art, it conjures up all kinds of things: the creative act—who produced it, where it's from, what the background is, what the artist's personality is, the times in which it was created. It's just endless what you can learn from a single work of art. You can fill up the crevices of your life, the cracks of your life, the places where the mortar comes out and falls away—you can fill it up with the love of art."

25

DURING THE EARLY years of television many film actors had scorned the new medium. Vincent, however, immediately understood its potential, and participated in several early programs, including *Pantomime Quiz, Lux Video Theater, Climax*, and the very first episode of the prestigious *Playhouse 90*. By 1950, he had appeared in over two hundred television programs. Mary remembered how, in that time, "The movie studios feared the new medium and any actor who signed with a major studio was told not to work on television. But Vincent was fascinated with it and was one of the first to work on it. On *Pantomime Quiz*, a charade-like game sponsored by General Mills, they didn't pay you but instead they gave you things that no one except the Hans Conreids and the Prices took home. We had more pancake flour than anyone." As Vincent wryly told one reporter, "There's very little money in television but I have more lighters than anybody."

However fascinating Vincent found working in television, he refused to own a set. He told Darr Smith of the *Los Angeles Daily News*, "Can't stand the stuff. I have friends who were terribly excited about television when they first got their sets. Now they rarely turn them on. When television gets wise to itself and realizes that it's a writers' medium and turns television over to the writers, then we'll be getting better stuff." But according to Mary, "He wouldn't buy one because they were too expensive. I finally bought one over Vincent's dead body."

While staying out at their Malibu Road beach house, Mary had a call from the studio to tell her that her husband had been injured on the set. In a fight scene, another actor had hit Vincent over the head with what was supposed to be a break-away chair. It wasn't, and for the fourth time in his life, his nose was broken. Once again, as he had done when Ted Thomas had elbowed him, Vincent simply put his nose back in place and carried on working. As before, the nose set crooked, and by the end of the shoot it was looking worse and worse. Mary noticed that her husband seemed very down. "He would go on and on about something as if all were lost—for example, how awful he looked. It was as if he had lost his mind. The timing coincided with his unemployment by the greylisting. It was easy for me to say, but it seemed to me that if he tried to address each problem one at a time, at the end of the line it would come together. When I first suggested a nose job, he was absolutely horrified. But gradually it began to make sense and he consulted Billy Brice's sister Fran Stark, who had always been very beautiful but was now even more beautiful after her plastic surgery. As it turned out, she had done in-depth research by having lunches with women who'd had their noses done and chose the nicest noses. All of the best ones had been done by Maury Parks. Vincent had his done when he wasn't working and Maury Parks told us afterward that he had almost canceled because he was so anxious. Parks had never put back a known public face. But he did a brilliant job. A few weekends later, Vincent made his first appearance on the *$64,000 Challenge*. It turned his life around."

By 1956, when Vincent Price had been collecting art for over thirty years and had become a significant force in the Southern California art scene, an event occurred that would transform him into a nationally recognized spokesperson for the visual arts. *$64,000 Question* was based on the premise that many people who make their living in one field have an area of expertise in another. It became one of the highest-rated television programs of all time. American audiences rooted for contestants such as psychologist Dr. Joyce Brothers, whose hobby was boxing, and, most popular of all, the jockey Billy Pearson, who was an art expert.

The producers followed up this hit show with the *$64,000 Challenge*, in which new competitors were brought in to take on the already established experts. As Vincent recounted, "The problem was who had the personality to compete along with the expertise in the subject. I was approached to challenge Billy Pearson and, having fallen under his spell, had great trepidations. His knowledge of art was prodigious and his way of handling the questions charmingly theatrical. I decided to do it for two reasons. One, I saw in that kind of exposure a public pulpit for my favorite subject, art. Secondly, I thought I might have a chance, if not to out-charm Billy's audience, at least to out-act him. I would play the kindly erudite professor to his boyish good nature. Where he answered questions with simple positiveness, I would elaborate, give background to the answers. My characterization proved just the right contrast to Pearson, and we became what America loves most—friendly rivals."

Vincent was performing in a play in Miami when he was invited to appear on the game show. He was given one week's notice. He bought two comprehensive art encyclopedias and began to study. When he arrived in New York the day before filming, he went to the Metropolitan Museum, where he quizzed himself on the pictures there. With so little lead time, Vincent had to rely on his long experience of looking at art along with his tremendous memory. Initially the contest was pitted between "the tall villain" and "the little jockey," but, as the weeks wore on, Vincent persuaded the producers to allow him to assume the role of art educator and his answers were soon peppered with little tidbits about the paintings and the artists. Week after week, the two contestants dueled on, reaching increasingly higher dollar plateaus. On the final Sunday, both contestants correctly answered their $64,000 questions. Consequently, they returned a week later, tied again, and split the prize.

Mary recalled, "During the week before each show, Vincent never stopped studying. He would walk up one side of the Metropolitan stopping at each painting—Leonardo, born, studied, died—like a machine. He had a photographic memory of everything he looked at when he was reading or in museums. He would leave for New York on Friday on the red-eye and be back to work on Monday morning. I went to New York for a few tapings, but mostly he would call me after the show to tell me how it came out and then Barrett, Hank, and I would watch it happily three hours later. It was on for many, many weeks and the publicity was *huge*. People rooted for you, like they do now for basketball stars."

As a champion, Vincent was given the opportunity to choose a challenger. He suggested his good friend Edward G. Robinson. The two proved the most popular team ever. Between thirty-five and fifty million viewers tuned in each Sunday for six weeks. On the final week, Robinson was asked his four-part $64,000 question first and incorrectly answered the third part, mistaking a painting by Bellini for a Van Eyck. Vincent then had the chance to win it all. He was asked to name every artist who had worked on the Sistine Chapel. He named all nine, but left out Daniel da Volterra, who was brought in by a conservative eighteenth-century pope to paint fig leaves over all of the nudes. The next day the press went wild, some grumbling that he had lost by a fig leaf, others accusing him of taking a dive for his friend, Robinson, so that the two could split the prize—a charge Vincent strongly denied. The end result, $64,000 later, was that the name of Vincent Price had become inextricably linked to art in the public mind. The Chicago art columnist Aline Saarinen (wife of architect Eero) described Vincent as the hero of the popular show: "At once urbane and appealing, he communicated to millions an infectious enthusiasm and adventuresomeness about modern art. When he said, 'You don't need $64,000 to be a collector or to enjoy art—it doesn't cost 64 cents to go to a museum,' he took art off its pedestal and showed it to be alive and pertinent." Further, as Mary put it, "For the first time, audiences saw that there was more to Vincent than just the famous voice. They saw his true charm, that he was quick on the draw, and what a gentleman he was."

For Vincent Price and Edward G. Robinson, the *$64,000 Challenge* represented simply another, more public, chapter in their long friendship. Vincent remembered, "When I first came out here I met Eddie, and thank God I met him. Actually, I had known him slightly in New York because I used to follow him around the galleries because I knew he had money. But I had knowledge and I was interested in what he would buy—and he bought superb things. He loved to *hondle*, Eddie did. He and Fanny Brice. He and Fanny admitted that half the fun was the game of buying. And the dealers, of course, all knew. It was all over the art world. So, they jacked up the prices so Eddie and Fanny could get them back down, which, of course, they did."

Over the years, Robinson accumulated an extraordinary collection of Impressionist paintings, a few Picassos, and the famous Grant Wood *Daughters of the American Revolution*. Vincent always felt that "Of all the stories about Hollywood that you've read and know, one of the true tragedies was the dissolution of the Edward G. Robinson collection. It was really a tragedy because Eddie came from a very humble background and his education was really his collection. He had a great knowledge of what he owned. For the most part his taste was safe, although it was rather adventurous to put up that kind of money on art at that time.

"It was a beautiful collection, beautifully shown in a house that was lived in and lovely. But when he came to getting a divorce from his wife, Gladys, she wanted to hurt him, and instead of letting him give her money, she made him sell his collection and give her that money. She said, 'I don't want your damn paintings. I want your money.' So he sold the whole collection to Niarchos, the Greek shipping tycoon, for, it was rumored, three million dollars. Well in the 1990s, it would be worth three hundred million dollars, because it was an incredible collection. She just blew the money on diamond buttons for fur coats and things. And it broke Eddie's heart.

"I used to go see Eddie and I'd have long talks with him. I'd say, 'You know, Eddie, so you got took. But you're not the first person in a divorce who got took. Why don't you start collecting the young artists that are around now?' He said, 'I don't know how to look at them.' And it was really true. One day I saw him really cry because he had nothing in his house that he loved any more. It had all been so much a part of his life. Sad story, because she destroyed him, which is what she wanted to do."

Vincent always felt that Robinson was the quintessential amateur, which was, in Vincent's mind, the greatest compliment he could give. He was also a dear friend. On one New Year's Eve in the mid-fifties, the Prices were throwing one of their usual extravaganzas—a formal dinner-dance for eighteen friends. Mary told the story: "I was up in the kitchen over the stove when Vincent came in late from the studio, yelling, 'Are you still cooking? Don't you have any idea what's going on?' We went to the front door where not a hundred yards up the canyon there was a wall of flames. It was the first of the series of Bel Air fires. The police quickly came by and asked us to evacuate. Vincent parked all the cars in front of the gate, then I said, 'Everyone takes the most important thing to them and then we go to work.' Barrett took his track medals, I took the photo albums, Vincent took his toothbrush; the caviar, because it had cost so much money; and a parking ticket, because he didn't want it to burn up and then have to pay the late fee. Then people began grabbing things. I carried the huge African mask—it was very heavy—halfway down the front stairs before someone took it out of my hands. There were media at the gate and I snarled at them. There was also a huge young man who I also snarled at until he said he was a member of the UCLA football team and he had heard that the art collection was in danger. Eddie Robinson and his second wife, Jane, had driven up Sunset in their pink convertible Cadillac when he was stopped by the police. He said, 'I've never used my clout, but this is my friend and he needs my help,' and they swept in."

In her autobiography, actress Cathleen Nesbitt recalled, "A number of us were drinking in the New Year with Clifton Webb and going on to a party at the Vincent Prices'. Clifton came back from a phone call white-faced. 'The Prices' place has been cordoned off, they are under notice to be ready to evacuate within fifteen minutes if necessary. The only guest there at the moment is Eddie Robinson. They *may* come down to us.' By one of those miracles that happened that night, the fire suddenly turned east and though some of the garden was roasted, the house was intact. When I asked Mary Price afterwards, 'What did you *do* when they said it might be on you in fifteen minutes?' she laughed.

" 'We rushed about like a colony of ants.'

" 'The *pictures!*' cried Eddie, and started pulling them down from the walls.

" 'My *Columbians!*' cried Vincent, who has a famous collection of pre-Columbian art."

At 10:30, an all-clear was given and everyone arrived. Presiding serenely over the scene was the Huastecan figure, dressed for the occasion with a sash and holding a bunch of helium balloons on fifteen-foot strings. When Mildred Jaffe came in, she said, "My God, it's Pompeii."

Vincent's interest in the arts extended far beyond himself. His desire was to become a spokesman for the arts. He had always sincerely believed that art had the power to change people's lives, and his experience on the *$64,000 Challenge* only whetted his already keen appetite to promote it. His appearance on the program had made him one of the most visible champions of the visual arts in the United States, thanks to his unique ability to communicate his knowledge and passion to an audience. His value was soon recognized, and he became increasingly busy with lectures, public appearances at museums, jurying shows, and writing books and articles.

But the shine of the *$64,000 Challenge* was tarnished by a new and unpleasant obstacle that hove into view in 1959, just as Vincent had begun to settle into his new role as spokesman for the visual arts. The United States Congress launched an investigation into television game shows, which would later come to be known as the quiz show scandal. Although the main focus of the investigation was the now notorious *Twenty-One*, all similar programs came under government scrutiny. The nub of their concern was that the shows were rigged, with contestants either given the answers beforehand or coerced into deliberately missing questions.

Vincent Price was called upon to make a statement, which he did in a letter dated October 14, 1959. "At no time was I given any answers or coached for my appearances on the *$64,000 Challenge*. I was invited to be on the program because I had started my career as an art historian, and because, during my acting career, my hobby has been the study and collection of art. When I was selected to challenge Billy Pearson, I agreed because of a sincere feeling that this would be a way to put across to a large portion of the American public what I had been talking about and working for my whole life—the encouragement of visual education—and pointing out that the museums of America contain the greatest art treasures of the world." He went on to state that he had received letters from museum directors across the United States attesting to the fact that museum attendance had increased, as had the sales of art books and the study of art in colleges and universities. He also claimed that despite tying for the win on both shows, he had actually lost money by not taking other work during the quiz engagements.

But the Congressional scandal raged on, and Vincent eventually employed the law firm of Pehle, Lesser, Mann, Riemer, and Luxford to draw up a "Memorandum of Factual Information Regarding Participation of Mr. Vincent Price on the *$64,000 Challenge*." This twenty-five page document begins by stating the actor's qualifications as an art expert and then goes on to detail his participation in the show. For the first two weeks of the show, Vincent simply showed up and answered the questions. On the third Sunday, however, the document notes that "an event occurred which was extraordinary and, to him, definitely disconcerting." He was called to the office of Mert Koplin, a member of the Cowan public relations staff employed by the producers of the *$64,000 Challenge*. "Mr. Koplin, without further ado and with no explanation of what he had in mind, showed Mr. Price a series of pictures and questions and asked Mr. Price to identify and answer them. This Mr. Price proceeded to do and Mr. Koplin, without in any way indicating whether or not Mr. Price's answers were correct, or even commenting further thereon, suggested that hereafter, and as long as Mr. Price was a contestant, he would like to see Mr. Price before each show at the same time. Mr. Price at the time did not know that these pictures and questions were to be used that night, but in fact they were the exact pictures and questions which were used."

The document records Vincent's concern about this routine. Because Koplin did not tell him whether or not the answers were right or wrong, Vincent "rationalized Mr. Koplin's conduct as follows: (i) permitting Mr. Price to see the pictures and questions in advance did permit Mr. Price to mull over in the hour or two before show time the amplifications he would make about each in his answer and not keep him under the intense pressure of having to identify the picture and add his educational remarks on the spur of the moment; (ii) Mr. Koplin was not in any way assisting him with the answers, which Mr. Price already knew, and was in no way indicating whether or not Mr. Price's answer was correct, and, most importantly; (iii) Mr. Price was satisfied in his own mind that if he did not know the answer to a question at the time he saw Mr. Koplin, it would by then be too late for him to ascertain the answer in the short remaining interval before he had to appear for the program. Therefore, Mr. Price, as an experienced actor, concluded that what Mr. Koplin actually was doing was giving him more time in which to give a more entertaining and informative answer without in fact affecting the basic integrity of the contest."

There were, however, a few notable exceptions to this peculiar routine. During the preparations for the $8,000 round, Vincent correctly answered all of the questions until he was called upon to identify approximately eight signatures or artist's marks. As the document states, "On one of these he was sorely perplexed. He finally floundered and gave the name of one of a German school of artists who made a practice of employing such marks. Mr. Koplin laconically stated words to the effect 'try the Italian school.' Mr. Price immediately recalled the mark as that of Michelangelo. Mr. Koplin, as usual, neither confirmed nor denied the correctness of this answer but it was unnecessary in any event since Mr. Price at once knew of his own knowledge that his second answer was correct. In this connection, Mr. Price states that if he had not known the answer to the question at that time, it would have been useless to try to check it between then and show time since so far as he knows there is only one reference work (which he did not have) which provides the key to art identification by such marks alone."

The document then discusses Vincent's reluctance to appear on the second round of the show, but maintains that as the champion and as a spokesman for art in America, he felt he could not refuse. In the Price v. Robinson match, the same routine again transpired with one exception—during his preparation, Vincent reversed artist and subject of two paintings and Koplin told him he had it backward. However, when they came to the final night of the show, something disturbing occurred. As had happened in the first show with Pearson, Vincent and Eddie had both correctly answered their $64,000 question, thus necessitating a run-off the following Sunday. During that week, Vincent had racked his brain as to what questions he might be asked. He had long been convinced that the Sistine Chapel would be a perfect topic and since it had not really been covered, he made sure to study it in detail. He was right—one of the questions dealt with the Sistine Chapel—and the document describes the events that followed: "Here Mr. Price's memory is somewhat confused as to one significant detail. He knows that at that meeting with Mr. Koplin he definitely answered correctly every part of the question except the last portion which, in effect, inquired as to who besides Michelangelo worked on *The Last Judgment* in the Chapel. There were, of course, a number of other artists who had worked *in* the Chapel but not *on* that mural. The answer was Daniel da Volterra who was ordered to put fig leaves over the private parts of some of the nude figures. What Mr. Price cannot now be certain of is whether he answered that question without help or whether Mr. Koplin had to assist him . . . Be that as it may, the most interesting part of this incident is not whether or not Mr. Price did know the answer to this precise part of the question. It is what immediately followed. Mr. Koplin turned to Price and said words to this effect: 'What if Eddie should miss this question? If he does, it is entirely up to you whether you win tonight or you tie.' This definitely came as a shock to Mr. Price."

Vincent's dilemma as he went to call Mary is then described. "It was a difficult question. The money did not mean too much to him in view of his high tax bracket. He was satisfied in his own mind, however, that he knew as much or more about art than Eddie Robinson, especially in the field of the Renaissance; on the other hand, something about it made him sorry to see Mr. Robinson lose. His wife counseled him that if he knew the answer to go ahead and win. Still he was deeply troubled. It did not seem quite right to him, under all the circumstances, to take all the money but, more importantly, to make Eddie lose. Finally, and only after he was in the booth, he decided to miss the question and this he decided after Mr. Robinson had missed not one but two parts thereof. They thereupon divided the money equally." As the document notes, Vincent used his winnings to buy a work of art for UCLA.

When the scandal broke, Vincent was quoted as saying that he felt Congress was making a terrible mistake in digging into quiz show scandals; he believed they were only "programs that were imparting knowledge, regardless of how they were phonied up." However, when it was intimated that he might be called up before a Congressional committee to testify, he was torn with doubt: Had he done something wrong by appearing on the show? In his mind, he had consistently tried to make ethical decisions. He treated the challenge seriously and studied hard each week. Furthermore, he had used his appearance on the show not for personal gain but rather to boost public awareness of the fine arts. Although he had had to work within the parameters of the show, he felt that he had always been honest and consistent. Viewed at a distance of more than forty years, certainly both this attitude and the legal document may seem disingenuous, but it is finally what my father came to believe.

In the fall of 1959, Vincent undertook a country-wide lecture tour, enduring the scrutiny of the local press and fearing the suspicion of the public. He wrote his wife, "I feel like Mata Hari—I've taped off my name on the Valpack and I know at long last why Garbo wore black glasses." More than ever he counted on his close friends and family. Once again, he relied on the advice of Mildred Coombs, whom he loved and whose guidance he profoundly respected. A very spiritual lady, she encouraged him to dig deeper within himself and to find strength. When times were particularly difficult, he often called her in New York or wrote or called Mary and Barrett. Mary observed how her husband stood up to the scrutiny of the press. She wrote him, "I have never been any happier or prouder to be part of your life than I have been since this last period of trial began. You have been more of a man over this whole ugly mess than about anything we have faced together. There has been nothing petty or illogical or resentful in your approach and there has been, consistently, gratitude, alertness, humility, and singleness of purpose. You have never been as impressive to me."

Fortunately, although the press raked mud, Vincent's friends remained staunchly behind him. In November 1959, Ralph Altman wrote to him, "It might please you to know that people here discuss the affair intensely and widely—the people in the shop, at UCLA, etc. I didn't hear *one* negative attitude expressed against you, only expressions of the conviction and the wish that you'll ride the storm out. People feel apparently that you did not betray—because one is aware that you really know something about art, and because you are an actor and not a professor."

Ultimately, of course, Vincent came out of the scandal completely clean and even profited from the heightened recognition it brought him. During the next decade, his name would be linked to the visual arts in a variety of interesting and exciting new ways, but perhaps even more than the public rewards, he reaped a few quieter ones. Throughout the tour he had received letters of support and encouragement from Barrett and, mostly, from Mary. The love that he felt from family, friends, and even from the public, gave him a confidence that he had not had before and the necessity for self-examination brought him new strength.

*   *   *

After his appearance on the *$64,000 Challenge,* Vincent conceived the idea of writing a book about his life in art. The premise was to chronicle his life as "a visual autobiography." Doubleday bought the proposal and Vincent settled down to write it, an undertaking that began a lifelong habit of jotting down his thoughts. Mary recalled, "That was one of the best periods of his life. He discovered the joy writing gave him. It was one of the few times I ever saw him calm and satisfied with what he was doing and not worried about work. He was happy at the end of the day and eager to start the next. Writing that book was one of the joys of his life."

In *I Like What I Know,* Vincent used the events of his life to discuss his evolution as a devotee of the visual arts, thus illustrating the paramount importance of art to him personally and in the world he inhabited. He wrote, "I've cherished my eyes, and I've seen, through my own and through the eyes of others. I still have much, much seeing to do, and one thing I know for sure, if I can continue to make my judgments on art out of my knowledge of it, and not just my preferences in it, I'll always have the pleasure of being alive in the most living experience . . . art . . . I know what I like—I like art—and I like what I know."

The book detailed many of Vincent's most significant contributions to, and most exciting moments in, the arts. But mostly, with his easy style and his ability to poke fun at himself, he sought to make art accessible, to make it fun. One of the stories he told against himself was that of his adventure with the Women Painters of the West. In the mid-1940s, when he was beginning to speak out in public about the importance of the visual arts, he was quoted as saying, "Art is essentially a man's medium. Women sometimes do excel, but . . ." This chauvinist remark incurred the wrath of a group called Women Painters of the West, who challenged the actor to a debate, held on Valentine's Day, 1946. As he told the story in *I Like What I Know,* "I walked into the luncheon a few minutes late . . . The program chairman led me to my seat, banged on a glass, and said, 'Well, girls, here he is.' No applause, no cessation of folding the peas into the creamed chicken. I sat down next to the president. I had always thought that one of the reasons women weren't particularly good painters was their delicate femininity, but Madame President looked as though she could have whipped off the Sistine Chapel in two days. She had vigor, and she looked at me as though she wished I had posed for St. Bartholomew—after his martyrdom! He was flayed alive as they intended to flay me. Luncheon over, almost without a word I was led to the auditorium, sat on the stage, and introduced thusly: 'This is Vincent Price, who says ladies can't paint. And now, Mr. Price, defend yourself!'

"I started out bravely with the assertion that women, being able to create physically, did not have the need to express themselves artistically—that they were the real creative force. Besides which, they were the most practical of God's creatures and ran the world in which men could dream and, dreaming, could create the beauty they could not give birth to, except mentally. I guess this left-handed compliment hit those ladies with a little less force than a good left hook, for after I finished my 'defense,' the storm broke loose, and I've never spent a more fascinating, stimulating, or quick-on-my-feet hour and a half dodging those dogmatic dames . . . It was a heated argument throughout, but one with great fun in it, for they knew they were using the weapons of wish-fulfillment against my defense of historical facts. They also knew that the final emancipation of women was imminent and that when women did enter the world of painting, without the tinkling shackles of femininity, they would really be on equal footing with men. And somehow I felt it would happen soon, which, indeed, it seems to have done. Women today are really painting—like men!"

Newspaper accounts of the debate, however, tell a slightly less rosy story: Vincent began to defend his claim by taking the tack that men can paint women better because they admire women so much and therefore can do a better job. He compared the paintings of horses by nineteenth-century French painter, Rosa Bonheur, to the seventeenth-century Spaniard, Diego Velázquez, noting, "You can pat the Bonheur horses in just the places where they should be patted, but it was Velázquez who really painted the spirit of horses." He did, however, note that women were winning new freedoms constantly and that he believed the leading theatrical artists were women. That said, he also stated that he believed that art, painting, sculpture are the only things that the human race leaves behind. It is our greatest achievement. The theater is a "nincompoop art" compared with painting and sculpture. After citing a few other women artists who clearly were not as talented as their male counterparts—Tintoretto's daughter never equaled the status of her father, etc.—he theorized, "Perhaps it is frustration on the part of men—they can't produce children so they must show their superiority by producing great art. Women, to me, have so much more to give than just as artists that it is difficult for them to paint with the abandon of Rembrandt or El Greco."

The Women Painters countered well, stating that "Women must be so much better than men to receive recognition." They discussed the economic inequities that existed between the sexes and even asked Vincent how he could know that some of the cave paintings weren't by women. They concluded by quoting Cicero, who said, "We can't allow women to be our equals—they immediately become our superiors." The newspapers seemed to feel that the women had won and indeed, Vincent would later say that he should have "shut my mouth." Late in his life, he came to understand, for most of the history of art, "The truth was that only the men had been able to dream."

Toward the end of *I Like What I Know*, he refers to an event in which he took a measure of pride. In November 1958, Gordon Washburn, director of Pittsburgh's Carnegie Institute, invited the actor to sit on the jury for the Pittsburgh International Exhibition, then the largest exhibition of contemporary art in the world. His fellow jurors were made up of a remarkable sampling of the art world, including artist Marcel Duchamp; critic Leonello Venturi; director of the Guggenheim, James Johnson Sweeney; artist Raoul Ubac; and sculptor Mary Callery.

Although he only devotes a page to his experience on the jury, in later life he would refer to it as "One of the high points of my life. I was chosen because of the *$64,000 Challenge*. It was terribly exciting because the Carnegie was a huge building and so each of us had a gentleman who pushed us around in a wheelchair. There were so many paintings and it was not a show where you chose the painter. You chose the work. Each artist submitted one painting and you made your selection based on that piece alone. We awarded the first prize to Antonio Tapies, a Barcelona artist who had never been shown in this country before. But it was fascinating to hear Marcel Duchamp argue the case for Magritte although the Magritte there that had been chosen by Gordon Washburn was not necessarily the best Magritte. It took us five days, but it was such fun to be on the jury, to be with those people, really incredible people. It was a marvelous experience. I loved it. While we were there, we were all asked to a party at a country club. The Heinz pickle people had taken us out to dinner and afterward we were all sitting in the lounge having a drink when we were told that someone wanted to meet us. And it was Jonas

Salk, who had just recently discovered a cure for polio. Amazing. I was terribly impressed with that. We all were."

Written in a style that combined the vernacular with the intellectual, *I Like What I Know* was very well received. In an open letter to the *New York Times Book Review*, Aline Saarinen wrote, " 'Why don't you write him a fan letter?' Eero kept asking me in exasperation as I kept telling him what a *wonderful* book it was. It is thoroughly unorthodox to tell an author whose book you are reviewing what you think about it, but I cannot resist. Bravo. I found you more challenging and fascinating than ever—a complete paradox, which is perhaps the definition of the twentieth-century man—an egghead with a huckster's vernacular, a man with both knowledge and love of art, and, God bless you, a man of courage and intensity and integrity."

Another happy result of the *$64,000 Challenge* was an invitation to appear on Edward R. Murrow's popular television program *Person to Person*. Because of Vincent's extremely high television popularity rating, Charles Collingwood had suggested to Murrow that he put the Prices on his show. Mary and Vincent were overjoyed at the idea of appearing on the prestigious program, but only after the initial elation wore off did the Prices realize what they'd committed themselves to. One of the show's gimmicks was that it linked Murrow's studio with a live broadcast from the guest's house, so first of all Mary had to make sure that the house looked its best. For a month, Hank, Harry, Mary, and Vincent finished up every project, cleaned every last inch of 580's nine thousand square feet, shone all the copper pots and molds, landscaped the grounds, and groomed the animals. But that merely kept Mary's mind off her real terror: "For me, the thought of appearing on television was truly alarming, let alone on live television. To make it easier for me, they gave us permission to write out a sort of script for me to follow so that I wouldn't have to answer Mr. Murrow's questions impromptu. I practiced it with everyone, day and night, until everyone, including Vincent, got in such an uproar, that when it came time to film, I knew my lines perfectly. But he was so concerned about me that he almost forgot his."

The Prices' appearance on *Person to Person* was filmed on one of the hottest days of the fall of 1958. As the mercury soared to 104 degrees, the crew came in to ready the house for the live shoot. Their first task was unshining all of the copper in the kitchen so that it wouldn't reflect the powerful lights used for filming. The shoot took all day and into the night, with Murrow asking them questions on a live feed from New York. The Prices were shown in various rooms around the house as well as outdoors on the patio by the totem pole. Setting up that shot, the crew worked next to the newest goldfish pond—a raised brick enclosure that featured flame jets that could be lit up at night. In the unbelievable heat, the crew watched in horror as, one by one, all the fan-tailed goldfish went belly up. No one could bear to tell Mary. Aside from the goldfish, though, the day was a success. The program went smoothly and both Mary and Vincent seemed wonderfully calm and at ease, their status as one of Hollywood's most elegant and interesting couples forever captured on film.

My father once remarked, "There's a saying, Ask a busy man to do something and he's the one to do it. I've just never felt that there were enough hours in the day, and I don't understand laziness. I think that if you're going to *have* a life, you might as well *use* it, and I have accepted challenges. I haven't done everything always the way I hoped it would be; I've accepted some things that I don't think were as good as they should have been, but for the most part I've kept busy and I've produced quite an amount of pretty good work. Some of it's been crappy, but at least I've kept working. I've accepted the challenge of lecturing because when somebody asks you to say something, by God, you've got to think about it!"

Along with all the other activities which filled Vincent's busy schedule, each year he spent the months of January and February on a lecture tour of colleges, universities, and town halls. He generally made sixty stops in sixty-five days during the worst travel months of the year, but felt, "A lecture tour is a way of revitalizing myself. I want to see what's going on in the world of art outside of New York and California." Since his early Broadway days, the actor had been asked to speak to various groups. He recalled, "I always loved talking to people. I started when I was in *Victoria Regina*. I went and talked about the theater to women's clubs, and then they came to see the play. It was a way of selling tickets. I'm good at speaking, good on my feet, as they say. After I got out to Hollywood and found that the original movie contracts were only for forty weeks, I started doing it professionally. I found out that not only did it stimulate me to have contact with students and with lots of different people—professors and academics around the country—but it also took up my time and gave me an added income, which I needed desperately. I really adored doing it. I never felt it was a waste of time."

W. Colston Leigh, a well-known and perspicacious lecture manager, persuaded the actor that he would be a natural on the national lecture circuit, and during the late 1950s he became the nation's second-most requested speaker (after Eleanor Roosevelt). Even during the 1960s, as unrest and protest hit American universities, Vincent remained extremely popular on campuses and in town halls around the country. Audiences loved him. From society ladies to university students, he struck a chord with everyone.

Vincent culled his early lectures from impromptu art talks such as the commencement addresses he had given at East Los Angeles College. In all of his lectures, he tried to combine his interest in the visual arts with his skill as an actor and a public speaker. In a lecture he called "Three American Voices," he discussed the creative contributions of three very different Americans—poet Walt Whitman, painter James McNeill Whistler, and playwright Tennessee Williams. Vincent had long been a Whitman aficionado—"I Sing the Body Electric" was his favorite poem—and he loved to lend his voice to the reading of his poetry. In addition to drama and poetry, he always injected humor into the evening. He recounted Whistler's long-standing feud with the most famous wit of the nineteenth century, Oscar Wilde: "Always in conflict, Whistler cultivated the gentle art of making enemies along with his onetime friend, Oscar Wilde, the most quoted man in the world. Whistler had a mind like a dagger and one of his favorite backs to plunge that dagger into was Oscar Wilde's. Wilde once heard Whistler make a witticism and, turning to him, said, 'Oh Jimmy, I wish I'd said that.' 'Don't worry Oscar,' Whistler replied, 'you will.' " But Whistler also became Vincent's platform from which to launch into his primary lecture topic—art. From Whistler, he would move on to his fellow St. Louisan, Tennessee Williams, first discussing the effects of success on creativity and then reading from his own favorite of Williams' one-act plays, *The Last of My Solid Gold Watches*.

Among his other popular lectures were "Paradise Lost: Letters from Paul Gauguin in Tahiti" and "Dear Theo," a reading of Vincent Van Gogh's letters to his art dealer brother. In both of these lectures, Vincent was able to expound upon his passion for the arts and his belief in their fundamental importance to society. "Dear Theo" began as a benefit for the UCLA Arts Council and became over time one of his best pieces. As he later recalled, "It made a wonderful evening of real drama. *Time* magazine, who reviewed it when I did it in New York as a benefit for the Archives of American Art, called it 'One of the great spiritual messages of our time.' Which it is. Van Gogh was as good a writer as he was a painter. Extraordinary man." One of Vincent's favorite written passages came from Van Gogh, who wrote his brother, "If one has more ambition and love of money than love, in my opinion there is something wrong with that man. Ambition and greed are partners within us that are very hostile to life. He who loves lives, he who lives works, he who works has bread."

In addition to his prepared lectures, Vincent often gave impromptu talks on art, particularly on the modern artists such as Jackson Pollock, Jasper Johns, Robert Rauschenberg, and Andy Warhol, who seemed little understood by audiences anywhere outside New York City in the early sixties. Although he took his role as a spokesman for the arts very seriously, sometimes he found the provincial attitudes of certain members of his audiences frustrating. He once remarked, "Some people say to me after I have given a lecture that I have made some very interesting points on contemporary art but that they will take the good old days. If there is one thing I'd love to give them, it's the good old days. They would die in a minute." Nonetheless, for the most part, he approached his audiences with respect. "For a long time, art was considered too difficult and elitist. Museums and galleries put a kibosh on the way we respond to art. It's such a pussyfoot approach, telling people, 'Don't scream and yell in front of a painting. Don't show your feelings.' In all my lectures I try to free people from that kind of intimidation so that everyone can enjoy art."

In addition to his art lectures, Vincent was frequently asked to perform with symphony orchestras all over the United States, among them those of Baltimore, St. Louis, Denver, Houston, Los Angeles, Philadelphia, and Seattle. For many years, he read poems by Poe, Wilde, and e. e. cummings, as well as narratives set to music. Then Leonard Slatkin set *The Raven* to music for Vincent, and this became one of his most-requested performance pieces. One reviewer wrote, "Price's voice is a treat to the ear. His delivery is conversational, his diction is impeccable, and his flair for drama is strong." Vincent later created another performance piece, which he also recorded, called *America the Beautiful*, which encapsulated a history of America through its verse.

Vincent loved the lecture tours. They gave him the opportunity to talk to people one on one, to see what was happening in cities, small towns, and universities around the country and, in essence, to pay his audiences back for his success. In 1973, he received a letter from David Niven, who was living in France. "This is an SOS from a voice from your past. W. C. Leigh has talked me into doing one of those tours. In a moment of drunken weakness I agreed and now I cannot get out of it. Please help me! Put my mind at rest. Is it absolute hell? What does one do about clothes, laundry, etc? And, above all, how does one get out of being mixed up with all the blue-rinse ladies after one has bashed one's brains out to make them happy. P.S. Is it advisable to hire a traveling companion to ease the path . . . ducking local newspapers, etc.?"

I can only imagine my father's amusement when he read Niven's letter, for all the things the debonaire British actor feared were precisely the things that appealed to my father about lecture tours. He traveled with one small suitcase containing an extra shirt, tie, pants, and clean underwear. He washed his clothes in the sink of his hotel room and wore the same navy blue blazer each night. Because he usually toured in the dead of winter, my mother insisted that he buy a cashmere blazer, cashmere socks, and a cashmere vest to keep himself warm. Those were the only luxuries he allowed himself. And as for the blue-haired ladies, they and the students were easily Vincent's main reason for the entire production. He never ducked a local newspaper in his life; he recognized the thrill local reporters got from interviewing a famous person, and he always took the time to give detailed and personal interviews.

This was one of the marvelous paradoxes that characterized Vincent Price. Although he understood that he could use his own fame as a tool for accomplishing important things, he was also remarkably unassuming, capable of becoming starstruck in the company of other famous people even long after he himself was a household name. Hank Milam recalled, "There were literally hundreds of times we would go into a restaurant and I never saw Vincent in any way say, 'I'm Vincent Price and when can I get a table?' Or 'I only want a table on the first aisle.' It was absolutely like he was an insurance salesman coming in from West St. Louis. . . . Of course, he had a voice that was instantly recognizable, and he would call up and ask for a reservation but he would call up and ask for a table just under the name of Price, because he would have seen it as a pretension to have said, 'This is Vincent Price.' We used to be down at the mailbox at the Glen when Marilyn Monroe was living across the street, and she would sometimes nod, and we would turn and walk back up the driveway and Vincent would say, 'Isn't it amazing? She's such a big star.' " (Mary told how, during the period that Monroe lived across the street, Vincent, Barrett, Hank, and Harry all found reasons to go check if the mail had come at least three times a day.)

Hank also remembered walking down the street in those days when "Beverly Hills was so charming, it was like a little community. We were coming out of Pioneer Hardware and there was this very fancy Mercedes limousine and this black lady in the back seat yelled, 'Vincent.' It was Ella Fitzgerald, and Vincent turned and said, 'Hello, how are you?' And she leaned out the window and Vincent leaned in and kissed her and they chatted for a few minutes until someone honked and they pulled away. And Vincent said, 'Isn't it amazing she remembered me?' I met her a few years ago at CBS.' "

26

VINCENT'S PUBLIC RECOGNITION for the *$64,000 Challenge*, his rewarding experiences as a lecturer, and the excellent reviews for *I Like What I Know* gave him a sense of fulfillment he hadn't had since his work in such films as *Champagne for Caesar* and *His Kind of Woman* in the early 1950s. He had made a few pictures that had done very well at the box office—most notably *House of Wax* and the two Castle projects—but his increasing identification as a one-note villain gave him some cause for concern. Although his visibility as a spokesman for the arts brought him enormous satisfaction, his screen roles remained a disappointment and he continued hoping for assignments of quality.

In both the United States and Great Britain, the horror movie renaissance that began in the late 1950s continued to boom during the following decade. Having achieved a regular cult following with its *Dracula* and *Frankenstein* series, England's Hammer Productions had two solid box-office draws in actors Peter Cushing and Christopher Lee. Cushing, an accomplished stage performer who had become one of Britain's first television stars, joined Hammer in 1957 when he was cast as the steely Dr. Van Helsing in *Dracula*. Lee, who had starred as the monster in *The Curse of Frankenstein*, became both an international sex symbol and a classic horror star following his appearance in the title role of *Dracula*. This modernized, sexy version of Stoker's classic story was a hit with America's baby boomer generation as well as audiences around the world. With headliners Cushing and Lee, Hammer became an extremely successful, not to mention profitable, film company during the sixties, and in 1968 the studio received the Queen's Award for Industry in recognition of its contribution to Britain's balance of trade—an honor unprecedented in the U.K. film industry.

American counterparts to Hammer were few and far between, but one studio that had capitalized on the sci-fi craze of the fifties hoped to do the same with the new wave of Gothic horror. American International Pictures had been founded in 1954 by Samuel Z. Arkoff and James Nicholson, two movie buffs who saw a way to make a buck in movies even as television took over and the old studio system began to crumble. They realized that independent theater owners, in particular drive-in operators, were desperately searching for affordable movies that would bring in customers. The major studios were making fewer and fewer pictures each year, mostly costly star-studded extravaganzas. Arkoff and Nicholson distributed cheaper genre films—action, Western, and, later, sci-fi flicks—to the smaller exhibitors. Their method was to arrange financing and distribution for independent producers. Among the most reliable of these was a young man named Roger Corman who had shot his first feature, *Monster from the Ocean Floor*, for $12,000, and then consistently made a profit for AIP thereafter.

During the 1950s, AIP and Corman formed a successful alliance, producing a variety of films that brought in quick cash—teen flicks and science-fiction features for the most part. But over the decade the market became crowded with imitators, and AIP was looking for a new hook. In 1960 Roger Corman approached Arkoff and Nicholson with the idea of making a cycle of films based on the stories of Edgar Allan Poe. Corman recalled, "At that time, there was a system that was working well, doing two low-budget pictures and sending them out as a combination—two science-fiction or two teen films and so forth. I had done a number of them for AIP and other companies. Then AIP had asked me to do two ten-day black-and-white horror films but I, frankly, was getting tired of this and wanted to do something better. Also, I thought that the idea had been repeated so much that it was losing some of the impact at the box office. So, I said, 'Instead of doing that, let me do one fifteen-day picture in color on a slightly bigger budget, and they asked me what I wanted to do and I said *The Fall of the House of Usher*, which I had read when I was a junior in high school and I had always loved. After some discussion, it was agreed that they would let me make that film. Vincent Price was my first and only choice for the lead role of Roderick Usher. It wasn't one of those things where you have a list and he was at the top of the list. He simply was the person I wanted and Jim Nicholson, who was more involved with the casting and that end than Sam Arkoff— Sam was more at the business end—agreed with me. It was the fact that I knew he was a very fine actor, that he had done one or two pictures in the horror bracket, but he had had a solid career in other types of films, and also I felt that he was right for the role. We sent the script to Vincent. He liked it and we had a meeting and got along very well."

Indeed, Vincent was very intrigued by Corman's slant on Poe. He had always loved Poe's work, considering him one of the great American literary masters; furthermore, he felt that he and the young producer/director had a very similar vision for the film. For the first time in years, the actor felt he might have found a genuinely challenging film-making venture. He later remarked, "Roger was a wonderful director. He was very intelligent and well-organized. He had a genius for hiring wonderful people, which is the secret of all great directors. He showed people how to make pictures fast and on a small budget, and they made money! Working for Roger was a gamble. But there comes a point in every actor's career when you think money isn't everything. I wanted to take a gamble on projects I believed in, and I believed that the works of Edgar Allan Poe hadn't been done properly on the screen. Roger's pictures were based on Poe's short stories. The problem is, it's very difficult to turn a short story like 'The Pit and the Pendulum' or a poem like 'The Raven' into a long picture. The stories had to be expanded in order to fit the movies. What Roger tried to do was to express some of the psychology of Poe's characters, and imbue our movie versions with the spirit of Poe. Richard Matheson, who scripted some of the films, captured the essence of Poe. I always tried to base my characters as much as I could on what Poe had written because it was a sharper clue to the character."

But before the partnership could begin, there was still one stumbling block—money. Once Vincent had expressed interest in doing the film, it was up to the studio to find a way to pay his salary. Arkoff recalled, "We paid Vincent Price $50,000 for *House of Usher* and by his last Poe movie he was making $80,000 per picture. That was a lot of money for AIP, and I wasn't sure we could afford Vincent. We were a very young company at the time we started out with Vincent and we didn't have the money and we really couldn't afford to buy Vincent. So we worked out a deal with him whereby we would pay him more, but we would only pay it over a period of time. And I sold him on the idea, which was true, that this was for his future. This was like laying aside money for the future. I know his agent didn't want to take the deal, but Vincent took it. He was a very bright man, and I can't say much for most actors in that regard. He understood that being an actor is not the best of occupations, and I think he recognized that you had to be careful."

With Vincent Price signed to a long-term contract that exclusively tied his right to appear in horror films to AIP, director and star got down to the work of making their first film together. Corman remarked, "He had some ideas; I had some ideas. I saw Roderick Usher then, and still do, as an extremely intelligent, extremely sensitive and very complex person, and I believe Vincent Price was that person. He was able to access that sensitivity very well." Indeed, Vincent had an affinity with Poe's characters. He was attracted to the Romantic ethos of these Gothic tales, in which hypersensitive men whose dark heritage combined with their refined sensibilities, doomed them to torment as outsiders. He would later say of *House of Usher*, "I loved the white-haired character I was playing because he is the most sensitive of all Poe's heroes."

If Corman saw Vincent as the ideal Roderick Usher, he also saw the true "monster" of the movie as the house itself. Sam Arkoff recalled, "Although Poe's tales were engaging and fascinating—just what AIP was always looking for—I had concerns. While French and British filmmakers had molded their own versions of Poe's *Fall of the House of Usher* (in 1927 and 1950), the American studios hadn't touched it, and I could understand why. 'Here are my worries,' I said. 'How can we turn Poe's stories into full scripts? They're just too short. The literati are going to be screaming that we've taken too many liberties with Poe if we stretch it into any eighty-minute picture.' . . . The brevity of Poe's work wasn't my only concern. AIP has always had a monster or a beast in its pictures to bring the audiences in . . . Poe didn't have them in his stories. Roger had an answer. 'In *House of Usher*,' he said, 'the house is the monster! Can't you see it? It's the house!' . . . In the middle of shooting, Roger made sure he had covered his bases. He asked Vincent Price to utter a couple of lines that he had written into the script at the last minute—'The house lives! The house breathes!' "

Vincent himself understood the importance of the house to the story and—taking his inspiration from the deathly pallor achieved by Conrad Veidt in the 1919 German Expressionist masterpiece, *The Cabinet of Dr. Caligari*—Vincent suggested to Corman that he bleach his hair, noting, "If you lived in that house, you'd be *very* strange!" With his white hair, pale skin, and pale blue eyes, he looked almost albino, as if the cursed place and tainted line of the House of Usher had stripped him of life itself. As the tortured and sensitive Roderick, Price delivered a restrained performance in the role of the cursed brother who tries to protect his sister and her suitor from the inevitable consequences of their ancestry.

Corman had assembled an extraordinary crew for the fifteen-day shoot, including Academy Award–winning cinematographer Floyd Crosby and production designer/art director Daniel Haller. Screenwriter Dick Matheson regarded *House of Usher* as his toughest screenwriting assignment. "Poe's story is very brooding and ruminating, and not too much plot, movement or dialogue, so I kind of faked the Poe touches. I wrote an extremely complex outline for it, and I think it turned out very well. American International was floored by the success of the film; it ran all summer—it played on a double bill with *Psycho*—and made all kinds of money. It was just intended to be a one-shot

Poe adaptation, but it was so successful that American International started a whole cycle of pictures."

Indeed, *House of Usher* was made for $270,000 and grossed 2 million dollars during the summer of 1960, in a run that lasted longer than that of any previous AIP film. Furthermore, after six years of making B to Z movies, the studio found that it had its first mainstream success. The *New York Herald Tribune* noted the film's "restoration of finesse and craftsmanship to the genre of dread." Arkoff, Nicholson, Corman, and Price were quick in deciding to capitalize on a good thing, and thus the Poe cycle was born.

Roger Corman and Vincent Price made eight films together: *House of Usher, Pit and the Pendulum, Tales of Terror, Tower of London, The Raven, The Haunted Palace, The Masque of the Red Death,* and *The Tomb of Ligeia,* six of which form the Poe cycle. *(Tower of London* and *The Haunted Palace* take their inspiration from Shakespeare's *Richard III* and a story by H. P. Lovecraft, respectively.) The Poe cycle begins with two rather subdued and serious Gothic tales, filmed with the integrity of the Poe stories kept firmly in view. The next two take a comic turn and are much farther removed from the dark essence of Poe. The final two come back to the feeling of the first two and are regarded as the most psychologically complex of the series. According to Corman, this was no accident: "There was a logic to that. We started out to do simply one film, *House of Usher,* which I felt was a classic horror story and I wanted to make in that style. We then continued through *Pit and the Pendulum* with this uppermost in my mind, that I was dealing with classics of literature that I respected and wanted to treat as well as I could. Vincent felt the same way but, by the third or fourth, all of us, including Dick Matheson, felt that we were getting into almost a formula. What had started out as something original and new was not new anymore, so we started introducing a little humor. *Tales of Terror* was three short stories and one of them we decided to do as a comedy. It worked very well and everybody liked it so much that we went all the way with *The Raven* and did that as a full comedy. Then, having recharged our batteries, we were able to return to the original concept and say, we are again dealing with classic horror stories."

Pit and the Pendulum began filming in January 1961. All the people who had made *House of Usher* a success were brought back for this next project, including Dick Matheson, who was asked to write the screenplay. Matheson recalled, *"Pit and the Pendulum* was ridiculous because we took a little short story about a guy lying on a table with that huge razor-sharp blade swinging over him, and had to make a whole story out of it. So, I just imposed a plot from an old suspense mystery on that basic premise." Vincent played Don Nicholas Medina, a Spanish nobleman grieving over the recent death of his wife. Set in sixteenth-century Spain, the plot centers on the investigation into the death of Medina's wife, Elizabeth who, he claims, died from "something in her blood." The inquiry is conducted by Elizabeth's brother, a physician, who uncovers much of Don Nicholas' morbid family history—the father, Sebastian (also played by Vincent), was a leader of the Inquisition, who not only murdered thousands of people in the house in which Elizabeth mysteriously died, but killed his own wife and brother who were having an affair, immuring his wife in a wall—all of which was witnessed by his son Nicholas.

Tortured by his past, Nicholas believes that his own wife has been buried alive. And when she appears one night as a ghost, he falls down the stairs of his father's subterranean torture chamber, apparently dead. But he returns, not dead but driven to dementia, only to find that the doctor and his wife are lovers and have conspired to kill him. In his madness, Nicholas brings the adulterous physician to the dungeon and straps him under the pendulum, in a climactic scene that would become a classic of the genre.

If Roger Corman was an expert at creating masterful films on limited budgets and very short shooting schedules, he was somewhat less adept at directing his actors, and Vincent's performance in *Pit and the Pendulum* was regarded as somewhat more over the top than his restrained turn in *House of Usher*. The *Hollywood Reporter* noted, "Vincent Price gives a characteristically rococo performance as the slightly mad Spanish aristocrat." Indeed, as Nicolas Medina teetered on the brink of madness before utterly losing his sanity, Vincent abandoned himself to the extreme passions of his character. It was an approach he would increasingly take throughout the Poe cycle. Nonetheless, the reviews were generally excellent and the film's grosses surpassed those of its predecessor.

After their two successes, AIP resolved to turn out at least one Poe film a year. The next was conceived as a trilogy of three short tales, each starring Vincent. Once again, Matheson was brought in to write a screenplay, adapting "Morella," in which Vincent once more played a widower haunted by the death of his wife; "The Black Cat," co-starring Peter Lorre, with Vincent as a wine connoisseur entombed for having an affair with Lorre's neglected wife; and "The Case of M. Valdemar," in which he plays a terminally ill man averting death by getting Basil Rathbone to place him in a trance.

Vincent and Peter Lorre worked together for the first time in *Tales of Terror*, which also reunited Vincent and Rathbone (the two had first worked together in 1939). Vincent liked both men immensely. He said of Rathbone, "Basil was an intelligent person and a brilliant actor. He was rather unhappy toward the end of his life about having been stuck in the Sherlock Holmes pictures. He had been a great Shakespearean actor in the theater, but most people thought of him as Sherlock Holmes or as a villain." And of Lorre he remarked, "Peter loved to make jokes and ad-lib during the filming. He didn't always know all the lines, but he had a basic idea what they were. He loved to invent; improvisation was a part of his training in Germany." All three actors had a strong sense of humor—after all, it was Rathbone and Boris Karloff who had dunked twenty-seven-year-old Vincent in a vat filled with Coke bottles and cigarette butts during the filming of *Tower of London* in 1939. And Vincent delighted in the opportunity to explore the comic elements of the Gothic horror films. He maintained, "Comedy and terror are very closely allied. We tried to make audiences enjoy themselves, even as they were being scared. My job as an actor was to try to make the unbelievable believable and the despicable delectable."

Tales of Terror did reasonably well at the box office, garnering $1.5 million. Although this was down from the two earlier films, the popularity of "The Black Cat" was enough to encourage AIP and Corman to continue in the comic vein. It had been more than a decade since Vincent had starred in *Champagne for Caesar* and *His Kind of Woman,* and he was delighted to return to comedy, particularly with the brilliant Peter Lorre as his partner in wit. Playing two drunks, Price and Lorre created a wildy funny wine tasting scene. Vincent later recalled, "Before we did it they brought in this very famous wine taster to show us how it was done. We enjoyed that enormously; we got very drunk in the afternoons. Roger really allowed us to comedy it up on that scene. I did it exactly the way the wine taster showed us, but added just a little bit more, and Peter was doing it the way they didn't do it, which made for a very funny scene."

AIP and Corman also felt that the new horror audiences enjoyed "discovering" some of the older horror icons such as Lorre and Rathbone, and for their next film AIP hoped to exploit this ingredient further. For this older generation of horror stars, the AIP films provided them both with work and with recognition from a new generation. And so for the next film in the Poe cycle, *The Raven*, Vincent and Peter Lorre would be reunited with another horror great: Boris Karloff.

The screenplay for *The Raven* was drawn from Poe's essentially plotless poem, leaving Matheson once again having to create a storyline out of thin air. Although it was intended from the start as a comedy, no one was prepared for quite the level of humor the film finally attained. Sam Arkoff recalled, "The picture didn't turn out the way it was meant to turn out at all. *The Raven* was a bastard in its own way, although a successful bastard. I remember going to see the rushes in the beginning and I thought to myself, 'What the devil are we breeding here?' But you see, Vincent and Peter did have a sense of humor. Boris Karloff was a typical English well-behaved gentleman. And he just went along reluctantly."

Roger Corman agreed. " I think Vincent probably liked the more classical approach, but he did comedy with great glee and with great good humor. Working with Boris Karloff and Peter Lorre in *The Raven*, he particularly helped to hold that picture together. Boris Karloff was a very serious actor who knew the lines and was prepared to give the performance that was written in the script; Peter Lorre was very much of an improvisational actor who vaguely knew the lines but came in to improvise and play around and make changes in the script. And Vincent was the one who could work both ways. He understood Boris, he understood Peter, and I think he helped to bring unity to that film."

Although Vincent thoroughly enjoyed working with both these men, whom he perceived as among the best actors of the century, it was his longstanding friendship with Karloff in which he took the most delight. Vincent said of his friend, "Boris was a great professional; I was very fond of him. He was a man who loved his work and knew exactly what he was doing. Off the set, he was a very funny man. An extraordinary thing about Boris was his gratitude for *Frankenstein*. He had great pride in it, even though it was something that plagued him his whole career."

Although *The Raven* featured an exceptional ensemble, it also brought together a group of actors with very different theatrical backgrounds and techniques. Not only was Lorre improvisational and Karloff traditional—Price fell somewhere in between—but there were two other actors with key roles, both of whom had very different acting styles—Vincent and Mary's friend Hazel Court, and a young actor named Jack Nicholson. Hazel, also a sculptor, was an actress in the English tradition; Nicholson had been trained in the Method style so popular in his era. Corman recalled, "I said to Jack, who was a young actor, 'You're good. I've seen you do improvisations in class. You are good with comedy. You can learn from Vincent and Peter and Boris because these are professional actors. They are good and they are funny and you can use your youthful vitality and your natural humor and combine it with them and learn to work with them." Boris and Vincent, however, were under the misapprehension that Jack Nicholson was the son of the producer, Jim, and assumed that he had gotten the part through the family connection. Arkoff remembered, "Vincent and Boris used to joke among themselves, 'Nepotism! Nepotism!' and roar with laughter."

Hazel Court maintained, "I don't think the picture was really meant to be a comedy; it evolved into one on the set," and Sam Arkoff described how he and Jim Nicholson were initially disturbed by the ad-libbing. However, as he said, "Most of the ad-libs worked, and they made it into the movie. Vincent added his own brand of humor to *The Raven*. He persuaded Roger to insert a running gag that would leave no doubt that this movie was something more than just a horror picture. So every time Vincent walked through his study, he 'accidentally' bumped his head into a telescope. It was a joke that got more laughs each time it appeared on screen." And Lorre's ad-libs amused Vincent no end: "In one scene we had together I said, 'Shall I ever see Lenore again?' And Peter said, 'How the hell should I know? What am I—a fortune teller?' "

Corman remembered that Vincent liked to have fun on the set. "It helped, as a matter of fact, because we were working under a lot of pressure. It helped to relax the crew, to relax everybody and keep everybody in a good mood, and particularly in pictures such as *The Raven*, and others that we treated as comic horror films." There was one part of filming *The Raven*, however, that Vincent found less than amusing. Corman told his star that he was bringing in a boa constrictor for a scene. Vincent hated snakes, and informed his director of that fact, adding that he particularly detested big snakes. Corman assured him this one was a mere eleven feet, he didn't think it was poisonous, and it would only be wrapped around the actor for a few minutes. Terrified, Vincent dreaded the day of the shoot. As Sam Arkoff related the incident, "With his knees knocking, Vincent finally agreed to proceed with the scene, figuring it would be over in just a few minutes. In fact, it dragged on for more than an hour and a half. Whenever Roger wanted the snake to slink to its right, it wouldn't move at all. Whenever the snake became overactive, Vincent needed a moment to catch his breath. Once the entire scene had finally been shot, the trainer required the help of two burly crew members to pull the snake off Vincent."

The last two films that Vincent made with Roger Corman were shot in England. AIP was increasingly filming on location in England and in Italy, where they were able to book more studio time for the same money. *The Masque of the Red Death* and *The Tomb of Ligeia* were shot at Elstree Studios just outside London in November 1963 and June 1964, respectively. Vincent relished the opportunity to work in England, but in Sam Arkoff's recollections, "Vincent wanted more money. We finally agreed that we would give him $1,000 a week, which was a lot of money in England at that time." Vincent took advantage of his increased expense allowance to spend more of his weekends in galleries and on the Portobello Road hunting for art.

This was the first time Vincent had worked as an actor in the U.K. since his debut at the Gate in 1936, and he welcomed the opportunity to reestablish his professional reputation in England. In turn, the British seemed to appreciate his work, both on screen and off. Film critic Paul Mayersberg noted, "Corman's Poe always offers a Gothic hero— a nonvirile aesthete. That's why Vincent Price has been the perfect interpreter of them. For Price himself, in real life, is an aesthete, an expert in the visual arts, an appreciator and a collector."

Moving the production to England had several beneficial effects on the Poe cycle, as Roger Corman explained, "I had a little bit more time, more time to rehearse, more time to go for more takes, to go for more intricate camera angles, and to go for a bigger look. We were able to raid the scene dock at the studio, where they had these magnificent set pieces left over from pictures like *A Man for All Seasons* and *Becket*, and, particularly in *The Masque of the Red Death*, we were able to assemble sets that we would never have had the money to build in the United States. We wouldn't have had the money to build them in England either."

The improved sets and more relaxed working atmosphere helped ease the transition back to a more serious approach to Poe. *The Masque of the Red Death* is now regarded as one of the best of the Poe cycle. Bruce Lanier Wright calls the film "One of the high-water marks of modern Gothic cinema . . . ambitious, original, uneven, sometimes pretentious, and ultimately brilliant." Utilizing a new writing team of Charles Beaumont and R. Wright Campbell, Corman fused two Poe stories, "Hop Frog" and "The Masque of the Red Death." Set in twelfth-century Italy, the film has a pronounced surreal feel that certain critics have attributed to the director's interest in Ingmar Bergman's work, particularly *The Seventh Seal*. Vincent plays Prince Prospero, a sadistic Satan-worshiper who tyrannizes the peasants of his village but becomes obsessed with one of them—a beautiful Christian woman named Francesca (a very young Jane Asher) whom he forcibly abducts to his debauched court, to the dismay of his mistress, Juliana (Hazel Court). Much intrigue follows, leading up to a climactic costume ball at court, at which a stranger dressed in red arrives. The countryside around the castle is being decimated by plague, the Red Death, and the wearing of red is forbidden because of its association with the dread disease. Prospero confronts the masked figure, who tells him, "Death has no master. Each man creates his own heaven, his own hell," before moving through the ball and casting the disease on the revelers. At the end, a dying Prospero strips off the stranger's mask only to reveal that the face of Death is his own.

Despite the elaborate sets and brilliant cinematography by Nicholas Roeg, the film—more complex and demanding than AIP's teen-oriented horror flicks—performed less well at the box office. As *Cinefantastique* noted, "Had the film been shot in a foreign language and subtitled, it would probably still play at art and revival houses today." Regardless of the drop in receipts, Corman and Price pursued their artful vision of Poe for one last film together, *The Tomb of Ligeia*, which many fans find the most satisfying of the cycle. Although the plot offers a love story, the film's theme is more psychological in its orientation. Clean-shaven and wearing a black wig and rectangular sunglasses, Vincent plays the intense and gloomy Verden Fell, who after the death of his first wife, Ligeia, falls in love with and marries his next-door neighbor, Rowena (both played by Elizabeth Shepherd). After their honeymoon, the lord of the manor begins evincing moody and obsessive behavior—the result, his new wife eventually learns, of his being hypnotized by his dead wife, whose body he keeps in a secret chamber and visits each night. When Verden is discovered in a compromising position with his dead wife, all havoc ensues, culminating in a conflagration in which Verden perishes. It seemed to Vincent that he was forever being immolated at the end of his movies. "The scariest thing about the horror films were all those fires blazing. Symbolical cleansing of evil by the fire is a horror-tale tradition. I have been singed many times. While making *Tomb of Ligeia*, in which the whole set was sprayed with liquid rubber, someone lit a cigarette and the whole thing went up. But then Roger's a fire fiend. He's a firebug."

The screenplay was by Robert Towne (who later wrote *Chinatown*) and constitutes a worthy contribution to the Poe cycle. Towne was apparently unhappy with the casting of Price, convinced that Verden should have been played by a younger actor such as Richard Chamberlain; nonetheless, Vincent's restrained performance was appreciated by critics. The London *Times* found that "Vincent Price gives one of his best performances as the tormented Verden," while the *Los Angeles Times* raved more generally: "The fluid camerawork, first-rate color, sumptuous period sets, and an impassioned performance from Vincent Price blend perfectly to bring a great Gothic tale of terror to life on the screen."

*   *   *

Over the course of their collaboration, Corman and Price developed an easy and excellent working relationship. In Corman's opinion, "Vincent required very little from the director. He, as all good actors do, researched, prepared, and studied. In general, I would talk with Vincent before each picture so that we were in unity on words that have almost become clichés—the motivation, the subtext—so that we would evolve and define the character before the picture started. Once having done that, Vincent came to the set prepared and was wonderful to work with. I really didn't have time to go for more than two or three or maybe four takes at the most and Vincent understood that and was able to give that performance from the beginning."

Though Vincent's professionalism made him ideal for Corman's fifteen-day shoots, it was his appeal to audiences that kept Arkoff and Jim Nicholson happy. Arkoff believed the actor was uniquely suited to succeed in the genre: "He was perfect in a number of ways. In the first place, he was an imposing man physically, and when he wanted to have an imposing look, he could really do it. You see, Vincent liked horror. It did something for him, and that wasn't really true of the others. Boris didn't really mind it. Peter Lorre didn't really like it. To Vincent, it was like doing Shakespeare; it really was. Vincent relished that."

Vincent himself said that he and his fellow horror stars all had "a very strong feeling they were Gothic tales and not horror stories. Horror stories are the ones that deal with reality, like *Marathon Man* and *Taxi Driver*. But ours were based on Edgar Allan Poe, and he was not a horror-story writer. Rather, he was the greatest American writer of Gothic tales."

Most of Vincent Price's fans feel that his success as a horror star was twofold. In the first place, he always played sympathetic characters—evil, yes; tormented, definitely; sadistic, possibly; but they were always human and thus always sympathetic in some manner. Second, one could always sense the humor beneath the surface, or at least the amusement he found in playing villains. As he later noted, "Villains are among the most challenging roles an actor can play. They're also the most fun to play." The light side of his villains were, as one critic noted, a major factor in his box-office popularity: "With the notable exception of Vincent Price, who keeps his tongue firmly in his cheek, few heavies grow rich."

In 1964, Susan Sontag elucidated the idea of "camp" as something which had always existed but had never been named. Camp, she wrote, is a "sensibility—unmistakably modern, a variant of sophistication but hardly identical with it . . . It is not a natural mode of sensibility, if there be any such. Indeed the essence of Camp is its love of the unnatural: of artifice and exaggeration." She goes on to define Camp as a "quality discoverable . . . in the behavior of persons . . . a particular kind of style. It is the love of the exaggerated, the 'off,' of things-being-what-they-are-not . . . As a taste in persons, Camp responds particularly to the markedly attenuated and to the strongly exaggerated . . . Camp is the consistently aesthetic experience of the world. It incarnates a victory of 'style' over 'content,' 'aesthetics' over 'morality,' of irony over tragedy . . . Camp taste is, above all, a mode of enjoyment, of appreciation." In the Poe cycle, Vincent Price brought camp to the horror genre, and the cult status enjoyed by both the films and the actor owe a great deal to his camp sensibility. Playing Poes' passionate, tormented, hypersensitive aesthetes, Vincent imbued his growing status as a horror icon with his own unique cultural sensibility as well as his wicked sense of humor. During the sixties, the growing awareness of the integral place of camp in cinema created a growing audience for Price's horror antics and the veteran actor ascended to true movie stardom for the first time in his thirty-year career.

With the success of the Corman-Price Poe cycle, Arkoff and Nicholson endeavored to capitalize on the concept by casting Vincent in other Poe-style films. Though these pictures did not always live up to Vincent's standards for the Gothic genre, he rationalized his ongoing involvement in a spirit of optimism, always finding a way to hope that something artistically worthwhile would emerge. And, as always, he was concerned about being a good provider—a concern that landed him in a number of contractual obligations he might have preferred to avoid. His initial willingness to take on a few films of lesser quality ultimately precipitated a gradual slide into precisely the kind of films he had always hoped to avoid—pure horror schlock. And yet he always believed there was no harm in what he was doing; "The horror films were entertainment," Mary recalled, "because the real horror is gang rape and so forth. And his were fantasy horror, fable horror—they were entertainment."

One of the first of these was *The Haunted Palace* directed by Corman, a classic horror picture based on a short story by horror master H. P. Lovecraft. The film was derived from a story called "The Case of Charles Dexter Ward," about the resurrection of the dead, but the success of the Poe cycle led AIP to title the film after one of the poet's works and promote it as "Edgar Allan Poe's *The Haunted Palace*." Originally slated to star Ray Milland, Hazel Court, and Boris Karloff, the film was transformed into a Vincent Price vehicle in order to make the most of his rising box-office stock; Court's role was given to Debra Paget, and Lon Chaney Jr. replaced Karloff. The film is hardly one of Corman and Price's best, but it did very respectably at the box office.

AIP also brought in other directors. In 1964 Jacques Tourneur made *The Comedy of Terrors*, in which Price was again joined by Karloff, Lorre, and Rathbone. If *The Raven* had attempted to display some restraint, *The Comedy of Terrors* went all out for humor. The idea for the film—a couple of rascally undertakers go out and kill people when business is slow—came from Dick Matheson. Vincent loved working with his friends on this film. He recalled, "Boris, Peter, Basil, all of us, we used to talk about what really scares people. One time, we were trying to figure it out, and Boris said, 'Cobwebs.' And I said, 'Oh, come on, Boris, cobwebs don't scare anybody!' And he said, 'They scare *men*. Men *hate* cobwebs!' And it's absolutely true, you know; they're *sticky*. Women don't mind them; they just think you're a bad housekeeper. But men *hate* 'em! So, we rigged up this huge cobweb, and I walked right into it, and this thing went right across my face, and the whole male audience went 'Yeeech!' "

The Comedy of Terrors was the last time the four actor friends worked together. Peter Lorre died on March 23, 1964. He was buried at the Hollywood Memorial Cemetery, where his honorary pallbearers included Irwin Allen, Sam Arkoff, Sir Cedric Hardwicke, Burl Ives, James Nicholson, and Vincent, who was asked to deliver the eulogy. He said, "A great actor of another era said of our calling that we are sculptors in snow, and yet at the final dissolution of this ephemeral image the whole world mourns. Something irreplaceable has disappeared, but if there is immortality, surely it is in the remembrance of man, and what the actor creates is a lasting memory, however insubstantial the material of which it is made. The memory of a great performer is elemental, and the elements are life. Peter had no illusions about our profession. He loved to entertain, to be a face maker, as he said so often of our kind. But his was a face that registered the thoughts of his inquisitive mind and his receptive heart, and the audience, which was his world, loved him for glimpses he gave them of that heart and mind . . . The snow statue of his work perhaps will melt away, but the solid substance of his self must last."

Despite his efforts to be seen as a kind of Renaissance man whose identification with horror was merely a part of a very full and rounded life, through the Poe films Vincent acquired a legion of movie fans who elevated him to cult status. Horror aficionado Bruce Lanier Wright assessed Vincent's work in the Poe cycle thus: "Was there ever an actor so seemingly custom-made for a series of roles? The Poe pictures, for better or for worse, sealed Price as a horror star forever, and they contain some of his all-time best work. At times in the series, Price can lapse into chest-thumping melodrama, but he usually goes over the top in a way that seems perfectly in keeping with Poe's own neurotic conceptions. And for those most familiar with Price's spoofy 'Uncle Vincent' persona—no one parodied Vincent Price better than Vincent Price—some of these performances, particularly his roles in *Pit and the Pendulum* and *The Masque of the Red Death*, are a revelation."

By the mid-1960s, Vincent Price was regarded as the reigning King of Horror. For the most part, he accepted this position with equanimity, perhaps understanding that, like his friend Peter Lorre, he was achieving a kind of immortality. But he could only accept his growing fame in the horror genre because of his continuing work in the visual arts. And certainly everyone who knew him well understood this about him. Sam Arkoff, thinking particularly of Vincent as art historian and collector, said, "As much as I appreciated all those veteran actors (Karloff, Lorre, Rathbone) for their talent in front of the camera, I particularly enjoyed being around Vincent. He was much more intelligent, sophisticated, and cultured than some people might expect from a horror star."

27

IN 1957 VINCENT Price was asked to become a dollar-a-year man for the United States government. As he later recalled, "I was invited to be on the Indian Arts and Crafts Board, which was founded at the time of the World's Fair in San Francisco in the late thirties by Rene d'Harnancourt, head of the Museum of Modern Art. It was a five-man board appointed by the Secretary of the Interior, each for a five-year term. All appointments were nonpartisan and our only recommendation was our interest in the American Indian. In other words, we were to try to find markets for their work, try to put them in touch with people who would give them a break. I was very excited about it because I thought it was a chance to do something for the American Indian. I was also terribly conscious of the fact that I was invited because I was the only person on the board who had publicity value, because I was an actor.

"I was appointed under the Eisenhower administration," Vincent explained, "which is kind of surprising since I am a Democrat." The board's effectiveness was hampered by changing administrations, as he recalled: "Each time a new secretary of the interior came in you had to restate the whole purpose of the board again and try to get the money and the power to go out and help the Indian." But it was gratifying work for Vincent, and under the most cooperative secretaries, such as Vincent's personal favorite, Stewart Udall of Arizona, he felt the board was able to make a difference. Vincent was appointed to three five-year terms; for the last, from 1967 to 1972, he was named chairman. Among the other members over the course of the fifteen years during which he served were Rene d'Harnancourt; director of the Museum of the American Indian Fred Dockstader; art dealers Erich Kohlberg, Royal Hassrick, and Mitchell Wilder; noted author and Native American activist Alvin Josephy; and artist/educator Lloyd Kiva New; each of whom brought a different level of interest and expertise to the Board.

Undoubtedly Vincent's greatest strength was his boundless gift for working with people. He thoroughly enjoyed touring the country in support of Native American arts; during his fifteen years of service he found time not only for regular meetings in Washington, D.C., but also for visits to Alaska, the Dakotas, Oregon, Oklahoma, New Mexico, and Arizona on behalf of museums, schools, and individual artists. He gave frequent readings with students and established a fund for student poets and other writers. One of his most rewarding experiences came about through fellow board member Lloyd Kiva New, who became the Arts Director of the Institute of American Indian Arts (IAIA) in Santa Fe, New Mexico, in 1962. New was particularly concerned with allowing his students to work on new variations of traditional forms that reflected their Indian heritage, which often included three-dimensional arts and crafts. Previous to the IAIA, the Santa Fe Indian School had strongly stressed a two-dimensional Western technique. New describes being "under great siege when we came up in '62 and I was the arts director," he recalled. "I was Indian, but I was a bad Indian, I was a traitor to my culture. So that was the battle that was going on and Vincent came in and sided with us. We would occasionally run into political things, funding problems, and public pressure, and Vincent was always on our side. Whenever we got into a difficulty, a phrase that he used over and over—and I remember him saying this on many occasions when I was crying on his shoulder about whatever was going on—was, 'We'll get there. We'll get there.' And it stuck in my head. It was very encouraging."

During his five years as chairman, Vincent was often asked to speak up for Native American issues, as well as to write about his beliefs. In 1968 he wrote the introduction to the first volume of *Native American Arts*, the official journal of the IAIA and the Indian Arts and Crafts Board: "To much of the world, one of the most important aspects of our oft-times challenged cultural prowess, past and present, is the contribution to the historic lore and the continuing cultural fact of the American Indian. If anyone chooses to question this they will have to admit that the Indian contribution to the world picture of America has been and still is the most glamorous, romantic, and intriguing. Sadly, the average American boasts an almost voluntary ignorance of factual Indian history and/or contemporary life. Sadder yet has been the insensitive disregard for the cultural as well as physical needs of a great people whom we seem to have tried quite consciously to beach along the swift current of modern life. The stultifying tendency we all have shared of cataloguing the Indian racially and culturally as an old people, apart and past, is being overcome by their own young people. They are proving themselves very much of the present, and have become living proof of that cheering proverb, 'The Past is Prologue,' and . . . the best is yet to come."

Vincent felt very strongly about using his celebrity status in any way he could to support and promote the arts, and he lent his name and his time to help with the founding of the Archives of American Art. He recalled, "Edgar Richardson—Ted—who was the director of the Detroit Art Institute, wanted to write a book on American art. But he found that in doing it, everything took him five times longer than it should have because it was so difficult finding anything about American artists. Everything was scattered all over the place." There had never been a project dedicated exclusively to documenting the working lives of artists—often as not, artists kept few records of their lives, and for those who did there was no well known repository to store and preserve them. "In the nineteenth century and the early part of the twentieth, American art was held in such low regard that there was no demand for his stuff. So Ted and a guy named Larry Fleischman, who was the son of a rug merchant in Detroit, decided to start something called the Archives of American Art. They were given a room in a basement of the Detroit Art Institute and the stuff started to pour in. They'd microfilm it and document it and then they'd keep some of it and give the rest back." Indeed, since its inception in 1954, the Archives of American Art have accumulated research materials in the form of letters, diaries, photographs, scrapbooks, and business records numbering over twelve million, as well as an oral history program that comprises over three thousand interviews. Today its collection can be found at the Smithsonian Institution.

*   *   *

In the early 1960s, an opportunity presented itself to Vincent that seemed to promise the culmination of his lifetime of work in the arts. Sears, Roebuck, the great American catalogue company and department store founded in the nineteenth century, had undergone a change of leadership. The new regime sought to change the company's image and bring it up to date. Their goal was to revolutionize their stores, and one of the first steps in this process was to hire spokespeople for each new department. For example, in 1962, a committee of leading sports authorities was formed by baseball great Ted Williams to advise the company on their sporting goods department. The committee included Bob Mathias and Sir Edmund Hillary. In line with this policy, the store turned its attention to the promotion of an art department designed to sell quality pictures to department store customers. Vincent was approached, he accepted eagerly, and the Vincent Price Collection for Sears was born.

Mary Price recalled her skepticism at the idea: "When Vincent first told me about the Sears deal, I rejected it out of hand, knowing that it would be a disaster which we would all regret. Neither he nor history took that position. Along with being a triumph for all concerned, it contributed a great deal to a great many people, notably me." Although Mary had always encouraged her husband's art projects and Vincent valued her opinion, this time he paid her naysaying no attention. The Sears offer gave him an opportunity to put his populist beliefs into practice, to bring art to the American public.

The Vincent Price Collection was initially the brainchild of Sears vice-president of merchandising, George Struthers. *Look* magazine described Struthers as "a Sears vice-president who likes to poke around art galleries. He decided that if customers believed in Sears minks, diamonds, and tractors, they would have faith in the Sears art collection, too." For Vincent, one of the program's most appealing aspects was its promise to make art affordable for middle-class families. "I felt that here at last was a chance to expose the U.S. public to fine art at reasonable prices. The average housewife doesn't realize that she can buy an original work of art for very little money. She reads in the papers how one Rembrandt recently cost the Metropolitan Museum of Art $2,400,000 and that the Somerset Maugham collection was auctioned off for another million or so, and art scares her. She equates it with millionaires like J. Paul Getty and J. P. Morgan. Well, it's not so. I've been a collector all my life and never having been a very rich one or interested in terribly expensive paintings for myself, I've learned to buy extremely well. I think 90 percent of the people I know around the country are scared to death to go into a gallery. They seem to be awed by it, which is nonsense of course, but that's the attitude we've had in America for decades. There are also hundreds of American cities without a single sizeable art gallery. And that's a pity, because we're a cultured nation, but until we have a cultural identity of our own, the rest of the world pays no attention to us."

In conjunction with Struthers, Vincent developed a program that went far beyond the company's original expectations. The September 30, 1962 issue of the syndicated Sunday national newspaper magazine *Parade* featured Vincent Price on its cover; behind the actor was a wall of framed paintings and drawings and below his picture was the caption, 'His goal: original art in every home.' In his article, Lloyd Shearer noted, "This coming week Sears, Roebuck will begin a monumental venture in American culture. Here in its Denver store it will hang for sale approximately 100 works of original art— Rembrandts, Chagalls, Picassos, Dürers, Bohrods, Whistlers, Legers—the works of the great masters as well as those of the best contemporary artists, domestic and foreign.

These works will range in selling price from $10 to $3,000, from watercolors to etchings. They will be offered on the installment plan for as little as $5 down and $5 a month. Each work will be guaranteed as an original work of quality, 'just as we guarantee our lawnmowers or TV sets or any other Sears product.' "

The Denver store had been chosen to launch the scheme because the Rocky Mountain city was felt to have a fairly strong artistic community. The choice proved a wise one for, as Vincent later recalled, "That first night in Denver we sold out. We sold way too many pictures the opening night and had no show for the next day—because I insisted on the policy that you could take the picture home. This terrible thing that they have in grand galleries, that you have to leave the thing on the wall till the show is done, drives the buyer and the art lover out of their minds. So, we had to fly things in the next day from the warehouse." The Sears management was ecstatic at the response, and the following week shows of 100 to 150 pieces opened simultaneously in ten more Sears stores around the country—at Hartford, Harrisburg, San Diego, Sacramento, Evansville, Madison, Pasadena, Birmingham, Oklahoma City, and Hayward.

In preparation for these openings, Vincent had spent six months buying paintings, drawings, and prints. Controlling the logistics of this initially proved difficult, as Sears thought about art as just more merchandise, but from the start Vincent tried to establish quality control. "I made certain provisions. If I bought from contemporary artists, living artists, I paid them on the spot. Well, that nearly killed Sears. But they gave me a checkbook, which they had never done in the history of Sears. And I was terribly careful. If I mailed a two-cent stamp, I put it on the bill or paid them back. And I had to try to gather a first show; I had to find out what the hell people would buy, what price range. I was able to buy some old-time collections of etchings. They were wonderful things, but they'd gone out of style. People weren't buying etchings. They were collecting oil paintings. The great etchings, of course, always sold. And that kind of gave me my clue of what to look for in the way of Old Masters. I bought Rembrandts; I bought Dürers."

Vincent took great joy—and some measure of amusement—in watching the Sears sales staff adjust to its new assignment. "We got to Denver and we had maybe one hundred items to sell, including some contemporary watercolors and drawings, and the man who was assigned to be in charge said—it was one of the greatest remarks I've ever heard—'My God, I started out in manure spreaders and now I'm in art.' Sears had a theory that if a man or a woman was a good salesperson of something, they could be a good salesperson of anything. In other words, if you could sell brassieres, you could sell art. And actually the last very good manager of the collection that we had in Chicago happened to have been a very excellent brassiere salesman." One salesman greeted Vincent in the midst of a china demonstration. "He was standing on top of a teacup to see whether it would break or not. It was Japanese porcelain and that was the way he would test it—by standing on the rim of it. And he was a big man. But he was also a nice man and he did a wonderful job" selling the Vincent Price Collection.

Although Sears was thrilled with the financial rewards they reaped from the Price Collection, Vincent's own goal went far beyond money. The week before the Denver show opened, he told reporter Lloyd Shearer, "I can't tell you what a revolution this project will inspire in the art world if it comes off. Just think of it! There are so many talented young people today who cannot earn their living as artists. If eventually we end up supplying only two hundred of our 755 stores with paintings, we will be providing artists with a ready market for their works. We'll be able to buy twenty, thirty, forty paintings from each artist, and he'll be able to make a decent living and confine all his energy to his art instead of working part-time in the post office to make ends meet." As a man who had come of political age during the Roosevelt administration, Vincent envisioned a private enterprise revival of such New Deal programs as the WPA. In the booming postwar years, he imagined himself as the middleman between big business and the arts.

Under the supportive leadership of George Struthers, everything flourished—though there were a few bumps in the road. One of the biggest problems for Vincent and for Sears was finding a way to frame thousands of works of art. Vincent later recalled, "Mary, thank God, came in and did the framing and, of course, got thoroughly criticized for spending too much money." As a designer, Mary believed that a work of art should be framed to its best advantage. As Hank Milam said, "Her point of view was that the art was quality and that it should be presented in its best frame, and Sears' point of view was that it didn't matter—if it's any good the painting will sell, so just put it in a black diploma frame." Mary's views were upheld when Charles Pearson asked her to get involved, agreeing to let her work from the vast and empty cellar at 580 Beverly Glen. Thereafter Mary Price officially took over and reorganized the framing department.

At first, the art world greeted Sears's venture into the fine arts with a certain skepticism. As Vincent remembered, "There were all sorts of jokes about Sears and art, because Sears was almost sort of a comedy thing—they sold everything. But the stores were really very elegant and they were trying to make them more elegant. It was an all-over-the-store project to raise people's standards. And one of the presidents of the company told me later on that we brought in something like six million new customers into Sears—the art thing alone. So, that was something not to fool around with. But there were jokes about it in the *New Yorker*—a man showing another man a Rembrandt etching and the caption was 'It's not generally known but we picked up this little Rembrandt etching at Sears, Roebuck.' There were cartoons in all the magazines and I was invited to be on every cover."

From 1962 to 1966, Mary and Vincent Price traveled across the United States and around the world on art buying trips for Sears. They loved it, particularly Vincent, who confessed to feeling like a Medici. In the course of their first five years of Sears work, the Prices bought art in the United States, England, France, Italy, Denmark, Norway, Mexico, Thailand, Japan, Hong Kong, Spain, Holland, and Australia. Whenever Vincent was filming on location, he used his free time to scour whatever city he might be in for new pieces for the collection.

Along with these initial buying sprees, work poured in for consideration from all corners; but quality was never sacrificed for availability. "Much material is also submitted to us by artists on their own," Vincent told reporters, "either by sending slides of their work directly to us, or through the stores at local levels, which are then passed on to us. The first criterion for selecting the work is honesty. By that I mean an artist following any trend who we feel is a serious and trained artist. Of course, many primitive and naïve painters have been included in the collection, but even these self-taught artists are generally completely serious about their work and have had long careers."

After the success of the Sears program, other department stores attempted to follow suit—among them Macy's in New York and Bullock's in Los Angeles. And yet without the cachet of the Price name and his unflagging efforts to buy or approve each work of art and to appear in person at as many local openings as possible—none of the competitors was able to touch Sears's art sales, which continued to skyrocket. Within less than two years of its inception one-day sales were reaching above the $150,000 mark, and artists began to become eager to have their work represented by the once-derided store. Vincent found himself screening the work of thousands of artists from around the world. Most notably, even artists of the highest international reputation participated in the project. Andrew Wyeth, then at the height of his fame, painted a number of canvases for Sears, as well as overseeing a series of lithographs. Perhaps the greatest coup was the sale of Salvador Dali's *Mystical Rose Madonna*, a canvas the surrealist master painted exclusively for Sears at Vincent's behest. Dali himself appeared at the New Jersey opening, and the painting became the highest single-ticket item ever sold at the store, fetching $25,000.

Vincent was overjoyed with the success of the venture and, despite the time and energy it consumed in his already busy life, he was always eager to do more. He later reflected, "What intrigued me about the Sears collection was that I was trying to make art a part of other people's lives. Sears, where they went to buy the necessities of life, the tools and implements of life, was also where they went to buy their art." Riding high on the success of his lifelong dream to bring art into people's lives, during the early sixties Vincent Price was perhaps the most visible and vocal spokesman for the visual arts the nation had ever had. And he loved every minute of it.

In April 1962, Vincent received a letter from a fellow member of Yale Class of '33, James Whitney Fosburgh. Fosburgh had stayed on at Yale after graduation to study at the nascent Yale art department and had gone on to become a curator at New York's Frick Museum. Because of their mutual interest in art, Vincent and Jim had become friends, although they had moved in very different circles at Yale. Vincent recalled, "He was one of those Eastern boys who was terribly well connected. His uncle was Kingman Brewster, who was president of Yale, and Jim was a Whitney. He was a bachelor, a very devout bachelor, and then he married Vincent Astor's ex-wife, Minnie, who was one of three famous sisters. Babe Paley and Mrs. Jock Whitney were the other two. So, they did all right, those three gals. But Vincent Astor was apparently a son of a bitch and beat Minnie. So, she divorced him and married Jim. It was an ideal, late-in-life love relationship. Mary and I saw a lot of them. They were very dear."

Jim had written to ask Vincent to sit on the White House Art Committee, which was the brainchild of Jacqueline Kennedy. As Vincent described it, "The White House had been sort of looted over the years by the first ladies, who had said, 'Let's just take this along as a souvenir of our presidency.' And also each president had felt compelled to add his own touch. Teddy Roosevelt was a great conservationist but also a great hunter. He had the lovely Georgian mantelpieces torn out and put marble mantelpieces in that had the heads of deer and buffalo. And Mrs. Garfield I think it was, had a Tiffany glass porch put on the back of the White House." The National Park Service and others had been lobbying for years to have 1600 Pennsylvania Avenue restored to its original state, but the timing was always impossible. Then, "when Truman was president, he had a piano upstairs in his private quarters. He was a thumper. One day one whole leg of it went right through the ceiling, which they found was full of termites. So Truman moved across the street to Blair House and the White House was gutted and restored. Truman never did get back into the White House. He preferred living at Blair House, which is very beautiful. But by the time the Kennedys came, it was all kind of a mishmash because there had been no organization in putting it back together. They thought it should be redone by experts and they started with the furnishings. Then they started the White House Art Committee, and Jim Fosburgh was appointed by Kennedy, who was a good friend of his." In the second year of the Kennedy administration, Fosburgh invited Vincent to join the new Committee."

The White House Art Committee, which was presided over by Mrs. Kennedy, set out to acquire a permanent collection of American art for the White House. A bill had been passed by Congress declaring the building a national monument and that anything given must remain on public view at all times, either in the White House or in the Smithsonian. Fosburgh wrote, "The ambition is to assemble a great collection of good pictures that might have been in any great American house over the years—it has been the President's residence since 1791—had there been a continuity of interest and taste. It is also hoped that it might be a reflection of the best in American painting and taste over those years. This is not intended to mean that all the pictures should be by great names, in fact they could be by unknown painters if they had sufficient interest—historical, as memorabilia, or of some special quality. The immediate objective is to get together a few people who would keep their eye out for possible pictures and possible donors."

Vincent eagerly accepted Fosburgh's invitation, and Mrs. Kennedy was delighted with his appointment. The committee proved immensely successful in soliciting donations; Vincent himself was instrumental in getting Sears, Roebuck to donate $40,000 toward the purchase of five portraits by Charles Bird King of nineteenth-century Native American leaders.

Mary and Vincent decided that they personally wished to donate a picture to the collection, and offered a small oil painting by nineteenth-century landscape painter Albert Bierstadt—a study of clouds. The First Lady approved of their choice and in August 1962, after going through all the governmental channels, the piece made its way to the White House. On September 30, 1963, almost a year later, Jim Fosburgh wrote to Vincent, "I went down to see Mrs. Kennedy last week and while we were talking, she said, 'Guess where the Bierstadt is hanging.' I, of course, said I didn't know, not having been there since May, and she said, 'Come and see.' The president has hung it at the end of his bed where it is the first thing he sees when he wakes up in the morning and he is crazy about it." When President Kennedy was assassinated in November 1963, Vincent was in London filming *The Masque of the Red Death*. Like millions of people all over the world, he was stunned by the tragedy. He recalled, "Great Britain and the world was at half-mast for this brilliant and beloved young man. The outpouring of sympathy to Americans was overwhelming. When I walked on the set that day, it was as though I had lost a close relative. I was asked to say a few words in tribute. It wasn't easy. Later, when I regained my senses, I couldn't help hoping that waking that fateful morning before boarding Air Force One to fly through similar clouds to his unexpected death, perhaps he derived some peace from that gift of mine he had honored by hanging at the foot of his bed."

During the Kennedy administration, Vincent and Mary were invited to several social functions at the White House. They also had the privilege of spending a quiet dinner at the Fosburghs' with Jacqueline Kennedy in December 1962. Mary recalled, "To our great joy Jim and Minnie invited us to dinner and the theater. The two other guests were Mrs. Kennedy and N. C. Berman, who had written the play we were going to see— about the legendary art dealer Lord Duveen, starring Charles Boyer and Agnes Moorehead. Mrs. Kennedy was just as charming as one had always heard, but I felt for her because she seemed to have a genuine fear of crowds. As we reached the theater, where her arrival was expected, she became increasingly tense and clearly it was very difficult for her. Like everyone else, Mrs. Kennedy was a fan of Charles Boyer and after the play, we returned to the Fosburghs' with Mr. Boyer—the first lady was not immune to Mr. Boyer's charm." On December 8, Vincent received a letter from his old friend Agnes Moorehead: "Not that I want to crowd J. Edgar Hoover out of his job, but didn't I hear your hearty laughter in the audience Tuesday night? If I'm right you selected a most exciting performance with Jackie Kennedy in the audience. I was told Marlene Dietrich was there too but nobody was aware of it until too late. When she can be overlooked I guess our First Lady is *glamorous*. Were you sitting anywhere near her?"

After her husband's death, Jacqueline Kennedy handed the reins of the White House Art Committee to Lady Bird Johnson, who tried to keep up the efforts of her predecessor. In March 1964, the first lady sent Vincent a letter thanking him for his work on the Kennedy committee and informing him that President Johnson had issued an Executive Order "establishing on a permanent basis the office of Curator of the White House and the Committee on the Preservation of the White House. We believe that this will ensure the perpetuation of the splendid achievements of Mrs. Kennedy and your committee. I know you made your contribution in hopes it would be preserved, and that is our purpose in following this course. We will continue to need your advice and assistance and, therefore, I want to personally ask you to be available to me and the Committee on the Preservation of the White House." Naturally, Vincent was eager to help in any way he could, and the rapport he established with the new president and first lady at the White House was as warm and positive as that he had had with Mrs. Kennedy.

During the early 1960s, Vincent came to be regarded as one of the most articulate and enthusiastic art experts in America, and his influence increased accordingly. But even as he became acquainted with more powerful people in the government and in the arts, he never lost sight of the fact that his greatest contribution was as liaison to the American public—a public he hoped could be made to feel as strongly about the arts as he always had.

28

IN JUNE 1958, Vincent Barrett Price graduated from University High School in Santa Monica, California. That summer he traveled to Europe on a bicycling tour. In Rome, Barrett received a telegram from Vincent informing him that he had been accepted to two universities—Arizona and New Mexico. Having visited both states more than once with his parents, his choice was easy; that fall, he left home to begin his freshman year at the University of New Mexico in Albuquerque.

Like his father, Barrett had been only an average student in high school, far more interested in running track than in academics. But where Vincent Sr. had enrolled his son in an excellent college preparatory school and had paid meticulous attention to his son's education, Vincent had not done the same for Barrett. Fortunately, Barrett ended up at the right university at the right time. After slogging through freshman year, he took an interest in anthropology and for the first time found himself engaged in his studies. During the summer between his sophomore and junior years, he went to Mexico City to study, and during his junior year the once-uninterested student was awarded a Ford Fellowship in anthropology.

In the summer of 1961, between his junior and senior years, Barrett returned home to Los Angeles to house-sit for Mary and Vincent, who were in Italy. Vincent had offered the use of the house to his brother Mort, who had been diagnosed with cancer. He and his wife, also named Mary, came out to Los Angeles to spend time with their daughter, Sara, and her family. Barrett recalled, "I stayed home for two months of the summer looking after the house. Actually, looking after Mort. He was a Southern gentleman with an accent. Very dapper, very charming." Though these were Mort Price's waning days—Barrett was aware that his uncle's cancer had spread through his body—he was grateful for the chance to spend time with his father's older brother, a true link to his St. Louis family history.

Vincent and Mary had embarked on another of their glorious adventures in the spring of that year, 1961. AIP had offered Vincent two films in Rome, and so with all expenses paid the couple picked up and moved to Italy for six months. Although Vincent knew the films he was slated for were mediocre fare, he was glad to exchange the work for the opportunity to be in Rome. It was the realization of a cherished dream—and what a time to have it come true. In the early sixties, Rome was at the height of its postwar glamour. It was the Rome of *la dolce vita*, of wealthy Americans living it up on the Via Veneto—a time when Italian movie actors such as Sophia Loren and Marcello Mastroianni, and directors such as Fellini and Antonioni, were becoming international su-perstars. And at the hub of Rome's thriving film industry was the famous Cinecittà studio, where Vincent would work.

The first of the films was called *Rage of the Buccaneers*, a costume picture pairing Vincent with Latin matinée idol Ricardo Montalban. Much of the filming took place in a small seaside town called Porto Ercole, which Roman society had recently discovered and was endeavoring to keep unspoiled. There Vincent and Montalban developed a great friendship which would last over the next thirty years.

Rage of the Buccaneers passed almost unnoticed on its release in the United States two years later; the second Italian movie, *Queen of the Nile*, took almost three years to make it to the big screen in the United States. Starring Jeanne Crain, the film was another costume epic, this time set in Egypt. Vincent played the villain in both films, got neg-ligible notices, and would later joke: "I made some dreadful pictures in Italy. They were terrible. But I bought so much good art."

Although Montalban and Vincent became friendly on location, the time they spent together in Rome itself was limited "because he [Vincent] was always hunting for things with Mary." Indeed, Vincent used every spare minute to track down treasures for Sears and to explore all the nooks and crannies of the city. By the end of their six-month stay, he boasted that he had visited every single church in Rome.

Although the Prices had been offered an apartment near the Via Veneto, Vincent disliked the snobbishness of the area and hated the idea of being surrounded by Americans. The couple settled on a small flat occupying the top two floors above a shoe store just off the Via del Corso, near the church of Gesu e Maria and a few blocks from the Piazza del Popolo. Mary and Vincent were delighted with their new "home," which had a 360-degree view of Rome from its rooftop garden. Sam and Mildred Jaffe were also living in Rome, and through them the Prices were introduced to a resident American businessman named Lee Engel who knew the city well and introduced his new friends to wonderful restaurants and lesser-known galleries and flea markets. Through the Jaffes and Lee Engel, Vincent and Mary finally came to know Rome intimately.

In late May, Francie and Sidney Brody flew over to surprise Vincent for his and Francie's mutual birthday on May 27. It was Vincent's fiftieth, and there was nowhere in the world where he would rather have celebrated it. Living in Rome, with the security of a film contract with AIP, and an art contract with Sears, Roebuck, Vincent Price, instead of dreading the milestone, felt it a cause for rejoicing.

Mary and Vincent would both remember their time in Rome as one of the best periods of their marriage. One of the many highlights of their stay occurred during a simple lunch at a local restaurant. Vincent recalled: "There was a lady sitting at a table down the way from us. She looked very familiar—wonderful face—a black lady sitting with three black men. And on the way out, she came by and said, 'Hello, cousin.' It was Leontyne Price, and she asked if we would like to come over and listen to her record Verdi's *Aida*. So, we went to the opera house where we were all alone in the auditorium with just the orchestra. They'd torn out all the seats. And the singers were on the stage, each with a boy or girl who told them when to kneel, when to stand, when to do everything, which was what gave perspective to the recording. It was just an extraordinary experience, because her recording of *Aida* is marvelous. I was in heaven."

In August, Barrett joined his father and Mary in Rome. The three had always loved to travel and explore together, and Barrett, with his recent training in anthropology and archaeology, found Rome more fascinating than ever. While Vincent was working, Barrett and Mary spent most of their days sightseeing or taking trips to places such as Siena, where they had a balcony view of the famous medieval horse race, the Palio. The two had never been closer. And yet, throughout their visit Mary was not feeling up to par. She frequently felt ill—queasy, with a peculiar appetite. She recalled, "I felt terrible all the time. Vincent kept telling me to take vitamins, which, along with Campho-Phenique, was his solution to everything."

For Barrett's twenty-first birthday, the Jaffes threw a party at their home. The end of August was always a festive time, with Mary and Vincent celebrating their anniversary three days before Barrett's birthday. This year was their twelfth. Toward the end of Barrett's visit in mid-September, the three flew to Paris, their first visit as a family. During the trip, Mary couldn't stomach the French cooking and found that all she wanted to eat was Chinese food. This sent her husband scurrying all over Paris in search of Chow Mein and other Asian delicacies, during which he discovered that Paris offered top-class Asian cuisine. However, with little sympathy for Mary's plight, he later remarked, "To eat Chinese food in that capital of French gastronomy is about on a par with dropping in at the Louvre just to buy postcards. You'll get what you went after all right, but oh, what treasures you will have missed!"

While in Paris, the Prices saw their good friends Charles and Deanna (Durbin) David, who were concerned with Mary's poor health. In late September, Barrett returned home while Mary and Vincent headed back to the States via Rome. In January 1962, Vincent wrote Charles and Deanna with an explanation for her troubles. "My poor Mary who, if you remember, was ailing that night (and throughout our stay in Paris) came home to find out that the cause of her complaint was proof that we aren't as old as we thought we were. She is presenting me with a Baby Price somewhere around the first of May. We're overjoyed at the prospect, naturally, and looking forward to being born again in it."

Deanna wrote back, "See what happens when you get too close to the Vatican? If it's a boy, start with his singing lessons immediately—I want him as a leading man for my comeback. If it's a girl, Charles would like her to come over and spend her finishing-school days with him—learning French!" The Prices tried unsuccessfully to keep the news quiet and several friends got in touch. Joan Crawford wrote, "I think your baby is being a very smart one already in choosing both of you as parents," while Vincent's old friend and mentor, Cecil Baldwin, speculated: "I think you will have more time to enjoy her babyhood than you had with Barrett."

II.

Father and Daughter

$\mathcal{T}$O BURN ALWAYS WITH THIS HARD, GEMLIKE FLAME,
TO MAINTAIN THIS ECSTASY, IS SUCCESS IN LIFE.

—WALTER PATER, *CONCLUSION*

29

On April 27, 1962, exactly one month shy of my father's fifty-first birthday, I was born at St. John's Hospital in Santa Monica, California.

A few months later, Barrett came home to meet his baby sister. He was twenty-one years old, had just graduated from college, and was newly married to Sandy Greenwald, a brilliant and beautiful student at the University of New Mexico. A few months before I was born, Sandy had learned that she was pregnant. My mother took the news badly. Struggling through the trying last few months of her own pregnancy, she found it hard to fathom that Barrett, whom she thought of as her son, was also going to be a parent. She felt confused and overwhelmed, but my father couldn't understand why his wife was having such a hard time accepting that she was going to be a mother and a step-grandmother within the same year. He found it marvelous. In October 1962, my nephew Jody was born; he was followed a year later by his brother Keir.

Over the years, when asked about having two children almost twenty-two years apart, my father liked to say that it was the perfect example of planned parenthood: Get one child through college and then have the next. Of course, that was just his witty way of explaining the inexplicable. In truth, I was completely unplanned and unexpected—though, paradoxically, very much wanted.

In the 1950s, during the early years of their marriage, my parents had considered adopting a war orphan. After Barrett came to live with them, however, my father decided that one child was more than enough. Nevertheless, I am told, when he found out that I was on the way he was overjoyed.

My parents had a marvelous marriage in many ways, and the addition of a baby daughter was only cause for celebration. But, in truth, the timing was not ideal. At a time of life when most people's children are leaving home or having children themselves, my fifty-one-year-old father and my forty-five-year-old mother were facing at least eighteen years of parenthood. Furthermore, they both had more professional responsibilities than ever before. The strain of these commitments on top of the stress of parenthood brought a thread of tension into their marriage that had not previously existed.

In her March 1, 1963 column, my parents' good friend Hedda Hopper wrote, "Vincent Price will be known by his daughter, Mary Victoria, as that man who comes to dinner every six months. No sooner had he lighted here after doing a picture in Europe than he was packing for a month's tour of the country to lecture on 'America the Beautiful.' Between stops, Vince writes the preface to an anthology of thriller stories and signs autographs for all the kids who are making *The Raven* a hit. His wife Mary stays home to mind the baby and frame all the paintings he bought in Europe for Sears. They're arriving by the boatload. In Paris alone he laid out $100,000 for paintings which will go on sale—from $25 to $4,000—in Sears galleries. Vince has made these grassroot stores the biggest art dealers in the world and is doing more to sell culture to the country than Jacqueline Kennedy." (This last sentiment may have been an exaggeration, but then Hopper was a staunch Republican and my father one of her favorite people.)

During the 1960s, my father made films for AIP; lectured around the country; traveled the world buying art for Sears, Roebuck; flew to meetings in Washington, D.C., Alaska, Oklahoma, South Dakota, New Mexico, and Oregon for the Indian Arts and Crafts Board; wrote five books, and took on a nationally syndicated column; meanwhile, my mother framed the Vincent Price Collection, designed and co-wrote two cookbooks with my dad, and oversaw the coordination of Sears's National Treasures. These were the years of my childhood. I grew up in a household bustling with secretaries, agents, art consultants, major domos, and nannies. Into this busy world, my parents entered as often as they could—my father as the bringer of gifts and teller of tales, my mother as the organizer and disciplinarian.

If my father was doting but largely absent, my mother was present but overly protective. All of her friends' children were long past the infant stage, so she had no one with whom to share her fears and concerns about raising a child. For years her husband had been away from home for lengthy periods, but she had always been able to join him on tour or on location whenever they had been apart for too long. Now not only was her flexibility in adapting to his busy schedule severely hampered, but his absence meant that she felt solely responsible for my well-being. Also, her own work for Sears required that she be available to travel to meetings in Chicago or on buying trips around the country. Though my father tried to help in my upbringing, he left it largely to my mother, who felt the weight of this responsibility. When I was a baby and her work for Sears was at its height, she tried her best never to be away from me for more than two weeks at a time. When she had to be absent, she made sure that I was left with the best caregivers.

As I grew older and her commitments to Sears lessened, it was my mother who picked me up from school and took me to art classes, cotillions, and riding lessons—but it was my father who charmed my friends when he came to my birthday parties or scared them when he took us trick or treating on Halloween. Although I loved them both, I, of course, warmed to my father's easy joy more than my mother's practical strictness. But even as a child I felt protective of her, sensing that she often got the short end of the stick.

Our household at 580 consisted of my mother and father, Hank, Harry, my father's secretary Wawona Hartwig, and a nanny or governess for me. These last seemed to come and go with amazing frequency. In advertising for the position, my mother wrote, "The value of a full-time nurse-housekeeper is that the Prices are free from anxiety about the security and well-being of Mary Victoria. At the same time, they wish the nurse-housekeeper to be able to have as much of a full, happy life with her husband as is compatible with her professional duties. This is why they are paying a complete salary and making available the apartment with all utilities included. It is their wish that although this is a 'Full Time Live In' position, that the nurse have the advantage of spending as many evenings with her husband as Mr. and Mrs. Price's schedules permit." Most of my nannies seemed to last about a year, but the first one I can clearly remember, because I really cared for her, lived with us in 1968, when I was six. Twenty-year-old Danielle Baumruk and her husband, Stanley, managed to escape from Czechoslovakia not long before the Soviet tanks rolled into Prague. After my years of "professional nannies," Danielle was the first person in the job whom I really loved. We all did. When she turned twenty-one, my mother threw her a party. We had a cake decorated with the Czech and U.S. flags and we celebrated her birthday together. Although no one, least of all me, wanted Danielle to leave, we were all pleased for her when she found a job better suited to her education and skills. After her departure, the procession of caregivers resumed as before.

Despite all this flux and change, there was a measure of continuity in my life. Sandy Sears was my babysitter, who filled in on evenings, weekends, and short vacations. She was a talented artist and craftsperson who made me toys, told me stories and, over the years, became a trusted confidante. She was a wonderful artist and I know my parents were pleased that I was being influenced by such a creative and kindhearted person. (For years, however, I thought that she was related to Sears of Sears, Roebuck—as if she were somehow part of my parents' benefits package.)

And I can't imagine what would I have done without Uncle Hank and Uncle Harry. (As a little girl, my sense of family was helped immeasurably by the fact that everyone to whom my parents were close became my "uncle" or my "aunt.") Harry Mullen lived with us until I was five, but even after he left I saw him regularly because he worked for the family of one of my very best friends. Hank Milam moved out before I was born, when he married the lovely writer-editor Marin Scott, but they both remained very much part of the family. Hank worked with Vincent Price Enterprises for Sears, so was frequently at the house. When my parents were away, Uncle Hank and Auntie Marin took me out to play with other children and kept a watchful eye on my various nannies.

Dad's secretary, Wawona, was also tremendously important to me. Every afternoon when I came home from school there she was, working in her tiny office at the bottom of our driveway. Near her desk, my father had hung a large and very colorful painting called *Three Farms*, by an American primitivist named Streeter Blair. I loved that painting. It appealed to my youthful imagination because it was bright and simple and had lots of cows and horses and snowcapped mountains. When I visited Wawona after school, we liked to play "our game"—pretending that we each lived in one of the farms. We constructed a wonderful make-believe world in which we rode our horses all over this brightly-colored countryside together having adventures. In fact, Wawona *had* grown up riding horses all over a brightly-colored countryside having adventures—her father had run one of the great hotels in Yosemite National Park. I loved the stories of her childhood, which were straight out of a Wild West storybook. The West captured my imagination far more than my hometown of Hollywood ever did. Even as the various nannies came and went, I counted on Wawona and her little poodle, Tinkerbell, who were always waiting for me after school.

Despite their hectic schedules, my mother and father were both dutiful parents. Whenever time permitted, they attended the school plays, ballet recitals, horse shows, and cotillion balls in which I took part. My mother was determined to provide me with all the lessons and classes and schooling of which she had been deprived as a girl. That, of course, meant hours of driving me back and forth and sitting through whatever activity I was engaged in. She always tried to be there, raising me as she would have designed a Broadway show—meticulously, efficiently, and with inspired creativity.

My father, on the other hand, was away much more than he was home. When I was a very little girl, my mother and I picked him up and dropped him off at the airport so often that I thought the airport was his office. It took me quite a while to grasp that it was actually a place of further departure. But it was precisely because my father was so absent that he became such a magical presence in my life. He didn't have to do any of the dirty work of being a parent. He simply showed up from time to time—this wonderful man whom I adored, who played with me, and who told me how much he loved me.

No one was more fun to be with than my father. I knew it, and from a very early age I could see that others felt the same way. Every time he walked into a room people's faces lit up with pleasure. He made them laugh, he made them feel special. But despite the fact that everyone seemed to love him, I believed he loved me most. He made me feel I was the most important person in the world to him, that we had a connection that nothing and no one could touch: I was his blond image and likeness whose face lit up when he came home. I was his reminder that he wasn't as old as he sometimes felt. I was the reason he worked so hard, cared so much, tried to keep giving back. I was the one who listened to all his stories as though they were the best fairy tales. I was the repository of his dreams, the match for his curiosity, the hope for his future.

I remember my childhood mostly as a series of vignettes, like a movie montage rather than as a straightforward chronology. My father managed to raise the most prosaic activities to high art. Together we walked on the beach looking for moonstone and driftwood, skipping flat stones on the water between the breaking waves; rode rolly coasters at amusement parks—the faster, the higher, the more stomach-sickening the better; bought stacks of books at wonderful Hunter's Books in Beverly Hills; went Christmas shopping; took long driving trips in the Clark Cortez; held hands; ate Tootsie Rolls and black licorice; drank root beer floats; went deep-sea fishing; played catch with a baseball and our well-worn mitts in the driveway while we waited for my school bus.

My favorite place to go was the beach house. When my parents were both home, we piled into the Clark Cortez after school on Fridays for the hour-long drive to Nicholas Beach. We always made one stop along the way—a trip to the beach house wasn't complete without a visit to the Tidepool Gallery, where my father added to his incredible collection of shells from around the world—brightly-colored shells, pointy and prickly shells, once-poisonous shells (usually the black-and-white ones), and huge conch shells that he blew like trumpets. Every visit yielded some new treasure from a far-off sea.

There were about ten houses on Nicholas Beach; ours was the last one at the end of a long driveway on top of a hill. Beyond us was Leo Carillo Beach, one of the best surfing areas in Southern California. From our porch, we loved to sit and watch the distant specks that were surfers riding into shore on their waves.

When my parents bought the little house on Nicholas Beach after selling their place on Malibu Road, it was just a simple stucco box. But my mother transformed it into the most glorious home, made of weathered wood turnings and corbels, old stained glass panels that formed shades for a large glass-enclosed porch, and lots of patinated copper. It was a truly mystical spot that seemed somehow to bring out the best in all of us. I don't think any of us was ever happier than when we were there.

*   *   *

"Once, when you were a very little girl, I decided to take you out for the day. And I asked you where you wanted to go. You said, 'Somewhere that's meant for children.' It was an extraordinary statement, because I couldn't think of one thing that was meant for children. Because what I liked were childish things partly, you know. Some things that I liked to do with you were, I thought, very appealing things." I have no memory of this incident, but this is how my father told it to me. I grew up on a gated half-acre in sedate Holmby Hills—not the kind of neighborhood where kids played on the street or walked over to their friends' houses. The children of my parents' friends were teenagers; my own brother was two decades older than I; my cousins were adults with children of their own. I actually looked forward to going to school because I had friends there that were my own age. But the absence of siblings, cousins, or neighborhood playmates was more than compensated for by the presence of an extraordinary group of adults. Even though ours was not a conventional family, we had a large family of friends.

Martha Amory decided I should have a godmother and that she should be it. She took her role very seriously, which was incredibly fortunate for me because we loved so many of the same things—horses, dogs, sports, theater, movies, travel. She had been a tomboy just like me and the fact that she grew up to be a glamorous, intelligent, and adventurous beauty seemed to bode well for my own future—both to me and to my parents. My Auntie Martha was a great dog lover; she had two Siberian huskies, Ivan and Peter, that I just adored. She walked them in Central Park twice a day, rain, shine or snow. During a massive blizzard in the 1970s, when the entire Eastern seaboard was shut down, the *CBS Evening News* ran its closing credits over stunning shots of a whitened Central Park, completely deserted but for my striking red-haired Auntie Martha striding purposefully in the distance with two matching dogs.

Her husband, my Uncle Cleveland, founded the Fund for Animals. As an animal lover I embraced his cause wholeheartedly at a very young age, emblazoning his bumper stickers on my school notebooks: "Real People Wear Fake Fur," "Support the Right to Arm Bears." Auntie Martha and Uncle Cleveland led photo safaris to Africa or India, trying to stem the tide of big-game hunters by showing people that animals should be appreciated and preserved rather than killed. The postcards they sent me from these journeys nurtured in me a lifelong fascination with Africa; how I longed to go on safari with them.

Mary Wickes was my second godmother. She earned her stripes the hard way, attending countless of my birthday parties, school plays, and graduations. Auntie Wicksie and my father loved to talk about being from St. Louis. Not one visit went by without some reference to their hometown. Over the years, however, I began to notice that everyone who came from St. Louis talked about their city—within minutes of meeting a native St. Louisan, some reference to their place of birth crops up in the conversation. People from St. Louis, I have come to understand, are born with an extraordinary pride of place. Wicksie also had a ribald sense of humor to rival that of my father, which gave me the idea very early on that people from St. Louis love to laugh.

Margo and Eddie Albert were two of my other favorite adults. Aunt Margo seemed to have a light that shone from deep within her and it touched everyone with whom she came into contact. She radiated incredible love and joy. I adored her, as did my parents. During the sixties she started a cultural center in East Los Angeles called Plaza de la Raza, which promoted and celebrated Los Angeles's Mexican heritage. Like my parents, whose art gallery was also in East Los Angeles, Margo had recognized a need and acted on it. Plaza de la Raza became an important L.A. cultural center and Margo an extraordinary cultural ambassador to whom my father often turned in his complicated political dealings at East Los Angeles College.

Whoever married Margo would have to have been a remarkable person, and Eddie Albert was. His interest and enthusiasm and joy matched hers. They were a terrific couple. Uncle Eddie often had the dubious honor of being my surrogate father when my own was away. From an early age I attended cotillion in Beverly Hills, where I learned deportment, manners, and ballroom dance. Twice a year, cotillion balls were held at elegant hotel ballrooms. Being Hollywood, these were glamorous events—lots of movie-star kids and movie-star parents. One of the highlights of these evenings was the father-daughter dance contest. The orchestra played waltzes, cha-chas, swings, and fox trots, and each pair was judged on their dancing ability. Uncle Eddie was the perfect substitute for my father, better than perfect since he had made a career performing in musicals such as *Oklahoma!* and dancing with his wife—who, after all, had introduced the rhumba to New York City. In our first contest we did quite well together, Uncle Eddie and I, until the band played a swing piece. To my great annoyance, Uncle Eddie didn't know the swing. As he told the story for years afterward, I looked up at him and, in a voice filled with disdain, said, "You mean you don't know how to do the swing?" It seemed woefully unfair to me to be saddled with someone who didn't know how to dance! I dragged him through the steps, but clearly he was out of his league. He found the whole incident hysterical.

Because my father was away so much, I grew attached to many of my parents' male friends. Frank McCarthy and Rupert Allen were two of the nicest men in the world, and I adored Lee Engel, who always took time to find out how I was doing in school and what my hobbies were. When I told him that I collected stamps, he sent me envelopes weighed down with stamps from all over the world. Jim Tritipoe spent an entire Easter Sunday teaching me how to skip. Of course no one could fill my father's shoes, but I did grow up surrounded by an extraordinary group with a vast capacity for fun.

I thought of all of these people—my parents' friends—as my family, but of course I also had "real" family. My first cousin Sally lived just up the Glen with her two children, Heidi and William Christian. Christian and I were only six years apart. He was the quintessential California boy—a blond, tan surfer—and I idolized him. The rest of the Price family lived back East. After Mort died in 1963, my father became even closer to his two sisters. We visited Aunt Hat whenever we went to New York and made special trips to Aunt Lollie's home in the Ozark Mountains. But I never really got to know any of their children. I felt closer to my mother's side of the family—my Aunt Clay and her children, and my Uncle John, who lived in San Francisco. Though my father's voice was one of his professional calling cards, it had nothing on my Uncle John's—he sounded just like Ronald Colman.

Neither the Prices nor the Grants were very big on family gatherings, but I was given a taste of what it was like to grow up in a big family by the Maitlands and the Dreyfusses, who embraced me as one of their own. The Maitlands—Walter, Ruth and their four children—lived in a spectacular turn-of-the-century ranch house in Colorado, two-storied and built of massive pine logs. At least once a year we visited Mountain Home Ranch, where I rode their old palomino paint horse named Sunny. Everyone knew my childhood dream was to have a horse of my own. Sunny was as close I got, so the Maitlands allowed me to think that he was mine, at least while I was there. I adored their four children. To me, they lived a picture-book life—they rode horses, lived on a ranch, and skied all winter long. Undoubtedly they thought the same of me. After all, I lived with their adored Aunt Mary and Uncle Vincent at glorious 580 amidst the palm trees of sunny Southern California.

Closer to home were the Dreyfusses. Though Henry and Doris's children were much older than I, there were lots of grandchildren who became my California cousins. Thanksgiving at the Dreyfuss house was a much-anticipated ritual. Each year Henry (he and Doris insisted that I call them by their first names) would measure us kids on a kitchen doorframe to see how much we had grown; I loved the gesture of being included with his own grandchildren. Then he would give us wonderful things he had made or drawn. One year he made us the most incredible masks out of brown paper bags. No ordinary masks these, they were elaborately constructed, beautifully colored animals—giraffes, lions, tigers, elephants. Even as a kid, it was clear to me that he was a uniquely brilliant man.

Henry and Doris were two of the kindest people in the world. In 1972, Doris was diagnosed with terminal cancer. Henry decided that he didn't want to go on living without her and they committed suicide together. I found a newspaper account of their deaths in the back seat of our car. When my mother saw that I was reading it, she took it from me. I pretended that I hadn't read the article because I didn't want to worry her. But I didn't feel sad for Doris and Henry. I just pictured them as they always were together, full of love for life and for each other.

After I was born, my parents continued to travel a great deal, perhaps more than ever because of their Sears work. My mother hung a map of the world above my bed and made four colored flags—blue, green, red, and yellow—one apiece for my father, my mother, my brother, and me. I kept track of their journeys on my map. Each time I received a postcard, I found the place and moved my flags. At a very young age, I developed not only a marvelous sense of global geography but also a burning desire to see all the pretty places on the postcards for myself.

As I got older, my parents brought me on trips during my school vacations. From 1968 to 1972 we traveled to Europe once a year, usually at Christmas. During this period my father shot a movie in England every November and December, and my mother and I would meet him there for the holidays. He stayed in hotels while filming, then rented a flat for the three of us. These ranged in size and splendor from simple three-room apartments to sumptuous homes, but all were in South Kensington near two of his favorite places—Harrods and the Victoria and Albert Museum.

Our London Christmases were memorable. We bundled up in unfamiliar winter clothing to listen to carol singers on Sloane Square or to attend elegant parties at the Sam Jaffes (they had moved to London in the mid-sixties) or the Joe Cottens. My father always bought a Christmas tree and decorated the flat. In retrospect, I think he liked those simple holidays we spent together almost as much as the elaborate Christmases at home in L.A.

Both my parents had the ability to make every place we visited seem like the most fascinating spot in the world. Of course, we spent a lot of time at museums. I'm afraid I didn't have my father's youthful eagerness to learn about art, but he had a way of telling me stories about what we were seeing that made anything interesting. When we stood in line for hours to see the Tutankhamen exhibition at the British Museum, my father recounted the life of this boy king so wonderfully that I couldn't wait to see the show. He made art fun. And yet I was really much more interested in books. When we drove out to visit Stonehenge my parents were terribly excited about showing it to me, but I had just discovered C. S. Lewis's *The Chronicles of Narnia* and could barely be bothered to get out of the car.

After one of our London Christmases it was decided that we should go to Switzerland to stay in a small village called Engelberg, where I took ski lessons. I can't imagine what they did. Undoubtedly, they shopped. I distinctly remember that New Year's Eve, which we spent in the great dining room of the hotel. We were sitting at a large table by the dance floor when someone came over to say hello to my father. Eager to show off his German, my dad beckoned to the waiter and asked, *"Bitte, bringen Sie noch ein Tisch."* Bring me another chair. The man was gone an inordinately long time and my father became a little annoyed. Suddenly, the couples on the dance floor parted like the Red Sea as two waiters carried a huge table over—*Tisch* being table, which is what my father had mistakenly asked for. How we laughed at him.

After this vacation, we were scheduled to fly home via London, but Heathrow was fogged in and the plane was forced to make an emergency stop in Paris, where we were to sit on the runway until the fog cleared in London. My father couldn't bear the idea of being that close to Paris without showing it to me. We stayed for three days. I loved my father not just for his spontaneous sense of adventure, but also for his ability to persuade my mother that it was all right for me to miss a few days of school.

I also adored our driving trips around the West—and not just because there were horses for me to ride. The "frontier spirit" brought out a different side of my parents. My father was definitely of the "if you've seen one tree, you've seen them all" school of landscape appreciation, but on these trips we visited Indian reservations, drove up into mountain ranges, ate outdoors under picture postcard blue skies, and watched the Big Dipper appear at night. We visited New Mexico a lot, both because Barrett lived there and because my father was on the Indian Arts and Crafts Board. We took other trips, too, to the Dakotas, to Oregon, Wyoming, and Colorado, and together we learned about Indian tribes and their histories.

Over the years, my parents had invested in pieces of land in various areas they had visited and liked. They briefly purchased a piece of beachfront property near the Mexican border, and in the late 1960s they joined an innovative Northern California coastal community called Sea Ranch, whose unique angular and weather-beaten wood houses were breaking new architectural ground in environmentally-conscious housing. These properties gave us a built-in excuse to get away.

Our family trips provided rare and perfect opportunities for the three of us to spend time together. My mother and father had a wonderful sense of fun, and when we spent time in places geared for kids, they found a way to make it fun for themselves too. Trips to San Diego were no longer just about crossing the border into Tijuana, but included visiting Shamu the Killer Whale at Sea World, and eating corn dogs and seeing the animals at the world-famous San Diego Zoo. Their appetite for travel was infectious; I loved their curiosity about everything. They encouraged me to emulate them in my own way— if I read about someplace that interested me, they made a point of taking me there. And while they collected Indian jewelry and pots on our Southwest trips, I collected arrow-heads and T-shirts.

My only negative memories of our travels were the arguments my mother and father had about my table manners. Not surprisingly, my mother was determined that I should learn to use a knife and fork properly, that I should clean my plate, use a napkin. I thought the whole idea ridiculous and rebelled furiously. Our meals frequently disintegrated into a round of arguments—my mother complaining about my manners, my father urging her to leave me alone. Of course I sided with my father, more than pleased to endorse his laissez-faire approach. But as time wore on, I no longer cared who was right or wrong. I just wanted them to stop arguing.

My ninth summer, we crossed the Atlantic from New York to Le Havre on Cunard's *Queen Elizabeth II*. It was a glorious crossing. I loved the ship because there were lots of other kids, and fun activities like swimming, shuffleboard, and bingo. My father simply loved being at sea. But the rest of the trip went quickly downhill. Two gourmets should never take a finicky child to France. They wanted me to find the same pleasure in food that they did. One restaurant on Mont St. Michel was world-famous for its omelets, but I hated eggs, cheese, and milk, and I refused to eat. Then I got sick as we drove across Brittany. It was a disaster. But there were good moments. I found a four-leaf clover in Versailles, which impressed my father no end. I showed off my schoolgirl French, displaying a remarkable adroitness for ordering ice cream of many flavors, and my mother was pleased that I seemed to have inherited her facility with languages rather than my father's dubious stranglehold on foreign tongues.

Food was a constant subject of discussion in the Price household. My father was always experimenting in the kitchen, and having a fussy eater for a child must have been the bane of his existence. When I was six or seven, he went through his ratatouille period; when he was home, we had ratatouille almost every night. For me, the height of culinary genius was a Bob's Big Boy double cheeseburger and a chocolate milkshake; the ratatouille period was a dark passage indeed.

I didn't spend much time in the kitchen. Clearly, my parents realized that it was a place where my talents didn't lie. I did, however, share my father's passion for breakfast foods—pancakes, waffles, bacon, popovers—the more fattening the better. I like to think my dad made the best pancakes in the world, and though I never have achieved his facility in the kitchen, he did manage to teach me how to make a pretty mean pancake. And popovers, a breakfast version of Yorkshire puddings, were his greatest breakfast treat, the making of which required very little more than patience. The batter was ridiculously simple, but too much opening and closing of the oven door meant that they wouldn't rise to their magically airy height. It took me a while, but I managed patience, and popovers too.

If my father was in charge of breakfasts and all major culinary adventures, my mother was the baker. She created the most extraordinary cakes. My personal favorite was a dark, dark chocolate cake with bittersweet chocolate frosting that was so thick it was almost like eating a soft Swiss candy bar. In between each layer—and there were four—was more of this sumptuous frosting mixed with bitter orange marmalade. On top was a dusting of shaved orange peel. Chocolate was my mother's great talent—she also made individual bittersweet chocolate *pôts de crème* for the parties that I longed to be old enough to attend.

My mother ruled the kitchen on holidays. Thanksgiving and Easter were her particular specialties. I still remember with mouthwatering joy her succulent clove-and-pineapple-studded Easter ham. But Thanksgiving was her favorite holiday. She never stopped being grateful for her life in America and her Thanksgiving feasts reflected that gratitude in abundance. Indeed, special occasions were my mother's stock-in-trade. By contrast, however, because my father was often away, I came to think of every day I spent alone with him as our own private special occasion, always imbued with a kind of magic. This extended to his cooking. I always loved to watch his enormous, yet elegant and gentle, hands breaking the eggs for a soufflé or tossing a salad. He made the most extraordinary soufflé—light, airy, pungent, rich—served with a garlicky salad made in a huge koa bowl, well worn from his use.

Though my parents patronized many fancy restaurants, our family favorites were simple—Ah Fong's, basic Chinese fare in a Beverly Hills basement; Uncle John's Pancake House in Santa Monica; and, of course, Hamburger Hamlet, where we all ordered the famous Number Eleven—a bacon cheddar cheeseburger.

As the child of a Hollywood actor, I met many famous people while I was growing up. I was never terribly impressed by them, perhaps because I didn't really understand what they were famous for. I did understand early, though, what it meant to be famous. I saw how my father was treated and how we, my mother and I, reaped the benefits of his fame. We were given the best tables at restaurants, the most luxurious rooms in hotels, free gifts, complimentary food, beautiful service. It was seductive. To her credit, my mother understood how confusing growing up like this could be, and she took pains to see that I didn't become spoiled like so many other movie-star children. When I was old enough to decide that I was somehow special because I was Vincent Price's daughter, my mother had the ability to change my point of view—permanently.

By Hollywood standards of the 1960s, my parents were very strict and, I thought, rather old-fashioned. They were particularly concerned about how much television I watched. I was allowed one hour a day by myself in addition to the shows we watched together—the *CBS Evening News* with Walter Cronkite, *The Flintstones, Flipper, Gentle Ben, Batman, Get Smart, Mission: Impossible, The Avengers,* and anything of historical significance, such as Neil Armstrong's first steps on the moon. Furthermore, as a family, we rarely went to the movies. Thus, I didn't really know who any of the actors or celebrities were who came to our house. Some of my classmates at the Buckley School had famous parents—Clark Gable, Nat King Cole, Bobby Darrin and Sandra Dee, Edgar Bergen, James Coburn, Eartha Kitt, Vicki Carr, and Quinn Martin. Of all of these, the only ones who really meant anything to me were Eartha Kitt, who played Catwoman on *Batman,* and Quinn Martin, who produced, it seemed to me, every other show on TV.

However, I did meet a few famous people who really impressed me. During my one allowed hour of television I often watched reruns of *I Love Lucy,* so when my father guest-starred on *The Lucy Show* in 1970, my mother took me to watch the taping. When Lucy came out to talk to the audience before the show started, she introduced my mother and me. I couldn't believe that this brilliant woman I watched every night knew my name! On the show, my father played a parody of himself—an actor who was also an art expert. In one scene, Lucy telephoned "our house" and, while talking to my father, she said, "And how are Mary and Victoria?" Lucille Ball had mentioned my name on the air! I had arrived.

A few years later, my father took me with him to tape an episode of *The Sonny and Cher Show.* I had seen the famous duo on TV, and was casually interested in meeting them. Their daughter Chastity was a baby, and I was introduced to both mother and daughter in what seemed more like an exotic boudoir than a typical studio dressing room. But much more exciting than meeting Cher was meeting their other guest star, George Foreman, who had just been crowned heavyweight boxing champion of the world. He seemed so big that when he shook my hand I was afraid he would crush it. But he had the gentlest handshake. I was thrilled to meet him because I was a sports fanatic. Growing up in Hollywood, I never idolized movie stars. I never found them glamorous because it seemed to me that they were simply my father's colleagues. But sports were another thing. And animals.

For my tenth birthday, I was taken to meet my favorite movie star—Lassie. We drove out to Rudd Weatherwax's ranch in the California desert where I met all of the dogs who played Lassie, some of whom, to my surprise, were male. Mr. Weatherwax showed me how they did their tricks and then he gave me one of Lassie's books, personally autographed with a pawprint. Later that year, at a benefit my father did for Sea World in San Diego, I met another childhood idol—Shamu the Killer Whale.

A year earlier I had met the president of the United States, though at the time I was not sure it was a privilege. My parents and I flew to Washington, D.C. to attend a White House function for the Indian Arts and Crafts Board. President Nixon spoke to a small gathering, after which we moved through a receiving line to meet the president and the first lady. This was May 1971; I was in the fourth grade, and Nixon's name was practically anathema in Hollywood. Every night I watched Walter Cronkite deliver the body count from the Vietnam War; I thought Nixon was a "bad man," and I told my parents I didn't want to shake his hand. They in turn informed me that I had no choice. It was an early lesson in life's moral compromises. More surprising, this "bad man" was very nice to me.

Of my parents' many famous friends, a few did stand out. Chief among these was Helen Hayes, whom both my mother and father gave me to know was very special, and treated with a great deal of respect. She was always very kind to me—even after I played poker with her one night and blatantly cheated, which I was wont to do as a child. Indeed, I judged my parents' friends not by their fame, but by their capacity for fun. The winner in that category was undoubtedly Red Skelton.

But if I didn't know who most of the movie stars I met were, everyone certainly seemed to know who my dad was. When I was in the fifth grade he made a television commercial for children's vitamins in which he played on his villainous persona, pretending that he kept his children locked up in his basement. The gag was that, despite being a bad guy, he still fed his kids these children's vitamins, in the shapes of various monsters. For years people asked me if my father kept me in the basement. My dad got a real kick out of keeping current. He liked the fact that my friends—a whole new generation—knew who he was, but he also stayed "hip" for me, guest-starring on all of my favorite TV shows—*Get Smart, The Lucy Show, The Carol Burnett Show, The Brady Bunch* and, best of all as far as I was concerned, *Batman*, in which he played the show's classic villain, Egghead, who peppered his sentences with topical puns like "eggzactly" and "eggstraordinary." My friends were suitably impressed.

I was four years old when I first saw my father act. He was playing Captain Hook in a local production of *Peter Pan*, and my mother took me to see it. Throughout the whole first act, to the discomfiture of everyone around me, I had a very audible fit. I thought something had happened to my father's hand. I couldn't understand why he had a hook. During the intermission, my mother had to take me backstage where my father showed me that the dreaded hook was nothing more than a coat hanger. It never got much easier. I hated my father's horror movies. And it wasn't just the blood and gore. He died. In all of his movies, he *died*. I couldn't bear it.

As a little girl, I unreservedly adored my father. Ultimately it didn't matter to me how little time he spent at home, because the time we did spend together was so extraordinary.

He was fun and funny, handsome, enveloping, full of joy and his infectious love of life. Everything I did, everything I wanted to be, the life I hoped to have and the kind of person I wished to become, was derived from my father's singular and seductive way of being. I wanted to walk on a beach and find intense fascination in a brightly colored stone. I wanted to eat a meal and discover pure satisfaction in its flavors. I wanted to look at a painting and derive deep pleasure from its beauty. I wanted to move through the world and experience utter joy in its and my own existence. This was my childhood vision of Vincent Price, this man who was my father and whom I loved more than anyone in the world.

30

IN 1964, MY father's beloved dog, Joe, died at age seventeen. Later that same year, Vincent remembered his canine companion in an interview for *Pet Life* magazine: "Joe was once best described by a houseman of ours as 'a dog who was short on looks but long on disposition.' He was built like a coffee table with Duncan Phyfe legs, had a multicolored coat and great sorrowful brown eyes through which the beauty of his spirit shone." When asked what he and Joe had liked to do best, my father replied, "I liked to sit where Joe could lie at my feet."

Vincent had two consolations for Joe's passing. The first was that they had had a long and marvelous life together; the second was that he had immortalized Joe a few years earlier in a book, *The Book of Joe: About a Dog and His Man*. Having discovered how much he loved to write while working on *I Like What I Know*, Vincent next embarked on *The Book of Joe* with gusto; it not only chronicled his life with Joe, but also related stories about all the other animals in his and his family's lives. *The Book of Joe*, published by Doubleday in 1961, was dedicated "To the memory of my mother and father whose love for pets and people gave purpose to their lives and their children's."

My own mother and father, in turn, passed their love of pets on to me. I don't remember Joe, who died when I was two, but I loved our poodles, Prudence and Pasquale. Before I was born, there was some concern that Prudence might not take to me. Over the years her attachment to my mother had intensified, and my parents thought she might feel jealous of a new baby. But they needn't have worried—Prudence looked after me as if I was her own puppy. One of my most treasured photographs shows me, at six months, sitting on my nanny's knee with Prudence's head resting on my lap. But Pasquale was my favorite. He was a huge, living, breathing, huggable and playful stuffed toy of a dog.

When Prudence and Pasquale died my parents gave me my first dog, a Skye terrier named Paisley. Alas, she turned out to be untrainable, although she loved me and the family. When she got a little rough with a friend's baby, though, Paisley had to be given away to a trainer. The next dog, Puffie the pug, went to my father. Puffie was a big success, and even appeared with him on Betty White's television program about celebrities and their pets. But even though she was my dad's dog, I took care of her, or, perhaps, the other way around.

But no dog would ever touch my father's heart quite as Joe had. He wrote that *The Book of Joe* was "a tale of how I went to the dogs or, to be numerically correct, to the *dog*. Now please do not expect this book to end with a glorious proclamation of rehabilitation. Not a chance. After fourteen years I'm incurably hooked on, intoxicated by, and addicted to my dog, Joe." Written in what the jacket noted was a "merry and mellow" style, the book sold well and created a new school of Vincent Price fans among animal lovers.

Through his association with Sears, Vincent soon found another opportunity to put pen to paper. In 1964 he and Mary produced *The Michelangelo Bible* for the company. Touted as "a plan to put the family Bible back on the table in the living room as a work of art," it was published on the 400th anniversary of the death of Michelangelo. An elaborate, ornate, and oversized tome, it utilized fine-art photographs of Michelangelo's oeuvre, from the Sistine Chapel to statues of biblical characters, to illustrate biblical scenes. It was Vincent's idea to use Michelangelo's artwork to bring the Bible to life and he wrote all the copy for the book, but it was Mary who oversaw the design, working with photographers who were sent around the world to photograph Michelangelo's work and picking out all the paper and leather samples. *The Michelangelo Bible* contained 121 reproductions of the artist's work, a parchment paper section for noting family births, marriages, and deaths, a concordance, and maps of the Holy Land. Available in both the King James and the Revised Standard versions, it was sold at a cost of $30 in a presentation box that depicted the Sistine Chapel ceiling. Vincent expressed the hope that it would "help restore the Bible to its ancient and rightful place in the center of family living."

My parents made an excellent team, and after the success of *The Michelangelo Bible,* they approached Sears about producing a cookbook, an idea to which the company happily agreed. Throughout their extensive travels, they had collected recipes from the many restaurants in which they had eaten. *A Treasury of Great Recipes* was published in 1965 by Ampersand Press in association with Sears. As my father wrote in the book's introduction, "The purpose of this book is to invite you to dine, wine, break bread with us, to partake with us of our favorite dishes gleaned from kitchens all over the world. We have gone straight to the source, to the great chefs and to those dedicated to seeing to it that the world eats well. Mary and I have accepted not only their invitation to eat, but also the challenge of trying to find out what we were eating, why it was so good, and how it got that way. Behind the scenes we've met the alchemists in tall white hats who have initiated us into their mysteries. So far they've all been wonderful to us, and not a skillet has been raised in high dudgeon when we invaded their domain. Somehow it has gotten around that we are collectors of everything, all the arts, folk art, decorative art, fine art and the art of enjoying food—and preparing it.

"When we come back home from any trip to anywhere we try to bring something of that place with us. Sometimes there has been some aspect of a place that made us feel we could do something more to decorate our house when we returned, to remind us of that place. Or there came a day when we got home and it occurred to us how lovely it would be if we could have a meal such as the one we had in that tiny old restaurant in Spain. Then we would have fun cooking it and telling our guests where we first had it and how ours was different. The whole thing was a wonderful glamorous recreation of the experience. And that is what we really want to try to do for people with this book."

A Treasury of Great Recipes represents the cuisine of nine countries—France, Italy, Holland, Denmark, Norway, England, Spain, Mexico, and the United States. The recipes came from such world-renowned restaurants as the Tour d'Argent in Paris, the Ivy in London, and the Whitehall Club in Chicago; lesser-known establishments in places such as Puerto Rico, Brooklyn, and Memphis; and a few of my parents' favorite culinary haunts—Chavez Ravine (Dodger Stadium) in Los Angeles, Harrods' Food Halls in London, the Santa Fe Super Chief, and the Hotel Hana-Maui.

My mother was responsible for designing the book and was determined to preserve the principle on which it was based. As she said, "The principle of the book was that gourmet is where you find it and ambiance is what makes the occasion. Every time the publishers would bring in an idea, something that veered from that principle, I said no. For example, they were determined to have a suckling pig and I said that Vincent and I would never do that. Nothing that anyone couldn't make in their own kitchen was included and so it was completely consistent. The cookbook was a huge thing in our life. We did it in six months and we were all very tense."

Sears made efforts to cut costs on the project, but my mother stuck to her guns and the final product was a handsome and lavish volume with a copper and gold cover, its recipes printed on heavy paper, and illustrated with over seventy full-color photographs. The book was the first of its kind and even at the then high price of $20 it did extremely well. In just over a year it sold 50,000 copies, and has since become a collector's item, fetching up to $500 at book auctions.

Much of what appealed to the public was the style of the book, which included photographs of many of the restaurants featured along with some wonderful pictures of our own home. For each country, there was a two-page description of the gastronomic pleasures written in my father's colloquial tone. Italy, for example, he described as "surely one of the most beautiful countries in the world, a place where every vista is a feast for the eye. Time seems to have sustained it through all the ages only, I suspect, because it has been so loved by those who live there. When the orchards produce their first fruits, when the old earth yields a new crop of vegetables, Italians thank God for these fresh proofs of His bounty. This gratitude is one of the secrets of Italian happiness, and this seasonal respect for the good things of the earth is what makes each meal in Italy a special feast. The waiter peeling a red orange from Sicily, the first little pencil-thin stalks of asparagus, rich red ruby cherries, tender baby lamb, all are celebrated as they are eaten. In time with nature, never out of step, one can taste the months go by in the simplest or most elegant places to eat."

The cookbook attracted national and international audiences, and Vincent was soon being treated as a culinary expert. This new identity opened the door to friendships with many chefs around the world. In December 1965 Martha Deane, host of a popular television cooking show, wrote Vincent: "My husband and I were in Madrid last month and a friend took us to Botin for dinner. The proprietor came over and sat with us for a little while and talked about food in which my husband has a great interest, as you know. Finally, Bill hinted around that he would like to have the recipe for Botin's Andalusian Cold Soup. The owner started to write the recipe but, without looking up, he said, 'Do you know Vincent Price?' With some pride I told him that you have been on my program several times and that we have your superb cookbook. 'Well,' he said, 'the recipe is in Vincent Price's cookbook.' The rest of the evening was spent in singing your praises, each of us trying to outdo the other."

Much of the impetus for the cookbook clearly derived from the Prices' wonderful dinner parties and grand functions. In 1965 Vincent was named International Ambassador for California Wines, and later that year he and Mary threw a gala evening in honor of his appointment. Their guest list was a virtual who's who of Hollywood: In addition to their intimate circle and regular social acquaintances, it included the Dominick Dunnes, Andre Previn, Norton Simon, Angie Dickinson, the Ray Starks and their guest Ronald

Reagan, John Frankenheimer, Lee Remick, Vera Miles, Ann Sothern, Judith Evelyn, Angela Lansbury, Charlton Heston, Ray Milland, Maureen O'Hara, Eva Marie Saint, David Niven, Fred Astaire, Joan Fontaine, Herbert Bayard Swope, Mel Ferrer, the Sam Goldwyns, Merle Oberon, Gene Tierney, and Richard Basehart. The event was a huge success, and Vincent continued to host elaborate wine tastings on behalf of the California vineyards.

In 1967, Vincent was invited to become a founder-member of the American Food and Wine Institute. He spoke on behalf of the new organization in an effort to raise awareness of the quality of domestic wines, delivering a message not dissimilar to the one he carried on behalf of the visual arts: "The love of wine is a case of constant discovery." The American Food and Wine Institute grew steadily in prestige from its small-scale beginnings, and my father continued to derive great pleasure from his association with it for the rest of his life.

My parents' reputation as accomplished hosts and patrons of the arts frequently afforded them the opportunity to entertain distinguished guests, including foreign visitors. One of these, who came to dinner at 580 in the late 1950s, was the German Expressionist artist Max Beckmann. Beckmann spoke very little English, leaving his wife Quapi to interpret. At the end of the visit, as my father told it, "Quapi said, 'Thank you so much. It's just meant so much to Max. He would like to send you a drawing.' Beckmann went up to Mills College in San Francisco to teach, and then went back to New York and died. To my amazement, Beckmann's dealer, at Quapi's behest, did indeed send me a drawing. Whether Beckmann picked it or not, I don't know, but it's a wonderful drawing of an accordion player from the thirties when he was in Berlin."

In November 1965 my parents were asked to host a private dinner for Princess Margaret and Lord Snowden, whom they had met in England. Arranging the event required careful and detailed organization. The guests had to be approved and the house security-checked. The guest list was very small—Lord Snowden's private secretary, Princess Margaret's lady-in-waiting, a few distinguished guests from the British embassy, the Brices, and the Dreyfusses. It was one of the smallest of Price dinner parties, but it required more time and effort than any other. As a child, I was naturally too young to be included in such events. I was, however, usually brought down as Exhibit A to curtsey to the assembled company before being sent off to bed. Army Archerd once wrote that I looked "for all the world like Alice in Wonderland."

In 1966 Vincent received yet another exciting offer, this time as a result of his growing success as an author: He was invited to contribute a regular column on art in the Sunday *Chicago Tribune*. Naturally he jumped at the chance, and for over four years he wrote a weekly column which soon became syndicated nationwide. He covered a large range of topics. The opening article was on the *Venus of Cyrene*, the ancient marble statue that Vincent referred to as "a beautiful girl from a small town in northern Africa, who finally made it to the big city, Rome." Over the years the articles would discuss particular pieces of art, as well as individual artists from Rubens to Giacometti. Some dealt with controversial topics such as the high prices paid for paintings at auction, the historic preservation of old buildings, or the unjust neglect of American Indian art; in others Vincent lent his light tone to ruminations as diverse as flowers, dogs, or the ocean, places like Hawaii and Rome, even, on occasion, his own friends—Tallulah Bankhead, for example, or the Milams and the beautiful home they had created.

Inspired by the possibility that each week he might be able to convert one more newspaper reader to his love of art, Vincent wrote in a vernacular style that combined knowledge and erudition with a down-home approachability, even when dealing with touchy subjects. In an October 29, 1967 article entitled "Why a Furor over Nudity in Art?" he wrote, "Objections to nudity in art are hard to explain. Art's first subjects were nudes and animals, and the human male and female were portrayed, naturally, without clothes. Nakedness is something else, but the nude in art is the portrayal of the unself-conscious human body." He always tried to entertain as well as to inform his readers. His September 22, 1968 piece was titled "Why 'Junk' Sculpture?" "I sympathize with the tyro art viewer who is baffled by the 'inventiveness' of the modern sculptor. It helps to know that the use of scrap metal, junk, and the 'found object' can be attributed in part to the economic chaos in which so many sculptors find themselves. It may also help to realize how little sculpture is understood by even the most supposedly knowledgeable art collector . . . I sympathize with the lack of understanding of, and the collecting of, sculpture, and yet I know of no other art form that can give such complete aesthetic pleasure. Perhaps one of the reasons for this column is to try to get more people to understand and share that pleasure, and to encourage the sculptors of America."

Writing a syndicated column became one of Vincent's favorite assignments in his long and varied career. He welcomed the wide-reaching forum the column provided for sharing his ideas about art with thousands of readers around the country.

31

VINCENT PRICE'S AFFILIATION with Sears was an unqualified success during its first years; so much so, in fact, that it quickly became apparent both to him and to his employer that, with his acting commitments, he could not be expected to continue doing all the buying himself. Nevertheless, he maintained that if his name was attached to the collection, some way had to be found by which he could keep control, which meant approving each piece of art sold by the company. George Struthers had introduced him to a well-known Chicago entrepreneur and collector of French Impressionism named Harry Sundheim. Sundheim, Vincent's agent Lester Salkow, and Vincent thus formed Vincent Price Enterprises, which oversaw and made all decisions regarding the collection. A young Yale graduate named Jeffrey Loria was hired as "a consultant seeking works of art on Vincent Price's behalf," acting as Vincent's eyes and legs for initial forays into possible ventures on the East Coast. Back in Los Angeles Hank Milam also became closely involved, but it quickly became clear that what Vincent needed was a full-time secretary.

A simple office at the end of the long driveway at 580 became the West Coast headquarters of Vincent Price Enterprises. There, Vincent and Hank each had a place to work and room was made for a secretary. But after a few less-than-successful hires, it seemed as if they were never going to find someone whom they could trust and who could handle their hectic and idiosyncratically creative style of running a business. Then Wawona Hartwig came to temp at 580. Wawona had originally come to Hollywood as a stunt rider, but was no longer in the movie business. She had never really worked as a secretary, but as a favor to a friend who had just left the post for a more conventional job, she agreed to fill in answering the phone for a week or so.

After a few days at 580, not yet having met either Vincent or Mary, she was asked by Hank Milam to type some galleys for the cookbook. At the end of the week, she received an invitation to a Sunday luncheon at the Prices' poolhouse. She recalled, "I don't know why I got invited to their party, but I think they were testing me out to see if I got along and if I knew my manners or something. They had invited a bunch of Democrats to raise money, and somehow Mr. Price knew I was a Republican. We were almost through the whole dinner and he stood up and he banged on the glass and then he called for contributions for Hubert Humphrey. Then, at the very end, he said, 'But I must tell you, we have a spy in our midst.' And everybody murmured. And then he looked at me and then looked away. And I thought, 'Goldarn you, that's a dirty, lousy trick. I'm embarrassed enough with all these movie people. I'll fix you.' So, I just stood up and said, 'Yes.' And he came over and gave me a big kiss on the cheek. After that, any time he could befuddle me in any way, he did it, just to see how I was going to get out of it."

The day after the party, Vincent offered Wawona a permanent full-time job. She remembered, "I told him I didn't think I was qualified and that I wasn't really interested. And he said, 'We'd like you.' And then I said, 'Well, I don't know anything about art and I don't want to learn,' and then he said, 'Well, that's all right. Do you think I want somebody down here who knows more than I do?' So then I told him, 'I don't take dictation and I'm not really a secretary.' But he said, 'I don't want to spend all my time dictating. Do you think you can write your own letters?' I said I thought I could but that I didn't like Dictaphones. And he said, 'I don't like using those machines.' Well, he wore me down. I had no more excuses, so I told him I'd think about it. Eventually I gave in, and I'm sure glad I did."

By mid-1964, with Jeffrey Loria on the East Coast, the Prices, Salkow, Milam, and Wawona Hartwig on the West, and Sundheim in Chicago, Vincent Price Enterprises was running in high gear. After a year or so, my parents' workload for Sears had so increased that it was necessary to hire an assistant for Wawona. The association of Vincent Price Enterprises and Sears, Roebuck was booming.

In 1964, Sears and the Prices joined forces for a new program—National Treasures. Mary explained, "Our third venture for Sears was National Treasures, which was also George Struthers's idea. The premise was to research and reproduce items used, although not necessarily manufactured, in America from the earliest days through 1900. It was an ideal concept for Sears because in those days the company had a department for almost everything used in daily life, and National Treasures consisted of furnishings in all sizes, shapes, and forms. What made it an exciting project was that they appointed a committee to research in museums, historic sites, catalogues, contemporary magazines, and private collections. The committee consisted of Letitia Baldridge, a well-known writer of etiquette books who was social secretary to Jacqueline Kennedy; Marvin Schwartz, who was then the antiques editor for the *New York Times* and curator of decorative arts at the Brooklyn Museum; Dick Butler, head of design for Sears; a representative from Winterthur, the great design museum; and myself. In many cases we were able to have certain items manufactured at their original sources. For example, we had Delftware made in Holland. The quality of all the merchandise was extraordinary."

The National Treasures were organized into five periods of American history: Early Eastern Settlements (struggle for survival years, 1607–1730), Spirit of '76 (years of independence and elegance, 1730–1800), Spanish Colonial (mission years, 1600–1850), Ante Bellum (splendor of the South years, 1800-1850), and American Victorian (man and machine years, 1850–1900). The National Treasures were carefully reproduced to exacting standards, and in limited editions; all pieces were stamped with the manufacturer's mark as well as a special hallmark representing Vincent Price and Sears' National Treasures. Vincent and Mary promoted the new line by touring the country with a slide presentation called "Portals of the Past."

Having spent over a decade scouring the antique stores and junkyards of Southern California for forgotten treasures, the Prices simply continued these expeditions on behalf of their new venture. Usually accompanied by Hank—and sometimes Marin—Milam, they would set off in the Clark Cortez in search of inspiration. At one antique store,

Mary, Hank, and Marin decided to go in while Vincent stayed in the Clark Cortez—a common occurrence whenever Mary thought they could get a better price if her famous husband stayed out of sight. When Mary and the Milams came out of the store, they found a small crowd had gathered. The Clark Cortez was one of the first motor homes of its kind, and wherever it appeared it was greeted with curiosity and interest. As they approached the vehicle, the group of onlookers asked if they could see inside. Mary agreed and opened the back door. A woman was the first to peer in whereupon she recoiled with a scream, for lying on the floor of the vehicle, stretched out like a corpse, was Vincent Price, the King of Horror. My father was taking one of his beloved ten-minute naps: He would stretch out on whatever floor was handy—on a set during lunch, in his trailer, at an airport—drop off immediately, and wake up ten or fifteen minutes later completely refreshed. The poor woman had quite a shock, but once startled from his nap, Vincent gave the group a tour of the home on wheels. My parents and the Milams gleefully recounted the incident for years afterward.

Hank Milam, who went on to become one of Southern California's most successful designers, found his work for National Treasures very exciting. "It was one of the world's most fabulous ideas. What we were looking for were things that were really tasteful and good-looking, but could be expanded into every department of Sears and that most households could absorb. For example, if you could find a precedent for a wonderful table lamp or an object that could be made into a table lamp, then Sears would commission the lamps to be made and sold. And, of course, at that time, Sears had about nine hundred retail stores, so it was a wonderful opportunity. George Struthers felt it would be wonderful for the prestige of the company."

The public response to National Treasures was tremendous, and Struthers was immensely pleased. Under the auspices of National Treasures, Sears and the Prices decided to exploit the popularity of *A Treasury of Great Recipes* by creating the *National Treasures Cookbooks*. Based on the premise that "To all men at all times a journey to a new country has been an adventure," the small series of beautifully designed books chronicled the history of the United States through its food, including such recipes as Kentucky soup, Shaker pease porridge, Lone Star chicken, and stuffed tortillas. In 1965 the association between the Prices and Sears reached its creative pinnacle.

My father circled the globe buying art to sell through Sears. A January 1965 article in the *Los Angeles Times* quoted him as saying, "In the last four weeks in London I've bought $30,000 worth of graphics, watercolors, oil paintings, and drawings. So far this year I've bought artworks worth nearly three-quarters of a million dollars. I guess no one's been buying on this scale since the Medici." Vincent continued to purchase art at this remarkable pace and on an amazing scale. Most of the initial purchases had been made in galleries, but warehouses were later set up and filled with pieces for Vincent to review. In Japan, a whole room of Haniwa ceramic figures was assembled for his approval. This became a usual practice. Wawona Hartwig recalled, "They were ready for him when he'd get to wherever he was going. There were whole warehouses full of art that he would just go in and see, and in L.A. they'd line paintings up all the way down our driveway and he'd point, That one. That one. That one. I couldn't figure out why he'd pick that one over this one and finally I said to him, 'Would you tell me why you don't want this one.' Maybe I could learn from that. And I did."

Needless to say, the logistics of buying and selling for Sears were often overwhelming and the potential pitfalls alarming. On June 16, 1965 the *Los Angeles Herald Examiner* ran the headline VINCENT PRICE ART COLLECTION STOLEN.'' The $135,000 Vincent Price

Art Collection was reported missing en route from the Sahara Hotel in Las Vegas, where it had been shown, to a Sears warehouse near downtown Los Angeles. Among the missing items was Salvador Dali's $25,000 *Mystical Rose Madonna*. Wawona recalled, "Mr. Price was home alone, because Mrs. Price was in Chicago. When the van went missing, the authorities called him, and the calls went back and forth with Chicago and the police and the FBI. Everyone in God's green earth was there at the house. Mr. Price was just sitting in the office and all I could say was, 'No comment, no comment.' That's all I could say.

"Now when Mrs. Price wasn't there, she asked me to be sure that he got himself dressed right for things. He would go to film *Hollywood Squares* and he had to take clothes for five shows, and once he had gotten together some really weird combinations. He wore just the most dilapidated clothes. Never any socks, just old tennis shoes, and always he would rumple up his hair. He would do it purposely sometimes, and I would ask him, 'Why do you do that?' 'Oh, it likes that. It likes to grow that way,' he said. So, here he was in the office, looking just terrible, and the press was gathering at the front steps down the driveway, and I had to tell them Mr. Price wasn't home.

"Finally I said to him, 'You've just got to talk to them. Sooner or later somebody's going to wander back here. You've got to get upstairs and change.' But there was no way to get upstairs without the reporters seeing, so I made him climb up the hill and go in the back way. I didn't want anybody to see him looking like that. And all the time I was thinking about Mrs. Price. She'd *die* if anybody saw him looking like that, especially picture-takers. I was kind of on her side. I was used to people behaving and he didn't always behave. So I went down to tell the press he was coming, and the door opens and he comes down the steps and he's dressed just like a million dollars. Leisure clothes, but just that perfect poise. I was so mad at him, I just could have killed him."

The following morning, the *Los Angeles Times* reported that the missing van had been found. As Jack Smith, then a young staff writer, noted, "The truck driver who left $135,000 worth of art in a parked van while he toured local beer galleries for two days, was sleeping it off Thursday—but still has his job. 'He's too dependable a man to let go,' said Watson's boss. Besides, he pointed out, Watson has seven children. The FBI, as usual, declined to comment."

The Vincent Price Collection continued to flourish and, in addition to the traveling collection, Sears began marketing it through a special mail-order catalogue which featured the work of thirty-two artists, including Rembrandt, Dürer, Picasso, Chagall, Goya, and Piranesi. Prices for this special collection ranged from $30 to $2,000, with the majority falling in the $30 to $175 range. Certain pieces were commissioned by Vincent, including an edition of one hundred lithographs by Man Ray called *Still Life*.

Although Sears was popularly recognized as a legitimate purveyor of fine art, certain mainstream dealers resented the idea of "department store art" and began voicing public concern about the authenticity of the collection. Among the most vocal of these was Frank Perls, a prominent figure in the Los Angeles art world, and a friend of Vincent's for over twenty years. My father recalled that, when he had to relinquish exclusive control of the buying, he was "very concerned that things be as good as possible, but you could only do that as long as you had complete control. The minute they brought in other buyers I had a terrible time, because they didn't really care whether it was the five-thousandth strike of a Picasso etching or an original Salvador Dali."

Despite a certain laxity that crept into quality control, my father continued to believe that the Sears project was fulfilling its larger goal of providing art to the masses. When Frank Perls aired his concerns to the press, my father was devastated and felt betrayed by his friend. Bill Brice recalled, "He was really upset and hurt by some of the response to his working at Sears and to the Vincent Price Collection. It was really an uncommon idea, that you'd buy your Goya or your Rembrandt at Sears. But Frank Perls had reservations about that because it was encroaching on the uniqueness of the gallery scene. The dealers felt that, as the project developed, it wasn't certain whether Vincent had chosen all the works himself, and there was some question as to whether the buying process was honestly represented. A rather unattractive kind of thinking, and Vincent was really upset by it. On one level, he knew all about people and all about life, but he also had a lot of idealism, and I've always felt that the risk for idealists is disillusionment. I truly believe that what attracted him most to the Sears project was the opportunity to realize his ideas about the democracy of art. He was really anti-elitist in that sense. Vincent was passionately devoted to the arts and yet he was totally devoid of arrogance." Indeed, my father was thoroughly bewildered by Frank Perls's objections to his efforts to enlarge the audience and the market for art. He felt that if Perls had had a problem, he should have talked to him in private instead of publicly attacking the Vincent Price Collection. Though Perls eventually backed down, not only did the dealer irreparably damage a twenty-year friendship, but my father felt he also tainted the standing of the Sears venture. But this was only the beginning of the end.

Although each of Mary and Vincent's artistic endeavors garnered a reputation for inventiveness and originality, they were somewhat ahead of their time; they were certainly ahead of Sears's time. For four years, beginning in 1962, they had been steadfastly championed by George Struthers and a few other key executives, but when Struthers died suddenly in 1966, problems arose. Mary was the first to experience the sting of the new administration, when her work on the framing became the initial stumbling block between corporate America and creative enterprise. Sears began quarreling with the expense of providing quality frames for the collection, and Mary resigned.

Her departure was just the tip of the iceberg. Struthers' replacement, J. W. Button, viewed art as a commodity no different from tractors or frying pans, and expected the same price stability and profit margins. Thus, he quickly lost patience with the ebb and flow of the art market and encouraged his company to invest their funds and energies elsewhere. In 1966 Button began moving the Vincent Price Collection into a "second phase," pushing to replace the countrywide traveling shows with permanent galleries at strategically placed stores.

Aside from Button's desire to market art for maximum profit, he demanded that Vincent guarantee authenticity to Sears art customers. As Vincent saw it, "I became a middleman for the arts in the Sears thing. And it all just fell apart in the greed of modern business." In 1967, Button decided that efforts should be concentrated on one Sears art gallery, choosing Chicago, where the company headquarters were located. It quickly became clear, however, that the new administration at Sears was far less enthusiastic about art than their farsighted predecessors had been. A few months later, Vincent received a letter from J. W. Button informing him that the gallery would not be proceeding as planned, but asking him to "ride this out with us and then in a few months we both can review our desire to continue the art phase."

Although Vincent did continue his association with Sears through the early 1970s, his unique position in making art accessible and available to the public at large came to an untimely end. Sears also terminated National Treasures. Although the new administration was responsible for the dissolution of these visionary projects, my father, in some small way, played his part. By nature a man of quick enthusiasms, he nonetheless required that those enthusiasms be nurtured by the wholehearted response and support of others. After George Struthers died, as Hank Milam told me, "Vincent got bored with it. He hated the paperwork. It was not in Vincent's background, the regime and the routine, although he took it very seriously at the beginning." My mother agreed that, "Vincent got bored with the business of Sears. Except for art and acting, he had no stick-to-it-ness, no discipline." My father had spent a lifetime avoiding the nuts and bolts of commercialism, and he deeply resented Sears tarnishing, as he saw it, the ideals with which he had embarked on the enterprise.

32

IN THE EARLY sixties, Vincent's association with AIP had been immensely fruitful for all parties. Although Arkoff and Nicholson mostly utilized and promoted the actor's popular horror persona, they nonetheless cast him as Robur the Conqueror, a nineteenth-century inventor and pacifist, in 1960's *Master of the World*, an epic adventure inspired by two Jules Verne novels. The picture reunited most key members of the *House of Usher* production team, with one glaring exception: Roger Corman.

Vincent costarred with *House of Wax*'s Charles Buchinsky, by this point well-known as Charles Bronson. It was generally considered that Bronson was miscast in the film, and according to screenwriter Dick Matheson, he knew it. "Bronson was very unhappy. Testy is more the word. Vincent Price, who could make friends with a dead man, said, 'I can't get through to this guy. I cannot make friends with him.' " Directed by William Witney, the film had a cheap feel to it, but Vincent's reviews were nonetheless reasonably favorable, and the film proved very popular, particularly with teenagers. It grossed upward of $2 million.

In January 1963, AIP sent Vincent to Rome to shoot *The Last Man on Earth*, a science-fiction thriller in which he played, with commendable restraint, the only man on earth immune to a plague which is transforming the human race into vampires. (Charlton Heston starred in the film's more popular 1971 remake, *The Omega Man*.)

Although AIP held the sole rights to his horror persona in the Poe cycle, this didn't prevent Vincent from finding work with other studios as an independent contractor. In 1961 he made two films for Allied Artists, *Convicts 4* and *Confessions of an Opium Eater*. In the first, he had what amounted to little more than a cameo role, but the subject matter of the picture was right up his alley, and he was one of a cast that included Rod Steiger and Sammy Davis Jr. *Convicts 4* was based on the true story of John Resko (played by Ben Gazzara), an incarcerated murderer who, while in jail, discovers that he is a gifted painter. This talent eventually leads to his rehabilitation. Vincent played author and art critic Carl Carmer, who visits a prison art class and "discovers" Resko.

The second Allied Artists film, *Confessions of an Opium Eater*, was more of a star turn for Vincent but one that, in retrospect, he could happily have done without. He played Gil de Quincey, an early nineteenth-century gentleman who infiltrated the Tong sub-culture in San Francisco in order to help expose the inhumane practice of auctioning girls into slavery. Vincent was the hero of this action thriller, but the script was poor; worse yet, the film was caught in unwelcome controversy when the Los Angeles Committee against Defamation of the Chinese protested its release. When it reached theaters in June 1962, its appeal was summarized by the British *Monthly Film Bulletin*: "This crude claptrap has to be seen to be believed."

Over the course of the next year, Vincent signed on for three films made by Admiral Pictures and released through United Artists. With his burgeoning reputation as cinema's reining horror star, these films sought to take advantage of his command of the genre. In early 1962, Roger Corman's brother, Gene, announced that he would produce "a psychological study of Richard III" to be directed by Roger with Vincent Price starring. Though it was originally intended as a color movie, at the last minute Admiral decided on black-and-white, a fact which severely limited the film's success. With the same title, *Tower of London*, as the 1939 Universal version in which Vincent had also appeared, the film chronicled Richard's murderous rampage in pursuit of the throne. Reviews were mediocre, but the campy trend of horror films of the 1960s was by now hard to miss; as the *Los Angeles Times* reflected, "Mr. Price has a field day as the miserable monarch, particularly when his ghostly 'pals' return to taunt him. There's a strong possibility that you might chuckle here and there at the hysterical goings-on, but dyed-in-the-wool horror devotees should have a quivering good time."

Vincent appeared in *Diary of a Madman* directed by Reginald LeBorg for Admiral Pictures during the summer of 1962. It was a dull adaptation from Guy de Maupassant, in which the actor played a turn-of-the-century French magistrate who kills in self-defense when attacked by a man whom he condemned to death. The magistrate ends up setting fire to his house and himself—a typical Price demise.

At the end of the year, Vincent Price and Admiral made their final film together: *Twice-Told Tales*, a trilogy based on the stories of Nathaniel Hawthorne. Filmed by Sidney Salkow on a pitiful budget, the film was a miscaluculation of sorts, as *Newsweek* noted: "Vincent Price has almost single-handedly restored the works of Edgar Allan Poe to the screen, but one man can't carry everybody. Price has tried to make a horror writer out of Nathaniel Hawthorne. Despite a strenuous lot of tinkering with the material, Hawthorne doesn't have the stuff." But Vincent was never one to look a gift horse in the mouth; if there was an audience for his movies, he would continue to make them.

In 1964 Vincent signed a new contract with AIP, which gave him a considerable increase in salary. And yet not long after, as Arkoff recalled, "There was a period when horror movies weren't working. We had this commitment with Vincent, so we put him in pictures which, frankly, Vincent wasn't too happy with." With the appeal of the horror genre suddenly (but, happily, temporarily) on the wane, Vincent's contract with AIP, which required that he appear in at least three films a year for the company, saddled him with a string of pictures that he initially approached with good humor, but gradually came to regret. From 1963 to 1967, he appeared in a bewildering succession of AIP gems: *Beach Party, Taboos of the World, War Gods of the Deep, Dr. Goldfoot and the Bikini Machine, Dr. Goldfoot and the Girl Bombs*, and *House of a Thousand Dolls*.

Fortunately, most of these films merely required AIP's chief breadwinner to make a cameo appearance or supply a narration. *Beach Party*, the first of an immensely lucrative series of sixties teen flicks from AIP, starred Robert Cummings, Frankie Avalon, and Annette Funicello, with Vincent briefly appearing as Big Daddy, the guru of the beach. Throughout most of the action, Big Daddy is seen sitting in a corner of a bar, wearing a loose-fitting white suit, striped T-shirt, and large straw hat, completely out of it, while the kids in the film wait for him to wake up and give them "The Word." Vincent got a kick out of being featured in the groovy role, and it was he who came up with Big Daddy's immortal line: "The Pit! Bring me my pendulum, kiddies—I feel like swingin'!"

Vincent's initial willingness to appear in cameo roles spoofing his movie persona made him the ideal actor for AIP, who used him to narrate their "shockumentary" *Taboos of the World* and cast him in the title role in the teen-oriented Dr. Goldfoot series. The first of these, *Dr. Goldfoot and the Bikini Machine*, a high-camp sendup of the James Bond movie *Goldfinger*, was silly but successful, and Vincent seemed to be enjoying himself on screen, playing the mysterious doctor who tries to capture the world's richest men with the help of bikini-clad robots. AIP's attempt to cash in with a sequel proved catastrophic, however, and Vincent was at sea in the bizarre company of teen singing sensation Fabian and the team of Ciccio and Franco, the Abbott and Costello of Italy. Though Deke Heyward was brought in to do rewrites and co-produce, Vincent grew increasingly depressed—and with good reason. Heyward recalled, "We had one person speaking Portugese, several of them speaking Italian. Vincent would shake his head in disbelief and say, 'What is happening to me?' Not only did he not understand the Italians or the Portugese or the Spanish; he didn't understand Fabian."

Unfortunately, the Dr. Goldfoot sequel was merely one of many abysmal films in which Vincent's contract now obliged him to appear. In November 1964, he had flown to England for a four-week shoot at Pinewood Studios with director Jacques Tourneur. The result was *War Gods of the Deep*, a thinly disguised version of *Journey to the Center of the Earth*, that paired Vincent with teen idol Tab Hunter in another disaster. At least Vincent was able to console himself in London by indulging in an extensive art-buying spree for Sears. But by 1967, when he found himself in Madrid to shoot *House of a Thousand Dolls*, he had grown more than disillusioned with his work for AIP. Costarring Martha Hyer, this West German–Spanish co-production about white slavery featured numerous deaths and the brutal flaying of a scantily clad woman. Unbeknownst to Miss Hyer and Vincent, as he later discovered, "They were making a dirty version of the film at the same time. Every day we'd have off, they'd make a dirty version. We went visiting on the set one day and there was everyone naked!"

Although my father was in despair about the sorry run of films he was being forced to make, at the same time he was in the most visible and popular era in his career. As an actor in his mid-fifties, he did not take his growing appeal for granted, and from judging the Miss America Pageant to appearing as Grand Marshall of the Santa Claus Parade in Hollywood, he brought grace and charm to every event with which he was associated. He also continued tireless in his support of charities and causes, and he remained an active supporter of the Democratic party—though after his difficulties during the McCarthy era he tried to distance himself from overtly radical political associations. But, as my mother told me, "He came to feel, as did a great many people in the industry, that unless an actor was politically knowledgeable, he could do more harm than good in that arena." Nonetheless, during the turbulent sixties, he did make an effort to lend his support to the Civil Rights movement and other liberal causes whenever he felt he could be of genuine assistance.

For the most part, however, my father preferred to concentrate his efforts in support of the visual arts. He was invited to sit on a number of distinguished boards and committees around the country, including the National Committee for Manhattan's new

Whitney Museum. Headed by Jacqueline Kennedy, the committee also included Cleveland Amory, members of the Warburg and Vanderbilt dynasties, and Vincent's old friend Edward G. Robinson. As an ongoing trustee of the Archives of American Art he continued his efforts to gather materials pertaining to the history of American art, serving the organization along with Mrs. Edsel B. Ford, Al Capp, Senator J. W. Fulbright, and Joseph Hirschhorn. He also sat on the National Advisory Council of the National Society of Arts and Letters and the National Council of the Museum of the American Indian. He frequently lent his famous voice to public service announcements on behalf of museum and art groups throughout the United States, including the St. Louis Art Museum, the Albright-Knox Gallery in Buffalo, the Denver Art Museum, and the Los Angeles Natural History Museum.

My father also continued to devote two months a year to lecture tours. He genuinely enjoyed the interaction with students and faculty, and also found in the tours a measure of personal freedom from his endless professional obligations. Surprisingly, for a famous and sophisticated public figure, he was sometimes unable to cope with the simplest situations. Wawona collected a fund of stories about these tours. "One time he got off the train and it was snowing and nobody met him. And he called and said, 'What'll I do, Wawona?' You know, a grown man, intelligent as all hell! So I said to get a taxi, and he said that there weren't any. So then I asked if there were any cars around, and he said that some other people had been met at the train. So I said, 'Well, why don't you just go introduce yourself and ask them if you can get a ride into town with them.' So, later, the phone rang again and he had done that and he said, 'You know they were just so nice. They didn't mind taking me at all. It was just like they'd always known me.' Didn't he *know* that he just had to put his face in the car?! Sometimes he had no conception of who he was. No conception at all."

But even the fulfillment he derived from his work on behalf of the visual arts could not offset my father's fears about his declining acting career. Thus it was with great pleasure that he accepted a 1967 offer to star in a new Broadway musical, *Married Alive*, with music and lyrics by the incomparable Jule Styne and E. Y. Harburg. For the first time in ages he was hired not for his horror persona, but for the cultivated and artistic image that had been his earliest drawing card. The show was a musical adaptation of Arnold Bennett's *Buried Alive*, which concerned an early twentieth-century English landscape painter who despises the phoniness of the art world. When his butler dies the painter takes his place and goes into hiding, but soon runs into problems when a kindly widow (played by English actress Patricia Routledge) discovers his true identity.

His delight and excitement at the prospect of starring in a Broadway musical, however, would prove short-lived. The show previewed in Toronto in early December before moving on to the Shubert Theatre in Boston, where my mother and I joined him for Christmas. I was only five and had a wonderful Christmas with my parents in snow-covered Boston. I thought the show was wonderful, but then my opinion was hardly the one that mattered.

When the show reached New York in early January 1968, the producers made every effort to promote it—Vincent and Pat Routledge even appeared on *The Ed Sullivan Show*—but the advance was weak and, despite the fact that Routledge won a Tony award for her superb performance, *Darling of the Day*, as the show had been retitled, ran for a paltry thirty-two performances at the George Abbot Theatre before it closed.

The failure of the show could have been predicted after its troubled history. In his book *Not Since Carrie: Forty Years of Broadway Musical Flops*, Ken Mandelbaum notes, "Arnold Bennett's novel, which had already been adapted to the stage and screen, might have been the basis for a decent musical, but *Darling of the Day* was one of the most ill-starred projects in Broadway history. The book was first written by Keith Waterhouse and Willis Hall, Peter Wood was set to direct, and Geraldine Page to star. But E.Y. Harburg, the lyricist, did not see eye to eye with that team, so S. N. Behrman wrote a new book, and Albert Marre was hired to direct. That grouping did not work out either, and it fell to Nunnally Johnson to write yet another book and Steven Vinaver to direct. Before rehearsals started, Vinaver was fired, replaced by Marre, and then rehired. After bad reviews in Toronto and Boston, Noel Willman was brought in to replace Vinaver, Roger O. Hirson was brought in to revise the book, and Johnson removed his name from the credits; there was no author listed when the show opened on Broadway.

"The most interesting thing about *Darling of the Day* is that it was a flop that got good reviews—but the good reviews came too late. Because first-string *Times* critic Clive Barnes wished to cover a dance event, the *Times* assigned its second-stringer, Dan Sullivan to cover it. Watts in the *Post* and Chapman in the *News* liked it, but Sullivan didn't. A few days later, Barnes wrote about the show favorably in his dance column, and in the Sunday *Times*, Walter Kerr also approved; but the damage was done, and business never picked up. *Darling of the Day* closed as the costliest Broadway failure to date, losing over $750,000 on an initial investment of $500,000."

My mother remembers: "It was a big disappointment. It ought to have been a very successful production, because the music was composed by two men with a long reputation behind them. But everything in the production was mediocre. The score was in no way memorable, the visual was disappointing, apparently hampered by an impossibly low budget. That was especially upsetting to me because the costumes had been done by Raoul Pene du Bois, my old employer for whom I had enormous admiration. The main flaw was in the direction, as the critics were quick to note. In its earlier form as a British movie, it was charming. I saw it three times when it came out. And the musical should have been equally entertaining, but it missed the bus. In my mind, Pat Routledge and Vincent were perfectly cast in the lead roles, but they were laboring away in a show in which everything else was second rate. Vincent was extremely upset by the failure of *Darling of the Day* because, to him and to everyone else, its demise was totally unnecessary. It was devastating to Vincent. It was a very sad time."

After the play's closing night Vincent wrote Hank and Marin Milam: "I guess this ain't my year—it's all over but the postmortems and the next person who says 'That's show biz' is going to get my fist some highly uncomfortable place. Saturday just as the curtain went up on the matinée they told us we would close that night. It was the culmination of some of the most unbelievably bad planning ever—no ads, no last eight performances which would have packed the house what with the best notices of any musical this year. Oh well. It was a sixteen-week mess and I'm delighted it's over."

Wawona Hartwig recalled, "I got the phone call that it was going to close and they wanted me to come. And I thought that was awful nice. Of course, they made up lots of excuses and I had to cart my portable typewriter with me, but they were just making excuses. They were just being nice. And it must have been so sad for them. I saw the closing performance." Although he was feeling miserable, Vincent, true to form, remained generous and thoughtful in his determination to show Wawona around town. "One day they hired a car and driver and drove all different places, such as the United

Nations. And I wanted to see Wall Street, so we drove down and then Mr. Price said, 'We'll get out and walk.' It was marvelous. Then I wanted to see Broadway. So, after the shows were all over, we went in every theater on Broadway. I was introduced to all these people—I remember Ingrid Bergman was one of them. Then we went over to Sardi's and he plunked himself down in front of his picture. It really was quite an experience."

33

IN DECEMBER 1967, *House and Garden* featured an article on our house entitled "A Talent for Christmas." Indeed, although my parents adored any excuse for a special occasion, Christmas certainly got their fullest attention. The article noted, "Mr. and Mrs. Vincent Price live with style and humor in a wonderfully theatrical house, 'Spanish, more or less' on the outside, pure Price within. Omnivorous collectors of practically everything, they adore clutter and know exactly how to make it both delightful and, in an amusing way, outrageous. For Christmas, their favorite holiday, they bedeck their house with a fantasia of lights and garlands and baubles, and sit amid it with their five-year-old daughter, Mary Victoria, singing one carol after another, happy as three Tiny Tims.

"The Prices' preoccupation with Christmas has deep roots. Mrs. Price was born in England, the daughter of an army officer who believed in Discipline—at home as well as in the barracks. The only time he allowed his children to kick up their heels was during the twelve days of Christmas. 'That's why I'm such a child about it,' says Mrs. Price. 'To me, Christmas is an embrace, the warmer the better. And I love the spectacle of it all.' Mr. Price had the father of all fathers—a candy manufacturer. The little Prices didn't bother with mere sugarplums, they had life-size Santas and reindeer of solid chocolate—for as long as they lasted. 'Quite understandably, we were very popular kids. It's a lovely feeling, and every Christmas I resurrect it. Of course, chocolate won't get you very far with grownups, but champagne figures.' "

Our holiday rituals centered on the tree. Each year we picked out a twenty-foot fir, which we then decorated, sometimes taking days to attach the various ornaments my mother had collected. Christmas Day was a family affair that included Hank and Marin. Opening the gifts took us all day; as my father liked to say, "Mary thinks that if a little is good, a lot is better." But no one liked giving gifts more than my dad. Marin remembered, "One Christmas Vincent gave me a white fur coat, full-length with pink satin lining. Vincent and Hank had gone shopping for it together, having had a lot of drinks, and Vincent paraded around Joseph Magnin wearing it, saying, 'If it fits me, it will fit Annie,' as he called me. It was rabbit, and as it came out of the box, we all fell back. He was always so generous." It always seemed to me that my father derived far more pleasure from the giving than the receiving of gifts.

Harry Mullen was an integral part of our holiday festivities. Over the course of the twelve years he had lived and worked at 580, Harry had become virtually a member of the family. In May 1967, however, my father had been forced to ask him to leave, which was a great blow both to him and to us. Harry was an inveterate gambler. Over the years, my parents had helped him numerous times by agreeing to pay off his debts against the money he was earning. Unbeknownst to Harry, my father had even begun buying savings bonds for his future, but by 1967 the situation had become untenable. During a very busy period Harry suddenly became erratic in showing up for work, had made and broken a number of agreements, and my mother and father decided to let him go. My mother was very upset and left it to my father to handle things. He arranged for all that Harry owed them, which amounted to two thousand dollars, to be paid off by means of the savings bonds and severance pay. He wrote Harry a letter which, in part, said, "I must say how sorry I am, we both are, to end so many years in this impersonal way. We both feel too upset once again to argue this out face to face, which apparently does no good. We both hope that the future will see us on more friendly terms and that we will be able to remember all the pleasant things that have happened in the past. We are both extremely upset about this, Harry. We have long cherished our association and appreciated greatly what you have contributed to our lives. But when trust in each other is lacking, it is time to end it." My parents gave Harry letters of reference and their business managers helped him declare bankruptcy. By November of that year, he was working almost around the corner for the Bowles family, whom we all knew. He quit gambling, got out of debt, and continued to work for the Bowleses, where I saw him often, until he retired. Years later, when I was in high school, my mother and I were at a Christmas party at the Bowleses when Harry pulled my mother aside and said, "Mrs. Price, I always wanted to thank you. You did the right thing. If you hadn't, I would never have amounted to anything."

Barrett remained in Albuquerque after graduating from the University of New Mexico. He became a successful poet, journalist, and professor. But his marriage to Sandy Greenwald had fallen apart by the mid-1960s, and she was given custody of their two boys. After his divorce from Sandy my parents worried about Barrett, so when he called with the news that he was remarrying, they were overjoyed. He had fallen in love with a wonderful woman and talented artist called Rini. We all went to their wedding in Albuquerque in January 1969 and, though I was only six, I remember sitting on the plane when a woman came down the aisle who I was told was Barrett's mother. It was the first time Edith and my mother had ever met. The wedding was a happy occasion and an apt beginning to Barrett and Rini's long and happy marriage. As a wedding present, my parents gave them the down payment on a small house and a honeymoon trip to Hawaii.

In August of that year, my mother organized a family party to celebrate her and my father's twentieth wedding anniversary, which coincided with Barrett's twenty-ninth birthday. Rini recalled her first trip to our house. "It was some place! Barrett had told me something about the house, but even so it was pretty mind-boggling. I remember Vincent's grilled pepper steak, thoroughly black on the outside and just delicious. And Mary gave Barrett a pair of Adidas, because she paid attention to track when he was in high school." We all loved Rini from the start and welcomed her as part of the family. My mother had planted a tree for each of us at the beach house and bought one for Rini, which we all planted together. My new sister-in-law was the ideal addition to our family games of penny-ante poker—to my father's delight, she actually gave him a run for his money.

Although Vincent and Edith's meeting at their son's wedding was amicable, and he had continued to support his ex-wife financially, he had rarely seen her since their acrimonious divorce. As Wawona recalled, "She would ask for money every once in a while and he didn't want to talk to her, so he let me talk to her. And then I would be sent over to her house in Santa Monica with the money. Then I would take her to the bank, because she didn't have a car, and then take her back. She always had tea for us. She was very much the grand actress. She was always dressed just perfect with the right jewelry when she knew I was coming. She did everything just perfect and she was very dramatic, every move she'd make. Very gracious, very sweet, and pitiful. And he couldn't handle it at all."

Although her duties for Sears had decreased, Wawona had remained with the Prices and soon found herself busier than ever with Vincent's travel arrangements, the typing of his syndicated art column, and even some of the booking of his lecture tours. He relied on her for everything. In 1969 *Architectural Digest* proposed to publish an article on our home. According to Wawona, "*Architectural Digest* was just started back in that time and they wanted an article about the house and, of course, anything that was about the house Mrs. Price did most of. But they wanted Mr. Price's byline, and it must have killed her never to get the credit. She would get the credit from the people who knew, but most people would never know what credit she should have had. So he wrote an article and I typed it and sent it. Then the editor had his girl type up the things he wanted, and then that went to Mrs. Price, and there were things that she didn't want in there, and things she added. So, we had three versions. And Mr. and Mrs. Price were leaving the country, and so Mr. Price said to me, 'Well, do the best you can.' And so I put it together. And when it came out, the magazine was folded out on my desk with a note from Mr. Price: 'Great article, except it has the wrong byline.' "

Vincent counted on Wawona's efficiency and reliability. Once he called her from the studio and asked her to look three things up, saying he needed the information within the hour. She stopped everything, did what he asked, and was ready when he called back. When she gave him the information, he said, "I knew you could do it. I bet these fellows out here that I could give you three things to find in an hour and that you could do it." He won a hundred dollars, which he gave to Wawona when he got home.

No matter how busy he was, my father always found time to play. In 1966, he filmed a commercial for Airstream and my mother came up with the idea of having the company buy him a car in lieu of his fee. She located a secondhand Silver Cloud Rolls Royce and, though my father had chosen to drive a variety of less than impressive cars his whole life, he got a real kick out of the Rolls. Wawona remembered, "He telephoned down to me in the office and said, 'You haven't had a ride in it yet.' And I said that I hadn't but that I didn't care. So, when he came downstairs, he had on a dark suit coat and of course his old tennis shoes and things on underneath. And he had the cap that Harry wore when he played chauffeur for them. He came in the door and he said, 'Mrs. Hartwig, I'm James, and I'm applying to work as your chauffeur. Would you like to come for a drive now?' Of course, by this time I knew that I had to playact with him, so I said that would be fine. So, Pasquale and I got in the back and he asked where I would like to go, and he called me Madam. And I wanted to go up on Mulholland to see how he drove in the hills and then I wanted to go to the beach. We went to the beach. Oh, we were gone a long time. Then he said, 'Would Madam like to return to the house?' And I said, 'No, I'd like to drive through Beverly Hills.' And he turned around and looked at me because he knew exactly what I was doing. I was hoping somebody would recognize him, I was just hoping with all my heart and soul. And we went up and down the streets and pretty soon somebody did—Oh, there's Vincent Price! And I said, '*Now* we can go home.'

And he gave me another dirty look and then he held the door and Pasquale and I got out and he disappeared. He never missed a chance to have fun!"

By the early 1970s, the decline of the Sears venture, bad movies, constant touring, and film location work put my father under a kind of stress he had never experienced. As he neared his sixtieth birthday he began to worry that, to keep up his overhead, he would have to work forever—although in many ways he would have liked that. For years, however, the business managers had been persuading my parents to move to a smaller house. After looking at many homes all over Los Angeles, they finally settled on a smaller Spanish-style home situated on a spectacular promontory in Beverly Hills with a phenomenal city view. Though the business managers urged them to sell 580, my mother felt that, given their miniscule mortgage payments of $225 a month, it would be far more profitable to rent out the 9,000-square-foot house. Her logic prevailed, and in 1971 we moved out of 580. For almost a year, we rented a small, two-bedroom tract home at the top of Beverly Glen while my mother remodeled the new place. I remember that year with great fondness. I loved living in an ordinary house, with real neighbors, on a street where kids rode their bikes and we waited for the ice-cream truck every afternoon. I was nine, and for the first time I felt like a regular kid.

Situated above Coldwater Canyon, directly across the street from the glorious Rock Hudson estate, the new home we finally moved into was much more manageable than 580, with smaller grounds and no pool. For years my parents had engaged the services of many different people to oversee the running of 580, of Vincent Price Enterprises, and of me. After Harry's departure, and following the rash of violence in Los Angeles that culminated in the Manson murders, they had also employed a full-time security guard. (One night we had driven out to the beach house and found it ransacked, the furniture slashed, and all of our belongings covered in catsup. We never knew whether it was the doing of an unstable horror fan or a more serious threat.) My parents' decision to downsize reflected a desire to lessen their financial responsibilities as well as an urge to simplify their lives. The smaller house would be easier to maintain and much less help would be required to run it. Nonetheless, my mother had taken great pains to transform their new abode into a beautiful home. As Rini recalled, "We saw it before she had done everything to it, and after she was done it was smashing, glorious. The things that woman could do were just amazing. She just had such skills. It was a wonderful thing to see that." Little did any of us know how short-lived our tenure there would be.

34

FOLLOWING *THE MASQUE of the Red Death,* Roger Corman felt that he had exhausted the cinematic possibilities of Edgar Allen Poe and ended the cycle. A resurgence of public interest in the horror genre in mid-decade thus left Vincent in the position of fulfilling his horror obligation to AIP in films of increasingly poor quality. So when he was sent a well-written script based on the real-life exploits of Matthew Hopkins, Oliver Cromwell's "witchfinder general," Vincent seized the opportunity to play a part of substance again. During the interregnum of 1649 to 1660, Matthew Hopkins and his assistant John Stearne roamed the countryside for God and Cromwell, sadistically torturing and killing confessed "witches." Producer Deke Heyward had bought the rights to Ronald Bassett's novel *Witchfinder General,* and hired Tom Baker and Michael Reeves to adapt it to the screen. AIP agreed to co-produce the film and distribute it in America, on condition that Vincent Price would star.

Vincent arrived in England at the beginning of September 1967 and filming began shortly thereafter. The brash and brilliant twenty-four-year-old Michael Reeves was directing the film—and, from the start, he and his star were at odds. Reeves hadn't wanted Vincent for the lead—he had had Donald Pleasence in mind—and made no effort to mask his dissatisfaction. As Vincent later said, "Reeves hated me. He didn't want me at all for the part. I didn't like him either. It was one of the few times in my life that I've been in a picture where the director and I just clashed." This was more than discomforting for Vincent, who liked nothing less than controversy on a set and always endeavored to keep things as harmonious as possible. The open hostility that existed between him and Reeves made him very anxious; nonetheless, despite these difficulties, he managed to remain his usual gracious self: When one day on location at Bury St. Edmunds the catering truck didn't show up, Vincent took the hired Rolls assigned him, went into the nearby town to purchase fresh vegetables, pasta, and shrimp at his own expense, and cooked lunch for sixty people in the hotel kitchen.

Filming took place during October and November in several locations around the English countryside. It was a very difficult shoot for the actor who, at age fifty-six, was forced to spend much of the time in his least favorite pursuit—galloping around on a horse. On the very first morning of shooting, Vincent took a fall and had to spend the remainder of the day in bed. Reeves refused to visit his star, but in order to comply with production insurance codes, sent one of the producers in his stead. Though some felt that Reeves chose not to check up on Vincent in order to goad him into anger and thus a more menacing performance, Vincent himself simply felt it was a matter of poor communication skills and lack of experience on Reeves's part. The actor later maintained,

"Michael Reeves didn't really know how to deal with actors. He would stop me and say, 'Don't move your head like that.' And I would say, 'What do you mean?' And he'd say, 'There, you're doing it again. Don't do that.' He was only twenty-four years old and had done two other films. He didn't know how to talk to actors. He hadn't the experience and all the actors on the picture had a very bad time. Afterwards, I realized what he wanted was a low-key, very laid-back, menacing performance. He did get it, but I was fighting with him almost every step of the way. Had I known what he wanted, I could have cooperated."

Despite the tensions on the set, Arkoff, Nicholson, and Heyward were pleased with Vincent's work. Arkoff thought, "There was a malevolence, a malignance about Vincent in that role." Vincent himself felt it was one of the best performances he'd given in some time. After seeing the film, he magnanimously wrote Reeves, "Congratulations! The contrasts of the superb scenery, and the brutality, the action the hero forces against the inexorable, almost pedantic inaction of the forces of evil, make for a suspense I've rarely experienced. So, my dear Michael, in spite of the fact that we didn't get along too well, I do think you have a very fine picture, and what's more, I liked what you gave me to do!"

The film was released as *Witchfinder General* in the U.K. and attracted strong reviews for its tyro director. The *Times* of London noted, "There is much in the film which would win Michael Reeves an important reputation if he were dealing with some more pretentious, but fundamentally no more serious, subject. Mr. Reeves is no longer merely promising. He already has real achievements behind him: not merely good horror films, but good films, period." In the U.S., AIP opted for its usual ploy of "Poeifying" the film, deciding to retitle it *Conqueror Worm* after a poem by Poe which Vincent read over the final credits. Happily, after his spate of poor films, the critics lauded this performance as one of his best, and Vincent returned to England in November 1968 to shoot *The Oblong Box*, another period horror film for AIP, once again to be directed by Michael Reeves. Shortly before the cameras rolled, however, Reeves was fired and Gordon Hessler was brought in.

Reeves became very ill following his dismissal and underwent shock treatment; not long thereafter he overdosed on barbiturates and alcohol, a probable suicide. Vincent later spoke of Reeves's death: "That poor boy! He was so talented and had such a bright future, but he was a deeply troubled young man. I realized only after I saw *Conqueror Worm* how talented he was. It was a great loss to the cinema. Had he been disciplined, he could have become a very good director. Believe me, this profession takes enormous discipline. You're out there at six in the morning, and you're up until midnight and back at six the next morning. There's no fooling around if you want to last."

Reeves's replacement, Gordon Hessler, found himself with a script of dubious quality. Set in England in 1860, the plot of *The Oblong Box* revolves around the revenge wreaked on Sir Julian Markham (Price) by his hideously mutilated brother Edward (Christopher Lee). For Vincent there was some compensation for the dreadful script in working with Lee, Hammer's horror great. He later recalled, "Before we first met, I had heard he was very pompous, and I was really a little worried about meeting him. Well, we took one look at each other and started laughing." Although they only shot one scene together, *The Oblong Box* was the start of a great friendship between the two tall, handsome horror stars. Vincent said of Lee, "We find each other hysterically funny. We spend our lives screaming and laughing at each other, and having a wonderful time. I'm really devoted to him. I think he's one of my very few good friends in the business."

Christopher felt the same. "Vincent had a wicked sense of humor combined with an appreciation of the ridiculous. He always saw the humor in everything."

After his restrained performance in *Witchfinder General*, Vincent reverted to camp in *The Oblong Box*. Although Hessler could have reined the actor in, he felt that Vincent's tendency toward melodrama might be the only thing that could breathe life into their dull script. Once again AIP misleadingly slapped a Poe title on the picture, but the ploy failed and the film earned just over a million dollars.

Vincent was now in the increasingly uncomfortable position of having to act in films he did not choose. His only consolation seemed to be the fact that most of them were shot in England, where the longtime Anglophile reveled in being one of the few American actors granted a work visa year after year. Whatever the quality of the film, Vincent found continual pleasure in exploring London's art galleries and flea markets on weekends, even as he enjoyed working with British actors and film crews during the week. And when Hessler, Price, and Lee joined forces again a year later for *Scream and Scream Again*, Vincent had the pleasure of finally meeting Hammer's other master of the genre, Peter Cushing, who appeared in a cameo role. AIP promoted the picture as the first joint venture of the three reigning kings of horror, though in truth the trio spent very little time together in front of the camera. However, the off-screen camaraderie between them proved lasting, particularly since Christopher and Vincent shared the same birthday and Peter's was a day earlier—a fact which gave them all childish pleasure.

Scream and Scream Again was a contemporary horror film–cum–thriller in which Vincent played a doctor engaged in creating a super race out of the bodies of living people. In his first role in years in a contemporary picture, he earned *Variety*'s accolade as "the rock generation's Boris Karloff," a label that must have pleased him. Reviews for the film and for his performance were strong, with the *Los Angeles Times* calling *Scream and Scream Again* a "superb piece of contemporary horror, a science-fiction tale possessed of a credibility infinitely more terrifying than any of the Gothic witchery of *Rosemary's Baby*. Above all, it is a minor masterwork of style and suspense, so unusual and so all-of-a-piece that it really can't be reviewed at length without spoiling its impact." Its critical success notwithstanding, Gordon Hessler felt that *Scream and Scream Again* was never a film in which Vincent took much pride. "I don't think Vincent really liked the films I made. He didn't understand *Scream and Scream Again*. He didn't know what he was doing in the picture; he thought it was all weird and strange. Nobody understood it. But it took off with the young people; it was an enormous success. Vincent liked the more traditional horror film, Gothic, classical. But it never affected his performance; he was into it, whatever he was doing. He was wonderful to work with." Hessler was right; Vincent himself said of the picture, "I never knew what it was about!"

Gordon and Vincent reunited for one more film, *Cry of the Banshee*, but unlike *Scream and Scream Again* the film was disastrous from the outset. It was yet another period horror movie in which Vincent played a seventeenth-century witchhunting magistrate, who incurs a curse upon himself and his family. The picture's only point of interest was the return of the legendary German actress Elisabeth Bergner, who emerged from retirement to play an avenger from the grave. As Hessler recalled, "It was the most appalling script! It was about the worst script I've ever worked on. Everybody realized it was disastrous. All we could do with that film was try to make it cinematically interesting: strange angles, moving camera, that sort of thing."

Cry of the Banshee was the final straw for Vincent, who had had enough of unsatis-factory parts in worse than awful films. His contract with AIP had expired, and though Arkoff wished to renew, Vincent, feeling frustrated and impotent, refused to negotiate. Though he later acknowledged that the scripts offered to Vincent were inferior, at the time Sam Arkoff wasn't pleased. Gordon Hessler maintained that Vincent was so angry with Arkoff that he refused to show up for AIP's wrap party on *Cry of the Banshee*, which was being promoted as the actor's 100th film to garner publicity. Hessler recalled, "Arkoff had this big birthday cake, where he had a naked girl inside and she was going to burst out. Just about an hour before, Vincent called up and said, 'If Arkoff's there, I'm not coming!' So I said, 'Vincent, you've got to come—you're the guest of honor.' Finally he showed up. I said to Arkoff, 'You've got to make the introduction speech to Vincent.' I went to Vincent and said, 'You've got to cut the cake.' So we start the ceremony for cutting the cake; we're looking for the knife; I said, 'Where's the knife?' and Vincent said, 'Take the knife that's in my back.' "

During this period, Vincent tried to offset his disappointment with AIP by working for other studios in non-horror pictures, but the roles grew fewer and farther between. In the fall of 1966 he had flown to South Africa for Twentieth Century-Fox to film *The Jackals*, a remake of the 1948 Western, *Yellow Sky*, set in the Transvaal at the turn of the century. Vincent played Oupa, a veteran miner and grandfather who preserves his honor, his mine, and his granddaughter in the face of a takeover by outlaws. It was a rare opportunity to play the good guy, and he enjoyed both the change of image as well as the chance to explore South Africa and to discover the local contemporary artists, both black and white.

In late 1967 Vincent appeared in United Artists' *More Dead Than Alive*, a morality tale set in the Wild West and starring hunk-of-the-moment Clint Walker. Vincent, second-billed, played another good guy, a traveling showman. Nonetheless, he was given a death scene worthy of any of his horror movies as, pumped full of bullets at close range, he expired bloodily and in very slow motion.

The Trouble with Girls for MGM in 1968 teamed Vincent with Elvis Presley, but only on the screen: They never met during its making. In this tale about a medicine show, Vincent played Mr. Morality, a character producer Lester Welch felt "represents the dedication and high purpose of the outstanding and authentic Chatauqua lecturer as they actually were at the height of the Chatauqua movement in this country." Despite high expectations, Vincent's role was essentially a cameo in an ultimately forgettable Elvis picture. After this, it would take long years before he would find work outside AIP.

Vincent Price and Sam Arkoff eventually managed to settle their differences, and the actor returned to England in November 1970 to shoot *The Abominable Doctor Phibes*, a film which would become a surprising cult classic. Vincent played a musicologist and theologist who is maimed and mutilated in a car crash while racing to be with his dying wife. When the charred corpse of Phibes's chauffeur is mistaken for the good doctor, Phibes spends the next few years reconstructing his battered body and planning his re-venge on the surgeons whom he holds responsible for the death of his wife.

Robert Fuest, art director turned movie director, took the helm. His design back-ground helped to give the film, set in a very "mod" 1929, a decidedly groovy and artistic feel, which Vincent—who, at age fifty-nine, had endeavored to remain decidedly groovy himself—appreciated and enjoyed. Producer Deke Heyward remembered working with Fuest as "a total delight. The creativity was flowing like crazy. Everybody contributed, because Fuest encouraged that. You'd do a funny little shtick during the walkthrough, and he'd say, 'Keep that in!' " Vincent himself thought Bob Fuest "one of the best directors I've ever worked with in my life because he was making *mad* films. He's a *mad* man!"

The film, which also featured Vincent's old friend Joseph Cotten, was shot in eight weeks. For the first time in many years, Vincent was once again thoroughly enjoying his work, despite spending hours each day in very heavy makeup. In 1973 the actor told a reporter for *The Guardian* that "*Phibes* was something I had to take very seriously when I was doing it so that it would come out funny. All the same, it was just agony for me because my face was covered with plastic, and I giggled and laughed the whole time, day and night, and the makeup man and I were practically married because the makeup kept dissolving and he had to patch me up every five minutes." As in *House of Wax*, Phibes's face was really a mask covering his horribly burned skull. Underneath this mask, Vincent was immobile, and the character spoke out of a voice box in his neck.

By the time the film wrapped, everyone involved was very high on its potential. Indeed, the studio was so pleased with the picture that they decided to launch it with a catchy ad campaign. In a play on the memorable tagline for the recently released *Love Story*—"Love means never having to say you're sorry"—AIP released its ad with a picture of the "beskulled" Vincent holding his female lead (Virginia North) in a romantic pose. The caption read, "Love means never having to say you're ugly." Although the campaign was a big success in Hollywood, the movie did very poor business on its opening weekend. Realizing that the traditional horror audience took their films quite seriously, Arkoff and company took a more conventional approach on the second weekend and business boomed.

Of course, AIP immediately rushed to prepare a sequel, and Vincent returned to Europe the following fall to film *Dr. Phibes Rises Again* in London and on a desert location in Spain through January 1972. Unfortunately, and predictably, the script was a pale shadow of its predecessor, overloaded with camp and short on restraint. Furthermore, the good humor and creative spirit that had reigned on the first set failed to carry over to the second shoot. Robert Quarry had been cast as Dr. Phibes' 150-year-old nemesis, Darius Biederbeck. Unbeknownst to Vincent, Quarry was being groomed by AIP to replace him as their new horror star.

Shortly after shooting began, recalled Quarry, "They had a big cocktail reception. An English publicist came up to Vincent and asked, 'How do you feel about Mr. Quarry coming in as your replacement at AIP?' Vincent told me what happened. He wasn't happy about it. He was hurt. So I went to the producer and told him what happened. Well, it was too late. The damage was done. This publicist made it sound as if I were out to dethrone the king. That made a rift between us. I never saw Vincent socially after that incident, not ever." Director Robert Fuest remembered, "In makeup, Robert Quarry used to sing Gershwin, and Vincent Price looked around the corner and Quarry said, 'Didn't know I was a singer, did you, Vincent?' And Vincent said, 'Well, I knew you weren't a fucking actor!' "

In addition to the tension between the two actors, Vincent was burdened by the realization that this would be his last picture for AIP. His contract had expired, and though he had grown increasingly upset by their treatment of him and with the parts he was being given, he was fearful of what would happen to him without the steady pay-check provided by his contract. With his association with Sears, too, coming to a close, the sixty-one-year-old actor was facing a difficult crossroads.

Although Sears continued to honor Vincent's contract, worth approximately $90,000 a year to him, they never made any effort to restart the art program. Rather, they coerced Vincent into the role of spokesman for a wide range of products, ranging from bathroom carpet and draperies to bedroom furniture, towels, and electric blankets. Though he hated the fact that he was passed around from department to department, he remained loath to give up his association with the department store. He continued to pour new ideas into the company, suggesting programs to promote art, books, even furnishings—most of which came to naught. As Wawona Hartwig told it, "They started using him for every darn thing in the world—perfume, men's cologne, some sports thing. They were just using him. It was awful. And I think that Mrs. Price was getting pretty upset over that, but he just went along with it. One time, he said, 'They're trading me around like a baseball player.' And he was mortified. It detracted from what he was supposed to be. Mr. Price was looking frazzled and I don't think feeling well. And he was hurt. He would say he was hurt. He was hurt enough that he didn't try to hide it. And Mrs. Price was very tense."

By 1970, it had become clear to both the Prices and Wawona that there was no longer enough work for Sears to warrant her staying on. As with Harry, it was extremely difficult to let her go. She worked through the early fall and then, as a thank-you present, my parents gave her a trip to the United Kingdom. Wawona recalled, "It was the sweetest thing in the world. He wrote all this stuff out for me—everything I had to see and about tipping and everything else I needed to know. I was always so thrilled when they were going places and I'd ask a thousand questions when they came back. But I knew I'd never get to go. So, it was just wonderful. I sent them cards because I was supposed to let them know what I was doing. They gave me plenty of money and when I got back to my friends in London after traveling around the country, there was a letter from them and more money. They were afraid I was running out of money. I wasn't running out at all. It was such a wonderful thing to do because they knew I probably was never going to have the kind of money to do that kind of thing again."

Only after the Sears association ended did Vincent give vent to his feelings. "I'll never forget them saying, 'We really don't need you anymore, because we can make just as much money selling schlock,' as they call it. Or shit, as I call it. So, it ended up very unhappily. Actually, I've found that most art things end up unhappily because people are dealing with a product that shouldn't be merchandised."

Nonetheless, he contined looking for creative outlets. In 1970, Stravon Education Press, a division of Rand McNally, published *Mary and Vincent Price's Come into the Kitchen Cookbook*. Essentially a reworking of the National Treasures cookbooks, the volume featured a collection of "America's great recipes." With illustrations by the brilliant Charles M. Wysocki, the cookbook linked the emerging awareness of American folk art with a down-home look at America's culinary heritage. But my father was perhaps even more excited about his next book project, *The Vincent Price Treasury of American Art*, coedited with his son Barrett.

In his foreword to the lavish *Treasury*, my father used Ralph Waldo Emerson's aphorism, "There is properly no history, only biography," to introduce his biographical approach to the history of American art. He wrote, "This book is in small part a history of American art, but above all, and most vitally, it is about people. This volume is also a biography of America. Each one of these artists represents something of this land." In a series of two-page spreads, the book featured a full-color reproduction of a painting along with biographical information about the artist and commentary on the work. My father included well-known artists such as John Singleton Copley, Winslow Homer, Thomas Eakins, James A. McNeill Whistler, John Singer Sargent, Frederic Remington, and Edward Hopper, as well as modern artists such as Willem de Kooning, Jackson Pollock, Robert Motherwell, Richard Diebenkorn, Mark Rothko, and Jasper Johns; remedying his *faux pas* of the forties, he also selected a good number of women, including Mary Cassatt, Georgia O'Keeffe, Henriette Wyeth Hurd, Isabel Bishop, and Helen Frankenthaler. He also included a few prominent Native American artists such as Fritz Scholder and Oscar Howe. He not only enjoyed the task of compiling the volume, he was immensely proud of its contribution to public awareness of American art and happily went on the road to plug it as an element of his favorite cause.

Although Vincent constantly fretted over typecasting, he nonetheless took advantage of all the work his popularity as a horror star brought him, particularly on television. Drawing on the same skills that he had brought to radio, theater, and film, Vincent was always well prepared, eager to try anything, and generous with his time.

He guest-starred on most of the popular television sitcoms, game shows, talk shows, and variety hours of the 1960s and 70s including *The Red Skelton Show, The Mod Squad, The Mike Douglas Show, Truth or Consequences, Laugh-In, The Ed Sullivan Show*, and, of course, *Hollywood Squares*. He appeared on over nine hundred episodes of the latter, becoming one of the most popular "regulars," and providing an erudite foil to the likes of Paul Lynde and Charlie Weaver. The appeal of the show was based on a blend of humor and knowledge, and Vincent generally managed to get just the right mix. In June 1969, Cleveland Amory reviewed the show in his weekly column for *TV Guide*. He wrote, "Our No. 1 favorite is the peerless Vincent Price, who, on one show, was asked: if he had committed regicide, what would he have done? 'I would,' he answered,' have killed Regis Philbin.' Receiving no favorable sign, he continued hopefully, 'Or Regis Toomey.' When there was still no response, he said, 'I would have killed my grandfather.' 'Not,' replied the moderator sternly, 'unless he was a king.' 'But he was,' Mr. Price protested, 'He was king of St. Louis. I thought everybody knew that.' "

Vincent was consistently asked back to appear on most of the variety and talk shows, becoming a choice guest on such popular programs as the *Carol Burnett Show* and the *Tonight Show*. He adored appearing on Burnett's variety hour, where he was asked to perform a wide range of roles. From reading poetry to appearing in send-ups of his horror persona, he loved working with Burnett's celebrated ensemble of Vicki Lawrence, Tim Conway, and Harvey Korman. Carol Burnett remembered, "We had these adorable cue-card guys who, every Thursday, would cook a meal when everyone else went to the truck. When Vincent's cookbook came out, which was very major, they got the cookbook and did one of his complete dinners and they invited Vincent and me. They set everything up in the dressing room and it was absolutely incredible. I don't know how they did it on a hot plate in the hall, all in between blocking and orchestra. But he flipped, we both flipped. Everybody loved him."

Vincent was also a hit with Jack Paar and his successor, Johnny Carson, on the *Tonight*

Show. Not only was he an easy and amiable guest who seemed to roll easily with Carson's humor, but Carson enjoyed promoting the actor's culinary skills on the show by asking Vincent to cook—which he did, eagerly and often. He prepared salads, baked bread, and, on November 21, 1975, on what would become one of the most talked about episodes of the Carson show, Vincent introduced an innovative dish that "any fool can prepare": Before a delighted studio audience, he proceeded to cook a fish in a Westinghouse dishwasher. For years thereafter, he would be asked for the recipe. The trick was to season the fish lightly with salt, pepper and lemon, wrap it in foil, place it in a dishwasher, and put it on regular cycle—without dishes and, of course, without soap. The end result was always a perfectly steamed fish.

Although he was working consistently and earning a healthy income, my father grew increasingly despondent about the state of his career. He was particularly sensitive to the fact that his friends and colleagues didn't seem to respect his work in the horror genre. He worried that his work was taken less than seriously by his fellow actors; few of them went to see his films, and many seemed to make excuses for his horror work. Jane Russell noted, "The horror movies were strictly a way to make some money, period. Had nothing to do with Vincent. You make money any way you can, to take care of your family. You do what you need to do." Jane Wyatt remarked, "Vinnie had enough sense of humor to do those horror pictures. He wanted the money to buy the art. A lot of actors wouldn't have been able to do that. But Vinnie had a wonderful sense of humor. He got fun out of life. He really did." And Norman Lloyd believed, "There was a decency about him no matter what you put him into. So, even if he was a villain, it was only just for the time you were watching him."

Certainly all this was true. My father himself frequently claimed that he made movies for the money, for the exotic foreign locations, for the chance to see and to buy more art. But, paradoxically, he still craved the respect of his fellow actors even as he was willing to do whatever it took to remain in the public eye.

While many of his friends and colleagues may have failed to appreciate his work in horror films, Vincent did attract an immensely large, loyal, and diverse following, including many members of the movie industry's younger generation. Director John Waters recalled that he was "obsessed" by Emergo—the gimmick used by William Castle in *House on Haunted Hill.* When he was ten years old, he went back to the theater over and over again to see the film and was equally hooked on the actor's next effort with Castle, *The Tingler.* As Waters remembered, "People went beserk in the theater. It's a childhood memory that's one of my best." And my father was certainly popular among his European peers. Screenwriter Bruce Villanch recalled working with Marcello Mastroianni on the Italian actor's first American film in 1971. One evening, he asked Villanch, "Have you ever heard of this actor—Vincent Price? He is my favorite American actor. I know he does these genre films, but I think he is so good. He can do so much with his words. He is serious but funny. This Vincent Price, he is always so good because the tongue is in the cheek."

Indeed, though he complained about typecasting and lack of respect, my father knew a good thing when he saw it. He understood that his popular association with villainy could carry his career when most of his peers rarely worked. It was a tradeoff: If he had bitten the proverbial hand that fed him by refusing to appear in horror films, with hard work and a little luck he might eventually have been able to find satisfying roles outside of the genre. That, however, might have entailed falling out of favor with his public, and that was a risk he wasn't willing to take. Ultimately he had decided that the best course of action was to embrace villainy on his own terms—to raise it to the level of art, or at least to a standard in which he could take pride.

Consequently, much as he had done when performing in *Angel Street*, he began giving interviews about his villainous roles—interviews that reflected his sophistication and his knowledge of the history of villainy. He also began defending his choice in playing the bad guys by discussing the art of making horror movies. "You can take it from me," he said, "that horror films are hard work. In the movies that I made, whether the scripts were great, mediocre, or even sometimes downright bad, we all worked terribly hard to make them good. And it isn't true at all what people say about comedy or horror films not being serious art. Those people think only in terms of problem dramas, but every single work of art that is ever done has to have some form of seriousness behind it. All the classic horror pictures really had a serious intent. Those films put together three of my great passions—art, mystery, and villainy. The plot can be as twisted as you like, but the horror film must be pure logic, like mathematics. Pure evil, as much as pure good, is poetic. I'm always evil in a keen, clean way. You have no identity with the audience if you play a man who is one hundred percent a black character. You have to have shades of grey. And the 'heavy' who loves beauty always makes the most terrifying villain!"

Vincent, of course, thought of his films as "Gothic tales with an unreality." When the media raised the issue of whether horror films were bad for children, Vincent responded, "I once went around and asked a priest, a rabbi, and a child psychologist if they thought horror movies were bad for children, and not one of them had a bad thing to say about them. They said they were like a catharsis, like a fairy tale, and they have the effect of shifting the child's hate away from the parent and transferring it to the villain."

Claiming that "everyone in Hollywood is typecast," Vincent frequently discussed the finer points of playing villains. "To be a villain in horror movies, you have to walk a tightrope between horror and humor. You've got to make the audience scream and then giggle. But God help you if they giggle and then scream. Villains are so interesting, while most leading men are boring in comparison. And you get better as you grow older. Those crinkles and cracks help." This was pure Vincent Price: taking an intellectual approach to a subject others would take for granted—and taking pains to put a smiling face on a difficult circumstance.

In the early 1970s, Vincent came up with an idea for a lecture about villainy, which he called "The Villains Still Pursue Me." This talk, which he performed around the country for almost twenty years, ran the gamut from anecdotes about his villainous roles to his tales of Hollywood; from an assessment of current villainous actors to a description of the place of villainy within Aristotle's dramatic theory; from a retelling of *Angel Street* to a speech from *Richard III*. He always concluded the evening with the interchange between Don Juan and the Devil in George Bernard Shaw's *Don Juan in Hell*, which gave him the opportunity to deliver what he felt to be "almost the most beautiful speech in modern theater":

"Is man any the less destroying himself for all this boasted brain of his? Have you walked up and down the earth lately, Don Juan? Well, I have. And I have examined man's wonderful inventions, and I tell you that in the Arts of Life, man invents nothing. But in the Arts of Death, he outdoes Nature herself and produces, by chemistry and machinery, all of the slaughter, of the plague, the pestilence, and the famine . . . I could give you a thousand instances, Don Juan, but they all come down to the same thing. The power that governs the earth is not the power of Life but of Death."

When Don Juan retorts that the Devil is taking man at "his own evaluation of himself"—that he is, in truth, a coward—the Devil responds, "Oh, go to Heaven, Don Juan. I prefer to be my own master and not the tool of any blundering life force. I know that beauty is good to look at, that music is good to hear, that love is good to feel. I know that to be well exercised in these sensations is to be a refined and cultivated being. And I also know, Don Juan, that whatever they say about me, the Devil, in churches on earth, it is universally conceded in good society that the Prince of Darkness is a gentle man."

35

IN 1972, VINCENT Price's old friend and former agent, Sam Jaffe, offered the actor an exceptional role in a film he was co-producing to be called *Theatre of Blood*. The part was that of Edward Lionheart, an aging Shakespearean actor who has spent a lifetime maligned by the critics. The final straw comes when he is denied the coveted Critics Circle Award for Best Actor. Outraged at this injustice, Lionheart fakes his own suicide; then, with the help of his daughter (played by Diana Rigg), he murders each of the critics who slighted him. But Lionheart is not content simply to kill. Rather, he exacts dramatic and painful deaths, killing each critic by replicating the death scene from the play in which he or she had particularly panned him. This gave Vincent his longed-for opportunity to essay an extract from eight of the great Shakespearean roles.

Diana Rigg recalled, "I got cast in this horror movie and it was a very good script. At the time I was working at the National Theatre doing a couple of classics, and it struck me as witty and wonderful and funny to be doing the classics on one hand and a spoof of the classics on the other. I didn't meet Vincent before we started working, so we were thrown into the deep end together in a way. We hit it off immediately. His manners were impeccable, and his enthusiasm for the part and the project was very great and he obviously loved doing it. Frankly, I can't find a bad thing to say about Vincent. First of all, he was a wonderful actor. This is acknowledged. What people don't know unless they have seen the film, and tend to forget because of his horror movies, is what a great classical actor he would have been. Listening to him deliver some of those Shakespearean speeches, I remember thinking, 'God, what a missed opportunity.' He was wonderfully humble, sort of deeply impressed that I was at the National and doing these things, and I found it so sweet in a way, because he was a very eminent man in his own right. And it was only later that I discovered that he was, of course, a very great art expert, because he was so modest he'd never talk about it. He'd convey his enthusiasm and he'd convey his scholarship, but he'd never talk down to you, so it was only later that I began to understand what an important part he'd played in this vein."

To enhance the project further, the ill-fated critics were played by several of Britain's finest actors: Robert Morley, Jack Hawkins, Arthur Lowe, Michael Hordern, Harry Andrews, Robert Coote, and Dennis Price. Vincent's London agent, Otis Skinner (Dick) Blodget, remembered, "When Vincent was doing that picture, he came here for dinner one night and I said, 'How's the filming going?' He said, 'Oh, you don't know what it's like! Years ago I had the position, especially at Fox, of working with the finest and the best. Then your career bounces around and lately I haven't been. Since the horror films stopped being with Peter Lorre and Boris Karloff, since that time, I haven't had really great performers to work with. And now here I am working with these ladies and gentlemen of the English stage—it's wonderful!' He went into paroxysms of honorifics about it."

Indeed, after years of wading through the bottom of the AIP barrel, Vincent was ecstatic to be playing a modern character, a Shakespearean actor to boot, and to be in such elevated company. From the outset, *Theatre of Blood* promised to be a positive experience. What he didn't know was that it would change his private life as well: for, playing the only female critic, was the inimitable Coral Browne.

Coral Brown (she added the *e* later) was born in 1913 in Melbourne, Australia, a place she couldn't wait to leave. Early pictures show her as a plump, pretty, dark-haired girl with a determined expression. The daughter of a restaurateur father and an overbearing mother, Coral was educated at Claremont Ladies' College and later studied painting. By the time she was seventeen, though, she had found her way onto the Australian stage. Under the direction of Gregan McMahon, who ran the Melbourne repertory company, she played a variety of roles, including Ibsen's Hedda Gabler and Orinthia in Shaw's *The Apple Cart*. Of McMahon she would later say, in the idiom which famously characterized her, "He taught me everything I knew about acting and a great deal about fucking, too."

Even at an early age, what Coral wanted Coral got—and what she wanted more than anything was to come to London to make her name in the British theater. For her twenty-first birthday her father gave her fifty pounds and a round-trip passage, on condition that she return home as soon as the money was spent. Coral, however, left Melbourne determined never to return. Her early years in England were fraught with difficulty. As an Australian, she had a tough time finding work or being taken seriously, and eked out a living as an understudy and playing small roles in small productions. One of these was *Basalik*, the 1935 experimental play starring Paul Robeson.

As Roddy McDowall told me, "There's a whole legend about Coral and Paul Robeson. She always claimed that it was Robeson who made it possible for her to stay in England, that his kindness and support kept her from the streets. He was a great womanizer and, of course, one of the most ravishing-looking people and one of the most talented. So I suspect there was a liaison. You see, coming from Australia, you were considered dreck. I mean, the class system was just deplorable. You were just really a third-class citizen, so survival for those women was either in the dance halls or being a fancy girl, to put it in the terms of the time. Attempting to survive it was horrendous. Also, Coral never really lost her accent. As much as she became elegant, there was still the sound of that flat twang. And inside the theater mores of the time, that really was unacceptable; it made you common. And, of course, that's one of the reasons ultimately that she was so absolutely galvanizing in *Mrs. Warren's Profession*. That's one of the ten greatest female performances I ever saw. She had all of her experience, all of her elegance, all of her tawdriness, all of her bawdiness, all of her fear and anguish to put into that role, and she made it just spin."

Indeed, the actress's friend Noel Davis confirmed, "Paul Robeson asked Coral what she was going to do after the play they were in ended. And she said, 'I think I'm going back to Australia.' And he said, 'I think you'd be unwise to do that. I think you have a future,' and she said, 'Nothing much has happened.' He asked her to give it a little more time and then sent her a cheque for fifty quid. It came three days later. I remember her saying, 'I'd never met a black man in my life. And when he shook hands with me, I was quite surprised that his hands felt like a white person's hands. I thought they'd be scaly or something.' Of course, that was nineteen-thirty-something, and you didn't meet black people. And he was very kind to her. He was a very big star. I don't know whether they became lovers, but I suspect they did."

After her first difficult years in England, Coral slowly established herself as an actress, largely through her association with impresario Firth Shephard. She acted in drawing-room comedies on stage and film and her reputation began to grow—initally, perhaps, more for her offstage activities than for her acting abilities. Roddy McDowall recalled meeting her when he was a child actor working in England. "She was a creature of such terror to me as a child because of what she represented. We first met on the set of a film called *Yellow Sands* with Marie Tempest. That would be 1938, and she was this gloriously imperious creature and I was told not to go near her because she had such a reputation. Coral was considered a scarlet woman, which, of course, she was. And it took me years to become her friend. I used to see her here, there, in New York or in London and so forth in the fifties, and there was this continual come-hither. I stayed charmingly polite, of course, but I was frightened of her." Indeed, by the late 1930s, Browne's reputation as a beauty, an outrageous wit, and a determined seductress was reaching epic proportions.

She was both the leading lady and the longtime mistress of Shephard, who ran London's famous Savoy Theatre. Under his watchful eye, the striking actress became a popular star, headlining at the Savoy during World War II, while keeping a suite with her lover in the exclusive hotel next door. Already noted for her aphorisms, Coral said of her lover, "Firth is my shepherd, I shall not want. His rod and his staff they comfort me." In theater circles, Coral was referred to as "Shephard's Bush" (a pun on a central London suburb). But as much as Coral gained by being Shephard's lover and leading lady, she contributed equally to his success. McDowall noted, "The plays that she persuaded Shephard to do—*Arsenic and Old Lace* and *The Man Who Came to Dinner*—nobody else thought would work in London. She made a great deal of money on that." Adrienne Corri concurred. "Coral was a pretty shrewd businesswoman. A lot of the things that Firth bought, like *No Orchids for Miss Blandish*, to do Coral justice, she made him buy."

However, while Coral was with Shephard, she was also having other affairs—with matinée idol Jack Buchanan, French singer-actor Maurice Chevalier, photographer and designer Cecil Beaton—all of which became the talk of London. As Adrienne Corri told it, "Firth Shephard had a nervous breakdown over Coral and Cecil Beaton. That happened during the war, and she used to ring up Firth and say, 'There's been an air raid warning and I'm going to be stuck for two or three hours, and I can't get back.' But what she didn't know was that Cecil's secretary, who had a crush on him, rang up Firth and told him. I once asked Coral what it was like being with Cecil Beaton. She paused for a bit, and then she answered me very thoughtfully, 'It was a bit like being a sailor.'

"She was a one-off, that dame. You see, she came over from Australia determined to be a star. 'I don't care who I sleep with,' was the kind of line. 'I'm going to be a star.' You know, she got around. Consequently, when she landed Firth, he put on one show after another for her at the Savoy . . . One of my first jobs in town was a play at the Savoy with Alec Guinness, which coincided with Firth Shephard's death, and everybody in the cast went to his memorial service, where Mrs. Firth Shephard sat on one side of the aisle in St. Martin's-in-the-Fields and Coral sat on the other. As the service ended, they got up and Coral gave a very grand nod to Mrs. Firth Shephard, who went up the aisle first with her sons. And then Coral went to the nearest fashionable Italian restaurant and regaled everybody with funny stories. I thought she was incredibly glamorous—this woman with a little black pillbox hat, and you can imagine the stories. And she was having a sort of hilarious lunch. Coral got a hell of a lot of jewelry and I think she got the rights to a lot of plays. That's where her money came from."

Shephard left Coral a large portion of his estate and she became a woman of means, free to pursue a more distinguished if less lucrative career. During the 1940s she was a popular star, but, as her friend Sir Alec Guinness remarked, "I don't know that one did regard her highly as an actress, though her performances were always elegant and she was wonderfully dressed. But then she did work at the Old Vic and with Tony Guthrie that was surprisingly good." Indeed, fortified by a large bank account, Coral was able to pursue her dream of becoming a serious actress. She had made it financially. Now she desperately wanted to earn the respect of her fellow thespians.

Acting did not come easily to Coral. Though she had an electric stage presence, she required sheer willpower to overcome her nightly battle of nerves and step in front of an audience. Actress Jill Melford, who first met her during the 1960s and became one of her closest friends, recalled, "I remember Coral saying she hated first nights. She always had a heart attack on first nights, sort of organized heart attacks in terror. And she was also terrified because she couldn't remember lines. She was always saying she had to pay somebody to listen to lines." Becoming a serious classical actress required Coral Browne to battle all of her demons. Indeed, after taking over shortly before opening night for an ailing Edith Evans in *Nina*, Coral took an absolute critical beating. One critic wrote, "Miss Browne's soufflé falls." She herself would later recall, "I was terribly hurt. Hurt, hurt, hurt, and I felt I could never face this again. I said, 'I will never act again.'" But when Tyrone Guthrie invited her to Canada to appear in his production of *Tamburlaine*, she decided to try the classics far away from England. During the first days of rehearsal it was clear to her director that this was not the indomitable Coral Browne he knew. While the rest of the cast broke for lunch, Guthrie worked with the actress, coaching her through her fear, and when opening night arrived, she turned in a remarkable performance. Her costar, Paul Rogers, recalled that the actress came alive when the play opened: "Coral had a love affair with a live audience." Her confidence restored, she went on to become a highly regarded classical actress during the fifties and sixties, appearing in London and on Broadway as well as traveling the world with the Old Vic and the Stratford Memorial Theatre company. She played many of the great Shakespearean women. Dame Judi Dench remembered, "She was wonderful as Gertrude—not to be forgotten. She was extraordinary as Lady Macbeth."

In addition to her newfound status as a serious actress, Coral Browne would always be admired as a beautiful woman and an elegant clotheshorse. Naturally, she became a favorite of many couturiers, and was more than once voted one of the ten best dressed women in England. But, more notably, her reputation as a great wit grew to legendary proportions. "Coral stories" became a staple of the London theater world, and gossip columnists competed to be first with the latest Browne bon mot. A number of the best loved of these tales center on her reputation as a woman who knew what she liked to wear and how she thought she should be seen. As Coral herself recalled, "Designers like me. I had one altercation with Cecil Beaton when he made me a red dress which I thought looked absolutely alarming. The last thing I wanted was to come on as a scarlet woman in *Lady Windermere's Fan* in a scarlet dress! And I said that I looked like a fire hydrant. What I really meant was that any dog that passed me by would lift his leg." In another memorable incident, a dress rehearsal for Guthrie's *Tamburlaine*, she put on a wig that had been sent over from England. "I nearly had a fit. You could see this much of my face and the rest was hair, hair, hair. Because I think the wigmaker loved me very much and if the wigmaker loves you very much, they put a lot more hair in. So, Guthrie said, 'What is that?' And I said, 'I feel as though my face is coming out of a yak's ass.' "

More than once, however, her wit got her into trouble. During the 1950s, a contretemps developed between columnist Radie Harris and Coral, who regarded Harris as a bitter woman given to emotional blackmail in her columns. The feud came to a head one evening at a London restaurant where Coral was dining with friends. Harris walked in with her entourage, and a hush fell over the room. The columnist had a wooden leg, a fact known to all but always politely ignored—not, however, by Coral, who turned to her dinner companions and in a voice that could be heard in the kitchen, pronounced, "Oh look, there's Radie Harris, with all of London at her foot." Though her fellow diners roared with laughter, Harris sued Coral for libel and won.

In 1950, the actress married actor/agent Philip Pearman. Although many questioned the ability of this tempestuous and sexually rampant woman to settle down, particularly with a man who was well-known as a homosexual, by all accounts the two enjoyed a full and happy marriage. Pearman was devoted to his wife and she to him. Noel Davis, who was briefly one of Pearman's clients, observed, "Coral adored him. Philip was a very good agent and had very, very good people. He was charming, attractive, very nice, and much loved." When Coral and Philip married, he had been working as an actor, but during their marriage, he became a very successful theatrical agent. With the assistance of his wife's unerring eye for talent, he made a number of significant "discoveries"—most notably Albert Finney and Julie Christie. By the 1960s he was, as his former client Michael York put it, "the top of the tree."

When Pearman died of cancer in 1964, Coral was absolutely distraught. Jill Melford, who was performing with her in *The Right Honorable Gentleman* during Philip's illness, recalled, "She was very shattered when he died. I mean, very shattered. She only missed one performance, and she came and stayed with me and Albie Finney came back for supper. It was one of the funniest nights I ever remember having in my life. I mean, I never heard laughter like it. Because Albie sort of did a cabaret because he worshipped Philip. And we just sort of looked after her." It was just after Philip's death that Coral and Alec Guinness became friends. The actor remembered, "I had always been alarmed by her and I didn't know Philip well at all, but when he died we were playing across the street from one another—I was at the Haymarket and she was at Her Majesty's. After he died, she went on playing, so I went over because I thought she might need some human contact . . . Coral meant a lot in one's life. My wife was always a shy short of person and she was a bit apprehensive the first time she was to meet Coral because this glamour lady was coming over. But she found her lovely and helpful and sweet. And afterwards she said, 'I think she's the most beautiful woman I've ever seen.' "

After her husband's death, Coral underwent a period of transformation. Although she continued to work—giving perhaps her most famous performance in *Mrs. Warren's Profession* for the National Theatre at the Old Vic—her personal life was turned upside down. As Melford told it, "She had a very, very pretty apartment with very, very pretty antiques and all that, and she suddenly decided to be a sort of trendy teenager and the whole apartment was suddenly done over and it was very modern and all the antiques were chucked out; all the pretty things went and it ended up sort of parrot-shit green and orange, which was very trendy at that time. You could have performed an appendectomy in that apartment. It was the most sterile place. It had nothing to do with Coral at all. I mean, it was brilliant, of its kind, if you like that sort of modern with white plastic sofas and that sort of thing. It had overhead lights. Adrienne Corri and I looked at each other and I said, 'You look a hundred.' And she said, 'You look two hundred. Everybody looks as if they're about to get the curse in this room.' Coral loved it. Absolutely loved it. Her whole past had gone and she was determined to start again. She changed her image daily and she reinvented herself and it was wonderful, because so many people plod on, but not Coral. We adopted the gypsy look, we had the Marsha Hunt frizz, we became a blond, we were all sorts of people. And then she met Vinnie and that was sort of magic time. She was like a twelve-year-old, absolutely hook, line, and sinker. I honestly think they fell in love like a couple of teenagers."

There are many accounts of Coral and Vincent's courtship. Coral herself told me that my father brought her champagne on her birthday, when they were filming in a graveyard. Others seemed to think that she had her eye on him from the start. Both were certainly willing participants. To my father, Coral seemed the way out of the underlying depression some might call a midlife crisis. Here was a woman who seemed to love the spotlight as much as he. They made a striking couple and they knew it. They both approached life with panache and a great deal of humor.

During the filming of *Theatre of Blood* it was apparent to all that Vincent was infatuated with Coral. Diana Rigg recalled, "I was instrumental in bringing Coral and Vincent together, insomuch as I think Vincent would not have made the first move. And I must also say in hindsight that he had not spoken about a wife and children, so I had absolutely no idea that there were other people involved. As far as I knew, he was separated. And so, in the light of that, my action appears something less than laudable. But I had absolutely no idea. Here was an absolutely adorable man who seemed quite lonely. I think you are, if you're on location somewhere and you're in a flat or a hotel somewhere and you don't know a vast number of people." One night Vincent asked Rigg to accompany him to a charity benefit performance. "I thought, 'My God, this man's got stamina.' After all, he was working from six in the morning. I suppose, in a way, he demonstrated his enormous relish for life. And I went with him to this do and Coral was there. I'm not sure if they had played their scene together in the film. In the interval, she and I both went to the lavatory and she said, 'It's a long time since I've fancied a man my own age, and I fancy Vincent Price.' Well, in the car home, Vincent volunteered that it was Coral's birthday the following week and he didn't know what to do about it. So, I think they must have eyed each other. And I said, 'Well, I think you can take her out to dinner. If you proffer an invitation, I think it would be looked kindly upon.' And from then on, they never looked back. I think they fell into bed and I think it was a wildly sexual relationship. Incredibly sexual. I remember Coral saying that they had worked out their combined ages were 120-something, and when you saw these absolutely shagged out people on the set, it was really quite funny. And that was the start of it all."

Although Diana Rigg assumed that my parents were separated, in fact, my mother and I came to London that summer. My father had rented a large flat at 1 Eaton Square, just around the corner from Coral Browne, who lived at 16 Eaton Place. It was a difficult summer, and my mother thought my dad seemed peculiar and distracted. He had promised to take us on a driving trip to the South Wales coast, where we were to visit my mom's birthplace. Throughout the trip, he was irritable and not at all himself. Back in London, my parents' friends hinted that my mother should watch out for Coral, that the actress had her sights set on my father. But my mother chose to trust her husband, as she had for the past twenty-three years.

*   *   *

When the filming of *Theatre of Blood* was completed, Vincent returned home to the States. By all accounts, Coral was devastated. Adrienne Corri remembered, "When he went away to America, she cried an awful lot and said, 'I'll never see him again. He's out of my life. I'll never see him again.' And then he came back to do a voice for a cartoon character, and that's when they met up again. After that, it was sort of for good."

Once my father was back with us, his odd behavior was still apparent to my mother; though he discussed nothing with her, he was corresponding with Coral Browne and planning their next rendezvous. He wrote her, "It's lovely to be in love and to love and to be loved. I really know you so little and feel very inadequate, humble and oh so grateful. Sixteen Eaton Place is a dream shrine with a beautiful face out the window marking me up the street and around that goddamn corner." He remained at home in L.A. only briefly before leaving on a month-long lecture tour.

While on the road he and Coral called or wrote almost every day, and he soon returned to London, flying in for a week of dubbing on *Theatre of Blood* and to work with animator Richard Williams on his full-length feature, *Nasrudin*. Vincent was very impressed with Williams's beautifully intricate animation, and recorded the part of the evil Grand Vizier with great enthusiasm and inventiveness. Williams later wrote the actor that he had "never expected such a *relentlessly* creative and wildly unique contribution." Although Vincent had booked a hotel room in London, he ended up spending every night at Coral's flat, and their relationship rapidly intensified.

A few days before he was due home, my mother received a business call that required her to get in touch with him. She tried to reach him at his hotel late at night London time, but he was not there. Because the matter was urgent, she tried contacting him on the set and through friends, but he was nowhere to be found. This was very unusual, since my father was meticulous about giving us his whereabouts and staying in contact. When he returned to Los Angeles, my mother confronted him as to where he had been. He was unforthcoming until she asked him straight out if he had been with another woman. When he said yes, she succumbed to her first hurt and angry impulse—she offered him a divorce. To her shocked surprise, he agreed.

In the midst of all this turmoil, Ralph Edwards and the producers of *This Is Your Life* decided to celebrate the life and career of Vincent Price. They called Mary to ask for her help in arranging to surprise her husband for the show. Because their separation was not yet public and she knew that the show was a big honor, she agreed to help, and was able to procure the appearance of many of my father's closest friends and most distinguished colleagues. On November 9, 1972, Vincent was signing copies of *The Vincent Price Treasury of American Art*, when his old friend Hans Conried dropped by. Vincent laughed to see his friend, but when Conried proceeded to introduce him to Ralph Edwards, who produced the leather-bound *This Is Your Life* script, he was stunned. With everything else that was going on in his life he didn't know how to react but, always the consummate professional, he gamely went along to the studio.

The show began with Hans Conreid reminiscing about their early days on television, and went on to chronicle Vincent's life as a Renaissance man. There were appearances by an old friend from St. Louis Country Day, Robert McCulloch, the head of McCulloch Oil who had recently moved the London Bridge to Lake Havasu; his Yale roommate

Ted Thomas, who recalled their misfortunes when trying to make grape juice into wine during Prohibition; AIP producer Sam Arkoff came on, and in the audience were many of Vincent's best friends and favorite leading ladies, including Jane Wyatt, Dorothy McGuire, Ann Seymour, Kay Medford, and Mary Wickes.

Ralph Edwards brought on two Native American artists whose lives and work had benefited from my father's efforts on the Indian Arts and Crafts Board: poet Donna Whitewing and painter Oscar Howe, who said, "Every American Indian is forever in Vincent Price's debt." Also attending was Wilma Victor, the special assistant for Indian Affairs to the Secretary of the Interior, who presented Vincent with the Department's highest civilian honor award in recognition of his service to the Indian people; and Vincent Graham, executive vice-president of Sears, Roebuck.

Then my mother came on, introduced as my father's coauthor, creative collaborator, and wife. When Ralph asked her, "Who really does the cooking in the Price home?" she responded, "Well, Ralph, we each have our specialties, and together, we add up to *one* pretty good cook. We are very pleased and proud to be Vincent's family—all of us." Barrett, Rini, and I then came out to greet our father. But the show was not over yet, as a voice-over was heard, saying, "I'd like to add just one more memory. May I come in, Albert?" And Helen Hayes, who normally eschewed appearances on such programs, came out to a standing ovation. She told her old friend and leading man, "You know, Vincent, playing with you in *Victoria Regina* was one of the truly happy experiences in my life." Turning to Edwards, she continued, "Ralph, if I may quote some Vincent Price philosophy—A man who limits his interests, limits his life. The more specialized his activities, the more restricted his mind becomes. Vincent says that, for him, the theater, the film, is one art among many. There's a whole world on stage and screen, but a bigger one off them."

The show was an unqualified success, but it was a very difficult and painful day for my parents. Not even the family knew about their impending separation, though my sister-in-law Rini sensed the tension between them. "It was a strange time. There was a party after the show in the green room. And Dad was drinking quite a bit and you could tell that he was not at all at ease with this situation. And, at one point, he was standing near a bar and I went over to get something and he gave me a hug and he held on to me like a drowning man. It was really strange. It was different. It wasn't just a familial warm hug and it wasn't a come-on hug. It didn't have the overtones of any hug I'd ever had before and it went on a long time and it felt like he was just hanging on. It might have been that he picked me because I brought no baggage with me, no old friendship, he had no anything with me. It might have been that I was the only safe person."

On Thanksgiving Day 1972, my mother told me that she and my father were divorcing. I remember feeling that it was important for me to be brave for my mother and so I said, "Well, it won't be that different. He's never home anyway." But like so many children I blamed myself for my parents' divorce; I even remember thinking that my dreadful table manners might have been the cause. Meanwhile, my father was attending three days of meetings for the Indian Arts and Crafts Board in Washington, D.C., where he had arranged for Coral to meet him and where they resumed their passionate affair. But he was back home by Christmas. Though the divorce proceedings were underway, my parents had agreed not to separate officially until I had finished my sixth-grade year. My father had admitted to being with another woman, but he hadn't told my mother or any of their friends that the affair was continuing. Before Christmas, my dad and I shopped for presents together in Beverly Hills. He was in very high spirits, and I remember our day together as being very special, filled with funny, imaginative adventures. Unbeknownst to my mother and me, a week before Christmas Coral came to L.A., where she and my father celebrated the holiday early at the nearby home of their friend Robert Hanley.

In early January 1973, Vincent left for his usual winter lecture tour. Although he and Coral were exchanging wildly sexual letters and cards on a regular basis while he was arranging divorce proceedings, Mary never knew about Coral. Vincent didn't want Mary to know that he was leaving her for another woman. Roddy McDowall thought, "It was terribly cowardly of Vincent not to tell Mary about Coral, but he didn't want to hurt anyone and he wanted everybody to love him."

After twenty-four years of marriage, sorting through the vast material accumulation of their lives together was not only an arduous and emotional task for my parents, but one that dragged on for many months. Burdened with guilt about Coral, my father took particular care that everything was as equitable as possible. The estate was divided in half, with each party claiming the pieces and objects they loved best. It was agreed that my dad would keep the beach house. My mom, on the other hand, wished to sever all ties with the past and wanted to move. After looking near San Diego and La Jolla, she finally chose a development on the westernmost edge of the San Fernando Valley called Calabasas Park, where we were to move at the end of my school year.

The business managers had urged my parents to sell both the house on Beverlycrest and the big house on Beverly Glen. Although my mother agreed to the former, she wanted to hold on to 580, sensing that the real estate market was just beginning to climb. The business managers and my father, however, overrode her, and in 1974, 580 North Beverly Glen sold for $245,000. Not many years later, my dad sent my mom a clipping from the *Los Angeles Times* real estate section, listing the "former Vincent Price estate" for over a million dollars. Enclosed was a note of apology. A contrite letter from Vincent's business managers soon followed. When the house went on the market for over six million dollars in the mid-1980s, my dad sent yet another rueful note and clipping. By this time, however, my mother had turned her design and real estate expertise into a happy and profitable career.

My father's lack of acumen regarding real estate excepted, he ensured that my mother received a generous alimony settlement, with child support until my eighteenth birthday. Though my mother was given full custody of me, my father retained visitation rights and input into my education.

I think of my childhood as coming to an end during the summer of 1973. I went away to riding camp with my friends, as I had every summer for the past three years. But when camp was over, I came home to an apartment in the San Fernando Valley, twenty-five miles away from where I had grown up. For the first time I understood that my father was never coming home again.

Once the separation was official, my father moved to the beach house, a place he had always loved. At various times during his life he had lived by the ocean, and he found much solace in those surroundings during this difficult time. But he was lonely. His new lover remained in London while the divorce was underway, and, living an hour's drive from town, he felt isolated from friends. To exacerbate matters further, his hectic professional schedule had noticeably slowed down. So it was that, during the summer of 1973, which he spent mostly alone at Nicholas Beach, he felt himself on the brink of a new life, at once terrifying and thrilling.

For almost a year after agreeing to a divorce, my father kept his relationship with Coral a secret. Guilt-ridden, and terrified that he would have to relive his custody battles over Barrett with me, he never told any of us that he had left for another woman. As far as we all knew, he was very much single. More than the money or the terms of the divorce agreement, my father was apparently very worried that the divorce would ruin his extremely close relationship with me. In countless letters to Coral he fretted over each interaction and visit with me, anxious lest I might start to treat him differently. Coral, who, of course, hadn't yet met me, tried to comfort him. "She really is yours. Despite the fact I'm sure you are a super Dad, girls really do love their male parent most. Just be *happy* with her in a natural manner and she will be doubly so with you. One brings children into the world but they are *not* yours—God lends them to you for a few years then when he feels they are ready for the trials and tribulations—the reason he has given them life—He sees they move on to fulfill their own destiny. I don't think you will allow yourself to face the fact that it is not in the nature of things that Toria should be your all, your lover, your beginning, your end. It kills me to see you torn to ribbons, and I *have* seen it, you know—despite the fact that you seem to think I just wander from room to room semi-nude with my brains and my eyes shut. I know how much you miss her."

I hardly remember seeing my father during this time at all. I was engrossed in my new life—starting a new school, making new friends, living in a new neighborhood. I was far more worried about my mother, for whom that first year of transition was terribly hard. I think I assumed that my sporadic yet special relationship with my dad would carry on as before, except that I would go to him instead of waiting for him to come home. In fact, during that first year, my father seemed the least of my concerns.

It was quite different for my brother. Barrett's initial reaction to Mary and Vincent's divorce was one of anger. "I was totally stunned. I was devastated. I thought, 'Oh fuck, here we go again. I'm not going to get in the middle of this again.' It was terrible. I was pissed off at him and I didn't know what to do. I was crushed. And then they sold the big house and I was totally pissed about that. I loved that house. They never talked to me about it once. He was down at the beach house and he told us that he was getting a divorce, but didn't say why. Then we kept on hearing that it was this wonderful person that he had fallen in love with. But he was always sort of coy about it."

As an adult, Barrett had grown increasingly close to his father. After he worked as a contributing editor on Vincent's last art book, the two embarked on a new project—a book about monsters. Vincent came to look upon his son as perhaps his only true confidant, sharing with him the doubts and fears that he wouldn't confide in anyone else. Thus, it may have been most difficult for him to hide his exuberant feelings about Coral from Barrett. But he did. As Rini recalled, "We found out about Coral long after the divorce, and Dad was living in the beach house, and we went out to visit him. He wanted us to come out and, when we were there, he said something about someone new in his life. But he wouldn't tell us who she was. He just said to go and see *The Ruling Class*. And we didn't know who he meant. We were looking at all these women in the film, and we didn't know for sure. But one thing Dad did say was, 'Don't worry, Barrett, I'm not giving you another mother at this age.' The next thing we heard he was married."

And my brother told me, "We saw it in the *National Enquirer* at the market. I really thought that he'd met her after the divorce."

My mother also found out about my father's relationship with Coral while standing in a supermarket checkout line. The October 14, 1973 cover of the *National Enquirer* featured a picture of Vincent and Coral eating dinner together. The headline announced "Vincent Price Admits He's Fallen in Love." In an "exclusive interview" with Henry Gris, Vincent admitted, "I certainly am in love with the lady—that's for sure. It is a very happy romance. I think that one is never too old to be in love. But I am going to need an elixir of youth if I am going to be around Miss Browne for very much longer." Amazingly, he also commented, "I think I am still going to have to be a bit discreet because I am not divorced yet. The divorce won't be final until about six months from now. I don't feel much like talking about this because I don't want to hurt my family."

Following the publication of the *Enquirer* article, my father confirmed the truth of its report to his ex-wife. Although my mother's first instinct was to tell me about Coral herself, she ultimately decided to leave it up to my father, but he said nothing for a long time. Shortly after the *Enquirer* came out, however, Barrett flew to L.A. where he finally met Coral. He initially thought her "charming and utterly, staggeringly beautiful."

Although devastated by Mary and Vincent's divorce, Barrett at first made every effort to support his father's new relationship, even writing to Coral to tell her how glad he was to see his father so happy. Later that fall, Vincent brought Coral to New Mexico to spend time with his son and daughter-in-law, as well as to show her one of his favorite places. Barrett and Rini arranged a day-long driving trip to a few of their favorite sites, some of which were unfamiliar even to Vincent. They went to the beautiful Anasazi ruins in Quarai and then drove down the scenic Turquoise Trail to an old mining town for dinner. Barrett remembered, "We brought them to Quarai. We had no idea how much she would hate that. It was a terrible day. She kept asking, 'How far is it?' Then we drove all the way up to Cerrillos for supper because I thought they wanted to see New Mexico. But all she said was, 'How far is it now?'" Rini recalled, "Barrett and I were just doing our thing, showing folks around, but she thought it was a pretty long way to go for anything. They were head over heels. They were like a couple of teenagers. They would goose each other and run around."

Vincent and Mary's divorce became legal in April 1974, after which Coral saw no reason why she and Vincent shouldn't live together. During their long periods of separation, she had constantly written to tell him how much she missed him, how she longed for the time when they could be together forever, but she had remained patient as he worked through the details of his divorce. Now she began to pressure him about living together. Though my father apparently considered moving to London, for a variety of reasons, including his desire to be near me, his lecture tours, and his television obligations, as well as Coral's interest in promoting her own movie career and, of course, the lovely California climate, the couple decided that Coral should move to Los Angeles.

Claiming that the damp sea air got into her bones, Coral lobbied for a place in town. Vincent was reluctant to leave the beach house, but his decision was made for him when Governor Ronald Reagan decided to reappropriate Nicholas Beach as a state beach. Although Vincent had certainly found it glamorous to own a portion of the beautiful California coastline, he at first saw no problem with the government's decision. After all, Leo Carillo Beach, which formed the other half of Nicholas Beach, was already a very popular public stretch. But when Vincent and the other residents were told that not only would their beach become public property, but they would no longer be allowed to live in their homes, he grew irate. The state government claimed that it was working toward making the whole coastline public; as a first step, they would be demolishing all the homes on Nicholas Beach and paying homeowners the price of the land. Vincent immediately began to fight the issue, and for almost a year engaged in a furious exchange of letters with the future president. But it was to no avail. Much to both Mary and Vincent's great sadness, the beach house was demolished by a wrecking ball in 1975.

Meanwhile, Vincent began to look for his "honeymoon house." After searching from Santa Monica to Beverly Hills, he settled on a modest Spanish-style house in the hills above West Hollywood, which bore a marked resemblance in size and feeling to his long-ago adobe at 1815 Benedict Canyon. He paid $90,000 for the two-bedroom home with a guest house, a small garden, a pool, and a panoramic view of the city below. He set about making everything ready for Coral's arrival, but her move was a gradual one. She made several trips from London to Los Angeles bringing her clothes and furnishings until, in the late summer of 1974, she arrived with her Chihuahua, Tiggy. It was the final act of commitment, for Coral would never return to live in London where Tig would have to endure a six-month quarantine.

Almost as soon as Coral had settled in at 1359 Miller Drive, she made it clear that she intended to become the next Mrs. Vincent Price. She complained, "I'm sick of being introduced as Miss Browne." Indeed, many of her friends felt that it was she, not Vincent, who wanted to marry. He seemed quite content to have them be Vincent Price and Coral Browne. After two divorces, the thought of entering into yet another marriage was daunting for Vincent. He preferred to let their relationship remain a "love affair," and when asked about his newly "liberated lifestyle," he joked that he and Coral had formed "a permissive society for the elderly." Indeed, at the beginning of their affair, Coral and Vincent seemed to enjoy the idea that two "elderly" people could be passionately and sexually involved. In one oft-told story, shortly after they fell in love the couple went to Peter Jones, the London department store, to order a new bed. Having chosen it, they asked a salesman how long it would take to deliver. When he replied that it might be over a month, Coral was aghast. "Look at the two of us," she said. "Do you honestly think we have that long to live?"

By the time she moved to California, Coral Browne was desperate to be married. Adrienne Corri remembered that, once Vincent's divorce was finalized, Coral rang her up with a command: " 'Tell him he's got to marry me.' So I said to Vinnie, 'Coral wants you to propose to her.' 'I'll marry the old bat when I'm ready,' he said, and then he suddenly surprised her by saying we're going out to Mexico. And she didn't want to go to Mexico, but she didn't realize he was taking her off to marry her."

Even after she tumbled to his plan, Coral didn't want to marry in Mexico, where Vincent had married Mary. Furthermore, as a staunch convert to Catholicism, she wanted a church wedding but didn't know how to get ecclesiastical approval for marriage to a twice-divorced man. Then she had an idea. She suggested to Vincent that because he and Mary were married in Tijuana, perhaps it hadn't been entirely legal and she began urging him to have that marriage annulled. In 1974, a Catholic priest came out to Calabasas and asked my mother to agree to an annulment of her former marriage on the grounds that it had been conferred by a Mexican justice of the peace. My mother, understandably, was horrified. She could hardly grasp that her former husband was not only willing to disregard their partnership of twenty-four years, but was, in effect, asking her to agree to make their daughter illegitimate. Naturally she refused to acquiesce, asking the priest only one question, "Does Vincent know about this?" He didn't answer, but returned a few months later with a document that he urged her to sign, informing her that Vincent not only knew about this, but requested that she comply. She stood her ground a second time.

Coral Browne had converted to Catholicism after World War II. Her close friend, Alec Guinness, himself a Catholic convert, recalled, "Ernest Milton was an old English-American actor. He was eccentric but he was one of the two or three best actors I have ever seen. He was a Jew who became a Catholic, and he and Coral were in something together and she became fascinated by him. He was instrumental in her becoming a Catholic in the late forties or early fifties." She was remarkably devout. As Noel Davis observed, "I'm a Catholic of a sort, and I was always amused by her Catholicism because she was much more devout than fitted in with her obscenities. She never missed mass on a Sunday." Nonetheless, her devotion to the faith did nothing to deflect her humor regarding the church. Complaining to Adrienne Corri about a long wait for a confessional, Coral groused, "There was some old bird in there keeping me waiting on the priest. I don't know what *she* had to confess to." Another oft-told Coral story reflects her unique attitude toward her religion. Exiting the Brompton Oratory one Sunday morning, Coral was accosted by a theatrical queen with the latest gossip. She stopped him in midsentence, exclaiming, "I don't want to hear such *filth*, not with me standing here in a state of fucking grace."

In October 1974, almost a year after the *Enquirer* article had made their relationship public, Coral Browne and Vincent Price were married in a civil ceremony in Santa Barbara, California. Shortly after their marriage, Vincent began disappearing every Thursday, coming up with various excuses for his absence. Coral tolerated it for a while, but she grew increasingly worried by this and finally demanded to know where he was going. He hedged for a few weeks before announcing that he had been taking instruction at St. Victor's, the nearby Catholic church. Although Vincent had been raised by a mother so vehemently anti-Catholic that he had donated Gauguin's handwritten diatribe against Catholicism to the St. Louis Art Museum in his parents' memory, he seemed sincerely moved by Coral's devotion to the religion. Thus, as his wedding present to his new wife, Vincent Price, at the age of sixty-three, became a Catholic.

Throughout his life my father was always concerned with what others would think of him, so it was only to be expected that he worried about how his friends would react to his divorce and remarriage. For almost two years after he and Coral had fallen in love, he saw less and less of his old circle of friends. As Hank Milam told me, "We hadn't seen Vincent but we heard that he and Coral were an item. I remember calling him in London and I said, 'By the way, we've heard about you and Mary.' And he said, 'What? What about Mary?' He was very defensive, so I just let it go. Then, after another stretch of several months, suddenly he called and said 'Let's have lunch.' And when we sat down he said, 'The most wonderful thing has happened.' He looked so exuberant and he said, 'I've met the most wonderful woman and I've fallen in love.' And I was so stunned because he was validating the rumors and putting a name to what I saw as the end of the relationship with Mary. And he said, 'She's just so wonderful and I'm happy to be with her.' I also remember him saying so many times in the conversation that she was fun."

However, once the divorce was finalized, both Mary and Vincent made every effort to handle it with grace. Wawona Hartwig recalled that almost three years after she left their employ, "Mrs. Price called and told me that it was going to be in the papers the next day and that she didn't want me to read it in the papers. And then Mr. Price called. They both called. That really touched me, because I would have been flabbergasted."

Mary and Vincent Price had been a Hollywood institution, much loved and well respected by the community. But Hollywood likes good publicity and the autumn romance between the elegant, sixty-three-year-old Price and the rambunctious, sixty-one-year-old Browne proved irresistible to the press. News of the divorce came as a shock to Vincent and Mary's friends. As Bill Brice commented, "I don't think Mary and Vincent's marriage disintegrated, I think Coral just sort of popped up. I think that Mary brought to Vincent a grounding that was useful to him, but it was a grounding. If he was a kite when she first met him, she taught him to fly more within his own control. But there may have been a part of him still wanting to be a free-floating kite. And I would think that Coral was a kite, too, a comet-kite, with a motor. We were all surprised, and I think that Vincent was, too. I think that, in that abandoned way, he really fell in love. Because love and flying—Chagall doesn't have his brides upside down in the air not on purpose—it's all about being free. Vincent was always a sparkler. Mary initially was much more casual than she became. She became a bit more constricted in herself, a bit more pulled together. And you could see them begin to diverge. Their qualities became qualities of contrast rather than fusion, and she grew less comfortable with Vincent's wide-open, all-folks thing. Coral was stunning. Like a whirlwind. So engaging. She could be very frightening, but very amusing. But it was Vincent's enjoyment of her that made it possible to be with her, otherwise it would have been very hard to tolerate her. He really did make her possible. There was another value, though. I think that he respected her professional opinion and I think he knew that she had integrity in her art and that was useful to him. But, of course, Mary had that integrity, too."

Certainly Coral's rapier wit and often cruel humor took some getting used to. Jane Wyatt remarked that Coral was "very different from Mary. The last person I would have thought Vincent Price was going to marry, but she was a very good actress and fun. A rollicking sense of humor." Norman Lloyd noted, "There is a certain world of the British theater that I'm not attracted to. There is an overall bitchiness, and although it may exist in the New York theater, I've never been attracted to it or been a part of it. When Vincent married Coral, I thought, Well now, Vincent was never a part of that world to my knowledge and now he is a part of that world, so it will be interesting to see what happens. Then, after a long time, I saw him, and Vincent was warmer and sweeter than he'd ever been, I thought. And I got on with Coral because she was Vinnie's wife and that was all right with me." Indeed, as Barbara Poe felt, Coral eventually "captivated everyone with her incredible sense of humor."

Even as Vincent's friends slowly warmed to Coral, her circle came to know and care for him. Jill Melford's response to him was typical. "I absolutely adored him. He was so sweet. He was fascinating and funny. But not sort of cabaret funny like Coral was, because he was so laid back. She was always telling him, 'Oh shut up, you don't know what you're talking about.' But it was quite obvious that he did know exactly what he was talking about." Adrienne Corri, too, was "very, very fond of him. There was an immediate openness about Vinnie. Everybody did like him." Only Alec Guinness perceived the paradox in Vincent, noting that though he had beautiful, charming manners, and always seemed warm and interested, "one felt one knew him better than one did." Indeed, as Guinness grasped, Vincent's innate interest in people and his ability to convey a sense of openness and intimacy often belied his ability to achieve real intimacy. Even with the friendships that lasted most of his life, he rarely divulged his innermost thoughts and feelings. He found it almost impossible to be openly vulnerable with anyone outside his immediate family, and even then, it went against his natural grain.

Thus, with so few people in his life whom he really allowed to know him, it was, perhaps, not surprising that he wanted to maintain a friendship with my mother. After all, she knew him so well and they had been through so much together; but it was my mother who actually facilitated their subsequent friendship. The deceptions she had endured notwithstanding, her hurt and anger gradually healed. Initially, my parents' only real contact was through and for me, but over the years they developed a warm friendship based on genuine affection—a tribute to my mother's forgiving and generous spirit.

Although Coral tolerated their continued relationship, it certainly did not please her. She could hardly forbid her husband to talk with his former wife on the phone or to see her occasionally, but that didn't mean that she refrained from aiming her pointed (and often nasty) wit in Mary's direction from time to time. Coral's close friends believed that Vincent's desire to retain a friendship with his ex-wife must have been terrifying to Coral. Jill Melford felt sure that "she was quite frightened that her marriage to Vinnie wouldn't work, and she was dotty about him. It would scare her that Vincent and Mary were friends because it would unnerve her." Joan Rivers agreed, "She would have been terrified that he was going to decide—Mary's softer, I like her better. *I* would have killed. You want to hear that she's the Wicked Witch of the North, the meanest white woman that ever lived and, honey, am I lucky to have you! I could see where she was threatened."

But Coral need not have worried. For Vincent and Mary there was no turning back. Though Mary had initially been devastated by the divorce, she went on with her life and, in time, stopped looking back. After having spent two decades informally designing homes, she became a professional architectural designer, turning her prodigious talent into a lucrative and exciting career, designing and refurbishing buildings and homes around the country. Vincent remained interested in and proud of Mary's work. As the years passed, my parents and I were comfortable spending time together and, in later years, they no longer needed me as a buffer, or as an excuse to see one another. They remained lifelong friends.

36

THE EARLY SEVENTIES brought Vincent Price his fair share of both highs and lows. On the one hand, he was madly in love, and he and Coral quickly became known as a glamorous couple, acquiring a whole new set of cosmopolitan friends in Los Angeles. On the other hand, with his AIP contract and his association with Sears both over, he had to face that which he had always feared—becoming an aging actor, with a diminished earning capacity, beginning to fade from the public eye.

During the mid-1970s, Vincent's movie work steadily decreased. Following *Theatre of Blood* he didn't make another film for almost two years, but in late spring of 1974 he returned to London for yet another excursion into horror. Jim Nicholson had died, but Sam Arkoff produced *Madhouse*, one last Price horror picture for AIP. It starred Peter Cushing, Vincent's perceived nemesis Robert Quarry, and Adrienne Corri, with Vincent in the lead. He played a has-been horror-film star trying to make a TV comeback following the murder of his fiancée and his subsequent nervous breakdown. In an unusual variation, both Vincent and Peter Cushing played the nice guys they really were beneath their assumed horror personae. The reviews were mediocre.

Later that year, Vincent also filmed *Percy's Progress*, a lamentable sequel to a 1971 comedy about the world's first penis transplant; Leigh Lawson starred as Percy, with Elke Sommer and Denholm Elliot, and featuring Vincent as the world's richest man. The film was released in London in September 1974 to rather poor reviews, and didn't make it to the United States until five years later, retitled *It's Not the Size That Counts*.

Vincent and Coral flew to Italy for July and August. There Vincent filmed *Journey into Fear*, a mediocre thriller with a stellar cast—Shelley Winters, Sam Waterston, Zero Mostel, Yvette Mimieux, and Donald Pleasence—and a talented director, Daniel Mann, whose credits included *Come Back, Little Sheba* and *Butterfield 8*. Vincent, needless to say, played the main villain, an Arab mercenary killer. The chief benefit of the film for him was an all-expense-paid vacation in Italy with Coral.

That busy summer of 1974 saw an end to Vincent's filmmaking for almost five years. With Coral's encouragement and support, he finally began turning down the depressingly poor scripts he was offered, and concentrating on restoring his dignity and rebuilding his legitimate acting career. Not surprisingly, he began to focus his efforts on the stage. If Vincent had hoped that, in marrying Edith, they might become an American theatrical institution à la the Lunts, he now had similar hopes for his liaison with Coral. Certainly this was what many of his friends assumed when they heard about his divorce from Mary in favor of the flamboyant English actress. Norman Lloyd believed that when Vincent met Coral, "He saw another career, another thing happening. What was the alternative?

He'd come back here and make another horror movie, because by that time, that's what there was. And suddenly he had another entrance into a world of theater that he admired and wanted to be a part of. Any actor of his generation was enamored of the English theater. In a sense, both Vincent and Coral saw an opportunity, and who is to say who benefited, really?"

The couple's first venture together, however, proved ill-fated—a West End production of *Ardèle*, a difficult play by Jean Anouilh, which ran during the summer of 1975 at the Queen's Theatre. The idea was Coral's, and she approached her good friend producer-director Frith Banbury about putting together the production. Banbury recalled, "Coral had been saying for some time that she wanted to do a play with Vincent, and she thought up *Ardèle*. The idea was to take the play on the road in America, then go to New York and then to London. The play is bitter as hell and had run only three nights in a previous New York production. So Coral's chum, Robert Whitehead, and Vinnie and Coral and I converged in New York to see about doing the production in the U.S. But we had trouble getting backing and this dribbled on for nine months. Finally, I talked to Coral and Vinnie about doing the play in London, but the strange thing was that it was difficult to raise the money. I had already told Vinnie that he couldn't be paid what he was used to in the U.S., and in the end, he took the deal for very little money."

There were many in the London theater world who found the choice of *Ardèle* a curious one, but an interview with Michael Leech of the *Times*, Coral noted: "I'm what's called a sucker for Anouilh. I love the way he writes and the things he has to say—I did the Broadway production of *The Rehearsal* and last year *The Waltz of the Toreadors* here in the West End—and I like this play. It's not an ideal play for Vincent and myself to do because we have almost no dialogue at all alone together. We are husband and wife in the piece, but we're not actually opposite each other; we each have a lover."

As for Vincent, he told Leech, "It's a great luxury for me to do a stage play, even for a short time. I can never believe what stars make at the National Theatre! I think in my career's forty years I've joined every American attempt at a national theater and in the process I've done about fifty plays, mostly subsidized by my 104 movies!" Most of those fifty plays had been performed in regional theaters around the country; the actor had not been on Broadway in a straight play since the 1950s and had never appeared in London's West End. Thus, *Ardèle* was more than a luxury, it was the chance to become part of a world which he very much admired. Sadly, the experience would become one of the most disheartening of his stage career.

Frith Banbury said, "Vinnie and Coral weren't from the same world of theater. Vinnie started there but then went off into films. Sad to say, he was really rather lost in *Ardèle*. During the first week of rehearsals, Vinnie kept looking at the other actors and saying how good they were in their parts and I said, 'Think about yourself.' But after three or four days, Coral came to me and said, 'What are we going to do? He can't do it, can he?' I told her that I thought it was a bit early to know that, but Coral said, 'You and I have to support him in every way we can.' Coral's feeling was correct. There was a part in the first act where Vinnie had to give snarky one-liners, which he did in a very amusing, rather Clifton Webb style. But in the second act, the chap has a sort of aria and all the technical virtuosity is necessary. For about twenty minutes he had to carry the whole thing on his shoulders and he couldn't cope with it. If he hadn't gone to Hollywood and had remained a stage actor, he could have coped with it, but he was sixty-four. Vinnie never got fussed, but I had to give the sort of direction one doesn't expect to have to give an international star. We had a session alone and Vinnie took it as a first-term student. Vincent Price was a commodity and that blunted his sensibility as an actor. He got into a rut, and so he fell back on what he could do.

"Vinnie never behaved like anything but that terrible expression—a gentleman. It was a flop, but I wouldn't put it all down to him. Vincent Price wasn't a draw for a stage play. There was a queue at the stage door waiting for autographs, but one felt that they hadn't bought tickets to the play. Vinnie later wrote to me, 'I feel as though I've let you and Coral down.' But Coral was not disappointed in him as a human being, but rather in herself for having miscalculated."

Ardèle proved a disastrous experience for Vincent. He was all too aware of the problems inherent in taking on the West End stage for the first time at his age. Not only did he have trouble with the range that the role demanded, but he also came up against difficulties he had never before encountered. One night, while the play was trying out in Brighton, Vincent was given the wrong cue and, for the first time in his life, he went up on his lines, skipping four pages of dialogue. Given his generally excellent memory, this was more terrifying than anything. He began having nightmares and soon found that he had to take sleeping pills every night to calm his anxiety. During the run, he began complaining of stomach pain. In 1962, he had collapsed on a set after persistently ignoring a severe ulcer, and doctors had removed a large portion of his stomach. This time a malignant tumor was found in his digestive tract and the actor underwent an operation. The procedure was totally successful; the cancer had not spread, and Vincent, Coral, and the doctors felt completely optimistic about his full recovery. He was advised, however, to allow two weeks to rest and recuperate. After a week he could no longer stand the inaction and went out to a museum, but he ruptured his sutures in the process and was forced back into bed for even longer.

The summer of 1975 was an extremely trying one. And yet, as usual, Vincent was able to find something positive in the experience; after *Ardèle*'s closing, he quipped, "Coral and I have survived a play together. I guess this marriage will last forever." Despite the play's failure, it did give him an entrée into the English theater, and he socialized with the great English actors and actresses he had so long admired. Later on, when visiting Los Angeles, Laurence Olivier, Ralph Richardson, John Gielgud, Alec Guinness, and Michael Redgrave all spent time with Coral and Vincent, and to Vincent's unending delight, their coterie of friends also came to include Maggie Smith, Eileen Atkins, Jean Marsh, Judy Parfitt, Joan Plowright, Alan Bates, Cyril Richard, and Lynn Redgrave.

If Vincent hoped that his liaison with Coral would allow him the opportunity to break away from the horror movies and move back to the live theater, it is equally safe to say that during the first years of their marriage, Coral hoped to take Hollywood by storm. And, at first, it seemed as if she might. In 1976, she was cast in two plays in repertory at Los Angeles's prestigious Mark Taper Forum—Wilde's *The Importance of Being Earnest*, in which she played Lady Bracknell, and the West Coast premiere of Tom Stoppard's *Travesties*. The productions received excellent reviews, and Coral won the Los Angeles Drama Critics Award for Best Actress. Naturally she hoped that this recognition would remind the film industry of her talents. She had, after all, made a great splash in the fifties playing Vera Charles opposite Rosalind Russell's Mame in *Auntie Mame*, and during the late sixties and early seventies she had appeared in such films as *The Roman Spring of Mrs. Stone, The Ruling Class,* and *The Drowning Pool.* But Coral was largely discouraged during her first years in L.A. While in England she had been aware of her husband's fame, but had not fully grasped the extent of his public recognition in the United States. Vincent was more than just a Hollywood fixture; he had become a cult figure, a household name recognized by three generations. It fell to Coral to assume the role of wife rather than respected actress; soon it came to seem that no one particularly cared who Coral Browne was, and yet everyone was interested in Mrs. Vincent Price.

Although she found it difficult not to be taken seriously as an actress by Hollywood, her reputation as a wit soon made itself felt in Los Angeles. When Charlton Heston was about to open in *Macbeth* at the Shubert, Coral and Vincent decided to go—not to see Heston, whom Coral held in fairly low esteem as an actor, but rather to see Vanessa Redgrave as Lady Macbeth. Coral had been friends with the Redgrave family for a very long time. She called the box office for opening night tickets, only to be told that the production was sold out. She asked to speak with the box-office manager, but he explained that there was absolutely nothing he could do about getting her seats. With immaculate timing, she responded, "Well, what about something for the second act?"

Of course, the most famous of Coral's "commentaries" on various theatrical productions had occurred years earlier in London. She had gone to the opening of *Oedipus Rex* at the Old Vic. The production had gone, as Coral later noted "smoothly, boringly but smoothly, until the last scene and on came a *huge* golden phallus, fifteen feet high. Unbelievable. Around it a chorus of people singing, 'Yes, we have no bananas.' It was too much for me, and I turned to my companion, Charles Gray, and said, 'It's nobody we know.' "

In the eyes of Hollywood Coral's wit and glamour provided the perfect complement to Vincent's casual sophistication, and the couple soon found themselves invited to all the A-list parties and events. Away from home, they maintained an elegant lifestyle, staying at the top hotels, sailing on the best cruise ships, dining at the finest restaurants. And they generally managed to do all this with all expenses paid, having perfected the technique of traveling as the guests of many of the cruise lines and hotel companies in exchange for personal appearances. For Vincent, who loved people, enjoyed performing, and always tried to save money, this was ideal. He could see the world, provide Coral with the high-quality accommodation she had come to enjoy, and remain in the public eye. In this manner, they criss-crossed the globe, from Greece to Egypt to Africa, from the South Seas to Hong Kong to China, and from Brazil to Haiti to Mexico.

Although the seventies saw the couple frequently on the road, they nonetheless adored their home life at Miller Drive, where they frequently entertained visiting friends from England as well as their growing circle in Los Angeles, which included Christopher Isherwood and Don Bachardy, David Hockney, John Schlesinger and Michael Childers, Marti Stevens, Gus Schirmer, Joe Hardy, Harry Mines, Robert Hanley, Gloria and Ricardo Montalban, George and Joan Axelrod, and Roddy McDowall. Among the closest of these new friends were Joan Rivers and her husband, Edgar Rosenberg. As Joan recalled, "Vinnie and I became friendly on *Hollywood Squares* and I adored him. I remember seeing Coral the first time she showed up. I remember this woman—I didn't know who she was—she was in a grey dress and a grey stole just over her shoulder and grey shoes and I went, 'Oh my God, who is that woman? She is so elegant!' And then Vinnie said, 'You have to come and meet my wife.' She had the most style of any person I've ever known. At first I was scared of her. Edgar, my husband, said to me, 'Don't you know she loves you? Talk to her!' But it took me months.

"My husband was English, so he and Vinnie had a great affinity. They both read, read, read, so there was always that bond of reading, there was always that bond of art, there was always that bond of—I hate the term—culture. You could go out with them for an evening and they knew there was an art exhibit, they knew that someone had written this book and they had read it! They were like a semi-family to me at the end, but in the beginning the bond that was always there was that there was so much to talk about, and it wasn't just the business. And that was so refreshing! The intelligence, the verbiage, the word choice was so exact, was so perfect; the humor, and the many, many, many interests. And he was so smart. He understood what it was to survive in the business and on a level that nobody else did. But he did it with such style that you didn't realize that he was doing it. He kept himself viable long after he should not have been viable. I found that astonishing. I had such admiration for him."

The Rosenbergs and the Prices gradually did become like family to one another. As Joan Rivers put it, "We had no family and they really became as close as family, especially for our daughter Melissa. Every year I always threw a Passover dinner and that meant everybody had to read and I always made sure that Vinnie and Coral read because it sounded so beautiful. The Jews read like [flatly] *And God said, Be good. Seven plagues.* Okay, enough! And now here's four pages of what happened with Pharaoh—Vinnie? . . . Poor Vinnie! These tones would come out. When someone is going to tell me the story of Egypt, I want it coming out of Vincent Price's mouth, I don't want it coming out of Larry Gelbart's. I'm sorry.

"You know, everyone's so busy and so full of themselves in Hollywood. And it takes so long, when you reach a certain age, to become closer and closer and closer. And it would be wonderful because they would come over on a Sunday night and they were probably one of the only couples that would sit in my kitchen and eat and talk. Or we could just say, 'We're going to eat at Spago, why don't you meet us down the hill?' And it meant so much that we were that close that we could just pick up the phone and it was easy. Or tell them the truth. There are so few people that you dare, in our business, to tell the truth. And you could tell them the truth and you knew you'd get great advice. You knew they were on your side. There was no question about that.

"And the other thing, the sweetness of it—wherever Vinnie went, he decided that he was going to bring Melissa money. Wherever he went, without fail, he would bring her foreign money, like a dollar from Thailand, and she began to get this amazing collection. He never, never, never went somewhere when he didn't bring it back for her. And he always had it laminated. He had it done up. And I always thought, How sweet to remember that. And he always made a point, which I loved about him, when he came to our house and there would be, oh I don't know, who's hot at the moment—Al Pacino and Sharon Stone—and he would sit down and talk to Melissa and be interested in what she had to say. Not, I have to talk to the kid for a few minutes; he actually went over and treated her as an adult and treated her as an equal. And I thought, this is what it's all about. He was fabulous."

Despite the failure of *Ardèle* in London, Vincent and Coral continued to work together in the theater, albeit on a much smaller scale than they had anticipated. In 1976, Roddy McDowall helped to put together a touring company of an old theatrical chestnut, *Charley's Aunt*, starring himself, Vincent, Coral, Joanna Gleason, and Annie Potts. Roddy felt that "when Coral did *Charley's Aunt*, it was an act of great, great generosity. For *that* actress to play Dona Lucia! And she did it just because she wanted Vincent to be legitimate. That was her big quest. And I must say she did achieve that. Her fury about the fact that 'the old boy' was wasting his gifts in 'these fuckin' horror films!' She couldn't stand that. I mean, there's no doubt about the fact that she loved him and admired him, and the one thing that Coral couldn't abide was the fact that she felt he'd squandered his acting talents. She was right because, even when we did *Charley's Aunt*, he still wasn't really with it. He was still trading on his personality. I don't think Vincent, in that sense, was an actor. It's a very difficult thing to discuss, because his appetites weren't for the pain of acting. He didn't have to act at any cost. By the time of the Poe films, he was immersed in a preconceived notion and had given in.

"I've always thought that Vincent so doubted his capabilities that he made less of himself in the acting area because then he couldn't really be brought to task. But Coral said, 'Wait a minute, fuck off, you are capable!' And he *was* capable of much more than he gave himself credit for. He wasn't a lightweight, he just considered himself a lightweight, until Coral berated him. He had this incredible quest to be liked. He had to be liked, and yet he didn't realize how much he was respected and admired."

Indeed, Vincent Price never lost his need to be seen, to be applauded, to remain in the public eye. To that end, he took whatever work came his way, almost without hesitation and regardless of physical hardship. After his knees collapsed when he took a jump from a raised platform down to the stage floor, he continued to perform in *Charley's Aunt* though pain and lack of mobility continued to plague him throughout the run. Nonetheless, he kept as rigorous a schedule as always. He traveled anywhere and everywhere that an audience might be interested in seeing him perform or hearing him speak. As Coral later remarked to playwright Alan Bennett, "You know Vinnie. He'd travel halfway across the United States to open a manhole." As film offers dwindled through the 1970s, he filled his time with lecture tours, jurying art exhibitions, and performing in summer stock around the country, headlining in *Oliver, Damn Yankees,* and *Charley's Aunt.*

However, *Charley's Aunt* was the last play in which Coral and Vincent appeared together. In 1976, Coral was quoted by Nancy Smith in the *Dallas Morning News* as saying "I don't think it's a terribly good idea to do plays together. The Lunts somehow managed marvelously in some strange way to live together and work together. But if you have a rotten night, there's nobody to come home to who'll listen." Nonetheless, the couple continued to work together on television, appearing in countless commercials. In 1979, an offer came their way to star in a midseason replacement television series, *Time Express,* a fantasy-adventure program. Coral and Vincent played Jason and Margaret Winters, an elegant couple who serve as the hosts on a "time train." As described in the original script, Jason Winters is "dapper and elegant, he's loftier in manner and more cynical in his thinking than Margaret, but she has a way of warming him up and bringing him down to earth. As a couple they're made for each other. Margaret Winters is beautiful, elegant, and lovingly devoted to Jason, though she's not above chiding him for his occasional lapses into cynicism. She's warm, intuitive, and emotionally supportive of the passengers." Written by Ivan Goff and Ben Rovers of *Charlie's Angels* and *Mission: Impossible* fame, and produced by *Hawaii Five-O* veteran Leonard B. Kaufman, each program featured a number of stories about passengers on the Winters' train. The plots demonstrated how individual lives can be altered with circumstances, and events changed at the moment of decision. On their train journey, passengers were "given a chance to relive their lives in those alternate styles"—a gimimick that would later be resuscitated for shows like *Quantum Leap* and *Early Edition*. Reviews for the series were shaky from the start, though Vincent and Coral were treated well by the press. One critic wrote, "Let's say five nice words about *Time Express*: Vincent Price and Coral Browne. The real-life married couple promise wit, sophistication, and a certain droll, Darling-we're-only-in-it-for-the-fun leavening for the time travel anthology." The series was not picked up for the following fall.

Although he was finding work in summer stock, on television, or in the occasional horror film, the 1970s proved a time of reckoning for Vincent Price. His acting career remained financially viable, but he nonetheless felt that his professional standing had diminished. Thus, when an offer came his way in 1976 to play Oscar Wilde in a one-man show, he was both intrigued by and fearful of the challenge presented by John Gay's marvelous script. Gay had received recognition for his screenplays *Run Silent, Run Deep; The Courtship of Eddie's Father;* and *Separate Tables.* For *Diversions and Delights,* he devised an effective conceit in which Wilde, released from prison and living in Paris under the assumed name of Sebastian Melmoth, decides to undertake the indignity of a lecture in order to earn some much-needed money.

From this premise, the playwright constructed two contrasting acts—the first rich in Wilde's epigrammatic wit, the second a poignant examination of his fateful relationship with Lord Alfred Douglas. The script provided for an acting tour de force, but Vincent, still smarting from the failure of *Ardèle,* was not confident that he still had what it took to carry a play, let alone a one-man show. He did, however, trust Coral's genius for finding the right material for the right actor, and when she encouraged him to do it, he said yes.

Coral had urged her husband to take the role, and also found him an ideal director in Joe Hardy. Hardy, who had received a Tony Award for his Broadway and London productions of *Child's Play* and a nomination for *Play It Again, Sam,* had directed such stars as Richard Chamberlain, Michael York, Dorothy McGuire, Charlton Heston, Jean Stapleton, and Glynis Johns. But his task with Vincent was considerably more daunting. Not only did Vincent fear another failure, he was also aware that, after years of playing horror and melodrama, he had virtually replaced real acting with skilled but facile camp. Hardy, however, managed to coax a brilliantly understated and deeply moving performance out of Vincent—a performance that doubtless drew on his talent as a dramatic monologuist and lecturer as much as on his skills as an actor.

Diversions and Delights opened in the summer of 1977 at the Marines' Memorial Theater in San Francisco, under the auspices of the American Conservatory Theater. In a city of sophisticated theatergoers with a large gay community, the piece was almost assured of success, but audiences and critics alike were astounded by Vincent's extraordinary performance. The sixty-six-year-old American actor played the forty-five-year-old Irish genius and wit with understatement and pathos, as well as the appropriate flamboyance. Many of his fans, friends, and family felt he gave the greatest performance of his life; it was certainly the best acting I ever saw my father do.

Following its successful run in San Francisco, *Diversions and Delights* played one-to-five-week engagements in major cities around the country. At each stop, both the notices and the audience response were tremendous. *Chicago Daily News* reviewer Sydney J. Harris headlined his review, "Price could win an Oscar for his Wilde show," and began "I nearly disqualified myself from reviewing the Vincent Price one-man show because of my prior prejudice against the man. Price's public persona—as art collector, gourmet, and general culture-vulture—has grated on me so, that I didn't feel that I could give him a fair and objective appraisal. Well, we are both better men than I thought. I had absolutely no trouble in accepting him as Oscar Wilde in *Diversions and Delights* and he had absolutely no trouble in persuading me that he is the paradoxical poet and playwright whose trial, imprisonment, and death remain a blot on nineteenth-century British social history. Performing to a full and highly enthusiastic first-night audience, Price was nothing less than superb in the multifaceted role—by turns witty, poignant, impudent, gracious, condescending, insouciant, pathetic, and at the end, most winning." Harris continued, "Price never would have struck me as the man for the role, but he incontrovertibly is, hairpiece, costume, facial expression, bodily movement and all. He senses who and what Wilde was, at a level deeper than the merely verbal and visual, projecting the essentially likable man beneath the poseur, the jester, and what Whistler called the 'epigrammophone.' Last month I had lunch with a San Francisco producer who told me he had been offered a piece of the action and turned it down. 'I just couldn't see Price in the part,' he said, to his later regret. You, too, will regret it if you don't toddle down to the Studebaker soon and get a marvelous glimpse of Oscar Wilde, who is there every night. I can't imagine where Vincent Price is."

David Clive had been asked to stage manage *Diversions and Delights* for its San Francisco run. Along with his wife, Jan, who served as the assistant stage manager, the two remained with the show for the duration of the first tour. In Clive's opinion, "Vincent, though a St. Louisan by birth, is an actor in what I regard as the English tradition. They are professionals first and artists second. Their most urgent ambition is to keep working. Witness the biggest stars, Gielgud, Olivier, Richardson, all doing bit parts or 'potboilers' from time to time, with no discernible embarrassment or damage to their careers. Vincent, through the years, had done more than his share of 'potboilers,' and indeed his later career was pretty much built on them. He tailored his performances and his public persona to what people had paid to see, which tended to obscure what a bloody good actor he is. I must confess that at first, seeing how good he was in rehearsal, I tended to give all the credit to Joe Hardy, worrying that as soon as he left, Vinnie would begin to 'chew the scenery,' as the saying goes. In a year and a half, it never happened. I might also say that, in a year and a half, I never saw him give less than his best, many times under trying circumstances."

Following their successful run in Chicago, the play moved to Ford's Theater in Washington, D.C. for four weeks. Again, the show was a hit and was extended for a fifth week. Riding high on its notices and audience response around the country, *Diversions and Delights* went to New York—only, sadly, to fail on Broadway. David Clive recalled, "He was so terrified by the thought of a Broadway opening that he gave his worst performance ever in the role. The show was roundly roasted, and we closed after only two weeks. There had been a rash of one-character productions, and the critics jumped on us as the latest in a boring trend. Even if Vinnie had been brilliant that night, I suspect that the result would have been pretty much the same, but he blamed himself and was devastated. A party had been arranged at Sardi's and I, being absolutely certain we would be a hit and run forever, persuaded Jan that we should go. In any case, the party soon turned into a wake and Vinnie disappeared."

Following the show's failure on Broadway, its producers realized that their star needed a morale boost and so booked the show back into San Francisco, where it was again a great success, running at the Geary Theater for a month. Although deeply disappointed by Broadway's reception of the show, Vincent decided to continue touring with it. David Clive remembered, "Our little troupe gathered again, aboard a Dodge van, for a one-night-stand tour that lasted for four months and took us to such far-flung outposts as Redding, California, and Halifax, Nova Scotia. Our crew of two traveled in a Ryder truck, with minimal lights and scenery. Aboard the van were Vincent, his dresser Billy Malloy, our company manager Camille Ranson, our trouping Lhasa Apso Sam, Jan, and myself. Vincent displayed good humor and even temper, not to mention generosity, remarkable under the circumstances. There are not too many sixty-six year olds who will go bouncing around the continent in a van, giving five or six exhausting perform- ances a week, with equanimity. The reward for all of us, though, was audience enthusiasm for a splendid piece, superbly performed. A great many of our one-nighters were at colleges and universities around the country. Oberlin College in Ohio stands out as the single greatest audience ever. They laughed, they clapped, they stamped their feet, till the ancient auditorium quite literally vibrated. In December 1978, *Diversions and Delights* finally closed in St. Paul, Minnesota. As we left the theater, the temperature was 11 degrees below zero. We found a Howard Johnson Restaurant and gathered there to toast, with hot chocolate, the fact that, after all of the vicissitudes, we were all still friends."

After the "official tour" had ended, Vincent put together a scaled-down version of the show and continued to tour with it on and off well into the mid-1980s. He took Wilde to more than 250 cities in the United States as well as to Australia, New Zealand, Hong Kong, and Canada. The opportunity to play Oscar Wilde had allowed him to tap talents long unused and served to remind him why he had wanted to become an actor in the first place. Touring with his one-man show gave him back the theater.

In a decade that witnessed so many one-person shows, many came to feel they were overdone. But my father explained his eagerness to appear in *Diversions and Delights*: "There are very few famous men or women whose character, humanity, humor, or even tragedy can survive the scrutiny of a 'one-man show.' Oscar Wilde is the ideal personage to be examined by this all-revealing kind of theater presentation. The fame of his wit is enough justification, but underneath the brilliant façade is a very human being, vulnerable to his own fame, his own strengths and weaknesses, and a being who inspires a kind of very real and identifiable audience admiration and appreciation. For the actor, the as- sumption of such a volatile personality is not only challenging but thrilling. Wilde, and through his genius the actor, seems to have something to say to everyone. Wilde is a joy to play. For his personal tragedy is as universally appealing as his private-public wit is individually enchanting."

Playing Oscar Wilde proved a turning point for my father. His success in a very difficult role changed his view of himself as an actor. He regained his confidence and found an authority he never knew he had. He even returned to New York with the production, appearing at off-Broadway's Roundabout Theater to generally excellent re- views. Though much credit must be given to the superb direction of Joe Hardy, in the end it was Coral who opened the door for him, and then made sure he walked through it. She constantly encouraged him. She made him believe not only in his talent, but in his deservedness. She made him think of himself as more than a horror film actor, and forced him to make the kind of commitment to his craft that he had avoided for so many years. As Joan Rivers said, "She made him do it. He needed that—a very strong woman who said, 'This is what we're going to do.' And 'Vinnie, don't you let them treat you like this, no one takes advantage of you.' Because she was very tough. She always had him busy. Whatever they were doing, she kept him moving."

My father found such joy in playing Wilde. After years of despair, he began to view his work as an actor with growing pride. Even though the Wilde piece was not a success on Broadway, it was a huge success everywhere else. But most important, it was a success in my father's life and career, as he came to realize that he didn't need the Broadway critics or the New York audiences to validate him. For the first time in many years, he had validated himself as an actor.

37

THE EIGHTIES WERE a fruitful, if trying, time for Vincent and Coral. Both struggled with illness, even as they saw their careers bring the sort of recognition they had long deserved. Vincent returned to film work, as well as continuing to travel the lecture circuit and tour as Oscar Wilde. For virtually the first time in his life as an actor, he felt in control of his acting career. Coral, however, felt that she had stagnated since moving to America. Moreover, since 1978, her life had become complicated by cancer.

Since her first husband, Philip Pearman, died of cancer in 1964, it is fair to say that Coral had become obsessed with the disease. Adrienne Corri recalled, "She was convinced when Philip died that she would have cancer, and she had tests practically every week. She got this very morbid thing about dying. She came here once for dinner and I said, 'If you say the word cancer, you're out the door. I'm not going to listen to it.' She couldn't speak for about half an hour because she couldn't think of anything else to speak about. I thought that when she married Vinnie she would get over this and it would change. But it obviously didn't, although it did for a time." Indeed, during the first years of their marriage, Coral remained in robust good health.

Then in 1978, she discovered what she believed to be a cancer on her leg and had a large chunk of her left calf removed. Thereafter the glamorous clotheshorse wore only pants, which she managed to elevate to a high art. But, as Adrienne Corri told it, there was some doubt among her close friends as to whether the operation was truly necessary. "That leg business was ridiculous, because it wasn't malignant. I remember saying to Vinnie, 'For God's sake, get her to come across to England for a second opinion.' I talked to Coral about it and I said, 'You were a bloody fool. Why did you let them do it?' And she said, 'Well, he was a friend of mine.' And I said, 'No surgeon is a friend of yours if you're a rich hypochondriac.' But that sort of started the whole thing. Later I remember somebody saying, 'Isn't it terrible, Coral's had a mastectomy.' I said, 'No she hasn't. She's had a small lump taken away.' I used to shout at her, because I was fond of her, and I could see that this was getting a grip. And I was worried about Vinnie." Certainly, from the late 1970s, Coral's health became a central focus of the marriage.

Coral's leg surgery made it difficult for her to manage the many stairs of their multi-level house on Miller Drive, so the couple decided to relocate. They settled on a more modern, single-story home in the Doheny Estates—an area of town locally known as Birdland, as all of the streets were named after birds—where they moved in 1979. Their new home on Swallow Drive featured sweeping views of the city, even more panoramic than those on Miller Drive, but it didn't have much room for a garden, nor was there a pool. Both said that it was perfectly suited to their need for a simpler existence, and in many ways it set a new tone for their lives. As the hip Hollywood of the sixties and seventies became the power-suited, elegant, Reaganized Hollywood of the eighties, Coral and Vincent changed along with it. Gone was their quirkily homey "honeymoon house"; in its stead was a sleek, streamlined residence, smartly decorated in whites set off by marble. Gone, too, were the couple's "liberated lifestyle" caftans and seventies perms. In their place were Armani, Missoni, and Chanel.

Coral claimed to loathe living in Los Angeles. She complained regularly to her husband that she despised the lack of culture in Southern California, along with most of its inhabitants. She railed against Vincent's friends, the film community, the traffic, the smog, the shops, the restaurants. Alec Guinness recalled that she frequently warned him about Hollywood films and Hollywood people, whom she referred to as "total rubbish." She particularly hated being left alone in the city during her husband's lengthy professional absences. Jill Melford said, "She hated all the bits that we all hate about California. But I said to her one day, 'Well, as you're banging on about all that you hate about California, why don't you come back and live in England?' But she said, 'I don't want to live there in the freezing cold.' And, of course, their house was ravishing. Also, I think by that time she was quite a contented woman. I mean, she really adored Vinnie. Complained a lot, said what a fool he was, and all that. But Coral would do that about anybody. I think she had a very happy life, because he spoiled her rotten, which she loved. There was a lot of 'I have to be Mrs. Vincent Price because nobody's ever heard of Coral Browne.' There was a lot of that. But she quite liked it."

Indeed, once Coral realized that there was no turning back, she set about finding her niche in Los Angeles by moving in a circle where her beauty, wit, and elegance would be appreciated. Although she was not as well known in Hollywood as she might have liked, she was extremely well known just down the hill from Swallow Drive in West Hollywood. Whenever her films, particularly the camp *Auntie Mame* played at the revival theaters in town, the gay community would turn out in droves. One day Coral came home and announced that, while scanning the shelves of the West Hollywood Safeway for chicken broth, she had been approached by an employee: "Oh Miss Browne," said the young man, "I have to tell you it's such a divine coincidence that you're here today!" "Really!" replied Coral in her inimitable accent. "Why, thank you! Why's that?" "Well," the clerk responded, "with Halloween coming up, me and my friend Jeffrey picked your film, *Auntie Mame*, as our theme and we are going as Mame and Vera Charles!" "How nice!" Coral rejoined. "But can you afford the frocks?" "Oh, we're making them—exact replicas, and the folks helped with the materials. Jeffrey and I drew lots to see who would play who and *I won!*" "Oh," Coral said, "So you're going as Mame." "*N-o-o-o!* I'm going as *you,* Vera Charles, actress!"

Many of Coral's closest friends were homosexual. She also had a million acquaintances whom Jill Melford described as "a lot of screaming old queens who laughed every time she opened her mouth." Of course, Coral's first husband had himself been gay until he married her; as her friend Noel Davis noted, "I don't think I would be indiscreet to say, his feet had not touched the ground in a very long time." Of course, Philip's sexuality soon became the source of a classic Coral story. At the time of their marriage, Philip had been an actor. One night they were in bed together and Coral was going over the script of *King Lear* for a new production in which she was to play Goneril. Philip asked if she thought there was a part that he could play. Coral quickly leafed through the script and, pointing at the stage directions, said, "Yes, dear, this is perfect. A Camp near Dover."

Among her most significant affairs had been the openly gay photographer Cecil Beaton. As she told Frith Banbury, "I can't stand macho men." But more than that, she felt gay men understood and appreciated her. She said, "Women feel very comfortable with homosexuals. There's a certain delicacy. We don't want to be pounced on every thirty seconds by some hairy ape." Thus, she began to cultivate a circle of gay male friends in Los Angeles, who invited her to elegant parties and good restaurants, and through whom she began to see the city in a different light.

In the early to mid-1980s, when the AIDS crisis hit West Hollywood, Coral knew it was her turn to give something back. Though many members of the film world turned their back on the gay community during the early days of the crisis, Coral spent a great deal of time visiting sick friends, dropping off food baskets, stopping by to brighten up a day with a well-timed Coral story. In 1985 she wrote Alan Bennett, "Am off now to don my red cape and hood and fill my basket with the local cotton-wool strawberries and visit sick folk. One death a day in L.A. from AIDS—very soon I won't know a soul here." She also encouraged her husband to do his part. In 1986, when AIDS was still thought of as a "gay disease," Vincent did a public service announcement: "I know how to throw a good scare into people. I understand fear. Especially fear of the unknown. That's healthy. And that could be why you're afraid of AIDS. But getting AIDS from talking on the telephone, food, shaking hands, or even being coughed on shouldn't frighten you. Because you can't get AIDS from everyday things like that. If you're living in fear of AIDS, I hope I've made some of your fear disappear."

Coral's "checkered past," her reputation as a "scarlet woman," and her circle of prominent gay friends gave rise to many rumors that her marriage to my father was one of convenience. Like so many Hollywood couples, Vincent and Coral were grist to the gossip mill, a fact of which they themselves were fully aware. It never bothered them. As Roddy McDowall noted, "Obviously, from dropped remarks by both Coral and Vincent, they both had bisexual experiences, but I don't know the importance of those. And I don't know of their moral response to the situation. But certainly Coral, and the mutual jokes that she and Vincent sometimes shared, were highly sophisticated." Although these jokes, which took the form of witty and worldly-wise innuendo, were mostly initiated by Coral, Vincent took great pleasure in his wife's ribald humor. However, neither she nor Vincent every spoke directly to McDowall about their sexual experiences. Rather, as he saw it, Vincent and Coral enjoyed presenting the worldly facade of an extremely liberal and liberated couple who were comfortable with their own, and unjudgmental about other people's, sexuality.

Coral's rumored bisexuality mostly derived from her appearance in the 1969 film *The Killing of Sister George*, in which she played a broadcasting executive who forms a liaison with a very young Susannah York. In the film, she made love to Susannah York on screen, a scene both actresses found highly uncomfortable to shoot. One critic wrote, "Miss Browne was seen grimly twiddling the naked chest of Susannah York, as though trying to find Radio Three." However, Coral did have at least one significant lesbian relationship while still in her twenties. The five-year relationship came to an end when Coral's lover asked her to move in with her. After years of struggling to establish herself as an actress, Coral was terrified that her career would be doomed and so broke off the relationship. She would later say that it was the hardest thing she ever did. After this, there is no evidence that she ever had another affair with a woman, though her many affairs with men certainly did nothing to damage her career. Rather they seemed to enhance her reputation, at least within the theater community.

Similarly, many people in both the gay and film communities seemed to find it self-evident that he was bisexual. As with Coral, much of this reputation sprang from his film and stage work. In 1977, when he opened in San Francisco as Wilde, Anita Bryant was making headlines with her denunciations of homosexuality. For Vincent Price to play Oscar Wilde was seen as a strongly pro-gay statement. And, of course, much of my father's horror work was overtly campy, a fact which seemed to "prove" gayness—like his interests in art and cooking.

Both my father and Coral had many close gay friends. He was extremely comfortable in those friendships and thought nothing of embracing or kissing a male friend, gay or straight. Like his wife, he was never judgmental about other people's sexual preferences. One of the things he seemed to enjoy most about Coral was her sexual bravado and colorful past. After her death, when John Schlesinger was planning her London memorial service, he asked my father if Coral had had any favorite hymns. "Yes," said my dad, "and quite a few hers."

My father often complained that none of his wives had ever allowed him to have close male friends. He claimed that they felt threatened by his strong emotional ties to certain men. As Roddy McDowall saw it, "Vincent had the ability to intellectually romance you, and it wasn't by design. It was just what he was. But I'm not certain what sexual expression meant to either him or Coral." Indeed, my father craved the frisson of intellectual, artistic, and creative exchange, and it did not matter with whom he found it. To him, the sharing of artistic and intellectual passion was as profound an expression of love as existed.

Although my father was emotionally drawn to both men and women, I will never know whether he thought of himself as bisexual. But I do know that the rumors that he and Coral had a marriage of convenience were completely unfounded. The sexual passion that brought them together was as real as anything either had ever experienced. In the long run, they were a unique couple, capable of relating to both men and women with humor, grace, and passion.

Indeed, Vincent and Coral, who displayed a unique combination of elegance, humor, kindness, and concern for others, were acknowledged as a remarkable pair. As Joan Rivers recalled, "They were the perfect dinner guests. You knew he was going to be a gentleman, with manners that California still doesn't understand, and great stories. And you also knew that there would be something going on at the other end of the table, that Coral was going to be the firecracker. So they were a great combination."

Reggie Williams, who became my father's personal secretary during the mid-eighties saw the couple as "meticulous in the Old World courtesies of friendship, acknowledging favors, and extending sympathies and encouragement not only in telephone calls but also in handwritten missives, penned punctually on personalized stationery or on carefully selected cards. Although both of them had led transient lives in their profession, because of their respective wit, intellects, and good looks, and, moreover, their concern and all-consuming interest in their fellows and in the arts, they had retained a circle of friends who endured throughout their lives."

*   *   *

In 1981 Vincent Price turned seventy. In 1985 he celebrated his fiftieth year as an actor, and in 1988 his fiftieth year in movies. Throughout the decade he was increasingly accorded the status of Hollywood legend. He enjoyed the fanfare, cheerfully attending retrospectives and film festivals in the United States, Spain, Italy, and France. He gleefully clipped a cartoon featuring three frames of people watching horror movies on television, with the caption: "Somewhere around the world, a Vincent Price movie is playing on television." And when *The New York Times* made him the subject of their crossword puzzle, he exclaimed, "Now I really know I'm famous."

Following the three mediocre films he made in 1974, though, he was absent from the screen for five years—until, in 1979, he appeared in a cameo role in *Scavenger Hunt*, a Twentieth Century-Fox production featuring Richard Benjamin, James Coco, Scatman Crothers, Ruth Gordon, Cloris Leachman, Cleavon Little, Roddy McDowall, Robert Morley, Richard Mulligan, Tony Randall, and Meat Loaf. Though he appeared in only one scene, Vincent's character provided the premise for the picture—a scavenger hunt for a $200 million estate. In 1980 it was back to horror, with John Carradine, Donald Pleasence, and Britt Eklund in *The Monster Club*. For the first time in his career, Vincent played a vampire. He described the picture as "a sort of vampire disco, a fun picture for children. It is scary but not frightening. My vampire, for instance, is quite kindly. I have insisted on a line in the script to explain that I have retractable teeth. This was necessary because I found I couldn't talk with the vampire fangs in my mouth."

The producers of *The Monster Club* had hoped for a monster reunion of sorts, to feature Peter Cushing and Christopher Lee with Vincent and Carradine; but neither Lee or Cushing was available. In 1982, however, *House of the Long Shadows* brought the four of them together. Loosely based on the oft-filmed novel and play *Seven Keys to Baldpate*, the film script was irredeemably mediocre. This was nothing new for the four veteran actors, and yet they managed to enjoy themselves hugely in each other's company. As Lee noted, "We never had the advantages, in these films, of having the top scriptwriters, the top directors, the top budgets, the top locations. We really did have to create the proverbial silk purse out of the proverbial sow's ear. We did it because of the kind of *people* we were. As people, we were *proud* of our profession. We were dedicated and very, very, very determined."

In 1983, again in England, Vincent appeared in *Bloodbath at the House of Death*, a little-seen spoof of the horror genre; in 1986 he took part in the horror anthology *The Offspring*. Neither film was well received; in a publicity interview at the time Vincent, rather testily but with some justification, complained, "I'm bored talking about horror. I'm too old. Do you ask Al Pacino how he likes doing gangster roles? I'm bored talking about it." Yet Vincent's cult status continued to grow.

In the late 1970s, Vincent received a gold record for his work with Alice Cooper on his album, *Welcome to My Nightmare*. He enjoyed the fact that he seemed to be popular among musicians and counted Gene Simmons of Kiss as one of his friends. Then, in 1983, Vincent Price's name once again danced on everyone's lips as the inspiration for, and the voice behind, Michael Jackson's new album, *Thriller*, which went on to become the best-selling record in history. Vincent had met the Jackson Five in the 1960s on a television show; always eager to appeal to younger audiences, he was delighted when Michael Jackson asked him to perform the "rap" on the album's title song. Sadly, however, the experience proved a mixed blessing. In his usual eagerness to work, Vincent agreed to lend his famous voice for what amounted to a small honorarium; if only he had secured a royalty arrangement, the album's phenomenal sales might finally have brought his pecuniary paranoia to an end.

This experience typified my father's financial foibles. In *I Like What I Know* he had criticized his forebears for their lack of monetary acumen, but he sold himself short just as often as his relatives had done. His desire to remain in the public eye often led him to accept paltry fees. His work on *Thriller* simply followed this pattern; but when the album began making its millions he was irate, feeling that Jackson should have materially acknowledged his significant contribution to the album's success. In truth, he was also angry with himself for not having made a more sensible financial arrangement—another evidence of his tendency to obsess over money troubles.

Word eventually trickled back to Michael Jackson that my father was upset about the money. One day I answered the door at my father's house to find three members of Jackson's entourage. They came bearing a gift—a letter of thanks from Jackson and a large frame containing a poster of the pop star and one gold and two platinum albums, all dedicated to Vincent. When I brought this "gift" in to my father, he didn't know whether to laugh or cry; at first he opted for the former by turning it into a faux altar surrounded by candles and flowers. But, as Reggie Williams observed, the whole experience continued to irk him. "There were few things that totally displeased him, but one item of memorabilia around the house began to rile him—the framed gold and platinum records for his contribution to *Thriller*. When a move was made to obtain payment for Vincent for the video usage, his agent was referred to the small print of the recording contract where a video clause was buried, and further payment was refused point blank. Vincent agitated to have the gold disc auctioned, with the proceeds to go to his gallery at East Los Angeles College. When it was reported that Michael Jackson had made a multimillion-dollar payment in respect of charges of his possible misconduct with a young boy, Vincent channeled the ill feelings about his own mistreatment into a joke: 'All I can say is that Michael Jackson fucked me—and I didn't get paid for it!' "

Vincent's exposure on *Thriller*, however, paid other kinds of dividends. By being associated with Jackson and heard on radio stations around the world, he attracted a new audience among the younger generation; so he was delighted when, in 1983, Disney asked him to provide the voice for the villain in their first full-length animated feature in many years. The animators had screened *Champagne for Caesar* with the idea of using Ronald Colman's voice as the model for the villain's. When they heard Vincent, they decided to ask him to read for the role. Supervising animator Glen Keane remembered that as soon as they heard his audition, "We realized we had found the perfect actor for the role. Price's expressive voice and attitude inspired us to further redesign the character."

The Great Mouse Detective is a wonderful takeoff on the Sherlock Holmes adventures, featuring Basil of Baker Street, a mouse detective who must go up against the great rat villain, Professor Rattigan. Vincent got a big kick doing the part, remarking, "Rattigan is the *ultimate* villain. He's got a huge sense of humor about himself, but dead seriousness at the same time about crime." Vincent was proud of his work on the film, not only of his vocal characterization, but of his influence on the animation and his work on the soundtrack, where he sang as Rattigan. Indeed, the veteran actor thoroughly enjoyed working in animation, a new field in which he began to develop an outstanding reputation. Susan Blu, one of the industry's leading animation directors and voice-over teachers, worked with him in 1985 during his recurring guest role on *The Thirteen Ghosts of Scooby Doo* for Hanna-Barbera. The actor played Vincent Van Ghoul, the good leader of the ghosts and goblins, a character drawn to look like the actor himself. Blu said of working with Vincent, "As a director, I always say, 'Get the words off the page.' With Vincent, they flew off to become full three-dimensional characters. His vocal uniqueness was matched only by his superb talent as well as his childlike enthusiasm."

Through his successful association with the studio, Vincent was asked by Disney Television to host the children's series, *Read, Write, and Draw*. He thought the program a wonderful extension of his lifetime interest in the visual arts, noting, "I think it's fascinating to be able to see how different children's imaginations develop. I also find *Read, Write, and Draw* very challenging as an actor. I don't ever wish to sound condescending and I don't want to read down to the young ones. I want to share their stories and their art with them, as a friend."

Vincent's burgeoning fame with younger audiences endeared him to new generations of college students. Throughout the 1980s he continued his grueling lecture tours, making many return visits to his favorite institutions. One of these was Northeast Missouri State, now called Truman State, in the small town of Kirksville. He had first visited the college during the 1970s, where he was struck by the evident enthusiasm and interest of the student body. Over the years, he developed a rapport with the staff, faculty, and students of the college, and soon began annual appearances at the small school. He became a close friend of the then-head of the Department of Speech and Communications, Ed Carpenter, who recalled that Vincent was always more than generous with his time and money. The actor not only gave the scheduled lecture, but also performed such diverse tasks as giving interviews for communications students' videotapes, riding in the Homecoming Parade, and sponsoring an annual scholarship. He often dined with Ed and his wife, Nettie, and seemed to find the college town and its intellectual denizens gave him the respite he needed from his life in Hollywood.

During the 1980s, Vincent also devoted more and more thought and energy to the Vincent Price Gallery at East Los Angeles College, continuing to donate time, money, and works of art to it. He frequently visited the campus to look at students' work, gave graduation speeches and lectures, and always visited the fine gallery exhibitions mounted by director Tom Silliman. During the late seventies, California tax cuts in the form of Proposition 13 threatened the gallery, even forcing it to close for a year in 1979. My father was enraged. "I called the president of the college and I said, 'What the hell is this? I didn't get this stuff to be put in the closet. Let's use it. Or let's give it to somebody else if you all don't want it.' And he said, 'Oh no, my God, we want it.' And he did a tremendous job of bringing back interest into it."

In his efforts to reopen the gallery, the actor turned to Wallace Albertson, widow of actor Jack Albertson and then head of the Los Angeles County Community College District board of trustees. With Mrs. Albertson's help, the gallery was placed under the care of the Vincent Price Art Gallery Foundation, a nonprofit organization free from the restrictions and politics of the school or of the community college system. During this difficult time, Vincent maintained almost daily contact with Tom Silliman and Wallace Albertson in working to create a lasting artistic legacy.

Over the years, however, he had grown increasingly frustrated as mainstream Los Angeles newspapers ignored the gallery. In 1990 recognition finally came in the form of Huell Howser's *Videolog*, shown on L.A.'s prestigious public television station, KCET. Howser's popular program brought attention to one of Southern California's "hidden gems." Following the transmission, the gallery was at long last written up in the *Los Angeles Times*. Vincent was thrilled with the attention. The article acknowledged the collection as one of the finest of any community college in the nation, and spoke with various alumni who had been influenced by the gallery and the program. Among these was actor Edward James Olmos, who said, "It definitely molded and shaped my career, especially having access to the kind of artworks that I was exposed to. It really elevated my awareness. What that gallery has meant to the community in the east part of Los Angeles is overwhelming. It has created some extraordinary people."

In the early eighties, Vincent began an eight-year stint as the host of *Mystery!* for PBS. This venture was the first to combine the several elements of his disparate public personae, marrying his association with villainy to his image as an intelligent, sophisticated, and cultivated spokesman for the arts.

Produced by WGBH in Boston, in conjunction with Mobil Corporation, the program featured British-made mystery stories, for which a large audience had already been created by the popular *Masterpiece Theatre*. After hiring the incomparable Edward Gorey to create the sets—"Gorey Mansion"—and the wonderful title art, the next task was to find a host. In an effort to duplicate but not imitate the popularity of *Masterpiece Theatre*'s Alistair Cooke, the program's inaugural season was hosted by NBC's *Today Show* arts and film critic, Gene Shalit. When Shalit left after the first year, executive producer Joan Wilson knew exactly who she wanted to bring in as his replacement. As Ron Miller has noted in his book on the popular series, "Price became America's favorite mystery man, the gentle giant of Grand Guignol. That's why Executive Producer Joan Wilson couldn't wait to sign him up as the series' new host. Price loved hosting *Mystery!* and said so to virtually everyone he met during his eight years on the job. He became the program's walking, talking trademark. Price so clearly belonged to Gorey Manor that you often wondered if he wasn't a Gorey illustration come to life. His approach was to have fun with the genre and to do a lot of winking at the audience. That's exactly what Wilson, and her successor Rebecca Eaton, wanted, because it expressed the spirit of the show. He was their willing accomplice from the start. Price happily strolled through make-believe cobwebs, dodged dangling spiders, and ducked out of the way of nearsighted bats while doing his intros."

Vincent adored hosting the classy, well-produced *Mystery!* series, and greatly enjoyed his trips to Boston each summer and fall to film the intros and extros. He got along famously with executive producer Joan Wilson, and they were quite close until her death in 1985. Fortunately, he also liked her successor, Rebecca Eaton, very much.

Aside from the pleasure of doing good work, undoubtedly one of the reasons Vincent so enjoyed his eight-year stint on *Mystery!* was the close friendships he made with two members of the WGBH staff, Sandy Leonard and Dali Cahill. As Leonard recalled the beginning of their friendship, "Joan Wilson asked me if I would like to write Vincent's introductions. And I said, 'Of course, but why are you asking me?' And she said, 'Well, you have a twisted sense of humor and I think that you would bring to this something that would be good.' And writing for Vincent and working for him was the best thing I've ever done. When he arrived for the first time, the first thing we worked on was *Reilly, Ace of Spies*. And I wrote these pieces that were very long, heavy and historical and we had to cut them down. But after I got to know his voice, it became very easy, and he never changed anything I ever wrote. I was very proud of that. When we started talking for the first time, I think he must have realized that we shared an interest in art. He would say, 'Let's go to the museum.' And it was just very comfortable. So after that, when Vincent came to town, he and Dali and I would have dinner, go to museums, go for walks. We had a great time."

My father loved being identified with the distinguished series. He felt the British programming was of the highest caliber, and after years of being associated with schlock, he enjoyed being *Mystery!*'s answer to his old friend Alistair Cooke. He said, "I'm a grand fan of English mystery movies. All the great mystery writers are English. American mystery stories are a bit too obvious. I think the English do it better than we do—ours are full of car chases. But theirs are so extraordinarily well thought out." He also believed that PBS offered the American public the best television programming, and he liked to think that his wide audience appeal might help popularize public television. The job proved to be the best of both worlds—a distinguished and consistent gig as well as a form of public service that ideally suited the lifelong popularizer of the arts.

By the early eighties Coral and Vincent had lived in Southern California together for almost ten years. However, although Coral had left London permanently in 1974, she kept her flat in Eaton Place, unwilling to completely sever her ties to England. While the couple were on a trip to Venice in the mid-1980s, the flat was robbed and Coral lost a great many valuable and sentimental items. The couple returned to London and took an inventory of what was missing. One of the items they feared stolen was Coral's silver, until Vincent opened a drawer and found a cutlery service for eighteen. He called to his wife to tell her that he had found the silver, but when she reached the drawer her face fell: "That isn't my silver. Look at it." Vincent picked up a spoon and glanced at the inscription, The Ritz, Paris. He picked up a fork, The Savoy. A knife, British Airways Concorde. He dined out on the story for years.

Not long afterward, Coral decided to sell the apartment, though she continued to make trips to London, where her mother lived in a nursing home until her death at age ninety-nine. Victoria Brown was, by all accounts, a tyrant. Jill Melford remarked, "Coral looked after her mother, who was a vicious old cow. I once said to Coral, 'I'll do anything in the world for you, but don't ask me to deal with that woman. She's the most unpleasant woman I've ever met.' She would do anything to put Coral down. She was a really embittered lady who was horrible to Coral, and Coral took it. Coral could be deflated like that. Her mother used to come into the dressing room and say, 'You look fat and old.' She was seriously evil to Coral." Nonetheless Coral always supported and visited her mother, enlisting the help of her friend Rosemary Merrick to look after her needs. This wasn't easy. At ninety-two, Victoria Brown had gone missing for two days. She was found in France, having organized a trip across the Channel for herself and few of her fellow nursing-home residents. Victoria was indefatigable. In 1986, after Coral had come through an eight-week bout with pneumonia, she wrote Alan Bennett, "I don't go anyplace except hospitals for X rays and blood tests. Vinnie has thyroid trouble and is not himself *at all*. Mother is fine!!" Difficult as others justifiably found Coral's mother, my father and she got along famously—a fact that understandably annoyed Coral.

Whenever she returned to England, Coral was greeted warmly by the press as well as by her friends. She worried, however, that she was being forgotten. When other actresses of her generation received choice roles on stage or in film, she often resorted to nastily witty remarks in an attempt to deflect her worries about the state of her own career. In a 1979 London article chronicling one of Coral's brief visits to London (dinner with Alec Guinness and Laurence Olivier at the Connaught, supper with Maggie Smith at Chez Solange), columnist Michael Owen noted that the actress missed the London theater and her old home in Eaton Place with accessible shops but also quotes her as saying, "I cannot leave my husband for too long. He is a complete workaholic. Unless he gets five offers a day he looks forty years older."

Though she worried about her career, friends seemed to feel that Coral had relaxed somewhat into her California life as Mrs. Vincent Price. Jill Melford believed, "She mellowed enormously. She still kept you on your toes, but it was a lot mellower than when she was unhappy and on her own and frantically ambitious. I don't think she was particularly ambitious towards the end, but I think she was competitive." Despite her willingness to take a back seat to her husband's career, Coral tried to work whenever possible. In 1981, she received a script in the mail from English playwright Alan Bennett, to whom she had told the story of meeting exiled British spy Guy Burgess during her 1958 tour of Russia with the Shakespeare Memorial Company. As Bennett wrote, "The picture of the elegant actress and the seedy exile sitting in a dingy Moscow flat through a long afternoon listening again and again to Jack Buchanan singing 'Who Stole My Heart Away?' seemed to me funny and sad, but it was a few years until I got round to writing it up. It was only when I sent the first draft to Coral Browne that I found she had kept not merely Burgess's letters, thanking her for running him errands, but also her original notes and measurements, and even his cheque (uncashed and for six pounds) to treat her and one of her fellow-actors to lunch at the Caprice."

In a November 20, 1981 diary entry, Bennett has noted a phone conversation with Coral. "We talk about the Burgess piece and discuss who should play him, and we go through various names while it becomes increasingly obvious that we haven't talked about who is to play her. Eventually I hear myself saying, 'Would you like to do it?' 'But aren't I too old?' 'Well,' I say, 'what do you think?' 'I'm not sure, dear. You see, in a way, age didn't come into it.'" In fact, Bennett had some doubts about the wisdom of sixty-nine-year-old Coral Browne playing her forty-five-year-old self. "I was scared of her, but I wouldn't have dared say no. And I can't think of anybody who could have played her and also anybody who would have dared play her. And I was very glad she did, obviously."

Coral loved the idea of seeing this story from her life filmed and followed the playwright's revisions with enthusiasm. After showing the script to her friend, director John Schlesinger, she wrote Bennett, "John S. put himself up as director (which pleased me no end)." To star opposite Coral Browne, she, Bennett, and Schlesinger settled on Alan Bates. Coral had wanted the actor from the beginning, but his agent had told her that, after playing Diaghilev, he would never play another homosexual. Then, as Coral later recalled, "The next thing I got was a telephone call from London saying, 'Alan Bates is absolutely delighted.'"

An Englishman Abroad was set to shoot in January 1983 in Glasgow and Dundee. Coral flew to England while my father chose to stay home in L.A. where I was spending my semester break from college. Shortly before filming began, my father received a phone call from Coral. Concerned by a growth under her arm, she had gone to the doctor where a malignant tumor had been discovered. Naturally we were both terribly worried, but when the doctor told Coral that it would be perfectly safe for her to have the surgery after filming, she decided to go on with the shoot and reassured my father that she would be fine without him. In truth, filming was always a strain for Coral and she found it easier not to have her husband on or near the set.

Several people felt that it was, perhaps, the realization that this could be her last film that inspired Coral to give what many consider one of her finest performances. Be that as it may, she also simply reveled in another opportunity to star in a superb production. And, as Bennett recalled, there was never any doubt that she *was* the star. "We went to Nathan's, the costumiers, to fit her clothes and something happened that I'd never seen before. All the sewers and fitters came out to look at her, because she was a legendary figure, really. She wore clothes in a way that people had forgotten how to wear clothes. She was very, very picky about them. She was very particular. Wouldn't settle for just anything."

An Englishman Abroad received extraordinary reviews in both England and the United States, where it was shown on *Masterpiece Theatre*. The British Academy of Film and Television Arts voted Browne and Bates best actress and actor awards, and Schlesinger best director, while Bennett won the screenwriting award. Though Coral called their fistful of awards "frightfully vulgar," she was, in fact, thrilled to be the object of such acclaim at the end of her career. Almost ten years after her last performance in London's West End, Coral Browne had returned in greater style than she could ever have hoped, her talent more than intact.

Then, in 1985, having recuperated successfully from cancer, she was once again in the spotlight. The seventy-two-year-old actress was cast as Alice Hargreaves in *Dreamchild*. Written by Dennis Potter and directed by Gavin Millar, the film costarred Peter Gallagher and Ian Holm. Alice Hargreaves was the original Alice in Wonderland, the ten-year-old girl who had inspired Reverend Charles Dodgson (Lewis Carroll) to write the children's fantasy. Against a background of extraordinary "Wonderland" creatures made by Jim Henson, Coral played Hargreaves at eighty when, as an old lady, she was invited to receive an honorary degree from Columbia University in 1932, in honor of Carroll's centenary. Because Coral looked at least twenty years younger than her age, she was forced to wear a considerable amount of makeup to play a woman only eight years older than she. Stripped of her glamorous facade, she appeared both vulnerable and imperious, delivering an extraordinarily moving performance that won her the *Evening Standard* Best Actress award. In America the film received marvelous reviews, but only a limited theatrical release from Cannon. The star was furious, particularly as she had to pay her own airfare to promote the film. She glowered, "If it was up to them, I'd have to work the engine and serve the tea." Nonetheless, she was extremely proud of the critical response. *Newsweek*'s David Ansen wrote, "The magnificent Coral Browne gives as entertaining a performance as any I've seen this year: one moment the picture of frosty nineteenth-century hauteur, she seems to light up from within when Gallagher touches her girlish vanity." And in the *New York Times* Stephen Holden wrote, "As Alice Hargreaves, Coral Browne gives a performance of indomitable dignity, in which reserves of warmth and vulnerability are constantly cracking through the chilled exterior of Victorian propriety."

Following her acclaim for *An Englishman Abroad* and *Dreamchild*, Coral found herself very much in the public eye, emerging from the twilight shadows of her role as Mrs. Vincent Price. But when approached about writing her biography, she remarked, "I disapprove of most biographies. I find it offensive to read about these people having affairs and who they did it with. The books are not a success unless you have been to bed with eighty-two people in the first three chapters. No, I shan't do that."

*   *   *

My father was thrilled that his wife's career was enjoying a renaissance, frequently expressing gratitude that these two glittering projects had come her way. As a man who struggled with an overwhelming sense of guilt, he felt the pressure of Coral having "given up her career" for him—a state of affairs to which she herself often alluded to anyone who would listen. Joan Rivers echoed Coral's sentiments when she told me, "She gave it all up for him. She gave up the position, she gave up who she was. She never made it in the United States. They didn't let her in. She adored him, and never complained, though she may have complained to poor Vinnie!"

Coral even went so far as to tell friends in America that the British government had offered her a DBE, provided she would undertake a national tour of Australia. She further claimed that she had refused the offer rather than return to the place of her birth, hinting strongly that Australian soprano Joan Sutherland, who was happy to sing in her native land, was given the honor instead. When I told Coral's English friends this story they were utterly amazed—not to mention thoroughly skeptical, particularly since Coral had quite happily accompanied my father on his own national tour of Australia in the early 1980s. Fantasy or no on Coral's part, her assertions only served to heighten my father's feeling that he had somehow deprived her of her rightful place.

Interestingly, many of Coral's English friends felt that she was happy to leave Britain when she did because she knew that the style of acting for which she had been trained had fallen out of fashion. As Alan Bennett remarked, "She was a grand dame of the theater when the theater was still very old-fashioned really. There weren't parts for people like that in the sixties and early seventies. And they hadn't started revivals yet. Her elegance wasn't the elegance of that time."

Although Vincent was genuinely pleased that his wife had been given two extraordinary roles, he secretly hoped that there would be similar opportunities for himself. While his work in other arenas was distinguished, his film work no longer was. His turn finally came in 1986, with an offer for a good part in an excellent film with an extraordinary cast. In the early eighties producer Mike Kaplan had set about securing the rights and funding for a film version of David Berry's play, *The Whales of August*. The story of two sisters living out the end of their lives on an island off the coast of Maine, it was purchased as a vehicle for veteran actresses Lillian Gish and Bette Davis. Along with these two great ladies of American film, the costarring roles were to be played by Ann Sothern and Sir John Gielgud. Two years later the film had yet to be made, though, and when the money at last came through Gielgud was no longer available. Thus, British director Lindsay Anderson took a chance on Vincent Price in the role of the charming Russian gentleman, Mr. Maranov, who has spent a life of exile in the United States, living on the kindness of strangers. Though many considered Anderson's choice risky, the director said, "In England, we're not so completely blinkered by Vincent's horror reputation."

Vincent accepted the offer with enthusiasm. His late brother, Mort, was his inspiration for the role: "He was an enchanting man, but he never took advantage of all his opportunities. I used my memories of him to show a man who is very charming but in no way working toward anything." The shoot, however, proved extremely difficult, with cast and crew having to spend a very cold autumn on an island off the coast of Maine. Vincent remarked, "Bette kept calling it *The Whales of November*, because it kept getting colder and colder. We were really very uncomfortable. We couldn't get onto the mainland without a forty-five-minute water-taxi ride. It wasn't the jolliest picture I've ever been on, but then the jolliest pictures are sometimes the ones that turn out worst." He treated the difficulties with equanimity, although Coral worried about his health. The shoot was additionally difficult because Bette Davis was frequently temperamental with cast and crew alike. Vincent, however, who had worked with her in *Elizabeth and Essex* almost fifty years earlier, got along quite well with her. He loved to tell how, when Coral heard about the film, she asked him the name of the production company. When he said it was called Alive, she replied, "With you and Bette Davis and Lillian Gish? It should be called Almost Alive!"

The Whales of August was released in the fall of 1987 to excellent reviews. *Newsweek*'s Jack Kroll felt that Price "in his ravaged handsomeness, gives his best performance in years." And the London *Evening Standard* noted his performance had "all the nuances that his horror roles have left dormant for years." Vincent's name was soon being bandied about as a possible Oscar nominee for Best Supporting Actor. Though he didn't receive the nomination, he nonetheless relished the attention. The syndicated magazine *Parade* chose Vincent Price as the subject of a May 1988 cover story. Chronicling the history of the actor's career, the article endorsed Vincent's status as a Hollywood legend and a latter-day Renaissance man.

His followup to *The Whales of August*, however—a cameo role in *Dead Heat*, starring Treat Williams and Joe Piscopo—proved disappointing. He thought them both good actors, but nobody came out ahead in this run-of-the-mill film about two cops investigating the apparent resurrection of dead criminals.

A year later, Vincent played another cameo role in *Backtrack*, a film directed by his old friend Dennis Hopper, and starring Hopper and Jodie Foster. Vincent was cast as Mafia Don Lino Avoca, who sends Hopper out to kill an artist (Foster) who has witnessed a mob execution. The picture was not shown in the United States until 1991, when it appeared on the Showtime cable network. Vincent enjoyed working with Dennis Hopper, and appeared with him a few years later in *The Heart of Justice*, a Turner Pictures production starring Eric Stoltz, that also premiered on television. Vincent and Dennis had remained good friends since their first meeting in the 1950s when Hopper was a teenager, and one of the last art exhibitions Vincent attended was an opening of Dennis's work, where he bought one of the younger actor's pieces. As for Hopper, he never ceased to be grateful to Vincent for introducing him to art, noting that "my whole life would be enormously diminished without having met Vincent Price."

Even as Vincent and Coral seemed to be experiencing a career renaissance, each made an effort to spend more time at home with the other. They loved the simplicity of the house on Swallow Drive, where Vincent grew a beautiful garden and Coral had time to read and do her needlepoint. Vincent's personal secretary, Reggie Williams, noted, "Their domicile was precisely fashioned to their taste and interests. Their active lives— if they were on their feet, something was always in the offing—was reflected in the fact that there was only one truly comfortable easy chair in the entire household—and that was a large burnt-orange Queen Anne just inside the front door, in which no one ever sat. They did no big-scale entertaining at home and the neighbors knew to involve them only in courtesy exchanges in the driveway, so they preserved their little world in complete privacy. Marika Kiss, a Hungarian emigrée, executed the heavy household chores a couple of days each week. Graced with something of a Mother Earth demeanor, Marika would react to Coral's incisive comments, sometimes heavily barbed, with a faint, bemused smile."

As ever, dogs were a significant part of the Price household. In the mid-seventies, Vincent and Coral had bought Tiggy a Chihuahua companion, a delicate black puppy from Hawaii, whom they named Maile after the tropical flower. In 1980, Tiggy died suddenly on my father's sixty-ninth birthday, and he consoled his wife with another Chihuahua to keep Maile company. They named this one—a long-haired, snub-nosed, feisty little girl—Fendi, for her motley-colored coat. When Maile died in 1989, at age fifteen, Fendi, too, became forlorn. While walking by their favorite pet store on Santa Monica Boulevard, the couple saw three Schipperkes in the window and decided to buy a friend for Fendi. Their first choice among the lovable black dogs had just been sold, so they settled on her sister, who they named Wilhelmina, or Wili, after the breed's origin as Dutch barge dogs. A few weeks later, Coral noticed that Wili seemed to grow unduly tired after brief periods of play. When the vet diagnosed the little puppy with a hole in the heart, the Prices decided to pay for the expensive operation.

Wili came through perfectly, but shortly thereafter the pet shop called to say that my father and Coral's first-choice puppy had been returned and they offered her gratis to the couple by way of apology for Wili's defect. The household soon boasted two puppies, Wili and Kiki, as well as Fendi. Vincent adored the rambunctious Schipperkes, while Coral remained solicitous of Fendi's well-being, making sure that the puppies didn't hide Fendi's favorite grey rat. Coral found it endlessly amusing that, as Fendi grew older, her only real pleasure was humping her stuffed grey rat. As Reg recalled, "Coral's frequent cry was, 'Where's the rat? Fendi wants to fuck!' "

During the 1970s, Vincent and Coral had become regular parishioners at St. Victor's Church on Holloway Drive in West Hollywood. In 1984 they celebrated their tenth anniversary with Coral's long-awaited church wedding at St. Victor's, in the presence of a small circle of friends. Over the course of the decade, the couple devoted more time to church attendance and the sermons and guidance of Father Parnassus, as well as the company of fellow parishioners such as Christopher Hewitt and Gus Schirmer. As Reg Williams noted, however, "Services there put no rein on Coral's spontaneous declarations. Soon after Betsy Bloomingdale's husband's S&M sex scandals had hit the front page, Betsy was seen by Coral entering the church. "There goes Betsy," Coral pronounced, "thin as a whip!"

But the highlight of the 1980s for Vincent and Coral was their social life, which blossomed even as their careers had done. In the seventies they had become regulars at Patrick Terrail's trendy Ma Maison, but when chef Wolfgang Puck left to open his own restaurant in an unlikely location above Sunset Boulevard, Vincent and Coral were among his first devotees. Spago was conveniently located just down the hill from Swallow Drive, and the two frequently enjoyed dining there with friends such as Joan Rivers and Edgar Rosenberg, Roddy McDowall, David Hockney, Sammy and Tita Cahn, Billy Wilder, and many others. In 1983, Vincent agreed to be Puck's celebrity host for an American Wine and Food Festival to benefit Meals on Wheels. Over the decade, the event grew in popularity as chefs from around the U.S. were invited to cook on the Universal Studios Western back lot, while diners paid $100 to walk around in Santa Fe style, eating and drinking some of the country's finest fare. By 1988 the festival had raised

$600,000 for Meals on Wheels, and had become one of the best-attended charity events of the year. Coral and Vincent were regularly seen around town at film premieres, benefits, art openings, and myriad parties, and in 1989 they were asked to appear on the Academy Awards together during an opening number which celebrated the elegance of Hollywood. During the eighties, the couple seemed to epitomize the glamor to which Hollywood aspired.

As well as their busy social life in L.A., Vincent and Coral loved traveling the world on cruise ships. Coral, unlike my father, disliked Christmas, and often tried to arrange for them to be at sea during the holidays, preferably in a very warm climate. Many of their friends found it curious that a woman so notoriously choosy about the company she kept would enjoy cruising, but she did, keeping up a correspondence with several friends made on these excursions. Vincent continued to enjoy the socializing, the joy of being at sea, and the opportunity to visit foreign ports of call, while Coral relished the luxury, the shopping—the *idea* of seeing the world.

On dry land, Coral and Vincent particularly liked staying at the Kahala Hilton outside Honolulu, where Vincent was actually able to unwind on a beach vacation. Most of their trips together, however, were geared around mutual interests such as art and theater. They enjoyed weekend getaways to San Francisco, a city that appealed to Coral so much that she refused to believe it was in the same state as Los Angeles. They often traveled to New York to visit friends and catch up on the latest exhibitions and plays. Of course, London was another frequent destination, for both work and pleasure. And Venice became one of their most beloved ports of call. Coral encouraged her husband to take Marcella and Victor Hazan's course on Italian wine and cuisine and, although Vincent rarely spent money on vacations for himself, he later admitted that the week-long course at the Cipriani with the Hazans was one of the best things he had ever done. The Prices adored Marcella and Victor, and no trip to Italy was complete without visiting them in Venice.

Despite the strength of their relationship, there was one significant area of conflict between them. Coral was certainly not the easiest person to live with, and although my father generally found a way to humor her, she had an opinion about everything, particularly her husband's friends and family. She tended to disapprove of both. For a man to whom friends and relations were so important, this proved very trying. His initial enthusiasm for her caustic wit soured when it turned vicious and nasty. As the years went on—particularly once she was ill—she fought with my father frequently, usually over money or his children. He generally backed down, but never all the way. Roddy McDowall felt that Coral's "raging jealousy was formidable. Of course, one of the most affecting things about her was that inside of this brutally factual gorgon was this child, who was always looking for someone to take care of her; but if they started to take care of her, she cut their head off because she couldn't trust them. I really adored Coral, and the only time I ever felt her behavior to be unconscionable was in relation to Vincent's children. But he was catholic enough, and I don't mean in the religious sense, to understand that area of her impossibility and that it bore no relation to common sense. Vincent's most remarkable achievement was that he would not let her kill his relationship with his children."

As Reggie Williams remembered, "Vincent's love, concern, and contact with his two children was not overtly paraded before his spouse. Warm and humane though Coral was to generous extreme, children—anybody's children—were anathema to her. One wonders whether, having sacrificed any maternal instinct she might have had for her profession, she deemed it somewhat boorish to procreate."

In actual fact, Coral did manage to take an interest in a few of her friend's children; it was, more precisely, her husband's children with whom she had real difficulty. She made her opinion about Barrett and me very clear, and as a consequence, my father, who refused to let her cut us out of his life completely, often had to to sneak behind her back to spend time with us. It was worst for Barrett and Rini, who gradually found themselves shunted to the sidelines of my father's life when Coral decided that she simply didn't like my brother—whom she disparagingly referred to as "the Albuquerque poet"—or sister-in-law, and they were never invited to visit again. My father's solution to the rifts she was manufacturing was to invent projects such as book collaborations or lectures in Albuquerque, which would allow him "legitimate" time with his son. Barrett soon found himself using the same ploy, creating writing assignments in L.A. which would allow him to have what he later referred to as "a $250 dollar lunch" with his father (airfare included). But their visits grew increasingly sporadic as Vincent found himself forced to choose between his children and his wife. And unbeknownst to my father, when Barrett's oldest son, Jody, called to speak to his grandfather one day, Coral told him not to call the house again. Because Jody and Keir had been raised in New Jersey, my father had spent very little time with his grandsons. He had spoken at Jody's high school graduation in 1980 (two weeks after speaking at mine!) but, with his calendar so tightly controlled by Coral, he barely ever saw them again.

Curiously, the longer Coral and Vinent were married, the more possessive Coral became. As Adrienne Corri observed, "She kept everyone who liked him away from him. I very rarely saw him alone apart from a couple of times when he came over to England without her, and we went out to dinner and talked. But when she was here, it was very much a case of only 'Coral's friends.'" Through her jealousy, Coral ended up destroying many of my father's relationships, rebuffing even old friends such as Hank and Marin Milam, Jane Russell, and Diana Rigg.

Marin recalled, "After the marriage to Coral we had one dinner at their house and when we called to ask them in return they were busy—always. So it all died away. Every once in a while, in a mood of nostalgia, we would send a birthday card and Vincent would usually answer with a brief note, not the newsy kind we were used to. The ties that bound us had obviously been severed. The new Madame Price was calling the social shots and we had not made the cut. One Christmas, many years into the marriage with Coral, I decided to call anyway. She answered the phone, very on, 'Hello-o-o', in that sort of gritty English way she had of talking, anticipatory. I said, 'Coral, it's Marin Milam calling to say Merry Christmas.' There was a pause and then, 'Oh.' No longer anticipatory. Dismissive. Disappointed. And then nothing more. Silence while she obviously handed the phone to Vincent and there followed a very awkward, very short conversation, as if Coral's reaction to me had registered with him. I cried afterwards. Because I was hurt at first and then angry. If I had had a plum pudding handy and she was within throwing distance, I would have hurled it at her. Instead I said, 'Bitch,' and went back to cooking our Christmas dinner." After over twenty years of a close friendship that was more like family, my father never saw the Milams again.

Diana Rigg remembered the dissolution of her friendship with Coral and Vincent. "Coral was in hospital for cancer in her leg, and I remember ringing her up and getting the frost at the other end of the telephone. After that, when I rang or sent cards and messages, I always got the frost. I could never understand this. It was completely inexplicable to me. I didn't really know Coral well. I wasn't part of her coterie or her group or anything, so it was really Vincent that I cared about. I was not laying claim to anything other than a great fondness for him, but I was frozen out, and I think the same applies to a lot of other people that I've talked to. What her motives were behind it, I can't begin to conjecture. Nothing happened between us, absolutely nothing. It was simply that I was persona non grata to Coral for reasons which I could not understand. My feelings of affection were chiefly for Vincent, and probably that is what she sensed."

Most of those friends who were spurned by Coral, and consequently faded out of my father's life, found it hard to believe that he could be party to her actions; but they also couldn't believe that he could have been entirely ignorant of her behavior. Indeed, it is difficult to understand why he put up with his wife's mercurial behavior unless, as Diana Rigg believed, he was unaware of it. Sandy Leonard, however, talked with my father about his friendship with Diana. According to him, my dad said, "She stopped calling. When she used to come to California, she'd call all the time. But she stopped." When Leonard asked why, my father replied with a slight smile, "I think it may have been something Coral said." And Bill Brice believed, "Vincent was essentially not a confrontational person. He wanted everybody to love everybody and when they didn't, he wasn't sure how to deal with it." Though my father must, on some level, have known what Coral was doing, he so hated conflict that he buried his head in the sand, naïvely hoping his friends would understand and forgive him.

And so Coral's friends became the couple's "family." Where Coral could seem ungenerous toward her husband's friends and family, she could not have been more kindhearted within her own circle. In a curious way, over the years Vincent quietly took a back seat to his gregarious wife. Alan Bennett recalled, "They came here once to supper and I'd never met him before. I was quite nervous, meeting such a big star. And he was the most courteous man I think I've ever met. His manners were so old-fashioned, in a way, that he just made it very easy. And such a contrast with Coral squawking away, who really didn't take any account of anything like that. She wanted to make me a needlepoint cushion. And while she was talking, without disturbing anybody, he found some scissors and made a pattern of the chair it was going to go on and cut it out. And he was so unobtrusive that you hardly noticed." Indeed, though Coral took the lead in social matters, Vincent found a place in the hearts of her friends.

38

THROUGHOUT THE 1980S, Coral's health fluctuated as she battled the cancer that manifested itself throughout her body. However, after she underwent a series of operations and courses of chemotherapy, she seemed, somehow, to emerge feeling and looking better than ever. Jill Melford recalled, "When she had chemotherapy, she said, 'I look horrendous.' But I said, 'Coral, I have to tell you, if I were you, I'd stay on chemo for a very long time because you've never looked better.' She looked wonderful. When Coral was young and sort of a juvenile, she was not very pretty at all. She said one day, 'I hit sixty, dear, and turned into a raving beauty.' And she sort of did. Because she'd had a moon face. She always had a great body, and a lot of style. But she became beautiful in her old age."

However, Coral's frequent bouts of illness gradually took their toll on the marriage, as both she and Vincent became increasingly anxious about their health. Adrienne Corri told me: "I think she was very, very frightened. She was frightened of your mother, she was frightened of you, she was frightened of anyone who would take the interest and attention away from her. And she had this very morbid thing about dying, and it was a great attention-getter. After she married Vinnie, I never knew whether it was the faux grandeur or the illness that changed her so much. But I remember saying to Marti Stevens that the Coral we first knew changed quite a lot. I think the first one was kinder, was much kinder, was less self-obsessed. I think she became more and more obsessed with herself. That was partly also the illness, or the wishing to be ill, or the hypochondria even. Whatever it was, it turned her more in on herself. Because, after all, you know, the best part of her life really was when she married your dad. But if you're a woman who has always been regarded as very beautiful and witty and you think you might be getting older, then you think of another way, and I think she thought of the illness as another way of keeping him. I mean, she was the disaster queen of all time. I remember she thought Maggie Smith's teeth looked very good and she said, 'Who was her dentist? I want to get all my crowns done.' So she went to this dentist and the telephone rang about three days later and not only had she gone to the dentist and had all the teeth done, but the teeth all fell out and the dentist had absconded. I shrieked with laughter, and she was very angry with me: 'You've got no sympathy for anyone. All my teeth have fallen out!' I mean, she spent a fortune. She didn't have to have her teeth done, but she decided she liked Maggie Smith's teeth, so she was going to *have* Maggie Smith's teeth."

Coral frequently went under the surgeon's knife of her own accord—for many different forms of plastic surgery. And she encouraged my father to do the same. As

Adrienne also remarked, "Coral played about with her face like you'd alter a dress. She'd say, 'I'm having Vinnie get those bags taken away from his eyes.' I said, 'What do you mean? His face is wonderful. Leave him alone.' And she said, 'Oh, they do it in a dentist chair in America.' So she hauled him off and had the bags taken away from his eyes. This was a hobby with Coral. She was always looking for new doctors and new nips and tucks. Once she came to England and had another face lift and something went wrong, so she had to have it redone and she'd had to sit up all night. And her back went out. I went visit her and Vinnie was sitting outside her door saying, 'Why did you let me do it? Why did you let me do it, Corri?' And I said, 'Don't blame me. If another person blames their marriage on me . . .' That was the day her dreadful little mother came up. We escorted Coral out of the nursing home and back to the Grosvenor House, and she lay on one bed and her dreadful little mother lay on the other and were outdoing each other with the hypochondria. The mother was saying, 'My poor daughter's so ill, but I'm much worse!' And Vinnie and I started to laugh and we laughed till tears ran down our faces. Vinnie had too much sense of humor. Often when things got too much, which would have driven another person mad, Vinnie just collapsed with laughter. Because it was ridiculous. It was funny."

Coral used plastic surgery to keep the aging process at bay and encouraged her husband to do so as well. The effects were extraordinary; both seemed to look better with each passing year. Jill Melford noted, "Coral did it terribly well and enjoyed every second of it. Every time she had something tweaked, it really cheered her up no end. She fancied herself as Nefertiti; she made it work." But between my father's bad knees, feet, and teeth, Coral's recurring cancer, and their dual plastic surgeries, much of the eighties seemed to be spent going in and out of hospital and then slowly recovering.

During the mid-eighties, Coral and Vincent's marriage went through an extremely difficult period. Many of their friends seemed aware of the situation, but ignorant of the precise cause. As Alec Guinness noticed, "There was an upset in later years, but I don't know what it was." Coral told only a few of her closest friends that she believed her husband was having an affair. Joan Rivers recalled, "It was awful. It was terrible. They were both older. Vinnie was in his seventies and there was a lady involved. I got a call when I was playing Las Vegas and Coral called and she just cried and cried and cried. She couldn't stop crying on the phone. I never saw Coral so vulnerable. And it was stopped. Vinnie stopped, because she found out about it."

Not long after Vincent's alleged affair had been discovered by Coral—and, under the threat of a very public divorce, terminated—his health seemed to decline drastically. He very rapidly grew weak and thin and fragile and underwent a barrage of tests to determine the cause of the illness. Various possibilities surfaced. In 1986 he was encouraged by his doctors to take a radioactive pill to destroy the thyroid; from then on, he relied on thyroid medication. But this did nothing to improve his general health. There was concern for his heart, and he was subjected to an exploratory procedure to examine and unblock his arteries, during which his doctors decided to implant a pacemaker. But these efforts also did nothing to increase his stamina. Added to this, the arthritis which had so crippled his father and which Vincent had feared his whole life, began to render him increasingly less mobile. Though he tried reducing the acid in his diet and even undertook baking bread as therapy, his health continued to deteriorate.

By 1988, with both of them in such precarious health, Coral decided that it was time to make practical provision for the future. She talked her reluctant husband into spending the money to build a small guest quarters over their two-car garage, with an eye to hiring someone to live there and take care of them when they became too ill to take care of themselves. As Vincent continued to deteriorate, Coral felt unable to tend for him herself. In May 1988, after the couple returned from a cruise through the Panama Canal, she wrote Alan Bennett, "Vincent put on twelve pounds and is much stronger, but it's all rather sad. I see him 'leaving me' day by day. He fell apart so suddenly really and I hoped and prayed it wasn't for keeps but now I'm beginning to realize how difficult it is to die—not that he's on the verge, but one can see it's inevitable. He's always been able to bounce back, but I fear not any more. Vincent is very forgetful and needs constant attention and it takes all my hours coping. I'm trying to get permission to pull down our carport and erect a garage with a 'servant's quarters' above—some dwarf who can clean and drive a car."

In the meantime, she encouraged my father to hire a personal secretary to take care of the details of his life and to help with the correspondence—particularly the fan mail, each and every letter of which he insisted on answering himself. While doing publicity for *Dreamchild*, Coral had worked with entertainment publicist Reggie Williams. The English-born Williams had previously been involved with her West End run of *Waltz of the Toreadors* and was one of the few people at Cannon who had enthusiastically tried to promote Coral's brilliant performance in the art house film. After the studio folded, Williams had bowed out of the publicity business and Coral conceived the idea of bringing him in two or three days a week to work with Vincent. Reg agreed—he had previously been actress Ava Gardner's personal assistant for three years—and his presence immediately went a long way toward easing my father's lot.

During Reg Williams's first year with the couple, they received clearance to build their guest house. After its completion, they began asking friends if they knew of any young, unattached British man or woman who might be suitable as a live-in caretaker. They also asked Reg if he knew anyone who might be right for the job. In due course, he told them that all of his friends had suggested that he was the most suitable for the job and, if they were agreeable, he would be happy to take up the challenge. My father and Coral were overjoyed and Reg moved in.

In the fall of 1988, Vincent informed WGBH that this upcoming eighth season would be his last as the host of *Mystery!* As usual, he flew to Boston to tape the introductions. Sandy Leonard recalled picking the actor up at Logan Airport. "This small propeller plane pulled in and they let down the staircase to the tarmac and Vincent was having difficulty with stairs at that point. He had to go down those stairs and had to walk up another set to get into the airport. It was awful, and when he finally arrived, I said, 'Let's just sit for fifteen minutes.' He looked very tired, very beat. It was interesting, I always felt that he didn't mind looking like an old man around me. Then, when he finally got it all together and we walked down to the baggage claim, he became Vincent Price. I'll never forget that transformation."

It was with great regret that Vincent withdrew from *Mystery!*; he said he'd "never had a job I've enjoyed so much," but both he and Coral felt that he needed to concentrate on regaining his health. For the first time he virtually stopped working, even canceling his fall lecture tour. After almost forty years of lecturing, it seemed he had at last "retired."

However, despite having released himself from his obligations, there was no improvement in his health, and the doctors were mystified.

Finally, in September 1989, Vincent was rushed to the hospital and placed under the care of Dr. Richard Wulfsberg, a close friend of Joe Hardy, the director of *Diversions and Delights*. It was Wulfsberg who asked Vincent to walk down the hospital corridor and, in observing his movement, realized that he had Parkinson's disease, which was debilitating his nervous system. Tests confirmed the diagnosis, and Vincent was placed on L-DOPA, a drug that had just recently been approved by the FDA. For almost a year the drug seemed to have a miraculous effect, and after four years of illness Vincent's life reverted almost to normal as he regained much of his strength and drive.

In 1982, Vincent had received a call from a Disney executive telling him about a talented young animator who had put together a six-minute short called *Vincent*, about a boy who wants to grow up to be Vincent Price. The executive asked, on the animator's behalf, if the actor might be interested in seeing the piece and even lending it a voice-over. Naturally my father said yes. Thus began an important friendship between Vincent Price and Tim Burton. Growing up in Burbank, Burton had been a huge Price fan: "There was a connection, an emotional link for me, growing up and watching the Poe films. Vincent's characters had a sensitivity. There was an energy he had; it was evident in everything. I liked *believing* Vincent; I *believed* him."

Tim Burton went on to become one of Hollywood's most successful and iconoclastic directors, after following his auspicious *Pee-Wee's Big Adventure* with *Beetlejuice* and *Batman*. In 1989 he finally got the green light on the project closest to his heart, *Edward Scissorhands*, and asked Vincent to play the cameo role of Edward's inventor. Although Vincent still appeared alarmingly frail, the new drug gave him the strength to get through the small role, and he was delighted to accept the offer. As he soon discovered, working with Burton and Johnny Depp proved a further and wonderful antidote to illness. He loved their energy and youth and kept up both friendships until his death. Johnny Depp recalled, "He called me every year on my birthday—he was a Gemini, too—and left me these beautiful messages. One of the most incredible moments I've ever had was sitting in Vincent's trailer, showing him this first edition I have of the complete works of Poe, with really amazing illustrations. Vincent was going nuts over the drawings, and he started talking about *The Tomb of Ligeia*; then he closed the book and began to recite it to me in this beautiful voice, filling the trailer with huge sounds. Such passion! I looked in the book later, and it was verbatim. Word perfect. It was a great moment. I'll never forget that!"

Edward Scissorhands was a fitting finale to Vincent's long and varied movie career. He was marvelous as the kindly, quirky inventor who creates Edward but dies before he can give him hands. Ensconced in a marvelously Gothic castle, Vincent exuded the warmth and sympathy that for so many years had lain just under the surface of his horror movie creations. He and the film were very well reviewed and he was always grateful to Tim Burton for providing him with such a satisfying last piece of work.

Not long after Vincent finished shooting *Edward Scissorhands*, Coral was diagnosed with breast cancer. She said to her husband, "Well, old boy, I've looked after you for the past four years. Now I'm afraid it's your turn to care for me.' " As Reg Williams remembered, "It was the start of the Christmas season. With her unconcern for children and a lifetime of slog in the theater, where all the festivities added up to little more than a meal and a chance to snooze between shows, Coral had always shown little patience with Yuletide celebration highjinks. Conversely, Vincent, with his strong family ties, really loved the whole festive business. Now with the threat of the Big C hanging over them, he cajoled Coral into a traditional Christmas and the household wore an ironic air of merriment, which even Coral managed to enjoy."

Life with Coral and Vincent during the difficult years of their illnesses was both harrowing and remarkable; even during their most trying moments, humor somehow managed to prevail. Shortly after Coral went down with her final bout of cancer, she telephoned Reg at 2 A.M. to tell him that Vincent had lost his footing on his way back from the kitchen and, in trying to regain his balance, had leaned on the large, five-paneled ornamental screen in the front hall. This had fallen on top of him and he was now pinned to the floor. Grabbing the first items of clothing to hand, Reg rushed down to find Vincent trapped on his side, "stunned and scared to move. The weight of the screen requiring several strong hands to maneuver, I got onto the floor face down and wriggled under the screen parallel to Vincent." While Reg hoisted the screen onto his back, Coral pulled Vincent out. "An anxious few moments passed while Vincent regained his breath; to our relief, he had escaped with only a few slight bruises. As the Prices turned to shuffle off to the bedroom, there was a pregnant pause: all three of us tacitly acknowledged that this was the start of the downward spiral—no going back now! Never one for somber musing, Coral looked me up and down, taking in my Coca-Cola night-shirt, hastily buttoned shorts, and fuzzy white socks, and fired off, 'So this is boudoir attire for the West Hollywood smart set!' This salvo even set Vincent grinning."

Coral still received friends during the first year of her illness. As Reg recalled, "Joan Rivers, whose TV chat show was then at its peak, would never fail to pay bedside visits to Coral whenever she was in Los Angeles. In fact, there were occasions when Joan flew in from New York for the sole purpose of seeing her friend, engaging her with the latest gossip, the pick of the new books, cassettes of her show, an occasional houseplant, and such munchies as muffin baskets and noodle casserole." Joan was a devoted friend, and although Coral could be difficult during her illness, Joan's visits always cheered her up and my father never ceased to remark how grateful he was for their close friendship.

Other visitors included Maggie Smith, Alan Bates, John Schlesinger, and Joss Ackland from England. Tita Cahn would visit at least once a week, Roddy McDowall kept the front hall filled with beautiful flowers from his garden, dresser Eric Harrison brought shepherd's pie, and costumer Lily Fonda knitted caps when Coral's hair fell out during chemotherapy. As Reg put it, "If Coral did not get out into the world, the world—or at least her special portion of it—certainly came to her."

Indeed, despite the well-known acidity of her tongue, Coral succeeded in attracting wonderful friends because she was herself capable of being a very good friend to others. Jill Melford maintained, "She cared if you were unhappy or if things had gone wildly wrong and would kill whoever had been beastly to you. Deeply loyal. Coral kept friends. The old queens were all sort of sycophantic, and husbands and lovers come and go. The mates who kind of get you through it are usually girlfriends, and I think Coral was very aware of that."

Indeed, she was famously outspoken in defense of a friend or a cause in which she believed, and some of her outbursts, which entered the mythology of her wit, were not intended to be funny. After *An Englishman Abroad* was shown on *Masterpiece Theatre*, Coral met a second-rate screenwriter at a party in L.A. He said how marvelous he thought her performance was, but he "wasn't too sure" about Alan Bennett's script. Coral replied, "You weren't too sure about the *script?*" her voice rising. "You weren't too *sure* about the script? *You* couldn't write *fuck* on a dusty Venetian blind!" Her ability to find humor in almost any situation became one of her mainstays while battling cancer. Sandy Leonard, who frequently sent flowers during her illness, said, "She always sent a thank-you note, but they would go on from there and say things like, 'How nice of you to send cut flowers instead of some terrible arrangement put together by a color-blind Mexican.' She always found a way to bring somebody down." Furthermore, illness did nothing to dull Coral's vanity. Reggie said, "As she became steadily more housebound, then bedridden, her poise and hauteur did not escape her. She retained her majesty."

Coral's favorite photograph of herself was taken by Helmut Newton in the mid-eighties. It showed the elegant actress in profile, holding a long strand of pearls and wearing a fur coat. When Christopher O'Hare, a young American living in London, saw this photograph at John Schlesinger's house, he was mesmerised by it. He wanted to know more about Coral and, after talking to a few of her friends, realized that she was the ideal subject for a documentary film, which he undertook with John Schlesinger's sponsorship.

Caviar to the General aired in England in December 1990. O'Hare had interviewed many of Coral's friends and colleagues—Robert Morley, John Schlesinger, Alan Bennett, Nora Swinburne, Anna Massey, Paul Rogers, Ned Sherrin, Judi Dench—as well as Coral herself. It is perhaps these latter segments that are the most revealing, as she talks candidly about herself in her last filmed interview, not sparing the viewer her famous expletives. Asked about her colorful vocabulary, Coral remarked that it was something she had learned growing up in Australia: "They had small vocabularies. They were practically still off the convict ships, weren't they? To make any form of emphasis—I know this happened in my father's case, and I caught it from my father—instead of saying 'It's a lovely day today!' they'd say, 'It's a *bloody* lovely day today!' " Referring to her childhood in Australia, she averred, "I remember always wanting to leave. That was the height of my ambition." Discussing the famous "Coral stories" and remarking on her own wit, she seems almost remorseful about the damage her sharp tongue had sometimes caused. But it is the end of the film that is most moving. Asked by the interviewer, who is her friend John Schlesinger, whether she has any regrets, she says with a wry and vulnerable smile, "No, no regrets. Do you want me to say I'd rather be in Sydney with a kookaburra or something?"

Coral battled with cancer for almost a year and a half. For the most part, she was able to remain at home, although she spent frequent periods of time in the hospital undergoing tests and treatments. It was during one of these stays that one of the last great "Coral stories" emerged. Her nurse came in to Coral's hospital room to find the actress dressed and ready to leave. She had not been officially discharged, so the nurse asked what she thought she was doing. Coral looked at the woman and said, "My dear, there's a sale at Chanel," and promptly left.

In December 1990, Vincent and Coral spent a quiet Christmas together and celebrated the New Year. Though the illness and the treatments had taken their toll on her appearance, she seemed somehow more beautiful than ever. But by the beginning of 1991, though her hair had begun to grow back, she became progressively weaker and often had to rely on an oxygen tank in order to breathe.

As her health failed, Vincent and Reg realized they needed to hire a nurse. Vincent moved into the guest room, and the house was soon filled with a procession of nurses. Vincent began to feel like a stranger in his own home, and found sleep difficult. Joan Rivers remembered, "I went there all the time when she was in bed and that was very, very hard for him. But she was very smart. You've got to give her credit. She knew what was happening. She made him build that garage house. She made him get Reg. She made sure everything was in order and thank God she did." Indeed, Coral did everything she could to make sure all their bases were covered. Reggie recalled, "Over the years, Coral's closets had become a library of patent medicines gleaned the world over. She was rarely caught with her medications down. Sly cajoling of all the doctors she knew, and a crafty accumulation of the necessary medicines, had allowed her to compile a death-dose mixture of pills in a small phial, secreted only she knew where. However, there was no fear of death, so she turned neither to religion nor medical extremes to evade it. Nor, once a morphine drip sublimated her severe pain, did she think of resorting to her quick way out."

Although Coral faced death bravely, she found less comfort in her religion than she had hoped for. Though a devout Catholic since her conversion, during her illness her faith seemed to wane. Williams remembered how, "Once Coral became bedridden, Father George Parnassus would visit occasionally to hold private mass for the two of them. As her physical strength failed, something of a disillusionment with the Faith set in and Coral opted less and less to have the mass."

In mid–May 1991, Coral seemed to have decided that she was going, and she stopped talking altogether. On May 27, her husband came into the bedroom to tell his wife that it was his eightieth birthday. He never knew whether she heard him or not.

Two days later, he drove to the Vincent Price Gallery at East Los Angeles College to begin filming a documentary about his life, produced and directed by Tim Burton. Though Wednesday was normally a half-day off for Reg, because of Coral's condition, he stayed at home. During the morning she rapidly worsened. Reg called the gallery to find that Vincent was already on his way home. Coral passed away with Reg, Marika, and her nurse at her side. Marika then chose one of Coral's favorite Armani suits so that the ever-elegant actress could leave for the mortuary dressed as she would have wished. When Vincent arrived home to find that his wife had finally passed on, he seemed to understand that she had been unable to die in his presence.

Vincent had two more days of filming on Burton's documentary. He chose to fulfill his obligation and told no one on the set except Tim that his wife had died. Work was, as ever, his best medicine. Coral had wished to be cremated at the Hollywood Cemetery, the final resting place of many Hollywood luminaries, which was situated almost directly behind Paramount Studios. There, my father, Reg, and I attended an open-casket viewing and my father finally broke down; it was the first time I had ever seen him cry. The next day, Father Parnassus conducted a small service for Coral's closest friends, including Joan Rivers and Roddy McDowall, and her ashes were then placed beneath a special white rose tree in the grounds of the cemetery. My father said, "I'll always know it. It will be the tree on which all the roses are nodding their heads with laughter!"

Coral's obituaries in both the English and American papers reflected her extraordinary life. Richard Bebb in *The Independent* called her "one of the most elegant and stylish players of the last fifty years. She was blessed with great good looks rather than outstanding beauty, and it is to be doubted that any other actress in the long history of the British theatre had the art of making more of the gifts she was given by God." Kenneth Hurren in *The Guardian* said she was "a lady in whom the voice of the turtle and the buzz of the wasp were most endearingly conjoined to make a more interesting and diverting character than any she played." Charles Champlin of the *Los Angeles Times*, who had become a friend, wrote "Browne was a remarkably beautiful woman who could manage an elegant hauteur and a madcap insouciance with equal conviction. Yet the hauteur seemed more a pose than the insouciance, which, combined with a warm generosity of spirit, earned her a wonderful circle of friends in and out of the theater."

Naturally, Coral's death also brought an outpouring of affection in letters to her husband from friends and admirers. William F. Buckley, Jr. wrote, "She was *so* splendid, bringing dignity and warmth and mirth into every situation." David Hockney remarked, "Coral had a wonderful life being herself and gave pleasure and inspiration in a very rich way. I am very grateful for her life." Eileen Atkins noted, "I know she was witty and glamorous and fun but I will always remember how *kind* she was to me." Alec Guinness wrote Vincent, "She was a dear dear friend whom we shall sorely miss; I was proud of her friendship and always rejoiced to see her and hear from her. One of the really *rare* people." And from John Gielgud, "You must know how dearly she was loved and missed in London. To have achieved such a big range of acting successes in every field and to combine the hard work with such wit and resilience was a unique combination of qualities for which everyone loved and respected her. I have so many enchanting memories of her, the elegance and beauty and her devotion to you."

On July 23, 1991, which would have been Coral's seventy-eighth birthday, my father organized a celebration of her life to be held at St. Victor's. Compiling stories about, and tributes to, Coral from the letters he had received, with Reg's help he created a fitting and touching memorial program. After a short sermon by Father Parnassus, my father rose to speak: "Today is her birthday and we are here not so much to mourn her death as to celebrate her birth, her life, which was so full of living, of loving, of laughter. She lives in our hearts and in our minds for the laughter she brought to a too often troubled world. She will live for the talent she lent everything she touched—her incomparable artistry in the theater and on the screen, her wit and charm, her personal beauty. She shared her joy of life with all who met her; she was a presence wherever she happened to be." Then Gus Schirmer read from the scriptures, followed by excerpts from the letters read by Joe Hardy, Roddy McDowall, and by me. After the service, my father broke down briefly while talking to old friends. But he pulled himself together and, though in frail health, drove off to Spago to enjoy Coral's last birthday party.

Later that fall, John Schlesinger, Noel Davis, and Jonathan Altaras organized a memorial mass for Coral in London. Once my father realized that he was not physically up to making the journey, it was decided that John Schlesinger would read a letter from him at the service. On September 5, 1991, Coral's many friends and colleagues gathered at the Church of the Immaculate Conception to remember her in a mass of thanksgiving for her life. The scriptural selections and prayers were read by Alan Bennett, Sir Alec Guinness, and Jean Marsh. At the end of the traditional service, John Schlesinger read the letter from Vincent, and Alan Bates delivered an address. Bates began his eulogy, "I can hear Coral now saying 'So you got stuck with the address did you, darling, good luck; and don't think I won't be listening.' " My father had asked Alan not to tell "a lot of legendary Coral Browne stories." Instead, he gave a touching insight into the actress's character. "We all knew Coral Browne the superb actress, witty, stylish, powerful, classical, and of course beautiful. We all knew the Coral Browne that she presented to us socially, a great personality, mischievous, alarming, unpredictable, outrageous. It could be said that this Coral Browne was one of her great performances, one she certainly relished, and reveled in. I think there is another less well known Coral Browne. I was invited to present her *Evening Standard* award for that superb performance in Dennis Potter's *Dreamchild*. I made a rather extravagant announcement, as one does on these occasions, and she came to the stage, suddenly a Coral I had not reckoned with before. The supremely confident Coral Browne was nervous, she forgot the name of someone she thought highly of and very much wanted to thank and was, in short, suddenly vulnerable. I think the reason why we all loved her was perhaps because we all sensed that underneath her wicked sense of humor was this vulnerability, and it made all her outrageousness wonderfully acceptable. She was kind, she was generous, she was loyal, she was extremely sensitive to other people's condition, their bereavements, and *their* vulnerability. She loved people—she could see right through us all, and of course we loved her because she dared to say what she saw.

"When I think of the alarm one always felt when leaving a party before Coral, at what she might be saying about oneself, it makes me wonder now that *she* has left the party first, what she is saying to the powers that be; if she's true to form we'll never get in! Or perhaps it is simply that we will have no need for confession ourselves—we will just have to say 'Anything you wish to know about me, please refer my case to Coral Browne.' "

Many agreed that the most touching moment of the beautiful service was when John Schlesinger read Vincent's letter: "Dear John, When I was courting Coral, the first gift she gave me was a photo of herself simply signed: 'Remember Coral'—not really a challenge, as the problem was, how could you forget her. I've come to believe remembering someone is not the highest compliment—it is missing them. I find I miss every hour of Coral's life—I miss the morning cloudiness, noon mellowness, evening brightness. I miss her in every corner of our house, every crevice of my life. In missing her, I feel I'm missing much of life itself."

39

AND WHERE WAS I during the eighteen years of my father's marriage to Coral? Roughly right where I am now—on the outside looking in. From the time my father met the woman who would become my stepmother, I became strangely peripheral to his life. The three of us spent time together, but I was largely excluded from anything or anyone significant in their lives. My father's last agent, Pearl Wexler, didn't even know he had a daughter until I was in my late twenties. And it wasn't until Coral's memorial service that I met many of their closest friends.

Although Joan Rivers was my stepmother's best friend, we didn't formally meet until six years after Coral's death. During the eighteen years that my father and Coral were married, I encountered Joan only once. I introduced myself to her one night at Spago where I was having dinner with a friend. She and Edgar were eating across the restaurant. She looked up at me dubiously as I approached her table, but when I told her my name, her face lit up and she turned to her husband, saying, "Edgar, it's Tor!" I remember being thrilled that she even knew who I was. We chatted for a few moments and I returned to my table. I was twenty-seven.

In the summer of 1997, I visited Joan at her New York apartment. I immediately felt as though I had known her my whole life. After listening to her glowing memories of my father and Coral, we finally broached the touchy subject we knew we had to face—my difficult relationship with my stepmother. Joan said to me, "Coral was very protective. I know you were a big threat to her. It was a big love-hate thing. She thought you were terrific, but she knew he loved you. And you were going to 'get his money,' which we now know wasn't sitting well with Coral at all. It was very interesting—she liked you, didn't want to like you. It was like another woman. Truly, I think if you had been my daughter, you would have been fabulous. But you were the other woman in his life, and if he did leave her, you would still have been there. Of course she was jealous. She was jealous of anybody. Who's going to get close to Coral? And you were never included. Never! Were you sitting at my Passover table? I never would have thought to ask you. She did not make you part of the unit. I'm sixty-four years old and I wouldn't want Coral to come in and be my stepmother."

And yet there were times when my father, his wife, and I formed a curious kind of family. My first memory of Coral—though I'm fairly sure I must have actually met her before this—is seeing her sunbathing topless by the pool at the house on Miller Drive. With that famous figure that rivalled any of Gaston Lachaise's voluptuous women, she left an indelible impression.

At first my father told me that Coral was his house guest. I was a fairly naive eleven year old and because of that, and because when my parents were married we had always had a house full of people, I didn't find it odd that she never left.

My father and Coral lived together in the house on Miller Drive, which was quite wonderful—quirky yet cozy, with panoramic city views and a beautiful multilevel garden filled with my father's plants and flowers, a goldfish pond, and a small swimming pool. It was smaller than anywhere we had lived when my parents were together, which was one of the things that my father loved about it. That, and the significant fact that it had once belonged to Greta Garbo.

During the first year they lived there, whenever I came to visit I shared my father's king-sized bed. Coral slept in the guestroom, which I assumed she always did. I now realize that the arrangement must have infuriated her. I did, however, find it odd that his "house guest" hadn't chosen to stay in the much more spacious and private pool house, which had its own kitchen, living area, and bedroom. But, on the whole, I opted not to give any of it too much thought.

Then one evening in October 1974, in the house on Calabasas Lake where my mother and I were living, I came downstairs to ask my mom a question about my home-work. She was on the phone, and so I stared absently at the local news while waiting for her to finish her conversation. I saw my father's face flash up on the screen, but the vol-ume was turned down so I rushed closer to hear what the anchorman was saying. Though I missed most of the story, I grasped its essence—my father had married the "house guest" in Santa Barbara earlier that day. I had long since learned to roll with my father's punches, so I don't remember being particularly shocked. What I do remember is the terrible pit in my stomach as I realized that when my mother got off the phone I would have to tell her. A few hours later my father called, very apologetic that he hadn't reached us. He had asked the justice of the peace who had married them not to release the information to the press, and he told us he felt terrible that we had had to find out from someone other than him. Needless to say, the next time I went up to Miller Drive, I slept in the guestroom.

Coral and I really didn't know what to make of each other. For me, it was like having a cross between a British Auntie Mame and Cruella DeVil step off the pages of a novel and into my Southern California childhood. Certainly I had never met anyone like her, and by then I knew a number of unusual and extraordinary people. In the beginning, Coral and I both tried our best with each other, but we had very little in common except our love of dogs.

Tiggy (short for Antigone) was a golden Chihuahua who looked like a Labrador retriever that had somehow been shrunk down to fifteen pounds. I thought she was a great dog. She was also an unusual one; having been raised in London by Coral's cat, Tiggy had learned to walk on the backs of chairs and sofas just like her feline friend had. Tig and I got along famously and I was very grateful to her for being the first bridge between me and Coral. When I was about thirteen, my father and Coral brought Maile home from Honolulu. Compared to the robust and adventurous Tiggy, Maile was rather timid. She was particularly terrified of tackling the steep staircase to the bedrooms, so I took it upon myself to teach her how, and I spent hours helping her down and up, one step at a time. At first, Coral seemed very impressed by my patience and interest, but later, when Maile's back legs grew in somewhat crooked—bandy-legged as Coral called them—I was held, only partially teasingly, to blame.

Away from the dogs, Coral and I were left to improvise our tenuous stepmother-stepdaughter relationship. I remember rainy afternoons playing gin rummy in the living room, which we both seemed to enjoy. We went to movies from time to time, we swam in the pool. But, on the whole, Coral was almost completely unprepared for a teenager—a blond Southern California tomboy whose chief interests were horses and books. Moreover, this teenager was Daddy's girl.

When I was in my late twenties, Coral said to me, in a tone that somehow encompassed jealousy, regret, and admiration all at once, "I think your father loves you more than anyone in the world." Whether this was true or not, it seems to me that sometime around my thirteenth birthday Coral suddenly tumbled to just how close my father and I really were; I think it threw her completely. Though he had always told her how important I was to him, somehow she hadn't quite grasped the depth of his love for me. By nature a jealous and possessive woman, she hadn't a clue how to share her husband with his daughter. At sixty-two, the last thing she wanted to be was anybody's stepmother, let alone mine.

Looking back, I can see that we all felt trapped. Coral wanted her husband to herself, I wanted to keep my happy relationship with my father, and he wanted us all to love each other. But I also wanted Coral to like me, for though she could be terrifying and intimidating, I was as enamored with her as I was scared of her, and wanted to win her approval. But I always seemed to be doing something wrong.

Once, quite early on—I couldn't have been more than twelve or thirteen—my father and Coral gave a dinner party. I was staying with them and so naturally was included. I don't remember who was there, but I have the sense that it was someone very distinguished, someone from England whom Coral wanted to impress with her new life as Mrs. Vincent Price. It was an intimate evening and I thought everything went quite well; I even remember contributing something to the conversation. But dinner dragged on a long time, long enough for me to begin to fall asleep at the table. Coral was appalled at my rudeness; she never forgave me for falling asleep. I was never included at a dinner party at their home again. Never. Until the day Coral died.

After that evening, Coral kept me very separate from their lives. I was only allowed to spend time with their "everyday" friends. Of those friends I did come to know—Robert Hanley, who had harbored them during the early days of their secret affair; Harry Mines, the journalist who had been so important in promoting my father's early career—my favorite was Marti Stevens, a wonderful singer who had been Coral's neighbor in London and had moved back to L.A. in the seventies. She had grown up in Hollywood, too, the daughter of movie mogul Nicholas Schenk. Marti seemed to understand just how difficult it might be to have Coral Browne as a stepmother, and always took great pains to champion me. But, on the whole, I came to feel as though I traveled on the very edges of my father and Coral's lives.

As time wore on, Coral and I developed a somewhat combative relationship. Both hardheaded, we argued a great deal—over what, I now no longer remember. But I do recall a day when I was no more than fourteen, driving down Sunset Boulevard with my father, when he pleaded with me to make peace with Coral. He said, "When you and Coral have a fight, she forgets about it right away, but you're like an elephant. You hold onto things forever." I wanted to say to him, How am I supposed to forget? But I didn't. I also wanted to ask how I could forgive this person who was wrong, who should know better. In retrospect, I'm sure Coral and I each had a big stake in our respective stubbornness, and it took me years to understand that my father's plea was really for himself. He felt trapped between his wife and daughter.

Nonetheless, after that conversation, things seemed to get better as I tried to find new ways to get along with my stepmother. When I entered high school, I became very interested in the theater, and so I continually asked Coral questions about the London stage and her famous friends. I adored her stories and loved hearing her definite opinions about various actors, actresses, playwrights, and productions. Knowing that the theater world eagerly anticipated each new "Coral story," I reveled in being so close to the epicenter of her wit—if not all too often the brunt of its cruelty. But I don't think she ever understood that what I really wanted was to be included in her world.

And so things continued on rather tenuously between us until I suddenly had an insight which became my saving grace. One day, when I was still in high school, Coral announced that she was going to give me two Cacharel shirts that no longer fitted her. I had no idea what Cacharel was; I remember thinking that it must be some kind of fabric like corduroy. But one thing was very clear—this gift was a big deal to Coral. When she gave me the shirts I knew to appear suitably grateful, but I didn't really see what all the fuss was about. They were brushed cotton, one puce and one rose pink. Then I saw the label—Cacharel. Something clicked. I understood that the designer label was important to her, and I decided to make fashion our common ground.

My mother had been a costume designer, and I had spent countless tedious hours of my early childhood standing for fittings for long dresses for cotillions, short dresses for special occasions—altogether too many fancy clothes for my taste. As a little girl, my mother made sure that I always looked perfect—my hair combed within an inch of its life and held back in bows that matched my outfits. But whenever I got free of my mother—at school, at summer camp, at friends' houses—off came the bows and on went the jeans and tennis shoes. One summer, when I was ten, I went to camp for four weeks and purposely didn't comb my hair once. Once we were living on our own, my mother relented somewhat and we struck a deal—I dressed the way she wanted when she was around and I dressed my own way on my own time. When Coral gave me those Cacharel shirts, I was firmly entrenched in my blue jeans ethic. But all that changed as I began to read her fashion magazines and learn about the designers that mattered. When Coral went into her espadrille phase, so did I. When she donned power suits, I wasn't far behind. Hers were Armani and Chanel; mine cheap knockoffs. Every Christmas and birthday, I saved up enough money to buy Coral a fifty-dollar gift certificate from her favorite designer of the moment. For the first time, I felt we might be moving closer.

Coral's presence in my father's life irrevocably changed my own relationship with him. Because she refused to embrace his family, he continually felt guilty about wanting to spend time with Barrett or me. It was as though, in marrying her, he had handed her the reins of his life. She was in control in an almost parental way, and so he snuck behind her back—calling us when she was out of the house, arranging ways for us to meet him when he was working away from home, surreptitiously slipping or sending us money so that she wouldn't know. Our once easy companionship labored under the weight of his guilt and Coral's jealousy.

I eagerly anticipated any time I could spend alone with my dad, either when Coral was away from home, or when I was able to join him out of town. As a teenager, I often met up with him when he was doing summer stock or touring in the Wilde show. When we were alone together, it was like old times between us—happy, lighthearted, close, fun. I loved it and I loved him.

Although my dad was in his sixties when I was a teenager, my presence seemed to give him license to allow his childlike joy in simple things to resurface. As he had done with Barrett, he loved to take me to amusement parks. We never left until we had been on every roller coaster, water ride, and Ferris wheel, played a few games of chance, and eaten far too many hot dogs and sweets. We tried out every new ride, but ultimately our loyalties remained with the big, old-fashioned rolly-coasters. Less than an hour from home was Magic Mountain's Colossus, a grand wooden coaster—a purist's coaster—and it became a tradition for us to ride it for my birthday.

On one of those birthday excursions, he decided to give me a very special present: He refused to sign autographs for the entire day. I had been raised to stand patiently by while he signed autographs and talked with fans. He explained to me that this was a part of his job description, and had told me more than once about Helen Hayes's credo that an actor is a public servant. That birthday I found myself feeling a little sorry for those fans who had had the bad luck to pick the one day of my father's whole life when he wouldn't sign autographs. But I knew he thought it the best gift he could give me.

Although my father and I didn't take as many trips as I would have liked, I treasured each one. When he was in a play, I loved living on his schedule—waking up late, finding a wonderful restaurant for lunch, shopping, going to a museum, taking a nap, and then going to the theater. Afterward, we usually had dinner with someone interesting—a member of the cast, a journalist, a local friend. I always left any town we visited together feeling that I knew it intimately, for my father left no stone unturned in his quest to see and experience each new place. Together we reconnoitered Baltimore, Boston, Dallas, Denver, New Haven, New York, San Francisco, St. Louis, and Seattle.

We both loved these outings with just the two of us, but he kept trying to find a way for he, Coral, and me to be a family. Sometimes I met up with the two of them on their travels, most often in San Francisco. They both loved the city and together we developed a happy routine, which inevitably included Italian food at Mama's. We always stayed at a nice hotel on Nob Hill or near Union Square, and I was free to explore on my own while Coral shopped and my dad worked. If my dad was in a play, Coral and I often went to see it, or we would go to another theater. I learned a lot sitting next to Coral at a play. Sometimes we even went out to dinner, just the two of us. She was so attached to San Francisco that even being stuck with "the kid" couldn't dampen her spirits. Those were some of our best times together.

When we were getting along well, no one was more amusing or more fun than Coral. Sitting at a restaurant with my father and her, I hardly said a word. I just sat back and listened to their banter. It was like dining with Noel Coward and Tallulah Bankhead. Their mutual wit was devastating and they liked to put on a show. Over dinner, Coral would start in on the clothes of the diners next to us, and she wouldn't stop until she had gone clear round the room, playing off my father who jumped in from time to time. Shaking with laughter, I picked at my food, loath to miss a single brilliant word.

But other trips were less successful. During spring break of my freshman year at college, I joined them for a week in St. Louis, where my father was doing the Wilde show. He always loved performing in his hometown and he was terribly excited to have his wife and daughter with him, but Coral had a severe ulcer and was absolutely miserable.

She could only eat bland foods and, since one of their great mutual pleasures was eating out, she was in a black mood all week from pain and annoyance. When she felt too ill to go out, my dad and I rushed to the museum where he showed me the collection he had so loved as a child. But on the whole, our week together was very tense, and I was glad to leave for Los Angeles to see my mother and my friends.

When I got back to college, I was greeted by a three-page letter from Coral, which was the single most extraordinary piece of correspondence I have ever received. In it she called me every name in the book. I thought I had heard them all, but Coral could have written a lexicon of scatology. If it hadn't been so upsetting, it would have been hysterically funny. The reason for this outpouring of anger was the fact that I had neglected to write a thank-you note for the week in St. Louis. This unthinkable faux pas caused her to regard me as the most selfish and ungrateful person she had ever had the misfortune to know, and she told me so in no uncertain terms. Ironically, just before the St. Louis trip, we had been getting along swimmingly. I was at Williams College in Massachusetts, a world away from the house on Swallow Drive, living my own life, and distance had improved our relationship. But it always happened that way between us—just when I felt she had opened a door, she slammed it good and hard in my face.

That breach was a long time in mending. Fortunately, my dad and I were able to arrange visits whenever he was in New York or Boston, and he even lectured at my college. Thus, despite the tension between me and Coral, he and I grew closer during those years. When my visits to Los Angeles coincided with one of Coral's trips to England, my father and I were inseparable. As Coral was always on a perpetual diet, he took her absence as permission to eat at will, with no regard for anything but taste. The winter that Coral was filming *An Englishman Abroad*, my father and I were making vats of crème brulée. As exemplified by his earlier ratatouille period, my dad got on "food jags." He would make the same dish again and again until he felt he had perfected it—or until he couldn't stand it any longer. That January it was crème brulée cooked in large Pyrex pans and topped with a thick crust of burnt sugar. There was much to master in making crème brulée—the consistency, the crust, the flavor. So no sense in letting it lie around— we had to eat our way through a whole Pyrex pan in a day or two, so we could move on to the next batch. I was his willing accomplice until I noticed that my jeans were getting very tight. When I professed concern about the fattening nature of the dish, he scowled disparagingly, and announced, "There are no calories in crème brulée." A glance at the trash can and my heart sank. It contained three used cartons of heavy cream and a large empty sugar bag. I tried to reproach him with this, but he would brook no argument; I was forced to slog through two more weeks of crème brulée before waddling back to college.

As I grew older, my father and I engaged in a lively correspondence. Although I had been accepted by his alma mater, Yale, I had decided to break with family tradition to go to Williams, which had superb art history and theater programs. Although my father was initially a little disappointed, he supported my decision, and was pleased with my course of study. In college, I was eager to share each new discovery with my dad and felt that my blossoming intellectual curiosity brought us even closer. For my twenty-first birthday he gave me a trip to Europe, just as he had done for Barrett. I planned an action-packed three-month journey that included two summer programs—one in art, one in theater—as well as plenty of free time for exploring on my own. I spent a few weeks traveling through northern France, and then headed toward Germany to visit the family I had lived with as an exchange student for a year when I was sixteen. My father had met the family's youngest daughter, Ilka, whom he liked very much, and so he gave me money to take her on a trip to Denmark for her birthday. He also sent me armed with gifts for her family and sufficient funds to take them all out to dinner. En route to Germany, however, I unknowingly initiated a rivalry that would become one of my father's and my great joys.

I decided to make a detour to the little town of Colmar on the French-German border to see Matthias Grünewald's *Isenheim Altarpiece*. Though I had studied the piece in school, nothing prepared me for its extraordinary beauty—the power of its imagery, the vibrancy of its color, its sheer scope and size. Grünewald's palette was so saturated and resonant that, even though the altarpiece dated to the fifteenth century, it looked as though it had been painted the day before. The altarpiece was housed in a Gothic gem of a museum filled with countless other treasures, but I was so transfixed by it that I stayed for four hours: I could barely drag myself off to see the rest of the collection. Of course, I immediately sat down to write my father a postcard about what I had just experienced.

When I called him from Germany a week later, he said, "I got your postcard, and I'm green with envy. I can't believe you saw the Isenheim altar and I haven't!" And so our rivalry began. For the rest of the summer—indeed, for the rest of his life—we played a game of artistic one-upmanship. I spent two months in Italy, studying art history in Rome and journeying around the country. My father sent me lists of things to see and I went—to countless lesser churches which required patience and a given amount of fortuitous timing just to gain entry—so that I could try to match him. From Italy I went to England, and the rivalry continued. From then on we tried to outsee and outpostcard one another as art became our safety net, our own world, our intimate language.

After the St. Louis debacle, my father skated on very thin ice between Coral and me. During my senior year of college, I went down to New Haven to join him at Yale, which was holding a festival of his films. During my childhood, I had studiously avoided his horror pictures—but even into my twenties, I found they still scared me too much. And in those days before video, his earlier films were hard to find. So I had not seen many of his hundred movies, and I was blown away by his early work, particularly in *Laura* and *Dragonwyck*. My dad seemed very proud that Yale had sponsored the retrospective, and terribly pleased that students seemed to know and care about him and his career.

At the end of the festival he invited me to take the train down to New York with him, where he was meeting Coral. But then a strange thing happened. He asked me where I was going to stay. I had thought, since he had invited me, that I would be staying with them, but I improvised and told him that I could get a room at the YWCA or the Williams Club—but I didn't tell him that I had no money to pay for it. We took the train to Penn Station and went up to the Wyndham Hotel where Coral was waiting. The three of us had a drink and went out to dinner, after which we went back to their suite. It was getting late and when I said I had to leave, Coral asked me where I was staying. I confessed that I didn't know, whereupon she immediately picked up the phone and called down to ask the front desk if they had a room for me. Happily they did, just down the hall, and I remained at the Wyndham for three nights on my father's tab. Once Coral had given her permission, my father seemed to relax, and the three of us had a wonderful time. They took me to the Russian Tea Room where I had my first blinis.

Two hundred and fifty dollars later, my dad and I had to stop for a pretzel on the way back to the hotel because we were so hungry.

It took me years to understand that Coral could be one of the most generous people on earth, as long as it was on her own terms. During my twenty-first summer, while I was in London, she was very concerned that I see every play, and if anyone she knew was in the cast she sent me backstage to see them. After years of longing for an entrée into Coral's world, I found myself sipping champagne in Alan Bates's dressing room. A few years later, when I was putting myself through graduate school in New Mexico, Coral was the only member of my family who would agree to cosign a loan for three thousand dollars. During that period, she often confided in me about difficulties in her marriage to my father and expressed loving concern for his health. And she also encouraged me through difficult periods in my own life, expressing confidence that I would get to the other side.

It was in 1986, while I was visiting L.A., that Coral asked me to meet her at their local Hamburger Hamlet for lunch. It had been years since the two of us had had a meal alone and, as soon as I arrived, it was clear that she had something on her mind. My father, she said, had been having an affair. And then she told me more about their sex life together than I ever would have wished to know. She wouldn't tell me who the affair was with, but she did say that she had demanded that my father put an end to it and that he had. She even insinuated that his lover was a man. Nevertheless, she enlisted my sympathy and somehow she got it.

He, of course, never knew that she had said anything to me about their marital difficulties. I never told him and neither did Coral, and although I didn't judge him for his behavior, I felt confused. I wasn't sure why Coral had told me. Shortly thereafter my father became very ill, and as I watched his health deteriorate I became terribly worried that whatever it was that had actually happened was now taking a horrible toll on him. If there had indeed been an affair, its ending seemed to have precipitated this decline. The anger I felt toward my father quickly turned into concern.

By 1987, he was in such poor health that doctors thought he had less than a year to live. So I put my Ph.D. on hold and went back to L.A. I wanted to be near my father at the end of his life, but not having lived in L.A. since high school, I failed to take into consideration the degree to which Coral had come to control my father's every move. All my visits had to be prearranged according to her schedule.

The next four years were among the most difficult of my life. I was living in a city with which I had a decided love-hate relationship, and the purpose for my moving there was being thwarted. But still I stayed. As my father's health fluctuated, so did my relationship with Coral, who kept a vigilant watch on his health and his time. Fortunately, my father did not succumb to the doctors' gloomy predictions. Though often weak and increasingly fragile, he was still able to drive, to see friends, and even occasionally to travel. My dad and I saw each other sporadically when Coral allowed it, but because we never had time alone, our relationship felt the strain.

Meanwhile, the rapport Coral and I had developed when I was living in New Mexico had completely disappeared. As it had when I was a teenager, her anger toward me surfaced at the slightest provocation. On my father's seventy-seventh birthday I took them out to dinner at an Italian restaurant. We had a lovely time and a very good meal, but when we came home, Coral started in on me. The topic? Her favorite—my lack of financial responsibility. This was always a difficult, confusing, and upsetting topic for me. I had grown up with parents who were extremely comfortable financially, but whose attitudes toward money were contradictory and bizarre. On the one hand, they would spend fortunes on luxuries that suited the moment; on the other, they cried poor and made quite sure that I should have no doubt that money didn't grow on trees. Thus, in my early adulthood, I had little idea how to deploy such funds as I had, particularly as these were often in short supply.

I genuinely made a mess of things—more, I like to think, because I had adopted my father's sporadic habit of extravagance than because I was fundamentally irresponsible. However, because Coral had cosigned my student loan, I had made the mistake of regarding her as an ally. I was very wrong. That night, her venom mounted until I suddenly burst into tears—something I rarely did. Across the living room, my father looked as though he wished the floor would swallow him up, but he gamely tried to defend me. "Stop picking on her. Can't you see she's crying?" Coral looked at me with great disdain and said, "Oh she cries easily. Just like the Gielguds." It was the most ridiculous thing I had ever heard and I almost burst out laughing. But it broke the spell. I decided that I would never let my stepmother get the best of me again.

Things went from bad to worse. After I had been in L.A. for about two years, I decided that I wanted to settle a question for myself once and for all. Did I want to be an actress? I had attended graduate school in acting right after college, but had dropped out a semester after I had begun, realizing that although I seemed to have talent, I didn't have the drive. Then I had moved to New Mexico and immersed myself in academia while working on my Ph.D. But living in Hollywood reawakened my desire to act and I rang my father up to tell him. He was surprisingly enthusiastic. My mother had once told me that my father came from a generation of Hollywood actors for whom nepotism was the ultimate dirty word. She said, "He wouldn't recommend a relative to sweep the stage." So I was amazed when he suggested I call his agent. Although he told me that he would feel uncomfortable phoning her himself, he said I could do it and use his name.

I called Pearl Wexler of the Kohner Agency and introduced myself. Although she took my call, she professed total shock, saying that she had never known Vincent had a daughter. I sent her my head shot and résumé; she invited me in for a meeting and then offered to represent me. That's when all hell broke loose.

Coral decided that my father and I had been plotting against her. She raged against him and she raged against me. Everything I had ever supposedly done wrong was paraded before me—falling asleep at the dinner table, neglecting to write a thank-you note, being financially profligate. I had, it seemed, been a disaster from the beginning and this heinous act was simply the final straw. But as bad as it was for me, it was far worse for my father. In her fury, she threatened to divorce him, but for the first time in his life he stood up to her. "Fine," he said. "If that's how you feel, if you want me to leave, I will." That threw her. Of course, she didn't want him to leave. In fact, she didn't really know what she wanted. Later, my father and I hypothesized that she had been so outraged because the Kohner Agency had once refused to take her as a client and now had signed me. How absurd, I thought, that a brilliant actress like Coral Browne, then at the height of her acclaim, should believe she had anything to fear from me.

After my father refused to back down, peace descended. Coral told me that she had felt left out and hurt that my father and I hadn't included her in our plans. I told her there hadn't been any plans. We more or less apologized to one another, and we never fought again.

* * *

In the fall of 1989, I came home from a weekend at a friend's ranch to find a message from Coral on my machine to say that my father was in the hospital. I called her right away and was told that he had suddenly begun to feel much worse and had been checked in for more tests. I asked her where he was, how long he would be there, what the prognosis was. She told me nothing except he had been admitted under an assumed name at a hospital in the San Fernando Valley. I don't think I have ever felt as impotent and angry as I did at that moment. I spent an anxious week waiting for someone to call me. When they finally did, the news was mercifully good: This was the visit when his Parkinson's disease was diagnosed, and the new drug he was prescribed soon brought him back almost to his old self.

Then Coral got sick. Life for the next two years on Swallow Drive was a catalogue of treatments, symptoms, wigs, and brave, funny stories. There was something remarkable about Coral when she was ill. In a way, she relaxed because she knew she was the center of attention. Somehow, battling cancer, she was in her element, describing in gorily witty detail each step of and reaction to chemotherapy, talking about what the doctors said, describing the food she could and couldn't eat. At one point she told everyone that, since she was so desperately ill, she might as well drink champagne. Soon the house was flooded with cases of Cristal, which she adored and drank with great pleasure. Even when her hair fell out and she wore the funny knitted skullcaps made for her by Lily Fonda, she looked beautiful. She moved through each successive stage of her illness with grace and astounding good humor—at least around those of us who didn't live with her.

But the situation was hard on my father, who did. Like most men, he found illness hard to bear, and the rigors of his wife's hospital stays and treatments, not to mention her almost obsessive concern with the course of the disease, were particularly trying to him at a time when he felt he was finally coming through his own difficulties. So whenever Coral went into hospital, I inevitably came home to a message on my machine. With opera blaring in the background, my father's voice would say, "Coral's in the hospital again, as you can hear. Let's have dinner." And the two of us would head out to one of our favorite restaurants for long and intimate repasts.

It was at one such meal, after a considerable amount of Chianti had been consumed, that my father decided to talk to me, heart to heart, in a way he had never done. He told me about his fears, his hopes, his own illness, his difficulties with Coral, his loves, his wives. And he told me about a friendship he had had a few years before with a man— a very well-read and interesting man who, he said, knew nothing about art. My dad told me that he had loved sharing his own passion for and knowledge of art with his new friend. He said, "It was like a love affair, but without the sex," but that Coral had felt threatened by the friendship and he had ended it. Five years later, he still seemed desperately sad. As he spoke, I realized that this was "the affair" of which Coral had told me. But I said nothing about that; I simply told him how sorry I was. In retrospect, however, I have often wondered which version of the story to believe. Given my own experience of Coral's jealousy and possessiveness, it seems more than likely that *his* story was the truth, and that when Coral accused him of having an affair, he did what he had always done—sacrificed an important friendship for the sake of peace and quiet.

I never felt closer to my father than I did that evening. I had longed to share that kind of intimacy with him since I had moved back to L.A. four years earlier. But throughout the evening, although I was overwhelmed with emotion, I knew that if I revealed how much his words were affecting me, he would stop. And so, at least six times during the course of dinner, I excused myself, went to the bathroom, had a good cry, pulled myself together, and came out for more. The next day my father called to tell me how much he had enjoyed himself. "I loved our talk," he said, "It was so real, so close, but best of all, it was so unsentimental . . . But you sure did have to pee a lot!'

Thinking back over my relationship with my father during those years, it is curious that so much of my memory is consumed by Coral. My brother, however, has said the same of his years with Vincent and Mary—that when he thinks about his parents, he thinks of Mary, that it was she who raised him. Coral didn't raise me, of course, though she became a significant influence on my life. So what was it about my father that has caused him to withdraw to the edges of both my brother's and my memories, while these powerful women come to the fore? Barrett has said to me, "I think he was afraid of all of them. His constant complaint was that they kept him away from his friends. He complained about them all in the same way, but I don't know what that was about."

My father hated conflict, and would almost always back down in any situation in order to avoid a confrontation. Or he would go away—on location, on tour—anywhere that he felt he could be himself. Certainly Barrett's experience of Mary was vastly different from mine of Coral, but our experience of our dad was oddly similar. He was capable of having more fun, being more jolly than almost anyone either of us has known. He was generous, interested, supportive, loving. He confided in us, he told us he needed us, he told us he loved us. But, in the end, we were both left wanting more. That bothered me for years until I came to see that my father carried a perpetual sense of his own inadequacies and failures, which burdened his relationship with his children. With strangers, with casual acquaintances, even with friends, he could keep his guilt at bay by virtue of his ability to have fun, to make fun for others, to be open and spontaneous and charming. But with his own family, particularly with his children, whom he felt he had in some way failed, that was much harder. He didn't know how to bridge the gap between his two sides—his happy-go-lucky, fun-loving self and his privately doubting and fearful self. So, with Barrett and me, he often swung from one extreme to the other in a way that usually precluded intimacy and trust.

When I was a little girl, it was easy for us both. He was best when he could come in and out of my life according to his schedule. It was an ideal relationship—he could play the wonderful dad and I the adoring daughter. He never had to punish me or get angry because he wasn't around enough. And I was usually at my best when I was with him because I so loved being with him. I always justified his absences with the thought that one day, when I grew up, we would have all the time in the world to be together. And then I wouldn't be a kid anymore, but an adult who would become his best friend. It never happened that way. Though the depth of our love for each other never waned, neither he nor I was capable of sustaining an intimate friendship with the other. I wanted more and he couldn't give it. He wanted more and couldn't ask me for it. And so we were forever trying to relive my childhood, even as we had both long outgrown it.

For my father's eightieth birthday, Barrett, Rini, and I took him out to a glorious dinner. When Coral died two days later, his three children were all nearby and able to be with him. It was the first time the four of us had ever been together in the house on Swallow Drive, and the first time that Rini had ever been there at all. Coral had cut my brother and sister-in-law out almost completely, and now that she was gone none of us knew quite what to do or how to act. After years of floating on the edges of my father's life, waiting for odd moments when he might be available or when Coral might be away, there we all were, a family again, the way it once had been. We had our father and he had his children, though so much had conspired to damage those relationships that they had become fragile. And so, even as we mourned Coral's passing and our father's loss, we prepared to take our first tenuous steps together. A new dance was about to begin—a cautious waltz with each of us taking turns to lead.

40

FOR ALMOST THREE years before his death on October 25, 1993, Vincent Price was preparing to die. He did this systematically and unsentimentally—by cataloguing, selling, donating, and giving away much of his beloved art collection, saying goodbye to friends and family, and tying up loose ends. Mostly, however, he tried to make sense for himself of the long and remarkable life he had lived. He had predicated his entire existence on work, travel, action, and accomplishment, but the gradual dissolution of his abilities through illness eventually took away his will to live. For Vincent Price, a life of inactivity was no life at all.

In the late 1980s, during the early stages of his illness, he had tried to keep his spirit alive by writing his memoirs. He never finished—his work halted as much by infirmity as by his ultimate inability to reconcile his private feelings with his public face. But completed or not, a record remains—hundreds of pages containing marvelous stories of his life in art, film, theater, and radio, anecdotes about famous acquaintances, and reconstructions of family history. Among these singular tales are the troubled musings of a man who feels his life is drawing to a close. These reflections reveal his efforts to resolve the varied impulses that drove him, and to arrange the many facets of his life into a workable perspective. Looking back on his extraordinary journey, he sought to allow himself an unfamiliar honesty, one perhaps too ultimately discomforting for a man who had spent a lifetime measuring his words, with one eye always on his public, ever to be able to release during his lifetime.

He wrote, "That I am concerned is what concerns me most—that I remain concerned about what matters most—the Art of Living. Time consumes me; it has a way of consuming all of us. Some get spat out, and fortunate are those who end up on a canvas, a stage, in poetry, or prose, in the shape of things to be, to be used, to be wondered at. To neglected by ourselves is to die. To be neglected by others for neglecting ourselves is living loneliness. I refuse it still awhile.

"The fiction of one's life is the truth. There is no lie in living. I have been human to the point of madness, have attempted rejection of my humanness, to the edge of nonacceptance of myself as myself. Only one escape, not passion and not love, only through the illumined exit of the arts have I been anchored in my life."

After Coral died, three or four afternoons a week I would climb into my car and drive up into the Hollywood Hills. There, in the cooler, cleaner air above the smog, in the salmon-pink house on Swallow Drive, I talked with my father. I suppose I had always thought that once we could have some real time together I would come to know this man, this glamorous figure I had adored and admired since childhood. Now, as an adult, I found myself wanting to find the substance behind that seductive image. In turn, I believe my father, too, thought that we could rediscover our common ground. After years of waiting for this time together, there was so much we wanted to say to one another.

I remember coming into his bedroom one afternoon during those last years. He was propped up by four or five pillows, staring out into the garden. He seemed preoccupied. Almost immediately, our conversation, imperceptibly but surely guided by my father, who clearly had something to say, turned to television. We began to talk about how much one can learn from television, if one put one's mind to it. And then he said, "I couldn't sleep last night, so I turned on the telly, and I found myself watching one of those made-for-TV movies. There was this young man in it, and slowly I started to realize that I could identify with him. And when the movie was over, I thought to myself that his problem had been my problem, too, my whole life, and that if I were only younger I might be able to work it out."

During this brief monologue, my father continued to stare resolutely out at his garden. He never made eye contact with me. And when he stopped speaking, I felt the space between us both loom and shrink. A hundred responses formed in my head, but I couldn't even ask the most basic question—what problem did you both have? And so I sat there paralyzed, completely mute. I didn't know what to do. I realize now that I didn't know what he wanted from me, and I was terrified of transgressing our boundaries. Of course, in retrospect I can see that crossing that line was exactly what he wanted, but he couldn't do it himself. And neither could I. I was, and would forever, be his daughter. How could I be the one to take the first step? So, instead we sat in uncomfortable silence until the moment passed and I heard him say, with that familiar insouciant lilt, "But I'm too old." And with that he raised himself up higher on his pillows and launched into one of his marvelous stories.

I will always be grateful that, during those last years, my father and I had the chance to mend our relationship and regain some of our former closeness, even as my memories of that time we spent together will always be tinged with regret.

My father had always imagined that the end of his life would be a marvelous adventure: Freed of the responsibility of work, he would travel the world and be surrounded by his family and friends. But first his health failed him, rendering him less and less mobile, then Coral died. After spending fifty years of his adult life as a married man, albeit with three different women, he now found himself alone.

Coral's illness had taken its toll on my father. After he was diagnosed with Parkinson's in 1989 he had rallied with the help of L-DOPA, but the drug's effect was short-lived. Even as Coral was declining, so was he. Years of smoking had given him emphysema; his arthritis became crippling; and Parkinson's attacked his nervous system. He began to feel as though he was on the way out, and most of the time after Coral died, he wanted to go. But, as he had always done, he rallied periodically and sometimes even seemed his old self.

My dad's old college friend, Ted Thomas, had given him a small needlepoint pillow, which he placed prominently on his bed; it read, "Screw the Golden Years." Not only did he miss the company of the provocative and difficult woman he had so loved, but he felt betrayed by his now frail body. And so he turned to family and old friends, only to realize that he had sorely neglected many of them during his life with Coral.

Fortunately, Coral had managed to tolerate a handful of my father's old friends, notably Jane Wyatt, Norman Lloyd, Bill and Shirley Brice, and Barbara Poe Levee. After Coral's death my dad saw a lot of them, particularly Barbara and Shirley, on whom he began to rely much as he had in the old days. After all, they had known each other for almost fifty years. Bill Brice, of course, also visited, and my dad always looked forward to their animated conversations about art.

Other old friends who came to see him included Hazel Court and Don Taylor, Lily Fonda, Tom Silliman, Ted Thomas, and Sam Jaffe. Of my father and Coral's mutual friends, John Schlesinger, Joan Rivers, Eric Harrison, Judy Parfitt, Maggie Smith and Jean Marsh, Marti Stevens, and Roddy McDowall kept in regular touch after Coral's death. Roddy, a frequent visitor, often invited my dad to intimate dinner parties at his nearby home. He famously entertained a diverse collection of film and theater people across the generations. His guest list could include familiar faces such as Christopher Hewitt or Dennis Hopper, old colleagues like Jessica Tandy and Hume Cronyn, foreign guests Joan Plowright and Luise Rainer, even members of the younger fraternity such as Winona Ryder. There, in easy and familiar surroundings, Vincent kept up with old friends and made a few new ones. After one of Roddy's evenings, my dad returned home full of enthusiasm about the encounter he had witnessed between Winona Ryder and Jessica Tandy. "They could have been one and the same person, with the younger actress just starting out confronting herself at the end of a fabulous career."

My father treasured his friendships with "young people" such as Michael Feinstein, Johnny Depp, and Tim Burton. He was particlarly close to Michael, who had been introduced to him and Coral by composer Sammy Cahn and his wife Tita. After Coral's death, Michael frequently dropped by the house where he and my dad listened to music together, talked about mutual friends, and shared show business stories. My father was deeply touched by Michael's friendship and, although they were more than two generations apart, they developed a mutual understanding and respect.

My father also kept up with Sandy Leonard, who recalled, "I never visited until after Coral died, but we would talk regularly and write back and forth. And I remember at one point he said, 'Why don't you come out and visit me?' I arrived and he picked me up at the airport. This is my first time flying to Los Angeles and a movie star picks me up at the curb! I grew up in New Jersey! The next day we drove to Santa Barbara. He wanted to show me the mission in Santa Barbara. On the way, he showed me Jayne Mansfield's house, Bob Guccione's house, and all along, he would tell me stories. We cooked together. He made a celery risotto once and introduced me to grits."

With Coral gone, my father also lost no time reaching out to his children and to other members of his family with whom he had had little contact in recent years. His niece, Sally Santschi, to whom he had been so close during the fifties and sixties, received a letter from him, saying, "I'm so sorry. Now that Coral is gone, I feel so weak. It's my fault that I cut myself off from all of you and I regret it so much that I didn't come to see you and William and that I didn't stay in touch with you. But Coral did not like family and I went along with it and I just feel terrible about it. Please forgive me." Sara recalled, "He wrote that out of the blue about a year before he died. I was really hurt and angry because we had been such a part of each other's lives, but I thought what the hell. So I called him up and said, 'I just called to see how you're doing. I know you're not well and I'm sorry.' And then we stayed in touch until he died. After all, he was the reason that I changed the direction of my life."

Barrett and Rini began coming to L.A. once a month. My dad was so proud of Barrett, telling everyone about his son's accomplishments and latest projects. But he was perhaps most surprised at the friendship he developed with Rini, whom he had hardly seen during the last decade. Because Rini had struggled with a serious illness, she seemed to understand his condition better than anyone else; in a sense, she was able to give him "permission" to feel depressed and frightened and then to help him through those difficult emotions.

Having his family around allowed my dad to enjoy some of the spontaneous fun we had all so missed. He reveled in each holiday as he hadn't been able to for years—buying silly gifts for family and friends, cooking marvelous meals, decorating the house, playing holiday music, dressing up in hats and festive clothing, carving Halloween pumpkins, dropping Easter lilies at friends' houses, sending out greeting cards, being the life of the party.

The first Christmas after Coral died, my dad and I went out and bought a tree, which he and Reg and I decorated. On Christmas Eve he felt well enough to take me to Roddy's traditional party, where he introduced me to many of his old Hollywood compatriots. On Christmas Day friends dropped by, we opened gifts, and we prepared a turkey dinner together. That day I saw my father's childlike joy resurface. Though he had tolerated Coral's hatred of holidays and her insistence on choosing her own gifts for him to wrap, he had missed having his kind of Christmas. We could never fully recapture our past, but seeing him surrounded by piles of gifts, tying red and green bows on the dogs, singing along to Christmas music, and entertaining friends, I was happier than I had been in a long time, for both of us.

My father was physically weak, but mentally he was as sharp as ever, and we found we enjoyed playing all sorts of games together. This was an unexpected turn of events, for, during my entire childhood I only remember ever playing one game (other than poker) with him—a board game called Masterpiece. My mother gave it to me for Christmas when I was eight or nine, doubtless because of my whining that other kids got to play games like Monopoly at home, but we never played anything. Masterpiece was a game based on accumulating works of art at auction, and I'm sure my mom chose it thinking my dad would also enjoy it. When we finally settled down to play the game, it lasted all of fifteen minutes, ten of which were taken up with reading the instructions. Then the game deteriorated rapidly when my dad began disputing the auction prices of the paintings as listed on the game cards, and we never played Masterpiece again.

At the end of his life, however, he found that he enjoyed games, probably because, despite his fear that his mind might go the way of his body, he always won. When he was sent a prototype for a game that involved identifying famous faces as they were slowly revealed from behind plastic dividers a section at a time, he proceeded to beat us all soundly (and one of the "all" was Roddy McDowall, who, after all, had known and photographed many famous faces). Whether it was an eyebrow or the corner of a mouth, my dad showed an uncanny ability to guess the famous person while the rest of us floundered hopelessly. To win the game, one last card was hidden for him behind the closed dividers. My father revealed one small section of this card and suddenly burst out laughing. He looked at us and said, "You've done this on purpose." We didn't know what he was talking about. We hadn't done anything on purpose. He pulled the card out of the holder and displayed a photograph of himself. Needless to say, he won.

He was particularly gifted at games of knowledge. We watched *Jeopardy!* together on television each evening that I was with him. Sitting on his king-sized bed, we stared at the television intently and played to win, which he usually did. When Barrett and Rini visited, we took to playing Trivial Pursuit, with my brother, father and I forming one team, and Reg, Rini, and my friend Lora the other. Without my father, Barrett and I would probably always have lost—all three members of the other team were crack players—but Dad always saved the day. He would remember the name of an obscure midcentury newspaperman, of Robert Taylor's costar in some movie, or of a long-since-forgotten political scandal. He had a stupendous memory. Lives of painters, German *Lieder*, Poe poems, Shakespeare sonnets, and operatic arias were all stored in the repository of his remarkable mind.

We played our most memorable Trivial Pursuit game one night when my father was feeling very weak. He was lying back on his pillows, drifting in and out of sleep, contributing only the occasional answer. The game was neck and neck, but Barrett, Dad, and I reached the championship question first. The other team picked our final category, which was, needless to say, Science and Nature, never our forte. They pulled out the card and gleefully asked the question, "What does a man have more than two of if he is polyorchid?" My father was almost asleep on his pillows, and so Barrett and I pondered the question carefully, meticulously examining the etymology of the word. From the looks on the faces of the opposite team, we could tell we were meandering far and wide from the correct answer. Just as our time was about to be up, my father gasped, "Balls!" We thought he'd lost his mind. Why was he cursing in the middle of the game? "What?" I asked. He raised himself up slightly on his elbows and said it again, "Balls!" The other team shrieked in anger. Of course, he was right. And, as usual, we won.

When Coral died on May 29, 1991, it was exactly four years to the day since I had moved back to L.A. to be with my ailing father. Now, although I was eager to leave the city, with Coral gone, my father had all the time in the world to spend with me. And I wanted to be with him.

My father experienced a baffling range of emotions after Coral's passing. In many ways, he was relieved that she was no longer suffering, and that he would no longer have to live in a house filled with death and dying. He was happy, too, to have his house and garden free of the nurses and visitors who had interfered with his privacy, but still, he missed her dreadfully.

In early June, Coral's will, of which my father was co-executor, was read. It was one of the most profoundly shocking moments of my father's life. Throughout their marriage, Coral had complained frequently and loudly, to anyone who would listen, about money—how expensive things were, how little money my father gave her, how poor she was—a perpetual catalogue of financial woes. But when the will was read, my father learned that his wife's estate was worth in excess of 6 million dollars. She had over a million dollars in the bank in the U.S. and 3 million pounds sterling tax free on the Isle of Wight.

Reg recalled, "The startling thing which came to light on Coral's death was that she had been much richer than anyone could have believed. She bequeathed to Vincent her share of the community property, but she chose to put her personal fortune out of reach. At first, she wanted to donate it to an animal foundation, but she was advised that bequests to the Motion Picture Home and her cancer hospital would be more seemly. In fact, this proved to have its own complication and embarrassment as Coral had specified the John Wayne Clinic. She intended this medical tribute to go to the UCLA Cancer Center, but the two foundations were jumbled together in most patients' minds, the John Wayne Clinic seeming to be the name of the wing occupied by the UCLA operation. Vincent had a delicate course to pursue to undo the error. He knew that neither Coral nor he would want to honor the legacy of redneck, iron-cast Republican John Wayne."

My father was traumatized by Coral's will. Not only would the probate prove complicated, but he was absolutely stunned that his wife had never told him about her money. For eighteen years he had worried about their finances while listening to her bellyache about his stinginess. To all of us who knew her, Coral's harangues about money were a fact of life. The revelation of her will left my father feeling utterly betrayed.

At first, he was angry. Gradually, however, anger gave way to hurt and embarrassment. As soon as he could bear it, he began asking Coral's friends about the money, trying to find a reason for his wife's deception. Jean Marsh thought it "one of the saddest things I have *ever* heard about a close friend. When Vinnie told me, he did it in such a funny way. God, I choked on my drink. He said, 'Do you know how much money she left?' And I said no. So I guessed half a million dollars. He said, 'A million and something dollars and three million pounds,' and that he didn't know until she died. I couldn't believe it. It is one of the biggest lies between a couple I have ever heard of, especially when it wasn't necessary. I mean, they *both* had money. She had enough money that she need never ask him about money again, especially considering her age. I felt so tearful for days. And then I thought, it's the saddest tale I ever heard about her. Vinnie must have been hurt and angry, but the true emotion of it is hers. How detached and sad. I mean, what was the point? What was the money for? It's one of the strangest tales I've ever heard."

Several other old friends of Coral's, however, maintained that it was always apparent that she was rich and that her curious attitude toward money preceded her marriage to Vincent. Jill Melford said, "Obviously she had money. She lived very well. Actors are funny because they're always going on about being broke, which she did all the time. But quite obviously she wasn't. I don't know where she kept it or what she did with it, but Marti Stevens and I always used to scream with laughter because Coral's will was always in the back of her address book and beneficiaries came and went with alacrity." And Diana Rigg remarked, "I could have told Vinnie. Anyone could have. Coral was constantly moaning about the price of everything, but there was no shortage of anything in her life. And I knew, as did most of her acquaintances, that when Firth Shephard died, and then her first husband, they both left her money. And she was a very canny woman. I'm pretty certain that just about everyone else knew except Vincent. She never picked up the bill for a dinner or a lunch or anything. I suppose she did this in order for Vincent to pay for as much as possible. Vincent must have felt very betrayed."

Joan Rivers also recalled her friend's curious behavior with regard to money. "At one point Edgar and I said, 'They're just never going to pick up a check, so we have to make up our minds. Do we love them enough to say they're like our family and that's Coral and Vinnie?' And we said, 'Yes we love them enough.' One dinner in fourteen there would be a half-hearted attempt to pick up the check. They were not generous that way. It was like a joke to us, but we loved them, so the hell with it. We literally had to say to ourselves, this is part of the deal."

When Joan told me this, I was really astonished. Not to hear that Coral was cheap—I knew that—but that my father seemed to have been so brainwashed by her. Although he lived much of his life deluding himself that he was on the brink of financial ruin, he was paradoxically very openhanded. As my mother reminded me, during the years of their marriage he unfailingly picked up the tab at restaurants with an almost reckless generosity that generally characterized his relations with other people. It will always remain beyond my comprehension how he could have sat by with Coral while others picked up every check. I can still hear Coral admonishing my father before they went out to eat, "Don't you dare pick up that bill. They're *rich*. They can afford it." However, I never knew that he actually allowed himself to be ruled, and thus completely transformed, by her meanness.

In due course, my father came to terms with Coral's will. Though she had left her money to charity, she had at least stipulated that while her husband lived, he should receive all of the interest from the capital. Thus, with characteristic humor, he told everybody that he was *determined* to live long enough to "get some of that money!" Meanwhile, he began sorting her effects.

My father, Reg, and I had to face the daunting task of disposing of Coral's countless possessions, which my dad hoped to put behind him as quickly as possible. We started with her clothes—closets and closets filled with Jean Muir, Armani, and Chanel. From the start, my father insisted that I take as many of Coral's clothes as fitted me. To my amazement, although she and I had totally different figures, we took the same size suit. It gave my father (and me) no end of pleasure, therefore, that I was able to wear almost all of her Armani and Chanel suits—though I couldn't help thinking that Coral wouldn't have been too thrilled.

The clothes were the easy part. Coral had raised makeup to a fine art and had literally hundreds of bottles, vials, boxes, tubes, and jars of cosmetics. After the makeup came the medicine, a veritable pharmacy of pills and potions, most of which had long since passed their expiration date. Next we set about fulfilling her bequests, sending paintings, drawings, jewelry and other collectibles to friends around the globe. My father added his own gifts from her estate, sending items that had been of sentimental value to friends such as Joan Rivers, Adrienne Corri, Jill Melford, Jean Marsh, and Marti Stevens.

Coral's gifts to me were generous, but I really valued them far more for their sentiment—sometimes humorous, sometimes thoughtful. A pearl necklace, for example, was left to me as a counterpart to one my mother had given me for my sixteenth birthday. I loved my mother's gift, but every time I wore the necklace, Coral said, "Those are the smallest pearls I've ever seen. With all the money your father gives her, can't your mother afford to buy you bigger pearls?!" Accordingly, she left me a very long strand of very large pearls, along with her Cartier watch, three gold bracelets she had had made out of my grandfather Vincent Sr.'s cigarette case, and an African sculpture.

Once we had fulfilled the conditions of the will, we began cataloguing my father's art collection. This was fascinating work, because for each painting, drawing, sculpture, pot, ring, or bracelet, my father had a story to tell. It was this undertaking that led to our next project—writing a book about art.

*　　　*　　　*

In the late eighties, my brother had been approached by a publisher to write a biography of our father. Barrett suggested the idea to Dad, who inveighed so vociferously against biographers that my brother quickly and permanently dropped it. Therefore, when my friend Danae suggested that, since my dad and I were spending so much time together, we might enjoy collaborating on a book about art, I pooh-poohed the whole idea. She kept at me; finally, to humor her, I tentatively broached the idea to my dad, expecting it to be shot down in flames. To my surprise, he said yes—an immediate, excited, and heartfelt yes. He insisted I go out and buy a tape recorder so as not to miss a word, and the next day we began the project that would carry us both through the next year.

"The first thing I want to bring up is the fact that this is a time when the arts are in great danger. They've been in constant danger since the first time man drew something on a wall, but now they're really in danger of being destroyed by ignorance and fear, which again is proof that the arts are enormously powerful and influential in shaping man's life and times." So began our yearlong "conversation" about art.

My father knew he was dying. On many levels, he wanted to die. He certainly did not want to linger on, becoming increasing immobile and dependent on other people. He had lived a long and fruitful life, but he still had a lot to say about the one thing that had mattered most to him—fine art. My father felt that "art is the hope of everything, of growth," and he was very worried that all the good that had been accomplished during his lifetime was going to be wiped out by right-wing politicians. The controversy surrounding the National Endowment for the Arts angered him to his very core, and he was determined to speak out about the vital importance of the visual arts to civilization. He said, "I think it's very important that people make the effort to see. The wonderful thing about art is that it does take a certain amount of effort. It doesn't just happen. You can never say that you know everything about art, because you don't." I asked him, "What are your hopes for the future of art?" He replied, "I hope that it retains its vitality and usefulness for the human mind and the human imagination. I hope that it doesn't die of censorship. I hope that man remains free in his expression of art. It's a very bad time, so it's a very good question, what with all the people saying, This is dirty. This is smutty. It may be, but people have a right to see it if they want to see it. I just hope art remains free and vital."

The political aspect aside, he liked the sheer fun of talking about art. One day he said to me, "I have an idea. We'll call it artistic instant assessments. You name an artist and I'll try to come up with a quick assessment of them." And so we began. Alexander Calder: "An inventive kid with a pair of wire cutters." Caravaggio: "An evil man looks at the good life and finds it evil." Hieronymous Bosch: "A man who went to hell, saw what should be recorded, and brought back the news that it was worse than you think." Paul Gauguin: "He would have been among the unemployed had he not known how to paint." David Hockney: "A boy of his time." Henry Moore: "Found a theme and punched a hole in it that he couldn't get out of." Caspar David Friedrich: "A painter who, one suspects, if he took one more footstep, would have arrived in heaven." Paul Cezanne: "The painter that everyone thinks they understand and nobody does." August Rodin: "The artist who, even when he played with himself, was making love with someone else." Leonardo da Vinci: "The human enigma solved."

My father also looked ahead to a century he knew he would never see. His vision was somewhat apocalyptic. "Tell me how you imagine the twenty-first century," I asked. "Well, I think the world is in for a terrible bath of fire because of over-population and lack of concern for the ecology—for the air and water and everything else. I think there's going to be a sort of dying off, as there was of the dinosaurs. You know, it wouldn't be the first time that a whole civilization or species has stopped. Because whenever it was that the dinosaurs were here, they were as populous as we are in their own way. And they just disappeared. Eventually, we'll do the same thing.

"I think there will be things left over of our civilization which will be desirable. But you wonder what is going to last—the sophisticated part of it, the knowing part of it, or the unknowing. Are the simple people going to last? I don't think so, because they have not kept up with what's going on. It's going to be a terrible time, I think. I don't envy you." And then he spoke of his own "future." "Right at this moment I only want silence. I believe that the end of life is silence in the love that people have for you. I've actually been running through what people have said about the end. Religion says that the end is one thing, because it serves their purpose. But great thinkers haven't always agreed. Shakespeare knew how to say it better than anyone else. Hamlet says, 'The rest is silence.' And when you think of the noises of everyday life, you realize how particularly desirable that is. Silence."

I found the year that we spent working on the book very exciting, and also quite trying. Every day that I drove up to the house on Swallow Drive, part of me was still looking for the image of my father that I had carried with me since childhood. And when I came in the front door and looked out on the courtyard filled with cymbidiums and roses and geraniums, when I walked past the drawing of the Gaston Lachaise nude woman with her leg playfully and seductively kicked high in the air, when I played with the three nutty dogs my father absolutely adored, I saw the signs of that wonderful mythical man all around me. This was the man who could riff on the High Renaissance, saying, "Michelangelo was always in trouble. He was irascible, difficult, sexually mixed up, a runt. But he had enormous power. Raphael was the exact opposite. He was beautiful, adored, sexually exactly the way he should be. The popes loved him; the painters loved him. Everybody loved him. The beloved Raphael. The thing that was wrong with him is that he died young. He walked into the wrong room where the black plague was sitting at the end of the table and he got it and was gone. Michelangelo lived to be a tremendous age. And Titian was the exact opposite of all of them, because he was a courtier, the most worshipped painter of his time. He was one of the greatest painters, and he knew it. But those last pictures of his are as free as Monet. This is what I think has always filled my life with art. It's the facts and stories about these people. It's absolutely incredible to learn about a man with a God-given talent. It makes you believe in God more than almost anything else." I loved these passionate reflections on the highways and byways of art, and I loved my father's continuing curiosity and enthusiasm for life. This was the father I had always adored.

But sometimes, when I entered his bedroom, I came face to face with someone else altogether—a weak, old man in a faded pink nightshirt who was angry that life had dealt him such an unfair blow. After a lifetime of attempting to control his temper, he was now simmering with rage, and had no idea what to do about it. He knew there was no one to blame, but still he lashed out—sometimes at himself, sometimes at others. And when he was consumed by that anger and that fear, he wanted nothing more than to be released from his misery. This angry, bitter, weary man bore absolutely no resemblance to the man I had thought of as my father. But though I could understand his frustration and his fear, neither he nor I knew how to help each other. We simply didn't know how to talk about hard things together, and so, inevitably, we sought refuge in the lighthearted, easygoing, often intellectual discourse with which we were both most comfortable. But the sense of having failed, both ourselves and each other, lingered palpably between us.

My father had always hoped to make one last trip to Italy, but he finally realized that he would never be able to manage the twelve-hour plane journey. Unwilling to surrender completely to his physical condition, he decided to ask Barrett and Rini to go to Hawaii with him. He wanted to spend time alone with his son and daughter-in-law, by way of "apology" for all the time missed during his marriage to Coral. Sadly, Barrett felt it was too little too late. "That last trip to Hawaii was so weird. By this time, he was this old man and my feelings for him were so different. It was terrible because he did not feel well and he wanted to have a good time and he was pushing himself and he was doing it for us, no question about it. And this was a place where he and Mary and he and Coral had spent time. It was very peculiar. We went down to dine and he was huffing and puffing and he was hiding in the elevators because he thought he looked ugly. He would wear his hat down and he was so embarrassed about his looks. We drove him around the island. We went out on the beach, but he never did. I think he stayed in his room. At night, we went down and listened to someone play all those wonderful tacky Hawaiian songs and we all got very drunk—which he could do a lot easier the older he got—and he sang Hawaiian songs. But where there ought to have been a kind of camaraderie, there wasn't. And it was largely because of me, because by that time I had to fake it, because I didn't feel that way. I wanted to, but I didn't."

My dad and I were also making up for lost time, for despite our disappointments in each other, we loved each other, perhaps more than ever. I tried to organize my life around him as far as possible. For his birthdays, I arranged parties which consisted of my father, Reg, myself, and my circle of closest friends, all of whom, happily, he liked very much. His eighty-first was held at Susan Feniger and Mary Sue Milliken's hip and popular City Restaurant, which was one of his favorite places. He loved the adventurous food, and he loved Susan, who often came to the house to cook for him or sent dinner from the restaurant.

We tried to enjoy L.A.'s cultural offerings together. When the Los Angeles County Museum had a blockbuster show of Mexican art, I arranged for a private tour and invited a few of my friends along. Moving through the half-empty museum, he told my friends and me stories of his trips to Mexico, relishing his own intellect and remembering his adventurous life. Whenever something appeared in the paper that interested him, Reg and I tried to find a way for him to get there—the Diebenkorn retrospective, where he was able to see the oeuvre of a man whose successful career he had helped to launch; a new play at the Music Center; a new restaurant or shop. He and Reg discovered a few special stores where he could indulge in his lifelong passion for discovery. At Sonrisa, a small gallery specializing in folk art from Mexico and Central America, he continued to buy pieces that interested him. Out in Santa Monica, he discovered a man who was importing wonderful pottery from Afghanistan and immediately began a collection.

My father's credo had always been that if one remained curious about life, one would never be bored. His failing health tested this belief severely, but to the very end he remained engaged by the world around him. And if he couldn't go out, he would have the world come in. He invited friends over and plied them with questions about the latest movies, books, and restaurants. Knowing that I was as curious as he, he sent me to places he had always wanted to go, or to art exhibits he would have loved to see. Armed with a video camera, I went to the great Mayan ruin of Tikal in Guatemala where I tried to absorb every inch and every fact about the area. When I returned, we watched the video over and over again, poring over photographs and literature as he quizzed me about everything I had learned. When the Titian show opened in Paris, off I went, notebook in hand, ready to immerse myself in the riches of the artist's long and glorious career. I spent almost a whole day at the show, making extensive notes so that my father and I could enjoy the catalogue together when I returned.

He also found that the television still could be a marvelous learning method. He ordered videos such as Kenneth Clark's *Civilization*, religiously watched PBS, kept up with current films through the videos sent each year by the Motion Picture Academy, watched the Dodgers all summer, and checked with CNN for the latest news. He was an avid watcher of CNN's *Crossfire*, railing angrily against the conservatives and rooting for the liberals.

Having had three wives who were never as passionate about music as he, my father was finally able to indulge his wide gamut of musical tastes. Reggie recalled, "Vincent had set up an elaborate sound system throughout the house, but, in Coral's presence, music was aired as little more than soothing background. Coral liked music, but really appreciated opera only in the opera house and show music only in the theater. Now Vincent would vie with me in discovering CD glories for daily jaunts to the musical stratosphere and Swallow Drive became, in turn, La Scala, Milan; and Theatre Royal, Drury Lane. Vincent followed the burgeoning careers of Thomas Hampson ('He has it all: the looks and the voice. How dare he!') and soprano Cecilia Bartoli."

Now that he was alone, my father also transformed the garden into a riot of color. Reggie noted, "The house at Swallow Drive was set on rock and the grounds had been devoid of any fertile soil. A rectangle of imported loam accommodated the rose garden, while the remainder of the grounds at the back of the house were flagstoned, providing a carpet for the many hundreds of pots in which Vincent's beloved cymbidium orchids and complementary assorted plants flourished. Coral wanted a garden filled with only white flowers—at which Vincent and I had shared the joke that this was probably because she wanted herself to be the only orchid in their midst. But Coral at least had to bow to the beauty of Vincent's cymbidiums. Now, with Vincent devoting as much time to his garden as his health and stamina allowed, the color bar disappeared and the patio burst into vivid and flamboyant bloom." My father, however, cut one white rose every week, which he placed in a bud vase next to Helmut Newton's photograph of Coral.

As his health deteriorated further, Vincent came to rely ever more heavily on Reg, but insisted that the hardworking Williams have at least part of each afternoon and evening free before returning to ready him for bed. My father still liked to cook for himself or have friends over who cooked with him. Gradually, however, he ceased to be able to do this, and so I came to spend two or three afternoons and evenings with him each week and a couple of Sundays each month. Having been more or less exiled from the kitchen since childhood but for the making of pancakes and popovers, I was not noted for my culinary skills. Although my dad's tastebuds were now impaired and his always sensitive stomach had become more troublesome, one of the foods that still gave him pleasure was the risotto he had learned to make in Venice with Marcella Hazan. He taught me how to make it—an arduous undertaking, since my father was not only an excellent cook, but an exacting one. Nonetheless I eventually learned to make a decent risotto, and was soon experimenting with ingredients ranging from saffron to celery to champagne. I think it gave him pleasure to watch me learn how to cook something well.

Fortunately for him, however, I was not the only chef around. As it became apparent that my dad would need someone else to help when Reg or I couldn't be there, I asked my friend Denis Adair if he could spend a few nights a week cooking for my father and keeping him company after dinner. Denis readily agreed and the two got along brilliantly. Denis had been an actor who was now working in the restaurant business, so they had lots of common ground. We all were delighted with the arrangement until Denis moved to San Francisco. My father was getting gradually worse and I knew we had to find someone else. Happily, more of my friends came to the rescue, forming a kind of care-taking tag team.

At the end of his life, my father was surrounded by an amazing group of interesting men who looked after him: Jim Phipps, a writer whose cooking skills were minimal, but who regaled my father with marvelous stories and was one of the only people who could give him a run for his money at *Jeopardy!*; Mitchell Anderson, an actor whose cooking was much better than Jim's, and who shared the vicissitudes of his "actor's life" with my dad, who was always willing to listen; Rick Mitz, a television writer and a very funny man, whose humor seemed to tickle my father; Chris Jakowchik, a young nursing student; and Paul Brown, another writer, and one whose highly idiosyncratic view of life and limited culinary ability made my father laugh more than almost anyone else could. My dad was particularly fond of discussing and, whenever possible, exploiting Paul's unique photographic "abilities," which he discovered when Paul brought over a picture he had taken of his two standard poodles. In the forefront was an indistinguishable curly gray mass which Paul proudly announced were his dogs. But, as my father gleefully liked to point out, in the background of these so-called dogs, the titles on the spines of the books sitting on a shelf across the room were in perfect focus and completely legible. Paul was frequently called upon to take group photographs, which often resulted in missing limbs, severed heads, and very fuzzy faces.

My father really loved having all of these young men around; indeed Roddy McDowall took to calling them, quite appropriately, "the angels." Not only were they a wonderful audience for the lifetime of stories my dad had to tell, but they made him feel as though he could still give something back—whether career advice or just friendship. On his eighty-second birthday, Mitchell, Jim, Paul, Reg, my best friend Cynthia, and I all gathered for a celebratory dinner at home. By then my father had such trouble walking that he used a motorized scooter at home and a wheelchair for outings. That evening he was propped up in his scooter wearing his pink nightshirt and an old bathrobe, but he was paid loving court by his "angels" as though he were in white tie and tails. Cynthia, a tall blonde who reminded my father of his favorite women—wickedly witty and statuesque—brought a bottle of very expensive vodka, and my father proceeded to get hellaciously drunk with his friends, who took funny photographs and toasted everything and everyone imaginable. It was the happiest I had seen him in years and years.

*   *   *

Despite Dad's increasing reliance on a wheelchair, Reg managed to persuade him into taking regular outings. Reg recalled, "My deliberately repeated observations that 'No one ever looks at the occupant of a wheelchair' and 'The new precinct at Santa Monica is the most attractive development in Los Angeles' finally combined to break down his resistance, and once the waters were successfully tested forays in the chair were the order of the day. He really enjoyed our visits to the best of the farmers' markets, sparking his depleting appetite with the fruit and vegetables of his choice and, of course, with an eye open for another attractive plant to try in his precious garden.

"The alleged anonymity of a wheelchair held true, and Vincent, despite his unmistakable visage and jaunty straw hat with ethnic necklace embellishment, still escaped largely unnoticed and certainly not bothered. Close up, the market vendors acknowledged their good fortune in having such a celebrated customer by selecting choice produce, and the management at the home store would always give him a good deal on the papier maché tulips. He purchased dozens over the months for the hallway at Swallow and for gifts to special friends. 'They are particularly attractive,' he declared, 'because the designer has not attempted to capture total reality but presents an impression of the tulip which happens to have its own appeal and symmetry.'

"His weekly sorties to Santa Monica stood in for any European idyll. Over his extra-large cup of cappuccino at the Third Street espresso bar, he fancied himself on the Via Veneto, the Champs Elysées, or the Ramblas of Barcelona. I was ever solicitous of avoiding Vincent being trapped in his wheelchair by any untoward intrusions, but I proved somewhat overanxious one time in the Italian deli, where Vincent enjoyed ordering antipasto misto sandwiches on crusty French bread. I noticed a dubious, bejeaned and tattooed young man fixing his attention on Vincent and attempting to move closer. I swung his chair around to impede the intruder, who shook back his long black hair and challenged, 'It's Vincent, isn't it?' Having to now take a second look, I recognized Johnny Depp. A reunion with a delighted Vincent then transpired, Johnny Depp having been cautious over his approach, as he had not realized that the veteran he so admired now needed a wheelchair."

My father lived in Los Angeles for over fifty years, and the devoted son of St. Louis became an avid Angeleno. In April 1993, when the Rodney King verdict came in, my father, Reg, and I watched dumbfounded as the rioting broke loose. It was a spectacularly clear day and, as Reg recalled, "The panorama of the city was clear in vivid detail. As property was torched and looted, white plumes of smoke billowed up ominously, moving steadily nearer. Vincent, in sad disbelief, alternated his attention between closeups of looting on television and the overall picture from his windows, where the mayhem had an eerie unreality. One of his last sorties around Los Angeles was to view some of the destruction. He contributed to the fund of attacked truck driver Reginald Denny and shook his head sadly. His adopted city appeared to be crumbling and falling apart, just as he knew himself to be."

My father always stayed abreast of political news, and he became an ardent Clinton supporter during the 1992 elections. He was ecstatic when Clinton was elected, and I always felt that he would have been uneasy about dying while Bush and Quayle were in office. On Clinton's inauguration day, my father and I took in all the festivities on television. He liked Clinton's youth and intelligence and pop culture appeal, and he got a big kick out of seeing so many Hollywood faces in Washington for the inaugural balls.

That afternoon in early January 1993, as I was preparing my father's lunch, I suddenly heard the frantic ringing of the bell he kept by the side of the bed to signal in case of emergency. I raced to the bedroom, imagining that he had fallen. Instead, I found a man with a mile-wide smile ringing his bell in the direction of the television. "What's wrong?" I gasped. "They're ringing the bells for liberty," he jubilantly replied. I looked at the TV and saw the president and vice president ringing the Liberty Bell. As other bells from around the country joined in, so did my father.

Although his health and stamina were frail, my father always found a way to delight his audiences, whether at a dinner party or propped up in his bed greeting visitors. Always a gifted storyteller, he now honed his skills as a raconteur, infusing his tales with great wit and charm. He recalled, "We were at a dinner to mark Estelle Winwood's ninety-eighth birthday. I reacquainted myself with her by reminding her of how we had worked together in T. S. Eliot's *The Cocktail Party*. 'Cocktail party?' she said. 'What cocktail party? I don't go to cocktail parties!' And then she nodded inquisitively toward fellow guest Jean Marsh, who had co-created and starred in *Upstairs, Downstairs*. I attempted to define her by saying, 'You know, Estelle, *Upstairs, Downstairs*! To which she replied, 'Upstairs, downstairs—can't she make up her mind?' "

Eventually, however, the time came when he no longer felt able to entertain. Reggie recalled, "Vincent was not a person to dabble, and when his failing health and stamina cut down on his ability to socialize with those dear to him, he opted to withdraw, signing off in style by personally visiting as many of his friends as he could to give them a painting or a treasured object as a token of the joy he had known in their company. Then he said good bye to them, one by one."

Sandy Leonard remembered, "When I left Vincent's house the last time I saw him, he was in a wheelchair. He was at the door and he took my hand and said, 'We'll never see each other again.' And I thought, 'Oh my God.' And I was really shaken up but I thought, 'Of course, he's probably right.' I learned a lot from Vincent, and I realized that when you get old, you can say things like that. You just kind of accept things that you never accept when you're younger."

As Vincent grew weaker still, Reg described how "he would find himself powerless, unable to eat or react and able to breathe only with difficulty. Arthritis, emphysema, nausea, depression would gang up on him, leaving him an anxious shell. When it was conjectured that marijuana might help, in despair, but still managing the smile of a kid trespassing in the apple orchard, he ventured to try the drug in tablet form, but the only result was yet more nausea. Friends then contributed a jar of cut, prime pot and even baked a couple of hash brownies. The jar remained untried and hidden in the far reaches of a closet and, when a sampling of the hash tarts produced only sickness, the baked goodies were buried in the freezer. A few months later, knowing the end to be near, Vincent ordered the jar returned to its donor and the volatile cakes to the garbage disposal in whispered, guarded tones, as if dispatching a master spy on a secret mission."

Although Father Parnassus sometimes came by to give Vincent private mass, after Coral's death his faith had waned. Sandy Leonard remembered, "Once, when Vincent was in Boston, he asked me where there was a Catholic church near the hotel. It became clear that he wanted me to go with him to mass. So I did. We went to St. Paul's Church in Harvard Square to the 11 A.M. mass that features the boys' choir and is musically very entertaining. I remember telling Vincent that he would always be my mother's hero, not because of any of the films he'd been in, but because he'd gotten me to go to mass again. He told me that he found great peace in the faith, great comfort; but after Coral's death, he said that he thought I would be very happy to learn he'd given up on Catholicism. I smiled. He told me that when Coral had died, he couldn't understand how her 'loving God' could have allowed her to linger for so long and in such misery. After her death, he had asked the priest how this could be. 'He couldn't give me a good answer,' Vincent told me. That was enough for him, and he was no longer interested in Catholicism."

When my father became too ill to rely on a bunch of amateurs—which, essentially, we all were—he knew that he should hire a nurse. But, with memories of the disruptive stream of caregivers, he resisted for as long as possible. When we realized we could no longer put off the inevitable, Reg and I began searching for just the right person. We found her. Peggy Powell's expertise and matter-of-factness proved to be just what was needed. By the fall of 1993 she had moved into the guest room. Though my father refused to let her bathe him—that was the last relic of his modesty—he counseled Peggy on exactly what he wanted—how he wanted to die and how he wanted to be dressed for the mortuary. And he prepared for death.

My father once said to me, "Being elderly is a miserable period of life—from the physical standpoint, I mean. Mentally, there are great rewards. You have an entire lifetime during which, if you have spent your time on Earth profitably, you have accumulated enormous amounts of knowledge. You understand things now as you could not when you were younger. You have gained wisdom and perspective. Now that I'm coming to the end of my life, everyday I think of something that's beautiful. The garden, the juxtaposition of leaves and plants, the variety of shapes of leaves and shades of green. Those are the things that are really worth cultivating in your life, and you must keep your eyes open for them and keep your imagination open to being surprised."

In late October 1993, I planned a trip to New York to meet with publishers regarding our art book. The night before I left town he said to me, "You know, they say I could go any time." I asked him if he wanted me to stay, but he was adamant that I should make the trip and excited that we might sell our book. He had started taking morphine, and that night, as we watched a rough cut of the documentary Tim Burton had made about my father two and a half years earlier, he faded in and out. I sat on his bed and held his hand.

I was in New York when my father started to drift away, and I caught the last plane home out of the city. As we taxied to the runway at Kennedy, I watched huge jets from all over the world lumbering around us; suddenly I heard the thrust of engines and saw a plane ascend into the night—Alitalia—and I imagined my father, free of his failing body, taking one last swing over Rome before heading on to his next adventure. He died while I was flying home. Reg told me that my dad's immense will to live made it hard for him to go, but I knew he couldn't have gone while I was in the house any more than Coral could have while he was there. I knew that I would miss him forever, but I was glad that he was finally free.

EPILOGUE

FOR THE LAST ten years of his life, my father was an avid obituary reader. Ever the actor, he saw obituaries as reviews of a sort. He had been pleased with Coral's "reviews," and I like to think he would have been happy with his own. In England, he was remembered by the *Times* as "the king of modern horror movies" who brought "complexity to his high-camp villains, making them seem wronged or misunderstood and to be pitied as much as reviled." The *Guardian* noted that he had begun as a distinguished stage actor, but "if this were all, Vincent Price might have been lucky to merit a few paragraphs in the posh papers to mark his death. However, it was the other Vincent Price—the suave, mocking, degenerate, and ghoulish villain who will be remembered and cherished. Unlike other malefactors of the screen, Price's polished evildoing was more likely to raise screams of laughter than of terror."

His hometown paper, the *Los Angeles Times*, printed two tributes—one a lengthy career retrospective by staff writer Myrna Oliver, and the other a more personal reminiscence by his friend Charles Champlin. The *New York Times* noted his many accomplishments, but my father would undoubtedly have been much more flattered by his tribute in *People* magazine, who called him "The Gable of Gothic." And film critic Leonard Maltin said, "Other actors may have made better movies, but few lived better lives, or touched so many people with their warmth and gentility." But it was Steve Persall of the *St. Petersburg Times*, who had spent his childhood "staring in childish terror" at my father's films, who seemed to capture the marvelous paradox of his appeal to his many fans, citing a "mix of toney class and evil elegance that made Vincent Price a classic film character, a standard of silky cinematic evil that will continue its influence on movie villains long after his passing. For now, however, it's time to wish this wonderful actor exactly what his unforgettable, nightmarish films took away from a wide-eyed child of the theater when bedtime rolled around: Mr. Price, rest in peace."

With his impeccable theatrical timing, my father died three days before A&E was due to air its television biography of him. Then, five days after his passing, the country celebrated Halloween with Vincent Price film festivals on TV and in revival houses all over the U.S. As an actor who devoted so much energy to remaining in the public eye, he would have been delighted.

My father wanted to be cremated and have his ashes scattered in the ocean, but insisted that it be someplace other than Santa Monica Bay, which was, he told us, "already too polluted." We held a small service for family and friends at the Hollywood Cemetery and the next day we took my father's remains out to sea. After we left the polluted confines of Santa Monica Bay on a private boat, we chose a spot off Point Dume from which we could see Nicholas Beach. The captain said the Lord's Prayer and we scattered long-stemmed red roses on the water with my father's ashes. The roses and ashes mingled, forming a circle of color, and then began floating away, together with my father's trademark old straw hat. This hat, its brim adorned with a heavy wooden African necklace, was so much a part of him that we felt it fitting to send it with him. As the hat bobbed away, a baby seal swam up beneath it and began to play, almost swimming through the necklace. As hat and necklace slowly sank, the seal gazed up at all of us on the boat with what seemed a smile, then swam away among the roses.

Then we went fishing, which is just what my father would have wanted us to do.

My father had continually told me that he didn't want a memorial service. At first I argued with him; eventually I just humored him. But after his death I felt bound by his wishes, so we threw a party instead. In November 1993, the Vincent Price Gallery at East Los Angeles College had a bash to celebrate the life of its benefactor. Guests were invited to view two exhibitions—a retrospective of the many donations my father had made, and a marvelous show by a former student whose art career had flourished since leaving the college. I spoke at the gathering, followed by the college president, and then by Roddy McDowall, who gave a eulogy that reduced everyone to tears. Michael Feinstein played two songs, after which we enjoyed chef Susan Feniger's wonderful food. It was the kind of party my father would have loved—great food, lots to drink, interesting people, loving friends, and plenty of art on view.

There is an oft-told story about my father. As Alan Bates, who was there, recounted it, "A few of us were out to dinner with Coral and Vincent. A woman came up to Vincent at the end of the meal and said, 'Can I have your autograph?' And he said 'certainly' and signed it 'Dolores del Rio.' I said, 'Vincent, you cannot do that. She'll be back in a rage in a minute. She'll pour a bowl of soup over your head.' He turned to me and said, 'Before she died, Dolores said to me, "Don't ever let them forget me." ' "

INDEX

All photos courtesy of the Price Family Collection unless otherwise noted:

Insert page 4: The summer after graduation. (Collection of Vincent Barrett Price)

Insert page 7: Vincent and Anna May Wong. (Estate of Carl Van Vechten)

Insert page 9: Edith Barrett Price. (Collection of Vincent Barrett Price)
Vincent and Edi visit St. Louis. (Collection of Vincent Barrett Price)

Insert page 10: On the set of *Service de Luxe*. (Copyright © 1999 by Universal City Studios, Inc. Courtesy of Universal Studios Publishing Rights, a Division of Universal Studios Licensing, Inc. All rights reserved.)
Constance Bennett and Vincent Price. (Copyright © 1999 by Universal City Studios, Inc. Courtesy of Universal Studios Publishing Rights, a Division of Universal Studios Licensing, Inc. All rights reserved.)

Insert page 11: A delighted Marguerite. (Collection of Vincent Barrett Price)

Insert page 12: Vincent as Sir Walter Raleigh. (Warner Bros.)

Insert page 14: Vincent as Inspector Dutour. (Twentieth Century-Fox)
Laura. (Twentieth Century-Fox)

Insert page 15: In the Benedict Canyon abode. (Collection of Vincent Barrett Price)
Father and son. (Collection of Vincent Barrett Price)

Insert page 16: *Up in Central Park*. (Copyright © 1999 by Universal City Studios, Inc. Courtesy of Universal Studios Publishing Rights, a Division of Universal Studios Licensing, Inc. All rights reserved.)
Mary Grant. (Collection of Mary Grant Price)
A rare earnest moment. (Collection of Mary Grant Price)

Insert page 17: At home in Benedict Canyon. (Collection of Mary Grant Price)
Mary and Vincent in Palm Springs. (Roddy McDowall)
The spoils of a trip to Tijuana. (Collection of Mary Grant Price)

Insert page 18: *The Las Vegas Story*. (An RKO Picture)
House of Wax. (Warner Bros.)